Communications in Computer and Information Science   **567**

Commenced Publication in 2007
Founding and Former Series Editors:
Alfredo Cuzzocrea, Dominik Ślęzak, and Xiaokang Yang

More information about this series at http://www.springer.com/series/7899

Antonio Celesti · Philipp Leitner (Eds.)

Advances in Service-Oriented and Cloud Computing

Workshops of ESOCC 2015
Taormina, Italy, September 15–17, 2015
Revised Selected Papers

 Springer

Editors
Antonio Celesti
DICIEAMA
University of Messina
Messina
Italy

Philipp Leitner
Software Evolution and Architecture Lab
University of Zürich
Zürich
Switzerland

ISSN 1865-0929   ISSN 1865-0937 (electronic)
Communications in Computer and Information Science
ISBN 978-3-319-33312-0   ISBN 978-3-319-33313-7   (eBook)
DOI 10.1007/978-3-319-33313-7

Library of Congress Control Number: 2016936647

Printed on acid-free paper

This Springer imprint is published by Springer Nature
The registered company is Springer International Publishing AG Switzerland

Preface

This volume contains the technical papers presented at the six high-quality workshops associated with ESOCC 2015 (European Conference on Service-Oriented and Cloud Computing), held in Taormina, Messina, September 15–17, 2015. The workshops focused on specific topics in service-oriented and cloud computing-related domains: Third International Workshop on CLoud for IoT (CLIoT 2015), 5th International Workshop on Adaptive Services for the Future Internet (WAS4FI 2015), Second Workshop on Seamless Adaptive Multi-Cloud Management of Service-Based Applications (SeaClouds 2015), First International Workshop on Cloud Adoption and Migration (CloudWay 2015), First International Workshop on Digital Enterprise Architecture and Engineering (IDEA 2015), the First Workshop on Federated Cloud Networking (FedCloudNet 2015).

Moreover, this volume also includes papers presented at the European Projects Track (EU Projects 2015) in conjunction with ESOCC 2015.

There were a total of 48 submissions, from which 24 papers were accepted giving an acceptance rate of 50 %. The review and selection process was performed rigorously, with each paper being reviewed by at least two Program Committee (PC) members. Here, a brief description of each workshop is given.

The CLIoT 2015 workshop aimed at discussing the limits and/or advantages of existing cloud solutions for IoT and at proposing original and innovative contributions for enhancing real-world resources over cloud environments. Smart connectivity with existing networks and context-aware computation is becoming indispensable for IoT. Cloud computing provides a very strategic virtual infrastructure that integrates monitoring devices, storage devices, analytics tools, virtualization platforms, and client delivery. It supports enormous amounts of data generated for IoT purposes, which have to be stored, processed, and presented in a seamless, efficient, and easily interpretable form. The first part of this volume includes all the technical papers of CLIoT 2015.

The W4S4FI 2015 workshop focused on Future Internet (FI) technologies. The FI has emerged as a new initiative to pave a novel infrastructure linked to objects (things) of the real world to meet the changing global needs of business and society. It offers Internet users a standardized, secure, efficient, and trustable environment, which allows open and distributed access to global networks, services, and information. There is a need for both researchers and practitioners to develop platforms made up of adaptive FI applications. In this sense, the emergence and consolidation of service-oriented architectures (SOA), cloud computing, and wireless sensor networks (WSN) give benefits, such as flexibility, computing, scalability, security, interoperability, and adaptability for building these applications. FI systems will need to sense and respond to a huge amount of signals sourced from different entities in real time. WAS4FI addresses different aspects of adaptive FI applications, emphasizing the importance of governing the convergence of contents, services, things, and networks to achieve building platforms for efficiency, scalability, security, and flexible adaptation. WAS4FI

2015 covered the foundations of these technologies as well as new emerging proposals. The second part of this volume includes all the technical papers of WAS4FI 2015.

The SeaCloud 2015 workshop focuses on enabling an efficient and adaptive deployment and management of service-based applications across multiple clouds. Deploying and managing in an efficient and adaptive way complex service-based applications across multiple heterogeneous clouds is one of the problems that have emerged with the cloud revolution. The current lack of universally accepted standards supporting cloud interoperability is severely affecting the portability of cloud-based applications across different platforms. At the same time, even at the level of a single cloud, adaptation of cloud services to their execution environment is strongly desirable in order to take appropriate actions in response to changes in the highly dynamic environment of the cloud. Adaptations can be performed at runtime (dynamic adaptation) and at development time. In the latter case runtime and contextual data provided to business application developers can allow them to enhance their applications based on the actual operating conditions. The SeaCloud 2015 workshop covered solutions and perspectives of the ongoing research activities aimed at enabling an efficient and adaptive management of service-based applications across multiple clouds. The third part of this volume includes all the technical papers of SeaCloud 2015.

The CloudWay 2015 workshop focused on novel cloud service migration practices and solutions, and aims to identify future cloud migration challenges and dimensions. Major IT companies and start-ups envision cloud computing as an economic strategy to meet business objectives cost effectively and a way to remain competitive by exploiting technical resources efficiently. Given the potential benefits of cloudification, an increasing number of organizational business-critical applications – so-called legacy systems – are being migrated to cloud environments. Regardless of the benefits of cloudification, many organizations still rely on legacy software systems developed over the lifetime of an organization using traditional development methods. Therefore, migrating legacy systems toward cloud-based platform allows organizations to leverage their existing systems deployed (over publicly available resources) as scalable cloud services. The CloudWay 2015 workshop covered novel cloud migration practices and solutions to identify future cloud migration challenges and dimensions. The fourth part of this volume includes all the technical papers of CloudWay 2015.

The IDEA 2015 workshop focused on the digitization of enterprises in the cloud computing era in order to advance digital enterprise architectures. Digitization is the use of digital technologies for creating innovative digital business models and transforming existing business models and processes. On a technological level, digitization embraces the automation of processes and decisions. Advanced analytics provides the automation of decisions hitherto made by human beings. Typical elements of digital enterprise architectures are the use of decision automation, predictive or even prescriptive analytics. In this way, digital technologies such as service orientation, cloud computing, big data, mobile or the Internet of Things enable the creation of new options for enterprises and organizations. Owing to the high diversity of concepts, the complexity of systems involved, and the heterogeneity of stakeholders, a methodological foundation is crucial to the success of digitization. The IDEA 2015 workshop covered business with technological themes and applied methodical and engineering principles to the design of digital enterprise architectures (EA). The fifth part of this volume includes all the technical papers of IDEA 2015.

The FedCloudNet 2015 workshop focused on federated cloud networking services. Cloud federation enables cloud providers to collaborate and share their resources to create a large virtual pool of resources at multiple network locations. In order to support this scenario, it is necessary to research and develop techniques to federate cloud network resources, enabling the instantiation and provision of overlay networks across geographically dispersed clouds, and to derive the integrated management cloud layer that enables an efficient and secure deployment of federated cloud applications. Emerging topics in this research area includes cloud network federation models and architectures, cross-data-center software-defined networking (SDN), network function virtualization (NFV), data center interconnection, overlay networks, virtual private networks (VPNs), federated cloud network security, geographic location-aware networks with high availability and elasticity. The FedCloudNet 2015 workshop covered the latest research results on traffic engineering for cloud network federation. The sixth part of this volume includes all the technical papers of FedCloudNet 2015.

EU Projects Track 2015 aimed at presenting the major running European-funded projects highlighting the main industrial and academic trends in terms of research and innovation. The seventh part of this volume includes all poster papers of EU Projects 2015.

October 2015

Antonio Celesti
Philipp Leitner

Organization

ESOCC 2015 was organized by the Department of Engineering and by the Mobile and Distributed System Laboratory (MDSLAB) of the University of Messina (Italy).

Contents

IDEA Workshop Papers

FedCloudNet Workshop Papers

EU Projects Track

CLIoT Workshop Papers

Preface of CLIoT 2015

A new generation of embedded devices provide an opportunity to create new business and social models by exploiting a strong interaction with the environment. At the same time, the Internet of Things (IoT) seem to change the way we interact with the world around us. The IoT conceptual base aims to represent the physical world through uniquely identifiable and interconnected objects (things). These things have the capacity for sensing, processing, or actuating information about entities available from within the real world. They allow interactions or generate events about them. The generated information travels along heterogeneous systems, such as routers, databases, information systems, and the Internet. Consequently, there are enormous amounts of data that have to be stored, processed, and presented in a seamless, efficient, and easily interpretable form.

Cloud computing represents a very flexible technology, able to offer theoretically unlimited computing and storage capabilities and efficient communication services for transferring terabyte flows between data centers. Cloud technologies address two important goals for distributed system: high scalability and high availability. These features make cloud computing a promising choice for supporting IoT services. IoT has the potential to offer the killer applications of cloud computing, where the cloud allows one to access IoT-based resources and capabilities, to process and manage IoT environments, and to deliver on-demand utility of IoT services such as sensing/actuation as a service.

CLIoT 2015 was the third edition of the International Workshop on Cloud for IoT. It aims at bringing together scientists, practitioners, and PhD students in order to discuss the limits and/or advantages of existing cloud solutions for IoT, and to propose original and innovative contributions for enhancing real-world resources over cloud environments. The topics of interest for CLIoT 2015 included but were not limited to:

- Innovative models and system architectures for cloud-based IoT
- IoT Data abstraction and processing
- Mobile cloud
- Cloud storage for IoT
- Interaction between sensor networks and the cloud
- Discovery Service for IoT
- Cloud computing-based IoT technologies
- Wireless sensor networks into the cloud
- Big data management using clouds
- Smart environments for IoT
- Ubiquitous computing/pervasive computing for IoT
- Real-time communication with smart objects
- Applications based on IoT and the cloud
- Inter-cloud management: cloud federation serving IoT
- Security and privacy in clouds and IoT

All submissions were peer-reviewed by an international Program Committee, with the objective of having at least three reviews for each paper. The final acceptance rate of the manuscripts was 62 %.

The contributions accepted for presentation at the workshop include the work of Cavallo et al., who designed a context-aware Hadoop framework able to schedule and distribute tasks among geographically distant clusters minimizing the overall job execution time. Such a framework can be successfully used to process huge amounts of data generated in IoT scenarios.

Steffenel et al. presented CloudFIT, a PaaS middleware for the creation of private clouds over pervasive environments. Using a Map Reduce application as an example, the authors showed how CloudFIT provides both storage and data aggregation/analysis capabilities at the service of IoT networks.

Panarello et al. proposed a cloud federation-based system to support the increasing usage of mobile devices and social networks, where photo selfie sharing is gradually turning into video selfie. The proposed solution exploits the Hadoop-MapReduce paradigm to perform video transcoding in multiple formats and in a fast and efficient way.

Gaivoronski et al. presented modeling tools for evaluating business models of ISPs in the Internet ecosystem, also discussing some results of this analysis. In particular, they modeled the relationship between a content provider (CP) with significant market power and an ISP. Such a relationship is very important in the establishment of a real interconnection between IoT environments and cloud providers.

Massonet et al. presented the main security requirements of a generic federated cloud netwoking architecture analyzed in the Horizon 2020 BEACON project that aims to research and develop techniques to federate cloud network resources in order to derive an integrated cloud management layer that enables an efficient and secure deployment of federated cloud applications.

The workshop program also included a short paper presenting the research activity of Mulfari et al. on container virtualization on Linux embedded IoT devices. In particular, the work presents a tool designed to compose cloud facilities by means of a flexible federation-enabled communication system.

Moreover, the workshop program included a joint panel with the CloudWay Workshop, titled "Migrating to Cloud and IoT Solutions: Challenges and Perspectives," where several different approaches and features in the field were discussed.

Maria Fazio
Dana Petcu

Organization

Workshop Organizers

Maria Fazio — University of Messina, Italy
Dana Petcu — West University of Timisoara, Romania

Steering Committee

Nik Bessis — University of Derby, UK
Massimo Villari — University of Messina, Italy

Technical Program Committee

Liz Bacon	Greenwich University, UK
Francisco J. Blaya Gonzálvez	University of Murcia, Spain
Antonio Celesti	University of Messina, Italy
Erik Elmroth	Umeå University, Sweden
Teodor-Florin Fortis	West University of Timisoara, Romania
Horacio Gonzalez-Velez	National College of Ireland, Ireland
Brian Lee	Athlone IT, Ireland
Juan Manuel Murillo Rodríguez	University of Extremadura, Spain
Tommi Mikkonen	Tampere University of Technology, Tampere, Finland
Victor Muntés-Mulero	Universitat Politècnica de Catalunya, Spain
Zsolt Nemeth	MTA SZTAKI, Hungary
Bogdan Nicolae	IBM Research, Ireland
Leire Orue-Echevarria	Tecnalia Research and Innovation, Spain
Jose Luis Vazquez-Poletti	Universidad Complutense de Madrid, Spain

A Scheduling Strategy to Run Hadoop Jobs on Geodistributed Data

Marco Cavallo, Lorenzo Cusmà, Giuseppe Di Modica, Carmelo Polito,
and Orazio Tomarchio$^{(\boxtimes)}$

Department of Electrical, Electronic and Computer Engineering,
University of Catania, Catania, Italy
{marco.cavallo,lorenzo.cusma,giuseppe.dimodica,carmelo.polito,
orazio.tomarchio}@dieei.unict.it

Abstract. Internet-of-Things scenarios will be typically characterized by huge amounts of data made available. A challenging task is to efficiently manage such data, by analyzing, elaborating and extracting useful information from them. Distributed computing framework such as Hadoop, based on the MapReduce paradigm, have been used to process such amounts of data by exploiting the computing power of many cluster nodes. However, as long as the computing context is made of clusters of homogeneous nodes interconnected through high speed links, the benefit brought by the such frameworks is clear and tangible. Unfortunately, in many real big data applications the data to be processed reside in many computationally heterogeneous data centers distributed over the planet. In those contexts, Hadoop was proved to perform very poorly. The proposal presented in this paper addresses this limitation. We designed a context-aware Hadoop framework that is capable of scheduling and distributing tasks among geographically distant clusters in a way that minimizes overall jobs' execution time. The proposed scheduler leverages on the integer partitioning technique and on an a-priori knowledge of big data application patterns to explore the space of all possible task schedules and estimate the one expected to perform best. Final experiments conducted on a scheduler prototype prove the benefit of the approach.

1 Introduction

While the first wave of IoT has focused on delivering frameworks on which "smart" sensors can be implemented and connected to the Internet, focus now has shift towards the definition of backend services capable of managing the huge amount of data that those sensing frameworks, as well as the sensors that billions of portable devices are equipped with, produce every day [9]. The Cloud has been evoked by many as the "right place" where sensed data ought to be stored and mined [12]. The Cloud can scale very well with respect to both the data dimension and the computing power that is required for elaboration purposes. If on the one hand there is a strong trend that pushes for executing some data processing (such as filtering, cleaning, etc.) close to the place where they have

© Springer International Publishing Switzerland 2016
A. Celesti and P. Leitner (Eds.): ESOCC 2015 Workshops, CCIS 567, pp. 5–19, 2016.
DOI: 10.1007/978-3-319-33313-7_1

been sensed (on the smart sensing frameworks, indeed), on the other one there is still the need to run computationally heavy mining procedures on the Cloud, where data are conveyed after sensing, and may even happen to reside on data centers which are geographically distant to each other's [11].

Devising efficient mechanisms for storage, manipulation and analysis of such huge amount of data is currently one of the main research and technological challenges [14]. Application parallelization and divide-and-conquer strategies are natural computational paradigms for approaching big data problems, addressing scalability and high performance. The availability of grid and cloud computing technologies, which have lowered the price of on-demand computing power, have spread the usage of parallel paradigms, such as the MapReduce [3], for big data processing. But, despite getting additional computing resources has become very simple by using cloud computing technologies, in many big data scenarios several challenges are still not adequately solved. It is not uncommon the need to process data which are geographically distributed. In these scenarios, the data required to perform a task is often non-local. This may severely affect the performance of a MapReduce application. Hadoop, one of the most widespread implementation of the MapReduce paradigm, has been designed mainly to work on clusters of homogeneous computing nodes belonging to the same local area network; thus, data locality is one of the crucial factors affecting its performance.

In our work we address just this issue, trying to take into account the actual heterogeneity of nodes, network links and data distribution in order to optimize the job execution time [2]. Our solution follows a hierarchical approach, where a top-level entity will take care of serving a submitted job: the job is split into a number of bottom-level, independent MapReduce sub-jobs that are scheduled to run on the sites where data natively reside or have been ad-hoc moved to. The designed job scheduling algorithm aims to exploit fresh information continuously sensed from the distributed computing context (available sites computing capacity and inter-site bandwidth) to estimate each jobs optimum execution flow. Main focus of this work is on a study conducted on the "profile" of applications, i.e., the set of application features that may impact on the phases of the job execution, and on the definition of a job scheduling strategy that leverages on the integer partitioning technique to search for the best task schedule that guarantees the job's shortest execution time.

The remainder of the paper is organized as follows. In Sect. 2 we introduce the overall system design. Section 3 provides the details of the job scheduling algorithm and discusses the application profiling. Section 4 presents some preliminary results of the proposed job scheduling run on well known MapReduce applications. Finally, Sect. 5 presents related work, while Sect. 6 concludes the work.

2   Design of a Hierarchical Hadoop Approach

According to the MapReduce paradigm, a generic computation is called *job* [3]. Upon a job submission, a *scheduling system* is responsible for splitting the job in several *tasks* and mapping the tasks to a set of available nodes within a cluster. The performance of a job execution is measured by its completion time (some refers to it with the term *makespan*), i.e., the time for a job to complete. Apart from the size of the data to be processed, that time heavily depends on the job's *execution flow* determined by the scheduling system (the sequence of tasks that the job is split in) and the computing power of the cluster nodes where the tasks are actually executed.

In a scenario where computing nodes reside in distributed clusters that are geographically distant to each other's, there is an additional parameter that may affect the job performance. Communication links among clusters (inter-cluster links) are often disomogeneous and have a much lower capacity than communication links among nodes within a cluster (intra-cluster links). Also, clusters are not designed to have similar or comparable computing capacity, therefore they might happen to be heterogeneous in terms of computing power. Third, it is not rare that the data set to be processed are unevenly distributed over the clusters. So basically, if a scheduling system does not account for this threefold unbalancement (nodes capacity, communication links capacity, data set distribution) the overall job's performance may degrade dramatically.

To face these issues, we propose a hierarchical MapReduce framework where a *top-level* scheduling system sits on top of a *bottom-level* distributed computing context and is continuously kept informed about the dynamic conditions of the underlying computing context. Information retrieved from the computing context is then used to drive the generation of each job's optimum execution flow (or *execution path*).

The basic reference scenario addressed by our proposal is depicted in Fig. 1. *Sites* (data centers) populate the bottom level of the hierarchy. A Site may be composed of one or more cluster nodes that provide the overall Site's computing power. Each Site stores a certain amount of data and is capable of running plain Hadoop jobs. Upon receiving a job, a Site transparently performs the whole MapReduce process chain on the local cluster(s) and returns the result of the elaboration. The system's business logic devoted to the management of the geo-distributed computing resides in the top-level of the hierarchy. When a new Hadoop job is submitted that requires to process the data distributed over the Sites, the business logic splits the job into a set of sub-jobs, pushes them to the distributed context, gathers the sub-job results and packages the overall computation result.

Hierarchical MapReduce approaches are not new in the literature [5, 7, 13]. The novelty introduced by this work is the adoption of a scheduling strategy based on the *integer partitioning* technique and the inclusion of the *application profile* among the parameters that may influence the determination of the job's optimum execution flow. Such a novelty will be thoroughly discussed in Sect. 3.

The system's business logic is composed of the following entities:

- **Orchestrator**. It is responsible for the generation of a *Top-level Job Execution Plan* (TJEP). A TJEP contains the following information:

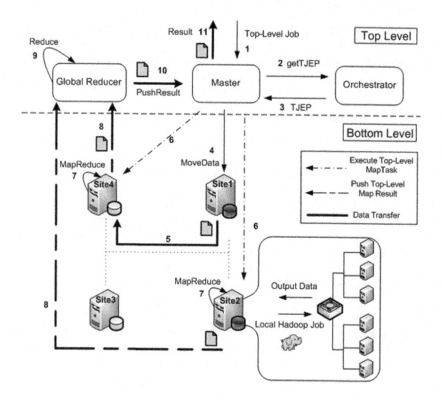

Fig. 1. Overall architecture

- the Data Logistic Plan (DLP), which states how data targeted by the job have to be re-organized (i.e., shifted) among Sites;
- the Sub-job Scheduling Plan (SSP), which defines the set of Hadoop sub-jobs to be submitted to the Sites holding the data.
- **Master.** It is the entity to which Hadoop jobs are submitted. It calls on the Orchestrator for the generation of the TJEP, and is in charge of enforcing the TJEP according to the information contained in the DLP and the SSP.
- **Global Reducer.** It performs the top-level reduction of the results obtained from the execution of Hadoop sub-jobs.

At design time two important assumptions are made. First, only one Global Reducer is responsible for collecting and reducing the data elaborated by bottom-level Sites. One may argue that this choice might impact on the job performance, nevertheless it does not invalidate the approach. Anyway, in the future this assumption is going to be relaxed. Second, being this a pure hierarchical app-roach, the top-level MapReduce job must be implemented in such a way that the applied operations are "associative", i.e., may be performed recursively at each level of the hierarchy and the execution order of the operations does not affect the final result [5].

In the scenario of Fig. 1 four geo-distributed Sites are depicted that hold company's business data sets. The numbered arrows describe a typical execution flow triggered by the submission of a top-level job. This specific case envisioned a shift of data from *Site1* to *Site4*, and the run of local MapReduce sub-jobs on two Sites (*Site2* and *Site4*).

One of the Orchestrator's tasks is to monitor the distributed context's resources, i.e., the Sites' available computing capacity and the inter-site bandwidth capacity. As for the monitoring of the computing capacity, each Site periodically advertises its capacity to the Orchestrator. Such capacity represents the overall computing capacity of the Site for MapReduce purposes (overall nominal capacity). Since the amount of computing capacity potentially allocable to a single job (slot capacity) may differ from Site to Site, Sites are also requested to communicate that amount along with the overall nominal capacity. The available inter-site link capacity is instead "sensed" through a network infrastructure made of SDN-enabled [10] switches. Switches are capable of measuring the instant bandwidth occupied by incoming and outgoing data flows. The Orchestrator periodically enquires the switches to retrieve the bandwidth consumption and elaborates statistics on the inter-site bandwidth consumption.

3   Job Scheduling Strategy

As mentioned in the previous section, the Orchestrator is the component in charge of generating the TJEP, which contains some directives on how data have to be re-distributed among Sites and the articulation of sub-jobs that have to be run on the Sites. In order to compute the TJEP, the Orchestrator will call on a scheduling strategy that explores the universe of all feasible execution paths for that specific distributed computing context. Each execution path is assigned a score, which is a function of its estimated completion time (the shorter the estimated completion time, the higher the score), and finally the execution path with the best score will be appointed TJEP.

If it may appear clear that the sites' computing capacity and the inter-site bandwidth affect the overall path's completion time, some words have to be spent on the impact that the type of MapReduce application may have on that time. We argue that if the scheduling system is aware of the application behavior in terms of the data produced in output with respect to the data taken in input, it can use this information to take important decisions. In a geo-distributed context, moving big amounts of data back and forth among Sites is a "costly" operation. If the size of the data produced by a certain application can be known in advance, this information will help the scheduling system to decide on which execution path is best for the application.

In [4] the authors introduce the α expansion/compression factor, that represents the ratio of the size of the output data of the Map task of a MapReduce job to the size of its input data. In our system focus is on the MapReduce process (not just on the Map phase) that takes place in a Site. Therefore we are interested in profiling applications as a whole.

We then introduce the data **Compression factor** β_{app}, which represents the ratio of the output data size of an application to its input data size:

$$\beta_{app} = \frac{OutputData_{app}}{InputData_{app}} \tag{1}$$

The β_{app} parameter may be used to calculate the amount of data that is produced by a MapReduce job at a Site, traverses the network and reaches the Global Reducer. Depending on that amount, the data transfer phase may seriously impact on the overall top-level job performance. The exact value of β_{app} for a submitted application may not be known a priori: Sect. 3.2 will discuss on how to get a good estimate of it.

We adopt a graph model to represent the job's execution path. Basically, a graph *node* may represent either a *Data Computing Element* (site) or a *Data Transport Element* (network link). Arcs between nodes are used to represent the sequence of nodes in an execution path. A node is the place where a data flow arrives (input data) and another data flow is generated (output data). Nodes are characterized by two parameters. The β_{app}, that is used to estimate the data produced by a node, and the **Throughput**, defined as the amount of data that the node is able to process per time unit. The β_{app} value for Data Transport Elements is equal to 1, because there is no data computation occurring in a data transfer. As for the Data Computing Element, instead, β_{app} strictly depends on the type of application to be executed. In the case of Data Transports Element, the Throughput is equal to the link capacity. The Throughput of a Data Computing Elements depends again on both the application type and the Site's computing capacity. Like for the β_{app} value, the exact Throughput value is not a priori known; Sect. 3.2 discusses a sample-based procedure employed to derive the Throughput of a computing node for a certain application. Finally, arcs between nodes are labeled with a number representing the size of the data leaving a node and reaching the next node.

The label value of the arc connecting node $j - th$ to node $(j + 1) - th$ is given by:

$$DataSize_{j,j+1} = DataSize_{j-1,j} \times \beta_j \tag{2}$$

In Fig. 2 an example of a graph branch made of two nodes and a connecting arc is depicted:

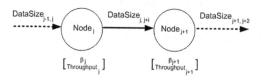

Fig. 2. Nodes' data structure

A generic node j's execution time is defined as:

$$T_j = \frac{DataSize_{j-1,j}}{Throughput_j} \tag{3}$$

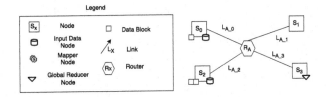

Fig. 3. Example topology of a distributed computing environment

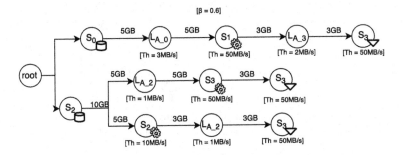

Fig. 4. Graph modeling a potential execution path

An execution path is then modeled as a graph of nodes. The hard part of the scheduling system's work is the generation of all the potential execution paths. The algorithm used to generate potential execution paths is discussed in Sect. 3.1. We now put the focus on how to calculate the execution time of a specific execution path.

Figure 3 depicts a scenario of four sites (S_0 through S_3) and a geographic network interconnecting the sites. A top-level job need to process a 15 GB data set distributed this way: 5 GB located in Site S_0 and 10 GB located in Site S_2. Let us assume that one of the execution-paths generated by the scheduling system involves the movement of 5 GB of data from S_2 to S_3, and that three MapReduce sub-jobs will be executed at S_0, S_2 and S_3 respectively. The Global reducing of the data produced by the MapReduce sub-jobs will be performed at $S3$.

In Fig. 4 the graph that models a potential execution path for the just discussed configuration is represented. Basically, a graph has as many branches as the number of bottom-level MapReduce (three, in our case). Every branch starts at the *root* node (initial node) and ends at the Global reducer's node. Next to node I is the node where the data interested by the MapReduce computation initially resides. In the example, the branch in the bottom models the elaboration of data initially residing in node S_2, that are map-reduced by node S_2 itself, and results are finally pushed to node S_3 (the Global reducer) through the links $L_{A.2}$ and $L_{A.3}$. In the graph, only the $L_{A.2}$ node is represented as it is slower than $L_{A.3}$ and will impose its speed in the overall path $S_2 \rightarrow L_{A.2} \rightarrow R_A \rightarrow L_{A.3} \rightarrow S_3$. Similarly, in the top-most branch the data residing in node S_0 are moved to node S_1 through link L_{A_0}, are map-reduced by node S_1 and results are pushed to node S_3 through link L_{A_3}.

We define the execution time of a branch to be the sum of the execution times of the nodes belonging to the branch; the Global reducer node's execution time is left out of this sum. Note that execution carried out through branches are independent of each other's, so branches will have different execution times. In order for the Global reducing to start, all branches will have to produce and move their results to the reducer Site. Therefore the longest among the branches' execution times determines when the global reducing is allowed to start.

The execution time of a branch is computed as the sum of the execution times of all the branch's nodes:

$$T_{branch} = \sum_{j=1}^{N-1} \frac{DataSize_{j,j+1}}{Throughput_{j+1}} \tag{4}$$

being N the number of nodes in the branch.

In particular, the execution time of the top-most branch of Fig. 4 is:

$$T_{top} = \frac{5\,GB}{3\frac{MB}{s}} + \frac{5\,GB}{50\frac{MB}{s}} + \frac{3\,GB}{2\frac{MB}{s}} = 3,27 \times 10^3\,s$$

The execution time of the Global reducer is given by the summation of the sizes of the data sets coming from all the branches over the node's estimated throughput. Let $DataSize(K)_{N-1,N}$ be the data size of the k-th branch reaching the Global reducer node. The execution time for the Global reducer will be:

$$T_{GR} = \frac{\sum_{K=1}^{P} DataSize(K)_{N-1,N}}{Throughput_{GR}} \tag{5}$$

being P the total number of branches in the graph. In the considered case, the execution time of the Global reducer (node S_3) will be:

$$T_{GR} = \frac{3\,GB + 3\,GB + 3\,GB}{50\frac{MB}{s}} = 180\,s$$

Finally, the overall execution time estimated for the specific execution path represented by the graph is defined to be the sum of Global reducer's execution time and the maximum among the branches' execution times:

$$T_{path} = \max_{1 \le K \le P} (T(K)_{branch}) + Throughput_{GR} \tag{6}$$

This concludes the computation of the execution time of the considered graph. We remind that the scheduling system is able to generate many job's execution paths, for each of which the execution time is calculated. In the end, the best path to schedule will be, of course, the one showing the shortest time.

In Sect. 4 a more complex scenario is shown and the result of experiments conducted on a real use case application are discussed.

3.1   Execution Path Generation

The scheduling system's strategy to identify the best execution path for specific top-level job is to generate all potential execution paths and find out the one with the shortest execution time. The scheduling algorithm just needs a few parameters in input: the network's topology, the list of Sites holding the data to be processed, parameters related to the MapReduce application (β_{app} and *Throughput*). All potential execution paths are explored by applying combinatorics operation. First, the algorithm analyzes all computing nodes (Sites) to find the best mapper nodes' combination. A combination is a way of selecting mapper nodes from the collection of all available Sites. The algorithm computes a *k-combination* of all nodes with k ranging from 1 to the number of available Sites, where K is the number of mappers. The overall number of *k-combination* is:

$$\sum_{k=1}^{n} C_{n,k} = \sum_{k=1}^{n} \frac{n!}{k!(n-k)!} \tag{7}$$

For each k-combination, the algorithm computes the needed data transfers. Those transfers consists in moving *data blocks* from the Sites that hold them to the mapper nodes. The basic assumption we make is that overall data to be processed must be divided into equally sized data blocks. Therefore, Sites holding data will hold one or more data blocks. Those blocks need to be re-distributed to mapper nodes. Of course, a Site holding data may also be a mapper, therefore will happen to be assigned one or more data blocks. In order to represent all possible assignments of data blocks to mappers, we call on the *Integer Partitioning* technique [1]. A partition of a positive integer n, also called an integer partition, is a way of writing n as a sum of positive integers. It is possible to partition n as a sum of m addenda, in which case we will refer to it as a partition of the number n of order m. Finally, our objective is to compute the partitions of the integer n of order m, where n is the total number of data blocks and m is the number of nodes candidates to become mappers.

By the notation $P(n, m)$ we refer to the number of partitions of the integer number n in the order m. The overall number of partitions of a number n in all the orders m $= 1, 2,..,$n is:

$$P(n) = \sum_{m=1}^{n} P(n, m) \tag{8}$$

Of course, the data blocks configuration tells us just the ways to "group" data blocks for distribution, but the distribution phase complicates the problem, as there are many possible ways to distribute group of data blocks among sites. So for the distribution of data blocks we have to call on the permutation theory. In the end, the calculus of the **number of all the execution paths** for a certain application must consider both the block data distribution configuration (Eq. 8) and the combination of mappers (Eq. 7). For example, in the case of $n = 7$ the number of generated paths will be around 18.000. For $n = 8$ more than 150.000 configurations were obtained. Treating the problem of the generation of execution paths as an integer partitioning problem allowed us to apply well known algorithms working in constant amortized time that guarantee acceptable time also on off-the-shelf PCs [15].

3.2 Application Profiling

The generation and evaluation of the best execution path is highly dependent on the data processing pattern of an application. The way an application manipulates data affects both the computing phase and the transfer phase of the overall job execution.

The parameters that can be used to best represent the application profile are the β_{app} and the *Throughput* discussed in the previous section. Since the exact values of those application parameters are not known at job submission time, we have to provide an accurate estimate. The estimate process consists in asking the Sites holding the data to run the job on a small portion of their data and provide back the nominal β_{app} and nominal *Throughput* computed on those data. Since the *nominal Throughput* indicates the amount of data processed per time unit, all Sites will have to compute it on a reference machine having an agreed computing power (e.g., equal to 1 Gflops). At the end of the nominal values estimate, the involved Sites send their estimates to the Orchestrator, where they will be appropriately averaged. The averaged values will be considered the application's official profile, and will be used in the definition of the graph.

The *Throughput* of a given computing node is computed by multiplying the application's official *Throughput* by the node's computational power expressed in Gflops. This estimate makes the assumption that the node's *Throughput* is a linear function of the computing power. To estimate the β_{app} we assume this parameter is not influenced by both the heterogeneity of the input data used for its estimate and the size of the data blocks that a node has to process. In order to support our assumption, we investigated on the behavior of this parameter in the case of two typical Hadoop applications: **WordCount** and **InvertedIndex**. The object of the investigation was to prove the independence of the β_{app} from the type and the size of the input data.

WordCount reads text files and counts how often words occur. The input and the output data are both text files. The output file is a list of words each followed by its occurrence in the input file. WordCount was executed on an input text file of a 4 GB Wikipedia dump. We started with a 500 MB sample, and then we considered samples of 1 GB, 2 GB and 4 GB size respectively. The observed result for the β_{app} are shown in Fig. 5(a). The graph shows that the variance between the maximum and minimum of β_{app} is negligible, so we can deduce that size of the input data does not affect the compression factor in an appreciable way. Let us now consider the analysis of the β_{app} evaluated on different data samples. We want to verify that whatever the particular data sample (split, in the figure), the β_{app} value is not influenced. The input data was then divided into splits of same size each time, and the compression factor for each sample was computed. Results are shown in Fig. 5(b). The experiment was run several times, each time with a different split size (from 500 MB up to 4 GB). Again, no appreciable variation of β_{app} can be observed.

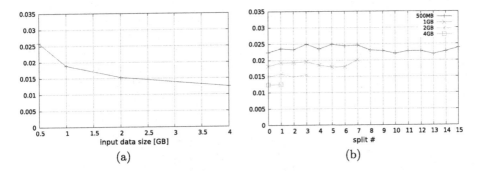

Fig. 5. Variations of beta in the WordCount application

InvertedIndex is a word-oriented mechanism for indexing a text collection in order to speed up the searching task. The inverted file structure is composed of two elements: the vocabulary and the occurrences. The vocabulary is the set of words in the text. For each word, a list of all the positions where the word appears is stored. The set of all those lists is called the occurrences. These positions can refer to either words or characters. We analyzed the execution of the InvertedIndex application on an input file originated from a 8 GB StackOverFlow dump. Figure 6(a) and (b) reports the obtained results. The considerations made for the WordCount application apply for the InvertedIndex as well.

To conclude, the investigation showed that the β_{app} is invariant to both the size and the type of the considered input data. This fact support the assumption made in Sect. 3 that the value of β_{app} computed on whatever small-sized data sample can be reasonably used as a good estimate of the β_{app} of a big data set as well.

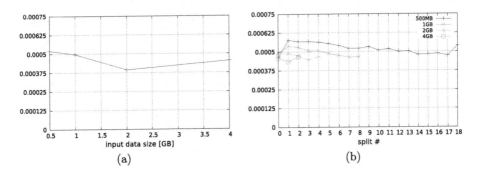

Fig. 6. Variations of beta in the InvertedIndex application

4   Prototype Implementation and Test Case

We implemented a prototype of the scheduling system in Java. With the proto-type, we ran a few experiments in order to test the effectiveness and efficiency of our scheduling approach. This section explains how a TJEP is generated for real use case applications. We chose to run experiments on the *WordCount* and the *InvertedIndex* applications, that we analyzed in Sect. 3.2, for which the esti-mated compression factors turned out to be $\beta_{app} = 0.015$ and $\beta_{app} = 0.0005$ respectively. The reference computing context is the network topology depicted in Fig. 7.

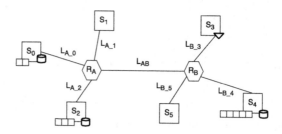

Fig. 7. Use case topology

The links connecting the computing nodes were configured to have the fol-lowing capacity: $L_{A\_0} = L_{A\_2} = L_{B\_3} = L_{AB} = 10\,\mathrm{MB/s}$; $L_{A\_1} = L_{B\_4} = L_{B\_5} = 5\,\mathrm{MB/s}$. Sites were assigned unbalanced computing capabilities in terms of Gflops. The Sites' computing power (Throughput) were estimated in a prelim-inary profiling phase (see Sect. 3.2). In the case of the WordCount, it gave the following results: $Throughput_{S0} = Throughput_{S2} = Throughput_{S4} = 10\,\mathrm{MB/s}$; $Throughput_{S1} = Throughput_{S3} = Throughput_{S5} = 50\,\mathrm{MB/s}$. The input data that both the applications need to process are organized in 10 data blocks of 128 MB. Data blocks reside in the network with this distribution: S_0 stores 2 data blocks; S_2 stores 3 data blocks; S_4 stores 5 data blocks.

When fed with the run the WordCount configuration, the scheduler generated 56376 potential execution paths in about 50 s[1]. The objective of the experiment was to compare the performance of the best execution path generated by our scheduler with that of the execution path of a plain hierarchical MapReduce, i.e., an execution path that makes use of no data transfer among sites, but just envisions to run MapReduce sub-jobs on the Sites holding the data and send the results to another Site for the Global reduce. Figure 8(a) depicts the graph representing the execution path of the no-data-transfer case for the Wordcount application. In Fig. 8(b) the graph modeling the best execution path (having the shortest completion time) is shown.

---

[1] The scheduler is a Java7 program running on PC with a 2.4 Ghz CPU and a 8 GB RAM.

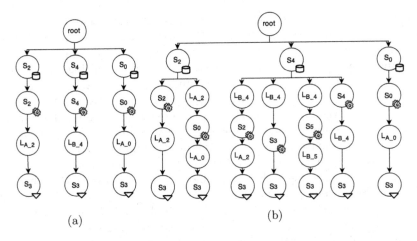

Fig. 8. Variations of beta in the WordCount application for (a) the no-transfer case and (b) the best case

Table 1. Completion time comparison.

	No-data-transfers case	Best case
WordCount	66.112 s	38.6304 s
InvertedIndex	64.0704 s	38.40768 s

The experiment result is condensed in Table 1. The result confirms that our scheduler is capable of finding an execution path which performs much better. In particular, in the WordCount case, the estimated completion time found by the scheduler is 58 % shorter than that of the standard path. In the case of the InvertedIndex application, the observed performance improvement is about 60 %.

5 Related Work

In the literature two main approaches are followed by researchers to efficiently process geo-distributed data: (a) enhanced versions of the plain Hadoop implementation which account for the nodes and the network heterogeneity (*Geo-hadoop* approach); (b) hierarchical frameworks which gather and merge results from many Hadoop instances locally run on distributed clusters (*Hierarchical* approach). The former approach aims at optimizing the job performance through the enforcement of a smart orchestration of the Hadoop steps. The latter's philosophy is to exploit the native potentiality of Hadoop on a local base and then merge the results collected from the distributed computation. In the following a brief review of those works is provided.

Geo-hadoop approaches reconsider the phases of the job's execution flow (Push, Map, Shuffle, Reduce) in a perspective where data are distributed at a geographic scale, and the available resources (compute nodes and network bandwidth) are not homogeneous. In the aim of reducing the job's average *makespan*, phases and the relative timing must be adequately coordinated. Some researchers have proposed enhanced version of Hadoop capable of optimizing only a single phase [6,8]. Heintz et al. [4] analyze the dynamics of the phases and address the need of making a comprehensive, end-to-end optimization of the job's execution flow. To this end, they present an analytical model which accounts for parameters such as the network links, the nodes capacity and the applications profile, and transforms the makespan minimization problem into a linear programming problem solvable with the Mixed Integer Programming technique.

Hierarchical approaches tackle the problem from a perspective that envisions two (or sometimes more) computing levels: a bottom level, where several plain MapReduce computations occur on local data only, and a top level, where a central entity coordinates the gathering of local computations and the packaging of the final result. In [7] authors present a hierarchical MapReduce architecture and introduces a load-balancing algorithm that makes workload distribution across multiple clusters. The balancing is guided by the number of cores available on each cluster, the number of Map tasks potentially runnable at each cluster and the nature (CPU or I/O bound) of the application. The authors also propose to compress data before their migration from one data center to another. Jayalath et al. [5] make an exhaustive analysis of the issues concerning the execution of MapReduce on geo-distributed data. The particular context addressed by authors is the one in which multiple MapReduce operations need to be performed in sequence on the same data.

6   Conclusion

The gradual increase of the information daily produced by devices connected to the Internet, such as smartphones, sensors, cameras and so on, combined with the enormous data stores found in traditional databases, has led to the definition of the Big Data concept. To efficiently process these heterogeneous data on a large scale, many distributed computing paradigms have been proposed, among which MapReduce stands out. In this paper we describe a solution based on hierarchical MapReduce that allows to process big data located in geodistributed datasets. Our approach involves the design of a scheduling system that, considering the available computational resources, the capacity of the links and the type of job applications to execute, is able to generate an execution plan that optimizes the completion time of a job. A prototype implementation is also discussed that proves the viability of the approach. Future work will focus on the development of other components of the presented architecture and on the implementation of a real large scale test-bed.

References

1. Andrews, G.E.: The Theory of Partitions, Encyclopedia of Mathematics and its Applications, vol. 2 (1976)
2. Cavallo, M., Di Modica, G., Carmelo, P., Tomarchio, O.: Context-aware mapreduce for geo-distributed big data. In: Proceedings of the 5th International Conference on Cloud Computing and Services Science (CLOSER 2015), pp. 414–421, Lisbon (Portugal), May 2015
3. Dean, J., Ghemawat, S.: MapReduce: simplified data processing on large clusters. In: Proceeding of the 6th Conference on Symposium on Operating Systems Design and Implementation (OSDI 2004). USENIX Association (2004)
4. Heintz, B., Chandra, A., Sitaraman, R., Weissman, J.: End-to-end optimization for geo-distributed mapreduce. IEEE Trans. Cloud Comput. **PP**(99), 1–14 (2014)
5. Jayalath, C., Stephen, J., Eugster, P.: From the cloud to the atmosphere: running mapreduce across data centers. IEEE Trans. Comput. **63**(1), 74–87 (2014)
6. Kim, S., Won, J., Han, H., Eom, H., Yeom, H.Y.: Improving hadoop performance in intercloud environments. SIGMETRICS Perform. Eval. Rev. **39**(3), 107–109 (2011). http://doi.acm.org/10.1145/2160803.2160873
7. Luo, Y., Guo, Z., Sun, Y., Plale, B., Qiu, J., Li, W.W.: A hierarchical framework for cross-domain mapreduce execution. In: Proceedings of the Second International Workshop on Emerging Computational Methods for the Life Sciences (ECMLS 2011), pp. 15–22 (2011). http://doi.acm.org/10.1145/1996023.1996026
8. Mattess, M., Calheiros, R.N., Buyya, R.: Scaling mapreduce applications across hybrid clouds to meet soft deadlines. In: Proceedings of the 2013 IEEE 27th International Conference on Advanced Information Networking and Applications (AINA 2013), pp. 629–636 (2013). http://dx.org/10.1109/AINA.2013.51
9. Miorandi, D., Sicari, S., Pellegrini, F.D., Chlamtac, I.: Internet of things: vision, applications and research challenges. Ad Hoc Netw. **10**(7), 1497–1516 (2012)
10. Open Networking Foundation: Software-Defined Networking: The New Norm for Networks. White paper, Open Networking Foundation, April 2012. http://www.opennetworking.org/images/stories/downloads/sdn-resources/white-papers/wp-sdn-newnorm.pdf
11. Petri, I., Montes, J.D., Zou, M., Rana, O.F., Beach, T., Li, H., Rezgui, Y.: In-transit data analysis and distribution in a multi-cloud environment using cometcloud. In: International Conference on Future Internet of Things and Cloud (FiCloud 2014), pp. 471–476 (2014)
12. Wright, P., Manieri, A.: Internet of things in the cloud - theory and practice. In: CLOSER - Proceedings of the 4th International Conference on Cloud Computing and Services Science, April 2014, pp. 164–169 (2014)
13. Yang, H., Dasdan, A., Hsiao, R., Parker, D.S.: Map-reduce-merge: simplified relational data processing on large clusters. In: Proceedings of the 2007 ACM SIGMOD International Conference on Management of Data (SIGMOD 2007), pp. 1029–1040 (2007)
14. Zikopoulos, P., Eaton, C.: Understanding Big Data: Analytics for Enterprise Class Hadoop and Streaming Data. McGraw Hill, New York (2011)
15. Zoghbi, A., Stojmenovic, I.: Fast algorithms for generating integer partitions. Int. J. Comput. Math. **80**, 319–332 (1994)

CloudFIT, a PaaS Platform for IoT Applications over Pervasive Networks

Luiz Angelo Steffenel[1(✉)] and Manuele Kirch Pinheiro[2]

[1] CReSTIC Laboratory, SysCom Team,
Université de Reims Champagne-Ardenne, Reims, France
`luiz-angelo.steffenel@univ-reims.fr`
[2] Centre de Recherche en Informatique,
Université Paris 1 Panthéon-Sorbonne, Paris, France
`manuele.kirsch-pinheiro@univ-paris1.fr`

Abstract. IoT applications are the next important step towards the establishment of mobiquitous systems, but at the same time these environments raise important challenges when considering data distribution and processing. While most IoT applications today rely on clouds as back-end, critical applications that require fast response or enhanced privacy levels may require proximity services specially tailored to these needs. The deployment of private cloud services on top of pervasive grids represent an interesting alternative to traditional cloud infrastructures. In this work we present CloudFIT, a PaaS middleware that allows the creation of private clouds over pervasive environments. Using a Map-Reduce application as example, we show how CloudFIT provides both storage and data aggregation/analysis capabilities at the service of IoT networks.

1 Introduction

Today, cloud computing is a widespread paradigm that relies on the externalization of services to a distant platform with elastic computing capabilities. Unsurprisingly, Big Data analytics profits from the computing capabilities from the cloud, making it the predilection platform for information extraction and analysis.

The emergence of Internet of Things (IoT) has naturally attired the attention of developers and companies, which mostly rely on cloud services to interconnect devices and gather information. Indeed, platforms like Carriots[1] or ThinkSpeak[2] now propose PaaS APIs to collect information, visualize and control IoT devices.

Contrarily to the case of Wireless Sensor Networks (WSNs), however, IoT has a much more complex data transfer pattern that is not always tailored for a cloud. While data from WSNs naturally flows from the sensors to a "sink" repository that can gather information and handle it to the analytics software,

---

[1] https://www.carriots.com/.

[2] https://thingspeak.com/.

© Springer International Publishing Switzerland 2016
A. Celesti and P. Leitner (Eds.): ESOCC 2015 Workshops, CCIS 567, pp. 20–32, 2016.
DOI: 10.1007/978-3-319-33313-7_2

IoT devices have M2M (Machine-to-Machine) capabilities beyond simple raw data transmission, as they are also information consumers and even actuators to the real environment.

Simply relying on a distant cloud infrastructure for data storage, processing and control imposes a non-negligible latency, a complete dependency on wide-area communications and the transmission of potentially sensible data across the network. From this point of view, it is clear that not all IoT applications would benefit from an external data handling.

Deploying a privative PaaS cloud for IoT is an interesting alternative to the complete externalization, as it ensures fast reaction and privacy levels tailored to the specific needs of an enterprise or application. Indeed, the omnipresence of IoT devices often raises questions about the dissemination of sensitive data, a problem that public cloud systems can minimize through the use of heavy layers of cryptography and anonymization, but never solve.

In this paper we present CloudFIT, a distributed computing middleware designed for pervasive environments that offers IoT applications both storage, data aggregation and analysis capabilities. In addition, CloudFIT does not require a dedicated infrastructure as a CloudFIT "grid" can be deployed over existing resources on the enterprise (desktop PCs, servers, etc.) and perform both the data aggregation, filtering and analysis required by IoT devices.

After describing CloudFIT, we illustrate its operation through the deployment of a data intensive application over a cluster. We deploy a MapReduce application over CloudFIT, and compare its performance against the well-known Hadoop middleware[3], a Big Data platform specially designed for dedicated clusters.

The paper is structured as follows: Section 2 discusses the challenges for the IoT applications and the reasons why a traditional cloud services is not always recommended. Instead, we emphasize alternatives for cloud computing that ensure both efficiency and data privacy. Section 3 focuses on the case of data-intensive problems and discusses the main challenges for its deployment over pervasive grids, analyzing some related works. Section 4 presents the architecture of CloudFIT and its characteristics related to fault tolerance and volatility support. This session also discuss how to interface IoT devices and applications with CloudFIT. Section 5 introduces our implementation of a MapReduce application over CloudFIT, discussing both implementation issues and performance evaluations. Finally, Sect. 6 concludes this paper and sets the lines of our next development efforts.

2   Cloud Services and IoT

2.1   Private Clouds, Cloudlets and the IoT

When the cloud computing paradigm started, we observed the development of middlewares and tools for the establishment of private and mixed cloud

---

[3] http://hadoop.apache.org/.

infrastructures. Most of these tools, like Eucalyptus [18], Nimbus [12] or Open-Nebula [17], are designed to provide IaaS on top of dedicated resources like clusters or private data-centers. While extremely powerful, the deployment of these environments is complex and requires dedicated resources, which minimizes their advantage against public cloud infrastructures like Amazon EC2.

Establishing on-demand cloud services on top of existing resources is also alternative to the complete externalization of services in a cloud. For example, [22] explore the limitations of mobile devices and the inaptitude of current solutions to externalize mobile services through the use of Cloudlets, i.e., virtual machines deployed on-demand in the vicinity of the demanding devices. Using cloudlets deployed as Wi-Fi hotspots in coffee shops, libraries, etc., the authors of [22] suggest a simple way to offer enough computing power to perform complex computations (services) all while limiting the service latency. Please note that these cloudlets do not work as a single entity/platform but instead act as detached handlers for specific demands.

Proximity cloud services can also be used to perform an initial processing on the data. For instance, [20] presents a platform where context information is collected, filtered and analyzed on several layers. This way, basic context actions may be decided/performed in a close area range, while a much deep analysis of the context information may be performed by external servers. This layered analysis can also be used to ensure privacy properties, for example by anonymizing the data that will be used to the global context analysis. As context my represent multiple and heterogeneous kind of information, this approach can also be implemented to general Big Data analytics on sensor data or access logs, for example.

Another usage for private clouds relates to the reinforcement of the security of a network [11]. In a mobile network (as well as in an IoT pervasive network), devices cannot rely in a single security device in the entrance of the network because multimodal connections may be established with outside devices via Wi-Fi, 3G, Bluetooth, etc. If nowadays similar procedures can be implemented through the use of 802.1x authentication or VPNs, their configuration complexity requires a high technical knowledge. A better alternative relies on a mutual monitoring system sharing information is created around a confidence zone (community). Joining a confidence zone is only possible if the device pass some control checks and, similarly, devices that become "dangerous" due to a virus or a Trojan can be blocked and removed from the community.

We consider that deploying cloud services for IoT over pervasive networks is a natural approach, as the heterogeneity and the dynamicity of the devices impose a frequent adaptation on both network interconnections and computing requirements.

2.2   Cloud Services over Pervasive Grids

Pervasive grids can be defined as large-scale infrastructures with specific characteristics in terms of volatility, reliability, connectivity, security, etc. According to [19], pervasive grids represent the extreme generalization of the grid concept, seamlessly integrating pervasive sensing/actuating instruments and devices together with classical high performance systems. In the general case, pervasive grids rely on volatile resources that may appear and disappear from the grid, according their availability. Indeed, mobile devices should be able to come into the environment in a natural way as their owner moves [6]. Also, devices from different natures, from the desktop and laptop PCs until the last generation tablets, should be integrated in seamlessly way. These environments are therefore characterized by three main requirements:

- The volatility of its components, whose participation is a matter of opportunity and availability;
- The heterogeneity of these components, whose capabilities may vary on different aspects (platform, OS, memory and storage capacity, network connection, etc.);
- The dynamic management of available resources, since the internal status of these devices may vary during their participation into the grid environment.

Such dynamic nature of pervasive grids represents an important challenge for executing data intensive applications. Context-awareness and nodes volatility become key aspects for successfully executing such applications over pervasive grids, but also for the handling and transmission of voluminous datasets.

Our approach to implement cloud-like services over pervasive networks relies on the use of an overlay network provided by a P2P system. In this approach, the P2P overlay provides all communication and fault tolerance properties required for the operation on a pervasive network, as well as some additional services like DHT storage that can help implementing additional services.

Indeed, if P2P systems are widely known for their use on storage and sharing applications, they can also be used as platforms for coordination and distribution of computing tasks. Solutions like CONFIIT [10], DIET [3] have demonstrated the interest of P2P to support computing problems in distributed and heterogeneous environments.

3   Data-Intensive Applications on Pervasive Grids

In spite of a wide tradition on distributed computing projects, most pervasive grid middlewares have focused on computing-intensive parallel applications with few I/O and loose dependencies between the tasks. Enabling these environments to support data-intense applications is still a challenge, both in performance and reliability. We believe that MapReduce is an interesting paradigm for data-intensive applications on pervasive grids as it presents a simple task distribution mechanism, easily implemented on a pervasive environment, but also a challenging data distribution pattern. Enabling MapReduce on pervasive grids raises many research issues, which we can decompose in two subtopics: data distribution and data processing.

There are two approaches to distribute large volume of data to large number of distributed nodes. The first approach relies on P2P protocols where peers collaboratively participate to the distribution of the data by exchanging file chunks [7, 15, 25]. The second approach is to use a content delivery service where files are distributed to a network of volunteers [13, 16].

Concerning data processing on pervasive grids, some authors have tried to improve the processing capabilities of Hadoop to take into account the volatility of the nodes. Indeed, Zaharia et al. [26] Chen et al. [5] or Ahmad et al. [1] deals with heterogeneity of the supporting infrastructure, proposing different scheduling algorithms that can improve Hadoop response time. Lin et al. [14] explore the limitations of Hadoop over volatile, non-dedicated resources. They propose the use of a hybrid architecture where a small set of reliable nodes are used to provide resources to volatile nodes.

Due to the simplicity of its processing model (map and reduce phases), data processing can be easily adapted to a given distributed middleware, which can coordinate tasks through different techniques (centralized task server, work-stealing/bag of tasks, speculative execution, etc.). Nevertheless, good performances can only be achieved through the minimization of data transfers over the network, which is one of the key aspects of Hadoop HDFS filesystem. Only few initiatives associate data-intense computing with large-scale distributed storage on volatile resources. In [4], the authors present an architecture following the super-peer approach where the super-peers serve as cache data server, handle jobs submissions and coordinate execution of parallel computations.

4   CloudFIT

In this work we present our efforts to enable MapReduce applications over the P2P distributed computing middleware CloudFIT [23]. The CloudFIT framework (Fig. 1) is structured around collaborative nodes connected over an overlay network. CloudFIT was designed to be independent of the underlying overlay, and the current version supports both Pastry [21] and TomP2P overlay networks [2]. Pastry is one of the most known P2P overlays and is widely employed in distributed computing environments. TomP2P is a more recent P2P library, enjoying an active development community.

An application for CloudFIT must provide a java class that implements two basic API methods: how many tasks to solve (`setNumberOfBlocks()`) and how to compute an individual task (`executeBlock(number, required[])`). When executing, each node owns the different parameters of the current computations (a list of tasks and associated results) and is able to locally decide which tasks still need to be computed and can carry the work autonomously if no other node can be contacted. Access to the storage is also provided through the API, if required. The status of completed tasks (optionally including the partial results from these tasks) are distributed among the nodes, contributing therefore to the coordination of the computing tasks and form a global view of the calculus.

The basic scheduling mechanism simply randomly rearranges the list of tasks at each node, which helps the computation of tasks in parallel without requiring

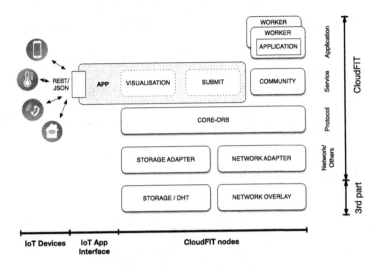

Fig. 1. CloudFIT architecture stack

additional communication between nodes. This simple scheduler mechanism was designed to allow idle processes to speculatively execute incomplete tasks, reducing the "tail effect" when a task is computed by a slow node. The scheduling mechanism supports task dependencies (allowing the composition of DAGs) and can be also be improved through the use of a context module [24] that provides additional information about the nodes capacities.

Finally, fault tolerance is ensured both by the overlay (network connections, etc.) and by the computing platform. Indeed, as long as a task is not completed, other nodes on the grid may pick it up for execution. In this way, when a node fails or leaves the grid, other nodes may recover tasks originally started by the crashed node. Inversely, when a node joins the CloudFIT community, it receives an update about the tasks current status and the working data, allowing it to start working on available (incomplete) tasks.

4.1 CloudFIT Services for IoT Devices and Applications

As previously stated, CloudFIT provides a pervasive PaaS for IoT applications. While we believe that CloudFIT can be deployed directly over IoT devices running Android (with the TomP2P overlay) or Linux on Raspberry Pi, the heterogeneity and limited resources of these devices make this approach very unreliable. Indeed, a node integrating the CloudFIT network must perform all the routing, storage and computing tasks as the others, and this can be both overloading and inefficient (please see Sect. 5.5).

A better approach, instead, is to use CloudFIT as a computing backend for IoT devices and applications. This mixed architecture, as illustrated in the left side of Fig. 1, allows an IoT application connected to CloudFIT network to act as an interface to gather data and launch computing tasks according to the application needs.

While the development of an interface for IoT devices can be provided through *REST/json* calls or even a direct a connection to the devices via Bluetooth or Wi-Fi, it is outside the scope of this paper. Instead, the next sections illustrate the deployment of a MapReduce application over CloudFIT. This is one of several computing intensive tasks that can be performed on CloudFIT to support IoT applications.

5   MapReduce over CloudFIT

5.1   MapReduce

MapReduce [8] is a parallel programming paradigm successfully used by large Internet service providers to perform computations on massive amounts of data. The key strength of the MapReduce model is its inherently high degree of parallelism that should enable processing of petabytes of data in a couple of hours on large clusters.

Computations on MapReduce deal with pairs of key-values (k, V), and a MapReduce algorithm (a job) follows a two-step procedure:

1. map: from a set of key/value pairs from the input, the map function generates a set of intermediate pairs $(k_1; V_1) \rightarrow \{(k_2; V_2)\}$;
2. reduce: from the set of intermediate pairs, the reduce function merges all intermediate values associated with the same intermediate key, so that $(k_2; \{V_2\}) \rightarrow \{(k_3; V_3)\}$.

When implemented on a distributed system, the intermediate pairs for a given key k_2 may be scattered among several nodes. The implementation must therefore gather all pairs for each key k_2 so that the reduce function can merge them into the final result. Additional features that may be granted by the MapReduce implementation include the splitting of the input data among the nodes, the scheduling of the jobs' component tasks, and the recovery of tasks hold by failed nodes.

Hadoop, one of the most popular implementations of MapReduce, provides these services through a dual layered architecture where tasks scheduling and monitoring are accomplished through a master-slave platform, while the data management is accomplished by a second master-slave platform on top of the hierarchical HDFS file-system. Such master-slave architecture makes Hadoop not suitable for Pervasive Grids.

5.2   Map, Reduce and Task Dependencies

In order to implement a MapReduce application under the FIIT model, tasks inside a Map or Reduce job must be independent, all while preserving a causal relation between Map and Reduce. Therefore, several tasks are launched during the Map phase, producing a set of (k_i, V_i) pairs. Each task is assigned to a single file/data block and therefore may execute independently from the other tasks in the same phase. Once completed, the results from each task can be broadcasted to all computing nodes and, by consequence, each node contains a copy of the entire set of (k_i, V_i) pairs at the end of the Map phase. At the end of the first step, a Reduce job is launched using as input parameter the results from the map phase.

In our prototype, the number of Map and Reduce tasks was defined to roughly mimic the behavior of Hadoop, which tries to guess the required number of Map and Reduce processes. For instance, we set the number of Map tasks to correspond to the number of input files, and the number of Reduce tasks depends on the size of the dataset and the transitive nature of the data. Please note that CloudFIT may optionally perform a result aggregation after each job completion, just like Hadoop *combiners*.

Because Hadoop relies on specific classes to handle data, we tried to use the same ones in CloudFIT implementation as a way to keep compatibility with the Hadoop API. However, some of these classes were too dependent on inner elements of Hadoop, forcing us to develop our own equivalents, at least for the moment (further works shall reinforce the compatibility with Hadoop API). For instance, we had to substitute the OutputCollector class with our own MultiMap class, while the rest of the application remains compatible with both Hadoop and CloudFIT.

5.3   Data Management, Storage and Reliability

As stated before, CloudFIT was designed to broadcast the status about completed tasks to all computing nodes, and this status may include the tasks' results. By including the results, CloudFIT ensures $n - resiliency$ as all nodes will have a copy of the data.

This resiliency behavior was mainly designed for computing intensive tasks that produce a small amount of data as result. On data-intensive applications, however, $n - resiliency$ may be prohibitive as not only all nodes need to hold a copy of all task's data, but also because broadcasting several megabytes/gigabytes over the network is a major performance issue.

In our efforts to implement MapReduce over CloudFIT we chose a different approach to ensure the scalability of the network all while preserving good reliability levels. Hence, we rely on the DHT to perform the storage of tasks results as {*task_key, task_result*} tuples, while the task status messages broadcast the keys from each task. As both PAST and TomP2P DHT implement data replication among the nodes with a predefined replication factor k, we can ensure minimal fault tolerance levels all while improving the storage performance.

5.4   Performance Evaluation Against Hadoop

In order to evaluate the performance of MapReduce over CloudFIT we implemented the traditional WordCount application and compared it against WordCount 1.0 application from Hadoop tutorial.

To make this first evaluation fair, we conducted this first experiment over 8 machines from the ROMEO Computing Center[4]. ROMEO cluster nodes are composed by bi-Intel Xeon E5-2650 2.6 GHz (Ivy Bridge) 8 cores and 32 GB of memory, interconnected by an Infiniband QDR network at 40 Gbps. Hadoop YARN nodes run with default parameters (number of *vcores* = 8, available memory = 8 GB), parameters that we reproduced on CloudFIT for fairness (i.e., by limiting the number of parallel tasks by node and setting the maximum java VM memory).

Two different versions of CloudFIT were tested, one using the FreePastry overlay with the PAST DHT at the storage layer, and the second one with the TomP2P overlay and its Kademlia-based DHT.

The experiments considered the overall execution time (map + reduce phases) of both CloudFIT and Hadoop implementations when varying the total amount of data (512 MB to 2 GB). The data was obtained from a corpus of textbooks from the Gutenberg Project and split in blocks of 64 MB to reproduce the size of an HDFS data block. The results obtained when running on an 8 nodes cluster are presented on Fig. 2, which shows the average of 10 executions for each data size.

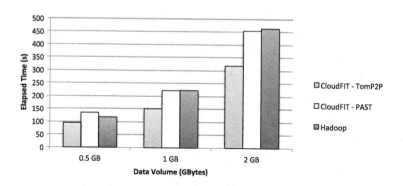

Fig. 2. WordCount MapReduce performance on 8 nodes

At first glance, we observe that the CloudFIT/TomP2P implementation easily outperforms both CloudFIT/PAST and Hadoop, which have aproximately the same performance. A deeper analysis of the CloudFIT/PAST implementation show that the PAST DHT experimented a performance bottleneck related to the use of mutable objects. Indeed, mutable objects are useful to gather $(k; V)$ pairs from different tasks but they force a non-negligible overhead at the DHT

---

[4] https://romeo.univ-reims.fr.

controller, which must scan the data for changes and trigger replication updates. One solution to improve the PAST performance is to rely on immutable objects that do not suffer from this problem, but this requires the usage of alternative data structures to reproduce the $(k; V)$ associations from MapReduce.

This is an encouraging result as it demonstrates the interest of CloudFIT as a platform for Big Data applications. Depending on the storage layer, we can provide good performance levels without sacrificing the platform flexibility. In addition, the modular organization of CloudFIT allows connecting other storage supports like BitDew [9], external databases, URLs, etc., according to the application requirements.

5.5 Performance Evaluation on a Pervasive Grid

As the previous section demonstrate that CloudFIT can execute MapReduce applications as fast as Hadoop in a HPC cluster, the next step in our experiments considered the creation of a pervasive cluster on top of common desktop equipments. For instance, we executed CloudFIT/TomP2P over a network composed by three laptop computers connected through a Wi-Fi 802.11 g network. The specifications for each model are presented in Table 1. Please note that these machines were not tuned for performance and indeed CloudFIT had to share the resources with other applications like anti-virus, word processors, etc.

Table 1. Specification of the nodes on the pervasive cluster

Laptop	Processor	GHz	Cores	Threads	Memory	OS
MacBook Air	Intel® Core™ i7-4650U	1.7	2	4	8 GB	MacOS 10.10.3
HP Pavillon dv6	Intel® Core™ i5-2450M	2.5	2	4	8 GB	Windows 7
Lenovo U110	Intel® Core™ 2 Duo L7500	1.6	2	2	4 GB	Ubuntu Linux 15.4

Figure 3 presents the execution of the WordCount application with three different data sets, and we compare the execution time obtained on the pervasive grid with the performance obtained over 3 nodes from the ROMEO cluster. Post-execution analysis indicated that in spite of the processors type and speeds, one factor that mainly influenced the performance was the network speed. Indeed, as the MapReduce application performs several read/write operation over the DHT, the network is a major bottleneck: to write 64 MB of data on the DHT using the ROMEO cluster (equipped with an Infiniband interconnection) we need in average 2 s, while the Wi-Fi connection used on the pervasive cluster required in average 15 s. Another element that contributes to the reduced performance of the pervasive environment is the competition between faster and slower nodes: while both node types have similar chances to draw tasks to execute at the beginning, faster nodes will complete their tasks first and finally re-execute the tasks from slower nodes, wasting computing resources.

While comparing both environments is not really fair, the conclusion is that one does need a dedicated environment to extract enough computing power for several applications. In fact, the flexibility of the pervasive cluster allows nodes to join or leave the cluster without interfering with the execution, making it a strategic tool for most organizations that cannot rely neither in a dedicated cluster neither in a distant datacenter/cloud infrastructure. Further, CloudFIT has the advantage that it can be easily run on Windows, contrarily to Hadoop, which reinforcing its ability to create pervasive clusters from the available resources.

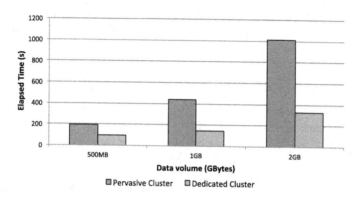

Fig. 3. WordCount MapReduce on 3 nodes: pervasive vs dedicated cluster

6 Conclusions and Future Work

IoT networks are the next important step towards the establishment of mobiquitous systems. Contrarily to Sensor Networks, IoT has a much richer M2M pattern that is not always adapted to the cloud computing paradigm. Indeed, moving data to distant platforms for filtering, analysis and decision-making is both expensive and time consuming, which not always fits the IoT applications requirements.

In this paper we present CloudFIT, a PaaS middleware that allows the creation of private clouds at the proximity of the demanding IoT devices. Using a P2P overlay, CloudFIT offers both storage and computing capabilities on top of pervasive networks.

We illustrate the usage of CloudFIT through the deployment of a MapReduce application and the comparative performance analysis with Hadoop. Indeed, we demonstrate that CloudFIT offers performance levels similar to those of Hadoop but with a better support for dynamic and heterogeneous environments.

Of course, the possibilities that CloudFIT offers to IoT are not limited to MapReduce applications. The CloudFIT API and its distributed computing model allow many other usages, as devices can use the platform as a storage support, data analysis support, intensive computing support, etc. By coordinating activities over CloudFIT, IoT devices and applications can elaborate a supply chain from data gathering to reasoning and actuation.

Acknowledgment. The authors would like to thank their partners in the PER-MARE project (http://cosy.univ-reims.fr/PER-MARE) and acknowledge the financial support given to this research by the CAPES/MAEE/ANII STIC-AmSud collaboration program (project number 13STIC07).

References

1. Ahmad, F., Chakradhar, S.T., Raghunathan, A., Vijaykumar, T.N.: Tarazu: optimizing mapreduce on heterogeneous clusters. SIGARCH Comput. Archit. News **40**(1), 61–74 (2012)
2. Bocek, T., et al.: TomP2P, a P2P-based high performance key–value pair storage library. http://tomp2p.net/
3. Caron, E., Desprez, F., Lombard, F., Nicod, J.-M., Philippe, L., Quinson, M., Suter, F.: A scalable approach to network enabled servers. In: Monien, B., Feldmann, R.L. (eds.) Euro-Par 2002. LNCS, vol. 2400, pp. 907–910. Springer, Heidelberg (2002)
4. Cesario, E., De Caria, N., Mastroianni, C., Talia, D.: Distributed data mining using a public resource computing framework. In: Desprez, F., Getov, V., Priol, T., Yahyapour, R. (eds.) Grids, P2P and Service computing, pp. 33–44, Springer (2010)
5. Chen, Q., Zhang, D., Guo, M., Deng, Q., Guo, S.: Samr: a self-adaptive mapreduce scheduling algorithm in heterogeneous environment. In: Proceedings of the 2010 10th IEEE International Conference on Computer and Information Technology, CIT 2010, pp. 2736–2743. IEEE Computer Society, Washington, D.C. (2010)
6. Coronato, A., Pietro, G.D.: MiPeG: a middleware infrastructure for pervasive grids. Future Gener. Comput. Syst. **24**(1), 17–29 (2008)
7. Costa, F., Silva, L., Fedak, G., Kelley, I.: Optimizing data distribution in desktop grid platforms. Parallel Process. Lett. **18**(3), 391–410 (2008)
8. Dean, J., Ghemawat, S.: MapReduce: simplified data processing on large clusters. Commun. ACM **51**(1), 107–113 (2008)
9. Fedak, G., He, H., Cappello, F.: BitDew: a programmable environment for large-scale data management and distribution. In: SC 2008: Proceedings of the 2008 ACM/IEEE conference on Supercomputing, pp. 1–12. IEEE Press, Piscataway (2008)
10. Flauzac, O., Krajecki, M., Steffenel, L.: CONFIIT: a middleware for peer-to-peer computing. J. Supercomput. **53**(1), 86–102 (2010)
11. Flauzac, O., Nolot, F., Rabat, C., Steffenel, L.: Grid of security: a decentralized enforcement of the network security. In: Gupta, M., Walp, J., Sharman, R. (eds.) Threats, Countermeasures and Advances in Applied Information Security, pp. 426–443. IGI Global, April 2012
12. Keahey, K., Tsugawa, M., Matsunaga, A., Fortes, J.: Sky computing. IEEE Internet Comput. **13**(5), 43–51 (2009). http://dx.doi.org/10.1109/MIC.2009.94
13. Kelley, I., Taylor, I.: A peer-to-peer architecture for data-intensive cycle sharing. In: Proceedings of the First International Workshop on Network-Aware Data Management (NDM 2011), pp. 65–72. ACM, New York (2011)
14. Lin, H., Ma, X., Archuleta, J., Feng, W., Gardner, M., Zhang, Z.: Moon: mapreduce on opportunistic environments. In: Proceedings of the 19th ACM International Symposium on High Performance Distributed Computing (HPDC 2010), pp. 95–106 (2010)

15. Marozzo, F., Talia, D., Trunfio, P.: A peer-to-peer framework for supporting mapre-duce applications in dynamic cloud environments. In: Antonopoulos, N., Gillam, L. (eds.) Cloud Computing. Computer Communications and Networks, pp. 113–125. Springer, London (2010)

16. Mastroianni, C., Cozza, P., Talia, D., Kelley, I., Taylor, I.: A scalable super-peer approach for public scientific computation. Future Gener. Comput. Syst. **25**(3), 213–223 (2009)

17. Moreno-Vozmediano, R., Montero, R.S., Llorente, I.M.: IaaS cloud architecture: from virtualized datacenters to federated cloud infrastructures. Computer **45**(12), 65–72 (2012)

18. Nurmi, D., Wolski, R., Grzegorczyk, C., Obertelli, G., Soman, S., Youseff, L., Zagorodnov, D.: The eucalyptus open-source cloud-computing system. In: 9th IEEE/ACM International Symposium on Cluster Computing and the Grid, CCGrid 2009, Shanghai, China, 18–21 May 2009, pp. 124–131 (2009). http://doi.ieeecomputersociety.org/10.1109/CCGRID.2009.93

19. Parashar, M., Pierson, J.M.: Pervasive grids: challenges and opportunities. In: Li, K., Hsu, C., Yang, L., Dongarra, J., Zima, H. (eds.) Handbook of Research on Scalable Computing Technologies, pp. 14–30. IGI Global (2010)

20. Rottenberg, S., Leriche, S., Lecocq, C., Taconet, C.: Vers une définition d'un système réparti multi-échelle. In: UBIMOB 2012 - 8èmes Journées Francophones Mobilité et Ubiquité, pp. 178–183 (2012)

21. Rowstron, A., Druschel, P.: Pastry: scalable, distributed object location and rout-ing for large-scale peer-to-peer systems. In: IFIP/ACM International Conference on Distributed Systems Platforms (Middleware), pp. 329–350, November 2001

22. Satyanarayanan, M.: Mobile computing: the next decade. SIGMOBILE Mobile Comput. Commun. Rev. **15**, 2–10 (2011)

23. Steffenel, L., Flauzac, O., Charao, A.S., Barcelos, P.P., Stein, B., Nesmachnow, S., Pinheiro, M.K., Diaz, D.: PER-MARE: adaptive deployment of mapreduce over pervasive grids. In: Proceeding 8th International Conference on P2P, Parallel, Grid, Cloud and Internet Computing, October 2013

24. Steffenel, L., Flauzac, O., Charao, A., Barcelos, P., Stein, B.: Cassales, G., Nesmachnow, S., Rey, J., Cogorno, M., Kirsch-Pinheiro, M., Souveyet, C.: Mapre-duce challenges on pervasive grids. J. Comput. Sci. **10**(11), 2194–2210 (2014)

25. Vazhkudai, S., Freeh, V., Ma, X., Strickland, J., Tammineedi, N., Scott, S.: Free-Loader: scavenging desktop storage resources for scientific data. In: Proceedings of Supercomputing (SC 2005), Seattle (2005)

26. Zaharia, M., Konwinski, A., Joseph, A.D., Katz, R., Stoica, I.: Improving mapre-duce performance in heterogeneous environments. In: Proceeding of the 8th USENIX Conference on Operating Systems Design and Implementation, OSDI 2008, pp. 29–42. USENIX Association (2008)

Design of an IoT Cloud System for Container Virtualization on Smart Objects

Davide Mulfari, Maria Fazio, Antonio Celesti[✉], Massimo Villari,
and Antonio Puliafito

DICIEAMA, University of Messina,
Contrada Di Dio, 98166 Sant'Agata, Messina, Italy
{dmulfari,mfazio,acelesti,mvillari,apuliafito}@unime.it
http://mdslab.unime.it

Abstract. Nowadays, container virtualization is a lightweight alternative to the hypervisor-based approach. Recent improvements in Linux kernel allow to execute containers on smart objects, that are, single board computers running Linux-based operating systems. By considering several IoT application scenarios, it is crucial to rely on cloud services able to deploy and customize pieces of software running on target smart objects. To achieve this goal, in this paper, we focus our attention on a Message Oriented Middleware for Cloud (MON4C), a system designed to compose cloud facilities by means of a flexible federation-enabled communication system. Its objective is to provide Internet of Things (IoT) services in a complex smart environment, such as a smart city, where smart objects interact each others and with the cloud infrastructure. More specifically, we discuss how MOM4C can be extended to support container virtualization on Linux embedded devices in order to easily deploy IoT applications in a flexible fashion and we present the design of related software modules.

Keywords: Cloud computing · Container based virtualization · IoT · Embedded systems · Linux

1 Introduction

Resource virtualization is one of the key concepts in cloud computing and it refers to the act of creating a virtual (rather than physical) version of "something", including but not limited to a virtual computer hardware platform, operating system (OS), storage device, or computer network resources. Virtualization consists of using an intermediate software layer on top of an underlying system in order to provide abstractions of multiple virtual resources. The latter software components are known as Virtual Machines (VMs) and they can be viewed as isolated execution contexts. Nowadays, several virtualization techniques are available. One of the most popular is the hypervisor-based virtualization, which requires a Virtual Machine Monitor (VMM) software module on top of a "host" OS that provides a full abstraction of VMs. In this case, each VM has its own

© Springer International Publishing Switzerland 2016
A. Celesti and P. Leitner (Eds.): ESOCC 2015 Workshops, CCIS 567, pp. 33–47, 2016.
DOI: 10.1007/978-3-319-33313-7_3

"guest" OS that is completely isolated from others. This enables us to execute multiple different OSs on a single physical host OS. Examples of such software solutions include: Xen, VMware, Oracle VirtualBox and KVM.

Recently, a lightweight alternative technology is the container-based virtualization, also known as OS level virtualization. This kind of virtualization partitions the physical machines resources, creating multiple isolated user-space instances [1]. Figure 1 depicts the key difference between the aforementioned virtualization technologies. While the hypervisor based virtualization provides a full abstraction for guest OS(s) (one per VM), the container based virtualization works at the OS level, providing abstractions directly for the "guest" processes. In essence, hypervisor solutions work at the hardware abstraction level and containers operate at the system call layer.

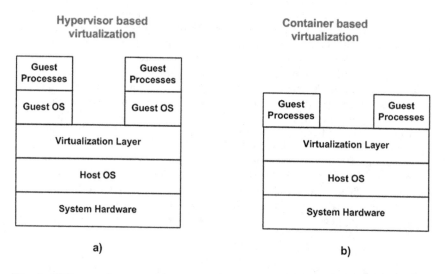

Fig. 1. Difference between (a) hypervisor and (b) container based virtualization.

As motivated in [1], all the containers share a single kernel; so the container based virtualization is supposed to have a weaker isolation when compared to hypervisor based virtualization. However, from the point of view of the users, each container looks exactly like a stand-alone OS. Additionally, by considering a cloud computing scenario, developers can deploy higher densities with containers than with VMs on the same physical host. Another advantage of containers over VMs is that starting and shutting down a container is much faster than starting and shutting down a traditional VM equipped with a guest OS.

Recent technological developments have allowed container-based virtualization technology to support Single Board Computer (SBC) devices equipped with a modern Linux kernel supporting a suitable virtualization layer. In these scenarios, container based software seems to be an interesting approach to deploy and to customize software applications running on a SBC. More specifically, in the present paper, we focus on Internet of Things (IoT) application scenarios and we define "smart object" a SBC embedded device equipped with a Linux based OS that runs specialized pieces of software in order to grab and process data from external sensors. We intend to distribute multiple smart objects in a complex environment, such as a smart city, where it is crucial to rely on a cloud service able to deploy and to customize pieces of software running on target smart objects.

In order to pursue our goals, we consider a Message Oriented Middleware for Cloud (MOM4C) [2], a piece of middleware able to arrange customizable Cloud facilities by means of a flexible federation-enabled communication system. The considered middleware has very innovative features, that make efficient, scalable and versatile the Cloud service provisioning. In addition, MOM4C enables the development of distributed services over an asynchronous instant-messaging architecture, which can be used for intra/inter-domain communications. In Cloud computing environments, MOM4C allows to compose Cloud facilities according to client requirements. MOM4C has been designed to act as a "planetary system model", where the central star includes the core, i.e., all the basic communication functionalities of the piece of middleware and the planets are the Cloud utilities that can be used. Such a service provisioning model guarantees high scalability and customization of the required service. In addition, besides the basic communication functionalities, the core includes security mechanisms for guaranteeing secure data exchange.

More specifically the main contribution of this paper is to discuss how MOM4C can support Linux based smart objects in order to allow software architects to dynamically deploy pieces of software on them by means of container-based virtualization techniques. The proposed hardware/software infrastructure uses Docker as containers engine platform; within the last year, such a software has emerged as a standard runtime, image format, and "build system" for containers on several distributed Linux environments.

The remainder of this paper is organized as follows. In Sect. 2, we discuss related works. In Sect. 3, we provide an overview about the container based virtualization for Linux environments and IoT devices. In Sect. 4, we discuss how we extended MOM4C in order to support the container virtualization in IoT devices. A system prototype with implementation highlights is discussed in Sect. 5. Finally, Sect. 6 concludes the paper.

2   Related Work

Nowadays, containers represents an interesting alternative to VMs in the Cloud scenarios [3]. Although the concepts underlying containers such as namespaces are very mature, only recently containers have been adopted and standardized in mainstream OS(s), leading to a renaissance in the use of containers to provide isolation and resource control. Linux is the preferred OS for cloud environments due to its zero price, large ecosystem, good hardware support, good performance, and reliability. The kernel namespace feature needed to implement containers in

Linux has only become mature in the last few years since it was first discussed in 2006 [4]. Several articles have focused on container based virtualization technologies by considering Cloud computing scenarios. Docker [5] is a lightweight virtualization based on Linux Containers (LXC) that can completely encapsulate an application and its dependencies within a virtual container. In [6], the authors discuss the design and the implementation of Cloud system based on Docker, especially intended for a Platform as a Service (PaaS). As motivated in [7], Docker has been deployed within a platform for bioinformatics computing that exploits advanced Cloud services. Authors investigate the security level of Docker by considering two main areas: (1) the internal security of Docker, and (2) how Docker interacts with the security features of the Linux kernel, such as SELinux and AppArmor, in order to harden the host system. The proposed analysis shows that Docker provides a high level of isolation and resource limiting for its containers using namespaces, cgroups, and its copy-on-write file system, even with the default configuration. It also supports several kernel security features, which help in hardening the security of the host [8].

Nowadays, Cloud computing has emerged in different application fields including energy efficiency [9], storage [10], Assistive Technology [11], dataweb [12] and so on. Several manuscripts deal with the development of Cloud pieces of middleware, addressing specific issues and exploiting different technologies. To support application execution in the Cloud, in [13], authors present CloudScale. It is a piece of middleware for building Cloud applications like regular Java programs and easily deploy them into IaaS Clouds. It implements a declarative deployment model, in which application developers specify the scaling requirements and policies of their applications using the Aspect-Oriented Programming (AOP) model. A different approach is proposed in [14], which presents a low latency fault-tolerance piece of middleware for supporting distributed applications deployment within a Cloud environment. It is based on the leader/follower replication approach for maintaining strong replica consistency of the replica states. If a fault occurs, the reconfiguration/recovery mechanisms implemented in the middleware ensure that a backup replica obtains all the information it needs to reproduce the actions of the application. The piece of middleware presented in [15] has been designed aiming at mission assurance for critical Cloud applications across hybrid Clouds. It is centered on policy-based event monitoring and dynamic reactions to guarantee the accomplishment of "end-to-end" and "cross-layered" security, dependability and timeliness. In [16], the authors present a piece of middleware for enabling "media-centered" cooperation among home networks. It allows users to join their home equipments through a Cloud, providing a new content distribution model that simplifies the discovery, classification, and access to commercial contents within a home networks. Mathias and Baude [17] focus on the integration of different types of computational environments. In fact, they propose a lightweight component-based piece of middleware intended to simplify the transition from clusters, to Grids and Clouds and/or a mixture of them. The key points of such a system are a modular infrastructure, that can adapt its behaviour to the running environment, and application connectivity requirements. The problem of integrating multi-tenancy into the Cloud is addressed in [18]. The authors propose a Cloud architecture for achieving multi-tenancy at the Service Oriented Architecture (SOA) level by virtualizing the middleware servers running SOA artifacts and allowing a single instance to be securely shared between tenants or different customers. The key idea of the work is that the combination between virtualization, elasticity and multi-tenancy makes it possible an optimal usage of data center resources (i.e., CPU, memory, and network). A piece of middleware designed for monitoring Cloud resources is proposed in [19]. The presented architecture is based on a scalable data-centric publish/subscribe paradigm to disseminate data in multi-tenant Cloud scenarios. Furthermore, it allows to customize both granularity and frequency of received monitored data according to specific service and tenant requirements. The work proposed in [20] aims to support mobile applications with processing power and storage space, moving resource-intensive activities into the Cloud. It abstracts the API of multiple Cloud vendors, thus providing a unique JSON-based interface that responds according to the REST-based Cloud services. The current framework considers the APIs from Amazon EC2, S3, Google and some open source Cloud projects like Eucalyptus. In [21], the authors present a piece of middleware to support fast system implementation and ICT cost reduction by making use of private Clouds. The system includes application servers that run a Java Runtime Environment (JRE) and additional modules for service management and information integration, designed according to a Service Oriented Architecture (SOA).

3   Container Virtualitation for Linux Environments

Container-based virtualization can be considered as an approach in which the virtualization layer runs within an application on top of the OS. In this approach, the OS's kernel runs on the hardware node with several isolated guest virtual environments called containers. In this Section, we describe the pieces of software needed to support the container virtualization by considering a generic Linux system. Looking at Fig. 2, a Linux host OS is normally deployed on the top of system hardware layer (including CPU, RAM, peripherals, etc.) and its kernel needs to work with a suitable virtualization layer. In this way, the OS-level virtualization does not require an additional hypervisor layer since the virtualization capabilities are part of the host OS. This technique allows to virtualize applications on top of the host OS itself. Therefore, the overhead produced by the hypervisor mediation is eliminated enabling near native performances. In addition, the host kernel provides process isolation and performs resource management. This means that even though all the containers are running under the same kernel, each container is a virtual environment that has its own file system, processes, memory, devices, etc. There are different host applications located on top of the Linux kernel. In particular, we focus our attention on the containers engine component that automates the deployment of any application as a lightweight, portable, self-sufficient container that will run virtually anywhere.

By considering several IoT services and applications, in this paper we mainly focus our attention on considering Linux-based Single Board Computers (SBCs)

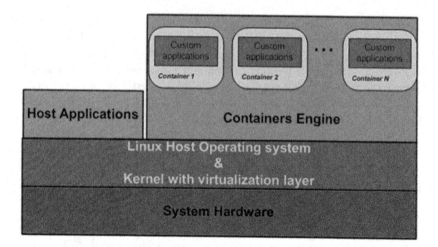

Fig. 2. Container-based virtualization.

that include several General Purpose Input Output (GPIO) extensions allowing our IoT device to interact with many different external sensors and actuators. More specifically, we consider the software structure shown in Fig. 3. Starting from bottom, our system hardware consists of a Raspberry Pi B+ model [22]. While the latter board is, in essence, a very inexpensive Linux computer, there are a few things that distinguish it from a general purpose machine. One of the main differences is that the Raspberry Pi can be directly used in electronics projects because it includes GPIO pins on the board. These GPIO hardware extensions can be accessed for controlling hardware such as LEDs, motors, and relays, which are all examples of outputs. As for inputs, the used Raspberry Pi can read the status of buttons, switches, and dials, or it can read data coming from sensors like temperature, light, motion, or proximity [23]. Our Raspberry Pi board is equipped with the Raspbian distribution that is the most popular OS for the considered piece of hardware; it also includes customizations that are designed to make the Raspberry Pi easier to use and includes many different software packages out of the box. In particular, in this paper, we are considering Raspbian 3.18.8 Linux kernel version that comes with the LXC extensions. As discussed in [24], this extension represents container-based OS virtualization and one of its major benefits is that it can run multiple Linux instances on a single physical host. With reference to the Fig. 3, host applications are deployed on the top of Raspbian OS and Linux kernel.

We consider the Docker Platform as container engine, which is an open platform for developers and system administrators to build, ship, and run distributed applications. Being the Docker Engine, a lightweight portable, runtime, and packaging tool it represents a valuable solution to implement a cloud service for sharing applications and automating workflows. In fact, Docker Hub enables apps to be quickly assembled from components and fulfil the gap between development

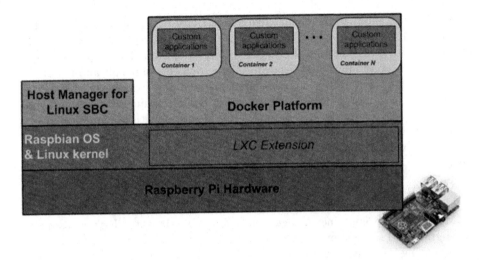

Fig. 3. Software architecture for container-based virtualization deployed on a Raspberry Pi board.

and production environments. As a result, cloud providers can fast ship and run the same application and service on VMs and IoT devices. Docker is also an open-source implementation of the deployment engine which powers dotCloud, a popular Platform-as-a-Service (PaaS). It directly benefits from the experience accumulated over several years of large-scale operation and support to hundreds of thousands of applications and databases. It relies on a different sandboxing method known as containerization. Most modern OS kernels now support the primitives necessary for containerization, including Linux with openvz, vserver and recently LXC containment features. Through a powerful API and simple tools, it lets Linux users to create and manage system or application containers.

In our context, at the same Docker's level, we can consider several services and applications allowing IoT devices to interact with the cloud, as it will be discussed in the next Section.

4 MOM4C Extension for IoT and Container Support

The MOM4Cloud architecture and its design choices have been already discussed in [2]. In this paper, our major contribution is to extend the piece of middleware's functionalities in order to support the management of container based environment on SBCs Linux devices, also known as smart objects or IoT devices. We can consider the container-based virtualization as a method for making available services and applications on IoT systems. For these reasons, our reference scenario includes a set of physical hardware resources i.e., embedded systems, where several types of container images are dynamically loaded according to their workload and other parameters. In this way, we aim to provide services into a complex smart environment, like a smart city where the objects can also interact with each others. Such environments are often pictured as constellations of instruments across many scales that are connected through multiple networks which provide continuous data regarding the movements of people and materials in terms of the flow of decisions about the physical and social form of the city. Cities however can only be smart if there are intelligent functions that are able to integrate and synthesise this data to some purposes, with the aim of improving the efficiency, equity, sustainability and quality of life in cities [25]. From a technical point of view, our cloud system has to guarantee the following basic operations:

- Monitoring the container environments behaviour and performance, in terms of CPU, memory and storage usage.
- Managing the container images, providing functions to destroy, commit, migrate and set network parameters.
- Managing the container resources, i.e., images discovery, uploading and downloading via a FTP repository.

Figure 4 summarizes our reference scenario and it shows a cluster of two kinds of nodes. Blade servers execute a cluster level management module, called Cluster Manager (CM), while each SBC piece of hardware supports both a host level management module, the Host Manager (HM), and a specialized Containers Engine component, like Docker. All these entities interact exchanging information by means of the communication system based on the Extensible Messaging and Presence Protocol (XMPP). The dataset necessary to enable the middleware functioning is stored within a specific Database deployed in a distributed fashion such as MongoDB; in addition, the depicted software infrastructure is equipped with a container repository that works with the FTP protocol. More

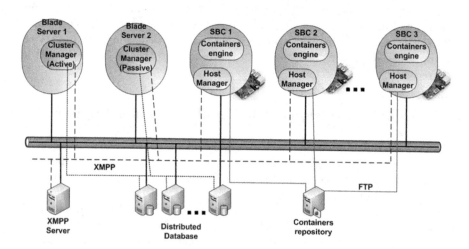

Fig. 4. Reference scenario. MOM4C architecture extended for IoT devices and container support.

specifically, core components of our infrastructure can be split into two logical categories: the software agents (typical of the architecture itself) and the tools they exploit. To the former set belong both the Host Manager and the Cluster Manager: The CM consists in as an interface between administrators (software entities, which can exploit the cloud services) and the HM agents. A CM receives commands from administrators, performs operations on the HM agents (or on the database) and finally sends information to administrators. It also performs the management of container images and the monitoring of the overall state of the cluster. According to our idea, at least one CM has to be deployed on each cluster but, in order to ensure higher fault tolerance, many of them should exist. A master CM will exist in active state while the other ones will remain in a monitoring state, although admin messages are listened whatever operation is performed. The HM performs the operations needed to monitor the physical resources and the instantiated container images: it interacts with the containers engine, the SBC's operating system and the FTP repository where the images are stored.

4.1   Architecture Overview

In this part, we focus our attention on the design of CM and HM software modules. Regarding CM, Fig. 5 highlights its functional blocks and their organization: the main components are described as follows:

- Database Manager: such a component interacts with the database employed to store information needed to the cluster handling. Database Manager must maintain the data strictly related to the cluster state.
- Performance Estimator: it analyses the performance dataset collected from physical assets (physical IoT devices), in order to provide a trend of performance estimation.
- Image Manager: it manages both registrations and uploads within the Cluster Storage System of the Docker images.
- Storage Manager: it manages the internal cluster distributed file system.

As previously mentioned, HM modules are deployed on each SBC piece of hardware. The HM's architecture is shown in Fig. 6. Its main components include:

- Monitor: it provides resource usage monitoring for each SBC. The pieces of information are organized and made available to the HM coordinator.
- Container engine interface: it is the middleware back-end of the container engine running on the SBC, for example the Docker Platform.
- Image Manager: it supplies to the container engine interface the needed container images by means of the FTP protocol.
- Network Manager: it gathers information about the host network state and it manages host network (at OS level) according to the guidelines provided by the HM Coordinator.

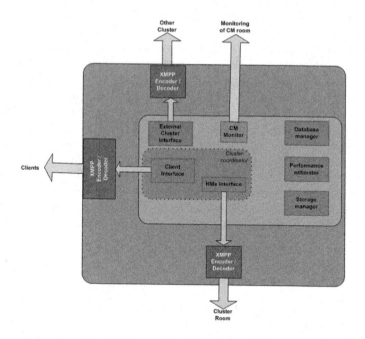

Fig. 5. Cluster Manager architecture.

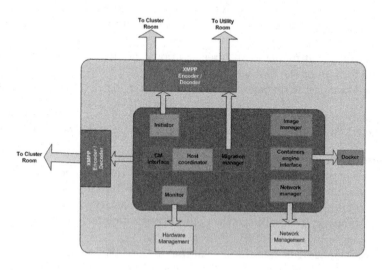

Fig. 6. Host Manager architecture.

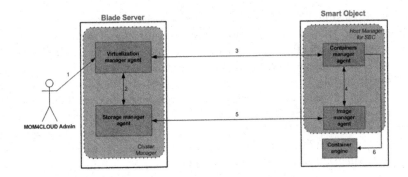

Fig. 7. Steps needed to load a container image on a smart object.

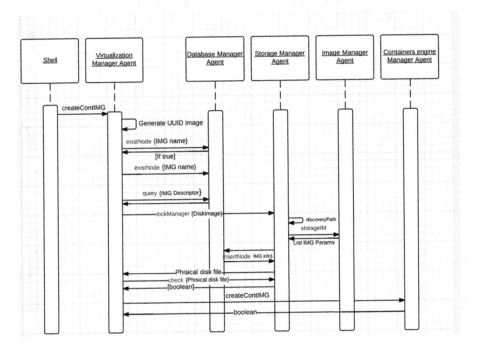

Fig. 8. Sequence diagram that shows the designed processes.

4.2 Technical Details

By looking at the Fig. 7, the dynamic load management of container images on a smart object requires six separate steps. Starting from left, the MOM4C administrator is a person who interacts with our piece of middleware by using a computer console program. The shell program sends user requests to the active CM running on a specialized blade server. More specifically, at the first step the Virtualization manager agent works on the received commands (step 1) and forwards the query to the Storage manager agent (step 2). The latter software module is responsible for managing the FTP repository that stores the required container image. If such an operation concludes successfully, an ACK message is sent to the Virtualization manager agent (step 3). After that, the active CM queries the Host Manager agent that executes on the smart object (step 4). The Virtualization manager agent sends suitable requests to the Containers manager agent to invoke the download of the required container images. Then, the SBC system connects to the Storage manager agent (step 5) in order to retrieve the needed data and information. Finally (step 6), the Containers manager agent calls the container engine (e.g., Docker) in a suitable way. In Fig. 8, we present the sequence diagram of the described process.

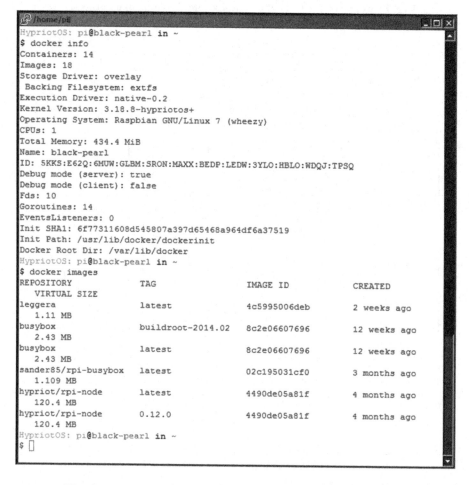

Fig. 9. Docker shell commands running on our embedded device.

5 System Prototype

A HM prototype was implemented on a Raspberry Pi B+ embedded system by using the Python high-level programming language. Our SBC device executes a custom Raspbian OS image with Docker 1.5 version, which adds support for IPv6, read-only containers and advanced statistics. Considering this environment, we relied on a standard Docker's command-line console as shown in Fig. 9 in order to monitor containers. In particular, our HM consists of a specialized XMPP client that accepts and processes container management messages coming from a CM deployed in blade server and that forward them to the container manager interface. This kind of communication has been managed through the XMPPPY libraries. In particular, the container manager interface interacts with the underlying Docker engine. In this way, the following basic operations can be performed on container images:

- Download an image from a FTP repository available on a blade server;
- Upload an image to a FTP repository available on a blade server;
- Start, stop, delete a given container image available on the embedded device.

6 Conclusion

Nowadays, container-based virtualization is a kind of OS-level virtualization that allows us to run multiple instances of the same OS user workspace sharing the kernel of the host OS. Technological developments have allowed such a technology to support SBCs, i.e., smart IoT devices equipped with a modern Linux kernel supporting a suitable virtualization layer. Considering multiple application scenarios, it is important to rely on cloud services able to deploy and to customize pieces of software running on target smart objects. To achieve such a goal, in this paper, we focused our attention on MOM4C, a flexible solution able to arrange customizable cloud facilities by means of a federation-enabled communication system. In this way, we aim to provide services into a complex smart environment, like a smart city, where objects interact each others and with the cloud. Therefore, we have discussed how MOM4C can be extended to support container-based virtualization on Linux embedded IoT devices. More specifically, we designed the two main software modules constituting our software infrastructure.

Since our prototype implementation is still at an early stage, we are already working to further extend the system functionalities according to our reference architecture. In future work, we plan to perform a set of experiments in order to evaluate the behaviour of the piece middleware and its performance when managing multiple containers on the same IoT device.

Acknowledgments. The research leading to the results presented in this paper has received funding from the Project "Design and Implementation of a Community Cloud Platform aimed at SaaS services for on-demand Assistive Technology".

References

1. Xavier, M., Neves, M., Rossi, F., Ferreto, T., Lange, T., De Rose, C.: Performance evaluation of container-based virtualization for high performance computing environments. In: 2013 21st Euromicro International Conference on Parallel, Distributed and Network-Based Processing (PDP), pp. 233–240 (2013)
2. Fazio, M., Celesti, A., Villari, M.: Design of a message-oriented middleware for cooperating clouds. In: Canal, C., Villari, M. (eds.) ESOCC 2013. CCIS, vol. 393, pp. 25–36. Springer, Heidelberg (2013)
3. Felter, W., Ferreira, A., Rajamony, R., Rubio, J.: An updated performance comparison of virtual machines and linux containers. In: 2015 IEEE International Symposium on Performance Analysis of Systems and Software (ISPASS), pp. 171–172 (2015)
4. Biederman, E.W., Networx, L.: Multiple instances of the global linux namespaces. In: Proceedings of the Linux Symposium, Citeseer (2006)
5. Bernstein, D.: Containers and cloud: from LXC to docker to kubernetes. IEEE Cloud Comput. 1, 81–84 (2014)
6. Liu, D., Zhao, L.: The research and implementation of cloud computing platform based on docker. In: 2014 11th International Computer Conference on Wavelet Active Media Technology and Information Processing (ICCWAMTIP), pp. 475–478 (2014)
7. Kacamarga, M.F., Pardamean, B., Wijaya, H.: Lightweight virtualization in cloud computing for research. In: Intan, R., Chi, C.-H., Palit, H.N., Santoso, L.W. (eds.) Intelligence in the Era of Big Data. CCIS, vol. 516, pp. 439–445. Springer, Heidelberg (2015)
8. Bui, T.: Analysis of docker security. arXiv preprint arXiv:1501.02967 (2015)
9. Giacobbe, M., Celesti, A., Fazio, M., Villari, M., Puliafito, A.: Towards energy management in cloud federation: a survey in the perspective of future sustainable and cost-saving strategies. Comput. Netw. 91, 438–452 (2015)
10. Celesti, A., Fazio, M., Villari, M., Puliafito, A.: Adding long-term availability, obfuscation, and encryption to multi-cloud storage systems. J. Netw. Comput. Appl. 59, 208–218 (2016)
11. Mulfari, D., Celesti, A., Villari, M.: A computer system architecture providing a user-friendly man machine interface for accessing assistive technology in cloud computing. J. Syst. Softw. 100, 129–138 (2015)
12. Celesti, A., Tusa, F., Villari, M., Puliafito, A.: How the dataweb can support cloud federation: service representation and secure data exchange. In: 2012 Second Symposium on Network Cloud Computing and Applications (NCCA), pp. 73–79 (2012)
13. Leitner, P., Satzger, B., Hummer, W., Inzinger, C., Dustdar, S.: Cloudscale: a novel middleware for building transparently scaling cloud applications. In: SAC 2012, pp. 434–440 (2012)
14. Wenbing, Z., Melliar-Smith, P., Moser, L.: Fault tolerance middleware for cloud computing. In: IEEE 3rd CLOUD 2010, pp. 67–74 (2010)
15. Campbell, R., Montanari, M., Farivar, R.: A middleware for assured clouds. J. Internet Serv. Appl. 3, 87–94 (2012)
16. Diaz-Sanchez, D., Almenarez, F., Marin, A., Proserpio, D., Cabarcos, P.A.: Media Cloud: an open cloud computing middleware for content management. IEEE Trans. Consum. Electron. 57, 970–978 (2011)

17. Manias, E., Baude, F.: A component-based middleware for hybrid grid/cloud computing platforms. Concurrency Comput. Pract. Exp. **24**, 1461–1477 (2012)
18. Azeez, A., Perera, S., Gamage, D., Linton, R., Siriwardana, P., Leelaratne, D., Weerawarana, S., Fremantle, P.: Multi-tenant SOA middleware for cloud computing. In: IEEE CLOUD 2010, pp. 458–465 (2010)
19. Povedano-Molina, J., Lopez-Vega, J.M., Lopez-Soler, J.M., Corradi, A., Foschini, L.: Dargos: a highly adaptable and scalable monitoring architecture for multitenant clouds. Future Gener. Comput. Syst. **29**, 2041–2056 (2013)
20. Flores, H., Srirama, S.N.: Dynamic re-configuration of mobile cloud middleware based on traffic. In: IEEE MASS 2012 (2012)
21. Nagakura, H., Sakurai, A.: Middleware for creating private clouds. Fujitsu Sci. Tech. J. (FSTJ) **47**, 263–269 (2011)
22. Maksimović, M., Vujović, V., Davidović, N., Milošević, V., Perišić, B.: Raspberry Pi as internet of things hardware: performances and constraints. Des. Issues **3**, 8 (2014)
23. Richardson, M., Wallace, S.: Getting Started with Raspberry Pi. O'Reilly Media, Inc., Sebastopol (2012)
24. Memari, N., Hashim, S.J.B., Samsudin, K.B.: Towards virtual honeynet based on LXC virtualization. In: 2014 IEEE Region 10 Symposium, pp. 496–501 (2014)
25. Batty, M., Axhausen, K., Giannotti, F., Pozdnoukhov, A., Bazzani, A., Wachowicz, M., Ouzounis, G., Portugali, Y.: Smart cities of the future. Eur. Phys. J. **214**, 481–518 (2012)

A Federated System for MapReduce-Based Video Transcoding to Face the Future Massive Video-Selfie Sharing Trend

Alfonso Panarello, Antonio Celesti[✉], Maria Fazio, Antonio Puliafito, and Massimo Villari

DICIEAMA, University of Messina,
Contrada Di Dio (S. Agata), 98166 Messina, Italy
{apanarello,acelesti,mfazio,apuliafito,mvillari}@unime.it
http://mdslab.unime.it

Abstract. The massive use of mobile devices and social networks is causing the birth of a new compulsive users' behaviour. The activity photo selfie sharing is gradually turning into video selfie. These videos will be transcoded into multiple formats to support different visualization mode. We think there will be the need to have systems that can support, in a fast, efficient and scalable way, the millions of requests for video sharing and viewing. We think that a single Cloud Computing services provider cannot alone cope with this huge amount of incoming data (Big Data), so in this paper we propose a Cloud Federation-based system that exploiting the Hadoop MapReduce paradigm performs the video transcoding in multiple format and its distribution in a fastest and most efficient possible way. Experimental results highlight the major factors involved for job deployment in a federated Cloud environment and the efficiency of the proposed system and show how the Federation improves the performances of a MapReduce Job execution acting on a additional parallelization level.

Keywords: Cloud Computing · Horizontal federation · IEEE P2302 · CLEVER · Big Data · MapReduce · Apache Hadoop · HDFS · Adaptive streaming

1 Introduction

Surely, one of the most tangible consequences of the advent of social networks has been their ability to replace the information brokerage with a direct, fast, emotional and one to one communication. This sudden innovation has brutally swamped the traditional media, journalism, brand communication and it has hugely accelerate the contents ageing. As just said acquires even more truthfulness if we go to consider the birth of applications that promise to broadcast live the life of every people belonging to a SN. The most famous examples are the new apps like *Periscope* purchased and launched by Twitter and *Meerkat*.

© Springer International Publishing Switzerland 2016
A. Celesti and P. Leitner (Eds.): ESOCC 2015 Workshops, CCIS 567, pp. 48–62, 2016.
DOI: 10.1007/978-3-319-33313-7_4

Periscope, substantially, opens a virtual window through which it possible to observe the reality: the users only need to start Periscope, to keep active the smartphone cam, broadcasting live right now in social streaming at time and any place. Other apps, that work apparently in a very similar manner to Periscope, are YouNow and Meerkat. Another kind of video applications that is following the current trend·is the well-known Dubsmash[1] tool. It is a simple video grub mobile application allowing you to mix video and audio together for a funny composition. These videos are easily shared among the SNs. We have foreseen the current trend of making selfies with photos will become the future trend to accomplishing selfies of video so, for this reason, clouds have to deal with the exigence to convert many videos at the same time for satisfying the even more increasing number of mobile customers. Therefore, to fulfil high adaptability of the systems to variable workloads, an elastic approach for resource management is required. Cloud computing, offers such a feature, by means of virtualization of resources that can easily scaled up/down. Parallelization capabilities of a computing system strongly depend on available resources into the working cluster. However, to overcome the problem of the strict link among available virtual resources/physical assets a CP can take part to a federated environment.

To this end, in this paper, we present a new solution to perform a MapReduce[2] video transcoding in a *Federated Cloud* ecosystem which is able to face the future massive Video-Selfie sharing trend. Our solution integrates the Hadoop functionalities into a Cloud middleware for federated environments called CLEVER [1].

To show the goodness of our approach, we tested it leveraging a video transcoding application on Apache Hadoop. Indeed, the video management use case provides us a real test case through which we drive our assessments.

The paper is organized as follows. In Sect. 2, we provide a brief overview of current works on the topic dealt in the paper. In Sect. 3, we highlight the benefits in adopting Hadoop in a federated Cloud environment in a context of video transcoding and distribution management. In Sect. 4 we introduce the technologies adopted in this work to arrange a real federated environment. Section 5 presents the proposed distributed processing service and one of many possible use cases, that is the video transcoding application. In Sect. 6, we analyse costs, in terms of delay and overhead, introduced by the federation management. In Sect. 7, our experimental results show the effective advantages of the processing in a federated environment. Section 8 concludes the paper.

2   Related Work

In the near future, but already from some time, the massive use of mobile devices and Social Networks (SN) have led to the explosion in the amount of data to be

---

[1] http://www.dubsmash.com/.

[2] Hadoop MapReduce is one of the most adopted implementations of the MapReduce paradigm developed and is maintained by the Apache Hadoop project, that also works on the parallel Hadoop File System (HDFS). http://hadoop.apache.org/index. pdf.

stored and elaborated. This problem, known as the Big Data problem, is becoming a crucial issue in the ICT world. The Cloud Computing Infrastructure as a Service (IaaS) level can be seen as a possible solution to solve the above mentioned Big Data problem. The computing power of the Cloud Computing, which is based on the virtualization concept, stands for the ideal solution to meet the management of these Big Data. In particular Big Data processing platforms, like Hadoop, can leverage the computation capabilities of Clouds relying on VMs. An example is given in [2], where Hadoop is installed into VMs exploiting the Public Cloud as Amazon EC2. Here the authors re-modelled the resources provisioning of the VMs in public Cloud platforms for Big Data applications. Hadoop uses the MapReduce paradigm, an high-level programming model for data-intensive applications using transparent fault detection and recovery, widely adopted in Cloud data-centers such as Microsoft, Google, Yahoo, and Facebook. Hadoop is an open-source implementation firstly developed by Yahoo. In our work, we advance the existing researches on that topic using the MapReduce high-level programming model even in federated and heterogeneous Clouds. Deploying VMs with Hadoop in federated scenarios is a challenge, as shown in [3]. Some authors in the past tried to optimize the Hadoop computation in heterogeneous environments, as discussed in "PIKACHU" [4], which looks at the paradigm attempting to optimize all processing tasks and, in particular, to the three main phases: *map, shuffle and reduce*.

Zhuo Tang et al. in [5] presents an algorithm that can dynamically determine the optimal to start time of the reduce tasks. This scheduling algorithm reduces the wastefulness of the time slots assigned to a reduced task thereby reducing the time needed to complete the job. "An Adaptive Auto-configuration" [6] faces the problem with the right Hadoop configuration. In the authors opinion this could easily lead to performance loss due to some misconfigurations. The [6] presents an adaptive automatic configuration tool (AACT), based on mathematical model, for Hadoop to achieve performance optimization. This model accurately learns the relationship that exists between system performance and configuration parameters and then configures Hadoop adapting the hardware and software dynamically.

All of the previous works have the common goal to optimize an Hadoop MapReduce job execution into a single cluster. Our work, following a similar approach to [2], has their same aims but we believe is much more challenging to set-up and to optimize a Hadoop environment in Federated Clouds. We get the optimization of the job execution going to split it on several clusters. Cloud Federation [7] represents a compelling opportunity in which IaaS Cloud Operators might achieve great business benefits, renting to others cloud operators the computation resources on-demand [8]. The well-know Hadoop platform can represent an appealing opportunity in this way because its architecture is well consolidated and widely used. Any Cloud Operator might offer Hadoop computation resources on-fly joining a federated cloud environment. In this way our work should not be considered only as an alternative to the previous works but as a new additional solution that works at a higher layer. The Federation adds another parallelization level to that already provided by a single hadoop cluster [9].

Another important aspect of the Federation is also the capability to leverage the communication infrastructure of Carrier Operators. The Federation might affect also these operators and mobile users might benefit of it. This paper looks even to Federation for Distribution (CFfD).

3 Motivation and Reference Scenario

In recent days we are watching a battle for the social live streaming application leadership. *Periscope* and *Meerkat* are fighting. Often when there is a battle there is economic interest too: just to think about the millions of users that populate the SN. Twitter now has about 302 million users of which about 80 % of the active users use a mobile device. Sharing live of videos through mobile devices is unquestionably the new trend. But besides sharing live, the users are interested to create *"viral"* videos and to share them with the virtual world so that they can be seen and seen again in off-line and on demand way. The latest smartphone generation has hardware resources that allow to watch and record High Definition videos. But not all users have got the latest model available on the market that has the high network transmission rate or HD support. Moreover the users do not in every moment have sufficient available bandwidth. So there is the need to allow all users to watch the shared video in the best format possible considering both their mobile hardware power and the network available bandwidth. We are talking about $Adaptive - bitrate - Streaming$ which is a technique used in multimedia stream over computer networks that, detecting user's hardware capabilities and bandwidth, $on fly$ adjusts the quality of a video stream accordingly. An important example is HTTP Live Streaming (HLS)[3] designed by Apple. Besides HLS we can cite other proprietary adaptive streaming technologies such as Adobe HTTP Dynamic Streaming (Adobe HDS)[4], and Microsoft Smooth Streaming[5] or not proprietary like MPEG-DASH[6].

Taking into consideration the *on-demand* provisioning videos, it is needed to transcode these shared videos in multiple formats. We are therefore talking about a panorama where millions and millions of users produce videos and share them at any time and each video has to be transcoded in several formats: in other words we are talking about *Big Data in Video Domain*. In order to keep up of this future trend, distributed computations, efficient data storage and aimed systems for manipulating of the greatest possible number of videos in the shortest possible time are extremely needed. One of the main problems of Video Big Data management is proving meaningful techniques able to process a huge amount of

---

[3] https://developer.apple.com/library/ios/documentation/NetworkingInternet/
    Conceptual/StreamingMediaGuide/StreamingMediaGuide.pdf.

[4] http://www.images.adobe.com/content/dam/Adobe/en/products/
    hds-dynami-streaming/pdfs/hds_datasheet.pdf.

[5] https://msdn.microsoft.com/en-us/library/ff469518.aspx.

[6] https://www.iso.org/obp/ui/#iso:std:iso-iec:23009:-1:ed-2:v1:en.

data involving even more computation resources in a distributed and scalable manner. Nowadays, Cloud Federation is emerging in different application fields including, for example, energy efficiency [10], storage [11], dataweb [12] and so on. We believe that Cloud Federation may provide advance features and capabilities useful for dealing with the massive data computation.

4   Integration of Hadoop in CLEVER

To deal with federated environments, the overall framework presented hereby is compounded from more complex parts. The core is represented by the CLEVER cloud. It is a challenging middleware because it fulfill many IEEE directives in the context of Cloud federation (see[7] and [13]). CLEVER accomplishes many features presented in these references. Other Cloud platforms like, OpenNebula or OpenStack have a weak approach in satisfying the federation. In this section we include a few information on Hadoop framework and how it is integrated with CLEVER.

4.1   CLEVER Overview

The CLoud-Enabled Virtual EnviRonment (CLEVER) is a Message-Oriented Middleware for Cloud computing (MOM4C), able to support several Cloud-based services [14]. Each CLEVER Cloud includes several distributed hosts organized in a cluster. Each Physical Machine (PM) is controlled by a management module, called Host Manager (HM), and only one host runs a cluster management module, called Cluster Manager (CM) that acts as interface between Cloud and clients. CM receives commands from clients, gives instructions to HMs, elaborates information and sends back results to clients. It also performs tasks for cluster orchestration. A CLEVER Cloud makes use of XMPP to exchange all communication messages and presence information in a near-real time fashion. A Jabber/XMPP server provides basic messaging, presence, and XML routing features within the Cloud.

In a federated environment, specific mechanisms for dynamic identification and service discovery have to be employed. We believe that the best way to accomplish all the above features is the adoption of strategic communication technologies, able to interconnect many different distributed entities and to provide an integrated platform. To this aim, we make use of the XMPP protocol. In fact it natively supports federation capabilities. With CLEVER, each Cloud involved in the federation is identified by a *Jabber ID* (JID). The utilization of a central server which maintains a list of JIDs can be avoided by structuring each JID as e-mail addresses, with *username* and *domain* names. In order to set up a federation, CMs belonging to Cloud Brokers of different administrative domains exchange messages through the Multi User Chat (MUC) with the unique room

---

[7] IEEE   P2302[TM]/D0.2.   https://www.oasis-open.org/committees/download.php/46205/p2302-12-0002-00-DRFT-intercloud-p2302-draft-0-2.pdf.

ID *Federation*. Only authenticated CMs, relying on XMPP Federated servers can access the MUC. The XMPP servers are responsible to manage the Federation Rooms and they can be entrusted by third part entities.

4.2 Hadoop Overview

Hadoop is a framework that allows for the distributed processing of large data sets across clusters of computers using simple programming models. It is designed to scale up from single servers to thousands of machines, each offering local computation and storage. Hadoop MapReduce is able to write and run applications in processing in parallel huge amounts of data (e.g., terabyte of datasets) on large clusters in a reliable, fault tolerant manner. A MapReduce job usually splits the input data set into independent chunks, which are processed by the map tasks in a completely parallel manner. Both the input and the output of the job are stored in a distributed file system, that is the Hadoop File System (HDFS). MapReduce components consist of a single master JobTracker and one slave TaskTracker per cluster-node. The master is responsible for scheduling the jobs' component tasks on the slaves, monitoring them and re-executing the failed tasks. The slaves execute the tasks as directed by the master. The master node of the HDFS is called *NameNode* whereas the slave node of the HDFS is called *DataNode*.

4.3 Hadoop and CLEVER

As we remarked above, to make the Hadoop functionalities Cloud-like, we make use of a virtual infrastructure provided by CLEVER. VMs run on HMs and work as slaves of the Hadoop cluster. Virtual Hadoop slaves are coordinated by the Hadoop Master arranged at the CLEVER CM. The first advantage of the integration of Hadoop in CLEVER is that, typically, Hadoop uses the TCP/IP layer for communication, and it is a problem during the inter-domain communication due to heavy usage of firewalls by each domain which take part to federation. In fact usually firewalls block inter-domain communications. So, integrating Hadoop in CLEVER, federation messages can be sent on port 80 thanks to XMPP technology. The second one advantage is that the system can automatically scale according to real time requirements. In CLEVER, the *Cluster Coordinator* (CC), inside the CM, is responsible for the cluster management and service provisioning. To this aim, it interacts with both the HMs into the cluster, by means of a *HMs interface*, and the Cloud clients which request a specific service by means of the *Client interface*. All these interactions are based on XML message exchange into XMPP MUCs. Through the *HMs interface*, the CC communicates with all the HMs in the cluster, exchanging information on available resources, running tasks, work specifications and offered services. The CC makes use of the *Client interface* to interact with Cloud clients, in order to receive client's requests, and to give back inquired services. The HM agent specifically designed to support the Hadoop activities in the Cloud is the *HMN Agent*. It provides the configuration settings to all the virtual nodes in the Hadoop cluster. The CLEVER HMN works as master for Hadoop cluster. Specifically, it implements the Hadoop functionalities to manage the Hadoop system. The *Network Manager (NM) Agent* allows to implement the virtual communications among Hadoop nodes through Notifications that arrives to the CM via the Dispatcher Agent. These notifications inform the *HMN Agent* about the presence or the absence of a host within the cluster.

4.4   Amazon S3

The Hybrid Cloud is accomplished using the Amazon S3 as Public Cloud storage service. It is designed to make web-scale computing easier for developers. Amazon S3 provides a simple web-services interface that can be used to store and retrieve any amount of data, at any time, from anywhere on the web. It gives any developer access to the same highly scalable, reliable, secure, fast, inexpensive infrastructure that Amazon uses to run its own global network of web sites. The service aims to maximize benefits of scale and to pass those benefits on to developers. In our work S3 represents the common storage shared among the Federated Cloud Providers.

5   Distributed Processing in Cloud Federation

Social Networks' (SNs) users have begun to abandon the photo selfies sharing, turning their interest toward a new way to share their life. The new trend is the movie selfies sharing, live or not, who allows to show virtual small fragments of their own daily lives to the friends. Mobile users want to share their produced video in the SN such as Twitter, Google+, Facebook, etc. In the work-flow we are considering here, all the time users require to share their videos. We are talking about hundreds of millions of users that will put their selfie videos into the web, and just as many users that will wish to follow one o more specific shared videos. The Social Network Cloud (SNC), received the users' requests for a video sharing, interacts with Clouds Storage Providers (CSPs) such as Amazon S3, Google Drive, Dropbox, etc. for storing these users' acquisitions. In this work we have adopted Amazon s3 only for practical reasons and because Amazon is at moment considered the most advanced Cloud Storage Provider. Only the selected Cloud Provider (CP) handles the entire work-flow; in the paper this CP is defined *Cloud Broker*. The choice to rely on external Public CSP as Amazon S3[8] was made to minimize the overhead associated to the data transmission between the federated CPs hence to be able to evaluate only the cost due to the federation management.

This scenario focuses on the off-line video sharing. The idea behind such a service is shown in Fig. 1. When an user requests to share a video-selfie, he contacts his Social Network (i.e. Twitter in the example in Fig. 1) and uploads his video. Twitter, in the future could not be able to fulfil all his user's video upload

---

[8] http://aws.amazon.com/it/documentation/s3/.

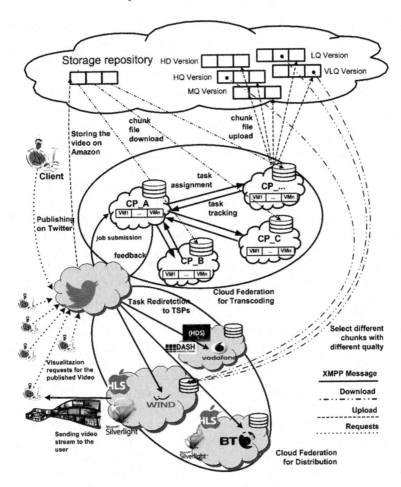

Fig. 1. Processing and distribution service management.

request, so we are supposing that it will vertically exploit the storage services of others CSPs (i.e., Amazon S3 depicted in Fig. 1) to face, in a scalable way, this growing demand for these kind of activities. We are supposing that CSP has multi-part download features. The SCN, after the storing, in order to allow to his users to watch the shared video in the best format possible, considering not only the users' mobile hardware power but also the network available bandwidth at a given time and place, has to transcode these shared videos in multiple formats and it has to be able to manipulate the greatest possible number of videos in the shortest possible time. To this end a processing service in Cloud Federation has been identified and exploited. In a federated Cloud environment, a CP can benefit of the storage and computational resources other CPs acting on other administrative domains. To satisfy the clients' requests, the SNs taking part to the Federation ask for available resources to the other federated CPs, which offer their unused resources at that time. In the examined case several CPs belonging to a Cloud Federation, can offer this kind of Processing Service. In Fig. 1 we call this Federation "Cloud Federation for Transcoding" (**CFfT**). There is a second Federation, called "Cloud Federation for Distribution" (**CFfD**) which aims to handle millions of requests for video visualisation, shifting his both hardware and software burden to the mobile operators that manage the users have made that request. To exploit this Federation service, after the storing of the video on Amazon, the SN contacts the broker to submit the transcoding task. For simplicity, in our scenario the broker(CP_A in Fig. 1) plays only the role of communication mediator, but it could have his own resources to be used for the transcoding tasks. More over we assume that each CP in the **CFfT** has an image of the VM including the piece of middleware for processing the task. The CP_A plays the role of broker. It retrieves information about the resources' availability of the federated CPs and sends them the instructions to fulfil their tasks. As soon as CP_n receives the file's URL information, it starts to downloads the file chunks and put them (HDFS-upload) in its HDFS cluster for local processing. At the end of the processing step, CP_n stores the result of its processing in the CSP and sends to CP_A an end task notification. Once CP_A has received all the end task notifications from all the involved CPs, it communicates to the SNC the new URLs of the multiple video streams and the necessary information for the client's player to reach the desired video streams. As it is possible to see in Fig. 1, and as previously mentioned, our scenario envisages the implementation of two different Federation. **CFfD** aims to lighten the system from the management of the video displaying requests. The current trend will lead to millions for video sharing requests, and an even greater number of video visualization requests. So a solution to make the system scalable has to be implemented. To this end, we decided to implement a second kind of Federation. When a user requests to view a specific shared video on "Twitter", he will first make a search for a specific #hashtag, and after he has found that video, he will attempt to display it. To avoid that, in the distribution process, Twitter will become the bottle neck of the system, it does not handle the transmission of the video streams in first person, but it redirects the that burden to the Mobile Phone Services Providers (MPSP) that has in managing the users requiring that service. Each provider to optimize the vision quality of the video, according to the user's actual hardware resources and network bandwidth, will manage the delivery by means of a Adaptive Stream Protocol (e.g., HLS or Microsoft Smooth Streaming). Also in this way, the provider will act as a cache for the system, going to download and locally store only the required video stream fragments, thereby significantly reducing the number of the accesses to the CSP (e.g., Amazon).

6   Cost Estimation of the Federation

With reference to the previous section, it is possible to identify eight steps of that federated transcoding process. It starts at time t_{t0} when a user sends a video sharing request to his SN to which he has a valid registered ID. At time t_{t1} the

SN, exploiting a software CLEVER agent that makes Twitter able to speak the XMPP language, contacts the broker of the Federation to communicate the need to transcode a video and all the necessary informations to correctly perform that task and at the same time it places the video to share and to transcode into the CSP Amazon S3. At time t_{t2} broker asks to the Federation, how many VMs each domain can provide. At t_{t3}, the Broker performs a task assignment involving the whole federated environment. At t_{t4} each involved federated CLEVER Cloud exactly downloads only a specific part of the movie file, using the multi-part download mechanism provided by Amazon APIs. At the time t_{t5} each domain starts to transcode the downloaded part. The t_{t6} indicates the starting time when each CLEVER Cloud begins to upload the transcoded part in multiple format on Amazon S3 and finally at the t_{t7} the broker, after receiving all responses from the foreign CPs, notifies the end of the transcoding process. As regards the distribution process, instead, it is possible to identify three steps: At t_{d0} the user, after made a #hashtag search, clicks on the video's previews to watch the movie. At t_{d1} the SNP (Social Network Provider), by analysing the users's IP, redirects the visualisation task to the appropriate MPSP. The MPSP a the t_{d2} begins the download from Amazon of the required stream, adapting it to the users' bandwidth by means e.g., the HLS protocol. Each MPSP stores in his own data-center only the required video stream chunks at the request time. The basic steps of the two processes are listed below:

- **Federation Set-up:** This step was not pursued in the previous section as it takes one-off at the time of taking part in the federation and therefore it does not affect the process previously described.
- **Service Discovery:** This step, albeit critical, has a negligible impact in terms of time. Our measurements show that this time increases by about 0.084 s for each participating domain in the Federation. It is negligible when compared to the sum of the downloads, computational, writing on HDSF and upload times process lifetime. This is a time that regards only the "Cloud Federation for Transcoding". In fact in the "Cloud Federation for Distribution" there is not the need of a discovery phase: the participants are statically known. In fact it is a dynamic environment where the CPs can take part and leave the Federation whenever they want. Regarding the Cloud Federation for Distribution, how we have already said, it is not true anymore because it is an a priori federated environment where all of the participants are statically known.
- **Communication Cost:** This is the time that a XMPP message takes to reach its destination. It is independent from the number of the federated CPs, therefore it is a negligible time.
- **Download + Upload from and to Amazon Costs:** These two phases of the process together have the strongest impact for the process. We are considering steps to download and upload together as both have similar features and despite some small difference in terms of time the two quantities are comparable. Considering a download speed of about 3 MB/s and file size equal to 512 MB we have download times about to 200 s. While considering a speed

of 2 MB/s we have a upload times that are in the neighbourhood of 270 s. Obviously increasing the number of the federated CPs these values of time decrease according to a pattern which can be approximated to the following function $y = a * x^{-c}$ (where y are the seconds and x is the considered chunk size).

- **Hadoop Cost:** This cost is related to the time needed to write data on HDFS and that one necessary to read from HDSF and write on the physical FS. It is well known that Hadoop works better with a few large files rather than with many small files. In other words, from the point of view of the performance is better to write a 1 GB file size instead to make 10 upload of 100 MB file size [15,16]. From our measurements it was observed that with files smaller than 20 MB and with block size equal to 64 MB (default Hadoop) the upload times into HDFS get highly comparable each others and therefore we do not get any more benefit from horizontal parallelization in terms of Hadoop cost.

- **Computational Costs:** This step of our analysis is just the cost due to the transcoding time. In our tests nevertheless, because the our paper's goal is not to do a video transcoding, but to demonstrate how the Cloud Federation can bring advantages if applied to whatever system which aims to provide a such service, we have not yet performed the video transcoding times measurements. However, we used the timing of OpenCV transcoding reported in [17], that focuses on measuring the total transcoding time varying several data's and cluster's parameters and Hadoop configuration files' values (block size and replication). The magnitudes involved are those ones that have the main impact on the whole federated transcoding process.

In the next section we analyse the times of the three phases of the process which, in our opinion, have the main impact on the entire transcoding federated flow.

7   Experiments

This section analyses several real experimental test-bed taking in consideration thirteen different CLEVER/Hadoop administrative domains. Twelve of them act as federated Cloud providers and only one of them acts as broker. This section also shows that by adding domains to the Federation the process' total time tends to the communication time between the broker and the CPs. So video transcoding is obtained in a time which is much smaller than it would have obtained without federation system. In fact, the federation allows to horizontally spread the workloads, significantly reducing the overhead and delays that the transcoding process as a whole introduces. Specifically, our studies show that only using the parallel processing provided by Hadoop it is possible to achieve a reduction of the computation time, instead by means more federated Hadoop-based environments, adding a horizontal cooperation, it is possible not only to reduce the computational time related to the video-transcoding but also that ones related to the delays and overheads introduced from the other phases of the process. With our testing we studied the behavior of the whole environment. We considered a parallel video transcoding use case involving several federated cloud providers. In particular, we arranged the test-bed taking in consideration 13 physical servers (one per CP). Each node of each cluster is a VM with the following virtual hardware and software: 1 CPU (1.3 GHz), 768 MB RAM, Ubuntu OS (12.04 server (32 bit)), CLEVER middleware including the Hadoop plug-in; Experiments were conducted with the following physical hardware configuration: CPU: AMD Opteron 2218 HE Santa Rosa with two Dual-Core 2.6 GHz processors; 8 GB RAM, running Linux Ubuntu 12.04 x86_64 OS and VirtualBox (version 4.1.12). The transcoding tool we are using in Hadoop (version 1.0.4) is the OpenCV framework converted in MapReduce shape. This physical hardware is located at the DICIEAMA department of the University of Messina. We redid each experiment 30 times in order to consider mean values and a low confidence intervals. In the following, we summarize the main phases involved in our experiments.

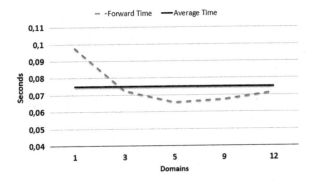

Fig. 2. Average time required to forward a request to Federated Clouds.

Figure 2 highlights that all the communications between Twitter and the broker and between the broker and the federated CPs have a very small magnitude. In others words Fig. 2 shows the time required to forward the video transcoding request to the other federated CLEVER Clouds domains. The CLEVER broker, obtained the network information regarding the federated CPs (by means a Discovery phase), distributes simultaneously the tasks that each of them has to accomplish. Thanks to the simultaneity of the communication, the forwarding time, that does not change if the number of the foreign domains does, assumes an average value of about 0, 075 s. How we said demonstrates that the Federation, by means of the XMPP communication technology, does not add any significant overhead. At phase $t_{t5} - t_{t4}$ each domain performs two tasks, at the first it downloads the assigned file block and then writes it into HDFS. Observing the Fig. 3(a) we can notice that, if there are more than one domains into the federation, each of them has to retrieve only a part of the original file. The Broker knows the number of the federated domains, and assigns to each of them a different block of the file. In particular Fig. 3(a), shows the download time from Amazon S3 varying both the file size and the number of the chunks. Observing the graphs, we can note that the download time for the whole 512 MB file takes roughly 200 s, while the times needed to download an eighth of file (64 MB) take roughly 30 s. Each download takes place in parallel, so we have a double benefit, the first one due to the smaller blocks size that a domain has to be download, the second one due to the parallelization of the download of these blocks. The Fig. 3(b), instead, shows the time needed to upload the transcoded files into Amazon S3 repository. The trend of such times is the same as that one shown in the graph in the Fig. 3(a). The upload time is not dependent on the number of chunks of the block.

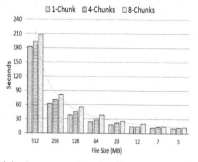

(a) Average download time of file blocks from Amazon S3.

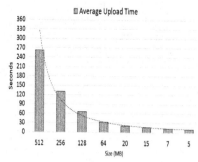

(b) Average Upload time of file blocks into Amazon S3.

Fig. 3. Average S3 download and upload time.

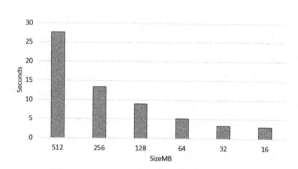

Fig. 4. Download time of file blocks from HDFS.

Figure 4 highlights that when the file size of the considered block decreases the time to read from HDFS and to write into the local FS decreases too but the obtained gain gradually lessens when the blocks become too small. A similar consideration is made for the upload to HDFS.

At the phase $t_{t6} - t_{t5}$, each federated domain performs the video transcoding. We have obtained from the paper [17] that, from the computational point of view, to have one domain with 4 available processing nodes is the same that to have 4 domains with only one available processing node. However, it is very important to emphasize that as just we said is true only from the computational point of view, in fact considering the whole federated transcoding process it is not true any more because in both cases the computational time is the same but in the first one the download from S3, the writing into HDFS and the upload to S3 times considerably increase.

It is clear that while the discovery time and the forward request time are small and negligible, the download + upload, Hadoop and transcoding time by means OpenCV tools are the most important impact for the examined scenario. At the phase $Ends - t_{t7}$ the broker sends a notification to the SN's CLEVER agent, that will communicate to SN to make available the video visualisation. Regarding the three steps of the distribution phase, we can assert that, a part the step $t_{d0} - t_{d1}$ that is outside of the federation scope, the steps $t_{d1} - t_{d2}$ and $t_{d2} - t_{d3}$ can be discussed similarly to the $t_{t4} - t_{t3}$ and $t_{t5} - t_{t4}$ of the transcoding federated process.

8 Conclusion

In this paper, we presented a federated Cloud environment which copes with future and just begun user trend to frantically share "viral" selfie videos. Our scenario hypothesizes two different *Federations*: **CFfT** and **CFfD**. The first one helps to achieve, as soon as possible, the video transcoding and sharing tasks. We applied the MapReduce paradigm exploiting the advantage of a Federation establishing between several CPs (managed by CLEVER) demonstrating how, by means of it, is possible to optimize the MapReduce Job execution and consequently to streamline and to speed the multiple video transcoding and sharing processes. The second one aims to face the increasing number of the "offline/on-demand" visualization requests for shared videos, assigning the transmission task of the video streams to the MPSP, avoiding that the SNC becomes the bottleneck of the system. In the future we will apply the Federation to other interesting use cases, so as to continue to demonstrate that the Federation in Cloud Computing environment is the key word for the future, and its advantages are not tangible only in the use case inspected in this paper.

References

1. Panarello, A., Celesti, A., Fazio, M., Villari, M., Puliafito, A.: A requirements analysis for IaaS cloud federation. In: 4th International Conference on Cloud Computing and Services Science, Barcelona (2014)
2. Yuan, Y., Wang, H., Wang, D., Liu, J.: On interference-aware provisioning for cloud-based big data processing. In: 2013 IEEE/ACM 21st International Symposium on Quality of Service (IWQoS), pp. 1–6 (2013)

3. Gahlawat, M., Sharma, P.: Survey of virtual machine placement in federated clouds. In: IEEE IACC 2014, pp. 735–738 (2014)
4. Gandhi, R., Xie, D., Hu, Y.C.: Pikachu: how to rebalance load in optimizing MapReduce on heterogeneous clusters. In: USENIX ATC 2013, pp. 61–66. USENIX Association, Berkeley (2013)
5. Tang, Z., Jiang, L., Zhou, J., Li, K., Li, K.: A self-adaptive scheduling algorithm for reduce start time. Futur. Gener. Comput. Syst. **43–44**, 51–60 (2015)
6. Li, C., Zhuang, H., Lu, K., Sun, M., Zhou, J., Dai, D., Zhou, X.: An adaptive auto-configuration tool for hadoop. In: 19th International Conference on Engineering of Complex Computer Systems (ICECCS), pp. 69–72 (2014)
7. Rochwerger, B., Breitgand, D., Epstein, A., Hadas, D., Loy, I., Nagin, K., Tordsson, J., Ragusa, C., Villari, M., Clayman, S., Levy, E., Maraschini, A., Massonet, P., Munoz, H., Tofetti, G.: Reservoir - when one cloud is not enough. Computer **44**, 44–51 (2011)
8. Toosi, A.N., Calheiros, R.N., Buyya, R.: Interconnected cloud computing environments: challenges, taxonomy, and survey. ACM Comput. Surv. **47**, 7:1–7:47 (2014)
9. Panarello, A., Fazio, M., Celesti, A., Puliafito, A., Villari, M.: Cloud federation to elastically increase MapReduce processing resources. In: Lopes, L., et al. (eds.) Euro-Par 2014, Part II. LNCS, vol. 8806, pp. 97–108. Springer, Heidelberg (2014)
10. Giacobbe, M., Celesti, A., Fazio, M., Villari, M., Puliafito, A.: Towards energy management in cloud federation: a survey in the perspective of future sustainable and cost-saving strategies. Comput. Netw. **91**, 438–452 (2015)
11. Celesti, A., Fazio, M., Villari, M., Puliafito, A.: Adding long-term availability, obfuscation, and encryption to multi-cloud storage systems. J. Netw. Comput. Appl. **59**, 208–218 (2016)
12. Celesti, A., Tusa, F., Villari, M., Puliafito, A.: How the dataweb can support cloud federation: service representation and secure data exchange. In: 2012 Second Symposium on Network Cloud Computing and Applications (NCCA), pp. 73–79 (2012)
13. Bernstein, D., Demchenko, Y.: The IEEE intercloud testbed - creating the global cloud of clouds. In: 2013 IEEE 5th International Conference on Cloud Computing Technology and Science (CloudCom), vol. 2, pp. 45–50 (2013)
14. Fazio, M., Celesti, A., Puliafito, A., Villari, M.: A message oriented middleware for cloud computing to improve efficiency in risk management systems. Scalable Comput. Pract. Exp. (SCPE) **14**, 201–213 (2013)
15. Dong, B., Zheng, Q., Tian, F., Chao, K.M., Ma, R., Anane, R.: An optimized approach for storing and accessing small files on cloud storage. J. Netw. Comput. Appl. **35**, 1847–1862 (2012)
16. Dong, B., Qiu, J., Zheng, Q., Zhong, X., Li, J., Li, Y.: A novel approach to improving the efficiency of storing and accessing small files on hadoop: a case study by powerpoint files. In: 2010 IEEE International Conference on Services Computing (SCC), pp. 65–72 (2010)
17. Kim, M., Cui, Y., Han, S., Lee, H.: Towards efficient design and implementation of a hadoop-based distributed video transcoding system in cloud computing environment. Int. J. Multimed. Ubiquitous Eng. **8**, 213–224 (2013)

Internet Service Provision and Content Services: Peering and Service Differentiation

Alexei A. Gaivoronski[1]([✉]), Per Jonny Nesse[1,2], Olai-Bendik Erdal[2], and Finn-Tore Johansen[2]

[1] Norwegian University of Science and Technology, Trondheim, Norway
Alexei.Gaivoronski@iot.ntnu.no
[2] Telenor AS, Bærum, Norway

Abstract. We consider the relationship of Internet service providers (ISP) like network operators and content service providers in the Internet ecosystem. Currently the position of ISPs is challenged by the emergence of powerful content service providers, especially with the spreading of bandwidth demanding video services. One issue here is that the further investment in the network capacity may be hindered by prevailing business models that largely exclude the ISPs from sharing in the major cash flows resulting from content provision.

We develop modeling tools for evaluation of business models of ISPs in Internet ecosystem and present some results of this analysis. In particular, we model the relationship between content provider (CP) with significant market power and an ISP. We show that it can be profitable for content provider to resort to paid content peering, thus transferring to ISP a part of his content provision revenue. The resulting business model may provide substantial benefits to all major participants in this ecosystem: network providers, content and service providers and end users. In addition, we consider the situation when ISP also engages in content provision.

Keywords: Business models for service provision · Connectivity provision · Content provision · Peering

1 Introduction

The current state of Internet ecosystems presents substantial challenges to telcos/network operators in their capacity of Internet Service Providers (ISP). Due to the introduction and explosive growth of services that are heavy on content (like video related services) their fast and mobile networks are experiencing substantial growth of traffic requiring more investment in network infrastructure [8]. At the same time the current Internet business models direct revenue streams towards content service providers, in particular those in possession of Content Delivery Networks and utilizing content peering. As the result, this revenue stream bypasses to a large extent the network providers (see, for example,

© Springer International Publishing Switzerland 2016
A. Celesti and P. Leitner (Eds.): ESOCC 2015 Workshops, CCIS 567, pp. 63–78, 2016.
DOI: 10.1007/978-3-319-33313-7_5

[7,9]). The growth of cloud based services has a potential to aggravate this situation even more. This jeopardizes the market position of ISP, which may result in future overall deterioration of network infrastructure due to lack of investment, something that will be detrimental to all the involved actors.

These issues has generated recently a substantial interest in academic and industrial literature, see [7–9] where one can find additional references and further discussion of policies for exchange of Internet traffic like peering. Proposals directed towards enhancement of position of providers of Internet connectivity (ISP) involve paid content peering, when content providers (CP) share their content provision revenue with respective ISP (By *peering* are usually understood agreements and principles that regulate the traffic exchange between different networks that comprise the Internet). Different ISPs consider introduction of policies that infringe on *network neutrality* (by which is understood the equal treatment by ISP of data packets from different sources), but allows them to collect additional revenue by differentiation of subscription fees according to usage. For example, [13] reports that Deutche Telecom considers differentiation of subscription fees that will limit the usage of video services from external CP, but not from its own video service. For in depth discussion of the economical network neutrality issues we refer to [1,4–6,10].

The literature cited above tries to find analytical relationships between different parameters of Internet ecosystem and understand to which actors the relaxation of the network neutrality is beneficial. We, instead, focus here on a relationship between ISPs and content service providers and develop tools for numerical analysis of their business models and policies. Another novelty is that we study the effects of uncertainty (particularly in demand), focusing on the analysis of paid content peering. First, we consider an important case: the relationship between a powerful CP and an ISP (Sect. 2). In such case the content provider can decide whether to transfer to the ISP part of his content provision revenue through paid content peering and the ISP accepts this decision.

We show that it can be profitable for the content provider to resort to paid content peering, stimulating the ISP to expand capacity. We show that this can happen in the case of efficient ISP (in terms of maintenance and expansion costs), not excessively high demand uncertainty and high elasticity innovative services. After this we proceed in Sect. 3 to analysis of business model, where ISP also engages in content provision, modeling the case of Deutsche Telecom, reported in [13]. We show that also in this case the paid peering can be beneficial to both ISP and CP and, in addition, removes part of the incentive to challenge the network neutrality.

This paper is motivated by the current largest source of traffic growth: real time video services and studies economic relationship between content provider of such services and ISP. For example, the results of the paper allow to evaluate the parameters of recent agreements between Netflix and Comcast [15] and between Netflix and some European ISPs. However, our results are also applicable to likely future sources of traffic growth and in particular to services in the context of the future Internet of Things (IoT). For example, survey [2] lists a number of applications of IoT which will contribute substantially to the growth of traffic. Our results can be used to analyze business models and economic relationships between providers of such services and providers of Internet connectivity.

2 Paid Content Peering with Strong Content Service Provider

Here we develop the leader-follower model based on Stackelberg game [14]. This model assumes that the leader annouces his decisions to the follower, which optimizes his objective using this knowledge. The leader chooses his decisions, taking into account this behavior of the follower. For transparency we begin with the case of a single service. The model considered here can be seen as a tool for approximate analysis of the agreement between Netflix and Comcast [15]. The case of several interacting services is considered in the next section.

1. *Profit model of the content provider.* We assume that the content provider maximizes his profit, which is the difference between content provision revenue net of paid peering fraction and costs. There are two types of costs: provision costs and opportunity costs resulting from not satisfaction of demand. This results in the following profit function.

$$P_{CP} = (p(1-x) - c) \mathbb{E}_\omega \min\{W_0 + W, D(p,\omega)\}$$
$$- e\mathbb{E}_\omega \max\{0, D(p,\omega) - W_0 - W\} \tag{1}$$

where p is the service price; c is service provision costs; x is fraction of the revenue transferred to the ISP; W_0 is existing network capacity and W is a possible capacity expansion. Besides:

e - opportunity cost for not satisfied demand; this cost is comprized of two parts: revenue immediately lost and part of the customer value that can be lost to *churn* (customer deserting to other provider or satisfying her needs in an alternative way), which is proportional to unsatisfied demand;

$D(p,\omega)$ - demand for service at price p. Besides the price, it depends on random variable ω that describes the demand uncertainty.

Here price p and paid peering revenue fraction x are the decisions of content provider that he takes in order to maximize his profit, W is the decision of ISP, demand $D(p,\omega)$ results from decisions of service users and c, e, W_0 are parameters.

2. *Profit model of ISP.* We assume that he takes the role of Internet Service Provider (ISP). His profit is the difference between his revenue (fixed subscription fees from customers plus the share of content provider's revenue obtained through paid peering) and his costs (network maintenance costs and network expansion costs). This yields the following profit function.

$$P_{ISP} = C + px\mathbb{E}\min\{W_0 + W, D(p,\omega)\} - rW - q(W_0 + W) \tag{2}$$

where C is subscription fee (we assume that all the user population is subscribed to Internet for flat fee); r is the cost of unit capacity expansion; q is the cost of unit capacity maintenance.

The ISP maximizes his profit by choosing the level W of capacity expansion.

3. *Demand function of user population.* There exists substantial empirical evidence that the demand function for ICT products and services exhibits constant elasticity γ with respect to price (see [12]). Then

$$D = \frac{M}{p^\gamma}$$

where M is population specific parameter that is interpreted as available budget. We modify this function in the following way

$$D(p, \omega) = \frac{M}{(a + p)^\gamma}(1 + \omega) \tag{3}$$

where a is opportunity price that plays the role of the stabilization parameter that prevents the demand function from excessive growth for small values of price p. Parameters a, M, γ are all uncertain and should be described by random variables with appropriate probability distributions. In order to admit the analytical treatment, we simplify the description of uncertainty here by assuming that a, M, γ are deterministic, but the demand function is multiplied by the term $1 + \omega$, where ω is a random variable with cumulative distribution function $H(\cdot)$ that has density $h(\cdot)$.

4. *Governance of the system.* We assume that the content provider due to his market power has the leading role in this relationship. Consequently, the decision sequence is the following.

   i. Content provider selects the service price p and the share x of his service provision revenue to be transferred to the ISP in the framework of content peering agreement.

   ii. Knowing price p, the users generate the demand for the service as in (3).

   iii. Knowing his revenue share x and the demand for the service $D(p, \omega)$ up to the random variable ω with known distribution H, the ISP decides the volume W of the network expansion that maximizes his expected profit.

   iv. The content provider selects at point i his decisions x and p in such a way, as to maximize his profit, taking into account the reactions of other actors described in ii, iii.

Now we can analyze the relationship of content provider and ISP, following the governance just described. The analysis consists of the following steps.

1. Maximization the profit of ISP (2), substituting there the demand function (3), this will yield the dependence $W(p, x)$ of the optimal network expansion on the decisions (p, x) of the content provider.

2. Maximization of the profit of the content provider (1), substituting there the demand function (3) and the optimal expansion function $W(p, x)$ obtained on the previous step. This yields the optimal policy (p, x) of content provider, his best profit and resulting profit of the ISP. Resulting optimization problems are the following.

1. *The optimal expansion program $W(p,x)$ of ISP.* It is obtained by solving:

$$\max_{W \geq 0} \left\{ px\mathbb{E} \min \left\{ W_0 + W, \frac{M}{a+p^\gamma}(1+\omega) \right\} - (r+q)W \right\} \qquad (4)$$

Compared to (2) we have omitted here the constant components of revenue and costs that do not depend on decision W of the ISP. Due to simplifying assumptions about the demand uncertainty, it is possible to derive its explicit solution.

Theorem 1. *The solution $W(p,x)$ of problem (4) is given by*

$$W(p,x) = \max \left\{ 0, \frac{M}{a+p^\gamma} \left(1 + H^{-1} \left(1 - \frac{r+q}{px} \right) \right) - W_0 \right\} \qquad (5)$$

2. *The optimal pricing p^* and paid content peering share x^* of content provider.* They are obtained by substituting (3), (5) into (1) and solving the resulting optimization problem:

$$\max_{p,x} (p(1-x) - c + e)\mathbb{E} \min \left\{ W_0 + \max \left\{ 0, \frac{M}{a+p^\gamma} \times \right. \right.$$
$$\left. \left(1 + H^{-1} \left(1 - \frac{r+q}{px} \right) \right) - W_0 \right\}, \frac{M}{a+p^\gamma}(1+\tau) \right\} - \frac{Me}{a+p^\gamma} \qquad (6)$$
$$p \geq 0, 0 \leq x \leq 1.$$

The proof of the theorem is obtained by analytical solution of optimization problem formulated above. This problem does not admit explicit solution like problem (4) and therefore we have to resort to numerical methods. We obtain the dependence of actors' profits and policies on significant parameters of the problem by solving this problem repeatedly.

2.1   Results of Numerical Analysis

We have solved the optimization problem from Theorem 1 numerically for different values of parameters and provide below a sample of representative results.

Free Versus Paid Peering: Efficiency of ISP. We illustrate here the following finding: paid peering can be beneficial to content provider, but only if ISP is efficient enough in terms of provision costs.

The relationship between free and paid content peering and their connection with the efficiency of ISP can be illustrated by looking at the dependence of profit of content provider on the service price on Fig. 1. The thin solid curve shows the profit of content provider with infinite available capacity, while the thick dashed line shows the case of limited capacity W_0 when only free content peering is admitted by the content provider. Both curves coincide when the price exceeds a certain level because the actual capacity needed for demand

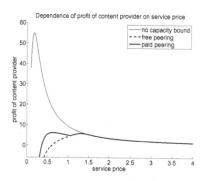

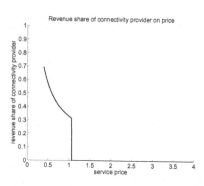

Fig. 1. Current cash flows and prospective cash flows

Fig. 2. Revenue share of ISP in paid peering

satisfaction becomes smaller than W_0. Both curves show a typical pattern of dependence of profit on price: the sharp increase in the region of low prices followed by slower decrease after attaining the maximal value.

The solid thick curve on Fig. 1 shows the case of paid content peering. It is positioned between the first two curves, coinciding with them in the region of high prices. Unlike the first two curves, it has a camel like appearance, having two maxima. The first maximum is found in the region of lower prices where it is profitable for content provider to resort to paid content peering, stimulating demand by aggressive pricing and stimulating the ISP to expand capacity to accommodate this demand. Another maximum is found in the region of the higher prices, where the content peering is unprofitable and the content provider admits only free content peering. For this reason in the region of higher prices this curve coincides with the curve of free content peering.

Whether the paid content peering will be actually employed by the content provider, depends on which of the to maxima is higher. One can see that on Fig. 1 the first maximum is indeed somewhat higher than the second one, so that it is profitable in this case for the content provider to admit the paid content peering because it yields about 6 % higher profit than the free peering. Figure 2 shows how the optimal share of the revenue accorded to the ISP changes with the service price in this case. One can observe that this share drops with the price increase because the demand decreases with the increase in price and less capacity is needed for its satisfaction, resulting in less stimulation of the ISP by the content provider. After the price passes a certain threshold it becomes no more profitable for content provider to resort to paid content peering and the share of the ISP abruptly drops to zero.

However, this advantage of paid peering exists only when the ISP is efficient enough in terms of expansion and maintenance costs. With less efficient ISP the left maximum drops below the right one which means that paid peering becomes unattractive to CP.

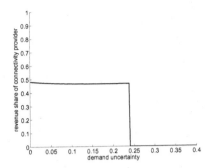

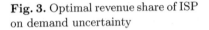

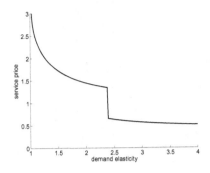

Fig. 3. Optimal revenue share of ISP on demand uncertainty

Fig. 4. Dependence of service price on demand elasticity

Dependence of Profits, Prices and Revenue Shares on Demand uncertainty. Here we show that high demand uncertainty induces risk averse behavior of content provider, caution with pricing and less interest towards paid peering.

We have studied the dependence of actor's profits and policies on the different problem parameters: costs c, e, r, q, initial available capacity W_0, demand parameters a, M, demand elasticity γ and variability σ. We show here these dependencies on the demand uncertainty/variability σ.

Figure 3 shows the dependence of optimal content provider's policy on demand uncertainty. When the uncertainty increases the content provider tries to hedge increasing risk by rising the price for his services. This has an effect of decreasing the demand and, consequently, also decreasing the demand variability and uncertainty as can be seen from the demand function (3). For low to moderate levels of uncertainty the content provider utilizes the paid peering because it is profitable to him to induce the ISP to expand the network capacity. In this uncertainty range the revenue share accorded to ISP is approximately constant and substantial. After the level of uncertainty passes a certain threshold the risk inherent in expanding capacity becomes too high and content provider rises his price substantially to limit the demand to already existing capacity, thus denying the ISP from any share of his revenue.

The profit of content provider decreases with increasing uncertainty. This is due to the combined effect of two causes. Firstly, the increase of price due to the effort to reduce risk leads to decreasing demand that has as a consequence contracted profits. Secondly, even for the constant demand the profit will decline with the increase of uncertainty. This is because in order to serve the same percentage of demand the content provider needs more capacity when the variation of demand increases. If, instead he lets the percentage of served demand to go down then he gets penalized by the opportunity costs. At the same time he gets the same or declining revenue because he get paid for the actual volume of service. To the contrary, the profit of the ISP grows because he gets incentivated more in order to install more capacity per unit of served demand. This is accompanied also by growth of his return on investment measured by the ratio of the

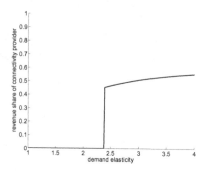

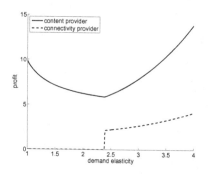

Fig. 5. Revenue share of ISP on demand elasticity

Fig. 6. Dependence of actors' profits on demand elasticity

profit and expansion costs. But, this happens only in the region of paid peering. After the content provider switches to the free peering the profit of ISP abruptly disappears and the profit of content provider continues to decline, albeit more slowly, because no part of his revenue goes to the ISP.

Dependence of Profits, Prices and Revenue Shares on Demand elasticity. Here we show that content peering is beneficial in the case of innovative high elasticity services.

Demand elasticity γ in the context of ICT services can be related to the relationship between basic, established, traditional services and innovative new services. For traditional services that cater to very basic communication needs viewed as indispensable, the demand elasticity is low. For example, there is considerable evidence in the literature that demand elasticity for the basic fixed net telephony is only marginally larger than 1. For new, innovative services that serve discretionary interests, like video on demand, demand elasticity can be high, exceeding 2 or more.

Figures 4 and 5 show how the optimal policies of the content provider change with increasing of the demand elasticity. If he caters to the basic services in the low to medium elasticity range then he sets the price relatively high. There is no need for paid peering in this elasticity range because the existing capacity is sufficient for their provision. While elasticity increases and the service consumption becomes more discretionary, the optimal price gradually drops. When the elasticity crosses a certain threshold, it becomes more profitable to the content provider to resort to paid peering in order to stimulate the ISP to install more capacity and obtain the capability to drop the price substantially in order to stimulate the demand. After the substantial initial drop the price continues to decrease slowly as the elasticity grows. The share of revenue accorded to the ISP starts from a relatively high level on crossing the threshold to paid peering and continues to increase slowly afterwards.

The profit of the content provider shown on Fig. 6 decreases with increasing of elasticity in the region of low to medium elasticities. This is because the decline

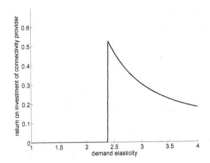

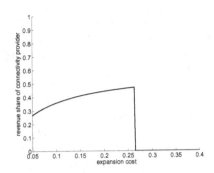

Fig. 7. Return on investment of ISP on demand elasticity

Fig. 8. Revenue share of ISP on the network expansion and maintenance cost

of prices is not offset sufficiently by increase of volume that remains capped by already installed capacity W_0 due to the absence of incentive to expand for the ISP due to free peering. When the content provider switches to paid peering the profit starts to grow with increasing elasticity because ever more capacity is becoming available. Also the profit of the ISP grows with increasing elasticity in the case of paid peering, even though not as steep as the profit of the content provider, while his return on investment shown on Fig. 7 decreases due to ever larger volume of capacity required to install.

Dependence of Profits, Prices and Revenue Shares on the Network expansion and Maintenance Costs. Here we come back to considering the dependence of actors' policies and profits on the efficiency of the ISP measured by the sum of the network expansion and maintenance costs $r + q$.

Similarly to Sect. 2.1, we observe that in the case of efficient ISP with low to medium expansion costs it is profitable to the content provider to accept paid peering. While the expansion costs of the ISP grow, he introduces less and less of additional capacity for the same share of the content provision revenue obtained. The content provider reacts to this in two ways. Firstly, he increases the service price in order to make the demand match the smaller available capacity. Secondly, he tries to incentivate the ISP more, transferring to him the gradually increasing share of his revenue (Fig. 8). Both these measures result in steep decline of his profit.

3   Content Peering and Service Differentiation

In this section we consider the situation when the ISP offers several internet provision services, which differ by the connection speeds and, consequently, differ by Quality of Experience (QoE) for the customers, which consume video services with high bandwidth requirements. More specifically, the connection speed decreases substantially for the basic connection package users after they exceed a specified download limit. Connection options without download limits are also available, but for higher price. In addition, the ISP provides his own content service in competition with existing video content providers (CP), but this service is exempt from bounds on downloading. This policy of ISP challenges the principles of network neutrality because it treats differently the data streams generated by similar services of different origin. It is similar to the policy announced recently by Deutsche Telekom regarding its own video service versus rival services like YouTube from Google, as described in [13].

We describe this situation by considering the population of customers to which three services s_i, $i = 1:3$ are offered. Each service is composed from two components, which together create the QoE for the end user: *content* and *connectivity*. Content can be provided by both ISP and CP, while the connectivity is provided only by ISP. More specifically:

- Service s_1, with content provided by CP. It is available to subscribers to the basic Internet connectivity package for a flat price C_1 with high speed V_1 until download limit $\bar{d}$ is reached and low speed V_2 beyond this limit.
- Service s_2 with the same content as in s_1 provided by CP. It is available to subscribers to the enhanced Internet connectivity package for a flat price $C_2 > C_1$ with high speed V_1 irrespective of download quantity.
- Service s_3 with competing content to s_1, s_2 provided by ISP. It is available to subscribers to the basic connectivity package for a flat price C_1, but the high speed V_1 is kept for this particular service without any download limit.

3.1   Service Selection by a Single Subscriber

Let us consider first services s_2 and s_3 taken in isolation. Suppose that p is a price that respective providers charge for the unit of content measured in bandwidth. Similarly to Sect. 2 we assume that demand d, generated by a single subscriber, has a constant elasticity dependence on the service price

$$d_i(p) = \frac{M}{(a+p)^\gamma}, \quad i = 2, 3 \qquad (7)$$

which conforms well with empirical data [12]. Here $a < 1$ is an opportunity cost for customer, associated with consumption of service unit, M is proportional to the income of subscriber, and $\gamma = \gamma_1$ for service s_2 and $\gamma = \theta$ for service s_3. We assume that elasticity γ describes the QoE, that is, the larger γ the better is the QoE. Indeed, with larger γ the consumption grows faster with the decrease in the service price and the limit consumption with $p = 0$ is higher, while for small γ the consumption will be low even for small prices. Thus, a service with larger γ is more attractive to consumers than a service with smaller γ. Let us assume further that QoE for service s_2 is higher than QoE for s_3. Indeed, they are provided with the same connection speed and one can expect that content of s_2 is in average superior to content of s_3 because content provision is a core business of CP. Thus, we assume that $\gamma_1 > \theta$.

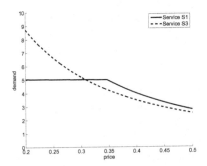

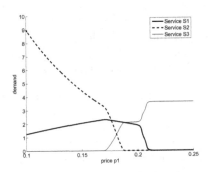

Fig. 9. Demand functions for services s_1 and s_3 with $\gamma_1 = 2, \gamma_2 = 0.1$, $\theta = 1.8$, $M = 1$, $a = 0.1$, $\bar{d} = 5$

Fig. 10. Dependence of population demand functions on price p_1 with $p_2 = 0.2$, $\gamma_1 = 2$, $\gamma_2 = 0.1$, $\theta = 1.8$, $a = 0.1$, $\bar{d} = 5$

Let us consider now service s_1. Until demand is smaller than $\bar{d}$, it is the same service as s_2, therefore its demand function is described by (7) with $\gamma = \gamma_1$. After demand exceeds $\bar{d}$ the connection speed drops, leading to substantially inferior QoE. Therefore we describe the demand function of s_3 when demand exceeds $\bar{d}$ by (7) with $\gamma = \gamma_2$, $\gamma_2 < \theta < \gamma_1$. This yields the following demand function

$$d_1(p) = \begin{cases} \frac{M}{(a+p)^{\gamma_1}} & \text{if } p \geq \left(\frac{M}{\bar{d}}\right)^{\frac{1}{\gamma_1}} - a \\ \frac{M}{(a+p)^{\gamma_2}} - M^{1-\frac{\gamma_2}{\gamma_1}} \bar{d}^{\frac{\gamma_2}{\gamma_1}} + \bar{d} & \text{otherwise} \end{cases} \tag{8}$$

These demand functions are shown on Fig. 9.

So far we have considered these services in isolation. The next step is to describe how a subscriber selects between these services, depending on their respective prices. Let us assume that consumer subscribes for just one of the services s_i, $i = 1 : 3$ and follow the approach of consumption theory of microeconomics [11]. This theory associates the consumption of service s_i with individual utility function of a consumer $\varphi_i(p, d)$. He selects the amount d of service to consume by maximizing this utility function with respect to d for given unit price p. For a risk neutral consumer this utility function can be further structured as follows:

$$\varphi_i(p, d) = \psi_i(d) - (a + p)d - C \tag{9}$$

where $\psi_i(d)$ is utility of consumption of amount d of service s_i, $(a + p)d$ is the cost of amount d of service and C is subscription fee. Demand function $d_i(p)$ is obtained from (9) by maximizing $\varphi_i(p, d)$ with respect to d. Substituting demand function $d_i(p)$ into $\varphi_i(p, d)$ we obtain the maximal consumer utility $\beta_i(p) = \varphi_i(p, d(p))$ associated with consumption of service s_i at price p. Having these functions for each service s_i, we can obtain the demand of consumer for service s_i by the following rule.

Consumption of services by single consumer. Suppose that services s_1, s_2 are offered at unit price p_1 and service s_3 is offered at unit price p_2. Then

- Find the highest value among $\beta_1(p_1), \beta_2(p_1), \beta_3(p_2)$, suppose that it is attained for service s_k.
- The demand d_k, for service s_k will be $d_k(p_1)$ if $k = 1, 2$ and $d_k(p_2)$ if $k = 3$. The demand for services s_i, $i \neq k$ is zero.

Observe that this operation of taking maximum between three utilities makes demand $d_i = d_i(p, C, M)$ for service s_i dependent on both prices $p = (p_1, p_2)$ and both subscription fees $C = (C_1, C_2)$.

In order to implement this rule we need to know expressions for utilities $\beta_i(p)$ and these are obtained from expressions for $\varphi_i(p, d)$. These expressions are obtained taking into account that demand functions $d_i(p)$ from (7), (8) are obtained by maximization of (9). They are summarized in the following theorem.

Theorem 2. *Suppose that demand functions $d_i(p)$, $i = 2 : 3$ are defined by (7). Then functions $\psi_i(d)$ from (9) that yield these demand functions are*

$$\psi_i(d) = \begin{cases} \frac{1}{1-\frac{1}{\gamma}} M^{\frac{1}{\gamma}} d^{1-\frac{1}{\gamma}} & \text{if} \quad \gamma \neq 1 \\ M \ln d & \text{otherwise} \end{cases}, \quad i = 2, 3 \tag{10}$$

$$\beta_i(p) = \begin{cases} \frac{1}{\gamma-1} \frac{M}{(a+p)^{\gamma-1}} - C & \text{if} \quad \gamma \neq 1 \\ M\left(\ln \frac{M}{a+p} - 1\right) - C & \text{otherwise} \end{cases} \tag{11}$$

with $(\gamma, C) = (\gamma_1, C_2)$ for $i = 2$ and $(\gamma, C) = (\theta, C_1)$ for $i = 3$.

Functions $\psi_1(d), \beta_1(p)$ are obtained similarly to (8) by gluing together at point $p = \left(\frac{M}{d}\right)^{\frac{1}{\gamma_1}} - a$ pieces of functions (10), (11) with $\gamma = \gamma_1, \gamma_2$. This theorem is proved by substitution of (10) into (9) and finding the maximum of obtained function with respect to d.

3.2   Demand Functions of Population of Subscribers

In order to obtain these functions $D_i(p, C)$ for the population of subscribers from demand functions $d_i(p, C, M)$ of individual subscribers let us recall that these latter functions depend on parameter M from (7), which is a proxy for the income of a given subscriber. Assuming that the subscriber income is representative of the household income in a given country, we can recover the distribution $H(y)$ of parameter M from the national statistics. For example, data reported in [3] show, that income of US households is approximated reasonably well by unimodal distribution with piecewise linear density $h(y)$, if we neglect the households in the top 5% bracket.

$$h(y) = \begin{cases} 0 \text{ if } y < 0, \ y > (1 + k_M)\bar{M} \\ y\frac{2}{(k_M+1)\bar{M}^2} \text{ if } 0 \le y \le \bar{M} \\ \frac{2}{(k_M+1)\bar{M}}\left(1 + \frac{1}{k_M} - y\frac{1}{k_M\bar{M}}\right) \text{ otherwise} \end{cases}$$

Here $\bar{M}$ is the maximal point of this density. This distribution is skewed to the right with $k_M \simeq 5$. Integrating the individual demand functions with respect to this density we obtain the population demand functions and shares $S_i(p, C)$ of subscribers to different services

$$D_i = U \int d_i(p, C, y) h(y) dy, \quad S_i = \int \mathbb{I}_{d_i(p,C,y)} h(y) dy. \tag{12}$$

where U is the total number of customers and $\mathbb{I}_z = 1$ if $z > 0$ and zero otherwise. Figure 10 shows an example of dependence of demand functions on p_1 for fixed p_2, which can be obtained through numerical integration.

3.3   Profit Maximization Problems for Actors

We assume here that the share of fixed subscription equal to the share of not satisfied demand is lost. Then the satisfied demands D_i^+ and respective subscription shares S_i^+ can be expressed as follows

$$D_1^+ = \min\{D_1, \max\{0, w - D_2 - D_3\}\}, \quad S_1^+ = \frac{D_1^+}{D_1} S_1$$

$$D_2^+ = \min\{D_2, \max\{0, w - D_3\}\}, \quad S_2^+ = \frac{D_2^+}{D_2} S_2$$

$$D_3^+ = \min\{D_3, w\}, \quad S_3^+ = \frac{D_3^+}{D_3} S_3$$

Similarly, we define nonsatisfied potential demand and missing subscription shares for $i = 1 : 3$ as

$$D_i^- = D_i(p, C) - D_i^+(p, C, w), \quad S_i^- = S_i(p, C) - S_i^+(p, C, w)$$

Let us define the following opportunity costs resulting from not meeting potential demand and possible churn

e_1 - opportunity cost for CP for not meeting potential demand for services s_1, s_2

e_2 - opportunity cost for ISP for not meeting potential demand for service s_3

g_i - opportunity cost for ISP for not meeting subscriptions for service s_i

Besides we have

c_1 - provision cost for CP for provision of content for services s_1, s_2

c_2 - provision cost for ISP for provision of content for service s_3

The service provision revenue of CP is

$$R_{CP} = R_{CP}(p, C, W) = p_1 \left(D_1^+ + D_2^+\right)$$

and we assume that share x of this revenue CP transfers to ISP in the context of paid content peering. Then the profit of content provider is expressed as follows

$$P_{CP} = (p_1(1 - x) - c_1)\left(D_1^+ + D_2^+\right) - e_1\left(D_1^- + D_2^-\right) \tag{13}$$

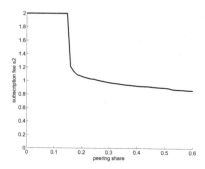

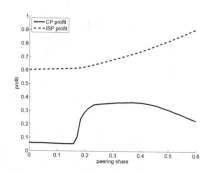

Fig. 11. Dependence of subscription fee for service s_2 on paid peering share

Fig. 12. Dependence of actor's profit on paid peering share

The revenue of ISP consists of revenue for provision of service s_3, subscription revenue and transfer of revenue from CP:

$$R_{ISP} = p_2 D_3^+ + C_1 \left(S_1^+ + S_3^+ \right) + C_2 S_2^+ + p_1 x \left(D_1^+ + D_2^+ \right)$$

and its profit is equal to revenue minus provision, opportunity, expansion and maintenance costs:

$$P_{ISP} = R_{ISP} - c_2 D_3^+ - e_2 D_3^- - \sum_{i=1}^{3} g_i S_i^- - rW - q \left(W_0 + W \right) \qquad (14)$$

System governance. In order to evaluate the possible impact of the paid content peering, we assume again that CP moves first, exercising his superior market power, selects price p_1 for his content and share x (if any) of his content provision revenue that he voluntarily transfers to ISP. ISP responds by selecting capacity expansion program $W = W(x, p_1)$, price for his content $p_2 = p_2(x, p_1)$ and subscription fee $C_2 = C_2(x, p_1)$ by solving the profit maximization problem

$$\max_{W, p_2, C_2} P_{ISP} \left(x, p, C, W \right). \qquad (15)$$

Anticipating these decisions of ISP, the CP selects his decisions (p_1, x) by maximizing his profit

$$\max_{p_1, x} P_{CP} \left(x, p, C, W(x, p_1) \right) \mid p_2 = p_2(x, p_1), \ C_2 = C_2(x, p_1) \qquad (16)$$

Thus, this is again the leader-follower Stackelberg game [14].

3.4   Some Results

We have solved the problems (15), (16) for different values of problem parameters, always keeping the attractiveness of content of the service s_3 provided by

ISP smaller than for the content of services s_1, s_2 provided by CP. The patterns obtained in the simpler case of a single service from Sect. 2 were confirmed and additional patterns emerged, regarding the impact of paid content peering on the degree of network neutrality. The main findings are the following.

1. ISP has an incentive to extract additional subscription fee for allowing customers to have the similar QoE for content provision service of CP as for his own content service. Thus, in the absence of regulation the network neutrality will be challenged (see Fig. 11). However, the extent of violation of network neutrality can be reduced substantially by resort to paid content peering. The difference between subscription fees can be halved, as shown on Fig. 11.

2. This increase of grade of network neutrality happens in parallel with increase in profit for both actors. One can see on Fig. 12 that profit of CP increases substantially with the share of content provision revenue accorded to ISP in the range of 0.3–0.4, compared to the absence of such share.

4 Conclusion

We have developed several game theoretical models for analysis of relationship between ISPs and content providers in Internet ecosystem. These models were used for analysis of paid versus free content peering and analysis of relationship between peering and network neutrality. We have shown that content peering can be mutually beneficial to content and ISPs even when the content provider has the market power to force the ISP to accept free content peering. We have provided an insight as to when this will happen: efficient enough ISP, not excessively high demand uncertainty/variability and innovative new services with high price elasticity. We have shown also that paid peering removes part of the incentive to challenge the principle of network neutrality.

References

1. Altman, E., Legout, A., Xu, Y.: Network non-neutrality debate: an economic analysis. In: Domingo-Pascual, J., Manzoni, P., Palazzo, S., Pont, A., Scoglio, C. (eds.) NETWORKING 2011, Part II. LNCS, vol. 6641, pp. 68–81. Springer, Heidelberg (2011)
2. Atzori, L., Iera, A., Morabito, G.: The internet of things: a survey. Comput. Netw. **54**(15), 2787–2805 (2010)
3. Bureau, U.C.: Current Population Survey. Annual Social and Economic Supplement (2011)
4. Cheng, H.K., Bandyopadhyay, S., Guo, H.: The debate on net neutrality: a policy perspective. Inf. Syst. Res. **22**(1), 60–82 (2011)
5. Economides, N., Tåg, J.: Network neutrality on the internet: a two-sided market analysis. Inf. Econ. Policy **24**(2), 91–104 (2012)
6. Krämer, J., Wiewiorra, L., Weinhardt, C.: Net neutrality: a progress report. Telecommun. Policy **37**, 794–813 (2013)
7. Krogfoss, B., Sofman, L., Weldon, M.: Internet architecture evolution and the complex economies of content peering. Bell Labs Tech. J. **17**(1), 163–184 (2012)

8. Labovitz, C., Iekel-Johnson, S., McPherson, D., Oberheide, J., Jahanian, F.: Internet inter-domain traffic. In: SIGCOMM 2010, New Delhi, India, pp. 75–86 (2010)

9. Liebenau, J., Karrberg, P., Elaluf-Calderwood, S.: A Critical Analysis of the Effects of Internet Traffic on Business Models of Telecom Operators: A White Paper of the Lse-etno Research Collaboration Programme. The London School of Economics and Political Science, London (2011)

10. Maille, P., Tuffin, B.: Telecommunication Network Economics: From Theory to Applications. Cambridge University Press, Cambridge (2014)

11. Mas-Colell, A., Whinston, M.D., Green, J.R.: Microeconomic Theory. Oxford University Press, New York (1995)

12. Mitra, D., Ramakrishnan, K.G., Wang, Q., Combined economic modeling, traffic engineering: joint optimization of pricing and routing in multi-service networks. In: Proceedings of 17th International Teletraffic Congress, Salvador, Brasil, Amsterdam. Elsevier (2001)

13. O'Brien, K.J.: Limiting Data Use in Germany. The New York Times, Berlin (2013)

14. Stackelberg, H.V.: The Theory of Market Economy. Oxford University Press, London (1952)

15. Wyatt, E., Cohen, N.: Comcast and Netflix Reach Deal on Service. The New York Times, New York (2014)

Security Requirements in a Federated Cloud Networking Architecture

Philippe Massonet[1(✉)], Anna Levin[2], Antonio Celesti[3], and Massimo Villari[3]

[1] Cetic, Charleroi, Belgium
philippe.massonet@cetic.be
[2] HLR, IBM Haifa, Haifa, Israel
lanna@il.ibm.com
[3] DICIEAMA, University of Messina, Messina, Italy
{acelesti,mvillari}@unime.it
http://www.beacon-project.eu/

Abstract. Cloud federation enables cloud providers to collaborate in order to create a large pool of virtual resources at multiple network locations. Different types of federated cloud architectures have been proposed and implemented up to now. In this context, an effective, agile and secure federation of cloud networking resources is a key aspect for the deployment of federated applications. This paper presents the preliminary security requirements analyzed in the H2020 BEACON Project that aims at researching techniques to federate cloud network resources and defining an integrated cloud management layer that enables an efficient and secure deployment of federated cloud applications. The paper analyses both how to protect the cloud networking infrastructure, and how cloud users can customize the network security for their distributed applications.

Keywords: Cloud computing · Federation · SDN · NFV · Security

1 Introduction

Federation enables cloud providers to collaborate and share their resources to create a large pool of virtual resources placed in multiple network locations. Different types of federated architectures for clouds and datacenters have been proposed and implemented so far (e.g., let us thing about cloud bursting, cloud brokering, and cloud aggregation architectures) with different levels of resource coupling and interoperability among resources, from loosely coupled to tightly coupled federation, according to the mechanisms that are involved to share resources. Typically tightly coupled approaches require more invasive mechanisms than loosely coupled ones. In this context, tenants (i.e., societies using federated cloud networking services) require to deploy their applications on multiple federated cloud providers. For this reason, an effective, agile and secure federation of cloud networking resources is fundamental to address the deployment of federated cloud applications. In order, to analyse the security requirements of

© Springer International Publishing Switzerland 2016
A. Celesti and P. Leitner (Eds.): ESOCC 2015 Workshops, CCIS 567, pp. 79–88, 2016.
DOI: 10.1007/978-3-319-33313-7_6

federated cloud networking architectures, in this paper, we focus on the Horizon 2020 BEACON project. The main goal of BEACON is two-fold: *(i)* research and develop techniques to federate cloud networking resources; *(ii)* define a cloud management layer that enables an efficient and secure deployment of federated cloud applications.

The paper is organized as follows. In Sect. 2, we briefly describe the BEACON architecture used as model to analyse the security requirements of a federation-enabled cloud networking system. In Sect. 3, we provide a security analysis considering both infrastructure and application levels. In Sect. 4, we discuss how to protect a virtual network infrastructure. In Sect. 5, we discuss how can be possible to achieve cross-cloud overlay network protection. In Sect. 6, we compare the BEACON security requirements with respect to other initiatives. Section 7 concludes the paper.

2   BEACON Overview

In this Section, we provide an overview of the BEACON federated architecture on which our security analysis is based. Figure 1 shows the BEACON federated architecture. The three main components are: the service manager, the cloud manager and the network manager. The Service Manager is responsible for the instantiation of distributed federated services. Each service component is typically deployed in a Virtual Machine (VM) according to a particular service manifest. The Cloud Manager is responsible for the placement of VMs into physical hosts. It receives requests from the Service Manager through the cloud interface in order to create and manage VMs and it finds where the best placement for these VMs is, satisfying a given set of constraints The Cloud Manager is free to place and move VMs anywhere, even on remote clouds within the federation, as long as the placement is done according to constraints. The Network Manager is responsible for allocating network resources to manage federated cloud virtual overlay networks across geographically distributed sites. Figure 1 shows two cloud stacks running on different cloud providers. Together they form a cloud federation. The middle part of the Figure shows that the Cloud Manager and Network Managers of the two cloud providers communicate to share federated resources. The top part of Fig. 1 shows two application level case of studies respectively focusing on flight schedule and cloud orchestration federated cloud applications. The bottom part of the figure shows the open source projects that are used to implement the federated architecture. The architecture has to manage cloud providers based on heterogeneous pieces of middleware. For example, the cloud provider on the left part of the picture is using OpenNebula, whereas the cloud provider on the right part is using OpenStack to manage its cloud infrastructure. The network managers of both cloud providers are both using the Open Virtual Network (OVN) technology to manage the network resources and communications between the two cloud providers by means of different Software Defined Networking (SDN) overlay networks.

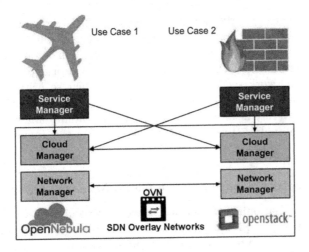

Fig. 1. BEACON federated architecture.

3 Security Analysis on the Federated Cloud Networking Architecture

Security issues are considered at both Cloud Manager and Network Manager layers. In addition, for each layer, we considered both infrastructure and application level security requirements. Infrastructure level security deals with securing the cloud infrastructure services provided by the Cloud Manager and the Network Manager, and protecting them from an unauthorized access of applications and users. Application level security deals with the security of the application when it is deployed in federated clouds. In our opinion, even the security requirements of the application level needs to be studied at both the Cloud Manager and Network Manager layers. In the following, we review the four categories of security issues that we identified.

3.1 Application Security at the Cloud Manager Layer

It involves the provisioning of security services from the Cloud Manager to applications. The Cloud Manager can provide security services for VMs such as an application level firewall service or a vulnerability analysis service. The application can also choose to deploy these services by itself. For example, an application can request that a vulnerability analysis has to be performed continuously on a given VM or could request that all HTTP traffic has to be analysed by application level firewall rules for a given HTTP session.

3.2 Application Security at the Network Manager Layer

It involves the provisioning of security services from the Network Manager to applications. The Network Manager can provide network level security services.

Applications have to provide their requirements according the network security services that they intend to use. The Network Manager will deploy and provide the security services as Network Functions Virtualization (NFV) and/or Sequential Function Chart (SFC). This allows applications to select the right combination of network security services to meet their security requirements. For example, the application may request either to apply network firewall rules on one or more overlay networks, to request a vulnerability analysis at the network layer, or to apply network intrusion detection to the application network traffic.

3.3 Infrastructure Security at the Cloud Manager Layer

It involves the provisioning of security services to secure the Cloud Manager. The threats to the Cloud Manager are both external and internal in nature. The Cloud Manager needs to be protected from unauthorised users who could try to access the Cloud Manager even though they are not authorised. Threats may also originate from internal sources. Internal threats come from authorised users deploying applications in the cloud. In this case the Cloud Manager must ensure a sufficient level of isolation of applications in the multi-tenant environment of the federated cloud infrastructure. This requires an in-depth analysis on how to secure the complete VM deployment lifecycle by the federated cloud infrastructure management, including issues related to credentials management. Internal threats can also come from the Cloud Manager layer of a provider that might try to access the federated applications instantiated by other providers without proper authorizations.

3.4 Infrastructure Security at the Network Manager Layer

It involves the provisioning of security services to secure the Network Manager. The main components of the virtual networks need to be secured. For example, the control plane of federated virtual networks need to be protected from applications. Another security challenge regards how to ensure a sufficient level of isolation and encryption of network traffic by automating the provisioning and configuration of secure on-demand SDN according to given security level agreements. From a security perspective, federated cloud networking provides the opportunity to monitor the virtualized compute, storage, and network resources across a federation. This provides opportunities to detect attacks to the federation level that could not be detected at an individual Cloud Manager layer. We can identify many security issues having a global picture of services deployed and executed in several federated clouds. The security issues that we are considering range from Intrusion Detections, to vulnerabilities scanning, even to distributed denial of service (DDoS) attacks. For example, DDoS attacks might be difficult to be detected by monitoring activities within a single cloud. However, DDoS attack patterns could be detected earlier by monitoring data coming from the cloud federation. In this context, enhanced monitoring capabilities provided by federated cloud networking systems can improve the detection of security threats.

4   Protecting the Virtual Network Infrastructure

In this Section, we discuss an access control system integrated into the generic federated cloud networking architecture depicted in Fig. 2. The main components of the networking architecture are the Federation SDN Management (MG), the Federation Agent (FA) and the Federated Data Path (DP). Each of these components has an Application Program Interface (API) that needs to be protected. In the following, we analyse how to protect these APIs in terms of access control. More specifically, our analysis focuses on these three main networking-related components and how their respective public APIs are protected. For simplicity, we assume that internal APIs will be protected by the local domain security policies. For this reason their description is out of the scope of this paper. The Federated SDN MG interacts with the FAs that are distributed in different federated clouds through public REST APIs. Each FA is connected to the SDN controller of its cloud. This connection does not need to be protected from external attacks because it is internal to the cloud. The south bound FA API allows the FA to configure the network forwarding rules in the Federated DP. The latter is responsible to query the corresponding FA when information is missing. All the collected pieces of information are stored by the Federated DP in forwarding tables that track network segments (e.g., VPN) among different federated cloud providers' sites. Since the FA-to-Federated DP interaction is made within the same domain it does not need to be protected from external attacks. An access control component may be integrated either within the Federated SDN MG or distributed among the different federated clouds. It depends on the fact if the federation is tightly coupled or loosely coupled. Figure 2 shows a cloud federation scenario where the Federated SDN MG is protected by an access control Policy Enforcement Point (PEP) and a Policy Decision Point (PDP) as well as a security policy database. The access control component also protects the FA API. In particular, Fig. 2 shows an example of cloud federation including two cloud sites where two network segments have been connected with an overlay network: network segment "123" from site 1 with "321" from site 2, and network segment "456" from site 1 with "654" from site 2.

5   Customizing Overlay Network Protection for the Deployment of Federated Applications

As previously discussed, in order to secure a federated networking application deployed in multiple federated clouds, a few security considerations have to be analysed at both the Cloud Manager and Network Manager layers. To this end, an application service manifest should specify the required security services that have to be provided by both Cloud and Network Manager layers to ensure that the federated cloud system meets the security requirements of the deployed federated cloud application. In doing that, the security requirements for the Cloud Manager must be separated from the security requirements for the Network Manager. In fact, these security requirements must be separately passed respectively

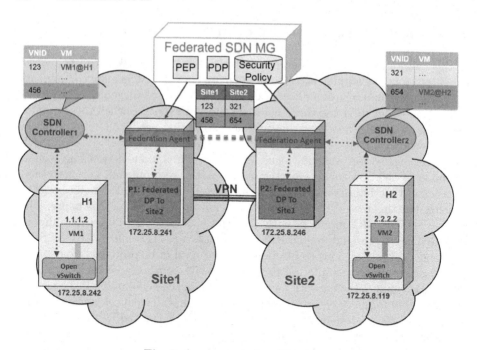

Fig. 2. Access control architecture.

to the Cloud Manager and Network Manager for enforcement. To this end, the security requirements must be translated into the appropriate security policies for the Cloud and Network Manager layers. This implies the Network Manager analyses of the considered pieces of middleware (e.g., OpenNebula, OpenStack, etc.) in order to design how they can exchange security policies. Another issue that has to be analysed is related to the location of the network services, e.g., to define which NFV firewall must be used when several are available. In addition, even the security mechanisms that allow VM migration within a federated cloud scenario have to be planned. In the following, we describe how to specify security templates for security functions and how to implement network security services as NFV.

5.1   Specifying Security Templates for Security Functions

In the following, we discuss how the service manifest could be extended to specify required network security services. The network security requirements could be passed to the Network Manager layer in order to customize the security services of each overlay network according to the security requirements of the application. Different applications have different security requirements on the environment in which they are executed, i.e. in this case the cloud, both in terms of computing and network resources. Commonly, it is difficult for a cloud provider to customize the physical infrastructure according to the applications' requirements of their individual clients. In this context the rapid evolution of network virtualisation technologies is simplifying things. For example, SDN and other network virtualisation technologies allow providers to customize virtual networks according to application requirements.

Cloud deployment requirements for applications have to be specified in the service manifest. The service manifest identifies the different application components, how they should communicate and how they should be deployed. The service manifest also specifies the Quality of Service (QoS) and security requirements. Figure 3 shows how the service manifest for an application is passed from a user to the cloud provider for the deployment of a federated application. The service manifest is parsed by the Service Manager that extracts security requirements and forwards them to the Cloud and Network Managers. The latter can use the network level security requirements to customize the security of the overlay network that is provisioned on-demand for the application.

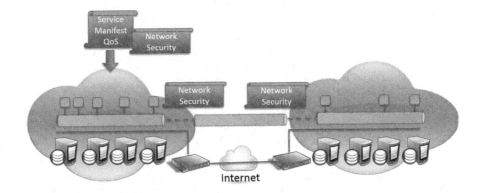

Fig. 3. Network security policies.

5.2   Implementing Network Security Services as NFV

Hereby, we discuss how the Network Function Virtualisation (NFV) and Service Function Chaining (SFC) technologies might be used to deploy virtualised network security services and mash-up them to provide the required level of network security for each application overlay network. Figure 4 shows how the security of overlay networks belonging to user A and B can be customised. NFV security services such as firewall (1), deep packet inspection (2) or intrusion detection (3) are deployed on the NFV infrastructure. The network security requirements of each distributed application are passed to the SDN controller. In order to meet the security requirements of the application, the SDN controller will set up each overlay network so that network traffic is routed through the required security services. For example, user A requires his/her network traffic to pass through security services (1) and (2) before leaving the cloud, whereas User B requires his network traffic to pass through security services (2) and (3) before leaving the cloud.

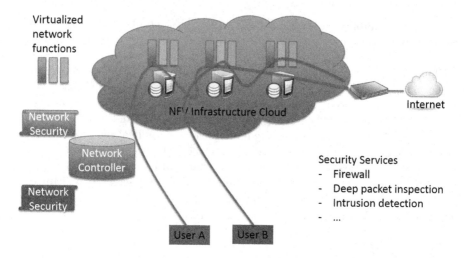

Fig. 4. NFV infrastructure with SFC.

6   Related Work

Cloud federation is a widely debated topic. In fact, there are many scientific works focusing on different fields including energy efficiency [1], storage [2], Assistive Technology [3], dataweb [4] and so on. A requirement analysis of federated Infrastructure as a Service (IaaS) clouds is discussed in [5], nevertheless the authors do not focus on security and virtual networking technologies. In [6], the authors analyse the main security threats for cloud computing infrastructures, as well as proposing a novel architecture in charge of reacting to security attacks in Infrastructure as a Service platforms. The basic idea is to migrate the attacked virtual appliance and to reconfigure the network by means of Software Defined Networking approach. The overhead due to data encryption in a message oriented middleware for cloud federation is discussed in [7]. A remote attestation approach to mitigate threats in cloud mush-up services is discussed in [8].

Currently, there are not so many scientific works focusing on federated cloud networking architectures. SDN enables the administrators to configure network resources very quickly and to adjust network-wide traffic flow to meet changing needs dynamically. However, there are some challenges for implementing a full-scale carrier SDN. One of the most important challenges is SDN security [9]. In [10], the authors design open-flow specific security solutions and propose a comprehensive security architecture to provide security services such as enforcing mandatory network policy correctly and receiving network policy securely for SDN. In [11], an Orchestrator-based architecture that utilizes Network Monitoring and SDN Control functions to develop security applications is proposed. In [12], the authors analyse the security attributes of the SN-Security Architecture (SN-SECA). In [13], the authors propose a network security approach which is aware of all existing systems and services hosted by at least one cloud provider.

The main idea is to maintain a logically centralized database that provides latest security related information about each system or service.

7 Conclusion

In this paper, we presented the main security requirements of a federated cloud networking architecture analysed in the Horizon H2020 BEACON project. The project aims to provide a homogeneous virtualization layer, on top of heterogeneous underlying physical networks, computing and storage infrastructures, even providing enablement for automated federation of applications across multiple clouds.

In particular, we first presented the reference federated networking architecture and then, we provided a security analysis of the major requirements. In addition, we discussed how the public interfaces of both Cloud and Network Manager layers should be protected. The paper also described how the overlay networks can be configured according to particular service manifests for the deployment of federated applications. In future works, we plan to optimize the impact of the security for the deployment of federated applications.

Acknowledgment. This research was supported by the European Union's Horizon 2020 Research and Innovation Programme Project BEACON under Grant Agreement No. 644048.

References

1. Giacobbe, M., Celesti, A., Fazio, M., Villari, M., Puliafito, A.: Towards energy management in cloud federation: a survey in the perspective of future sustainable and cost-saving strategies. Comput. Netw. **91**, 438–452 (2015)
2. Celesti, A., Fazio, M., Villari, M., Puliafito, A.: Adding long-term availability, obfuscation, and encryption to multi-cloud storage systems. J. Netw. Comput. Appl. **59**, 208–218 (2016)
3. Mulfari, D., Celesti, A., Villari, M.: A computer system architecture providing a user-friendly man machine interface for accessing assistive technology in cloud computing. J. Syst. Softw. **100**, 129–138 (2015)
4. Celesti, A., Tusa, F., Villari, M., Puliafito, A.: How the dataweb can support cloud federation: service representation and secure data exchange. In: 2012 Second Symposium on Network Cloud Computing and Applications (NCCA), pp. 73–79 (2012)
5. Panarello, A., Celesti, A., Fazio, M., Villari, M., Puliafito, A.: A requirements-analysis for IaaS cloud federation. In: Proceedings of the 4th International Conference on Cloud Computing and Services Science, pp. 584–589 (2014). doi:10.5220/0004945705840589. ISBN:978-989-758-019-2
6. Carrozza, G., Manetti, V., Marotta, A., Canonico, R., Avallone, S.: Exploiting SDN approach to tackle cloud computing security issues in the ATC scenario. In: Vieira, M., Cunha, J.C. (eds.) EWDC 2013. LNCS, vol. 7869, pp. 54–60. Springer, Heidelberg (2013)

7. Celesti, A., Fazio, M., Villari, M.: Se clever: a secure message oriented middleware for cloud federation. In: IEEE Symposium on Computers and Communications (ISCC), pp. 35–40 (2013)
8. Celesti, A., Fazio, M., Villari, M., Puliafito, A., Mulfari, D.: Remote and deep attestations to mitigate threats in cloud mash-up services. In: World Congress on Computer and Information Technology (WCCIT), pp. 1–6 (2013)
9. Scott-Hayward, S., O'Callaghan, G., Sezer, S.: SDN security: a survey. In: 2013 IEEE SDN for Future Networks and Services (SDN4FNS), pp. 1–7 (2013)
10. Hu, Z., Wang, M., Yan, X., Yin, Y., Luo, Z.: A comprehensive security architecture for SDN. In: 18th International Conference on Intelligence in Next Generation Networks (ICIN), pp. 30–37 (2015)
11. Zaalouk, A., Khondoker, R., Marx, R., Bayarou, K.: Orchsec: an orchestrator-based architecture for enhancing network-security using network monitoring and SDN control functions. In: IEEE Network Operations and Management Symposium (NOMS), pp. 1–9 (2014)
12. Bernardo, D., Chua, B.B.: Introduction and analysis of SDN and NFV security architecture (SN-SECA). In: IEEE 29th International Conference on Advanced Information Networking and Applications (AINA), pp. 796–801 (2015)
13. Seeber, S., Rodosek, G.: Improving network security through SDN in cloud scenarios. In: 10th International Conference on Network and Service Management (CNSM), pp. 376–381 (2014)

W4S4FI Workshop Papers

Preface of WAS4FI 2015

The Future Internet has emerged as a new initiative to pave a novel infrastructure linked to objects (things) of the real world so as to meet the changing global needs of business and society. It offers Internet users a standardized, secure, efficient, and trustable environment, which allows open and distributed access to global networks, services, and information. There is a need for both researchers and practitioners to develop platforms made up of adaptive Future Internet applications. In this sense, the emergence and consolidation of service-oriented architectures (SOA), cloud computing wireless sensor networks (WSN), and the new paradigm fog computing, give benefits, such as flexibility, scalability, security, interoperability, and adaptability for building these applications.

WAS4FI encourages a multidisciplinary perspective and welcomes papers that address challenges of Future Internet applications. The participation of researchers and practitioners from academia and industry is encouraged in order to promote cross-community interactions thereby avoiding disconnection between these groups. As the proud Organizing Committee and chairs of the 5th International Workshop on Adaptive Services for the Future Internet, we would like to take this opportunity to welcome you to the proceedings of WAS4FI 2015.

In this fifth edition, WAS4FI again aimed to bring together the community at ESOCC and addresses different aspects of adaptive Future Internet applications, emphasizing the importance of governing the convergence of contents, services, things, and networks in order to achieve the building of platforms for efficiency, scalability, security, and flexible adaptation. In this workshop, we cover the foundations of the aforementioned technologies as well as new emerging proposals for their potential in Future Internet services. To promote collaboration, WAS4FI has a highly interactive format with short technical sessions complemented by discussions on adaptive services in the Future Internet applications.

The broad scope of WAS4FI is reflected in the wide range of topics covered by the workshop, and the 21 members of the WAS4FI Program Committee from both academic and industrial research labs. During the workshop, four papers (three long and one short) were presented:

- "A Lightweight Method for Analyzing Performance Dependencies Between Services," by Arjan Lamers and Marko Van Eekelen (long paper). In this paper, the authors propose a methodology to describe and analyze performance dependencies between services.
- "Adaptive Architectural Model for Future Internet Applications," by Luigi Alfredo Grieco, Marina Mongiello, Massimo Sciancalepore, and Elvis Vogli (short paper). This paper proposes a model for runtime composition of software applications in sensors networks based on data, processes, and technology to design on the fly and architectures of a software system.

- "Automated Prediction of the QoS of Service Orchestrations: PASO at Work," by Leonardo Bartoloni, Antonio Brogi and Ahmad Ibrahim (long paper). In this paper, the authors illustrate the practical usefulness of a probabilistic analyzer of service orchestrations (PASO) by showing how it can be exploited to predict the QoS of service orchestrations.
- "A Workflow Service Mediator for Automated Information Processing and Scheduling Delivery to an Archive," by Salvatore D'Antonio, Giuliano Gugliara, Carlo Francesco Romano, and Luigi Romano (long paper). This paper describes a service mediator that addresses real-life digital preservation problems and an overview of the project's progress to date.

We believe this workshop was an enjoyable and productive opportunity for attendees to meet and discuss various adaptive services and Future Internet issues with their counterparts from other countries and other industrial segments.

We would like to thank all the people who contributed to make this workshop a reality, including the WAS4FI Program Committee, the ESOCC 2015 Workshop Organizers, Philipp Leitner and Antonio Celesti, and all the presenters, authors, and participants.

Javier Cubo
Juan Boubeta-Puig
Winfried Lamersdorf
Nadia Gámez
Marc Oriol

Organization

Organizing Committee

Javier Cubo	University of Málaga, Spain
Juan Boubeta-Puig	University of Cádiz, Spain
Winfried Lamersdorf	University of Hamburg, Germany
Nadia Gámez	University of Málaga, Spain
Marc Oriol	University of Pisa, Italy

Program Committee

Marco Aiello	University of Groningen, The Netherlands
Vasilios Andrikopoulos	University of Stuttgart, Germany
Antonio Brogi	University of Pisa, Italy
Florian Daniel	University of Trento, Italy
Valeria de Castro	Universidad Rey Juan Carlos, Spain
Gregorio Díaz	Universidad de Castilla La Mancha, Spain
Schahram Dustdar	Vienna University of Technology, Austria
Laura González	Universidad de la República, Uruguay
Alberto Lluch Lafuente	Technical University of Denmark, Denmark
Massimo Mecella	University of Rome La Sapienza, Italy
Andreas Metzger	University of Duisburg-Essen, Germany
Claus Pahl	Dublin City University, Ireland
Ernesto Pimentel	University of Málaga, Spain
Pascal Poizat	Université Paris Ouest, France
Franco Raimondi	Middlesex University, UK
Gustavo Rossi	Universidad Nacional de La Plata, Argentina
Romain Rouvoy	University of Lille 1, France
Quanzheng Sheng	The University of Adelaide, Australia
Massimo Tivoli	University of L'Aquila, Italy
Gianluigi Zavattaro	University of Bologna, Italy

A Lightweight Method for Analysing Performance Dependencies Between Services

Arjan Lamers[1,2] and Marko van Eekelen[2,3(✉)]

[1] First8 BV, Nijmegen, The Netherlands
a.lamers@first8.nl
[2] Open University of the Netherlands, Heerlen, The Netherlands
[3] Radboud University Nijmegen, Nijmegen, The Netherlands
marko@cs.ru.nl

Abstract. For many applications, performance is paramount. For example, to improve conversion rates in e-commerce applications or to comply with service level agreements. Current trends in enterprise level architecture focus on designing and orchestrating *services*. These services are typically designed to be functionally isolated from each other up to a certain degree. During the design phase as well as when the application is deployed, choices have to be made how services interact and where they need to be deployed. These choices have a profound impact on the responsiveness of an application as well as on which performance can be made. In this paper we propose a methodology to describe and analyse performance dependencies between services. The resulting model can then be used to assist in designing a service oriented architecture and improving existing solutions by pointing out performance dependencies of services.

Keywords: Services · Deployment · Architecture · Design

1 Introduction

Current trends in enterprise level architecture are focused on delivering true components. Service Oriented Architecture (SOA) and Microservices are trends that aim at delivering components (*services*) [7,8,14,16] that can be used as ready-made parts. Building software products should then become a matter of orchestrating these services. A service in SOA is defined by OASIS [14] as *a mechanism to enable access to one or more capabilities, where the access is provided using a prescribed interface and is exercised consistent with constraints and policies as specified by the service description.* Typically services are grouped together in a *domain* and each domain is isolated to some degree from other domains. This degree of isolation can mean that different domains are managed by different companies or departments, that they are hosted in different data centres, on different machines or that they don't share e.g. the same database schema. This degree of isolation has profound impact on the resulting software

© Springer International Publishing Switzerland 2016
A. Celesti and P. Leitner (Eds.): ESOCC 2015 Workshops, CCIS 567, pp. 93–110, 2016.
DOI: 10.1007/978-3-319-33313-7_7

product: it impacts how software changes can be managed but also has an effect on performance issues [11] such as latency and scalability.

The main goal of the methodology described in this paper is to analyse performance dependencies of services in an architecture. In general, not all parts of an architecture have the same performance constraints. Some areas can be more focused on latency, others on throughput. Some services may be governed by a service level agreement (SLA) while others are less business critical. If parts of a system can be isolated and have their own constraints, the resulting product can be simpler and cheaper. Moreover, to be able to guarantee that a specific part of a system has a certain level of performance, it cannot be influenced by parts of the system that are not under full control (e.g. public API's). This method does not attempt to quantify performance aspects; doing so would require a detailed knowledge on the actual implementation. These are either not yet known (in the design phase) or prone to change due to functional or hardware changes. Furthermore, not all services may be owned by the owner of the architecture or are exposed to third parties. For example, traffic on public API's might be possible to be estimated, but in the event of marketing campaigns or DDOS attacks, these averages are not representative anymore. In these events, even a low order relationship between the API and other services might still be enough to degrade the system performance as a whole. It emphasises latency (responsiveness) although it reveals information about throughput bottlenecks as well.

The method has been used by the author at different stages of various projects. During design it helped to determine how to design interaction between services as well as to define domain boundaries. It was also helpful with investigating performance problems in an existing architecture. Proposed changes were again validated using the model. Fellow architects in those projects were able to quickly explain performance issues more concisely using the methodology without having to invest in expensive tests or complex modelling. Business stakeholders were able to understand performance consequences of decisions and understand the reasoning behind the proposed changes. The methodology gives a more concise and formal output than the 'gut feeling' that a proposed change might improve the performance of an architecture.

The model assumes a given set of services. Higher level abstractions such as processes, or lower abstractions such as components are all flattened to basic services. By modelling the way the services interact it is possible to predict potential performance issues and solve them. It also helps in determine which services can be grouped together from performance point of view and as such can help in (re)defining domains. The interaction between services is described by making a distinction between a flow of information and a flow of initiative: is the information pushed or pulled? Rather than focusing on describing an algorithm or optimising a protocol between services, the method focuses on questioning if two services should be connected at all and, if so, which service should take initiative. In any sufficiently complex architecture, information can take a significant amount of time to travel through the system. Optimising that information latency while at the same time managing performance constraints is not trivial. The method first focuses on trying to solve this issue on the architecture level. The proposed abstraction is simple enough to allow discussion between software architects and domain experts, negotiating on performance aspects, while still expressive enough to meaningfully guide an architecture. Local optimisations can follow afterwards.

The methodology consists of three steps. First an *architecture* is defined in Sect. 2. This describes the services and their interactions. Also, isolation constraints can be formulated. Next, these services have to be run on machines, potentially having more than one instance of a service. This is described in the *deployment allocation* (Sect. 3) of the model. In Sect. 4 managing state is discussed. Based on the resulting optionality of connections, this deployment allocation can be configured by choosing which connections between machines are optimal. This results in a *deployment configuration* as described in Sect. 5. In each step, the isolation constraints of a service can be verified.

2   Architecture Layer

2.1   Service Interaction

In SOA, services are consumed by work flows or processes. Services can also be composed out of other services, making the model fractal. In this methodology, everything is flattened to a service. If a service consists of components that can be deployed by themselves (e.g. a service using a database), those components are considered services as well.

A service is considered a vertex in a graph. The edges represent *calls* from one service to another. There are two properties to be considered when describing interaction between two services. The first property is the flow of information, the second defines which service takes initiative. If service a has information that is required by service b, that information can be *pushed* from a to b (Fig. 1).

Fig. 1. a pushes to b   **Fig. 2.** b pulls from a

The initiative can also originate from service b. In this case, a is *pulled* by b (Fig. 2). Information still flows in the same direction, but the initiative is placed with the receiver instead of the sender.

A push from a to b is considered a fire-and-forget operation. It is assumed that even if b is busy, a can continue its work without significant delay. If a confirmation of a push which can have a significant delay (e.g. the confirmation contains a business result) is required information flows back from b to a. Therefore, an additional edge is required: a pulls from b.

Fig. 3. Gui and db   **Fig. 4.** Information graph   **Fig. 5.** Initiative graph

As an example throughout the paper, consider an online bookstore. In its basic form, it consists of a web application consisting of a graphical user interface (*gui*) and a database (*db*), as shown in Fig. 3.

In this scenario, the user interface allows users to enter new information or change information in the database. Thus, it *pushes* information as entered by the user to the database. The user interface also can query the database so it also *pulls* information from the database. Information flows in both directions (Fig. 4). All initiative, however, always originates from the user interface. In other words, this is a classical client-server setup; without a client, the server (*db* in this case) has nothing to do (Fig. 5).

Formally, an *architecture* A consists of a vertex set S for the services and an edge set C^A representing the *calls* between services. A typed edge (p, s, t) with $p \in \{push, pull\}$ going from source s to target t is defined as having s as the source of information. Thus, in the example above, $S = \{gui, db\}, C^A = \{(push, gui, db), (pull, db, gui)\}$.

This model can be translated to two different graphs, an information flow graph and an initiative graph:

The information graph I_{inf} for a given architecture A is defined as:

$I_{inf}(A) = (S, E)$, where S is the same service set of A. The edge set E is defined as: $E_{inf}(A) = \{(s, t) | (p, s, t) \in C^A\}$.

The initiative graph I_{int} for a given architecture A is defined as:

$I_{int}(A) = (S, E)$, where S is the same service set of A. The edge set E is defined as: $E_{int}(A) = \{(s, t) | (p, s, t) \in C^A \wedge p = push\} \cup \{(t, s) | (p, s, t) \in C^A \wedge p = pull\}$, reversing the *pull* edges.

2.2 Stress and Responsiveness

In this model, a couple of properties can be defined.

The first property is *stress*. The *stress graph* (Fig. 6) of a service s is defined as the subgraph of vertices that can reach the service s in the initiative graph, including s itself. This means that the amount of work to be done on that service s is influenced by all the services in the stress graph. For the example above, the *stress set STR* of vertices in the stress graph are: $STR(gui) = gui, STR(db) = \{gui, db\}$. This can be interpreted as follows: an increased load on *gui* will lead to an increased load on *db*, but an increase in load on *db* does not lead to more load on *gui*.

More formally, for a service S in an architecture A, the stress set STR is defined as:

$$STR(s) = \{s\} \cup STR_{push}(s) \cup STR_{pull}(s), \text{ with:}$$
$$STR_{push}(s) = \bigcup_{(p', s', t') \in C^A} \{STR(s') | s' = s \wedge p' = push\}$$

$$STR_{pull}(s) = \bigcup_{(p',s',t')\in C^A}\{STR(t')|t' = s \wedge p' = pull\}$$

To determine if a service can quickly respond to a request, the above properties are not enough. The stress indicates what impacts resource usage but the service might also require information from another service. If the database has a high load, it will still impact the user interface: retrieving information will be slower. To represent this a second property is introduced, *responsiveness* (Fig. 7), combining the stress on the service s with the stress of the services from which it *pulls*. For the example above, the responsiveness RES is $RES(gui) = RES(db) = \{gui, db\}$.

The *responsiveness set* (Fig. 7) is thus more formally defined as follows:
$$RES(s) = STR(s) \cup \bigcup_{(p',s',t')\in C^A}\{RES(s')|p' = pull\}$$

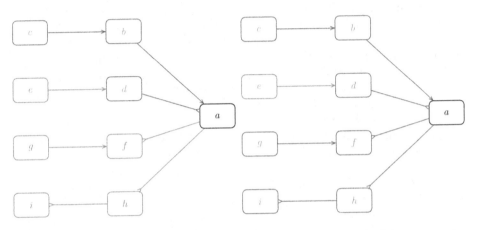

Fig. 6. $STR(a) = \{a, b, c, d\}$ **Fig. 7.** $e \notin RES(a)$

2.3   Analysing an Architecture

In any architecture, different services have different non-functional requirements. Typically, a user interface has to respond quickly to an end-user's actions. The model cannot give a quantitative measurement. However, it can reveal which services impact the user interface. This allows us to define constraints that enforce a disconnect in performance between two services. For example, consider a system with, amongst other services, a user interface and a public API. A typical constraint might be that the user interface should always be responsive, no matter the (uncontrolled) load on the public API. This constraint can be proven in the model by showing that the public API is not in the responsiveness set of the user interface.

We can thus define the following two constraints:

Definition 1. *A service a is* weakly isolated *from b if* $b \notin STR(a)$.

Definition 2. *A service a is* strongly isolated *from b if* $b \notin RES(a)$.

3   Deployment Allocation

The next step is to describe the machines on which the services will be deployed. Larger systems might require multiple (virtual) *machines*. If multiple machines are available, the option arises to deploy services isolated on machines or to combine a subset of them on a single machine. A service can even be deployed multiple times to be able to handle more traffic.

If two services are deployed on the same machine, they will share resources and thus their *stress* will be shared. A perfectly scalable architecture might thus be deployed in such a way that it looses its responsiveness properties. On the other hand, deploying two communicating services on separate machines will introduce additional network latency. Furthermore, since it is typically assumed that a network might fail, the two services will have to deal with CAP problems. To analyse this, a deployment layer will be added to the model.

A *deployment allocation* for an architecture A is a set of *machines* with each machine running a subset of A's services. The *calls* made between services in A are expanded to *connections* in the deployment: for each *call* from s to t in the architecture, a similar *connection* is made between every machine that runs s and every machine that runs t (Fig. 8).

Back to the bookstore example application. Initially, it might be deployed on a single machine, running both the *gui* and the *db*. If the bookstore is successful, the traffic to the website will increase. At some point, the single machine does not have enough resources to manage the traffic. Typically, the easiest way to scale up is to *vertically scale* by buying bigger hardware, or dividing the services over multiple machines as in Fig. 9. A next step, assuming that the bottleneck is the *gui* as it often is, could be to *horizontally scale* by deploying more than one instance of a service on multiple machines, as seen in Fig. 10.

In this example, machine *1* and *2* contain a deployment of the service *gui*. Machine *3* contains a deployment of the service *db*.

A deployed service σ for service s on machine m is defined as $\sigma = (s, m) \in \Sigma$. A deployment allocation D is graph with vertex set Σ of deployed services and an edge set of connections C^D.

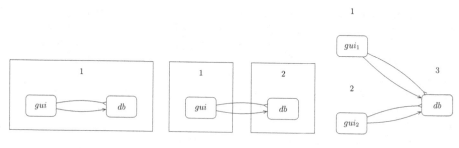

Fig. 8. 1 = {gui, db}   **Fig. 9.** 1 = {gui}, 2 = {db}   **Fig. 10.** 1 = 2 = {gui}, 3 = {db}

For convenience, the set of machines within D is defined as $M = \{m|(s,m) \in \Sigma\}$. The *deployment set* of a service s is defined as the set of machines that deploy s: $DEP(s) = \{m|(m,s) \in \Sigma\}$.

A machine holds a subset of services and all services should be deployed: $\forall(s,m) \in \Sigma : s \in S$ and $\forall s \in S : \exists (s,m) \in \Sigma$.

The edge set is derived from the services and holds a reference to the original call:

$$C^D = \bigcup_{(p_a,s_a,t_a)\in C^A}\{((p_a, s_a, t_a), s_d, t_d)|s_d = (s_a, m) \wedge m \in DEP(s_a), t_d = (t_a, n) \wedge n \in DEP(t_a)\}.$$

3.1   Analysing a Deployment Allocation

Similar to the properties STR and RES as defined in the context of an architecture, we can define analogue properties for machines and services in the context of a deployment. Services deployed on the same machine share resources such as memory or cpu. Therefore they share stress.

The isolated stress of a deployed service (s, m), i.e. the stress without considering other services on the same machine, is defined in a similar way to the stress of a service:

$$str(\sigma) = \{\sigma\} \cup strpush(\sigma) \cup strpull(\sigma)$$
$$strpush(\sigma) = \bigcup_{((p',s',t'),\sigma',\varsigma')\in C^D}\{str(\varsigma')|\sigma' = \sigma \wedge p' = push\}$$
$$strpull(\sigma) = \bigcup_{((p',s',t'),\sigma',\varsigma')\in C^D}\{str(\varsigma')|\varsigma' = \sigma \wedge p' = pull\}$$

The actual stress of a service s on machine m is thus simply the stress of machine m, $STR(s,m) = STR(m) = \bigcup_{(s',m)\in D} str((s', m))$.

We can now also define the responsiveness of a service *on a machine*. While stress is automatically shared between services (since they share resources), the responsiveness of two services on a different machine might still be different since they can pull from different sources. The responsiveness of a service s on the machine m is thus defined as the stress of the machine m united with the responsiveness of all deployed services that are pulled from service s. More formally,

$$RES(s, m) = STR(m) \cup \bigcup_{((p',s',t'),\sigma',\varsigma')\in C^D}\{RES(\sigma')|p' = pull\}$$

We can thus redefine the isolation constraints on deployment allocation level:

Definition 3. *A service a is* weakly isolated *from a service b if* $\forall_{m\in DEP(a)}\forall_{(s',m')\in STR(m)} s' \neq b$.

Definition 4. *A service a is* strongly isolated *from a service b if* $\forall_{m\in DEP(a)}\forall_{(s',m')\in RES(m)} s' \neq b$.

As an example, consider Fig. 10 again. The *gui*'s have been horizontally scaled, but how effective is that? The stress of the machines in this example is: $STR(1) = \{(gui_1, 1)\}, STR(2) = \{(gui_2, 2)\}, STR(3) = \{(gui_1, 1), (gui_2, 2), (db, 3)\}$

The responsiveness of the deployed services are: $RES(gui_1, 1) = RES(gui_2, 2) = RES(db, 3) = \{(gui_1, 1), (gui_2, 2), (db, 3)\}$.

The stress property indicates that all machines provide stress on the *db*, making it a likely bottleneck. Furthermore, while the *gui* deployments don't share stress, they still influence each other in responsiveness: if one *gui* puts a high load on the *db*, it will impact the other *gui*'s responsiveness.

Thus, both *gui* services are only weakly isolated from each other, not strongly isolated.

There are also some new properties to be discussed. In a distributed deployment (a deployment with $|M| > 1$), communication between two machines is done via network calls. These are orders of magnitude slower than local calls. Therefore, to reduce latency in a system, it is necessary to reduce the number of network hops. Secondly, since network connections are more prone to break, it is more important to define a consistency model which allows for faulty communication channels. To avoid network hops, one could collocate two services on the same machine. This, however, will result in them sharing stress.

A network hop or *non-local connection* is a connection that has its source and target services on different machines.

Thus for a connection c, with $c = (c', m', n')$:

$$local(c) = \begin{cases} 0 & \text{when } m' = n' \\ 1 & \text{when } m' \neq n' \end{cases}$$

There are two important properties that are impacted by the network hops. Firstly, the responsiveness is not only impacted by stress on the machines, network latency is an important factor as well: *responsiveness network depth*. The responsiveness network depth $RNET(s, m)$ for a service s on a machine m is defined as the maximum number of network hops to any other service which can be reached by s via *pull* requests. Note that if there are cycles in the graph, the network depth is defined to be infinite. More formally, assume a *pull-graph P* for (m, s) is a weighed graph derived from a deployment D with the same vertex set M. The edge set for P is defined as all the pull edges for s as well as all pull edges for the source vertices of those edges. An edge c in the pull-graph derived from edge c' in the deployment has weight $local(c')$. $RNET(s, m)$ is now the maximum of the sum of weights of each branch from s. If the graph is not a tree, $RNET(s, m) = \infty$.

Secondly, to accurately define a consistency model allowing for failing network connections, one needs to take into account the full source of information: *consistency network depth*. The first property to discuss is *consistency*. As with any system, there is a delay whenever information is passed from one point to another. As such, for a service to have a world view on its state consistent with the whole chain, any and all change in information it requires has to have reached the service. The subgraph of all vertices that can reach a service s in an architecture, including s itself, in the information graph is defined as the *consistency graph* for s. The *consistency set* for s is the set of vertices within the consistency graph. For the group of services in this set, consistency model limitations will hold (e.g. CAP limits). Either these services are deployed on a non-partitionable system, or availability/consistency limitations will arise. More formally, for a service s in an architecture A, the consistency set CON is defined as the set of vertices including s that can reach s in the information graph $I_{inf}(A)$:

$$CON(s) = \{s\} \cup \bigcup_{(p',s',t') \in C^A} \{CON(s') | s' = s\}$$

Similar to $RNET$, the *consistency network depth* $CNET(s, m)$ is defined as the maximum number of network hops to any service that provides information for s. The same definition applies, only using the information graph $I_{inf}(A)$ instead of the pull graph.

These properties can be used to analyse and reduce the number of network calls for a specific service. $CNET$ gives an indication from *how far* information has to come, thus increasing consistency model complexity, whereas $RNET$ indicates how much the network impacts the responsiveness.

4   State

When distributing a service, there is always the matter of synchronizing state. Changes in one instance of a service might impact another instance of a service. This impacts how an application can be deployed and which calls and connections are required. To reflect this, the model supports three kinds of *statefulness* for a service, *stateless*, *stateful* and *partitionable*.

These are defined as follows:

A service is *stateless* if, when there are multiple instances deployed of that service, they do not require any exchange of information between those instances to be able to fulfil all requests. In other words, each instance can be deployed fully isolated while still be able to serve all requests.

A service is *partitionable* if, when there are multiple instance deployed of that service, a specific instance can handle the request in isolation. The instance that is able to handle a specific call must be determined based on the content of that call. Each instance holds its own subset of the state and can manage that independently. A call is called *routable* if the correct instance can be determined based on the parameters of the call.

A service is *stateful* if, when there are multiple instance deployed of that service, they do require to synchronise state in order to be consistent with each other.

Recall that an architecture A has a vertex set of services S. A service $s \in S$ with name n and statefulness p is defined as a tuple (n, z) with $z \in \{stateful, stateless, partitionable\}$. For a partitionable service, it is further relevant on which dimensions it can be partitioned. To simplify, it is assumed there is only a single dimension on which a service can be partitioned if it is partitionable. If $s = (n, z), z = partitionable$ then its partitioning dimension should also be defined as $PART(z)$.

In the bookstore example, the architecture could be further refined to include an explicit business layer service. This might be deemed necessary due to an increase in features or due to a need for different front ends. The bookstore's architecture will then look like the following classical 3-tier architecture:

The graphical user interface can be scaled to have multiple instances. When a user logs in, he or she has a session at a specific instance and as such all requests related to that session can be managed by that single instance in isolation. Thus, the gui is partitioned by sessions.

Fig. 11. Partitioned gui (g), stateless business layer (b) and stateful database (d)

The business layer handles requests from the gui, interprets them, applies business rules and uses the database to store information. It does not keep any state between calls so if there are multiple instances of the business layer service, they can act isolated. The business layer is thus stateless.

The database stores the information as requested by the business layer. If there is more than one instance, these instances need to be synchronized in order to stay consistent. Thus, the database is stateful.

4.1 Deploying with State

When an architecture is deployed, the *statefulness* of a service determines how it affects the different connections resulting from calls between services. A call can be given as either *routable* or a *broadcast* in this model. Routable means that a single instance of a service is sufficient to handle the request and that it is known which instance this is. A broadcast means that all instances of a service need to handle the request. A routable call to a stateless or stateful service means that the request can be handled locally, a broadcast to these services is probably a cache invalidation or some other global effect. A routable call to a partitioned service means that by the nature of the request or its payload it can be determined which partition holds the subset of data required to process the request. A broadcast is necessary if it is unknown which partition holds the data, or all partitions are required to process the request. Graphically, this is indicated by the color of the service s (based on $PART(s)$) and the color of the connection (again based on $PART(s)$) where s is the source in the information graph.

Recall that an architecture A has an edge set C^A with a call $c = (p, s, t) \in C^A$. To represent the *routability* property, the tuple is redefined as $c = (p, s, t, r) \in C^A$ where $r \in \{routable, broadcast\}$.

When there is more than one instance of a stateful service, these instances need to synchronize. For that to happen, information has to be exchanged and that means that broadcast calls between all instances exist. By convention, these calls are designated as broadcasting push connections. For the properties as defined until now, it does not matter if it is push or pull since the call is from a service to itself. To indicate if a call is a broadcast or if it is routable, respectively double and single arrow heads are used in an architecture graph as in Fig. 12.

In extending a deployment graph from an architecture graph, connections are derived from calls. The connections will derive a new property *optionality* which can be *deployment optional*, *runtime optional* or *compulsary*, based on the type of service and if the call is routable or not.

A connection is by definition *compulsary* if the call is a broadcast, since all instances of a service have to be reached.

Fig. 12. Stateful database (d) needs to synchronize using a broadcast

A connection is *deployment optional* when, for all the connections in a deployment for a specific call, only one is necessary for the system to function correctly. All others can be left out of the deployment. If the target of a call in the initiative graph is either stateless or stateful, any of the deployed instances can be the target for the connection. Each instance can handle the request. This type of connection is considered *deployment optional*. A push to or a pull from any stateless or stateful service is considered deployment optional by default.

A connection is *runtime optional* when, for all the connections in a deployment for a specific call, only one connection is used in a specific instance. Which one it is, is determined at runtime. Other connections may be used for different calls. If the target of a call in the initiative graph is partitioned and the call is routable, only one connection is used runtime to the specific instance of the partitioned service. This type of connection is considered *runtime optional*.

A connection $c \in C^D$ is now defined as $c = (c', \sigma, \varsigma, o)$, with as before $c' \in C^A$ and having a deployed service $\sigma \in \Sigma$ as a source of information and $\varsigma \in \Sigma$ as a target. The new property $o \in \{runtime - optional, deployment - optional, compulsary\}$ is added.

As an example, consider deployments for the architecture as defined in the bookstore's 3-tier architecture (Fig. 11). If two instances for each service are created, the deployment as seen in Fig. 13 is the result. Here the dotted lines are deployment optional, the solid lines are compulsary. The two database instances are synchronized in what is generally called a master-master replication. Other database replication scheme's would require a change in architecture first. For

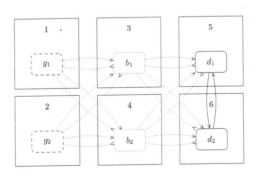

Fig. 13. Deployed partitioned gui (g), stateless business layer (b) and stateful database (d)

example, read-only slave configurations require that the client (in this case the business layer) knows which database to use for writes and which for reads. Thus, without changing the architecture, this is the resulting deployment.

If the statefulness of the business layer is changed, the connections will change as well. For example, assuming the business layer is partitioned as well, the graph will look like Fig. 14, where the dashed lines represent the runtime optional connections. Imagine for example that each business layer instance services different payment options (e.g., mastercard transactions go to b_1 and visa to b_2). In this example, the g and b services use different partitioning dimensions ($PART(g) \neq PART(b)$): the gui is partitioned by user sessions whereas the business layer by payment options. The connections from g to b thus have to be routable on $PART(b)$. As a last example, if the statefulness of the business layer is stateful, the graph will look like Fig. 15. This is quickly the case if the business layer manages its own state instead of delegating to the database.

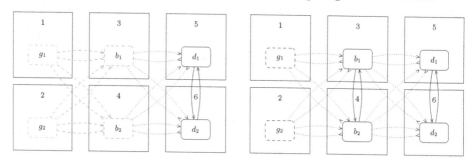

Fig. 14. Partitioned business layer   **Fig. 15.** Stateful business layer

5   Deployment Configuration

The deployment allocation assignes services to. machines. Given a deployment allocation, the optionality of the connections between machines is known and some of those connections are redundant. Based on this, non optimal connections can be pruned and configuration choices can be made. Some of these choices are obvious improvements, while others have both advantages and disadvantages. Choosing which connections to actually configure results in a *deployment configuration*.

5.1   Deployment Optional Pruning

In case of deployment optional connections, if one of the connections is *local* than that one is generally preferred; there is no obvious reason to use a non-local connection since all are equal. By picking the local connection, that connection is no longer deployment optional, there is nothing else to choose from. For example, considering the bookstore 3-tier architecture (Fig. 11). Due to budget constraints or other reasons, the gui and the business layer are to be deployed together on the same machine, resulting in a deployment allocation that will initially look like the graph in Fig. 16.

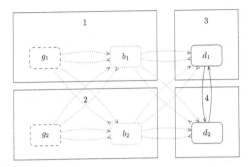

Fig. 16. Initial

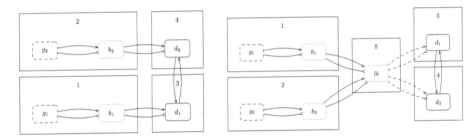

Fig. 17. Static load balancing   **Fig. 18.** Dynamic load balancing

The connections on the left side are all deployment optional and result from g and b having multiple instances. As such, all possible connections are derived from the architecture into the deployment allocation. However, since only one connection for each call is required, non-local connections can be removed, avoiding network calls when not required. For the deployment optional calls between the business services b_1 and b_2 to the databases instances d_1 and d_2, a couple of options are possible. One obvious choice is to assign each business service its own database. This would lead to Fig. 17 with each business service having compulsary connections to a dedicated database. Another is to dynamically load balance request between the databases. That would require an additional loadbalancer service (*lb*) which routes the traffic to one of the database instances (Fig. 18). The connections from the business service to the loadbalancer become compulsary, while the connections from the loadbalancer to the database will be runtime optional; only one is required. While having a load balancer might lead to a more evenly distributed load over both database instances, the load balancer by itself is another bottleneck and network hop.

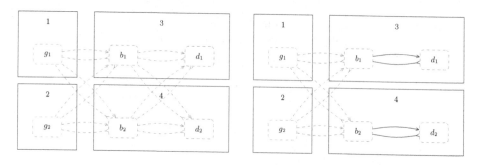

Fig. 19. Initial   **Fig. 20.** Pruned as processing units

5.2   Pruning Runtime Optionals

For runtime optional connections resulting from partitioned services, some pruning options are possible as well. If both the source s and the target t of a connection are partitionable, share the same partitioning dimension and are always codeployed, the deployment configuration can exploit that by assigning the same partitions for instances of s and t. The assumption here is that a call does not change routing. If the use case requires a different routing, it should be marked as a broadcast. If this assumption holds, the machine which holds both s and t can be treated as a "processing unit" which deliver all functionality for a subset of partitions.

As an example, recall the partitioned business layer architecture in Fig. 14. Each business layer served a subset of payment methods (e.g. mastercard to b_1 and visa to b_2). It might be beneficial to partition the database in a similar way, storing only mastercard transactions in one instance, and visa transactions in the other. This way, both database instances can operate independently, resulting in the deployment allocation as found in Fig. 19. The consuming services, in this case a differently partitioned user interface g, should be able to route its calls to one of the processing units formed by machines 3 or 4. Pruned, this could be reduced to Fig. 20.

6   Architectural Patterns

To resolve performance issues, there are a number of technical patterns available that will isolate service performance to some degree. In this section common patterns like caches and queues are discussed, modeled and compared using the method. The most basic patterns, *push* and *pull* have been discussed in the first chapter as they are the building blocks of the model.

A *cache* pattern is used to keep state readily available if it has been calculated or received before. This way, the consumer is decoupled from the performance of the producer. A cache can behave in a *lazy* way, and only retrieve values when they are requested as modelled in Fig. 21. Here, the consumer c pulls the information from a cache store (cdb). If this store does not contain the value, it retrieves it from the producer. While the *stress* of the consumer is decoupled from the producer, the model shows that the responsiveness is still dependent on the producer. In effect, the cache has no effect in the model since the producer and consumer are not fully isolated in the case of a cache miss.

Caches can also behave in an *eager* fetching way as modelled in Fig. 22. Here the *cdb* cache store is filled by an independent cache reader which pulls the original information from the producer. This can be a scheduled or an asynchronous task. In this scenario, the consumer's stress is isolated but the producers stress is depending on *cr*. The responsiveness of the consumer is now only dependent on *cr* and *cdb*. The *cr* service can thus be tuned to balance the stress on the producer versus the responsiveness of the consumer.

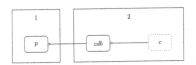
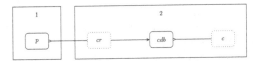

Fig. 21. Typical lazy cache   **Fig. 22.** Typical eager cache

A *queue* pattern is used to decouple a flow between services. One service pushes a message onto the queue, another service can pick it up at any time. See Fig. 23. The producer *p* can always deliver its messages and as such is unaffected by the performance of the consumer *c*. The model shows this as well: the stress and the responsiveness of *p* only depends on *p* itself. The consumer *c* also only receives stress from itself, but the responsiveness is impacted by both the queue (*q*) itself as well as the producer *p*. A queue reader or writer might be added (similar to the cache reader above, or even by adding a complete cache) to be able to improve responsiveness of the consumer.

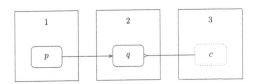

Fig. 23. A queue between p and c

In Table 1 presents a summary on how these architectural patterns behave according to this model. Note that the more performance isolation a pattern offers, the more elements are involved in maintaining consistency. For a queue, the consistency network depth also increases. As can be predicted, caches and push calls are excellent for improving responsiveness since they decrease the distance of accessing data (decreasing $RNET(s)$).

Table 1. Isolation levels of patterns

Pattern	p	c	$RNET(c,2)$	$CON(c,2)$	$CNET(c,2)$
Push	Strong	-	0	{c,p}	1
Pull	-	Weak	1	{c,p}	1
Lazy cache	-	Weak	0	{c,p,cdb}	1
Eager cache	Strong	Strong	0	{c,p,cdb, cr}	1
Queue	Strong	Weak	1	{c,p,qdb}	2

7 Related Work

In this paper we have presented a novel notation. Other notations, such as UML sequence diagrams or Petri nets, also exist. Sequence diagrams can express parallelism and ordering of actions, expressing interaction between services quite detailed. Petri nets allow concurrency and synchronisation analysis in distributed systems and as such require details on how state is synchronised. These details are very useful *within* a specific service or domain but less useful *between* domains since these are, by definition, reasonably isolated. Instead, our notation leaves out algorithmic details and focuses on expressing the distinction between the source of information and initiative on a higher abstraction. This allow a focus on the question whether the architecture or the deployment needs to change or whether some latency requirements can be loosened, before trying to optimise it in the implementation.

Research has been done which focuses on predicting a quantified throughput of a (workflow in a) Service Oriented Architecture, e.g. [3,4,6,10,17]. In general, these models require load functions, detailed descriptions or actual implementations for each service. Determining load functions and finding reasonable values for parameters of these models can be quite demanding and might be possible only quite late in the development process. Additionally, calculating the performance of the architecture might not be instant but requires a (relatively) long simulation. Instead, our work focuses on finding performance isolation between services without quantifying it. The properties can be quickly derived, even manually up to a certain complexity, and future tooling could extensively compare alternatives. SLAng [15] provides a precise way of defining SLA's for services. It would be interesting to see if some properties could be guaranteed by the model.

Software defined networks [13] decouple the network control decisions from the actual hardware, making it easier to change deployment configurations, either manually or automatically.

8 Conclusion

The described method gives insight into how services influence each other with regards to performance. This can be used to validate and assist in decisions both on architectural level as well as on deployment. Since the model does not require concrete details it can be used as a light weight method to drive discussion and validate performance requirements. Multiple implementations of a simple example, a bookstore website, were modeled and analysed, providing insight in difference in performance behaviour. Here the method provides a tangible result for performance related issues within an architecture. Possible solutions on both architectural (software) level as well as on deployment level can be compared and weighed.

Future Work

The methodology described can be applied to both small and larger architectures. For small architectures, this can be done by hand and the results are natural. For larger architecture tooling is required to derive results and these might be surprising. A tool is being build to automate calculation of the properties. This should aid in quickly discovering and analysing deployment scenario's and weighing the advantages and disadvantages such as balancing isolation versus network latency. It should also be able to point out possible areas where changes in the architecture could be beneficial and potentially detect (a subset of) performance anti-patterns [5]. Changing the initiative from one service to another, or edges that are suitable candidates for static or dynamic loadbalancing, could be auto detected and then alternatives could be compared. Other "Middlepipes" [9] related products such as circuit breakers as shown in e.g. [12] could be modelled as well, either as concrete specialisations or by deriving REO connectors [1]. The properties could be further formalised to derive optimisations for e.g. nested architectures and deployments. More research is to be carried out to see if we can help discover consistency models between services based on the initiative and information graphs, e.g. to help derive application invariants for [2].

To further validate the approach, the methodology should be applied at full scale projects in different stages of development or production.

References

1. Arbab, F.: Reo: a channel-based coordination model for component composition. Math. Struct. Comput. Sci. **14**, 329–366 (2004). http://journals.cambridge.org/article_S0960129504004153
2. Bailis, P., Fekete, A., Franklin, M.J., Ghodsi, A., Hellerstein, J.M., Stoica, I.: Coordination avoidance in database systems. Proc. VLDB Endow. **8**(3), 185–196 (2014). http://dx.org/10.14778/2735508.2735509
3. Bertoli, M., Casale, G., Serazzi, G.: JMT: performance engineering tools for system modeling. SIGMETRICS Perform. Eval. Rev. **36**(4), 10–15 (2009)
4. Brebner, P.C.: Real-world performance modelling of enterprise service oriented architectures: delivering business value with complexity and constraints. In: ACM SIGSOFT Software Engineering Notes, vol. 36, pp. 85–96. ACM (2011)
5. Cortellessa, V., Di Marco, A., Trubiani, C.: An approach for modeling and detecting software performance antipatterns based on first-order logics. Softw. Syst. Model. **13**(1), 391–432 (2014)

6. Ferrer, A.J., Hernández, F., Tordsson, J., Elmroth, E., Ali-Eldin, A., Zsigri, C., Sirvent, R., Guitart, J., Badia, R.M., Djemame, K., et al.: Optimis: a holistic approach to cloud service provisioning. Future Gener. Comput. Syst. **28**(1), 66–77 (2012)
7. Fielding, R.T.: Architectural Styles and the Design of Network-based Software Architectures. Ph.D. thesis, University of California, Irvine (2000). aAI9980887
8. Fowler, M.: Microservices. http://martinfowler.com/articles/microservices.html
9. Jamjoom, H., Williams, D., Sharma, U.: Don't call them middleboxes, call them middlepipes. In: Proceedings of the Third Workshop on Hot Topics in Software Defined Networking, pp. 19–24. ACM (2014)
10. Kounev, S.: Performance modeling and evaluation of distributed component-based systems using queueing petri nets. IEEE Trans. Softw. Eng. **32**(7), 486–502 (2006)
11. Kratzke, N.: About microservices, containers and their underestimated impact on network performance. In: Proceedings of CLOUD COMPUTING 2015 (6th International Conference on Cloud Computing, GRIDS and Virtualization) (2015)
12. Netflix: Hystrix. https://github.com/Netflix/Hystrix
13. Nunes, B., Mendonca, M., Nguyen, X.N., Obraczka, K., Turletti, T., et al.: A survey of software-defined networking: past, present, and future of programmable networks. IEEE Commun. Surv. Tutorials **16**(3), 1617–1634 (2014)
14. OASIS: Oasis soa reference model tc. https://www.oasis-open.org/committees/tc_home.php?wg_abbrev=soa-rm
15. Skene, J., Lamanna, D.D., Emmerich, W.: Precise service level agreements. In: Proceedings of the 26th International Conference on Software Engineering, pp. 179–188. IEEE Computer Society (2004)
16. The Open Group: Service oriented architecture: What is soa? http://www.opengroup.org/soa/source-book/soa/soa.htm#soa_definition
17. Zhu, L., Liu, Y., Bui, N.B., Gorton, I.: Revel8or: model driven capacity planning tool suite. In: 29th International Conference on Software Engineering, ICSE 2007, pp. 797–800. IEEE (2007)

Automated Prediction of the QoS of Service Orchestrations: PASO at Work

Leonardo Bartoloni, Antonio Brogi, and Ahmad Ibrahim[✉]

Department of Computer Science, University of Pisa, Pisa, Italy
{bartolon,brogi,ahmad}@di.unipi.it

Abstract. Predicting the QoS of a service orchestration is not easy because of the a priori undetermined behaviour of invoked services, and because of the non-determinism (alternatives, unbounded iterations, fault handling) and complex structure (dependencies, correlations) of the workflow defining a service orchestration. In this paper we illustrate the practical usefulness of a probabilistic analyser of service orchestrations (PASO) by showing how it can be fruitfully exploited to predict the QoS of service orchestrations.

Keywords: QoS · Service orchestrations · Probabilistic analysis · WS-BPEL

1 Introduction

Service orchestrations [1] provide an effective way to implement business processes [2] by suitably combining the functionalities offered by other (possibly third party) services. Quality of Service (QoS) [3,4] plays an important role in service-oriented computing, where it can be a key driver for customers' service selection and determine the achievement of business goals of both service customers and service providers. It is important to observe that the QoS of a service orchestration *does* depend on the QoS of the services it invokes. And the QoS of a (invoked) service can vary depending on different run-time conditions [5] such as servers' workload or network congestion [4]. The ability of predicting the QoS of a service orchestration is hence of primary importance both during the design of a service orchestration and for the definition of its Service Level Agreement (SLA) [6].

Unfortunately, predicting the QoS of service orchestration is not easy, mainly because of four characteristics of service orchestrations.

1. *Different results of service invocations.* Each invoked service can return a successful reply, a fault notification, or even no reply at all. If a fault is returned, the orchestration will execute a fault handling routine instead of the normal control flow. If no reply is received, the orchestration may get

---

Work partly supported by the EU-FP7-ICT-610531 SeaClouds project.

A. Celesti and P. Leitner (Eds.): ESOCC 2015 Workshops, CCIS 567, pp. 111–125, 2016.
DOI: 10.1007/978-3-319-33313-7_8

stuck waiting for a reply (unless some parallel branch throws a fault). In either case, the QoS of the orchestration will differ from the case of successful reply.

2. **Non-determinism in the orchestration workflow.** Different runs of the same orchestration can yield different QoS values since the control-flow of the orchestration workflow is non-deterministic. On the one hand, different runs of the orchestration can get different service invocation results (success/fault/no reply). On the other hand, some control-flow structures (alternatives and iterations) depend on input data which may differ in different runs.

3. **Correlations among workflow activities.** The above two characteristics suggest to employ a probabilistic approach. However, it is important to observe that the naive solution of assigning independent probabilities to workflow activities (e.g., as in [7]) can lead to incorrect results. For example, consider the case of a diamond dependency (Fig. 1a). We see that, after activity A will be executed, either B or C will trigger with 50 % probability, and then D will be executed with 100 % probability in either case. However, if the correlation among A, B and C is ignored (Fig. 1b), then there would be a 25 % probability that neither B nor C will be executed, which would lead to only a 75 % probability of D being executed — which is incorrect.

4. **Complex dependencies among workflow activities.** The control flow imposed by synchronizations on parallel activities (i.e., when a task needs to wait for another to complete before starting) is more expressive than what is allowed by parallel execution only (with synchronization barriers at the end of parallel tasks). This means that workflows which have complex synchronization structures (e.g., as those that can be specified with WS-BPEL synchronization `links` [8]) cannot be always decomposed in terms of parallel and sequential compositions [9].

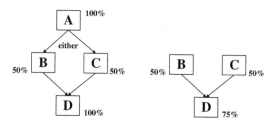

(a) With correlation.   (b) Without correlation.

Fig. 1. Example of correlation among activities.

In [10,11] we have presented an algorithm that employs Monte Carlo simulations to probabilistically predict the QoS of service orchestrations defined via WS-BPEL workflows. We have implemented such algorithm in F#.Net in an open source application named PASO (Probabilistic Analyser of Service Orchestrations).

In this paper we aim at illustrating the practical usefulness of PASO by showing how it can be fruitfully exploited to predict the QoS of service orchestrations. In particular, we will show how PASO can provide answers to various interesting questions.

– As we already anticipated, a first natural question is what will be the overall QoS of a service orchestration. For instance, what will be the response time, reliability, and cost of a given orchestration.
– A second type of interesting questions concerns assessing the effects on the QoS of an orchestration of replacing one or more of the invoked services with alternative services, e.g., offered by different providers.
– A further type of questions concerns assessing whether and how modifying the workflow of an orchestration impacts on its overall QoS.

It is worth observing that workflow designers are not interested only in getting estimated average values for the aforementioned questions (e.g., "What is the average response time of this orchestration?"). They are also typically interested in the distribution of values for such answers (e.g., "What is the probability that the response time of this orchestration will be more than 2 s?").

To illustrate the practical usefulness of PASO we will describe PASO at work on two examples of service orchestrations: A simple orchestration implementing a cloud-based storage service, and a business process defining how to start a manufacturing business. Although the two examples are deliberately simple, they illustrate how the analysis of the QoS of workflows defining service orchestrations is a time-consuming and error-prone activity even for simple workflows, and how such analysis can be fruitfully automated by PASO.

The rest of the paper is organized as follows. The two motivating examples of orchestrations are introduced in Sect. 2, along with a list of QoS-related questions on them. The PASO analyser is introduced in Sect. 3, and the results obtained by applying PASO to the motivating examples are presented in Sect. 4. Related work is discussed in Sect. 5, while some concluding remarks are drawn in Sect. 6.

2 Motivating Examples

2.1 Example 1: A Cloud-Based Storage Service

Let us consider a simple service orchestration (Fig. 2) that allows customers to store and retrieve data.

The orchestrator exploits two cloud storage services (C_1 and C_2) as follows:

– If the customer sends a *store* request, the orchestrator tries in parallel to store the data both on C_1 and C_2. If the first storage request on C_i fails (viz., a fault is returned), the orchestrator retries once (after some time) to store on C_i. If the data are successfully stored on both C_1 and C_2, the orchestrator replies positively to the customer. Otherwise it returns a fault to the customer.

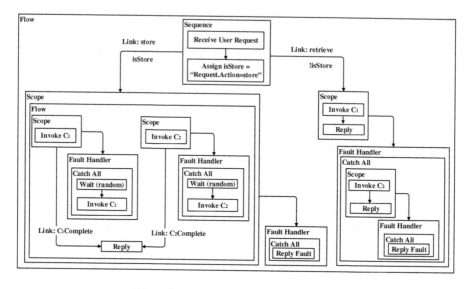

Fig. 2. A cloud-based storage service.

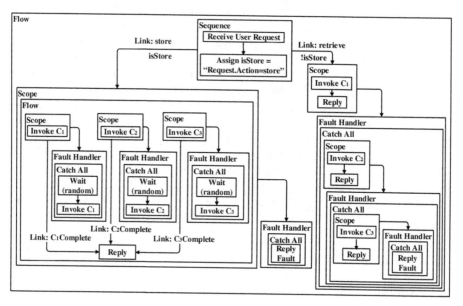

Fig. 3. Extended cloud-based storage service.

– If the customer sends a *retrieve* request, the orchestrator first looks up the data in C_1. If the invocation to C_1 fails, it looks up the data in C_2. If both invocations (to C_1 and C_2) fail, the orchestrator returns a fault to the customer. Otherwise it returns to the customer the result of the lookup.

Table 1. Probability distributions for the cloud storage services.

	Success	Fault
C_1	(99 %, 0.03$, 1 sec)	(1 %, 0$, 2 sec)
C_2	(90 %, 0.02$, 1 sec)	(10 %, 0$, 2 sec)

Let us assume the following probability distributions (Table 1) for the behaviour of the cloud storage services C_1 and C_2, in particular for their reliability, cost, and response time:

- C_1 cost is 0.03$ per invocation (for both *store* and *retrieve* requests), it is highly reliable and it completes almost always (99 %) in 1 s. Only in very few cases (1 %), it returns a fault in 2 s at no cost (0$).
- C_2 cost is 0.02$ per invocation, slightly cheaper than C_1, it is less reliable than C_1, and in most cases (90 %) it completes in 1 s. Only in few cases (10 %), it returns a fault in 2 s at no cost (0$).

Let us also assume that:

- 40 % of customer requests are *store* requests, and 60 % are *retrieve* requests, and that
- the random wait (before retrying to store on C_i) will last 0, 1, 2, 3, or 4 s, each with probability 20 %.

A first natural question is:

(Q1) *What are the estimated reliability, cost, and response time of the orchestrator using services C_1 and C_2 of Table 1?*

Other interesting questions on the QoS of the orchestrator of Fig. 2 are, for instance:

(Q2) *What is the probability that the response time of the orchestrator will be more than 5 s using services C_1 and C_2 of Table 1?*

(Q3) *Will the cost of the orchestrator exceed 0.04$ on average using services C_1 and C_2 of Table 1?*

Another class of interesting questions concerns assessing how the QoS of different external services may impact on the overall QoS of an orchestrator. Consider for instance the two alternative offerings for C_1 and C_2 illustrated in Table 2. An example of such questions is:

(Q4) *Which offering of Table 2 will yield the best QoS (reliability, cost, response time) for the orchestrator of Fig. 2?*

A further class of interesting questions concerns assessing whether and how modifying the workflow of an orchestrator will impact on the overall QoS of the orchestrator. For instance:

(Q5) *Extending the orchestrator (Fig. 3) so as to exploit one more cloud storage service C_3 (e.g., like the one described in Table 3) will increase the reliability of the orchestrator?*

Table 2. Two alternative offerings for the cloud storage services.

	Success	Fault
C_1	(90%, 0.02\$, 1 sec)	(10%, 0\$, 2 sec)
C_2	(90%, 0.02\$, 1 sec)	(10%, 0\$, 2 sec)

(a) Offering 1.

	Success	Fault
C_1	(99%, 0.03\$, 1 sec)	(1%, 0\$, 2 sec)
C_2	(81%, 0.01\$, 1 sec)	(19%, 0\$, 2 sec)

(b) Offering 2.

Table 3. Probability distribution of a third cloud storage service.

	Success	Fault
C_3	(81 %, 0.01\$, 1 sec)	(19 %, 0\$, 2 sec)

2.2 Example 2: Starting a Manufacturing Business

Let us consider a business process defining how to start a manufacturing business (Fig. 4). The process, after receiving a user request, starts three activities in parallel:

- It invokes a RentalAgency service to find a suitable location for manufacturing the desired product,
- It invokes a LoanAgent service to ask for a loan to fund the business start up, and
- It invoke a HumanResourceAgency service to find personnel with relevant skills.

Only after the LoanAgent secures the loan, a BuySupplies service will be invoked. Furthermore, the process will invoke a RentLocation service only after both invocations to the RentalAgency service and to the LoanAgent service will have completed.

Similarly, the process will invoke a HireStaff service only after both invocations to the HumanResourceAgency service and to the LoanAgent service will have completed.

Finally, the process will reply to the user only after the invocations to the RentLocation service, to the BuySupplies service and to the HireStaff service will have completed.

Let us assume the following probability distributions (Table 4) for the completion time of the aforementioned activities: For instance, the HireStaff service is guaranteed to complete within 2 to 15 days. In most of cases (35 %), it is completes in 4 days. It can also complete in 2, 6, 7, 10, 12 or 15 days with probability of 10 %, 10 %, 15 %, 15 %, 10 %, 5 % respectively.

A natural question for this example is to estimate the time needed to complete the execution of the whole business process. It is worth observing that, since

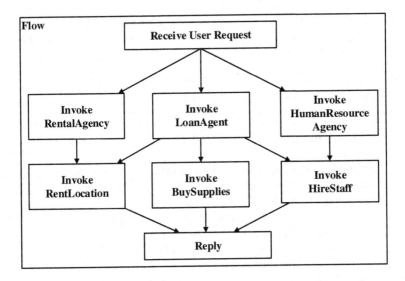

Fig. 4. Business process to start a manufacturing business.

Table 4. Probability distributions for the services invoked by the process of Fig. 4.

	1 day	2 days	4 days	6 days	7 days	10 days	12 days	15 days
RentalAgency		10 %	30 %	40 %		20 %		
LoanAgent	5 %	20 %	35 %	20 %	10 %	5 %	5 %	
HumanResourceAgency	10 %	30 %	10 %		30 %	20 %		
RentLocation				10 %	40 %	10 %		40 %
BuySupplies	20 %		15 %	35 %			20 %	10 %
HireStaff		10 %	35 %	10 %	15 %	15 %	10 %	5 %

all the invoked services have complex dependencies with each other, answering questions such as:

(Q6) *What is the expected time needed to execute the business process of Fig. 4 under the hypotheses of Table 4?*

(Q7) *What is the probability that the business process will not complete in time for the advertised launch date (e.g., in 24 days)?*

may be not easy.

3   Overview of PASO

PASO (Probabilistic Analyser of Service Orchestrations) is an open source application[1] developed in F#.Net which implements the probabilistic analysis

---

[1] The source code of PASO is available at https://github.com/upi-bpel/paso.

described in [10,11] to predict the QoS of service orchestrations. Unfortunately, space limitations allow us to include here only a very brief description of PASO[2].

In terms of input/output behaviour (Fig. 5), PASO inputs:

- A WS-BPEL [8] workflow[3] defining a service orchestration, and
- A file containing annotations of probabilities[4] for outcomes and costs of service invocations, as well as for the truth of the guards of if and while activities,

and it can output histograms and pie charts summarizing the results of the performed analysis.

PASO employs a structurally recursive function that associates each WS-BPEL activity with a *cost* structure, which is used to compositionally determine the QoS of structured activities. It is worth noting that, while determining the cost of a sequence of activities is pretty straightforward, the same does not hold for instance for flows, which cannot be always decomposed in terms of parallel and sequential compositions, as shown in [10,11].

To properly model **complex dependencies among workflow activities**, PASO employs two different cost composition functions: *Both* and *Delay*. Intuitively speaking, *Both(A,B)* denotes the cost of independently executing activities A and B, while *Delay(A,B)* denotes how to increase the cost of executing A with the cost of executing another activity B from which A depends. For instance, PASO models the cost of flow(A,B) as *Both(A,B)* only if A and B are not dependent one another, and it models the cost of sequence(A,B) as *Both(A,Delay(A,B))*.

To model **different results of service invocations**, PASO employs an *outcome* and an *environment* structure to store the outcome (success, fault, stuck) and the effects of previously executed activities.

Last, but not least, PASO models the **non-determinism in the orchestration workflow** and the **correlations among workflow activities** by employing Monte Carlo simulations to sample outcome and effects of service invocations as well as the conditions of alternatives and iterations. Monte Carlo simulation is useful for our algorithm in two ways. First, at each iteration of Monte Carlo we can sample the conditions of branches and loops (by using the sampling function) and deterministically decide what to execute. This, along with recursive sampling, allows us to address correlations, non-determinism and different invocation results. Second, many QoS properties (e.g., reliability, average cost and time) can be written as expectation queries.

---

[2] The interest reader can refer to [11] for a thorough description of the analysis implemented by PASO.

[3] PASO is able to analyse a subset of WS-BPEL structural (sequence, flow, if, while, scope, and faultHandlers) and basic (invoke and assign) activities. Other basic activities (like receive or reply) are considered by PASO successfully executable with zero cost.

[4] These probabilities may be deduced from Service Level Agreements (SLAs), or statistically inferred from data such as logs or performance counters if available.

Input   **Output**

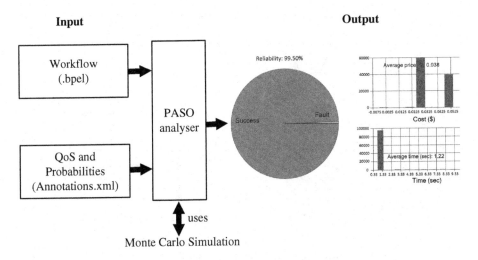

Fig. 5. Bird-eye view of the input-output behaviour of PASO.

4   PASO at Work on the Motivating Examples

In this section we show how the PASO analyser can be fruitfully exploited to get answers for the questions that we raised on the two motivating examples presented in Sect. 2.

4.1   Example 1: A Cloud-Based Storage Service

The first three questions raised in Sect. 2 concerned the quality of service of the orchestrator of Fig. 2:

(Q1) *What are the estimated reliability, cost, and response time of the orchestrator using services C_1 and C_2 of Table 1?*

(Q2) *What is the probability that the response time of the orchestrator will be more than 5 s using servicesl C_1 and C_2 of Table 1?*

(Q3) *Will the cost of the orchestrator exceed 0.04\$ on average using services C_1 and C_2 of Table 1?*

The results obtained by running PASO[5] on the orchestrator of Fig. 2 and on the offerings of Table 1 are illustrated in Table 5 and Fig. 6. The results reported in Table 5 are interesting as, for instance, we see that the estimated reliability of the orchestrator (99.53 %) is higher than the reliability of both C_1 (99 %) and C_2 (90 %). This is due to the fact that in the (less frequent, 40 % of times) case of *store* requests the orchestrator tries twice to store on each C_i (if needed), and in the (more frequent, 60 % of times) case of *retrieve* requests it succeeds if just one the C_i responds.

Moreover, the histogram of Fig. 6 shows that:

---

[5] We performed one million iterations of PASO for each group of questions.

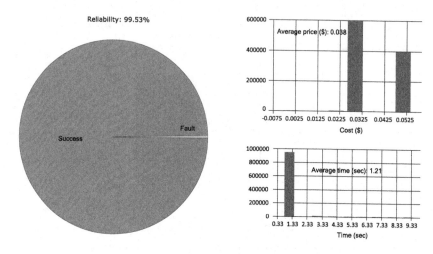

Fig. 6. Snapshot of PASO results for (Q1), (Q2) and (Q3).

Table 5. Results of PASO for (Q1).

Reliability	Cost	Time
99.53 %	0.038$	1.21 sec

- The response time of the orchestrator will be almost always (97.0 %) less than 5 s and that there is a noticeable probability (about 3 %) that it will exceed the maximum allowed time. Please note that this information is not evident just by looking at the average response time (1.21 s).
- The average cost is 0.038$, which is slightly below the target average expense of 0.04$.

Another class of interesting questions mentioned in Sect. 2 concerns comparing the effects of employing different external services on the QoS of an orchestrator:

(Q4) *Which offering of Table 2 will yield the best QoS (reliability, cost, response time) for the orchestrator of Fig. 2?*

The results obtained by running PASO on the orchestrator of Fig. 2 and on the offerings of Table 2 are summarised in Table 6. Also in this case the results are interesting as for instance, despite the different reliabilities of the two offerings (90 % and 90 % vs. 99 % and 81 %), we see that the reliability of the orchestrator is practically the same with either offering (while cost and response time differ).

A further class of interesting questions mentioned in Sect. 2 concerns assessing whether and how modifying the workflow of an orchestrator will impact on the overall QoS of the orchestrator:

(Q5) *Extending the orchestrator so as to exploit one more cloud storage service C_3 (e.g., like the one described in Table 3) will increase the reliability of the orchestrator?*

Table 6. Results of PASO for (Q4).

	Reliability	Cost	Time
Offer 1	98.3 %	0.027$	1.48 sec
Offer 2	98.4 %	0.034$	1.36 sec

Table 7. Results of PASO for (Q5).

	Reliability	Cost	Time
Offer 1	96.9 %	0.032$	1.82 sec
Offer 2	97.1 %	0.037$	1.66 sec

To answer this question, we used two alternative offerings for C_1 and C_2 (Table 2) and one offering for C_3 (Table 3). The results obtained by running PASO are summarised in Table 7. By comparing Tables 6 and 7, it is easy to conclude that adding a third storage service to the workflow is not a good idea as it decreases the QoS of the orchestrator.

4.2 Example 2: Starting a Manufacturing Business

The two questions raised in Sect. 2 for the orchestrator of Fig. 4 were:

(Q6) *What is the expected time needed to execute the business process of Fig. 4 under the hypotheses of Table 4?*
(Q7) *What is the probability that the business process will not complete in time for the advertised launch date (e.g., in 24 days)?*

The results obtained by running PASO on the orchestrator of Fig. 4 and on the offerings of Table 4 are illustrated in Fig. 7 and summarised in Table 8.

Table 8. Summary of the results of PASO for (Q6) and (Q7).

Probability of failing deadline	Average time
13.7 %	18.68 days

The results are interesting as, for instance, we see that the estimated completion time of the orchestrator is 18.68 days. The results also show that while the probability that the business process will complete in 24 days is 86.3 %, there is a noticeable probability (13.7 %) that it will not do so.

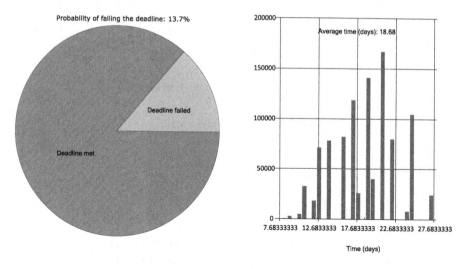

Fig. 7. Snapshot of PASO results for (Q6) and (Q7).

5   Related Work

QoS Prediction is not new and many approaches (e.g., [12,13]) and tools (e.g., Palladio [14], Kieker [15], Descartes [16]) have been proposed. We briefly discuss here only the work more closely related to ours.

Cardoso [17] proposed an algorithm to compute the QoS of a workflow composition. His approach employs a set of reduction rules to iteratively remove parallel, sequence, alternative and iterative structures until only one activity remains. A limitation of that approach is that some complex dependency workflow structures cannot be always decomposed in terms of parallel and sequential compositions, as shown in [9].

Mukherjee et al. [7,9] proposed a algorithm to estimate the QoS of WS-BPEL compositions. They convert a WS-BPEL workflow into an activity dependency graph, and assign probabilities of being executed to each activity. While the proposed algorithm can treat arbitrarily complex dependency structures, including fault handling, it does not take into account correlations among activities which do not have a direct dependency, and this may lead to incorrect results in some cases, as shown in Sect. 1.

Zheng et al. [18] studied QoS estimation for compositions represented by service graphs. They transform a service graph to remove loops, and then calculate probabilities of execution and QoS parameters for each path. Their approach however does not take into account fault handling and only partially deals with parallelism, not considering arbitrary synchronization links (only *flow*-like structures that can be decomposed in terms of parallel and sequential compositions are considered, as in [17]).

Ivanovic et al. [19] proposed a language to represent service compositions, and they address the problem of correlations. Some of the questions raised in this paper, for instance, what is the probability that response time of the orchestrator is between certain values or exceed a value, can be answered by their approach. However their language does not account for parallel execution.

Summing up, to the best of our knowledge, our approach advances the state of the art by handling workflows containing arbitrary dependency structures and fault handling, and by featuring a more accurate treatment of correlations among activities. Moreover, differently from all previous work, our approach is also able to handle unbounded loops.

6 Concluding Remarks

As we observed in Sect. 1, the ability of predicting the QoS of a service orchestration is of primary importance both during the design of a service orchestration and for the definition of its SLA.

In this paper we have tried to illustrate the practical usefulness of the probabilistic analysis featured the PASO analyser to predict the QoS of service orchestrations by answering interesting questions concerning the overall QoS of a service orchestration, the effects of replacing one or more of the invoked services with alternative services as well as of modifying the workflow of an orchestration. To illustrate the results of putting PASO at work, we have used two general examples of service orchestrations — a simple orchestration implementing a cloud-based storage service, and a business process defining how to start a manufacturing business — that show how the analysis of the QoS of workflows defining service orchestrations is, if performed manually, a time-consuming and error-prone activity even for simple workflows.

We see different possible directions for future work. One of them is to extend our approach to model other WS-BPEL constructs that we have not discussed in this paper, like `pick` or `eventHandlers`. It is also worth observing that while PASO currently inputs WS-BPEL workflows, the analysis it implements is not bound to WS-BPEL and it can be extended to analyse other similar workflow languages. Another direction for future work is to extend the number of QoS properties (beyond response time, reliability, and cost) supported by PASO. A further direction for future work is to improve the efficiency of Monte Carlo simulations performed by PASO by exploiting some of techniques proposed for instance in [20,21].

References

1. Papazoglou, M.: Web Services: Principles and Technology, 2nd edn. Pearson Education, Toronto (2012)
2. Weske, M.: Business Process Management: Concepts, Languages, Architectures. Springer, New York (2007)
3. Kim, E., et al.: Web Services Quality Factors. Candidate OASIS Standard Version 1.0. http://docs.oasis-open.org/wsqm/WS-Quality-Factors/v1.0/cos01/WS-Quality-Factors-v1.0-cos01.html

4. Kritikos, K., Pernici, B., Plebani, P., Cappiello, C., Comuzzi, M., Benrernou, S., Brandic, I., Kertész, A., Parkin, M., Carro, M.: A survey on service quality description. ACM Comput. Surv. (CSUR) **46**(1), 1–64 (2013)

5. Filieri, A., Maggio, M., Angelopoulos, K., D'Ippolito, N., Gerostathopoulos, I., Hempel, A., Hoffmann, H., Jamshidi, P., Kalyvianaki, E., Klein, C., et al.: Software engineering meets control theory. In: Proceedings of the 10th International Symposium on Software Engineering for Adaptive and Self-Managing Systems (2015)

6. Ravishankar, V., Baskaran, R.: A compendium on service oriented architecture and service level agreements. Int. J. Comput. Appl. **40**(1), 13–17 (2013)

7. Mukherjee, D., Jalote, P., Gowri Nanda, M.: Determining QoS of WS-BPEL compositions. In: Bouguettaya, A., Krueger, I., Margaria, T. (eds.) ICSOC 2008. LNCS, vol. 5364, pp. 378–393. Springer, Heidelberg (2008)

8. Jordan, D., Evdemon, J., Alves, A., Arkin, A., Askary, S., Barreto, C., Bloch, B., Curbera, F., Ford, M., Goland, Y., et al.: Web services business process execution language version 2.0. OASIS standard 11, April 2007

9. Mukherjee, D.: QOS IN WS-BPEL PROCESSES. Master's thesis, Indian Institute of Technology, Delhi, May 2008

10. Bartoloni, L., Brogi, A., Ibrahim, A.: Probabilistic prediction of the QoS of service orchestrations: a truly compositional approach. In: Franch, X., Ghose, A.K., Lewis, G.A., Bhiri, S. (eds.) ICSOC 2014. LNCS, vol. 8831, pp. 378–385. Springer, Heidelberg (2014)

11. Bartoloni, L., Brogi, A., Ibrahim, A.: Predicting the QoS of service orchestrations. Technical report, Dipartimento di Informatica, University of Pisa, Italy, March 2015. http://eprints.adm.unipi.it/2329/1/Unipi_TR.pdf (Submitted for publication)

12. Bouillard, A., Rosario, S., Benveniste, A., Haar, S.: Monotonicity in service orchestrations. In: Franceschinis, G., Wolf, K. (eds.) PETRI NETS 2009. LNCS, vol. 5606, pp. 263–282. Springer, Heidelberg (2009)

13. Leitner, P., Ferner, J., Hummer, W., Dustdar, S.: Data-driven and automated prediction of service level agreement violations in service compositions. Distrib. Parallel Databases **31**(3), 447–470 (2013)

14. Becker, S., Koziolek, H., Reussner, R.: Model-based performance prediction with the palladio component model. In: Proceedings of the 6th International Workshop on Software and Performance, pp. 54–65. ACM (2007)

15. van Hoorn, A., Rohr, M., Hasselbring, W., Waller, J., Ehlers, J., Frey, S., Kieselhorst, D.: Continuous monitoring of software services: design and application of the kieker framework. Research report, Kiel University, November 2009

16. Kounev, S., Brosig, F., Huber, N.: The Descartes Modeling Language. Technical report, Department of Computer Science, University of Wuerzburg, October 2014

17. Cardoso, A.J.S.: Quality of service and semantic composition of workflows. Ph.D. thesis, University of Georgia (2002)

18. Zheng, H., Zhao, W., Yang, J., Bouguettaya, A.: QoS analysis for web service compositions with complex structures. IEEE Trans. Serv. Comput. **6**(3), 373–386 (2013)

19. Ivanović, D., Carro, M., Kaowichakorn, P.: Towards QoS prediction based on composition structure analysis and probabilistic models. In: Franch, X., Ghose, A.K., Lewis, G.A., Bhiri, S. (eds.) ICSOC 2014. LNCS, vol. 8831, pp. 394–402. Springer, Heidelberg (2014)

20. Bhat, S., Borgström, J., Gordon, A.D., Russo, C.: Deriving probability density functions from probabilistic functional programs. In: Piterman, N., Smolka, S.A. (eds.) TACAS 2013 (ETAPS 2013). LNCS, vol. 7795, pp. 508–522. Springer, Heidelberg (2013)
21. Stuhlmüller, A., Goodman, N.D.: A dynamic programming algorithm for inference in recursive probabilistic programs. In: Second Statistical Relational AI workshop at UAI 2012 (StaRAI-12) (2012)

A Workflow Service Mediator for Automated Information Processing and Scheduling Delivery to an Archive

Salvatore D' Antonio[1], Giuliano Gugliara[2],
Carlo Francesco Romano[1(✉)], and Luigi Romano[1]

[1] Dipartimento di Ingegneria,
Università degli Studi di Napoli "Parthenope", Naples, Italy
{salvatore.dantonio, carlofrancesco.romano,
luigi.romano}@uniparthenope.it
[2] Comune di Afragola, Afragola, NA, Italy
g.gugliara@comune.afragola.na.it

Abstract. This paper describes our experience in building a service mediator to address real-life digital preservation problems and an overview of the project's progress to date. This article introduces the motivation for this work, describes the extensible technical architecture and places its approach into the context of the long term archive. The proposed framework is composed of configurations and control panels based on Restful WEB technologies, a data-analysis engine based on stream processing paradigms, and an asynchronous message delivery service which provides definition task types and effort driven scheduling. The framework has been implemented as a pilot application in Afragola, a municipality in Napoli (Italy).

Keywords: Stream processing · Message Driven · Long term archiving · REST · Business process manager · Grammar based parsing

1 Introduction

This paper describes our experience in building a service mediator designed to integrate heterogeneous document workflow into a long-term archive.

The impetus for our team comes from P.A. (Public Administration) and long term archives across Italy which have the legal responsibility to safeguard digital documents. While much progress has been made in digital preservation research, the current state of the art has shown a lack of integrated solutions for preservation of large-scale digital collections. A fundamental problem is that all workflow engines exist as stand-alone applications and are not geared to preserve digital objects. The main goal of this framework is to provide a common interface for document workflow engines that delivers the final record (eventually digitally signed) to achieve digital preservation and long-term archiving.

The rest of the paper is organized as follows. Section 2 reviews the technical approach especially the REST API design [1]. Section 3 presents the detail of a control

A. Celesti and P. Leitner (Eds.): ESOCC 2015 Workshops, CCIS 567, pp. 126–140, 2016.
DOI: 10.1007/978-3-319-33313-7_9

Panel, that supports a number of key preservation functions to provide an easily managed preservation system. Section 4 discusses the implementation of REST. With Sect. 5 we will provide an overview of related work in relevant areas and what we add in term of contribution to their work and we conclude with Sect. 6.

2 Technical Approach

The software architecture is rooted in the vision of a system that fully decouples any workflow from the archive, acting as a service mediator that translates the incoming document into a file compliant with the long term storage. A conceptual view of the framework is depicted in Fig. 1.

Fig. 1. A conceptual view of the framework

The whole process is divided into these transactional phases that characterize the life cycle of documents to upload:

1. A File including all records (eventually digitally signed) has to be generated
2. Temporary file mirroring to the Service Mediator database (local database), returning a receipt with an id-key
3. File delivery scheduling to an entrusted third-part

The engine key design concept is divided into three components: a documents acceptance system, a queuing and scheduling system and the connection interface to an archive. This decouples the workflow engine from the outsourced archival hub. A modular three-tier system is depicted in Fig. 2.

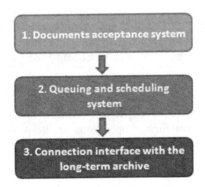

Fig. 2. Framework model

We have designed the system as a Restful (Representational State Transfer) [2] application rather than other architectural forms (such as SOA - Service Oriented Architecture) especially because it is XML-independent [3]. This allows exchanging information without adding overhead (i.e. encapsulation of several files within a soap message, encoded in base64). Due to the lightweight message format feature, REST also gives more space to system performance optimization. Furthermore the effort required to build a client to a RESTful service is very small as developers can test such services from an ordinary Web browser. In the Italian P.A. scenario, where consumer clients are mostly unknown, REST is a good choice because RESTful interface is more flexible to meet integration requirements and data are combined easily among different kinds of applications. A more in-depth discussion of these technologies is given by Pautasso et al. [4].

There are three kinds of actors in this scenario that can interact with the main resource "Archive":

- Uploader: can upload in certain category
- User: can search into certain category
- Operator: he is responsible for the long-term conservation. With the help of the dashboard described in Sect. 3, the operator must alert for problems and, in some cases, mitigate the criticality.

2.1 Documents Acceptance System

This layer collects the various document parts and its metadata [5], validates them, creates a file with an archive-compliant metadata and sends a receipt to the client (the upload technology is the multipart-form data over the HTTPS).

Entity "File". The "File" is the entity that abstracts away records and metadata to archive. The main metadata fields are referenced into a File column and XML data type is used to store metadata.

Upload Engine. As discussed above, we use a Restful approach to load and search documents. The upload service is invoked by the specific HTTP action POST:

```
POST /ServiceMediator/archive/insert/collectionX
Host: localhost:8080
URL:https://localhost:8080/ServiceMediator/archive/Collect
ionX/insert
```

Every "uploader" is linked to a specific workflow and the system will use the specific processor to perform further operations on it. A valid multipart/form-data contains these fields:

1. Text. User, Password
2. Text. Metadata
3. Binary/Octet. Record

The type of the message body is defined by a corresponding header field using MIME media types [6]. In this example /ServiceMediator/archive/CollectionX/insert/ calls the CollectionX processor and <<multipart/form-data>> is the record to process and validate. Hence, the CollectionX processor build the entity "File" to be stored locally (Service Mediator database), generate an unique ID (database side) and starts an asynchronous task (scheduled delivery); the client has a tracking device to get more details about the running task that is a resource with its own URI [7]. The server answer follows:

```
POST /ServiceMediator/archive/insert/
Server: GlassFish Server Open Source Edition 3.1.2.2
Host: localhost:8080
Content-Type: application/xml
...
<file id=3750>
   <deliveryOutcome>0</deliveryOutcome>
   <state>1</state>
   <stateDescription>...</stateDescription>
   <metadataXML>....</metadataXML>
   <user>UploaderXY</user>
   <timestamp>2015-02-23T13:21:20.449+01:00</timestamp>
   <MainRecord>
     <fileName>test.out</fileName>
     <mime>application/octet-stream</mime>
     <filesize>70304</filesize>
     <gzipcompression>true</gzipcompression>
   </MainRecord>
   <number>2</number>
   <year>2015</year>
   <type_registry>GENERIC</type_registry>
</file>
202 Accepted
Location:
https://localhost:8080/ServiceMediator/archive/Collection
X/3750
```

The response contains the marshalled entity "File" formatted in a variety of representation media types (i.e. the JavaScript Object Notation (JSON) [8] and the Extensible Markup Language XML) and the URI location, in this way each uploaded File is traceable. The client can execute a GET to the inserted URI to know the file current state or even use a DELETE to cancel it.

Search Engine. An authenticated User can retrieve easily a document into a File that belongs to CollectionX. A typical query is:

```
https://localhost:8080/ServiceMediator/archive/collection
X/query?year=2015&author=John Snow
```

It does retrieve all files based on query:

```
QUERY correlateInfo:
SELECT
  file name, metadata, blob_pointer,
FROM collectionX
WHERE
year='2015' and author='John Snow'
```

Blob_pointer is the pointer to the actual raw data.

Cataloging System. We have developed three Collection processors: Collection SUAP, CollectionSUE and CollectionDigitalContract used in the following applications.

1. SUAP workflow: a system used by local authority to register new business in Italy.
2. SUE workflow: a manage Planning Permission System.
3. DigitalContract workflow: contracts manager between local authority and third-parties.

Figure 3 shows the client upload schema.

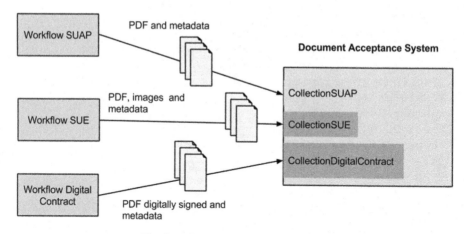

Fig. 3. Clients upload their documents

Once the file is uploaded a validation task takes place. This task can be easily upgraded to meet future requirements. In our case a syntactic engine (parser) analyses the correspondences between different information, such as.

- Number of attachments/annexes/annotations cited into the XML and number of them all actually uploaded.
- Digital signatures validity and/or double digital signatures.

The Documents acceptance system, through Collection processors, can generate from the original XML a new one for digital repositories interaction, integrating it with descriptive, administrative, and structural metadata. A Collection processor provides an engine (metadata-engine) for incorporating these various components from various sources under one structure and also makes it possible to aggregate these pieces together in a record in sync with METS (Metadata Encoding and Transmission Standard [9]). The core of this engine is based on JAXB (Java Architecture for XML Binding), a Data binding API that allows the programming to manipulate XML. JAXB can constitute the tree of Java content objects using an XML as input. The applications can access directly the Java objects, data content and structure. The whole process is called unmarshalling. Marshalling is opposite to unmarshalling. Marshalling is a process of generating XML instance document according to the Java content tree. The Collection processor unmarshalls the incoming XML, validate all digital records uploaded, and store and integrate information into a new Java Object. Hence the processor marshalls a single XML for interactions with long-term archive.

This functionality is depicted into Fig. 4.

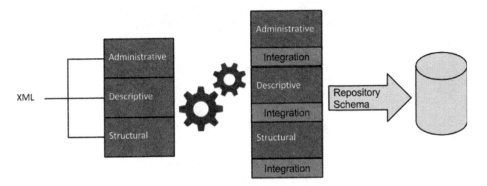

Fig. 4. Unmarshaller/Marshaller engine

Another problem solved is that each original metadata source provider may have used different metadata schemas, so it's possible to have a unified search engine that provides a single method and language of accessing data.

Finally, the file (records and metadata) is created and stored in the local database (Fig. 5).

2.2 Queuing and Scheduling System

The second layer allows delegating the message exchange management with server storage. Files are enveloped and a task is programmed, in order to send the message in a specified time. A simple schema is depicted in Fig. 6.

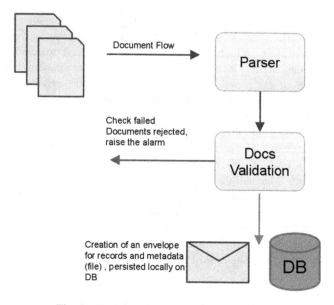

Fig. 5. Documents acceptance system schema

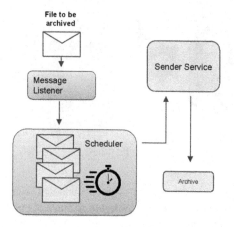

Fig. 6. Queuing and scheduling system schema

2.3   Connection Interface with Long-Term Archive

The last layer provides the communication interface to the archive, as depicted in Fig. 7.

As a timer programmed by the queuing and scheduling system expires, the system connects through the driver interface to the Archive, and then performs the upload.

The envelope contains information about destination, based on its metadata.

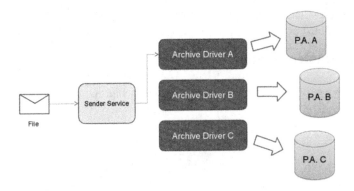

Fig. 7. Connection interface with long-term archive schema

2.4   File State and Delivery Outcome

The system is capable to make a self-decision and corrective action in case of failure, deciding whether to take further action. Every decision is logged. Possible states are:

1. INITIALIZED (0) file is initialized with empty parameters.
2. IN_PROGRESS (1), file has just been created with validated input and stored onto local database. The system will try to deliver it according configuration parameters.
3. SENT (2), the file has been sent to the archive.
4. PAUSE (3), the system will not take further action until the file state is in pause.
5. ERROR (4), the system will not take further action, whose is entrusted to an operator.
6. INITIALIZATION_ERROR (5); file is not properly initialized and will be never sent.

If an error occurs during transfer (connection error, network uplink down, etc.) the system updates the log with the exception information and reschedules delivery. After three errors logged, the system turns file state into "error". Possible states of delivery outcome are

1. TO BE SENT (0), File initialized.
2. SENT CORRECTLY (1), File sent without error.
3. SENT WITH WARNING (2), The archive receipt contains some warnings.
4. ERROR (3); an error occurred during transmission.

3   Control Panel

This system can be easily monitored through a control panel by Operators. It contains a web dashboard that provides visual control of different events, such as:

- Checking conservation status of each file proved by the Archive receipt.
- Managing conservation transaction and acting appropriate corrective action (e.g. forcing upload) in case of a negative outcome.

- Managing users and roles.
- Check scheduled task.

4   A Real Implementation

A bird's eye view of the entire system is depicted in Fig. 8.

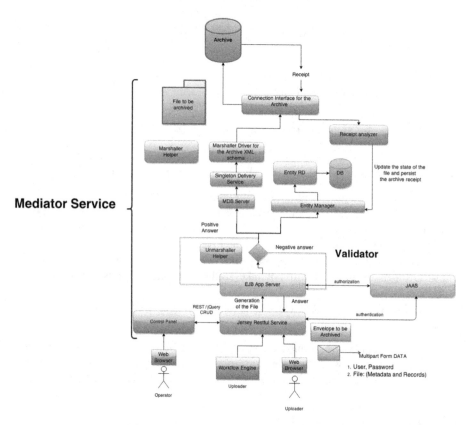

Fig. 8. Bird's eye view of the entire system

A client interacts with the system through a Jersey Restful service, consuming its resources (control panel and upload engine). An Enterprise JavaBeans (EJB) run in the EJB container, a runtime environment within the GlassFish Server. The EJB container provides system-level services, such as transactions and security, to its enterprise beans, which form the core of transactional Java EE application. After the file generation (see Fig. 8.) a validation task takes place. In case of success the file is sent into a Java Message Driven Bean (MDB) that mediates between the client and the long term archive [10]. The client always gets a receipt (in case of success or failure) and can track the state of its request from an URI that point to the task resource. This service mediator has been built with three goals in mind:

1. Modularity and Aspect-Oriented Programming (AOP): modularize crosscutting concerns, by using a concept called aspects [11].
2. Transactionality: the needs are to divide the entire project into transactional phases (upload and delivery).
3. Restful capabilities: REST does not allow for the overhead over a lightweight transport protocol such as HTTP and permits easy future system evolution with regard to scalability, performance, adaptability, etc.

For these reasons Enterprise Java Beans 3.1 and Glassfish have been the technological choices.

As depicted in Fig. 8, representation of identity and credentials are provided by the JAAS module (Java Authentication and Authorization Service) implemented in AOP. This modularization can ease the burden on developers, developing more secure applications faster. Whenever a client tries to access a protected resource, the application container activates the authentication mechanism. If the client is authenticated, he must be in role to consume that specific resource. Users and Roles are defined into the local DB.

4.1   Documents Acceptance System Implementation

The resource Archive, responsible for upload and search engine, is exposed by a Jersey Restful Web service framework that abstracts away the low-level details of the client-server. This framework decouples client-server interaction because it hides remote procedure calls. The client needs just the URL that represents the system state. This resource is implemented by a class FileService and exposed through the URL "*https://localhost:8080/ServiceMediator/archive/*". For every collection there is a processor that, with the help of an Unmarshaller Helper, validates the incoming record (s) and its metadata. Then the entity File is created (cf. Sect. 2.1). A scratch of code follows:

```
@Stateless
@Path("/CollectionX/")
public class FileService {
    @EJB
    Archive archive;
    @POST
    @Path("/insert")
    @Consumes(MediaType.MULTIPART_FORM_DATA)
    @Produces({"application/xml", "application/json"})
    public File insertFile(
    FormDataMultiPart formParams,
    @Context HttpServletRequest req) {
    //entity
    File initializedFile = inizializeFile();
    try {
        //check user and password
        if (!logged) {(req.login(user, pass));
        }
        //check role
        if (req.isUserInRole(role)) {
        //validate stream
        validateCollectionXRecords(metadataXML, record);
        //build the file
        initializedFile = do_buildFile(metadataXML,
record);
        //update the entity File with a local primary key
        archive.persist(initializedFile);
        // send the inizialized File to the Queuing and
scheduling system
        addQueue(initializedFile);
            }
        }
        // catch and  finally blocks
    }
    return initializedFile ;}
```

Validation is composed by a set of rules, such as:

- Number of attachments/annexes/annotations cited into the XML and number of them all actually uploaded.
- Digital signatures validity and/or double digital signatures.

4.2 Queuing and Scheduling System Implementation

This component has been implemented using Java EJB Message Driven Beans (MDB) and Java Timer technologies.

The message listener MessagingEngine implements the abstract method onMessage (Message message) which takes the file encapsulated into a java Message and schedules an intelligent delivery, driven by some configurable parameters:

- Weight: file with a blob less than X MB can be archived at the moment.
- Hand driven: an operator can manually activate delivery (e.g. after a failed transition).

Message Listener implementation sample code follows below:

```
//ScheduleDelivery is an EJB reosurce
@EJB
ScheduleDelivery scheduleDelivery;
public void onMessage(Message message) {
ObjectMessage objectMessage = (ObjectMessage) message;
FileMessage fileMessage= new FileMessage();
try {
    fileMessage = (FileMessage) objectMesage.getObject();
/*
The ActiveTask helper class is useful for scheduled deli -
very. It defines when deliver a File; it's driven by many
parameters
*/
ActiveTask at = new Activeask(fileMessage.getIdFile());
scheduleDelivery.insertCalendarTask(at);
        } catch (JMSException jmse) {
            jmse.printStackTrace();
            context.setRollbackOnly();
        } catch (Exception e) {
            e.printStackTrace();
        }}
```

ScheduleDelivery implements a method "sendFile" with the annotation @Timeout.

On timeout "sendFile" connects through the driver interface (DeliveryService) to the Archive, and then performs the upload.

4.3 Connection Interface with Long-Term Archive Implementation

This layer is implemented by an EJB resource, DeliveryService. It does accept a File, then marshalls its metadata into a new archive dependant XML-schema and delivers data through the right driver. This local resource is provided by Singleton Class which contains a @Lock (LockType WRITE) method. Below follows a sample code:

```
@Singleton
@Interceptors(CallAudit.class)
@TransactionAttribute(TransactionAttributeType.MANDATORY)
public class DeliveryService {
  @EJB
  Archive archive;
  private AtomicBoolean busy = new AtomicBoolean(false);
  //set lock in read
  @Lock(LockType.WRITE)
  public void send(long idFile)
throws InterruptedException {
      if (!busy.compareAndSet(false, true)) {
          System.out.println("Busy resource. ");
          return; }
      File file = archive.find(idFile);
      try {
/translate metadata into the archive-dependent XML-schema
String metadataXML =
GenericDriver.translateMetadata(file.getMetadataXml());
//get the answer from the Synchonous upload
String archive_receipt =
SynchronousUploader.uploadFileToArchive(file,
metadataXML);
  //updating State and delivery outcome
  file.updateFile(GenericDriver.translate_archive_receipt
(archive_receipt));
//add a log of transaction
LogDelivery logDelivery = new LogDelivery(file);
file.getLogCollection().add(logDelivery);
} catch (Exception ex) {
      } finally {
//update file into local DB
archive.update(file);
//Release resource as soon as task complete
busy.set(false);
```

During the busy time (resource locked), any other
scheduled delivery is discarded. The system retries as
soon as the task is completed.

4.4   The Control Panel Implementation

Every interaction with REST services in the control panel are done by a jquery interface using the Ajax common framework. For example, to retrieve all files, client must call the following function:

```
$( "#result" ).load(
"/https://localhost:8080/ServiceMediator/archive/all",
function( response, status, xhr ) {
if ( status == "error" ) {
var msg = "Sorry but there was an error: ";
$( "#error" ).html( msg + xhr.status + " " +
xhr.statusText );}});
```

5   Related Work

A common theme in much of this work is cataloging and hence recovering archived records using a search engine. Marcia Lei Zeng and Lois Mai Chan presented a comparative analysis between results of interoperability improvement efforts at different levels (Schema level, Record level, Repository level) [12]. In our work, the design rules responsible for dealing with interoperability are mapped at the Record Level. Hassan Mathkour and Ameur Touir presented XMed [13], a mediator that helps to aggregate heterogeneous data sources.

Our work consolidates these theories into an environment as end-product choosing technologies and a model, as adaptable as possible, in view of further tools/services developments that software vendors and service providers can implement and augment.

We built a system with additional functionalities and that fully decouples the internal workflow from the Digital Archive. It supports a number of key preservation functions adding these new features:

- The long-term archival hub might stop for maintenance, so we built a system that acts as buffer for on-line uploading.
- The system has been built with bandwidth optimization in mind, acting during non-peak hours.
- A mediation service integrates original XML schema into a new one in sync with METS (Metadata Encoding & Transmission Standard) for supporting long-term access requirements. Moreover, metadata can be refined according to business needs or future law compliances.
- The archival hub might change so we modularized the system adding a layer with a storage driver interface, then there's no need to rewrite code for the workflow engines.
- A monitoring panel has been designed to easily check records preservation state and performances.

6   Conclusion

A first prototype of the proposed framework has been implemented in Afragola, a small municipality in Napoli. This pilot application helps the management of long-term archive for digitally signed documents. It became a core application for all their workflow software as it integrates the workflow with:

1 The ability to schedule documents delivery that allows packets traffic optimization over the network, using continuously and optimally bandwidth.
2. Validation feature that can be made increasingly intelligent and adaptive, as it helps to identify human mistakes within the document generation chain.
3. A dashboard delivering greater visibility and control at a higher level into the process.
4. The presence of an aggregator node allowing homogenizing and adjusting heterogeneous document flows, making maintenance easier.

References

1. Haupt, F., et al.: A Model-driven approach for REST compliant services. In: 2014 IEEE International Conference on Web Services (ICWS), pp. 129–136 (2014)
2. Vinoski, S.: REST eye for the SOA guy. IEEE Internet Comput. **11**(1), 82–84 (2007)
3. W3C: Extensible Markup Language (XML) 1.0, 5th edn., 26 November 2008. http://www.w3.org/TR/REC-xml
4. Pautasso, C., Zimmermann, O., Leymann, F.: Restful web services vs. "big" web services: making the right architectural decision. In: Proceedings of the 17th International Conference on World Wide Web, pp. 805–814. ACM, New York (2008)
5. Perlin, N.: Introduction to metadata. In: 2006 IEEE International Professional Communi cation Conference, pp. 153–155 (2006)
6. Freed, N., Borenstein, N.: Multipurpose internet mail extensions (MIME) part two: Media types. RFC 2046. http://www.ietf.org/rfc/rfc2046.txt
7. Masinter, L., Berners-Lee, T., Fielding, R.T.: Uniform resource identifier (URI): Generic syntax. RFC 3986. http://www.ietf.org/rfc/rfc3986.txt
8. JSON.org: Introducing JSON, 11 Desember 2002. http://www.json.org/
9. IEEE: Recommended Practice for Learning Technology – Metadata Encoding and Transmission Standard (METS) Mapping to the Conceptual Model for Resource Aggregation. IEEE Std 1484.13.2-2013, pp. 1–73, 30 December 2013
10. Lohr, K.P.: Automatic mediation between incompatible component interaction styles. In: Proceedings of the 36th Annual Hawaii International Conference on System Sciences, p. 10 (2003)
11. Kiczales, G., Hilsdale, E., Hugunin, J., Kersten, M., Palm, J., Griswold, W.G.: An overview of AspectJ. In: Knudsen, J.L. (ed.) ECOOP 2001. LNCS, vol. 2072, pp. 327–354. Springer, Heidelberg (2001)
12. Chan, L.M., Zeng, M.L.: Metadata interoperability and standardization - a study of methodology Part I: achieving interoperability at the schema level. D-Lib Mag. **12** (2006). http://www.dlib.org/dlib/june06/chan/06chan.html
13. Mathkour, H., Touir, A.: An intelligent mediator for heterogeneous data sources. In: The 9th Asia-Pacific Conference on Communications, APCC 200, vol. 3, pp. 1002–1006 (2003)

Adaptive Architectural Model for Future Internet Applications

Marina Mongiello[(✉)], Luigi Alfredo Grieco, Massimo Sciancalepore,
and Elvis Vogli

Politecnico di Bari, Via E. Orabona, 4, 70125 Bari, Italy
{marina.mongiello,alfredo.grieco,massimo.sciancalepore,
elvis.vogli}@poliba.it

Abstract. Interoperability, flexibility and adaptability are key requirements of Future Internet applications. Convergence of contents, services,
things and networks seems to be the cornerstone to fulfill these requirements. In this paper we propose a model for runtime composition of
software applications in sensors networks based on data, processes and
technology, in order to design an "on the fly" architecture of a software system. The model is graph-based and composed by two control
levels: a formal model and the instantiation level. An algorithm extracts
a subgraph that identifies the applications to be executed according to
changes in the external context. The proposed approach has been instantiated in a use case example in a smart home environment, to evaluate
the usefulness of the approach and the applicability of the model in actual
scenarios.

Keywords: Formal model · Runtime architectural model · Sensor
networks

1 Introduction and Motivation

Future Internet applications should be able to handle dynamic changes in
user experience and interoperability between different technologies, data, and
processes. Convergence of contents, services, things, and networks seems to be
the relevant direction taken by these applications [2,4].

Such complex and composite source of data ranging from signals, raw data,
events and complex events needs technological and theoretical formalization. In
the light of all these novelties, adaptive mechanisms to develop and orchestrate
services and applications are emerging [3,5].

A formal approach for runtime composition of software applications in sensor
networks is proposed hereby. The approach is made of two control levels: a
technology independent level and an instantiation one. The first level catches
different configurations of adaptive software modeled using a graph structure.
Each node in the graph can be classified as a data or a process or a technology.
A data node represents information derived from the external context (e.g., a

© Springer International Publishing Switzerland 2016
A. Celesti and P. Leitner (Eds.): ESOCC 2015 Workshops, CCIS 567, pp. 141–148, 2016.
DOI: 10.1007/978-3-319-33313-7_10

data detected by a sensor). Data trigger processing of software applications, i.e. process node. Finally, technology node specify features of the devices (for example the state of the device where the application will be executed, the state of the memory of the device or the state of the middleware used to make software application interact with each other). At the instantiation level, instead, the graph model is contextualized to application context that are platform dependent and belong for example to Java, Android, and any other technology environment.

Data processing and technologies selection and management is driven by specification of operational requirements. On the graph model, hence at the first control level, we also define an algorithm to extract a subgraph from the graph by minimizing a cost function. The algorithm finds the best sequences of (data, process, technology) terns minimizing the cost due to resources utilization. Such sequences of nodes and the related paths correspond to the selected orchestration of services or application in response to the context behavior. The main advantage of the proposed approach is to possibility to delay architectural decisions at run-time and to build the architecture "on the fly", depending on the specified requirements.

The proposed approach has been instantiated in a use case example in a smart home environment, to evaluate the usefulness of the approach and the applicability of the model in realistic scenarios.

The remaining of this paper is organized as follows. Section 2 introduces background information needed for clarifying the proposed approach. The proposed formal model is defined in Sect. 3. Instantiation of the model with respect to a realistic use case scenario is described in Sect. 4. Conclusions and future works close the paper.

2   Background

In this section we introduce techniques and notions that will be used in the remaining of the paper. Specifically, Sect. 2.1 introduces the adaptive systems, Sect. 2.2 describes goals and operational requirements, and finally, Sect. 2.3 introduces REST Middleware.

2.1   Adaptive Systems

An adaptive system is an open system able to adapt its behavior according to changes in the environment or in parts of the system itself. Hence the adaptability is the ability of a software system to adapt efficiently and rapidly to any changes in the context or in the requirements.

Typically the development of a software system is completed within the life cycle where before delivery, requirements engineers, software designers and developers realize the system components. In modern software systems it is always difficult to predict the needs of users, so a single optimal configuration of the system is difficult to model and design.

It may be necessary to vary requirements run-time and then design the components of the application and implementation, all the same, always on the basis of changes arising from the external environment and the context, of course. For example, moving along a sensor network determines changes in the external environment that might trigger the execution of applications and software components not provided at design time.

2.2   Operational Requirements

Goals are objectives the system is intended to achieve through the cooperation of agents in the envisioned software and its environment [6]. A requirement is a goal assigned to an agent in the software design [1]. While functional requirements specify the functionalities to be implemented, generally non-functional requirements can determine decisions on the architectural model: for example, if the system must ensure security it is good to use a proxy to access protected data, if the system must integrate existing components it is good that has a distributed objects architecture and so on. A Operational Requirement captures the conditions under which a system component may or must perform an operation to achieve a goal. The operational requirements eventually belong to the set of non-functional requirements and describe the behavior of the system. They can be described by formal or semi-formal languages. Definition of operational requirements is basic in defining and describing the system analyzed in terms of the behavior more then the functionality to be provided.

2.3   REST Middleware

Nowadays many vertical M2M solutions have been designed independently for different applications, making the current M2M market very fragmented, which inevitably hinders a large-scale M2M deployment. To decrease the market fragmentation there have been many efforts from different standardization bodies to define horizontal service layers.

The European Telecommunications Standards Institute (ETSI) has defined with the SmartM2M standard a middleware which has a RESTful architecture [9]. On the other side, OneM2M, where are collaborating more than 200 standardization bodies and companies, is defining a RESTful middleware which will have a global validity [8].

The proposed solutions provide RESTful middlewares which separate the applications from communication domain. The middlewares are accessible via open interfaces and enable the development of services and applications independently of the underlying network. In addition they provide several service capabilities to enable machine registration, synchronous and asynchronous communication, resource discovery, access rights management, group broadcast, etc.

All the resources in the RESTful middlewares are organized in standardized resource trees and can be uniquely addressed by a Uniform Resource Identifier (URI). Their representations can be transferred and manipulated with verbs (i.e., retrieve, update, delete, and execute).

3   Model for Adaptive Applications Composition

In this section we propose a formal model for runtime composition of software applications in a sensor network.

The model is a graph based structure. The purpose of using a graph structure is to determine which apps to execute and how and where they will be executed, depending on variation in the contest and hence on data detected by the sensor. The main advantage of using a graph structure is the possibility to use rewriting or grammar graph techniques for extracting subgraphs satisfying a given requirement. Requirements to be satisfied are high level requirements (mainly Operational), that are hence modeled on the graph structure. The graph describes a snapshot of all the available software plugins mainly characterized by the data detected by a sensor in the network (Data), the functionality to be executed (Process) and by the state of the device where it will be executed (Technology). Each transition has a cost due to parameters involved in the context. Hence we can assume that each plugin is modeled as a triple of elements with a function cost associated.

Definition 1 (Resource Super Graph (RSG)). *A Resource Super Graph is a direct Acyclic Graph $G = \{\mathbf{N}, \mathbf{A}\}$, where nodes $\mathbf{N}$ are resources – $\mathbf{N} = \mathbf{D} \cup \mathbf{P} \cup \mathbf{T}$ ($\mathbf{D} = Data, \mathbf{P} = Process, \mathbf{T} = Technology$) – and arcs $a \in \mathbf{A}$ are such that:*

1. *$\mathbf{A} \subseteq (\mathbf{D} \times \mathbf{P}) \cup (\mathbf{P} \times \mathbf{T})$, i.e. "arcs connect data with process, process with technology, technology with data";*
2. *$a \in \mathbf{D} \times \mathbf{P}$ defines the variable cost v_c*
   $a \in \mathbf{P} \times \mathbf{T}$ defines the fixed cost f_c
   $a \in \mathbf{T} \times \mathbf{D}$ detection of a new data variation

Each node in the graph can be distinguished as: *Data, Process, Technology*. *Data* are those detected by a sensor network; *Process* is the operation performed on the data that can belong to one among the following: preprocessing, processing plugins, etc. *Technology* identifies the network type and the characteristics of the mobile devices. Arcs in the graph link pairs of nodes based on the value of a cost function. The cost computation depends on several parameters, that can be the type of node, the cost of the process and so on.

The cost function associated with the triple (Data, Process, Technology) depends on the features of the given plugin but also on the state of the devices. It is defined as $f_c(DPT)$ of the triple (DPT), and is given by the sum of the cost of the two arcs connecting respectively D with P and P with T, $f_c = v_c + fx_c$. The contribution of the variable cost depends on the characteristics of the available network and of the devices on which it is calculated. Where $v_c = device_c + network_c$. The cost of the network includes information about the state of the network at the time of receipt of the request of a plugin execution, such as connection delay, network bit rate, packet size, etc. The cost of the device is given by the amount of available RAM on the middleware, due to the number of active connections and by the cost of forwarding information when for example a middleware is not available so the request must be forwarded to another one. So $device_c = middleware_c - forwarding_c$. On the other hand, the costs of mobile device is given by the amount of available RAM and mass memory, the level of the device battery, as well as the geographic location (used to choose which middleware register).

The contribution of fixed cost fx_c depends on the characteristics of the plugin, such as size in bytes, computational complexity and so on. It remains unchanged if the plugin runs on the mobile device or if runs on the middleware.

Moreover, given a pair of starting and destination nodes, there are multiple paths connecting them, hence we can extract more "sub-graphs" from a SuperGraph. A path in the graph, i.e., a subgraph, identifies a sequence of apps to be executed with specifications concerning the features of the technology – the kind of network or of device–, and the type of process to execute each of them – where and how the app is executed. We need an algorithm to extract a subgraph according to the optimum condition, for example for extracting the subgraph that minimizes a cost function according to parameters depending on the nodes features.

A Resource SubGraph (RSubG) is the graph extracted by RSG by executing the DPT() algorithm to select the path in the RSG with minimum cost. Among all the possible subgraphs of RSG, hence all the possible sequences of plugins to be executed we need to find the best path, with minimum cost function in order to determine the best sequence of plugins as triggered by a set of data detected by sensors.

DPT Algorithm. Let us now define the proposed algorithm. The *Data Process Technology* (DPT) algorithm schedules, manages and monitors the data, technologies and processes execution on the devices. Suppose the hardware infrastructure of the sensor network is made up as described below. It is composed by motes, with a limited memory and computation capabilities. Physical motes are mapped onto logical ones, and have a virtual image at middleware level. The features of the middleware are those of a REST middleware whose functionalities can be extended through the implementation of adhoc plugins. Each plugin will encode functionalities that can be run-time loaded, depending on the specific requirement triggered by an event that occurred. Sensors detection is managed at middleware level, where subscribers have to registered and where updated data can be sent. At master level a scheduler plugin has to check and manage variations in the context and in data perceived from the sensors to decide which plugin or sequence of plugins to activate. The master plugin manages a runtime composition of plugins able to perform functionalities depending on data retrieved by sensors, but at the same time satisfying high level requirements modeled by triggering of events or being in a given state.

Communication among plugin occurs through the middleware that forwards requests, data, responses among pluging and sensors according to low level protocols while interaction is scheduled and managed by the high level master application.

To extract the shortest paths of the graph, and then the sets of nodes or sequence of plugins, we define the DPT algorithm to extract the shortest path made up of terns (Data, Process, Technology).

Data: A Resource SuperGraph (RSG)
Result: Resource SubGraph (RSubG)
1 $D \leftarrow$ data nodes;
2 $P \leftarrow$ process nodes;
3 $T \leftarrow$ technology nodes;
4 **foreach** $i = 1$ *to* $min(D\_length, P\_length, T\_length,)$ **do**
5     $ShortestPath(D, P)$;
6     $ShortestPath(P, T, cost_t)$;
7   select next data node;
8     $ShortestPath(P, D, cost_d)$;
9   *Evaluate plugin sequence*;
10 **end**

Algorithm 1. Algorithm Data Process Technology DPT()

Step 1 computes the shortest path following a stating node of Data type, Step 2 computes the shortest path following node of type P, step 4 computes shortest path following node of type T. Each step has as a parameter the function cost computed till the previous node. Shortest path extraction follows Djikstra algorithm [7].

The hardware infrastructure of the network is composed by motes, with a limited memory and computation capabilities. Physical motes are mapped onto logical ones, and have a virtual image at middleware level. The features of the middleware are those of a REST middleware whose functionalities can be extended through the implementation of adhoc plugins. Each plugin will encode functionalities that can be run-time loaded, depending on the specific requirement triggered by an event that occurred. Sensors detection is managed at middleware level, where subscribers have to registered and where updated data can be sent. At master level a scheduler plugin has to check and manage variations in the context and in data perceived from the sensors to decide which plugin or sequence of plugins to activate. The master plugin manages an run-time composition of plugins able to perform functionalities depending on data retrieved by sensors, but at the same time satisfying high level requirements modeled by triggering of events or being in a given state.

4   Model Instantiation

In this section we instantiate the model defined in Sect. 3 on the use case scenario that follows.

It is a cold winter evening, the temperature in the house is low, the heating system is activated to reach soon a temperature that will ensure comfort and well-being to Bob and Mary that are going to come back to after a busy working day. The blinds close to avoid the dispersion of heat. As soon as they get into the house the lights turn on. Mary goes into the kitchen and set about making dinner; she turns the oven on that will soon to bake tasty pork shank, in the laundry the washer and dryer are temporarily suspended to avoid overload. Bob comes into the living room where the lights turn on. He is very tired so decide to sprawl on the sof and enjoy some videos. So he prepares the projector for watching the video taken by of his GoPRO while skying the previous Sunday on mountain holiday. The video projection begins and the lights turn dim to create soft lights. Later, Mary later went – as every evening – to the basement to train on sports equipment while waiting for dinner to be ready. The daily news flow on the monitor of the tapis roulant on which Mary is training. Through headset she listens directives of the exercises to be carried out according to the training program as a result of the control of the calories consumed in the days and of the physical activity already performed. Mary wears her heart rate and distance walked monitors for physical activity. When the goal of training daily is going to be reached, in the bathroom the heating is switched on, the whirlpool is switched on to enable Mary to practice proper relaxation after physical activity. Mary goes into the bathroom and the lights turn on while the basement lights and sports equipment are turned off. Meanwhile, in the garden, video surveillance cameras found two suspicious individuals climbing on the first floor and forcing a window to enter the house, despite the presence of people in the house. The images sent to the nearby police station trigger the alarm that promptly active forces to stop the thieves intrusion. A spark caused by a failure of the electrical systems in the garage makes burst fire and soon the garage is filled with dense smoke. The high level of smoke triggers the fire alarm that immediately reaches the nearest fire department to active the necessary reliefs.

The Use case scenario is modeled in a Resource Super Graph with all the possible triples of Data Process and Technology nodes. The algorithm DPT() "on-the-Fly" extracts triples of nodes and hence activates plugins execution depending on the function cost.

For example the first situation: *It is a cold winter evening, the temperature in the house is low, the heating system is activated to reach soon a temperature that will ensure comfort and well-being to Bob and Mary that are going to come back to after a busy working day. The blinds close to avoid the dispersion of heat.* We have different paths that can be followed to orchestrate plugins. Modeled data node is temperature variation, but can also be light variation and position variation. Besides for each data node there exists different process nodes: if data retrieved is the temperature variation, process may be that of turning the heating system on, but can also be that of closing the blinds for avoiding dispersion of heat. After that, technology can be wi-fi, and the application can run on the house middleware or on the smartphone. Considering light variation as data node the process node can be the turning light on but also the closing of binds. So technology may be the execution of the process on the mobile phone or on a different device, the choice between several alternatives depends on the function cost. Different values of retrieved data and of function cost evaluation would determine different selections of path in the graph this means that the plugins to be executed and their orchestration is different depending on context behavior.

5 Conclusion and Future Work

In this paper we introduced a model for building "on-the-Fly" architecture of software systems based on data, processes and technology in context-aware environments.

The model is based on a graph structure to represent data, processing of context aware application and technological features and by an algorithm for extracting the sequence of applications to be executed.

We instantiated the model on a sensor network environment and validated the algorithm on a running example in a smart home use case scenario. We are currently working on performing wide and complex experiments to validate and test the model.

References

1. Alrajeh, D., Kramer, J., Russo, A., Uchitel, S.: Learning operational requirements from goal models. In: Proceedings of ICSE 2009, pp. 265–275. IEEE Computer Society (2009)
2. Cubo, J., Ortiz, G., Boubeta-Puig, J., Foster, H., Lamersdorf, W.: Adaptive services for the future internet. J. UCS **20**(8), 1046–1048 (2014)
3. Guinard, D., Ion, I., Mayer, S.: In search of an internet of things service architecture: REST or WS-*? A developers' perspective. In: Puiatti, A., Gu, T. (eds.) MobiQuitous 2011. LNICST, vol. 104, pp. 326–337. Springer, Heidelberg (2012)
4. Guinard, D., Trifa, V., Wilde, E.: A resource oriented architecture for the web of things. In: Internet of Things (IOT), 2010, pp. 1–8. IEEE (2010)
5. Ben Hamida, A., Kon, F., Oliva, G.A., Dos Santos, C.E.M., Lorré, J.-P., Autili, M., De Angelis, G., Zarras, A., et al.: An integrated development and runtime environment for the future internet. In: Álvarez, F., Cleary, F., Daras, P., Domingue, J., Galis, A., Garcia, A., Gavras, A., Karnourskos, S., et al. (eds.) FIA 2012. LNCS, vol. 7281, pp. 81–92. Springer, Heidelberg (2012)
6. Letier, E., van Lamsweerde, A.: Deriving operational software specifications from system goals. In: Proceedings of SIGSOFT 2002/FSE-10, pp. 119–128. ACM (2002)
7. Skiena, S.: Dijkstra's algorithm. In: Implementing Discrete Mathematics: Combinatorics and Graph Theory with Mathematica, pp. 225–227. Addison-Wesley, Reading (1990)
8. Swetina, J., Lu, G., Jacobs, P., Ennesser, F., Song, J.: Toward a standardized common M2M service layer platform: introduction to oneM2M. IEEE Wirel. Commun. **21**(3), 20–26 (2014)
9. Vogli, E., Alaya, M.B., Monteil, T., Grieco, L.A., Drira, K.: An efficient resource naming for enabling constrained devices in smartM2M architecture. In: IEEE International Conference on Industrial Technology (ICIT 2015), pp. 1832–1837, March 2015

SeaCloud Workshop Papers

Second Workshop on Seamless Adaptive Multi-Cloud Management of Service-Based Applications

Preface

The Second Workshop on Seamless Adaptive Multi-Cloud Management of Service-Based Applications took place on September 15, 2015, in Taormina, co-located with the 4th European Conference on Service-Oriented and Cloud Computing (ESOCC). The workshop was jointly organized by the CloudWave (EC-FP7-ICT-610802) and SeaClouds (EC-FP7-ICT-610531) European FP7 projects, represented by Dr. Francesco Longo and Prof. Ernesto Pimentel, respectively.

Deploying and managing in an efficient and adaptive way complex service-based applications across multiple heterogeneous clouds is one of the problems that have emerged with the cloud revolution. The current lack of universally accepted standards supporting cloud interoperability is severely affecting the portability of cloud-based applications across different platforms.

At the same time, even at the level of a single cloud, adaptation of cloud services to their execution environment is strongly desirable in order to take appropriate actions in response to changes in the highly dynamic environment of the cloud. Adaptations can be performed at runtime (dynamic adaptation) and at development time. In the latter case, runtime and contextual data provided to business application developers can allow them to enhance their applications based on the actual operating conditions.

The objective of the workshop was to provide a forum to discuss problems, solutions, and perspectives of the ongoing research activities aimed at enabling an efficient and adaptive management of service-based applications across multiple clouds.

The Program Committee of the workshop (please see later) included 20 internationally recognized experts from ten different countries (France, Germany, Ireland, Israel, Italy, Norway, Portugal, Romania, Spain, Sweden). Seven contributions were submitted in response to the call for papers. The originality and relevance of these contributions were evaluated during a peer-review process carried out by the Program Committee, which unanimously decided to accept three of those contributions as regular papers, and one more contribution was accepted as a presentation of work in progress.

The program of the workshop edition included an opening session with a brief discussion about cloud-focused European projects and the future of ICT in Europe. One of the conclusions of this discussion, also inspired by the earlier plenary round table organized within the main conference, is that start-ups and university spin-offs represent a precious resource for future European projects providing use cases and real business scenarios.

There was also an invited talk from Lan Wang (Imperial College, London) about "Cognitive Packet Network for Self-Aware Adaptive Clouds." The talk was indeed very interesting, focusing on the use of neural networks as a tool for intelligent and adaptive scheduling policies in cloud computing. After the talk, the four accepted papers were presented: three regular papers, and one short paper (on-going work).

The short paper, "Supporting Cloud Service Selection with a Risk-Driven Cost–Benefit Analysis," proposed a practical and simple approach to choosing a concrete cloud service (or a set of thereof) when several alternatives are available.

The paper "Axe: A Novel Approach for Generic, Flexible, and Comprehensive Monitoring and Adaptation of Cross-Cloud Applications" introduced a novel approach to monitoring and adaptation management that is able to flexibly gather various monitoring data from virtual machines distributed across cloud providers, to dynamically aggregate the data in the cheapest possible manner, and, finally, to evaluate the processed data in order to adapt the application according to user-defined rules.

The paper "A Model-Based Approach for the Pragmatic Deployment of Service Choreographies" discussed the problem of managing multiple choreographies in multi-cloud environments and advocated that sharing-aware deployment is a more effective and resource-efficient approach.

Finally, the paper "Multi-level Adaptations in a CloudWave Infrastructure: A Telco Use Case" described the CloudWave telecommunications application use case providing a proof-of-concept on how the QoS experienced by the application users can be improved thanks to the technologies provided by CloudWave.

The workshop concluded with a final wrap-up session highlighting how adaptive management of cloud infrastructures still represents a hot and promising topic as demonstrated by the number of submission and the high quality of the accepted papers.

We would like to thank all the people who contributed to the success of the workshop: the authors of the contributed papers, the Program Committee members, and the invited speaker.

Ernesto Pimentel
Francesco Longo
Program Chairs

Organization

Program Chairs

Antonio Brogi   University of Pisa, Italy
Ernesto Pimentel   University of Malaga, Spain

Program Committee

Marcos Almeida	Softeam, France
Antonio Brogi	University of Pisa, Italy
Dario Bruneo	University of Messina, Italy
Martin Chapman	Oracle, Ireland
Javier Cubo	University of Malaga, Spain
Francesco D'Andria	ATOS, Spain
Elisabetta Di Nitto	Politecnico di Milano, Italy
Nicolas Ferry	SINTEF, Norway
Giovanni Merlino	University of Messina, Italy
Andreas Metzger	Universität Duisburg-Essen, Germany
Boris Moltchanov	Strategy & Innovation, Telecom Italia, Italy
Simon Moser	IBM, Germany
Eliot Salant	IBM, Israel
Francisco J. Nieto de Santos	ATOS, Spain
Marc Oriol	University of Pisa, Italy
Dana Petcu	West University of Timisoara, Romania
Achim Streit	Karlsruhe Institute of Technology, Germany
Karl Wallbom	Cloudmore, Sweden
Chris Woods	Intel, Ireland
Marcel Zalmanovici	IBM, Israel

Publicity Chair

Giovanni Merlino   University of Messina, Italy

Webmaster

Adrian Nieto   University of Malaga, Spain

A Model-Based Approach for the Pragmatic Deployment of Service Choreographies

Raphael Gomes[1,2]($^{\boxtimes}$), Júnio Lima[1], Fábio Costa[1], Ricardo da Rocha[1], and Nikolaos Georgantas[2]

[1] Instituto de Informática, Universidade Federal de Goiás, Goiânia, Brazil
`raphael.gomes@ifg.edu.br`, `junio.lima@ifgoiano.edu.br`,
`{fmc,ricardo}@inf.ufg.br`
[2] MiMove Team Inria Paris, Rocquencourt, France
`nikolaos.georgantas@inria.fr`

Abstract. The development of applications using service choreographies is becoming one of the *de facto* standards for the Future Internet. However QoS-aware management of service compositions is usually performed without considering service sharing. This simplifying assumption makes choreography deployment less feasible in real scenarios, in which a single service is typically shared in many scenarios. In this paper we discuss the problem of managing multiple choreographies in multi-cloud environments and we advocate that sharing-aware deployment is a more effective and resource-efficient approach. We propose a model for the combined deployment of multiple choreographies on top of a shared set of services, and we further investigate the problem through experiments.

1 Introduction

Among its new features, the Future Internet is characterized by the evolution from content sharing to service sharing. In this new scenario, mainly facilitated by the adoption of cloud technologies, software modules of different complexities are provided on top of virtualized servers and consumed via the Internet [1].

Keeping centralized coordinators for these new types of applications is unfeasible due to requirements like fault tolerance, availability, heterogeneity and adaptability. For this reason, a promising solution is the use of decentralized and distributed services through choreographies. Choreographies are service compositions that implement distributed business processes in order to reduce the number of exchanged control messages and distribute business logic, without the need for centralized coordinators [2]. Building a choreography is usually a two-step task [3]. Firstly, the functionalities required from the participating services, i.e., their operations, are identified. Secondly, for each operation an appropriate implementation is selected and bound to it. The activity of performing the interactions and getting the expected results is named choreography enactment.

In most cases, service selection and choreography enactment are not based solely on functional criteria. Instead, they aim to satisfy non-functional requirements as well, in terms of Quality of Service (QoS) properties, which in turn

© Springer International Publishing Switzerland 2016
A. Celesti and P. Leitner (Eds.): ESOCC 2015 Workshops, CCIS 567, pp. 153–165, 2016.
DOI: 10.1007/978-3-319-33313-7_11

poses many challenges. For implementation selection, the growing number of alternative web services that provide the same functionality but differ in quality parameters makes service selection an NP-hard optimization problem [4]. On the other hand, along with choreography enactment, resource allocation plays an important role in QoS since almost all non-functional requirements are related to the resources used to deploy the services.

The problem of QoS-aware choreography enactment is usually solved using variations of the Knapsack Problem [5]. However, all these solutions assume that there are no conflicts between the services that are part of a choreography, such as heterogeneous communication protocols. They also do not take into account the fact that a given service may be part of more than one choreography, which in turn means that requests for the same operation of a service may come concurrently from different sources and with different QoS requirements. As a consequence, service implementation selection and resource management typically take into account QoS requirements that are specific to a single choreography. This is far from ideal, given the combined QoS-related constraints that arise from the sharing of services among multiple and diverse choreographies.

We argue that a pragmatic view of choreography deployment, based on service sharing and on management on a per operation basis, represents a more realistic perspective since each service can have different QoS requirements for the same operation depending on which choreography is generating calls to it. With this in mind, we propose a model-based approach that encompasses both choreography deployment and resource management. We first formalize a working terminology (Sect. 2) and discuss the effects of service sharing in choreographies based on some experimental results (Sect. 3). We then examine related work (Sect. 4), and propose a formal model (Sect. 5) to represent service choreographies taking into account a global view of service utilization and the associated non-functional requirements. We aim to use this model as part of a adaptive approach for choreography enactment, which is discussed in Sect. 6. Finally, Sect. 7 presents some final remarks.

2   Terminology

In our work, an **application** is a web-based computer program designed for a specific use, such as an application for setting up a doctor's appointment in the public health system. An application is composed using one or more services. A **service**, in turn, is an independent software component that executes one or more operations. An **operation** defines some action performed by the service. It requires some amount of computing power to be processed.

The composition of several services by means of their provided operations forms a **choreography**. As pointed out before, a choreography is a form of service composition where the interaction protocol (among services) is defined in a global way using a peer-to-peer approach. The services that compose a choreography can be described in an abstract way by means of the expected role that each service plays in the interaction. Such abstract services can be realized using concrete entities, i.e., by identifying a target implementation for each service. Abstracting services is particularly important in multi-cloud environments, as some implementations can be specific to a cloud provider/technology. In such environments, composition deployment may become overly constrained if concrete services are used instead to specify a choreography.

User refers to the person(s) responsible for application composition and administration, which includes service selection and resource allocation. Both tasks must be performed with the aim of satisfying the functional and non-functional requirements of clients. Another task performed by the user is to manage adaption of service selection and resource allocation in the face of changes in the system's conditions and in the client's expectations. The **client** in turn is an entity that interacts with the application. It mainly refers to the end-user.

Finally, a **system** is a set of interacting or interdependent components forming an integrated whole. We use this term to refer to the set of managed applications, together with the components required to implement our approach.

3   The Effect of Service Sharing

Nowadays applications are developed mainly by means of preexisting service compositions. QoS management in this composite scenario is even more difficult if we consider that a service may be used by many applications at the same time. For instance, a maps service can be used in applications such as driving directions guides, picture location tagging, and partner matching by location. For each of these applications, the service may have different QoS requirements.

As illustrated in Fig. 1, this scenario is equivalent to managing a dancer participating in a music mash-up choreography: she must be able to properly handle the multiple requests and perform the different dance rhythms with an expected quality. In the same sense, for a given application (which is analogous to the mash-up in our metaphor) there can be several choreographies (rhythms in our metaphor), with the same services (analogous to dancers) being shared among them with different QoS requirements. Therefore, it is not possible to manage services without considering all the choreographies in which they participate. To achieve this goal, we need to act upon resource allocation, as the majority of non-functional properties are related to the use of resources.

Fig. 1. Mash-up metaphor.

Thus, in our approach, QoS specification is done at two different levels: service and choreography. The first level specifies requirements regarding a specific service/operation, without taking into account end-to-end QoS. The second level concerns the quality of the choreography as a whole (i.e., end-to-end) and is evaluated in terms of the composition of all participating services.

We have performed a set of experiments to demonstrate the effect of service sharing on choreography QoS. Thereby, we aim to demonstrate the need for global resource management across choreographies for the effective satisfaction of QoS requirements. The experiments show that service concurrency does not make QoS satisfaction unfeasible, provided that proper resource management is performed. We present our analysis results in the following.

3.1   Evaluating the Effects of Service Sharing

Our analysis of the effects of service sharing is based on queueing theory. For this purpose, we used JINQS [6], a library for simulating multiclass queuing networks. We evaluated the execution of different choreographies composed by non-intersecting service sets, as well as choreographies that use shared services. In our experiment we generated random choreography topologies with sequential and branching control flow patterns. For simplicity, we assume that each service provides only one operation, whose processing time follows an exponential distribution with rate parameter μ taking values between 2 and 200 (meaning that the mean processing time is between 0.5 and 0.005 time units). By putting together generated choreography topologies, we create sets of choreographies. Considering the choreography topologies of a set separately and in combination, we model them as queueing networks and simulate them on JINQS. To each choreography we apply an external input load following a Poisson distribution with rate parameter $\lambda = 50$ requests per time unit.

We simulated different levels of service sharing among the choreographies, varying from 0 % (no sharing) to 100 % (all services are shared). With this in mind, we generated a service base of available services, from which we randomly selected 10 services each time in order to compose the choreographies, according to the chosen *service sharing level*. Note that this parameter only indicates the probability of having a specific number of services shared among the choreographies (it does not mean that all services are necessarily shared among all choreographies). We also analyzed different numbers of choreographies combined together, with 2, 4, 8 and 16 choreographies being enacted at same time.

As target metrics we first measured the number of served (completed) requests and the average response time (RT). The results are presented in Tables 1 and 2, which show the mean of the differences in the two metrics for running the choreographies in isolation and in combination, with a confidence interval of 95 %. Positive values indicate loss of QoS when executing choreographies in combination. Hence, negative values indicate better QoS. As expected, service sharing causes loss of QoS since both metrics are worse when we execute a higher number of choreographies concurrently. Another interesting result is that the number of served requests is less influenced by changes in the level of

Table 1. Mean difference (%) between the numbers of completed requests when running the choreographies in isolation and in combination.

Sharing/# Chor.	2	4	8	16
0 %	-0.02 ± 0.11	-0.04 ± 0.06	0.03 ± 0.05	-0.02 ± 0.03
25 %	-0.11 ± 0.11	-0.04 ± 0.07	0.00 ± 0.05	56.19 ± 0.05
50 %	-0.02 ± 0.12	-0.01 ± 0.08	41.32 ± 0.08	101.06 ± 0.05
75 %	0.01 ± 0.11	0.04 ± 0.07	41.34 ± 0.07	101.03 ± 0.05
100 %	-0.08 ± 0.09	-0.02 ± 0.07	63.20 ± 0.07	117.47 ± 0.06

Table 2. Mean difference (%) between the response times when running the choreographies in isolation and in combination.

Sharing/# Chor.	2	4	8	16
0 %	-9.88 ± 0.05	-12.20 ± 0.03	-13.32 ± 0.03	-13.42 ± 0.02
25 %	-7.68 ± 0.06	-4.31 ± 0.04	42.11 ± 0.18	199.94 ± 0.00
50 %	-2.80 ± 0.09	22.12 ± 0.11	199.93 ± 0.00	199.96 ± 0.00
75 %	3.60 ± 0.07	43.37 ± 0.11	199.93 ± 0.00	199.96 ± 0.00
100 %	13.46 ± 0.10	121.74 ± 1.16	199.95 ± 0.00	199.96 ± 0.00

Table 3. Mean difference (%) between the numbers of completed requests when running the choreographies in isolation and in combination (with the addition of more resources when running them in combination).

Sharing/# Chor.	2	4	8	16
0 %	-0.01 ± 0.12	-0.05 ± 0.07	-0.01 ± 0.04	-0.01 ± 0.03
25 %	-0.06 ± 0.10	-0.01 ± 0.06	-0.04 ± 0.05	0.02 ± 0.03
50 %	-0.12 ± 0.11	0.04 ± 0.07	-0.00 ± 0.04	3.77 ± 0.04
75 %	0.11 ± 0.13	0.06 ± 0.07	-0.04 ± 0.05	3.75 ± 0.05
100 %	0.04 ± 0.13	-0.00 ± 0.06	0.00 ± 0.05	27.07 ± 0.06

Table 4. Mean difference (%) between the response times when running the choreographies in isolation and in combination (with the addition of more resources when running them in combination).

Sharing/# Chor.	2	4	8	16
0 %	-9.96 ± 0.05	-12.22 ± 0.04	-13.30 ± 0.03	-13.42 ± 0.02
25 %	-25.68 ± 0.07	-28.79 ± 0.04	-28.61 ± 0.03	-24.13 ± 0.02
50 %	-43.85 ± 0.07	-46.98 ± 0.04	-43.54 ± 0.03	199.34 ± 0.01
75 %	-74.58 ± 0.06	-76.48 ± 0.04	-66.42 ± 0.03	199.36 ± 0.01
100 %	-106.46 ± 0.05	-101.48 ± 0.03	-77.25 ± 0.05	199.89 ± 0.00

sharing, while RT doesn't change significantly as the number of choreographies increases.

We also analyzed the impact of resource allocation. To this end we carried out the same experiment, now increasing resource allocation by a factor of 1 to 3 for combined choreography execution. Tables 3 and 4 show the results. The behavior is similar, although with a smaller difference between separately executing each choreography and executing all of them in combination. This reinforces the motivation for using a more precise resource allocation.

Motivated by these results, our proposal is to automate the management of service selection and resource allocation in multi-cloud environments taking into account service sharing. We propose the representation of services and resources in abstract models which are dynamically interpreted by the system. In the next section we discuss how this aspect is considered in related work. We then present the first step towards defining our approach, which consists in eliciting a formal model to represent combined choreographies.

4   Related Work

A number of research efforts reported in the literature have focused on the problem of providing QoS guarantees for service compositions [3–5]. However, most of these studies focus on service selection for a single composition. To the best of our knowledge, Nguyen et al. [7] carried out one of the first studies to deal with QoS guarantees for multiple inter-related compositions. The authors argue that if a service engages in a number of compositions, there will be a dependency between the levels of QoS that the service can contribute to these compositions. In the approach proposed by Ardagna and Mirandola [8], service composition is carried out based on groups of invocations where multiple requests are generated by multiple users. However, they assume that each service provider has fixed resources, thus not proposing resource adaptability.

Furtado et al. [9] present a middleware to support the enactment of web service choreographies in the cloud. Similarly to our work, resource adaptation is proposed to maintain the expected levels of QoS. However, they do not handle service selection. Huang and Shen [10] propose an approach for the deployment of multiple services in the cloud. They developed two types of graphs to model the communication costs and potential parallelism among the services of different compositions. However, unlike our approach, which focuses on service sharing, they aim at minimizing communication costs and maximizing parallelism.

In contrast, we propose an approach to deal with multiple inter-related service choreographies, taking into account their associated non-functional requirements and a global view of service utilization. We analyze the role each service plays in several choreographies and estimate the amount of resources needed to deploy each service in order to ensure the expected level of QoS.

5   Formal Model for Choreography Deployment

In this section we present a formalization of the problem of combined deployment of multiple choreographies. We focus on non-functional properties, although our formalization can handle functional properties as well. Our representation of choreographies is language-independent but contains the main components of commonly adopted choreography definition languages, such as BPMN2 [11].

The set of available services used to compose choreographies is defined as S, which contains n services $\{s_1, s_2, \ldots, s_n\}$, each represented by a group of operations $\mathcal{O}$. Each operation $o \in \mathcal{O}$ has resource demand d, which represents the amount of resources, e.g., number of CPU cores and their capacity, needed to compute the operation. Moreover, the set of available resources is represented as $\mathcal{V}$, which contains t virtual machine (VM) configurations $\{v_1, v_2, \ldots, v_t\}$. Each resource v has ρ resource units, each one with resource capacity ζ and a cost c for using it for a given time slice. The topology of a choreography can be abstracted using a process graph [12], which is defined as follows:

Definition 1 (Predecessor and Successor Nodes). *Let N be a set of nodes and $E \subseteq N \times N$ a binary relation over N defining the edges. For each node $n \in N$ we define the set of predecessor nodes $\bullet n = \{x \in N | (x, n) \in E\}$ and the set of successor nodes $n \bullet = \{x \in N | (n, x) \in E\}$.*

Definition 2 (Process Graph). *A process graph PG consists of a tuple $(b, Z, \mathcal{S}, L, t, E)$ where:*

- *b denotes the start point, $|b \bullet| = 1 \wedge |\bullet b| = 0$.*
- *Z denotes the set of end events, $|Z| \geq 1$ and $\forall z \in Z : |\bullet z| \geq 1 \wedge |z \bullet| = 0$.*
- *$\mathcal{S}$ denotes the set of services, $\forall s \in \mathcal{S} : |\bullet s| = 1 \wedge |s \bullet| = 1$.*
- *L denotes the set of connectors, $\forall l \in L : (|\bullet l| > 1 \wedge |l \bullet| = 1) \vee (|\bullet l| = 1 \wedge |l \bullet| > 1)$.*
- *t is a mapping $t : L \rightarrow \{AND, XOR, OR\}$, which specifies the type of a connector $l \in L$ as either a conjunction (AND), a disjunction (OR) or a mutually exclusive disjunction (XOR).*
- *E is a set of edges that define the flow as a simple and directed graph. Each edge $e \in E$ is a tuple $(\underrightarrow{e}, \overrightarrow{e}, o)$, where $\underrightarrow{e} \subseteq (b \cup \mathcal{S} \cup L)$ is the origin of this edge, $\overrightarrow{e} \subseteq (Z \cup \mathcal{S} \cup L)$ is the end of this edge, and o is the operation being requested. If $\overrightarrow{e} \in \{Z \cup L\}$, then o is null. Being a simple graph implies that $\forall n \in (b \cup Z \cup \mathcal{S} \cup L) : (n, n) \notin E$ (no reflexive edges) and that $\forall x, y \in (b \cup Z \cup \mathcal{S} \cup L) : |\{(x, y)|(x, y) \in E\}| = 1$ (no multiple edges).*

In our approach, each expected non-functional requirement is described in terms of a QoS property, which in turn is represented by one or more QoS metrics. These concepts are formalized in the following.

Our representation for QoS metrics is based on Rosario et al. [13]:

Definition 3 (QoS Metric). *A QoS metric is a tuple $m = (\mathbb{D}, \leq, \oplus, \wedge, \vee, \mathcal{U})$:*

- *$(\mathbb{D}, \leq)$ is a QoS domain with a corresponding set of ordered QoS values.*

- $\oplus : \mathbb{D} \to \mathbb{D}$ defines how QoS gets incremented by each new event. It satisfies the following conditions: (i) $\oplus$ possesses a neutral element 0 satisfying $\forall l \in \mathbb{D} \Rightarrow l \oplus 0 = 0 \oplus l = l$; (ii) $\oplus$ is monotonic: $l_1 \leq l'_1$ and $l_2 \leq l'_2$ implies $(l_1 \oplus l_2) \leq (l'_1 \oplus l'_2)$.
- $(\wedge, \vee)$ represents the lower and upper lattices, meaning that any $l \subseteq \mathbb{D}$ has unique lower and upper values $(\wedge_l, \vee_l)$. When taking the best result with respect to the ordering $\leq$, the lowest QoS is taken with $\wedge$. When synchronizing events, the operator $\vee$ takes the worst QoS as per the ordering $\leq$.
- $\mathcal{U}$ is a utility function $\mathcal{U} : (\mathcal{S}, \mathcal{V}) \to \mathbb{D}$, that gives the expected QoS value when a service $s \in \mathcal{S}$ is deployed on a specific resource $v \in \mathcal{V}$.

Definition 4 (Non-Functional Requirement). *A non-functional requirement (NFR) is represented using one of the following tuples:*

(1) (s, o, k, ϕ), *where* $s \in \mathcal{S}$ *is a service,* o *is the operation being requested,* k *is a QoS metric, and* ϕ *is the target average value for this metric* $(\phi \in \mathbb{D}(k))$;
(2) (k, ϕ), *where* k *is a QoS metric and* ϕ *is the target average value for this metric, with* $\phi \in \mathbb{D}(k)$. *This tuple is used to represent end-to-end NFRs, which means that the target value must be somehow split among the operations (and respective services) in the possible execution flows.*

To allow QoS-aware choreography enactment, we propose the representation of choreographies and NFRs in a structure called *QoS-Aware Process Graph*.

Definition 5 (QoS-Aware Process Graph). *A QoS-aware process graph consists in a process graph that is annotated with the expected load for each operation, along with the NFRs associated with the related service composition.*

Figure 2 shows two choreographies specified using this notation. At this stage, services are specified in an abstract way. They will be subsequently replaced by concrete implementations as a result of service selection.

Our proposal for choreography enactment is based on the combined representation of multiple choreographies using a structure called *QoS-Aware Dependency Graph*. This structure represents the services that are part of the choreographies, the dependencies among those services, and their NFRs.

Definition 6 (QoS-Aware Dependency Graph). *A QoS-aware dependency graph* $\mathcal{G}$ *is a directed graph represented by a tuple* $(\mathbb{P}, \mathbb{E}, \mathcal{Q})$:

- $\mathbb{P} = \{b \cup z \cup \mathcal{S}\}$ *is a set of vertices, where* b *and* z *represent the initial and end vertices, respectively.*
- $\mathbb{E}$ *is the set of directed edges. Each edge* $e \in \mathbb{E}$ *is a tuple* (p_s, p_r, o), *where* $p_s \in \{\mathbb{P} - z\}$ *is the send vertex,* $p_r \in \{\mathbb{P} - b\}$ *is the receive vertex, and* o *is the operation being requested.*
- $\mathcal{Q}$ *is a set of QoS properties. Each* $q \in \mathcal{Q}$ *is a tuple* $(k, \Omega, \lambda, \phi)$, *where* k *is a QoS metric,* λ *is the load* $(\lambda > 0)$, $\phi \in \mathbb{D}_k$ *is the target average value for this metric, and* Ω *is a set of pairs* $(s \in \mathcal{S}, o)$ *that represent the services and the target operations to which the metric must be applied.*

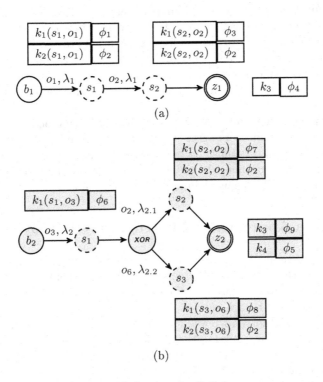

(a)

(b)

Fig. 2. Two choreographies specified using the QoS-Aware process graph notation.

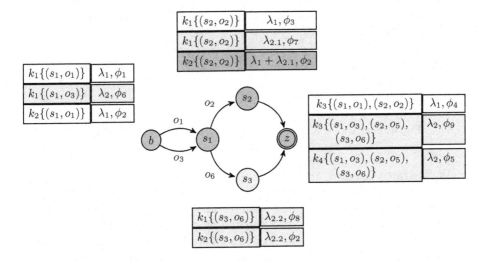

Fig. 3. QoS-aware dependency graph for the choreographies shown in Fig. 2.

Figure 3 illustrates the QoS-aware dependency graph for the two annotated choreographies shown in Fig. 2. We can find elements that remain the same as in the original choreographies (shown in lighter shades of gray) as well as elements that had some change in their load and target values (highlighted in darker tones). Changes are due to the increased load on services and to the aggregation of NFRs when they have the same target. In this structure the services represent concrete chosen implementations.

This formalization enables the representation of combined choreographies and the execution of more realistic service selection and resource allocation. Additionally, these aspects must be reexamined (i.e., adapted) during choreography enactment (at runtime). In the next section we outline the approach we are developing to do this using the model described here.

6   Adaptive Approach to Choreography Deployment

The preceding sections discuss the issue of managing multiple choreographies at the same time in the presence of service sharing. Users in charge of choreography management must take into account the different roles of services and select the resources needed to run each service. This must be done at deployment time, and needs to be constantly reviewed at runtime to match QoS requirements.

The formalization presented in the previous section can be used to deal with the service sharing issue during choreography enactment. It facilitates the initial resource allocation and its adaptation at runtime as outlined next.

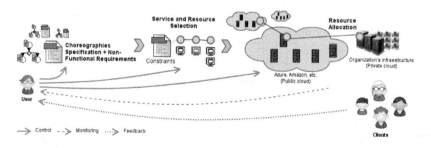

Fig. 4. Scenario of manual choreography enactment management.

As illustrated in Fig. 4, according to feedback from clients, such as regarding the level of satisfaction, or from the system, e.g., number of aborted requests, the user must manage service and resource allocation and adaptation. Every time some QoS violation is detected, the first attempt to deal with it is through adaptation of resource allocation. In cases where it is not possible to achieve the needed QoS by acting (solely) at this level, another strategy is to perform adaptation on service selection and resource configuration. As a last attempt, the user may be required to adapt the choreography and/or accept lower QoS.

Our approach to automate the above scenario is to use models at runtime [14]. The use of models at runtime allows the specification of services and resource requirements based on the current needs of applications; it also allows more precise management of the available computing power, especially compared to the allocation of resources based simply on profiles of virtual machines (VM). In doing so, service selection and resource allocation can be performed automatically according to abstract models and monitored data, thus facilitating adaptation.

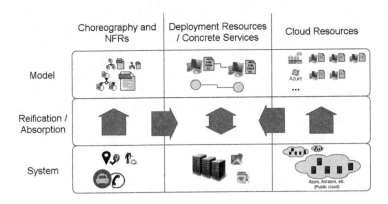

Fig. 5. Runtime models.

As can be seen in Fig. 5, our proposal relies on three different entities that are abstracted using models. The choreography model (upper left side in the figure) is represented using the QoS-aware process graph notation and is the input in our approach. It is then used to generate the deployment model (upper middle part in the figure), which is represented using the QoS-aware dependency graph notation (with concrete service selection). The dependency graph, in turn, is used to select the resources used to deploy/run the services. Moreover, the cloud resources model (upper right side) represents available resource configurations and is used as input for resource selection. The formalization proposed in this paper can be used to specify the first two levels of modeling. We aim to extend this formalization to represent cloud resources as well.

Although there is reification[1] of the running system in all models, direct absorption[4] only applies to the deployment model, since changes on it are directly reflected on the running system. Nevertheless, changes in the other two models are also reflected in a indirect way since they are used as input for service and resource selection. Note that this is ongoing work and an implementation of the

---

[1] Reification is the action of exposing the representation of a system in terms of programming entities that can be manipulated at runtime. The opposite process, absorption, consists in effecting the changes made to these entities into the system [15].

proposed approach is currently being developed. We are currently implementing the generation of dependency graphs by means of the combination of the target process graphs. Service and resource selection in turn are being implemented using a variation of the multiple-choice multi-dimension knapsack problem [16].

7   Final Remarks

The sharing of services among multiple service compositions has a significant effect on the overall provided QoS. Based on this observation, we advocate that performing choreography enactment without taking this into account is not a realistic approach. We present some experiments that demonstrate the problem and propose a formal model to represent QoS-aware service compositions.

We aim to use the formal model presented here to represent abstract service compositions. Taking these abstract compositions as input, we can automatically select the best services in order of satisfy associated non-functional requirements. Another important ongoing work is to extend the formalization presented here with a cloud resources model in order to provide a basis to implement the allocation of resources to run the selected services in a multi-cloud environment.

Acknowledgments. This work is supported by the Brazilian foundations FAPEG (calls # 04/2011, 12/2012 and 03/2013) and CNPq (grants # 249809/2013-3 and 473939/2012-6).

References

1. Strunk, A.: QoS-aware service composition: a survey. In: 2010 IEEE 8th European Conference on Web Services (ECOWS), pp. 67–74. IEEE (2010)
2. Barker, A., Walton, C.D., Robertson, D.: Choreographing web services. IEEE Tran. Serv. Comput. **2**(2), 152–166 (2009)
3. Zeng, L., Benatallah, B., Ngu, A.H., Dumas, M., Kalagnanam, J., Chang, H.: QoS-aware middleware for web services composition. IEEE Trans. Software Eng. **30**(5), 311–327 (2004)
4. Canfora, G., Di Penta, M., Esposito, R., Villani, M.L.: QoS-aware replanning of composite web services. In: Proceedings of IEEE International Conference on Web Services, ICWS 2005, Proceedings, pp. 121–129. IEEE (2005)
5. Peng, X., Changsong, L.: ESCA: evolution-strategy based service composition algorithm for multiple QoS constrained cloud applications. Int. J. Future Gener. Commun. Netw. **7**(1), 249–260 (2014)
6. Field, T.: JINQS: an extensible library for simulating multiclass queueing networks, v1.0 user guide (2006). http://www.doc.ic.ac.uk/ajf/Software/manual.pdf. Accessed 30 March 2015
7. Nguyen, X.T., Kowalczyk, R., Han, J.: Using dynamic asynchronous aggregate search for quality guarantees of multiple web services compositions. In: Dan, A., Lamersdorf, W. (eds.) ICSOC 2006. LNCS, vol. 4294, pp. 129–140. Springer, Heidelberg (2006)
8. Ardagna, D., Mirandola, R.: Per-flow optimal service selection for web services based processes. J. Syst. Softw. **83**(8), 1512–1523 (2010)

9. Furtado, T., Francesquini, E., Lago, N., Kon, F.: A middleware for reflective web service choreographies on the cloud. In: Proceedings of the 13th Workshop on Adaptive and Reflective Middleware, vol. 9. ACM (2014)

10. Huang, K.C., Shen, B.J.: Service deployment strategies for efficient execution of composite SaaS applications on cloud platform. J. Syst. Softw. **107**, 127–141 (2015)

11. OMG: Documents Associated with Business Process Model and Notation (BPMN), Version 2.0 (2011). http://www.omg.org/spec/BPMN/2.0/

12. Mendling, J., Lassen, K.B., Zdun, U., et al.: Transformation strategies between block-oriented and graph-oriented process modelling languages. In: Multikonferenz Wirtschaftsinformatik, vol. 2, unknown, pp. 297–312 (2006)

13. Rosario, S., Benveniste, A., Jard, C.: Flexible probabilistic QoS management of transaction based web services orchestrations. In: IEEE International Conference on Web Services, ICWS 2009, pp. 107–114. IEEE (2009)

14. Blair, G., Bencomo, N., France, R.B.: Models@run.time. Computer **42**(10), 22–27 (2009)

15. Kon, F., Costa, F., Blair, G., Campbell, R.H.: The case for reflective middleware. Commun. ACM **45**(6), 33–38 (2002)

16. Khan, S., Li, K.F., Manning, E.G., Akbar, M.M.: Solving the knapsack problem for adaptive multimedia systems. Stud. Inform. Univ. **2**(1), 157–178 (2002)

Supporting Cloud Service Selection
with a Risk-Driven Cost-Benefit Analysis

Aida Omerovic[✉]

SINTEF, Trondheim, Norway
Aida.Omerovic@sintef.no

Abstract. Our earlier work indicates feasibility of eliciting multi-cloud requirements and thus identifying selectable cloud services based on a risk-driven approach. Once an overview of the selectable services that treat a specific risk is obtained, a decision needs to be taken regarding the final selection. This position paper focuses on providing a practical and simple approach to choosing a concrete cloud service (or a set of thereof) when several alternatives are available. We propose a risk-driven cost-benefit analysis approach and exemplify how a decision maker, such as a business analyst or a multi-cloud architecture designer, can apply it in the context of cloud service selection. The strength of the approach is in its simplicity, since the approach is based on a set of relatively comprehensible guidelines. Still, we consider this to be work in progress, since an analysis of how to combine a set of interdependent cloud services (which address several respective risks) is necessary for enabling a full-scale design of a multi-cloud based architecture.

Keywords: Cloud service selection · Multi-cloud applications · Cost-benefit analysis · Requirements elicitation · Design · Decision support

1   Introducion

We have earlier reported on result that indicate feasibility of applying a risk-driven approach to identify selectable cloud services in the context of multi-cloud architecture design (Gupta et al. 2015b). The method is also supported by a tool which a decision maker can use to perform a risk-driven identification of the cloud services which are to be composed in a multi-cloud architecture (Gupta et al. 2015a). The services presented by the tool are those that meet the requirements which address the identified risks. We have moreover evaluated an approach to estimate and analyze cost, risk and quality when designing a system architecture (Singh et al. 2014). Based on this earlier work, we can perform a risk analysis and eventually obtain a set of risks as well as treatments that mitigate or reduce the respective risks. The treatments in our case will be requirements to cloud services which address concerns such as cost, quality or functionality. These requirements are then matched to the properties of the known cloud services (or cloud providers in general). Thus, for each risk, up to several independent

© Springer International Publishing Switzerland 2016
A. Celesti and P. Leitner (Eds.): ESOCC 2015 Workshops, CCIS 567, pp. 166–174, 2016.
DOI: 10.1007/978-3-319-33313-7_12

cloud services are suggested. The challenge in such a case is how to select the appropriate cloud service (or treatment alternative consisting of one or more cloud services that address a specific risk).

This position paper proposes a cloud service selection approach based on a risk-driven cost-benefit analysis. We provide guidance and exemplify how to select a specific cloud service when several alternative (independent) cloud services have been proposed in order to treat a specific risk. We assume two kinds of input:

1. A specification of risk and its treatment alternatives, both of which are identified through a risk analysis. The treatment alternatives are presented in the form of different cloud services.
2. A cost estimate of the original risk, a cost estimate of each treatment alternative, as well as a cost estimate of the associated remaining risk (that is, the risk that is left if we assume that the treatment alternative in question is adopted).

For both kinds of input, the existing state of the art provides guidance and models. For the cost estimation of risks and treatments, there are several existing models and approaches. COCOMO (Fenton and Pfleeger 1997) and SLIM (Fenton and Pfleeger 1997) are among the well-known models. For analysis of security economics, some of the known approaches are Net Present Value (NPV) (Daneva 2006), Return on Security Investment (ROSI) (Sonnenreich et al. 2006), the Cost Benefit Analysis Method (CBAM) (Kazman et al. 2002) and the Security Solution Design Trade-Off Analysis (Houmb et al. 2005). For risk analysis, some of the well known approaches include CORAS (Lund et al. 2011), CRAMM (Barber and Davey 1992), OCTAVE (Alberts and Davey 2004), Event Tree Analysis (IEC 1995), Cause-Consequence Analysis (Nielsen 1971) and Fault Tree Analysis (IEC 2006). For quality and architecture analysis, approaches such as PREDIQT (Omerovic 2012) and ATAM (Kazman et al. 2000) can be applied. One major challenge in the context of risk and cost models, is the uncertainty of the risk levels and the cost estimates. Uncertainty handling has, for example, been reviewed in (Omerovic et al. 2012a). There exists state of the art that we could adopt for uncertainty handling, based on various types of scales and approaches. Main distinction is made between possibilistic and probabilistic approaches. In PREDIQT, for example, uncertainty is handled based on intervals (Omerovic and Stølen 2011).

The target group of the approach is a business analyst or an architecture designer who needs a comprehensible decision support for service selection. Therefore, our objective has been to provide a practical and simple approach to choosing a concrete cloud service (or a set of thereof) when several alternatives are available. Note that the aim of the approach is not to provide a finite answer or choose the cloud service on behalf of the decision maker. Rather, the approach assists the user in making a more informed decision with respect to the goals specified through the risks and the acceptance criteria. Our approach is agnostic to the choice of the risk analysis method, or the approach to cost estimation. We argue that the strength of the approach is in its simplicity, since it is based on a set of relatively comprehensible guidelines. Still, we consider this to be work in progress, since an analysis of how to combine a set of interdependent cloud services (which address several respective risks) is necessary for enabling a full-scale design of a multi-cloud based architecture.

This paper is structured as follows. In Sect. 2 we outline the approach itself, including the guidelines to be followed during a cost-benefit analysis. In Sect. 3 we illustrate the application of the approach on an example. A discussion of the results is given in Sect. 4, before concluding in Sect. 5.

2   The Approach

This section presents the approach in general. We start by characterizing the input and prerequisites, and then provide guidelines for conducting a cost-benefit analysis which eventually proposes one treatment alternative (that is, one cloud service or a combination of thereof in case the treatment alternative is represented by more than one cloud service) to a specific risk which is not acceptable and needs to be reduced. Our approach is partially based on experiences from various case studies which have addressed treatment selection (Singh et al. 2014, 2015; Omerovic et al. 2012b).

Our starting point is a specific risk R_N (identified by a natural number N) and its original cost CR_N (i.e., cost of risk N). The risk is characterized by its known factors such as frequency of occurrence, consequence, type of threat that initiates it, etc. Based on a risk function which is an expression of how to deduce a risk level of risk based on the risk factors, we obtain level of risk N, that is, RL_N. Acceptance criteria, that is, a statement of to what degree a risk level is acceptable, need to be available[1]. We assume that the risk in question, according to the pre-defined risk acceptance criteria, is not acceptable and needs to be treated. The risk itself can be a textual description of how an incident caused by a threat scenario (that is, a threat exploiting a vulnerability and triggering a scenario) impacts something of value (a goal or an asset). Once the risk is described and the factors are denoted, we use the cost estimation approaches to estimate the expected cost of the risk (CR_N), that is the cost of the impact it may have on the goal or the asset.

In addition to the risk characterization and its cost, we assume that the cloud services $S_{X,N}$ (each identified by a natural number X) that treat the risk N are identified, along with their respective cost estimates $CS_{X,N}$. The cost of a cloud service should include all cost factors, such as licensing, operation, retirement, etc. Each cloud service represents an independent treatment alternative that addresses the risk. Only one treatment alternative is needed. Surely, some of the

---

[1] Best known acceptance criteria in practical use are colors shaded on a two-dimensional risk matrix – a table with frequency and consequence levels on the two respective axes, where the fields of combinations of the two factors are colored by for example green (acceptable), yellow (should be examined closer) and red (unacceptable).

services suggested can be dependent or one may wish to adopt several independent ones in order to achieve redundancy; in that case, the desired combination would be treated as one treatment alternative. For simplicity, we refer to each treatment alternative as an independent cloud service (although several could be combined to represent a treatment alternative). We also specify how much we can afford paying for a service that treats a risk and express that value as ACS_N. Each independent cloud service reduces the risk to some degree, resulting in a related risk level estimate $RL_{X,N}$ (that is, the estimated level of risk provided that service $S_{X,N}$ is adopted). The cost of the remaining risk ($CR_{X,N}$) (provided that the service X is adopted) is also estimated. Hence, for each selectable service, we will know how much it costs, what the resulting level of the related risk will be, as well as what the cost of the remaining risk will be. Hence, we operate with the following variables:

- R_N: risk identified by number N
- CR_N: expected cost of risk R_N without any treatment (that is, without adoption of any cloud service)
- RL_N: original level of untreated risk R_N. The risk level is based on a predefined function which combines risk factors such as frequency and consequence, to calculate risk level.
- $S_{X,N}$: a cloud service which is identified by a natural number X and addressing risk R_N
- ACS_N: affordable cost of a service that treats risk R_N
- $CS_{X,N}$: expected cost of cloud service $S_{X,N}$
- $RL_{X,N}$: expected level of risk R_N provided that service is adopted
- $CR_{X,N}$: expected cost of the remainder of risk R_N provided that service is adopted

With this as input, the following pseudo-code expresses our **guideline for service selection**:

If *there exists one or more cloud services $S_{X,N}$ such that*
($RL_{X,N}$ is acceptable) AND ($CS_{X,N} \prec CR_N$) AND ($CS_{X,N} \prec ACS_N$)
then *choose the cloud service $S_{X,N}$ which has $Min(CS_{X,N})$*
else *(that is, there is no cloud service reducing the risk to an acceptable level, or the alternatives which reduce the risk to an acceptable level are not affordable)*
If *there are other cloud services that reduce the risk to some degree such that ($RL_{X,N} \prec RL_N$) AND ($CS_{X,N} \prec ACS_N$) AND (($CS_{X,N} + CR_{X,N}) \prec CR_N$)*
then *$Min(CS_{X,N} + CR_{X,N})$ (that is, choose the cloud service which gives lowest sum of cost of service and cost of remaining risk).*

3   Applying the Approach to an Example

In this section, we exemplify the application of the approach on an example. We describe the target of the analysis and define acceptance criteria for our asset or goal. Then we consider one single risk and three independent cloud services that have been identified as possible alternatives for handling the risk in question. Finally, we apply the approach presented in Sect. 2 to select one of the three cloud service alternatives.

Our asset is performance of an online grocery store, and the risk analysis is performed from the point of view of the service provider. As a part of the context description (which is the first step of a risk analysis), we assume that the scales for consequence and frequency are defined with respect to the asset. Risk acceptance criteria are then defined through a matrix shown in Fig. 1. The red fields indicate the combinations of frequency and consequence of a risk that are not acceptable and must be treated. Similarly, the green fields show the acceptable risk levels, while the yellow fields show the risk levels that do not have to be treated but should be considered closer. Of course, the number of colors (risk acceptance levels) and their representation is specific to this example and can vary. The plotted values should be overseen at this stage and will be introduced later in the example.

		Consequence				
		Insignificant	Minor	Moderate	Major	Catastrophic
Frequency	Rare					
	Unlikely		RL3,1		RL1,1	
	Possible				RL1	
	Likely		RL2,1			
	Certain					

Fig. 1. Acceptance criteria for risks related to performance (Color figure online)

Assume that we have identified a risk to performance, namely: "R_1: Performance degradation due to inefficient storage". Frequency of R_1 is estimated to Possible and consequence is estimated to Major. We plot the original level of risk (RL_1) on the matrix that defines our acceptance criteria (Fig. 1) and see that the risk R_1 has a level which is not acceptable. Hence, a treatment is needed. Assume that cost of this risk is estimated to be 5000 EUR. Assume also that we can afford paying 3000 EUR for a cloud service that would treat the risk. Thus, RL_1 = (possible, major); ACS_1 = 3000 EUR; CR_1 = 5000 EUR.

Assume that we have identified three possible cloud services that can address the risk R_1:

- $S_{1,1}$: An SQL database from "ProviderX"
- $S_{2,1}$: A NoSQL database from "ProviderY"
- $S_{3,1}$: A hybrid database from "ProviderZ"

The corresponding estimates for cost of the service, cost of the remaining risk (assuming that the service is adopted) and remaining risk level after adoption of the service, are respectively:

- $CS_{1,1} = 1500$ EUR; $CR_{1,1} = 3000$ EUR; $RL_{1,1} = $ (unlikely, major);
- $CS_{2,1} = 2500$ EUR; $CR_{2,1}R = 1500$ EU; $RL_{2,1} = $ (likely, minor);
- $CS_{3,1} = 6000$ EUR; $CR_{3,1} = 200$ EUR; $RL_{3,1} = $ (unlikely, minor);

The estimated remaining levels of risk R_1 after adoption of each cloud service, are plotted on Fig. 1. Applying the guideline for service selection from Sect. 2, we find that:

- $S_{3,1}$ would make the risk acceptable, but it is more expensive than the original risk and it is not affordable. Therefore, we advise against $S_{3,1}$.
- In the case of $S_{1,1}$ and $S_{2,1}$, we see that both services reduce the risk level to the yellow area of Fig. 1 and both services are affordable. Hence, we consider the respective sums of cost of the service and the cost of the remaining risk. $CS_{1,1} + CR_{1,1} = 4500$ EUR while $CS_{2,1} + CR_{2,1} = 4000$ EUR. The sum of cost of service and cost of remaining risk is lowest in the case of $S_{2,1}$. **Thus, we recommend adopting the cloud service $S_{2,1}$.**

4   Discussion

Although the example indicates feasibility of applying the approach proposed in Sect. 2, there are threats to validity and reliability of the approach that need to be pointed out. To thoroughly assess the reliability of the approach, empirical evaluation of a realistic case is needed. In a practical setting, our original goals of comprehensibility and practical usefulness of the approach would be evaluated. Scalability of the approach with respect to the number of the cloud service alternatives, would also be better assessed in a practical setting.

Uncertainty of the risk frequency and therefore its likelihood of occurrence, makes it difficult to treat cost of adopting a cloud service and cost of risk equally. Naturally, it is more certain that the cost of adopting a cloud service will be materialized, than the cost of risk, since the risk does not have to occur while a treatment is assumed to be adopted as soon as a decision is made. Moreover, factors characterizing the risk are often to some degree uncertain since their estimates are based on incomplete empirical knowledge. At the same time, cost of a service is often made available by a service provider. That is also why the estimates of service adoption cost may be more certain than the estimates of risk.

In our example, both $S_{1,1}$ and $S_{2,1}$ ended in the different parts of the yellow area of the risk matrix. Their acceptance level was considered equal. However, in practice one risk level may have been preferred over the other. The example did not distinguish explicitly between the possible variations of the resulting risk within the same acceptance level. We did, however, take into account the differences of the remaining cost, that is the different values of $CR_{1,1}$ and $CR_{2,1}$ before providing the final recommendation.

One limitation of the current state of the approach, is that it does not take into account the multi-cloud aspects when performing the cost-benefit analysis. Only one risk is considered at a time. An obvious next step, is therefore to provide support for cost-benefit analysis when several interdependent services addressing multiple risks need to be combined in a multi-cloud architecture.

Once a cloud service is selected, new risks may be introduced. Some of those new risks also have to be treated. Hence, our approach also needs to support incorporating into the original model and handling of the new risks that occur due to the services selected.

Another challenge is how to take into account the risk attitude of the decision maker in the context of a cost-benefit analysis. A common way of expressing the risk attitude is through the acceptance criteria, which in the case of our example are expressed in the form of the colored risk matrix. The risk matrix of a *risk averse* decision maker would be more dominated by the red color, while the risk matrix of a *risk seeking* decision maker would be more dominated by green color. A *risk neutral* decision maker would define his or her risk matrix in a rather balanced manner. Note that, unless there exists a baseline definition of thresholds for risk attitude, it only makes sense to distinguish and compare the three attitudes and their respective acceptance criteria relative to each other. Risk attitude may be expressed in many forms through so-called risk function. Other (and more) factors than frequency and consequence may be involved. More than ove decision maker with varying risk attitudes may also be involved. Our approach should also be refined with more detailed guidelines which take into account varying risk attitudes.

Hence, we have managed to specify the guidelines and demonstrate feasibility of the approach, while the support for aspects such as multi-cloud handling and varying risk attitude still need to be included. Nevertheless, we consider the current results to be a first step towards a full-scale cost-benefit analysis for cloud service selection.

5   Conclusions

We have in this position paper proposed a risk-driven approach to cost-benefit analysis for selection of cloud services. The application of the approach has been illustrated on an example. The initial results indicate feasibility of specifying a guideline of the approach and applying it. The main strength of the approach is considered to be its simplicity and assumed comprehensibility for non-technical users. We have through the application of the approach on the example also identified several needs for improvement, such as support for analysis of multi-cloud aspects and better expressiveness with respect to uncertainty and risk attitude. Thus, our further work should be two-fold: (1) empirical evaluation on a realistic case to evaluate its practical usefulness and identify further requirements, and (2) extension of the approach with support for multi-cloud aspects handling, uncertainty handling, as well as capability of supporting a richer risk attitude function in the cost-benefit analysis.

Acknowledgments. This work has been supported by the MODAClouds project (Grant Agreement FP7-318484) funded by European Commission within the 7th Framework Programme.

References

Alberts, C.J., Davey, J.: OCTAVE criteria version 2.0. Technical report CMU/SEI-2001-TR-016, Carnegie Mellon University (2004)

Barber, B., Davey, J.: The use of the CCTA risk analysis and management methodology cramm in health information systems. In: 7th International Congress on Medical Informatics (1992)

Daneva, M.: Applying real options thinking to information security in networked organizations. CTIT Report TR-CTIT-06-11. Technical report, University of Twente (2006)

Fenton, N.E., Pfleeger, S.L.: A Rigorous and Practical Approach, 2nd edn. PWS Publishing Company, Boston (1997)

Gupta, S., Dominiak, J., Matthews, P., Mulero, V.M., Omerovic, A.: Decision Making Toolkit Prototype - Final Version. MODAClouds project deliverable D 2.3.3 (2015a)

Gupta, S., Muntes-Mulero, V., Matthews, P., Dominiak, J., Omerovic, A., Aranda, J., Seycek, S.: Risk-driven framework for decision support in cloud service selection. In: 15th IEEE/ACM International Symposium on Cluster, Cloud and Grid Computing (CC-GRID 2015), Shenzhen, Guangdong, China. IEEE/ACM (2015b)

Houmb, S.H., Georg, G., France, R., Bieman, J., Jürjens, J.: Cost-benefit trade-off analysis using BBN for aspect-oriented risk-driven development. In: 10th International Conference on Engineering of Complex Computer Systems, pp. 195–204. IEEE Computer Society (2005)

IEC: International Electrotechnical Commission. IEC 60300-3-9 Dependability management - Part 3: Application guide - Section 9: Risk analysis of technological systems - Event Tree Analysis. International Electrotechnical Commission (1995)

IEC: International Electrotechnical Commission. IEC 61025 Fault Tree Analysis Edition 2.0 (FTA). Technical report, International Electrotechnical Commission (2006)

Kazman, R., Asundi, J., Klein, M.: Making architecture design decisions: an economic approach. Technical report CMU/SEI-2002-TR-035. Carnegie Mellon (2002)

Kazman, R., Klein, M., Clements, P.: Method for architecture evaluation. Technical report CMU/SEI-2000-TR-004. Carnegie Mellon (2000)

Lund, M.S., Solhaug, B., Stølen, K.: Model-Driven Risk Analysis - The CORAS Approach. Springer, Heidelberg (2011)

Nielsen, D.S.: The cause/consequence diagram method as basis for quantitative accident analysis. Technical report RISO-M-1374. Danish Atomic Energy Commission (1971)

Omerovic, A.: PREDIQT: a method for model-based prediction of impacts of architectural design changes on system quality. Doctoral dissertation, Faculty of Mathematics and Natural Sciences, University of Oslo, Oslo (2012)

Omerovic, A., Karahasanovic, A., Stølen, K.: Uncertainty handling in weighted dependency trees: a systematic literature review. In: Dependability and Computer Engineering: Concepts for Software-Intensive Systems. IGI Global (2012a)

Omerovic, A., Solhaug, B., Stølen, K.: Assessing practical usefulness and performance of the PREDIQT method: an industrial case study. Inf. Softw. Technol. **54**(12), 1377–1395 (2012b)

Omerovic, A., Stølen, K.: A practical approach to uncertainty handling and estimate acquisition in model-based prediction of system quality. Int. J. Adv. Syst. Meas. **4**(1–2), 55–70 (2011)

Singh, A.G., Omerovic, A., Chauvel, F., Ferry, N.: An experience report. In: Proceedings of the 13th Workshop on Adaptive and Reflective Middleware, ARM 2014, pp. 7:1–7:6. ACM, New York (2014)

Singh, A.G., Omerovic, A., Chauvel, F., Ferry, N.: Towards feature-driven goal fulfillment analysis - a feasibility study. In: Proceedings of the 3rd International Conference on Model-Driven Engineering and Software Development, pp. 193–204 (2015)

Sonnenreich, W., Albanese, J., Stout, B.: Return on security investment (ROSI)-a practical quantitative model. J. Res. Pract. Inf. Technol. **38**(1), 45–56 (2006)

Multi-level Adaptations in a CloudWave Infrastructure: A Telco Use Case

Dario Bruneo[1], Francesco Longo[1(✉)], and Boris Moltchanov[2]

[1] Dipartimento di Ingegneria, Università degli Studi di Messina,
Viale F. Stagno d'Alcontres, 31, 98166 Messina, ME, Italy
{dbruneo,flongo}@unime.it
[2] Telecom Italia, Via G. Reiss Romoli, 274, 10148 Torino, TO, Italy
boris.moltchanov@telecomitalia.it

Abstract. CloudWave is a FP7 EU project whose aim is delivering novel technologies and methods for improving both the development of Cloud services and the management of their operation and execution. Such goal is reached by providing mechanisms and policies for coordinating multiple adaptations both at the level of the Cloud infrastructure and at the level of the hosted applications. In this paper, we describe the CloudWave Telco application use case and we provide a proof of concept discussing how the QoS experienced by the application users can be improved thanks to the technologies provided by CloudWave.

1 Introduction

Currently within ICT, cloud computing plays a key role and is recognized as one of the most significant technologies for boosting productivity, economic growth and job development [1]. As cloud computing takes hold, the challenges of fully realizing its potential become evident. In fact, nowadays, IT leaders increasingly consider the improvement of business agility as well as faster innovation the major strategic reasons for adopting this paradigm. Yet, the engineering methods and tools used to develop cloud services have not yet made the leap towards these expectations. Thus, there is a need to improve agility in designing software and operating cloud based service as well as to increase the cloud infrastructure adaptivity and the interaction between the higher level software & service goals and the lower level infrastructure (see NESSI [2]).

Moreover, cloud applications are often designed with incomplete knowledge about their actual usage profile, delivery model, and the reliability of the cloud infrastructure. This may lead to unforeseen runtime situations, resource utilization inefficiencies, and even performance degradation that can cause outages. These can result in loss of competitive advantage for service providers due to current and potential client's concerns about Quality of Service (QoS) and usage risks [3]. We believe that this issues are fundamental consequences of both application-level and infrastructure-level deficiencies: applications are not designed to explore the distribution, characteristics, and dynamic behavior

A. Celesti and P. Leitner (Eds.): ESOCC 2015 Workshops, CCIS 567, pp. 175–183, 2016.
DOI: 10.1007/978-3-319-33313-7_13

of cloud infrastructure while existing cloud technology stacks (such as Open-Stack [4]) do not provide concrete mechanisms to facilitate such cloud application development.

Thus, new, holistic, cloud-specific engineering methods are required. Such a novel paradigm should facilitate design and delivery of reliable cloud services and should support their continuous adaptation to changing environment conditions and market requirements, speeding up innovation cycles. The CloudWave project [5–7] represents an attempt to address this challenge by delivering novel technologies and methods for improving both the development of Cloud services and the management of their operation and execution. This new development and management paradigm is built upon new technologies and open standards, while leveraging assets and outcomes of other relevant FP7 EU projects, e.g., RESERVOIR [8], FI-WARE [9], Optimis [10].

In this paper, we provide a description of one of the use cases that the Cloud-Wave project is developing to prove the effectiveness of the proposed solutions. The use case is based on a Telco application that has been ported to a CloudWave infrastructure and adapted to leverage coordinated adaptation mechanisms both at the level of the Cloud infrastructure and at the level of the application itself. We discuss how the QoS experienced by the application users can be improved thanks to the CloudWave technologies and how we plan to actually implement the vision in future work.

2 Agile Software and Feedback-Driven Developments: The CloudWave Project

CloudWave: Agile Service Engineering for the Future Internet [5] is a European Commission Seventh Framework Programme (FP7/2006–2013) funded Integrated Project started at the beginning of November 2013 and still in progress.

In its mission, CloudWave takes inspiration from the emerging DevOps paradigm [11]. DevOps promotes communication, collaboration, and integration between software development and IT operations, recognizing the increasing necessity of more alignment between such two disciplines and their stakeholders for the production of high quality software ready for the Future Internet. CloudWave is the first holistic solution leveraging DevOps' principles, as shown in Fig. 1.

Specifically, the vision of the CloudWave project is based on three main innovation pillars that together contribute to the realization of a new generation software development environment, an innovative process, and powerful tools and methods for engineering high quality Future Internet applications.

Execution Analytics. (*Monitoring* in Fig. 1) - CloudWave exploits programmable mechanisms and specialized algorithms in order to dynamically introspect and analyze both the Cloud infrastructure and the application behavior. Data pertaining to physical resources, virtualized resources, IoT elements, exploited platforms, and the applications themselves will be integrated, supporting both application run-time adaptations and an agile incremental development process.

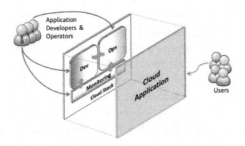

Fig. 1. The DevOps paradigm as adopted by CloudWave

Coordinated Adaptation. (*Ops* in Fig. 1) - CloudWave proposes and evaluates new distributed algorithms and data models that will enable Cloud infrastructures and applications to take coordinated adaptation actions across the system stack in response to dynamic changes in their execution environment. This will allow to optimize the quality of service and the resource utilization, while providing feedback on runtime adaptations to developers.

Feedback-Driven Development. (*Dev* in Fig. 1) - CloudWave is also a novel engineering paradigm and a set of modular platform services for agile development of new generation Future Internet applications. Developers will be provided with easy access to runtime data allowing them to enhance business applications for the sake of superior customer experience, based on observed user needs and context as well as application/infrastructure behavior and adaptations.

Based on those novel ideas, CloudWave goes significantly beyond the state-of-art in Cloud computing, investigating into emerging capabilities and mechanisms such as Cloud-aware applications, dynamic offloading of application code between Cloud, on-premise servers, and IoT devices, dynamic binary optimization of application code to support migration across the Cloud, integrated and coordinated multi-layer adaptations complementary addressing aspects such as service stability, availability, reliability, fail-safe provisioning, security and privacy. Overall, the project will provide solutions for delivering services in an effective, efficient and reliable manner across the future computing continuum embracing Clouds and IoT devices that the Future Internet represents, while utilizing and extending already existing, open-source, de-facto standard approaches such as OpenStack [4, 12].

3   CloudWave Telco Use Case

3.1   Application Architecture

One of the use cases selected for the project is a mobile telecommunication service scenario, which is built in the recommender class of services. This service accessible through a web-browser in a mobile terminal shows to the customer multimedia content chosen and selected based on the customers text or URI input and available data-bases connected to the services backend. The complexity of the service and its dependency on external data-sources explains significant delays in the service response given a certain text by the customers. The customers are equipped with mobile terminals connected to the mobile network and requests the service application via the same internet services URI. Potentially the number of the customers sending the request to the service at the same time could be extremely large. Each service request is processed separately; therefore the overall response time grows with the number of the customers using the service. The customers could be of two types: premium - paying customers, who pays for the service usage and so pretend to have certain QoS within certain Service Level Agreement (SLA) - and freemium - who are using the service for free and therefore are not guaranteed for any QoS. Although the freemium customers use full service functionalities, their service quality is not guaranteed as they are served by minimum resources allocated for the freemium customers. The service concept is shown in the Fig. 2.

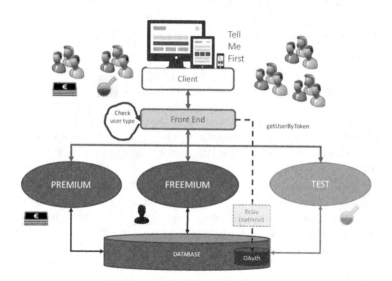

Fig. 2. Telco use case service scenario.

The premium customers are served with increasing service power, guaranteeing contracted by SLA QoS, nevertheless under certain conditions the service could degrade into a smaller set of mandatory features and breaks the SLA if increase further certain limit of numbers of requests per second. The power of underlying infrastructure allocated per service depends on the maximum infrastructural cost defined by the service provider within CloudWave platform. Therefore the overall service performance is limited by the limited IaaS resources dedicated to the service within the maximum allowed cup cost.

3.2   Application Deployment

The service is built in a way that its modular structure runs over many Virtual Machines (VMs) under CloudWave control, which measures the response time and, when the service usage increases, it tries first to split the customers traffic into Premium and Freemium VMs (PVM and FVM respectively), then instantiate new PVM until the total allowed expense is reached, then disables some optional features in the premium customers service and finally applies the QoS filtering rejecting the customers if requests numbers continues to grow. This behavior is possible due to the total control by CloudWave over the service components and number of requests, applying scale out/in techniques and application adaptation.

Detailed service integration into the CloudWave platform is shown in Fig. 3.

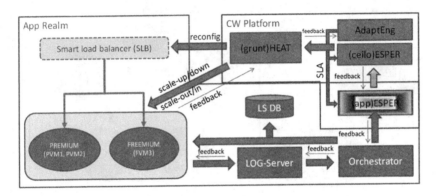

Fig. 3. Telco use case integrated into the CloudWave platform.

The CloudWave platforms components shown in the upper right corner of above picture receives the monitored metrics from the service components and once the monitored event is detected the CloudWaves Adaptation Engine release adaptation action corresponding to the detected condition at the infrastructural level (IaaS). Initial metrics coming from the monitored service components and VMs are intercepted by the appESPER module acting on the application level (PaaS/SaaS), which derives the aggregated metrics relevant for the CloudWaves internal ceiloESPER module, but could be also the adaptation requests released to the service components at the application level.

This scenario allows to split the total service control into two realms: application and infrastructural, where corresponding ESPER module activates actions for adaptation at the service application or the service infrastructure level. This permits to have application sensitive data hidden from the IaaS management and fetch the CloudWave underlying IaaS environment only with filtered data relevant for the IaaS level of actuations. The SLA defines the rules to be provided for both appESPER and ceiloESPER reasoners in order to take correspondent actions on separated respective SaaS/PaaS and IaaS levels, making the overall solution very fast reacting when each level is controlled by its own metrics, rules and action management tools.

4 Multi-level Adaptations: A Proof of Concept

In this section, we provide a proof of concept showing how multi-level adaptations can improve the overall QoS experienced by the Telco application users.

The state machine and the state transitions of the service behavior under different load conditions (L) defined by different threshold levels (L1..L4) is shown in Fig. 4.

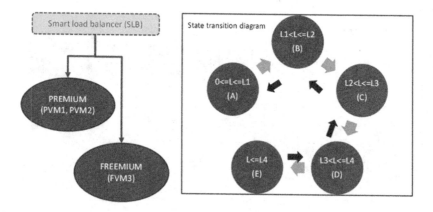

Fig. 4. States and state transitions of the use case.

The use case scenario run consists of the progressive scale up of the overall service performance by the following steps, as shown in Fig. 5:

1. run of a dedicated FVM and traffic split to the freemium and premium flows over dedicated FVM and PVM respectively;
2. run of an addition PVM serving increased number of the premium customers;
3. service degrade for the premium customers for reduced but mandatory (contracted) service functionality;
4. applying the QoS filter for the premium customers in order to serve certain number of the customers defined per allocated IaaS nodes.

The freemium customers are served at the best effort basis with very limited IaaS resources are their SLA is not defined.

The scenario behavior in case of the traffic reduction is straight backward, therefore the following adaptation steps are performed following the traffic decrease, as shown in Fig. 6:

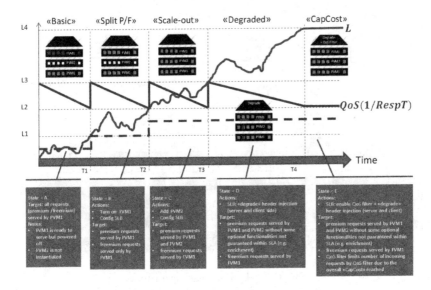

Fig. 5. Scale up use case run.

1. deactivation of the QoS filter;
2. restoring the full functionality and full features set for the premium customers;
3. removing of the second PVM;
4. joining the freemium and premium traffic in the same PVM and removing the FVM.

The adaptation actions configured in this use case scenario are on two levels:

– SaaS/PaaS: for the traffic split and QoS filter activation/deactivation;
– IaaS: for the launch of new VM and scale out and scale in of existing infrastructural resources.

This use case integrated into the CloudWave platform demonstrates the platform capability to monitor an application at the different cloud levels SaaS, PaaS and IaaS as far as generate decisions and take actions on its respective monitored levels. The decision making and action points are split into separated modules acting on their respective levels increasing the adapting flexibility and fine-tuning of the overall solution. Decoupling of the application and infrastructural level increased the reaction time of the controlled platform as application actions don't load the IaaS level and the decision making and action execution occur much faster performed totally in the SaaS/PaaS level without need to send raw application service data into the IaaS modules. Only IaaS metrics and actions are handled by the IaaS level as only there IaaS adaptations are possible due to the specificity of the hypervirtualization environment. However, at the end, this is only a first prototyping of a service use case in the CloudWave platform therefore the most relevant elements and actions are shown. A more powerful

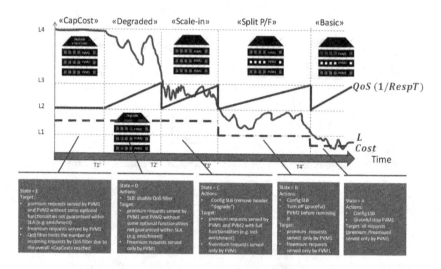

Fig. 6. Scale down use case run.

and more flexible use case run is a future work as well as the service trial and performance evaluation.

5   Conclusions

In this paper, we provided a high level view of the CloudWave project main innovation pillars. Then, we provided a description of one of the project use cases, namely the Telco application use case showing how it can take advantages of multi-level adaptations. Such adaptations can take place at the level of the infrastructure and at the level of the application itself and can be coordinated thanks to the mechanisms and policies provided by the CloudWave infrastructure. Future work will be devoted to the implementation of the use case and its evaluation from both a functional and non-functional point of view.

Acknowledgements. The research leading to these results has received funding from the European Community's Seventh Framework Programme (FP7/2007-2013) under grant agreement Nr. 610802 (CloudWave).

References

1. Communication from the Commission to the European Parliament: Unleashing the Potential of Cloud Computing in Europe (2012). http://ec.europa.eu/information_society/activities/cloudcomputing/docs/com/com_cloud.pdf
2. NESSI Cloud White Paper. http://www.nessieurope.com/Files/Private/120718_NESSI_Cloud_WhitePaper_July.pdf

3. Chang, W., Abu-Amara, H., Sanford, J.: Challenges of enterprise cloud services. Transforming Enterprise Cloud Services, pp. 133–187. Springer, The Netherlands (2010)
4. OpenStack Open Source Cloud Computing Software. www.openstack.org
5. CloudWave Project, funded by the European Commission Seventh Framework Programme (FP7/2006-2013) under grant agreement n. 610802. http://cloudwave-fp7.eu/
6. Longo, F., Bruneo, D., Villari, M., Puliafito, A., Salant, E., Wolfsthal, Y.: From vision cloud to cloudwave: towards the future internet and a new generation of services. In: 2014 International Conference on Intelligent Networking and Collaborative Systems (INCoS), pp. 641–646, September 2014
7. Bruneo, D., Fritz, T., Keidar-Barner, S., Leitner, P., Longo, F., Marquezan, C., Metzger, A., Pohl, K., Puliafito, A., Raz, D., Roth, A., Salant, E., Segall, I., Villari, M., Wolfsthal, Y., Woods, C.: CloudWave: where adaptive cloud management meets DevOps. In: 2014 IEEE Symposium on Computers and Communication (ISCC), Workshops, pp. 1–6, June 2014
8. Rochwerger, B., et al.: Reservoir - when one cloud is not enough. Computer **44**, 44–51 (2011)
9. Fi-ware: an innovative, open cloud-based infrastructure (2014). http://www.fi-ware.org/
10. Optimis - optimized infrastructure service (2014). http://www.optimis-project.eu/
11. Debois, P.: Devops: a software revolution in the making? J. Inf. Technol. Manag. **24**, 3–39 (2011)
12. The open source, open standards cloud, innovative, open source cloud computing software for building reliable cloud infrastructure. http://openstack.org/. Accessed Jan 2014

Axe: A Novel Approach for Generic, Flexible, and Comprehensive Monitoring and Adaptation of Cross-Cloud Applications

Jörg Domaschka, Daniel Seybold[✉], Frank Griesinger, and Daniel Baur

Institute of Information Resource Management, University of Ulm,
Albert-Einstein-Allee 43, 89081 Ulm, Germany
{joerg.domaschka,daniel.seybold,frank.griesinger,
daniel.baur}@uni-ulm.de
http://www.uni-ulm.de/in/omi

Abstract. The vendor lock-in has been a major problem since cloud computing has evolved as on the one hand side hinders a quick transition between cloud providers and at the other hand side hinders an application deployment over various clouds at the same time (cross-cloud deployment). While the rise of cross-cloud deployment tools has to some extend limited the impact of vendor lock-in and given more freedom to operators, the fact that applications now are spread out over more than one cloud platform tremendously complicates matters: Either the operator has to interact with the interfaces of various cloud providers or he has to apply custom management tools. This is particularly true when it comes to the task of auto-scaling an application and adapting it to load changes. This paper introduces a novel approach to monitoring and adaptation management that is able to flexibly gather various monitoring data from virtual machines distributed across cloud providers, to dynamically aggregate the data in the cheapest possible manner, and finally, to evaluate the processed data in order to adapt the application according to user-defined rules.

1 Introduction

Since the beginning of cloud computing, vendor lock-in has been a major problem. It is still around mainly due to the fact that cloud standards such as CIMI [6] and OCCI [16] have not been widely adopted by cloud providers. Tools abstracting the differences between cloud providers, and thus allowing *multi-cloud* deployment—the capability to deploy one application at different cloud platforms using the same application specification—have been a first step to overcome vendor lock-in. Yet, it is only *cross-cloud deployment*—the capability to spread a single application instance across different cloud providers—that enables users to take full advantage of different providers and their capabilities. In particular, it enables trading off the properties of application requirements against the offerings on a per-component or even per-component instance basis.

© Springer International Publishing Switzerland 2016
A. Celesti and P. Leitner (Eds.): ESOCC 2015 Workshops, CCIS 567, pp. 184–196, 2016.
DOI: 10.1007/978-3-319-33313-7_14

This for instance allows a *hybrid-cloud deployment* where a database containing sensitive data is deployed in a private cloud, while the rest of the application resides in different public clouds.

Both approaches, multi-cloud and cross-cloud, give the application operator the chance to change its current application deployment and to adapt to changed conditions such as the workload, e.g., more load than originally anticipated, and changed environmental conditions, e.g., the prices of other operators have changed. In order to benefit from these features, however, the application operators need to be able to actively judge the quality of the current deployment. For pure multi-cloud systems the application operator may refer to the monitoring tools of the currently selected cloud operator. While basic monitoring data may come for free on some cloud providers, often the user needs advanced metrics that either cost (Amazon, Rackspace) or require him to set up own monitoring tools. In addition to that, he has to familiarise with the user interfaces of various cloud providers.

For cross-cloud deployment using the providers' monitoring infrastructure is technically feasible, but tremendously increases the effort as multiple tools have to be used in parallel. Moreover, it is difficult to access metrics that involve the crossing of provider domains (such as network traffic from provider A to provider B). Furthermore is hard to access application-specific or component-specific metrics. Also, a sophisticated and configurable aggregation on the metrics is currently not easily possible. Finally, while most cloud providers support a simple approach to auto-scaling for application adaptation, e.g. metrics-based scale-out, there is currently no built-in mechanism that supports a cross-cloud adaptation of applications.

In this paper, we address these issues by introducing AXE, a generic, flexible, and extensible monitoring and adaptation engine for cross-cloud deployments. Besides the fact, that we introduce the tool, our contributions are as follows: *(i)* We present a powerful API that enables the specification of rules independent of the concrete deployment. *(ii)* We discuss a heuristic of how to reduce the cross-cloud provider network traffic and hence reduce costs. *(iii)* We introduce the first engine to deal with the *Scalability Rule Language* (SRL) [8,12]. All of the features are embedded in CLOUDIATOR, our cross-cloud, multi-tenancy deployment and application management tool [2,7].

This document is structured as follows: Sect. 2 introduces background on CLOUDIATOR and *Scalability Rule Language (SRL)* and further defines requirements towards our approach. Section 3 introduces our approach by presenting the individual tools of our platform and their configuration. It also discusses architectural options and introduces our architecture as well as the API. Section 4 exhibits the current status and upcoming tasks. Section 5 discusses related work, before we conclude with a report on our current status and open issues.

2   Background

The design of AXE has been heavily driven by constraints of cross-cloud environments. In addition to that, AXE builds heavily on earlier work. In the following, we first introduce the constraints and derive requirements from them. In the next step, we present our CLOUDIATOR tool that we use as the basis for the AXE implementation [7]. Finally, we roughly describe the Scalability Rule Language that constitutes the meta-model for our monitoring and scaling solution.

2.1   Requirements and Constraints

For supporting in-depth analyses of existing deployments, several requirements have to be considered: *(a)* The fact that on the one hand, the monitoring of large-scale applications does generate huge amounts of data and on the other hand cloud providers usually charge for network traffic that leaves their data centre gives motivation that as much of data processing shall happen within the domain of individual cloud providers. *(b)* In order to avoid single points of failures, the architecture of a monitoring solution should not rely on a centralised approach, but rather favour distributed approaches with no central entity. As the amount of monitoring data usually increases with the number of allocated *virtual machines (VMs)*, the resources assigned to monitoring shall increase with the size of the application. *(c)* The operators of a cloud application may discover that they have to monitor further high-level or even low-level metrics or need monitoring to happen at a higher resolution. Hence, it is necessary that monitoring properties can be changed also after an application has been deployed. *(d)* The same considerations that hold for monitoring, have to hold for scaling rules. In addition, it is necessary that rules can be defined in a generic way without having to know the exact number of instances per component in advance. *(e)* The monitoring platform has to be able to capture application-specific metrics.

2.2   The Cloudiator Tool

CLOUDIATOR[1] is a cross-cloud deployment tool that also supports adaptation and re-deployment. In this section, we present the CLOUDIATOR architecture to the extend necessary to understand how it embeds AXE. Figure 1 summarises the architecture as of the original CLOUDIATOR tool (green), but also the enhancements of AXE (yellow). The AXE specific components *Aggregation*, *Scaling Engine*, and *Visor* are introduced in detail in Sect. 3.

The figure shows that CLOUDIATOR consists of a *home domain* for which COLOSSEUM is the entry point offering a JSON-based REST interface. This is used by a graphical Web-based user interface, but can also be used by adapters and automatisation tools. It also comprises various registries that store the CLOUDIATOR users, information about cloud providers, the cloud accounts of the users, and meta-information about cloud offerings such as the operating systems of images. Moreover, the home domain contains a repository of application components together with their life-cycle handlers as well as applications composed of these components. In addition, the registries contain information about started VMs and the component instances deployed on them as well as about the

---

[1] https://github.com/cloudiator.

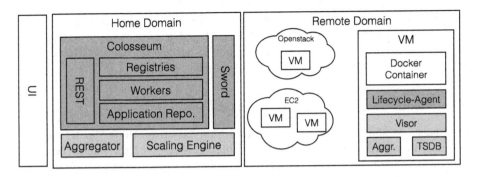

Fig. 1. The CLOUDIATOR architecture (Color figure online)

wiring between the component instances. Finally, they hold the workers syncing the registries with the cloud provider information, and executing the provisioning of virtual machines or the installation of application components on virtual machines. The SWORD abstraction layer realises the communication with the various cloud provider APIs based on Apache jclouds[2].

The *remote domain* comprises all VMs at various cloud providers as well as the component instances running on them. In addition to that it contains CLOUDIATOR's life cycle agent on each of the VMs that the home domain uses in order to distribute component instances over VMs and to poll the status of the component instances when it needs to be shown in the user interface.

2.3 Scalability Rule Language

The SRL [8] is a provider-agnostic description language. It provides expressions to define the monitoring raw metric values from VMs and component instances and also mechanisms to compose higher-level metrics from raw metrics. Moreover, it comprises mechanisms to express events and event patterns on metrics and metric values. Finally, SRL captures thresholds on the events and actions to be executed when thresholds are violated. A simple SRL rule in prose may be *add a new instance of this distributed database if* (i) *all instances have a 5 min average CPU load* $> 60\%$, (ii) *at least one instance has a 1 min average CPU load* $> 85\%$, *and* (iii) *the total number of instances is* < 6.

3 Approach

This section sketches our approach in order to realise a flexible monitoring and adaptation tool that satisfies the requirements imposed on cross-cloud tooling (cf. Sect. 2). Basically, our auto-scaling process maps to the MAPE loop [11,15] consisting of the following phases: monitoring, analysis, planning, and execution of changes. With respect to our setting, this means that first,

---

[2] https://jclouds.apache.org/.

we have to retrieve monitoring data from the virtual machines and component instances. In a second step, the raw data gathered there has to be aggregated and processed. Third, the rule processing has to happen on the aggregated data and finally, the resulted rule has to be executed.

3.1 Visor: Gathering Monitoring Data

In order to be able to gather the raw monitoring data from the VMs and component instances, we introduce VISOR as a monitoring agent to the remote domain. Just as the life-cycle agent, VISOR is deployed on every VM and provides a remote interface the home domain uses in order to configure a particular VISOR instance. This allows VISOR to adopt to the application and to only collect the required metrics, thus saving space and bandwidth. VISOR supports the capturing of data on a per component instance basis as well as on a per-VM basis. The sooner is achieved by sensors monitoring basic system properties on virtual machine level, e.g. by accessing system properties such as CPU load. The latter is done by exploiting the fact that all component instances are run inside a Docker[3] container and the resource consumption can be retrieved on a per-container basis. By default, VISOR offers various sensors supporting system metrics such as CPU load, memory consumption, disk I/O, and network I/O.

In order to support custom metrics, VISOR supports the implementation of custom sensors, by providing an easy-to-implement Java interface. It exploits the dynamic class loading properties of Java in order to be able to add those implementations at runtime. For supporting application-specific metrics that can only be retrieved from within an application such as the length of queues or the degree to which buffers have been filled, VISOR offers a `telnet`-based interface where applications can push their metrics data to. This interface is compatible with the carbon daemon of graphite[4], thus allowing an easy migration to VISOR.

3.2 Buffering Monitoring Data

A key element when computing higher-level metrics especially over larger time-windows is the need to buffer raw monitoring data. *Time-series databases (TSDBs)* have been designed to store timestamped data in an efficient way and also to provide quick access to the stored data. Many TSDB implementations support applying functions on stored data right out of the box what makes them a perfect match not only for buffering, but also for aggregation (cf. Sect. 3.3). The following paragraphs first derive a strategy on how to implement buffering including the constraints and then compares TSDBs found in literature and the open source community with respect to the required properties.

---

[3] http://www.docker.io.
[4] http://graphite.readthedocs.org/en/latest/carbon-daemons.html.

Strategy. With respect to our requirements (cf. Sect. 2) the buffering and therefore the TSDB approach needs to be able to work with limited resources, have no single point of failure, and increase available resources when more VMs are being used. In order to cope with these requirements, we use the following approach: from each VM acquired for an application, we reserve a configurable amount of memory and storage (e.g. 10 %) that we further split between a *local storage area* and a *shared storage area*. Both storage areas are managed by a TSDB instance running on the VM. The VISOR instance running on this VM will then feed all monitoring data to the TSDB. The TSDB will store data from its local VISOR in the local storage area and further relay the data to other TSDBs where it is stored in the shared storage area. This feature avoids that a TSDB becomes a single point of failure, but still enables quick access to local data. In order to keep network traffic between cloud providers low, any TSDB will only select other TSDBs running in the same cloud to replicate its data. If not enough instances are available to reach the desired replication degree, the maximum possible degree is used. Hence, this concludes to a ring-like topology that has been introduced in peer-to-peer systems [3] and is also used by distributed databases [13].

Selection of TSDB. Table 1 shows a comparison of established TSDB implementations [10] and several of their properties. The results are intermediate as our evaluation is this ongoing (cf. Sect. 4.1).

Table 1. Details of considered times series databases

Name	KairosDB	OpenTSDB	InfluxDB
Version	1.0.0	2.1.0	0.9.0
Datastore	H2/Cassandra	HBase	BoltDB
Distributed	no/yes	yes	yes
InMemory	yes/no	no	yes

The for us relevant details of the TSDBs are its maturity, available datastores, support of distribution and in memory storage. The TSDB should be in some mature state in order to provide a stable version, client libraries and an available documentation. Following the strategy exposed in Sect. 3.2 the datastores shall be lightweight and ideally support an in memory mode. Also they have to offer a distributed architecture to ensure horizontal scaling and replication.

OpenTSDB offers the best maturity regarding the version number. The underlying datastore HBase supports distribution but regarding the architecture of HBase [9] an in-memory mode is missing. Also, it is not a lightweight datastore [10] and an automated set-up as required in our scenario is not a trivial task and hard to script. Consequently, OpenTSDB is not an applicable solution.

From its capabilities InfluxDB seems suited for the outlined approach. Yet, the recently released version 0.9.0 comes with extensive changes in the storage architecture and API design compared to 0.8.0[5]. Given these changes there currently are no client implementations for version 0.9.0 available.

KairosDB also provides a mature version 1.0.0. It supports the single-site, in-memory datastore H2 and the distributed Cassandra datastore supporting scalable to a hundreds of instances [13]. While Cassandra's resource usage can be limited, in-memory storage is only supported in the commercial version[6].

Following this comparison KairosDB is currently the most appropriate TSDB to use in AXE based on maturity, distribution and the possibility to limit the resource consumption of Cassandra.

3.3   Aggregation

In order to make use of the time series produced by the various raw metrics, these have to be aggregated. Aggregation includes for instance the computation of average values, of maxima, minima, or simply the normalisation of values. In addition to that, aggregation may include merging of metrics, e.g. when computing the average of averages. Hence, aggregation is always application-specific.

Strategy. The strategy followed by AXE is based on the metric and metric aggregation concepts provided by SRL (cf. Sect. 2). In particular, it supports the hierarchical aggregation of metrics with an unlimited depth. In addition, it supports the use of time-bound or element-bound windows specifying the interval of a time series to be used for computations. Finally, the user may specify a schedule for each metric that defines how often a value of a metric shall be computed.

In order to satisfy the requirement for minimum network traffic and scale of the monitoring system, AXE performs aggregation as close to the data source as possible. Hence, all aggregations that require input data from a single VM will be performed on this VM. We refer to this computation to happen in the *host scope*. For this approach only the local storage is accessed and no communication is required which further reduces latency. Aggregations that need input only from VMs from a particular cloud are performed in *cloud scope*. Such computations exclusively access the shared space spanning a cloud. While it is desirable to distribute all computations of a particular cloud scope amongst the affected VMs the definition of a suitable heuristic is currently work in progress. Finally, computations that require input from multiple clouds happen in *cross-cloud scope* (or global scope). These are performed in the home domain of CLOUDIATOR.

It is important to note that values for higher-level aggregated, metrics have to be buffered just as the values of any other metric as well. Here, we use the following strategy to write to our storage platform: Values from local scope

---

[5] https://influxdb.com/docs/v0.9/introduction/overview.html.
[6] http://www.datastax.com/.

computations are treated just like values from raw metrics. Values from computations in cloud scope are written to the shared store of their cloud. The results from cross-cloud scope computations are stored in a possibly distributed TSDB operated at the home domain.

Using this set of hierarchical scopes, we expect to have effectively minimised latency and network traffic while at the same time having equally loaded all VMs with monitoring tasks and hence also equally spread the risk of failures. The deployment of the aggregation tasks onto the Aggregators residing in the system, and hence the decision which scope to use for it, is handled by the Scaling Engine component.

API. The API provided by COLOSSEUM in order to configure the monitoring and aggregation functionality of AXE as described above mainly supports the power of SRL. Yet, in order to ease the specification of sensors and aggregation functions independent from the number of deployed virtual machines and the cloud they are currently deployed on, we offer a richer interface.

```
Monitor doMonitorVms(AppInst app, Component comp, SensorDescription sens);
```

Fig. 2. API example. This method will trigger the monitoring of all VMs of this application instance where component `comp` has been installed using sensor `sens`.

The methods (cf. Fig. 2 for an example) for defining raw metrics consist of filters (e.g. by the component type) specifying all instances to be monitored, and a sensor description defining what to monitor. The sensor description consists of scheduling information and information which sensor type to be deployed on VISOR. The return value of such an invocation can be used in further methods to define higher-level metrics (cf. Fig. 3). Here, a map functionality is used to specify the high level metric: That is, for each ingoing (raw) metric a new metric is created (e.g. average CPU usage in the last 5 min). The API also supports reduce-like semantics where a single metric is generated from all input metrics (e.g. average of above averages).

```
Monitor mapAggregatedMonitors(FormulaQuantifier quantifier,
        Schedule schedule, Window window, FormulaOperator op,
        List<Monitor> monitors);
```

Fig. 3. API example. This method will install an aggregation triggered according to a schedule, based on an operator, and using a window of elements operating.

3.4 Auto-Scaling

In general, auto-scalers can be categorised in five different classes [14]. For AXE we adopt SRL which mainly belongs to the threshold-based rules as well as time series analysis class. SRL links a set of threshold-based conditions with each other using binary operators. In addition, any set of thresholds may be linked to the values produced by the metrics. Furthermore, any of such constructs has attached a set of scaling actions to be executed whenever the condition has been satisfied. So far, AXE supports to trigger the scale out and scale in of components. Yet, the implementation of further actions is underway. The triggering of rules leads to an invocation of the CLOUDIATOR functionality to bring up a new or shut down an existing VM.

Strategy. The auto-scaling functionality of AXE builds on top of the monitoring capabilities. In particular any of the conditions connected via Boolean operators is considered to be a metric on its own taking the values 0 or 1. When the metric turns to 1 the respective action will be triggered and forwarded as request to the other CLOUDIATOR tools, in particular COLOSSEUM. These tasks are executed by the Scaling Engine component.

API. The scaling API provides the capability to attach an action to a monitor. The action itself is described in terms of the component to deal with, the scaling type, and its parameters. For instance for horizontal scaling, the parameters are the amount of instances to add/remove, and the allowed maximum and minimum number of instances of that component.

3.5 Architecture

Above descriptions and discussions lead to the architecture from Fig. 1 and whose main components are (i) the Scaling Engine, (ii) the Aggregator, and (iii) VISOR. The latter has already been introduced in earlier work [2].

The Scaling Engine is the central managing environment of AXE that controls the distribution and outsourcing of the computation-heavy work to highly scalable and loosely coupled components, the Aggregators. Nevertheless, it is possible to scale the Scaling Engine up to having one instance per scaling rule.

The aggregations are managed and executed by the Aggregators in the system. Due to the design of the system, this can be done in parallel. Also, for their implementation, the focus has been set to minimise latency.

4 Current Status and Future Work

The following presents the current status and gives an outlook on our planned work. We distinguish these aspects for data collection in a TSDB, data aggregation, and scaling.

4.1   Time-Series Database

The current version of AXE uses KairosDB with the Cassandra as a datastore. Cassandra is configured to use only a low portion of a VM's resources to keep the impact on the components running on that VM small. Upcoming work comprises a performance-oriented evaluation of InfluxDB and other NoSQL databases focusing on their capabilities for managing time-series data. Further, the Zipkin framework[7] will be evaluated on its suitability for cross-cloud applications.

4.2   Aggregators

Currently, the aggregation functionality is implemented for KairosDB and supports aggregation from and to arbitrary KairosDB instances. We plan to extend these capabilities to fit all predefined operators of SRL. We currently implement aggregators for other databases as well to support the TSDB evaluation.

4.3   Scaling Engine

So far AXE supports horizontal scaling actions. Vertical scaling is currently being implemented. Furthermore, we work reducing the burden for the user when implementing scaling rules. Therefore, we plan to encapsulate SRL's complexity in a simpler language possible inspired from complex-event-processing languages [17].

While SRL and with it AXE adopts concepts from auto-scaling concepts based on threshold-based and time series analysis, other concepts exist that include queuing theory, control theory, and reinforcement learning [14]. Accordingly, AXE borrows all its strengths from SRL, but also the weaknesses and could profit from the integration of other techniques. For instance, reinforcement learning might be handled in external processing tools, that constantly adjust the scaling rules. Future work includes the evaluation of such approaches.

5   Related Work

We compare related work with respect to monitoring and auto-scaling.

Cloud Monitoring. Lifting monitoring to the cloud comes along with various requirements compared to traditional server monitoring [1]. Tools provided by cloud providers, such as Amazon's CloudWatch[8] suffer from vendor lock-in. Also, additional tools are required when data from different cloud providers shall be aggregated. Established open source monitoring tools such as Ganglia[9]

---

[7] https://github.com/openzipkin/zipkin.

[8] http://aws.amazon.com/en/cloudwatch/.

[9] http://ganglia.sourceforge.net/.

or Nagios[10] are designed to monitor large distributed systems, but struggle with the dynamic of cloud environments. More cloud-aware monitoring systems such as Zipkin—which is based on Dapper [18]—can cope with the dynamic cloud environment and offer a rich functionality. Yet, in order to scale the monitoring system manual actions or additional tools are necessary. Compared to AXE none of the mentioned tools supports a reduction of communication overhead for cross-cloud applications.

Auto-Scaling Techniques. In contrast to similar scaling engines [4], AXE is not tied to a specific language, but targets to be open for various approaches.

Cloud orchestration tools such as Apache Brooklyn[11], the rules are simple threshold-based and any more complex rules have to be defined in an external monitoring tool. AXE in CLOUDIATOR goes beyond this, as it provides an integrated and easy-to-use solution that even allows changes of the scalability configuration at runtime.

Several projects deal with integrated auto-scaling mechanisms for cloud services. One of them is the EU project CELAR [5]. Auto-scaling in CELAR is based on a multi-level description of combined metrics. By that metrics are assigned to a certain level and when violations occur, the scaling is based on the top level of the topology. While AXE also supports a multi-level description of metrics, it goes beyond the CELAR approach due to the fact that it realises metric aggregation and analysis in a distributed and hierarchical manner.

6   Conclusions

The integrated scaling solutions of current cloud orchestration tools lack an support for sophisticated implementations of auto-scaling techniques. Only such a solution can achieve highly dynamic applications, with the ability to adjust their configuration at runtime in order to cope with unexpected changes of workload. In this paper, we introduced AXE, a novel, cloud provider-independent approach of cloud application monitoring and application adaptation management. AXE supports distributed monitoring of cross-cloud applications and also comes with a distributed, hierarchical aggregation of monitored metrics reducing the network traffic across cloud providers. The adaptation of the *Scalability Rules Language (SRL)* enables the expression of powerful scaling rules based on hierarchical metrics, complex events and threshold. The platform is scalable in itself and hence also supports large-scale applications. It has been integrated in our CLOUDIATOR deployment tool[12].

Acknowledgements. The research leading to these results has received funding from the European Community's Seventh Framework Programme (FP7/2007-2013) under

---

[10] https://www.nagios.org/.
[11] http://brooklyn.incubator.apache.org/.
[12] https://github.com/cloudiator.

grant agreement number 317715 (PaaSage) and from the European Community's Framework Programme for Research and Innovation HORIZON 2020 (ICT-07-2014) under grant agreement number 644690 (CloudSocket).

References

1. Aceto, G., Botta, A., De Donato, W., Pescapè, A.: Cloud monitoring: a survey. Comput. Netw. **57**(9), 2093–2115 (2013)
2. Baur, Daniel, Wesner, Stefan, Domaschka, Jörg: Towards a model-based execution-ware for deploying multi-cloud applications. In: Ortiz, Guadalupe, Tran, Cuong (eds.) ESOCC 2014. CCIS, vol. 508, pp. 124–138. Springer, Heidelberg (2015)
3. Clarke, I., Sandberg, O., Wiley, B., Hong, T.W.: Freenet: a distributed anonymous information storage and retrieval system. In: Federrath, H. (ed.) Designing Privacy Enhancing Technologies. LNCS, vol. 2009, pp. 46–66. Springer, Heidelberg (2001)
4. Copil, G., Moldovan, D., Truong, H.L., Dustdar, S.: SYBL: an extensible language for controlling elasticity in cloud applications. In: 2013 13th International Symposium on Cluster, Cloud and Grid Computing (CCGrid), pp. 112–119, May 2013
5. Copil, G., Moldovan, D., Truong, H.-L., Dustdar, S.: Multi-level elasticity control of cloud services. In: Basu, S., Pautasso, C., Zhang, L., Fu, X. (eds.) ICSOC 2013. LNCS, vol. 8274, pp. 429–436. Springer, Heidelberg (2013). http://dx.doi.org/10.1007/978-3-642-45005-1_31
6. DMTF: Cloud Infrastructure Management Interface (CIMI) Model and RESTful HTTP-based Protocol (2013)
7. Domaschka, J., Baur, D., Seybold, D., Griesinger, F.: Cloudiator: a cross-cloud, multi-tenant deployment and runtime engine. In: 9th Symposium and Summer School on Service-Oriented Computing (2015)
8. Domaschka, J., Kritikos, K., Rossini, A.: Towards a generic language for scalability rules. In: Proceedings of CSB 2014: 2nd International Workshop on Cloud Service Brokerage (2014, to appear)
9. George, L.: HBase: The Definitive Guide, 1st edn. O'Reilly Media, Sebastopol (2011)
10. Goldschmidt, T., Jansen, A., Koziolek, H., Doppelhamer, J., Breivold, H.P.: Scalability and robustness of time-series databases for cloud-native monitoring of industrial processes. In: 2014 IEEE 7th International Conference on Cloud Computing, Anchorage, AK, USA, June 27–July 2, 2014, pp. 602–609 (2014)
11. Jacob, B., Lanyon-Hogg, R., Nadgir, D., Yassin, A.: A practical guide to the IBM autonomic computing toolkit. IBM redbooks, IBM Corporation, International Technical Support Organization (2004)
12. Kritikos, K., Domaschka, J., Rossini, A.: SRL: a scalability rule language for multi-cloud environments. In: 2014 IEEE 6th International Conference on CloudCom, pp. 1–9, December 2014
13. Lakshman, A., Malik, P.: Cassandra: a decentralized structured storage system. SIGOPS Oper. Syst. Rev. **44**(2), 35–40 (2010)
14. Lorido-Botran, T., Miguel-Alonso, J., Lozano, J.: A review of auto-scaling techniques for elastic applications in cloud environments. J. Grid Comput. **12**(4), 559–592 (2014)
15. Maurer, M., Breskovic, I., Emeakaroha, V., Brandic, I.: Revealing the mape loop for the autonomic management of cloud infrastructures. In: ISCC 2011, pp. 147–152, June 2011

16. Open Grid Forum: Open Cloud Computing Interface - Core (2011)
17. Paschke, A., Kozlenkov, A., Boley, H.: A homogeneous reaction rule language for complex event processing. In: 33rd VLDB 2007 (2007)
18. Sigelman, B.H., Barroso, L.A., Burrows, M., Stephenson, P., Plakal, M., Beaver, D., Jaspan, S., Shanbhag, C.: Dapper, a large-scale distributed systems tracing infrastructure. Technical report, Google, Inc. (2010)

CloudWay Workshop Papers

Preface of CloudWay 2015

Cloud computing has recently been the focus of attention both as academic research and industrial initiatives. From a business point of view, organizations can benefit from the on-demand and pay-per-use model offered by cloud services rather than an upfront purchase of costly and over-provisioned infrastructure. From a technological perspective, the scalability, interoperability, and efficient (de-)allocation of resources through cloud services can enable a smooth execution of organizational operations.

Regardless of the benefits of cloud computing, many organizations still rely on business-critical applications – so-called legacy systems – developed over a long period of time using traditional development methods. In spite of maintainability issues, (on-premise) legacy systems are still crucial as they support core business processes that cannot simply be replaced. Therefore, migrating legacy systems toward cloud-based platforms allows organizations to leverage their existing systems deployed (over publicly available resources) as scalable cloud services.

The First International Workshop on Cloud Adoption and Migration (CloudWay 2015) was held on September 15, 2015, in Taormina (Messina), Italy, as a satellite event of ESOCC 2015. The workshop's goals were to bring together cloud migration experts from both academia and industry; to promote discussions and collaboration amongst participants; to help disseminate novel cloud migration practices and solutions; and to identify future cloud migration challenges and dimensions.

In this first edition, four full papers and one short paper were accepted for presentation during the workshop. The first paper, "Migrating to Cloud-Native Architectures Using Microservices: An Experience Report," by Armin Balalaie, Abbas Heydarnoori, and Pooyan Jamshidi, reports on the experience and lessons learned in an ongoing project on migrating a monolithic on-premise software to a microservice-based cloud architecture. The second paper, "Cloud Computing for e-Sciences at Université Sorbonne Paris Cité," by Christophe Cerin, Leila Abidi, Marie Lafaille, and Danielle Geldwerth-Feniger, presents a methodology to assist e-Science researchers in assessing and adopting cloud technologies. The third paper, "Resource Distribution Estimation for Data-Intensive Workloads: Give Me My Share & No One Gets Hurt!," by Alireza Khoshkbarforoushha, Rajiv Ranjan, and Peter Strazdins, describes a machine-learning framework for resource distribution estimation of data-intensive workloads in a shared cluster. The fourth paper, "Supporting Partial Database Migration to the Cloud Using Non-Intrusive Software Adaptations: An Experience Report," by Caio Costa, Paulo Maia, Nabor Mendonça, and Lincoln Rocha, reports on an early experience of partially migrating a legacy application's relational database to a NoSQL storage service in the cloud. Finally, the fifth (short) paper, "Cloud Adoption by Fine-Grained Resource Adaptation: Price Determination of Diagonally Scalable IaaS," by Kevin Laubis, Viliam Simko, and Alexander Schuller, examines the resource reduction potential of diagonal scaling in comparison with conventional horizontal approaches.

In addition to the presentation of the accepted papers, a panel was jointly organized with participants of the Cloud for IoT (CLIoT) Workshop focusing on the challenges and perspectives of migrating to "Cloud and IoT Solutions." The panel members were Pooyan Jamshidi, from Imperial College London, UK, and IC4, Ireland; Maria Fazio, from the University of Messina, Italy; Orazio Tormachio, from the University of Catania, Italy; Luiz Angelo Steffenel, from Université de Reims Champagne-Ardenne, France, and Nabor Mendonça, from the University of Fortaleza, Brazil, as moderator.

We take this opportunity to thank all authors, members of the Program Committee, and workshop attendees, whose participation was invaluable to the success of the event. We also acknowledge the financial support provided by The Irish Centre for Cloud Computing and Commerce (IC4) and the University of Fortaleza (UNIFOR).

Claus Pahl
Nabor Mendonça
Pooyan Jamshidi

Organization

Program Committee

Aakash Ahmad	IT University of Copenhagen, Denmark
Vasilios Andrikopoulos	University of Stuttgart, Germany
Thais Batista	Federal University of Rio Grande do Norte, Brazil
William Campbell	Birmingham City University, UK
Fei Cao	University of Central Missouri, USA
Schahram Dustdar	Technical University of Vienna, Austria
Sören Frey	Daimler TSS, Germany
Wilhelm (Willi) Hasselbring	Kiel University, Germany
Tomayess Issa	Curtin University, Australia
Pooyan Jamshidi	Imperial College London, UK (Co-chair)
Ali Khajeh-Hosseini	RightScale, Inc., UK
Xiaodong Liu	Napier University, Edinburgh, UK
Theo Lynn	Dublin City University, Ireland
Paulo Henrique Maia	State University of Ceará, Brazil
Nabor Mendonça	University of Fortaleza, Brazil (Co-chair)
Claus Pahl	Dublin City University, Ireland (Co-chair)
Dana Petcu	West University of Timisoara, Romania
Américo Sampaio	University of Fortaleza, Brazil
Amir Shariffoo	University of Duisburg-Essen, Germany
Giovanna Sissa	Università degli Studi di Genova, Italy
Steve Strauch	University of Stuttgart, Germany
Michelle Zhu	Southern Illinois University, USA

Sponsors

Migrating to Cloud-Native Architectures Using Microservices: An Experience Report

Armin Balalaie[1], Abbas Heydarnoori[1(✉)], and Pooyan Jamshidi[2]

[1] Department of Computer Engineering, Sharif University of Technology, Tehran, Iran
armin.balalaie@gmail.com, heydarnoori@sharif.edu
[2] Department of Computing, Imperial College London, London, UK
p.jamshidi@imperial.ac.uk

Abstract. Migration to the cloud has been a popular topic in industry and academia in recent years. Despite many benefits that the cloud presents, such as high availability and scalability, most of the on-premise application architectures are not ready to fully exploit the benefits of this environment, and adapting them to this environment is a non-trivial task. Microservices have appeared recently as novel architectural styles that are native to the cloud. These cloud-native architectures can facilitate migrating on-premise architectures to fully benefit from the cloud environments because non-functional attributes, like scalability, are inherent in this style. The existing approaches on cloud migration does not mostly consider cloud-native architectures as their first-class citizens. As a result, the final product may not meet its primary drivers for migration. In this paper, we intend to report our experience and lessons learned in an ongoing project on migrating a monolithic on-premise software architecture to microservices. We concluded that microservices is not a one-fit-all solution as it introduces new complexities to the system, and many factors, such as distribution complexities, should be considered before adopting this style. However, if adopted in a context that needs high flexibility in terms of scalability and availability, it can deliver its promised benefits.

Keywords: Cloud migration · Microservices · Cloud-native architectures · Software modernization

1 Introduction

In recent years, with the emergence of cloud computing and its promises, many companies from large to small and medium sizes are considering cloud as a target platform for migration [9]. Despite motivations for migrating to the cloud, most of the applications could not benefit from the cloud environment as long as their main intention is to simply dump the existing legacy architecture to a virtualized environment and call it a cloud application.

One of the main characteristics of the cloud environment is that failures can happen at any time, and the applications in this environment should be designed

© Springer International Publishing Switzerland 2016
A. Celesti and P. Leitner (Eds.): ESOCC 2015 Workshops, CCIS 567, pp. 201–215, 2016.
DOI: 10.1007/978-3-319-33313-7_15

in a way that they can resist such uncertainties. Furthermore, application *scalability* would not be possible without a scalable architecture. Cloud-native architectures like *microservices* are the ones that have these characteristics, i.e., availability and scalability, in their nature and can facilitate migrating on-premise architectures to fully benefit from the cloud environments.

Microservices is a novel architectural style that has been proposed to overcome the shortcomings of a *monolithic architecture* [16] in which the application logic is within one deployable unit. For small systems, the monolithic architecture could be the most appropriate solution and could become highly available and scalable using simple load balancing mechanisms. However, as the size of the system starts growing, problems like difficulties in understanding the code, increased deployment time, scalability for data-intensive loads, and a long-term commitment to a technology stack would start to appear [16]. This is where microservices come to help by providing small services that are easy to understand, could be deployed and scaled independently, and could have different technology stacks.

Most of the current approaches on cloud migration are focused on automated migration via applying model-driven approaches [1,2], and reusing of knowledge by migration patterns [5,10,12] without having cloud-native architectures as their first-class citizens. Furthermore, microservices is a new concept and thus, only a few technical reports can be found about using them in the literature [15,17].

Migrating an application's architecture to microservices brings in many complexities that make this migration a non-trivial task. In this paper, we report our experience on an ongoing project in PegahTech Co.[1], on migrating an on-premise application named *SSaaS* to microservices architecture. Although the migration steps that we describe in this paper are specific to our project, the necessity of performing these migration activities could be generalized to other projects as well. Furthermore, we summarize some of the challenges we faced and the lessons learned during this project.

The rest of this paper is organized as follows: Sect. 2 briefly explains the background behind the microservices architecture. Section 3 describes the architecture of SSaaS before its migration to microservices. The target architecture to which we migrated SSaaS is described in Sect. 4. Section 5 then discusses our migration plan and the steps that we followed in our migration project. Next, Sect. 6 summarizes the lessons learned in this project. Finally, Sect. 7 concludes the paper.

2   Background

Microservices is a new trend that binds closely to some other new concepts like *Continuous Delivery* and *DevOps*. In this section, we first explain these concepts followed by the background on microservices architecture.

---

[1] http://www.pegahtech.ir.

2.1   Continuous Delivery and DevOps

Continuous Delivery [8] is a software development discipline that enables on demand deployment of a software to any environment. With Continuous Delivery, the software delivery life cycle will be automated as much as possible. It leverages techniques like *Continuous Integration* and *Continuous Deployment* and embraces *DevOps*. The DevOps is a culture that emphasizes the collaboration between developers and operations teams from the beginning of every project in order to reduce time to market and bring agility to all the phases of the software development life cycle. By adopting microservices, the number of services will be increased. Consequently, we need a mechanism for automating the delivery process.

2.2   Microservices

Microservices is a new architectural style [6] that aims to realize software systems as a package of small services, each deployable on a different platform, and running in its own process while communicating through lightweight mechanisms like RESTFull APIs. In this setting, each service is a business capability which can utilize various programming languages and data stores. A system has a microservices architecture when that system is composed of several services without any centralized control [11]. Resilience to failure is another characteristic of microservices as every request in this new setting will be translated to several service calls through the system. The Continuous Delivery and DevOps are also needed to be agile in terms of development and deployment [6].

To have a fully functional microservices architecture and to take advantage of all of its benefits, the following components have to be utilized. Most of these components address the complexities of distributing the business logic among the services:

- *Configuration Server:* It is one of the principles of Continuous Delivery to decouple source code from its configuration. It enables us to change the configuration of our application without redeploying the code. As a microservices architecture have so many services, and their re-deployment is going to be costly, it is better to have a configuration server so that the services could fetch their corresponding configurations.
- *Service Discovery:* In a microservices architecture, there exist several services that each of them might have many instances in order to scale themselves to the underlying load. Thus, keeping track of the deployed services, and their exact address and port number is a cumbersome task. The solution is to use a Service Discovery component in order to get the available instances of each service.
- *Load Balancer:* In order to be scalable, an application should be able to distribute the load on an individual service among its many instances. This is the duty of a Load Balancer, and in this case, it should get available instances from the Service Discovery component.

- *Circuit Breaker:* Fault tolerance should be embedded in every cloud-native application, and it makes more sense in a microservices architecture where lots of dependent services are working together. Failure in each of this services may result in the failure of the whole system. Leveraging patterns like Circuit Breaker [14] can mitigate the corresponding loss to the lowest level.
- *Edge Server:* The Edge Server is an implementation of the *API Gateway* pattern [16] and a wall for exposing external APIs to the public. All the traffic from outside should be routed to internal services through this server. In this way, the clients would not be affected if the internal structures of system's services have changed afterwards.

3   The Architecture of SSaaS Before the Migration

The SSaaS (Server Side as a Service) application was initially started at PegahTech Co. to be a service that provides mobile application developers a facility for doing the server side programming part of their applications without knowing any server side languages. The PegahTech Co. envisions SSaaS as a service that could be scaled to millions of users. The first functionality of SSaaS was a RDBMS as a Service. Developers could define their database schema in the SSaaS website, and the SSaaS service provides them an SDK for their desired target platform (e.g., Android or iOS). Afterwards, the developers can only code in their desired platforms using their domain objects, and the objects would make some service calls on their behalf in order to fulfill their requests. As time goes on, new services are being added to SSaaS like Chat as a Service, Indexing as a Service, NoSQL as a Service, and so on.

SSaaS is written in Java using the Spring framework. The underlying RDBMS is an Oracle 11g. Maven is used for fetching dependencies and building the project. All of the services were in a Git repository, and the modules feature of Maven was used to build different services. At the time of writing this paper, there were no test cases for this project. The deployment of services in development machines was done using the Maven's Jetty plugin. However, the deployment to the production machine was a manual task that had many disadvantages [8].

In Fig. 1, solid arrows and dashed arrows respectively illustrate service calls direction and library dependencies. Figure 1 also indicates that SSaaS consisted of the following five components before the migration:

- *CommonLib:* This is a place for putting shared functionalities, like utility classes, that are going to be used by the rest of the system.
- *DeveloperData:* This holds the information of developers who are using the SSaaS service and their domain model metadata entities that are shared between the DeveloperServices and the ContentServices components.
- *DeveloperServices:* This is where the services related to managing the domain model of developers' projects reside in. Using these services, developers could add new models, edit existing ones, and so on.

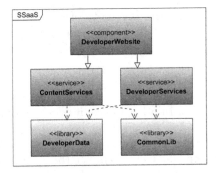

Fig. 1. The architecture of SSaaS before the migration

- *ContentServices:* This holds the services that the target SDK is using in order to perform the CRUD operations on the model's objects.
- *DeveloperWebsite:* This is an application written in HTML and JQuery and acts as a dashboard for developers. For this purpose, it leverages the DeveloperServices component.

3.1   Why Did We Plan to Migrate Towards the Microservices?

What motivated us to perform a migration to a microservices architecture was a problem raised with a requirement for a Chat as a Service. To implement this requirement, we chose *ejabberd*[2] due to its known built-in scalability and its ability to run on clusters. To this end, we wrote a script in *python* that enabled ejabberd to perform authentications using our system. After preparing everything, the big issue in our service was the *on demand* capability, otherwise our service was useless. In the following, we discuss the reasons that motivated us to choose the microservices architecture:

The need for reusability: To address the above issue, we started to automate the process of setting up a chat service. One of these steps was to set up a database for each user. We were hoping that this was also a step in creating RDBMS projects that we can reuse. After investigating the RDBMS service creation process, we recognized that there was not anything to satisfy our new requirement. To clarify further, there was a pool of servers in place. Each of these servers had an instance of the Oracle DBMS installed and an instance of DeveloperServices running. During the creation of a RDBMS project, a server was selected randomly and related users and tablespaces were created in the Oracle server. The mentioned design had several issues since it was just designed to fulfill the RDBMS service needs, and it was tightly coupled to the Oracle server. Nevertheless, we needed MySQL database for ejabberd and we should add this functionality to the system. After struggling a bit with the system, we recognized that we were just revamping the current bad design. What we needed

---

[2] https://www.ejabberd.im/.

was a database reservation system that both of our services could make use of. Thinking more generally, we needed a backing resources reservation system. This was the first step towards making cohesive services that can be reused by other parts of the system.

The need for decentralized data governance: Another problem was that every time anyone wanted to add some metadata about different services, they were added to the DeveloperData. In other words, it was kind of an integration point among the services. It was not a good habit because services were independent units that were only sharing their contracts with other parts of the system. Consequently, another step was to re-architect the system so that any services could govern its own metadata and data by themselves.

The need for automated deployment: As the number of services was growing, another problem was to automate the deployment process and to decouple the build life cycle of each service from other services as much as possible. This can happen using the Configuration Server and the Continuous Delivery components.

The need for built-in scalability: As mentioned before, the vision of SSaaS is to serve millions of users. By increasing the number of services, we needed a new approach for handling this kind of scalability because scaling services individually needs a lot of work and can be error-prone. Therefore, to handle this problem, our solution was to locate service instances dynamically through the Service Discovery component and balancing the load among them using the internal Load Balancer component.

To summarize, new requirements pushed us to introduce new services, and new services brought in new non-functional requirements as mentioned above. Hence, we got advantage of microservices to satisfy these new requirements.

4   The Target Architecture of SSaaS After the Migration

In order to realize microservices architecture and to satisfy our new requirements, we transformed the core architecture of our system to a target architecture by undergoing some architectural refactorings. These changes included introducing microservices-specific components as explained in Sect. 2 and re-architecting the current system as will be discussed in this section. The final architecture is depicted in Fig. 2.

The new technology stack for the development was including the Spring Boot[3] for its embedded application server, fast service initialization, using the operating system's environment variables for configuration, and the Spring Cloud[4] Context and the Config Server to separate the configuration from the source code as recommended by Continuous Delivery. Additionally, we chose the Netflix OSS[5] for providing some of the microservices-specific components, i.e. Service Discovery, and the Spring Cloud Netflix that integrates the Spring

---

[3] http://projects.spring.io/spring-boot.

[4] http://projects.spring.io/spring-cloud.

[5] http://netflix.github.io.

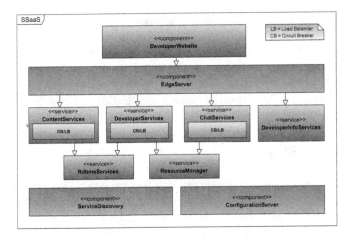

Fig. 2. Target architecture of SSaaS after the migration

framework with the Netflix OSS project. We also chose Eureka for Service Discovery, Ribbon as Load Balancer, Hystrix as Circuit Breaker and Zuul as Edge Server, that all are parts of the Netflix OSS project. We specifically chose Ribbon among other load balancers, i.e. HAProxy[6], because of its integration with the Spring framework and other Netflix OSS projects, in particular Eureka. Additionally, it is an internal load balancer, so we do not need to deploy an external one.

4.1 How Did We Re-Architect the System and Refactor the Data?

In the state-of-the-art about microservices [13,18], *Domain Driven Design* [4,19] and *Bounded Context* [4,19] are introduced as common practices to transform the system's architecture into microservices. As we did not have a complex domain, we decided to re-architect the system based on domain entities in DeveloperData. We put every set of cohesive entities into a service, such that the only one which can create and update that entity would be that service. For example, only the ChatServices service could update or create the chat metadata entities. Other services can only have copies of the data that they do not own, e.g., for the purpose of caching. However, they should be careful about synchronization with the master data as their copy could be stale. With respect to this discussion, the list of architectural changes to reach the target architecture is the following:

- Letting the ChatServices service handle its metadata by itself and not inside the DeveloperData.
- Introducing a new Resource Manager service in order to reserve resources like databases. The entities related to Oracle server instances will be moved from DeveloerData to this service.

---

[6] http://www.haproxy.org.

- Introducing a new service to handle developer's information and its registered services.
- Transforming DeveloperData from a library to a service. Therefore, DeveloperServices and ContentServices have to be adapted such that they can make service calls to DeveloperData instead of method calls. Please note that the remaining data in DeveloperData are just RDBMS entities like Table and Column.

5   Migration Steps

Migrating the system towards the target architecture is not a one-step procedure and should be done incrementally and in several steps without affecting the end-users of the system. Furthermore, as the number of services is growing, we need a mechanism for automating the delivery process. In this section, we describe how we migrated SSaaS using the following eight steps:

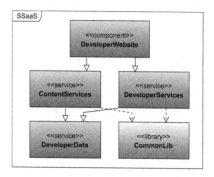

Fig. 3. Transforming DeveloperData to a service

5.1   Preparing the Continuous Integration Pipeline

Continuous integration is the first step for having an effective Continuous Delivery. It allows developers to integrate their work with the others' early and often, and helps to prevent future conflicts [8]. To this end, a continuous integration (CI) server, an as-a-service or self-hosted code repository, and an artifact repository is needed. We chose Jenkins[7] as the CI server, self-hosted Gitlab[8] as the code repository, and Artifactory[9] as the artifact repository (cf. Fig. 8).

By adopting microservices, the number of services will increase. As each of these services can have a number of instances running, deploying them by virtualization is not cost-effective and can introduce a lot of computational overhead.

---

[7] https://jenkins-ci.org.
[8] https://about.gitlab.com.
[9] http://www.jfrog.com/open-source.

Furthermore, we may need to use Configuration Management systems in order to create the exact test and production environments. *Containerization* is a new trend that is well suited for microservices. By utilizing containers, we can deploy service instances with lower overheads than the virtualization, and in isolation. Additionally, we would not hear phrases like "this works on my machine" anymore because we are using the exact environments and artifacts in both of the development and production environments. Another major benefit is *portability* since we can deploy anywhere that supports containerization without any changes to our source codes or container images. Many public cloud providers such as Google and Amazon now have a support for containerization.

Docker[10] is a tool for containerization of applications, and it is now becoming the de-facto standard for containerization in industry. There is a pool of ready to use images in the Docker Hub, the central docker image repository, that can be pulled and customized based on specific needs. Docker Registry[11] is another project that let organizations to have a private docker image repository. As we are going to use Docker, we need Docker Registry to be in our pipeline as well.

To summarize, in this step, we installed and integrated the Gitlab, Jenkins, Artifactory and Docker Registry as a CI pipeline.

5.2 Transforming DeveloperData to a Service

In this step, we changed DeveloperData to use Spring Boot because of its advantages (see Sect. 4). Furthermore as shown in Fig. 3, we changed it to expose its functionalities as a REST API. In this way, its dependent services would not be affected when the internal structure of DeveloperData changes. Since they have service-level dependency, the governance of DeveloperData entities will be done by a single service and DeveloperData would not act as an Integration Database [7] for its dependent services anymore. Accordingly, we adapted DeveloperServices and ContentServices to use DeveloperData as a service and not as a Maven dependency.

5.3 Introducing Continuous Delivery

A best practice in the Continuous Delivery is to separate the source code, the configuration, and the environment specification so that they can evolve independently [8]. In this way, we can change the configuration without redeploying the source code. By leveraging Docker, we removed the need for specifying environments since the Docker images produce the same behavior in different environments. In order to separate the source code and the configuration, we ported every service to Spring Boot and changed them to use the Spring Cloud Configuration Server and the Spring Cloud Context for resolving their configuration values (cf. Fig. 4). In this step, we also separated services' code repositories to have a clearer change history and to separate the build life cycle of each service.

---

[10] https://www.docker.com.

[11] https://docs.docker.com/registry.

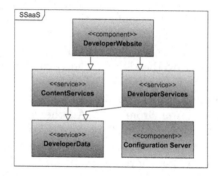

Fig. 4. Introducing configuration server

We also created the Dockerfile for each service that is a configuration for creating Docker images for that service. After doing all of the mentioned tasks, we created a CI job per service and ran them in order to populate our repositories. Having the Docker image of each service in our private Docker registry, we were able to run the whole system with Docker Compose[12] using only one configuration file. Starting from this step, we had an automated deployment on a single server.

5.4 Introducing Edge Server

As we were going to re-architect the system and it was supposed to change the internal service architecture, in this step, we introduced Edge Server to the system to minimize the impact of internal changes on end-users as shown in Fig. 5. Accordingly, we adapted DeveloperWebsite.

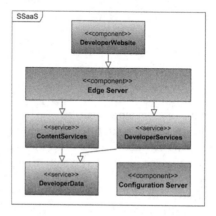

Fig. 5. Introducing edge server

---

[12] https://docs.docker.com/compose.

5.5   Introducing Dynamic Service Collaboration

In this step, we introduced Service Discovery, Load Balancer and Circuit Breaker to the system as shown in Fig. 6. Dependent services should locate each other via the Service Discovery and Load Balancer; and the Circuit Breaker will make our system more resilient during the service calls. By introducing these components to the system sooner, we made our developers more comfortable with these new concepts, and it increased our speed for the rest of the migration and of course, in introducing new services.

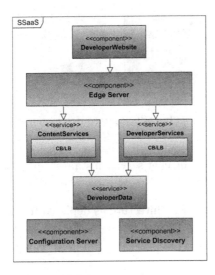

Fig. 6. Introducing dynamic service collaboration

5.6   Introducing Resource Manager

In this step, we introduced the Resource Manager by factoring out the entities that were related to servers, i.e. AvailableServer, from DeveloperData and introducing some new features, i.e. MySQL database reservation, for satisfying our chat service requirements (cf. Fig. 7). Accordingly, we adapted DeveloperServices to use this service for database reservations.

5.7   Introducing ChatServices and DeveloperInfoServices

As the final step in re-architecting the system, we introduced the following services:

– *DeveloperInfoServices* by factoring out developer related entities (e.g., Developer) from DeveloperData.

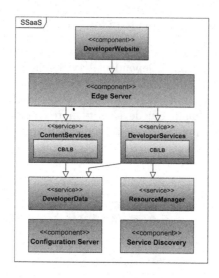

Fig. 7. Introducing resource manager

– *ChatServices* for persisting chat service instances metadata and handling chat service instance creations.

This led us to the target architecture as depicted in Fig. 2.

5.8 Clusterization

Compared to virtualization, one of the main features of containerization is its low overhead. Due to this feature, people started to make it more efficient by introducing lightweight operating systems, like CoreOS[13] and Project Atomic, that only have the minimal parts to host many containers. Google Kubernetes[14], that has a good integration with the CoreOS, is a tool for easy deployments of containers on a cluster. Using Kubernetes, a container can be easily fetched from a private repository and deployed to a cluster with different policies. For example, a service can be deployed with three always available instances.

In this step, we set up a cluster of CoreOS instances with Kubernetes agents installed on them. Next, we deployed our services on this cluster instead of a single server. The final delivery pipeline is shown in Fig. 8.

In Sect. 5, we described the incremental process of migrating the SSaaS application towards the microservices architecture. This migration was actually performed in three dimensions: re-architecting the current system, introducing new supporting services, and enabling Continuous Delivery in the system. The important point to note is that how we incrementally evolved the system in all these three dimensions together. Despite the smoothness of the explained process, we

---

[13] https://coreos.com.
[14] http://kubernetes.io.

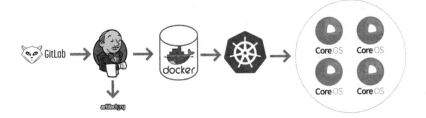

Fig. 8. The final delivery pipeline

faced several challenges in this process as well. Section 6 discusses some of the lessons we learned during this process.

6 Lessons Learned

Migrating an on-premise application to a microservices architecture is a non-trivial task. During this migration, we faced several challenges that we were able to solve. In the following, we share some of the lessons we learned in this process that we think might be helpful for others who are also trying to migrate to microservices:

- *Deployment in the development environment is difficult:* Introducing new services to the system will put a big burden on developers. It is true that the application's code is now in isolated services. However, to run those services in their machines, developers need to deploy the dependent services as well. For example, the service registry should be deployed as well in order to have a working system. These kinds of deployment complexities are not normal for a novice developer. Hence, there should be a facility in place for setting up such a development environment with a minimum amount of effort. In our case, we chose the Docker Compose to easily deploy dependent services from our private Docker registry.
- *Service contracts are double important:* Changing so many services that only expose their contracts to each other could be an error-prone task. Even a small change in the contracts can break a part of the system or even the system as a whole. Service versioning is a solution. Nonetheless, it could make the deployment procedure of each service even more complex. Therefore, people usually do not recommend service versioning in microservices. Thus, techniques like Tolerant Reader [3] are more advisable in order to avoid service versioning. Consumer-driven contracts [3] could be a great help in this regard, as the team responsible for the service can be confident that most of their consumers are satisfied with their service.
- *Distributed system development needs skilled developers:* Microservices is a distributed architectural style. Furthermore, in order for it to be fully functional, it needs some supporting services like service registry, load balancer,

and so on. Hence, to get the most out of microservices, those team members are needed who are familiar with these concepts and are comfortable with this type of programming.

- *Creating service development templates is important:* Polyglot persistence and the usage of different programming languages are promises of microservices. Nevertheless, in practice, a radical interpretation of these promises could result in a chaos in the system and make it even unmaintainable. Consequently, having standards is a must in order to avoid chaos. Different languages and data stores can be used, but it should be in a controlled and standard way. As a solution, having service development templates for each leveraged language is essential. It would reduce the burden of development since people can easily fork the template and just start developing.
- *Microservices is not a silver bullet:* Microservices was beneficial for us because we needed that amount of flexibility in our system, and that we had the Spring Cloud and Netflix OSS that made our migration and development a lot easier. However, as mentioned before, by adopting microservices so many complexities would be introduced to the system that require a lot of effort to be addressed. Therefore, these challenges should be considered before the adoption of microservices. In other words, maybe our problems could be solved more easily by applying another architectural style or solution.

7   Conclusions and Future Work

In this paper, we explained our experience during the migration of an on-premise application to the microservices architectural style. In particular, we provided the architecture of our system before and after the migration and the steps that we followed for this migration. Furthermore, we highlighted the importance of Continuous Delivery in the process of adopting microservices. Finally, we discussed the lessons learned during this migration.

In future, we plan to consolidate these practices and develop a set of reusable patterns for migrating on-premise applications to microservices architectural style. These patterns should generalize the process that we used in this paper, but in a well-defined structure that can be instantiated independently, similarly to the approach that we devised in [10].

Acknowledgments. The work of Pooyan Jamshidi has been supported by the Irish Centre for Cloud Computing and Commerce (IC4) and by the Horizon 2020 project no. 644869 (DICE).

References

1. Ardagna, D., di Nitto, E., Mohagheghi, P., Mosser, S., Ballagny, C., D'Andria, F., Casale, G., Matthews, P., Nechifor, C.S., Petcu, D., Gericke, A., Sheridan, C.: Modaclouds: a model-driven approach for the design and execution of applications on multiple clouds. In: 4th International Workshop on Modelling in Software Engineering (MISE), pp. 50–56, June 2012

2. Bergmayr, A., Bruneliere, H., Canovas Izquierdo, J., Gorronogoitia, J., Kousiouris, G., Kyriazis, D., Langer, P., Menychtas, A., Orue-Echevarria, L., Pezuela, C., Wimmer, M.: Migrating legacy software to the cloud with artist. In: 17th European Conference on Software Maintenance and Reengineering (CSMR), pp. 465–468, March 2013
3. Daigneau, R.: Service Design Patterns: Fundamental Design Solutions for SOAP/WSDL and Restful Web Services. Addison-Wesley Professional, Reading (2011)
4. Evans, E.: Domain-driven Design: Tackling Complexity in the Heart of Software. Addison-Wesley Professional, Reading (2004)
5. Fehling, C., Leymann, F., Ruehl, S., Rudek, M., Verclas, S.: Service migration patterns - decision support and best practices for the migration of existing service-based applications to cloud environments. In: 6th IEEE International Conference on Service-Oriented Computing and Applications (SOCA), pp. 9–16, December 2013
6. Fowler, M., Lewis, J.: Microservices. http://martinfowler.com/articles/microservices.html. Accessed 15 Jun 2015
7. Hohpe, G., Woolf, B.: Enterprise Integration Patterns: Designing, Building, and Deploying Messaging Solutions. Addison-Wesley Professional, Reading (2004)
8. Humble, J., Farley, D.: Continuous delivery: Reliable Software Releases through Build, Test, and Deployment Automation. Addison-Wesley Professional, Reading (2010)
9. Jamshidi, P., Ahmad, A., Pahl, C.: Cloud migration research: a systematic review. IEEE Trans. Cloud Comput. 1(2), 142–157 (2013)
10. Jamshidi, P., Pahl, C., Chinenyeze, S., Liu, X.: Cloud migration patterns: a multi-cloud service architecture perspective. In: Toumani, F., et al. (eds.) Service-Oriented Computing - ICSOC 2014 Workshops. LNCS, vol. 8954, pp. 6–9. Springer, Switzerland (2015)
11. Martin, R.: Clean micro-service architecture. http://blog.cleancoder.com/uncle-bob/2014/10/01/CleanMicroserviceArchitecture.html. Accessed 15 June 2015
12. Mendonca, N.: Architectural options for cloud migration. Computer 47(8), 62–66 (2014)
13. Newman, S.: Building Microservices. O'Reilly Media, Sebastopol (2015)
14. Nygard, M.: Release It!: Design and Deploy Production-Ready Software. Pragmatic Bookshelf, Raleigh (2007)
15. Calçado, P.: Building products at soundcloud. https://developers.soundcloud.com/blog/building-products-at-soundcloud-part-1-dealing-with-the-monolith. Accessed 15 June 2015
16. Richardson, C.: Microservices architecture (2014). http://microservices.io/. Accessed 15 June 2015
17. Borsje, S.: How we build microservices at karma. https://blog.yourkarma.com/building-microservices-at-karma. Accessed 15 June 2015
18. Stine, M.: Migrating to Cloud-Native Application Architectures. O'Reilly Media, Sebastopol (2015)
19. Vernon, V.: Implementing Domain-driven Design. Addison-Wesley Professional, Reading (2013)

Cloud Computing for e-Sciences at Université Sorbonne Paris Cité

Leila Abidi[1], Christophe Cérin[1(✉)], Danielle Geldwerth-Feniger[2], and Marie Lafaille[1,2]

[1] Université de Paris 13, LIPN UMR CNRS 7030, UMR CNRS 7244, 99, Avenue Jean-Baptiste Clément, 93430 Villetaneuse, France
{leila.abidi,christophe.cerin}@lipn.univ-paris13.fr
[2] Université de Paris 13, UMR CNRS 7030 - CSPBAT, UMR CNRS 7244, 99, Avenue Jean-Baptiste Clément, 93430 Villetaneuse, France
{danielle.geldwerth-feniger,marie.lafaille}@univ-paris13.fr

Abstract. The present paper relates the involvement towards migration and adoption of cloud computing at Université Sorbonne Paris Cité (USPC), a major french consortium of universities and higher education and research institutes. Migration to the cloud for a wide and diverse community of actors is nevertheless not straightforward. The ambitious interdisciplinary program 'Imageries du Vivant' (IDV or 'Life Imaging') at USPC, a key program dedicated to the development and use of life and biomedical imaging, constitutes our use case. It allows to sketch how cloud computing may change scientific practices and the landscape of computing, and to specify the steps to be followed for such purposes. The outcome of the paper is a methodology for accompanying adequate technological choices and acceptance by the users of the cultural changes when they migrate to cloud technologies. In short, we provide useful guidance for cloud adoption based on observations made for the IDV project.

Keywords: Cloud computing · Inter/multi-disciplinary projects · e-Sciences engineering · Methodologies for cloud migration and adoption

1 Introduction

Cloud computing technology potentially offers permanent access to data and services, from any device and anywhere at any time. Basically, it considers everything 'as a service': computing, storage, network, and infrastructure. As a generic term, cloud computing also describes a category of sophisticated, on-demand Internet Technology (IT) services, popularized through providers such Amazon, Google and Microsoft. Cloud computing puts the individual users at the center of the system, and allows him to deploy, on-demand, software, development platforms or even the infrastructure he needs.

A. Celesti and P. Leitner (Eds.): ESOCC 2015 Workshops, CCIS 567, pp. 216–227, 2016.
DOI: 10.1007/978-3-319-33313-7_16

Cloud computing may help to meet many challenges within educational institutions and research laboratories: data storage, computing, collaborative work, communication, mobility, on-line education, technical supports, costs, human resources management. Therefore, Université Sorbonne Paris Cité (USPC), a major consortium of french universities, decided to join efforts and to develop a capacity in the promising cloud computing technology area. To this end, USPC is currently funding several projects related to infrastructure and e-Sciences.

Our paper relates our experience in constructing the cloud technology for USPC, mainly by depicting current thinking related to cloud usage in our communities (researchers, teachers, technicians and engineers, decision makers). The paper deals with two main points. How - from a technical point of view - can we migrate to the cloud? To what extent do we share conception on cloud technologies in order to be able to design and adopt a cloud? This work focuses on migration towards the cloud for an ambitious interdisciplinary program at USPC, the Imageries du Vivant (IDV or 'Life Imaging') program.

The organization of the paper is as follows. In Sect. 2, we motivate our work by presenting the general objectives of cloud migration and adoption. In Sect. 3, we introduce the institutional context at USPC. We also present and analyze a survey related to the IDV program and summarize current pieces of work on cloud adoption. In Sect. 4, we present the main architectural choices of the USPC cloud infrastructure, and their adequacy to meet the needs of the IDV program. Section 5 concludes the paper.

2   The General Context of Cloud Adoption and Migration

The cloud industry forum[1] focused on the current individual practices that organizations need to address while designing their processes towards cloud migration and adoption. Four categories cleared up:

1. IT and data governance, which deals with maintaining data integrity and measuring data safety.
2. Architect solution, which deals with designing private/public cloud service provisions, architectures, technical standards and management tools.
3. Adoption process, which addresses the critical factors and steps towards ensuring effective cloud adoption
4. Security, which addresses access for remote users, and key factors like data privacy, device safety, regulatory compliance, business continuity.

Our empirical work mainly focuses on the category of Adoption process, and implements some of the recommendations from the cloud industry forum. We put emphasis on individual current practices i.e. the ways people use computers in their daily work, how they behave and on whom they rely. We are conducting this study because we are faced to a lack of methods for accompanying the changes associated with cloud adoption. USPC, as a big university and the Conférence des

---

[1] http://cloudindustryforum.org/knowledge-hub/preparation.

Présidents d'Université (CPU[2]) formulated in May 2015 ten general proposals for the digital area. Among those, the following items underline the relevance of our study and constitute our research gap: *Establishing infrastructure to deal with public data produced by research, teaching and training; Organizing open and participative sciences with data flows for research and innovation; Appropriating the new ways of work organization that are generated by the digital era.*

One limitation of our work is that we are not the decision makers at all the different steps of the process leading to cloud adoption. For instance, people managing the computing facilities are also legitimate to promote cloud technologies because they have technical skills in the choice of cloud middleware as well as in the administration of such large scale systems. USPC staff members manage the different budgets and allocate them not only for cloud platforms but also for other platforms. We are representing one large community (IDV members) and we need to negotiate and seek consensus with others. This explain why in this study we focus mainly on the discussions with the IDV members. One outcome of these discussions is a big picture of needs in order to calibrate in part the cloud infrastructure and the budget to allocate and to negotiate. Our current methodology is now reused to explore the needs of people in Social Sciences. Another outcome is the working group on data management setup in the spirit of what we are doing for the IDV project. New insights into technical and legal issues are under concern for data related to patients in hospitals.

3   The Université Sorbonne Paris Cité and the IDV Interdisciplinary Program Use Case

3.1   Institutional Context at Université Sorbonne Paris Cité

Université Sorbonne Paris Cité (USPC) is one of the major consortium of french universities. It gathers four Parisian universities and four institutes for higher education and research. In addition to 120.000 students, USPC hosts numerous research teams most often also affiliated to the different french public research institutions. USPC puts strong emphasis on the quality of training and on research development, and gathers approximately 17.000 researchers, teachers, engineers and technicians. The USPC infrastructures dedicated to experimental sciences present strengths and weaknesses that directly arise from the wide internal diversity. Some institutes greatly call for scientific computing, have access to national super-computing facilities, and have been using cluster/grid computing for a while. This is the case for IPGP but it is far less developed for practitioners from life and health sciences, that constitute most members of the IDV community.

3.2   The IDV Program and Network

Program Partnership and Organization. The IDV program is a multidisciplinary and interdisciplinary program centered on the development and use of

---

[2] http://www.cpu.fr/actualite/colloque-annuel-de-la-cpu-les-10-propositions/.

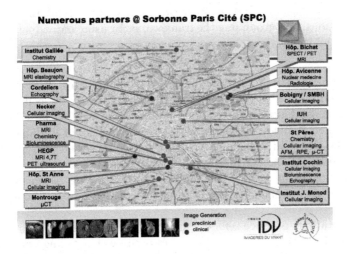

Fig. 1. The location of the different IDV participants working on image generation (non exhaustive list).

life imaging. It was founded at the end of 2014 for a 4 years period, and currently gathers approximately 200 researchers from USPC. USPC partly supports the operational expenses of the program, and the costs of some human resources, such as master and PhD students, post-docs, or support engineers.

The various partner teams belong either to academic research laboratories, to private chemical and pharmaceutical companies, to *in vivo* (clinical and preclinical) and cellular imaging core-facilities, as well as to hospital imaging departments (radiology, nuclear medicine, anatomy and histo-pathology). They are geographically widely scattered, as illustrated by the map on Fig. 1 which precises the location of the groups dedicated to image generation (i.e. developments in physical imaging set-ups and chemical imaging agents).

The Three Main Objectives of IDV. Building a smart multi-modality and multi-scale life imaging atlas is the first main objective of the IDV program. An integrative and advanced intelligent atlas should help unifying the growing body of images generated among the various partners of USPC, and should improve reuse of the data. It should allow to extract information from large image data-sets, as well as to integrate data from various individuals and instrumental origins, levels and complexities, connecting the project to the challenges and expectations of the 'Big Data'.

Validating imaging biomarkers for personal health and education constitutes a second main objective of IDV. Reflecting knowledge transfer from the level of a general population to the individual level, biomarker validation relies on large data sets analysis which warrants the development of precision medicine and education.

The third objective of IDV aims at providing ethical, legal and economical recommendations, and grounding the frameworks for using individual biomedical and imaging information.

Benefits Expected from Increasing Cloud Usage and Migration. Individual image annotations constitute the background work for constructing an advanced intelligent atlas. The various professionals within the IDV network have - from their individual training and/or with the help of loadable dedicated software - the technical skills and expertise to annotate their own images. Such annotation aims at defining high level semantic features that describe a given image or image set in a way that goes beyond extracting parameters strictly related to the image content as are pixel histograms, texture and morphological information.

The annotations produce semantic information associated with a given data set, and constitute the background for appropriately structuring knowledge in a given application field, most frequently by relying on the use of field dedicated ontologies. By associating detailed annotations at various levels of a common data base, and seeking for relevance feedback on a given query from others experts in a network, connected experts within the network become able not only to personalize their production, but also to improve the global performances of the community because of crowdsourcing and resulting mobilization of the collective intelligence.

The discovery and validation of imaging biomarkers generally require that researchers start from pre-clinical development on animal models, and further go on to translation towards clinical applications. Here also, fusion of data coming from different scales and/or imaging methods directly contributes to reach valuable and pertinent translation.

Last, acceding to and sharing data concerning individual human beings meet ethical and legal concerns. Besides technological solutions, it is necessary to elaborate guidelines to be taken into account while setting the rules that govern access to databases and defining their indexations.

3.3   Dedicated Survey for the IDV Program

Survey Settings. We set up a survey of our use case at USPC with the aim to provide, at the beginning of the project, an overview of all the scientific activities, methods and tools used by the IDV members, as well as the current life cycle(s) of the data used in their daily work. The 200 members belong to 30 different teams from research laboratories, imaging core facilities and departments from 14 hospitals. This community is very diverse in terms of initial training, background disciplinary fields and practice. The following fields are represented among the members: physics, chemistry, biology, medicine, psychology, pharmacy, mathematics and computer sciences for image processing, data sciences and humanities like law and applied ethics. The survey was divided into 3 main parts: the identity of the members, their scientific approach (what are the important processes in your work?) and the life cycle of their data (how, where, how much, whom is data produced? and how long is it conserved?).

The answers from participating members were collected using the Sphinx-Online (v3.1.2) platform which contains management tools of the survey such as a WYSIWYG editor, revivals by emails, classification of answers, statistics and tools for automatic chart drawing. The results presented below have been obtained during a seventeen-week period covering questioning to final analysis.

Survey Analysis. By mid-April 2015, we had collected answers from different structures which are well representative of the wide disciplinary diversity within the IDV program. Answers were indeed obtained from 20 teams in 18 academic research laboratories, 4 teams from 3 imaging core facilities and hospital departments, and one small company specialized in ethical and legal issues while using personal data.

What is the typical profile of an IDV member? Most IDV members (75 %) are researchers from public academic laboratories. Some teams are affiliated to the CNRS (47 %), to the INSERM (28 %) and to the 'Assistance Publique Hôpitaux de Paris - AP-HP' (16 %). The community can roughly be divided into 2 populations: on one hand, a 'biologist population', for whom experiences, observation and statistical analyzes are central to the research process; on the other hand, a 'computer scientist population', who very routinely uses theoretical calculations, models and numerical simulations. Respectively, half of the IDV members, and more than one third, work in teams from 3 to 5 and 5 to 10 researchers. Collaboration among scientists from different teams or even laboratories is widespread practice. Indeed, more than 70 % of answers confirmed that they needed sharing data with other teams in their daily work.

Image Formats and Software. Because of the wide disciplinary field coverage and because so many different structures are involved, many image formats as well software elements are currently used within the IDV community. Among the 20 different image formats counted, TIFF and DICOM are the most commonly used. More than 70 different software elements are daily used, with Matlab and ImageJ by far the most popular.

Data Characteristics, Storage Location and Data Preservation. In most cases (64 %), the volume of data annually produced by individual members is quite low (< 1 TB) and it rarely exceeds 100 TB (for 7 % of collected answers). Half of the image data contain tags or meta-data; image data mostly require post-treatment for full interpretation (80 %). Some kind of images are thoroughly analyzed (more than 14 extracted parameters, for 17 % of collected answers). Other images could be sources of additional information. Less than 5 parameters are indeed extracted for almost half of the images.

For data storage, local physical supports (i.e. hard drives) are widely used (more than 70 % of collected answers) at each step of the research process, i.e. before, during and after the data treatment. This practice does not allow easy nor efficient data sharing among scientists and laboratories. The spatial fragmentation leads to frequently under-exploited data, and hard drive crashes often generate data loss. Only few IDV members use online solutions, i.e. clouds (around 10 % of collected answers). Long term data preservation is far from current practices, with approximately one half of all the data produced by the IDV members deleted within the 10 years following production.

3.4   Current Reference Surveys About Cloud Adoption

Our IDV survey has been setup to avoid major overlapping according to what we know about the expectation of e-Sciences communities like with the XSEDE survey we now introduce. In our context, two surveys dedicated to cloud adoption technology and a research paper were used as general guidelines for gaining insight into the needs and practices of the IDV community. This selection of related works also allows a clear positioning of our work which is more focused and less general because the community has been identified by USPC before the project on cloud adoption.

The first work is the retrospective study carried out by the Extreme Science and Engineering Discovery Environment (XSEDE) on a large community of researchers in the USA. The second one is an advance poll recently initiated for educational purposes in Arab countries. It is designed by The Arab League Educational, Cultural and Scientific Organization (ALECSO), the Arab Regional Office of ITU (the United Nations agency specialized for information and communication technologies) and the Arab Telecom Regulators Network (AREGNET).

A previous analysis of the researchers practices and needs was carried out from September 2012 to April 2013, through XSEDE, a virtual system that scientists use to interactively share computing resources and expertise. The information collected therefore only concerns researchers, albeit from 80 different projects related to a wide range of knowledge and disciplines (sciences, engineering, humanities and fine arts). Reasons that emerged for using the cloud were mainly: (1) on-demand access for bursting resources; (2) high throughput scientific workflows and data analysis; (3) enhanced collaboration through data sharing and deployment of the individual Web sites of the research teams.

The qualitative feedback about benefits and challenges when using the cloud was inferred. Some technical dimensions of cloud usage were also quantified (number of cores used at peak/steady state, bandwidth in/out of the cloud, amount of data stored in the cloud). Building domain-specific computing environments emerged as one of the programming models sought in the cloud, with others such as high throughput, embarrassingly parallel workloads, academic research and teaching tools, current software, scientific portals, real-time event-driven sciences. Our proposal for cloud adoption by the IDV program at USPC mainly corresponds to the construction of a domain specific computing environment, relying on virtual machines for image analysis, as we will develop below.

The second survey, very recently started (June 2015), aims to anticipate the needs for computing based infrastructure, software and services for educational purposes. It focuses on a wider public than the XSEDE survey since it concerns not only researchers but all stake-holders in relation to education and research, namely also teachers and students, IT managers and decision-makers. Researchers, teachers and students all need to access to services and resources from any device, anywhere, at any time. IT managers are especially concerned by simplification in management and monitoring, as well as by the associated technical operations. Last but not least, decision-makers want to control the costs and to have actual plan and policies to concretely display the infrastructures, all purposes for which our own expertise was requested.

Reference paper [16] introduces scenario to illustrate how the researchers, teachers and engineers can benefit from the grid infrastructure.

4 Building the Dedicated IDV-USPC Cloud Infrastructure

4.1 Details of the Proposed Infrastructure for IDV

At least three big instruments related to computing coexist at USPC because of historical reasons: the S-Capad cluster at IPGP, the MAGI cluster at Paris 13 and the Cumulus cloud system located at Paris 5. The USPC board of governors decided to call for a common project aimed at federating all existing infrastructures.

USPC universities and institutes were asked to express their needs for common infrastructures and for sharing 'more than in the past'. A round table was organized to depict common needs from individual answers. Three projects aimed at consolidating the S-Capad, MAGI and Paris 5 infrastructures. S-Capad and MAGI received budgets to increase their nodes number for a total of about 2500 and 1000 cores respectively. Paris 5 received a budget for the Cumulus cloud for a storage capacity of about 1.5 PB, extensible to 2.3 PB, and for the production of approximately 500 virtual machines (VM). The choice of the cloud middleware for the Paris 5 infrastructure is OpenNebula[3]. Moreover, providing some technical support for OpenNebula is also a matter of negotiation.

The administrators of the three systems are presently working together to federate identities and procedures, in order to facilitate individual access and registration to the future pooled infrastructure. The current procedure for getting an account onto the MAGI cluster is very straightforward, and requires no authorization from the system administrator, even for requesters that are extraneous to Paris 13 university. In this later case, the requester is only required to provide the name, email and agreement of a sponsoring godfather to obtain an account. For historical reasons, the access procedure to the S-Capad cluster is less flexible, and requires validations by several intermediaries.

---

[3] http://opennebula.org.

USPC also hired a research engineer to perform the scientific animation of the pooled infrastructure, in particular for public not yet familiar with cloud usage. The research engineer will also propose social networking-like tools for the users of the infrastructure, federate the existing Web sites, and propose new policies. Last, he will also build the development policies of the pooled infrastructure, and analyze the whole bunch of accommodated data. Dealing with anonymous data from the patients in hospitals remains a hot topic, nevertheless out of the scope of this paper.

4.2　Impact of Cloud Migration on the IDV Program

The survey and discussions with the IDV members clearly indicate the necessity to focus first on image display and archiving. Image analysis and treatment, as well as matching between images, will be developed secondly. Thus, we consider below the storage and the VM system only (and not the renovated cluster systems available at USPC). This choice helps us to build a base to be enriched later on and to solve all remaining problems.

Basically, image visualization is straightforward: all you need is the right software for the right image format. This is easy when you work on your local computer with only two or three software packages. But, in a collaborative network with over twenty different formats and seventy different software packages, sharing image visualization becomes a problem. A first alternative consists to 'cloudify' all the software in order to be able to deal with all formats. This is technically feasible but costly in time and human resources. Moreover, the result is not guaranteed, especially in the case of proprietary software and the constraints on studying, distributing and modifying the source code. A second alternative consists to 'cloudify' a selection from the most frequently used software, such as ImageJ or OsiriX. ImageJ can display, edit, analyze, process and save images. It can read many image file formats, including TIFF, PNG, GIF, JPEG, BMP, DICOM and FITS, as well as raw formats [13]. OsiriX is the most widely used DICOM viewer in the world [14]. A third alternative would consist to display all the image formats with a single software, but this is highly challenging, if not unrealizable. We chose the second alternative and we are developing it as follows.

Cloudification. Our cloudification consists in providing software and infrastructure as services in the distributed architecture of the cloud. Technically, we chose to connect and make accessible pre-defined templates of VMs that will contain a certain number of pre-installed tools, the most frequently used ones, as depicted from our initial survey, like ImageJ. Nevertheless, we do not exclude the possibility for each individual user to further install other tools, and customize his own VM. We should thus be able to customize every working environment, starting from the tools provided by the operating system, and integrating individually all personal tools. Linux, in one of its versions, will be the operating system by default. The communication for downloading images between the VMs and our data center will occur through a secure protocol.

Presently, we are investigating which configurations are best suited to the future pooled infrastructure. We must decide how the desktop applications - for instance developed under the Java framework - will be worked out. There are indeed two possibilities for running them out. Either on the client browser, with data pushed from the server/to the client; or on the server side, through a VM in the cloud, and with transfer of all the computation work to the client browser through the network.

Atlas. As underlined above, the intelligent atlas should increase the a *posteriori* exploitation of the huge mass of images generated within USPC. Individual users should be able to perform queries for similarity to a given image or image set (so called the query image). The procedure for searching and extracting images as an answer to a given query should be intuitive, fast, pertinent and deliver the most relevant images from the data base.

All the query (question/answer) systems rely on: (1) query analysis; (2) dedicated search within the database; (3) display/extraction of the most matching documents. Using keywords for image searching and matching requires a good adequacy between those keywords referring to the various images in the database, and those provided by the user for a given query. The development of the so-called 'semantic approach' has offered a solution to this strong constraint. Indeed, the tools of traditional search engines are not efficient enough for life imaging clinical/pre-clinical data, because of the large amount of information contained in the digital images and their associated meta-data. The addition of sense to stored data, and creation of links - based on the additional pieces of sense - between all the data, not only strengthen the requirement for sophisticated search tools but also make them possible. Further enriched pertinent information becomes available for practitioners on their queries, like for diagnosis purposes, by enlarging the search for similar images and ensuring relevance feedback from connected experts within the network.

Our proposed global architecture offers to make VMs facilities available, in addition to the data storage system. Through these VM, access will be given to XNAT (eXtensible Neuroimaging Archive Toolkit), a server dedicated to images visualization and treatment. XNAT[4] is a web-based software platform that facilitates current management and routine tasks related to life images and associated data, thus increasing productivity for life imaging studies. It consists of an image repository to store raw and post-processed images, a database for storage of meta-data and non-imaging measures, and several user interface tools for accessing, querying, visualizing, and exploiting the data.

In order to use the XNAT tool, migration to a cloud is required, with collection of the data from multiple sources, centralized access and data treatment through a secure Web portal.

Positioning. The IDV program has the same goal as the Cloud and Autonomic Computing Center - CAC[5], namely to develop computational middleware

---

[4] http://www.xnat.org/.

[5] http://nsfcac.rutgers.edu/CometCloud/CometCloud/applications/imagereg.

and services for medical and life imaging. The IDV cloud program focuses on image acquisition and visualization tools. CAC is rather interested in mapping together images and data acquired in different conditions or through different methods and with 'traditional' architecture. Despite this difference, the architectures of two projects do present similarities. They share the same constraints and requirements, namely gathering a great number of collaborating research teams, dealing with many tasks to process, supplying medical images recordings, storage and visualization. The two infrastructures are designed on cloud conception, migration and adoption. Moreover, CAC and IDV both call on data centers and research teams that are able to develop new tools for the infrastructure exploitation. However, while CAC may use a public cloud for various tasks, the nature of IDV program requires only the use of a private, well secured and controlled infrastructure.

5   Conclusion

We thus share in this paper our experience in changing practices for doing e-Sciences at the scale of a large institution consortium, Université Sorbonne Paris Cité (USPC). USPC federates over 17.000 actors from several prestigious Parisian organizations. It also acts as a research agency that funds various programs for education, research and innovation, like the multi-disciplinary 'Imageries du Vivant' (IDV or 'Life Imaging') program. Sharing common computing infrastructure and daily-work services is especially important for all actors: users (researchers, teachers and students), system administrators and decision makers. The survey we initiated at the level of the IDV community ($\sim$ 200 individuals) allowed us to analyze the wishes, daily practices and the life cycle of data produced by the IDV members. The results convinced us to choose and set up a cloud infrastructure with a common storage repository, individually customizable VMs and access through a secure protocol. Such design, taking into account the needs of all the different actors, should allow increasing mutual sharing and understanding. We pretend that our work may serve as a use case reference to all actors working for cloud migration and adoption. The later is invaluable at the present and forthcoming digital era, especially at the scale of geographically distributed institutions.

Acknowledgments. Leila Abidi is supported by the IDV program and works with Laboratoire de Recherche en Informatique de Paris Nord, Institut Galilée, university of Paris 13, France. Marie Lafaille is supported by USPC for the scientific coordination and promotion of the digital infrastructures.

References

1. XSEDE Cloud Use Survey (2013). http://xsede.org/CloudSurvey/
2. National Science Foundation: Cyberinfrastructure for 21st Century Science and Engineering Advanced Computing Infrastructure: Vision and Strategic Plan, NSF 12-051, February 2012. http://www.nsf.gov/pubs/2012/nsf12051/nsf12051.pdf

3. Distributed and Parallel Systems Group: Cloud Computing (n.d.), University of Innsbruck. http://www.dps.uibk.ac.at/en/projects/cloud/

4. Intel Cloud Finder: service provider quick search (n.d.). http://www.intelcloudfinder.com/quicksearch

5. Foster, I.: CERN, Google, and the future of global science initiatives. HPC in the Cloud, 21 May 2013. http://www.hpcinthecloud.com/hpccloud/2013-05-21/cern_google_and_the_future_of_global_science_initiatives.html

6. Kar, S.: Gartner hype cycle for cloud computing: SaaS most promising technology, CloudTimes, 21 Aug 2012. http://cloudtimes.org/2012/08/21/gartner-hype-cycle-cloud-computing-saas/

7. Allen, B., Bresnahan, J., Childers, L., Foster, I., Kanadaswamy, G., Kettimuthu, R., Kordas, J., Link, M., Martin, S., Pickett, K., Tuecke, S.: Globus Online: Radical Simplification of Data Movement via SaaS, July 2011. https://www.globusonline.org/files/2011/07/Globus-Online-SaaS-Simplification-of-Data-Movement.pdf

8. Agee, A., Rowe, T., Woo, M.: Building research cyberinfrastructure at small/medium research institutions. Educause Review, 22 Sep 2010. http://www.educause.edu/ero/article/building-research-cyberinfrastructure-smallmedium-research-institutions

9. National Institute of Standards and Technology: Cloud Computing Synopsis and Recommendations (by Badger, L., Grance,T., Patt-Comer, R., Voas, J.), May 2012. NIST Publication 800-146. http://csrc.nist.gov/publications/nistpubs/800-146/sp800-146.pdf

10. High-throughput medical image registration on Comet framework(n.d.) Rutgers: The Cloud and Automatic Computing Center. http://nsfcac.rutgers.edu/CometCloud/CometCloud/applications/imagereg

11. Tudoran, R.: A-Brain: using the cloud to understand the impact of genetic variability on the brain [Web PPT] (2012). http://research.microsoft.com/en-us/um/redmond/events/cloudfutures2012/mondayLifeSciencesA-BrainRaduTudoran.pdf

12. NIST cloud specific terms and definitions, 31 Mar 2011. http://collaborate.nist.gov/twiki-cloud-computing/pub/CloudComputing/ReferenceArchitectureTaxonomy/TaxonomyTermsandDefinitionsversion1.pdf

13. http://imagej.net/

14. http://www.osirix-viewer.com/

15. Syed, J., Ghanem, M., Guo, Y.: Supporting scientific discovery processes in discovery net. Concurrency Comput. Pract. Experience 19(2), 167 (2007). doi:10.1002/cpe.1049

16. Jin, H., Shi, X., Qi, L.: Use case study of grid computing with CGSP. In: Shimojo, S., Ichii, S., Ling, T.-W., Song, K.-H. (eds.) HSI 2005. LNCS, vol. 3597, pp. 94–103. Springer, Heidelberg (2005). http://link.springer.com/chapter/10.1007/11527725_11

Resource Distribution Estimation for Data-Intensive Workloads: Give Me My Share & No One Gets Hurt!

Alireza Khoshkbarforoushha[1,2]([⊠]), Rajiv Ranjan[1,2], and Peter Strazdins[1]

[1] Australian National University, Canberra, Australia
`peter.strazdins@cs.anu.edu.au`
[2] CSIRO, Canberra, Australia
`{alireza.khoshkbarforoushha,raj.ranjan}@csiro.au`

Abstract. Robust resource share estimation of data-intensive workloads is integral to efficient workload management in a (virtualized) cluster where multiple systems co-exist and share the same infrastructure. However, developing a reliable resource estimator is quite challenging due to (i) heterogeneity of workloads (e.g. stream processing, batch processing, transactional, etc.) in a multi-system shared cluster, (ii) limited (in batch processing) or complete uncertainties (in stream processing) on input data size or arrival rates, and (iii) changing configurations from run to run. To address above challenges, we propose an inclusive framework and related techniques for *workload profiling, similar job identification,* and *resource distribution prediction* in a cluster. Our analysis shows that the framework can successfully estimate the whole spectrum of resource usage as probability distribution functions for wide ranges of data-intensive workloads.

Keywords: Resource estimation · Big data workload · Multi-cluster workload management · Distribution prediction · Data-intensive systems

1 Introduction

Datacenter-scale computing for big data analytics workloads has seen a surge in adoption due to availability and affordability of large-scale data processing systems which transform the traditional data mining and machine learning techniques into easy to program and deploy distributed analytics applications. In such an environment, robust resource usage prediction of data-intensive jobs is integral to make efficient workload management decisions in different scenarios such as workload migration between clouds or workload scheduling in a multi-system cluster.

Cost reduction is one of the main drivers for migrating the workloads between cloud providers (e.g. Amazon AWS) [10]. For example, the Azure Cost Estimator[1] has been designed to assist the infrastructure manager to either assess the

---

[1] http://www.microsoft.com/en-us/download/details.aspx?id=43376.

© Springer International Publishing Switzerland 2016
A. Celesti and P. Leitner (Eds.): ESOCC 2015 Workshops, CCIS 567, pp. 228–237, 2016.
DOI: 10.1007/978-3-319-33313-7_17

running cost of the existing on-premises workloads or analyse how much she can save by moving the hosted servers on other cloud platforms (e.g. AWS) to Azure. This class of tools typically does analysis irrespective of the workload resource usage patterns, thereby is not able to extrapolate the analysis beyond the current conditions of the workloads. However, robust resource usage prediction paves the way for predictive analysis of workload migration costs betweens clouds. From another standpoint, such estimation is integral to efficient workload scheduling in a multi-system cluster.

In a multi-system cluster, data-intensive workloads are typically classified as either productions or best effort jobs [5]. Production jobs (e.g. Oozie), unlike the best-effort ad-hoc jobs, are business-critical, meaning that missing their service level agreements (SLAs) can have substantial financial impact. State of the art workload scheduling techniques [5,8,14] focus on guaranteeing the SLAs for this class of workload subject to fairness, capacity, priority, and throughput maximization. Majority of these techniques [5,8] need *the cost of the workload* to be specified a priori to be able to define appropriate resource sharing policies.

However, developing a reliable resource estimator for production jobs is a hard research problem due to: (i) heterogeneity of workloads pertaining to each class of big data systems, (ii) limited (in batch processing) or complete uncertainties (in stream processing) on input data size/arrival rates and schema, and (iii) changing configurations (e.g. number of mappers/reducers or spouts/bolts respectively in Hadoop and Storm) from run to run. To address above problems, we propose an inclusive framework and related techniques for resource distribution estimation of heterogeneous big data workloads in a shared cluster.

To this end, the proposed framework first generates a set of data-intensive specific job templates (JT) by applying a clustering technique on a set of job characteristics. These templates are then used to identify similar jobs. Once the templates are generated, an statistical machine learning (ML) model is built for each of them by exploiting the past execution traces within the template. We argue that the existing single point resource estimator is not adequate for describing the whole spectrum of resource usage of big data workloads. Therefore, we introduce the novel approach of applying mixture density networks (MDN) as an underlying ML technique to approximate the probability distributions by means of finite mixture of Gaussians.

Therefore, the main contributions of the proposed resource estimation framework for big data analytics workload are: (i) Introducing appropriate techniques to profile and identify similar jobs within a heterogeneous workloads from both batch and stream data processing systems, (ii) Proposing a novel approach of estimating the full spectrum of resource usage in form of probability density functions (pdfs).

The reminder of the paper is organized as follows: The next section explores the related work. Section 3 presents the overview of the proposed framework. In this section, we propose our ideas on *how to define templates for similar jobs identification,* and *how to build resource distribution prediction models.* Section 4 presents initial results on distribution based resource modelling along with some discussions on how the predicted pdfs can be utilized in workload management scenarios. The paper ends with some concluding remarks and the plan for future work in Sect. 5.

2 Related Work

In this section we present a high level discussion on the past research done in the domain of job performance estimation. Following that, discussion of related work including performance estimation of declarative (SQL-style) and procedural (MapReduce style) data-intensive workload is presented.

Job Performance Estimation. Job performance estimation, in general, using historical information of *similar* job has been studied in the past in domain of parallel computing [17,18]. The key difference among the existing approaches is the way they tackle the problem of identifying similar jobs. In particular, authors in [18] focus on application characteristics such as user of jobs, jobs' submission time, jobs' arguments and on the number of physical servers on which the jobs are submitted for the definition of application similarity. Recently, authors in [17] propose the novel use of clone detection technique to determine the clone level of a newly submitted job with respect to the jobs in the execution history and to predict the resource requirement of the new job depending on its clone level.

High-Level Data Intensive Frameworks. There are a number of related work on runtime and resource usage estimation in the context of DBMS [1,13]. In the majority of related work, different statistical ML techniques are applied for estimating query performance. These approaches typically build statistical models using past query executions and a representative set of query features (query plan and/or operator level features) which possibly have the high predictive power in terms of resource or performance measures.

When it comes to MapReduce ecosystem, a major fraction of big data cluster workloads are generated by a handful of high-level frameworks such as Hive, Pig, Giraph [4]. This opens up an opportunity to train ML techniques against a set of finite recurring operators to estimate workload performance. For example, authors in [7] apply the Kernel Canonical Correlation Analysis (KCCA) to the Hive execution plan operators. They conclude that *only* a set of *low level features* pertaining to Hive query execution such as the number of maps and reduces, bytes read locally, bytes read from HDFS lead to accurate performance modelling. However, the provided low level features are *not* available before actual query execution. Therefore, above technique cannot be applied for performance prediction of new incoming workloads.

Similarly, authors in [16] propose a technique that predicts the runtime performance for a fixed set of queries running over varying input data sets. Specifically, it splits each query into several segments where each segment's performance is estimated using uni-variate linear regression. Next the estimates are plugged into a global analytical model to predict the overall query runtime. Since modelling a small and finite space of relational operators might not be adequate for all MapReduce workloads (e.g. iterative analytics), several studies focused on more fine-grained analysis of MapReduce job performance analysis as discussed next.

Procedural Data Intensive Workload. Herodotou et al. [9] propose a self-tunning system for Hadoop that uses performance models with the goal of workload tuning, finding the best configuration settings for a given workload and a cluster infrastructure. Along these lines, the authors in [20] first build the job profile from the job past executions or by executing the workload on a smaller data set using an automated profiling tool. Then, they apply the performance bounds of completion time of different job phases to predict the job completion time as a function of the input dataset size and allocated resources.

In terms of runtime prediction of ML algorithms executing on top of MapReduce ecosystem, authors in [15] present an experimental methodology for predicting the runtime of iterative algorithms written in Apache Giraph. To do so, they conduct sample runs for capturing the algorithm's convergence trend and per-iteration key input features.

Concluding Remarks. In summary, all of the above studies focused on single type of workload in particular Hadoop, while in reality big data workloads are heterogeneous consisting of multiple types of systems (e.g. Apache Hive, Apache Storm, etc.) and jobs. In contrast, our framework considers heterogeneous workloads where different jobs and queries from either batch or stream data processing systems running side by side. Moreover, existing approaches estimate resource and performance as a single point value which is neither expressive enough nor does it capture the possible variances due to resource contentions and interferences from other workloads. In contrast, we use a distribution prediction technique that describes the resource usage as conditional distribution functions.

3   Overview of the Proposed Framework

The problem of resource requirement estimation for future job in a multi-system cluster is decomposed in (i) characterizing the similar jobs that have executed in the past, and (ii) building a prediction model based on the collected statistics. The workflow in the proposed framework, as shown in Fig. 1, is as follows. Firstly, workload profiling is conducted in order to collect required information for defining similar jobs and building resource models. Secondly, a set of job templates are generated based on the collected features and their corresponding values. Finally, a distribution ML model is trained and built for each job templates which is responsible for resource prediction of a new incoming workload.

3.1   Similarity Definition and Template Generation

The routine nature of productions jobs allows us to build the resource model based on the past execution profiles of the *same* or *similar* jobs. Thus, building

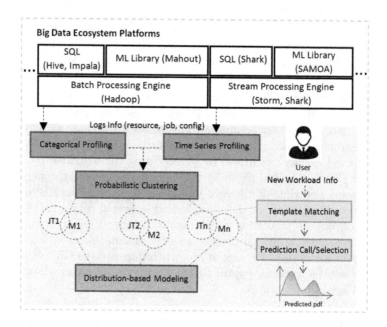

Fig. 1. Comprehensive framework for performance distribution prediction of heterogeneous data-intensive workloads.

profiles is the first step. Our framework considers both batch and streaming workloads, thereby the profiles will be logged as either categorical or time series files respectively. We next look into *what* to profile.

Resource usage r is the function of a job j that is executed on input data (stream) d using configuration parameter settings c:

$$r = f(j, d, c) \tag{1}$$

This means that resource modelling requires logging appropriate information about job, its data flow and configurations along with the resources in use, as follows:

- **Job Profile**
    - *Input Data Stats:* such as number of Input Records/Bytes (e.g. in Hive tables), Average arrival rates (in Stream processing), Data file format, etc.
    - *Job Metadata:* including Job Name, User who submitted the job, Submission time, File input path, and so on.
    - *Runtime Stats:* such as number of mappers and reducers per stage (as in Hive), Response time, Latency/Throughput (in stream processing).
- **Resource Profile** including CPU time and utilization, Memory usage, local/network I/O.

- **Configuration Profile**
  - *Compact[2] job configs:* such as number of reducers in Hive which can be set for a specific query using mapred.reduce.tasks property and override the cluster wide settings.
  - *Compact cluster configs:* such as the number of virtual CPU cores for each reduce task of a job which is set by mapreduce.reduce.cpu.vcores property in Apache Yarn [19].

The job profiling is a recurrent process, means that the mentioned profiles will be generated for every submitted job. However, to avoid any performance degradation, two design principles need to be realized. First, statistics should be collected passively, without affecting the performance. For example, in [12] we used *dstat* (http://dag.wiee.rs/home-made/dstat/) as a lightweight python-based tool that collects OS and system statistics non-intrusively. Second, profiling process should be tractable via enabling a feature to on/off profiling process. This means that every job is profiled unless it is deactivated by the user of the final prototype.

Upon extracting required information from job history and big data cluster logs, we now focus on the second challenge, that is characterizing the similar jobs that have executed in the past. We need to identify a set of classes of jobs (i.e. job templates) that exhibit a similar resource usage pattern.

Modern big data clusters run a diverse mix of applications and production workloads [19], thereby characterizing similar jobs is challenging. Although difficult, we argue that appropriate clustering techniques along with the proper job execution and big data system configuration profiles lead to formation of fitting templates.

In our problem domain the clusters (i.e. candidate job templates) need not be disjoint, and the same job can be associated to several classes. Because two jobs can be compared in many ways. For example, our initial analysis on synthetic MapReduce workloads of Facebook[3] [4] demonstrates that the (submit_time_seconds, hdfs_input_path) is a proper candidate job template since jobs with the close submission time and same input path have roughly same map input byte size, shuffle bytes, etc. Yet another template is (user, submit_time_seconds, hdfs_input_path) which is more restricted. Intuitively, a certain job can be assigned to both of these templates with respect to its characteristics.

Therefore, we use a probabilistic clustering technique, Expectation Maximization (EM) algorithm [6] which is a soft clustering technique. EM finds clusters by determining a mixture of Gaussians that fit a given data set. Each Gaussian has a mean and covariance matrix. The prior probability for each Gaussian is the fraction of points in the cluster defined by that Gaussian. These parameters can be either initialized by randomly selecting means of the Gaussians or by using the output of K-means algorithms for the initial centres.

---

[2] Due to the large number of configuration parameters, only a subset of settings which have substantial impacts on resource and performance measures need to be logged.

[3] https://github.com/SWIMProjectUCB/SWIM/wiki.

EM converges on a locally optimal solution by iteratively updating means and variances.

Once the candidate job templates (i.e. clusters) becomes available, different validity measures which falls broadly into internal, relative, and external validations are used to evaluate clustering results. The output of this step is a set of final job templates through which we are able to identify who belongs to whom. To do so, for a new job, the template membership probability is calculated. The higher probability seemingly shows the more the templates match the job's characteristics.

3.2   Distribution Prediction

Many workload scheduling studies [5, 8] formulate and optimize the policies subject to fairness, capacity, and priority, conditioned on having the cost of a workload a priori in a multidimensional space representing different resources. In contrast, there exists criticism of the off-line predictions [14] due to the interferences from other workloads concurrently running and sharing the same resources at runtime.

As stressed in related work, the state of the art resource and performance estimation techniques for data intensive workloads only provide the conditional mean of the point of interest. However, even running the same query on the same data with constant configuration show different performance and resource behaviour. In response, we argue that the *distribution* estimation provides an expressive description of the target values (e.g. runtime, CPU time) and the possible variances due to resource contention.

We adopt a novel approach of workload resource distribution prediction using Mixture Density Networks (MDN) [3]. An MDN fuses a Gaussian mixture model (GMM) with feed-forward neural networks. In MDN, the distribution of the outputs t is described by a parametric model whose parameters are determined by the output of a neural network, which takes x as inputs. Specifically, an MDN maps a set of input features x to the parameters of a GMM including mixture weights α_i, mean μ_i, and variance σ^2 which in turn produces the full *pdf* of an output feature t, conditioned on the input vector. Detailed discussion on the proposed approach are available in accompanying technical reports [11, 12] which discuss how to predict the resource and performance distribution for batch (Hive workloads) [11] and stream data processing (i.e. continuous queries) [12]. We will show the efficacy of distribution as opposed to existing techniques in workload resource modelling in the next section.

Note that due to the large number of profiles and historical logs, building a model could be prohibitively expensive, though we already showed [11] that the training time of the MDN linearly grows with respect to the training data size. Thus, enabling a *maximum history* feature as in [18] which indicates the maximum number of data points to be used for building/refreshing a model is inevitable.

Once the model is built and trained, it can then be invoked when a similarity measures assign a new job to one of the existing classes. Since the job templates overlap, a single job may be associated to multiple job templates and their corresponding ML model. Therefore, the prediction with the smallest confidence interval will be selected.

4   Initial Results

In this section, we present some compact yet lucid results on how the distribution prediction look like and how one can utilize them for appropriate policy setting across a shared big data cluster.

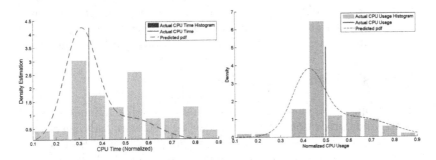

Fig. 2. (a) a sample predicted pdf for CPU Time of an input test from Hive workload. (b) a sample predicted pdf for CPU Utilization, selected from a test dataset of linear road benchmark (Color figure online).

Figure 2(a) plots a sample predicted pdf for CPU time for one of the experiments conducted on TPC-H in [11]. The predicted pdf is corresponding to a test input from Template-7 (Q7) of TPC-H against 100 GB database size. To demonstrate the whole possible range of CPU time values under Q7, the histograms for 30 instance queries based on Q7 from test set are shown as well.

As we can see, the predicted distribution adequately estimates the CPU time distribution in which they show high probability around the target value. More importantly, they provide information about the whole spectrum of resource usage. In particular, the predicted pdf shows highly probable CPU time in ranges (0.25, 0.4) which are consistent with the actual distribution. Note that the predicted pdf is concerned with one single input, thereby the resulted uncertainty of pdf for the range (0.6, 0.9) is justifiable.

In a similar manner, Fig. 2(b) depicts a sample predicted pdf and actual CPU usage in terms of normalized histogram for one of the experiments on linear road benchmark [2] queries conducted in [12]. As the figure indicates, the estimated pdf approximates the actual resource usage closely. The predicted pdf provides a complete description of the statistical properties of the CPU utilization through which we are not only able to capture the observation point, but also the whole spectrum of the resource usage. In contrast, a best estimation from the existing resource estimation techniques [1,7,9,13,20] merely provides the point which is visualized by solid red vertical line. Unlike pdfs, with such estimation we are not able to directly calculate any valuable statistical measures (e.g. variance, expectation) about the target data. Detailed evaluation of the proposed approach and its comparison with the state of the art single point estimator can be found in accompanying technical reports [11,12].

Once the resource usage distribution becomes available, it can then be used to define appropriate resource pool policy for critical SLA-driven workloads. For example, Cloudera Manager[4] provides the ability to statically allocate resources using Linux control groups through which one can allocate services (e.g. Hive, Storm) a *percentage* of total resources. Static resource pools isolate the services in the cluster from one another, so that load on one service has a bounded impact on the others. With distribution based resource estimation, we are able to determine appropriate percentage of resource shares for a workload before actual execution, without sacrificing the cluster throughputs and utilization.

5   Conclusions and Future Work

This paper proposed an inclusive framework and related techniques for resource usage distribution prediction of heterogeneous big data workloads in a cluster. To this end, our framework uses the clustering techniques along with the statistical machine learning algorithm to identify similar jobs and build a distribution-based prediction models. The initial results show that the approach is capable of estimating resource usage distribution accurately, through which we are able to define more reliable resource sharing policies aiming at guaranteeing SLA subject to fairness, capacity, priority, and throughput maximization.

As an ongoing work, we plan to complete and evaluate the template generation phase using real-world workload traces collected from our private CSIRO big data cluster and possibly more traces from other companies. Following that, we also plan to accommodate the distribution predictions in cost-optimized resource provisioning of big data analytics flows in a datacenter cloud.

References

1. Akdere, M., Çetintemel, U., Riondato, M., Upfal, E., Zdonik, S.B.: Learning-based query performance modeling and prediction. In: 2012 IEEE 28th International Conference on Data Engineering (ICDE), pp. 390–401. IEEE (2012)
2. Arasu, A., Cherniack, M., Galvez, E., Maier, D., Maskey, A.S., Ryvkina, E., Stonebraker, M., Tibbetts, R.: Linear road: a stream data management benchmark. In: Proceedings of the Thirtieth International Conference on Very Large Data Bases, vol. 30, pp. 480–491. VLDB Endowment (2004)
3. Bishop, C.M.: Mixture density networks (1994)
4. Chen, Y., Alspaugh, S., Katz, R.: Interactive analytical processing in big data systems: a cross-industry study of mapreduce workloads. VLDB 5(12), 1802–1813 (2012)

---

[4] http://www.cloudera.com/content/cloudera/en/products-and-services/cloudera-enterprise/cloudera-manager.html.

5. Curino, C., Difallah, D.E., Douglas, C., Krishnan, S., Ramakrishnan, R., Rao, S.: Reservation-based scheduling: if you're late don't blame us! In: Proceedings of the ACM Symposium on Cloud Computing, pp. 1–14. ACM (2014)
6. Dempster, A.P., Laird, N.M., Rubin, D.B.: Maximum likelihood from incomplete data via the em algorithm. J. R. Stat. Soc. Ser. B (Methodological) **39**, 1–38 (1977)
7. Ganapathi, A., Chen, Y., Fox, A., Katz, R., Patterson, D.: Statistics-driven workload modeling for the cloud. In: 2010 IEEE 26th International Conference on Data Engineering Workshops (ICDEW), pp. 87–92. IEEE (2010)
8. Ghodsi, A., Zaharia, M., Hindman, B., Konwinski, A., Shenker, S., Stoica, I.: Dominant resource fairness: fair allocation of multiple resource types. In: NSDI, vol. 11, p. 24 (2011)
9. Herodotou, H., Babu, S.: Profiling, what-if analysis, and cost-based optimization of mapreduce programs. VLDB **4**(11), 1111–1122 (2011)
10. Jamshidi, P., Ahmad, A., Pahl, C.: Cloud migration research: a systematic review. IEEE Trans. Cloud Comput. **1**(2), 142–157 (2013)
11. Khoshkbarforoushha, A., Ranjan, R.: Resource and performance distribution prediction for large scale analytics queries. TR-2015-01, ANU Technical report (2015)
12. Khoshkbarforoushha, A., Ranjan, R., Gaire, R., Jayaraman, P.P., Hosking, J., Abbasnejad, E.: Resource usage estimation of data stream processing workloads in datacenter clouds. arXiv preprint arXiv:1501.07020 (2015)
13. Li, J., König, A.C., Narasayya, V., Chaudhuri, S.: Robust estimation of resource consumption for sql queries using statistical techniques. Proc. VLDB Endowment **5**(11), 1555–1566 (2012)
14. Mace, J., Bodik, P., Fonseca, R., Musuvathi, M.: Retro: targeted resource management in multi-tenant distributed systems. In: NSDI. USENIX (2015)
15. Popescu, A.D., Balmin, A., Ercegovac, V., Ailamaki, A.: Predict: towards predicting the runtime of large scale iterative analytics. Proc. VLDB Endowment **6**(14), 1678–1689 (2013)
16. Popescu, A.D., Ercegovac, V., Balmin, A., Branco, M., Ailamaki, A.: Same queries, different data: Can we predict runtime performance? In: 2012 IEEE 28th International Conference on Data Engineering Workshops (ICDEW), pp. 275–280. IEEE (2012)
17. Sarkar, M., Mondal, T., Roy, S., Mukherjee, N.: Resource requirement prediction using clone detection technique. Future Gener. Comput. Syst. **29**(4), 936–952 (2013)
18. Smith, W., Foster, I., Taylor, V.: Predicting application run times using historical information. In: Feitelson, D.G., Rudolph, L. (eds.) IPPS-WS 1998, SPDP-WS 1998, and JSSPP 1998. LNCS, vol. 1459, pp. 122–142. Springer, Heidelberg (1998)
19. Vavilapalli, V.K., Murthy, A.C., Douglas, C., Agarwal, S., Konar, M., Evans, R., Graves, T., Lowe, J., Shah, H., Seth, S., et al.: Apache hadoop yarn: yet another resource negotiator. In: Proceedings of the 4th annual Symposium on Cloud Computing, p. 5. ACM (2013)
20. Verma, A., Cherkasova, L., Campbell, R.H.: Aria: automatic resource inference and allocation for mapreduce environments. In: Proceedings of the 8th ACM International Conference on Autonomic Computing, pp. 235–244. ACM (2011)

Supporting Partial Database Migration to the Cloud Using Non-intrusive Software Adaptations: An Experience Report

Caio H. Costa[1], Paulo H.M. Maia[1(✉)], Nabor C. Mendonça[2],
and Lincoln S. Rocha[3]

[1] State University of Ceará, Fortaleza, Brazil
caiohc@gmail.com, pauloh.maia@uece.br
[2] University of Fortaleza, Fortaleza, Brazil
nabor@unifor.br
[3] Federal University of Ceará, Fortaleza, Brazil
lincolnrocha@ufc.br

Abstract. This paper reports on an early experience of partially migrating a legacy systems' relational database to a NoSQL database in the Amazon cloud. The migration process involved converting part of the relational database data to the schema-less format supported by the target NoSQL database, and adapting the two software applications that make up the system (developed using Grails and Groovy, respectively) to transparently access both the relational database on-premise and the NoSQL database in the cloud. The required software adaptations were performed using a non-intrusive approach based on aspect-oriented programming (in the case of the Grails application) and meta-programming features (in the case of the Groovy application). This approach allowed the system to be easily adapted and tested, without the need to change its source code directly.

Keywords: Cloud · Database migration · Non-intrusive adaptation

1 Introduction

This paper reports on the partial migration of the relational database of a legacy system to a cloud NoSQL database aiming at solving performance issues originated from the exponential growth of its bigger and most important table. The system concerns vehicle monitoring and is composed by two applications: RastroBR, a Grails Web application, and RBRDriver, a Groovy standalone application. When this migration was carried out, the first author of this work was the system analyst of the company that developed the system and was responsible for performing maintenance tasks in both applications.

The applications share the concept of *position* in their domains. A position regards the georeferenced localization of a vehicle monitored by the system. The data corresponding to the vehicle position is constantly sent to the database

© Springer International Publishing Switzerland 2016
A. Celesti and P. Leitner (Eds.): ESOCC 2015 Workshops, CCIS 567, pp. 238–248, 2016.
DOI: 10.1007/978-3-319-33313-7_18

within intervals of one minute-time. As a consequence, the data volume stored in the `Position` table grew very fast and reached, at the time this paper was being written, approximately 200 GB. Due to this, database search and insert operations became slower.

The first attempt to mitigate this problem consisted of performing vertical scaling procedures in the database server, i.e., increasing the server's memory size. Although that solution attenuated the performance bottleneck, it was expensive and presented practical limitations to be implemented, since it demanded frequently memory improvement.

Another alternative considered was to apply a horizontal scaling to the database server, which comprises distributing the data among servers in a cluster. According to Costa et al. [1], if correctly implemented, that solution should provide read an write scalability. However, according to [2], relational databases have not been designed to be horizontally scaled. On the other hand, aggregate-oriented NoSQL databases can support great data volume through that kind of scaling. In addition, the resource elasticity feature brought by the cloud computing made the process of setting up a NoSQL server in the cloud easier and cheaper. Therefore, using a cloud NoSQL database was the most viable alternative to tackle the aforementioned problem. The Amazon DynamoDB [3] has been chosen as the NoSQL database server.

After that, it was necessary to adequate and migrate the `Position` table's data to a collection in the DynamoDB and to adapt the two applications that compose the system such that both of them could access the new database. However, the system adaptation should be as less intrusive as possible, since changing the application code directly could introduce new errors and could make future software maintenance more difficult. In addition, the programmers who developed both applications no longer worked for the company, making the process of adapting the applications more difficult for the new developers. The solution relied on using aspect-oriented programming (in the case of the Grails application) and meta-programming features (in the case of the Groovy application). Thus, the original code could be preserved without any modifications, making the tests and migration easier.

The rest of the paper is divided as follows: Sect. 2 discusses the main related work. Section 3 presents the architecture of the two applications that make up the system. Section 4 details the data migration from the `Position` table to a DynamoDB collection and the adaptions performed in the applications. Finally, Sect. 5 brings the conclusion, lessons learned, and suggestions of future work.

2 Related Work

Lessons learned during the transition of a big relational database to a hybrid model, which combines a relational and a NoSQL database, are reported in [5]. The system addressed in that paper is composed of services that collect and analyze information from Twitter posts related to natural disasters. The persistence layer of that system is a bottleneck due to performance issues of the

Hibernate framework when dealing with large volumes of data. Like the adaptation discussed in this paper, the adaptation described in [5] is preceded by the adaptation of the data previously stored in the relational database MySql in order to be inserted in the NoSQL data store. That system was adapted using a less intrusive approach which consisted of using the Spring's dependency injection mechanism to inject concrete implementation in references of abstract types at runtime. Although the RastroBR application also uses the Spring framework, its adaptation was performed using aspect-oriented programming in order to make the modifications more specific and granular.

In [4], a systematic review is conducted in order to identify, classify and compare research focused on plan, execute and validate migration of legacy applications to the cloud. Through a rigorous process, 23 studies were identified and classified. The authors classify the migration in: replacement, partial migration, whole stack migration, and cloudification. According to that classification, the migration presented here can be seen as a replacement. None of the studies discussed in the [4] is described as such.

In one of the works listed in [5], Vu and Asar [6] show an analysis of the main cloud platforms available in the market. A guide based on the lessons learned is presented and three examples of migration are described like concept proofs. Differently from our approach, those examples used intrusive adaptations, since they were not real running applications.

The paper in [7] describes the whole stack migration of the Hackystat tool to the cloud. The services that compose the tool are deployed separately in Amazon EC2 instances that use the cloud elasticity feature. The authors conclude that systems that divide the business logic between the application and the database layers (by using triggers or other functionalities) are more difficult to be migrated because the cloud should offer a database that allows the same artifacts to be executed. This is one of the reasons that imposed a partial migration of the RBRDriver and RastroBR's database, since it contains triggers that implement the business logic.

In [8], Vasconcelos et al. addresses the considerable development effort to adapt a legacy application to the cloud environment, which may contain many restrictive constraints, and the fact that the necessary changes in the source code can insert errors. Vasconcelos et al. suggests an event based non-intrusive approach to adapt the legacy application to the new cloud environment. That article mentions an example which consists in migrating the database of an application to a nosql datastore in the cloud, in order to achieve a better scalability.

3 System Architecture

In this section is described the architecture of the two applications that make up the system: RBRDriver and RastroBR. The former is a Groovy [9] standalone application whose main goal is to decode the packages sent by the monitored vehicles containing their current position and to persist that information in the Position table of a PostgreSQL relational database. In addition, it queries the

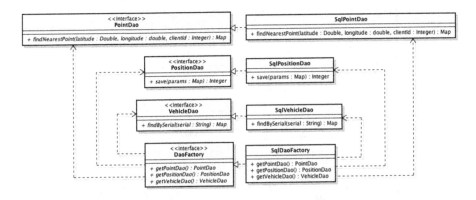

Fig. 1. RBRDriver's interfaces and DAO classes related to insert positions.

same database to extract the commands to be sent to the equipments installed in the vehicles.

The application uses the Data Access Object (DAO) and Abstract Factory patterns to access the database's tables. Particularly, the class `PositionCodec`, which is responsible for decoding and persisting the received data, requires to its `DAOFactory` attribute a concrete DAO object to query and store the vehicle positions in the `Position` table.

The concrete type of the DAO factory, which is the class `SqlFactory`, is defined in a configuration file as the standard factory of DAO objects. Therefore, all DAO objects returned by `DaoFactory` objects are specific DAOs that interact with a relational database (see Fig. 1). It is not possible to change this configuration such that a specific factory implementation of a particular NoSQL database can be used since this would imply in changing all DAO object family. This is not an interesting solution since the application, besides storing the vehicle localizations, also executes other functionalities that need the relationships and integrity offered only by the relational database.

RastroBR is a Grails Web application that allows the users to keep track of the vehicles routes, maintains the customers, users and vehicles information, and provides statistics and route reports. Likewise RBRDriver, RastroBR uses both DAO and Abstract Factory patterns to implement the database access layer. In RastroBR, the DAO classes uses the Grails Object-Relational Mapping (GORM) framework [10], which is implemented as an additional layer of abstraction upon the Spring and Hibernate frameworks.

The reports produced by RastroBR apply business rules on records of the `Position` table, having its performance affected by that table size. The report's services classes have a `DaoFactory` attribute, which is used to return specific DAO classes to access the database's tables. Due to the Spring's dependency injection capacity, the concrete class that implements the `DaoFactory` interface can be easily changed using a configuration script. At runtime, the obtained

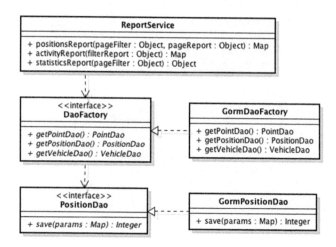

Fig. 2. RastroBR's interfaces and DAO classes related to query positions.

PositionDao reference is a `GormPositionDao` object that queries the positions contained in the `Position` table to create the required reports (see Fig. 2).

4   The Migration and Adaptation Process

In this section, the data migration from the relational to the NoSQL database and the adaptations performed in the applications are detailed.

4.1   Data Migration

It is possible to partition tables of relational databases to reduce the amount of data that must be searched when a query is submitted. The table partitioning also benefits insert operations because is easier for the Relational Database Management Systems (RDBMS) to find the correct position for the new data to be inserted when the volume of data is smaller. Even indexed table can benefit from the partition of a table because the index space will be smaller too.

But there is a limitation with this approach. In this type of partitioning, the wholes table, with all its partitions, still reside in the same node. Therefore, memory, CPU, and network resources are limited. So, even when a relational database table is partitioned, if the RDBMS is concurrently serving too many cliens, the limitaion of the aforementioned resources become a bottleneck.

Relational databases were not designed to be horizontally scaled. The features like referential integrity and ACID (Atomicity, Consistency, Isolation, Durability) properties makes difficult to distributed the database data among nodes of nothing shared system.

NoSQL datastores, since its conception, were designed to distribute its data among many nodes of a cluster. Consequently, to increase the database scalability new nodes can be added, as many as necessary to achieve the desire load balance.

The DynamoDB [3], an Amazon NoSQL aggregate-oriented database, has been chosen as a target migration database. The aggregate concept is quite appropriate to support horizontal scaling. An aggregate provides information to the database about what data should be handled as a single indivisible unit. Therefore, such data should be kept on the same server. However, two different aggregates, even belonging to the same table, do not need to follow that rule and can reside in different nodes of a NoSQL database cluster.

The lack of relationship among aggregates, such as those held by foreign keys in relational databases, makes possible the data partitioning and distribution across multiple sites. However, due to that data distribution, it is not possible, in a single query, performing joins between aggregates that belong to different collections. In the original version of the system, the data persistence was totally dependent on the relationship among entities provided by the relational model.

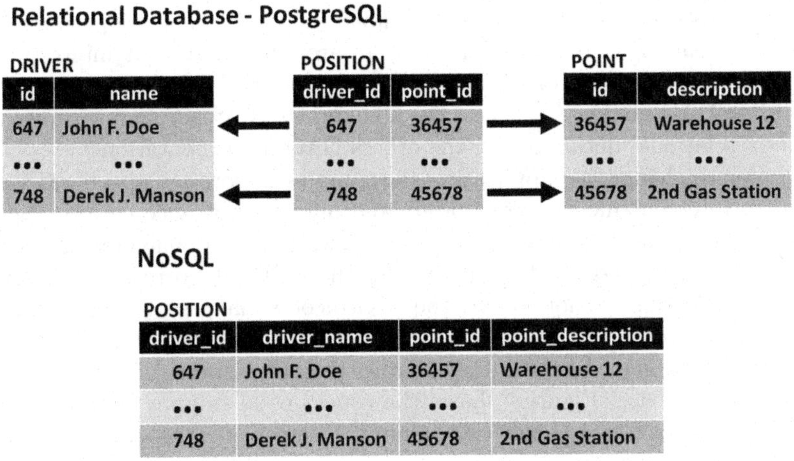

Relational Database - PostgreSQL

NoSQL

Fig. 3. Adapting the data of `Position` table to a NoSQL collection.

Despite of its importance, the `Position` table stores only not editable historical data. This particularity made possible the adaptation of its data to a NoSQL collection. The `Position` table has foreign keys which reference records in others tables as can be seen in Fig. 3. The data adequacy was carried out by joining in a single aggregate each record of the `Position` table and the necessary fields from records of other tables referenced by the its foreign keys[1]. Thus, the aggregates of the resulting collection provide, in a single query, all necessary data to produce the system reports. Figure 3 illustrates, in a simplified way[2], records

---

[1] It is out of the scope of this paper to address the consequences of the data normalization loss.

[2] The other table fields were left out since they are irrelevant to understand the solution.

from the Position table referencing records of other tables, and how their data have been adapted to form a new collection.

4.2 System Adaptation

The Spring Aspect Oriented Programming (AOP)[3] framework has been chosen as the aspect-oriented programming tool to support the adaptation of the RastroBR Web application because the Grails framework uses the Spring framework to implement many of its functionalities. In Spring AOP, the aspects are implemented as ordinary Java classes. An XML configuration file is employed to describe which classes implement aspects. In addition, inside each class, annotations are used to specify join points and advices.

In RastroBR, a DaoFactory implementation is injected in the dependent classes using the Spring dependency injection mechanism. Hence, when a dependent class requests a DAO instance, it is obtained from the same DAO "family" (i.e., instances that access the same relational database). The adopted strategy consists of creating an aspect containing an around advice that intercepts the getPositionDao method of the DaoFactory interface. This advice returns an appropriate DAO instance to access the DynamoDB, instead of an instance that accesses a relational database like the others DAO implementations.

In order to change the application's original behavior, an aspect was implemented to intercept method calls originated only from service classes that are dependent from the Position table. This aspect, named DaoFactoryAspect, contains an around advice that intercepts the pointcut corresponding to the getPositionDao invocation. Thus, the advice code changes the normal system behavior returning an instance of the PositionDao specific to deal with the Position collection in the DynamoBD rather than an instance designed to access a relational database. Figure 4 shows the aspect code snippet containing such advise. Line 13 of Fig. 4 shows the pointcut intercepting the getPositionDao invocation, while line 15 shows the instantiation and returning of a specific DAO implementation for DynamoBD.

```
10   @Aspect
11   class DaoFactoryAspect {
12
13⊝      @Around("execution(* rastro.br.dao.DaoFactory.getPositionDao())")
14      Object invoke(ProceedingJoinPoint joinPoint) throws Throwable {
15          new DynamoDbPositionDao(DynamoDbClient.instance)
16      }
```

Fig. 4. *Advice* returning a DynamoDB DAO rather than a relational DAO.

Considering the DaoFactoryAspect (Fig. 4) implementation in the system, a ReportService object calls the method getPositionDao of the DaoFactory

---

[3] http://projects.spring.io/spring-framework/.

object to obtain an instance of PositionDao suitable to access the Position table. In that moment, the DaoFactoryAspect advice intercepts that call and, instead of returning an expected PositionDao instance (i.e., instance that access the relational database), returns a DynamoDbPositionDao instance, which also implements the PositionDao interface. This process is depicted by the Sequence Diagram in Fig. 5. Therefore, no incompatibility is introduced and the ReportService code did not need to be changed.

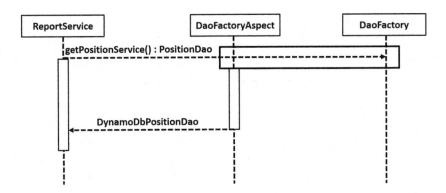

Fig. 5. Sequence diagram illustrating the behaviour of the aspect's around advice.

In order to make the aspect intercepting the pointcuts specified in its advices, it is necessary to indicate to Spring AOP which classes are aspects. This is carried out by the bean definition in the application Spring beans configuration script.

Similarly to the solution for RastroBR, an aspect was implemented in RBR-Driver, but now using the AspectJ framework [11]. It contained an around advice to catch the calls to the method getPositionDao of the DaoFactory interface. However, the advice was executed several times rather than only once for each method call. This was caused by the Groovy's dynamic functionalities that did not allow the correct working of the aspect.

A possible solution for that problem was pointed out in [12]. In a Groovy application, for each class loaded in memory there exists a correspondent metaclass that has the same properties and method implementations of the class that it is related to. According to the Groovy Meta Object protocol (MOP), a method call to an object is redirected to a metaclass instance of that object rather than to the method of the object itself.

An illustration of that process can be seen in Fig. 6. When an instance of the GroovySource class calls, through its "caller" method, the "called" method in an instance of the GroovyTarget class, the MOP layer redirects that method call to the invokeMethod method of the target metaclass. The invokeMethod calls the method which has the same signature of the originally called method.

Groovy also allows to replace a metaclass at runtime, thus dynamically changing the behavior of all instances of its corresponding class without modifying its

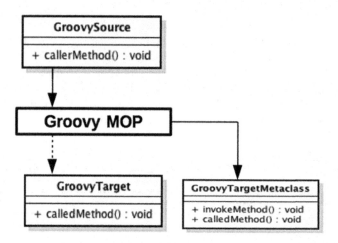

Fig. 6. Example of the Groovy metaobject protocol.

source code. One way to do it is to put the surrogate metaclass, adequately named, in a specific package, whose name and position in the package hierarchy depends on the class that will have its metaclass replaced.

Hence, considering the `SqlPositionDao` class, responsible for storing the vehicle positions in the `Position` table in the RBRDriver application, when its `save` method is called, what in fact happens is a call to the method `invokeMethod` of its metaclass, that calls the metaclass `save` method. Therefore, it was necessary to replace the standard metaclass provided by the Groovy compiler with a new one that accesses the DynamoDB. This was carried out by

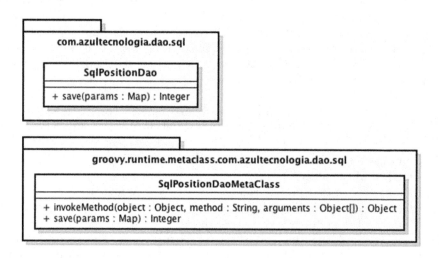

Fig. 7. Replacement of the standard metaclass by an appropriate metaclass for accessing the DynamoDB.

following the aforementioned steps: the `SqlPositionDaoMetaClass` metaclass was created and placed in the appropriate package; that surrogate class has a `save` method with the same signature of the `save` method from the `SqlPositionDao`, as illustrated by Fig. 7. But the new metaclass has a different implementation which used an instance of the `DynamoDbPositionDao` class to store the vehicle positions in the DynamoDB datastore. Therefore, that strategy simulated an around advice in an AOP language.

5   Conclusion

Aspect-oriented programming turned out to be a valid approach for non-intrusively adapting the RastroBR application. Although AOP was used to deal with a common crosscutting concern (persistence), it was not applied to intercept the calls to all tables of the original database, but rather to only one that had an expressive size and that was continuously growing.

It is difficult to adapt an application such that its relational database is completely migrated to a NoSQL database. According to [2], when an application uses a NoSQL database, its domain should be originally modeled taking into account the particular characteristics of that database, like the fact that NoSQL databases do not have many of the resources regarding relationship among entities and integrity rules available as in its relational counterparts. However, as shown in this experience report, it is possible to partially migrate the data that does not depends on the referential integrity feature.

The Groovy metaclasses have been used in a very similar way of aspects in order to achieve the objective of modifying an application non-intrusively. The Groovy's dynamic functionalities can be used as aspects in Groovy applications, thus avoiding adding an extra framework to the application code.

This work presented an experience report on partially migrating a relational database accessed by two legacy applications to a cloud NoSQL database via non-intrusive adaptations. For the Grails Web application, the Aspect-oriented Programming was the adopted solution, while for the Groovy application, the own Groovy metaclasses were used to promote the application adaptation. As a result, the two applications ended up being able to access both the relational or the NoSQL database, depending on whether the adaptions are active.

As future work, we plan to apply the techniques used in the migration described in this report to other NoSQL database servers and to carry out a comparison among them concerning performance and implementation facility, for instance. Other interesting work consists of using only the Groovy's features to catch the application's pointcuts and compare that approach to the current one reported here.

References

1. Costa, C.H., Filho, J., Maia, P.H.M., Oliveira, F.: Sharding by Hash partitioning. A database scalability pattern to achieve evenly sharded database clusters. In: International Conference on Enterprise Information Systems (2015)
2. Sadalage, P., Fowler, M.: NoSQL Distilled: A Brief Guide to the Emerging World of Polyglot Persistence. Addison-Wesley, Reading (2013)
3. Sivasubramanian, S.: Amazon dynamoDB: a seamlessly scalable non-relational database service. In: ACM SIGMOD International Conference on Management of Data (2012)
4. Jamshidi, P., Ahmad, A., Pahl, C.: Cloud migration research: a systematic review. IEEE Trans. Cloud Comput. 1, 142–157 (2013)
5. Schram, A., Anderson, K.M.: MySQL to NoSQL: data modeling challenges in supporting scalability. In: 3rd Annual Conference on Systems, Programming, and Applications: Software for Humanity (2012)
6. Vu, Q.H., Asal, R.: Legacy application migration to the cloud: practicability and methodology. In: IEEE Eighth World Congress on Services (2012)
7. Chauhan, M.A., Babar, M.A.: Migrating service-oriented system to cloud computing: an experience report. In: IEEE 4th International Conference on Cloud Computing (2011)
8. Vasconcelos, M., Mendonça, N.C., Maia, P.H.M.: Cloud detours: a non-intrusive approach for automatic software adaptation to the cloud. In: Dustdar, S., et al. (eds.) ESOCC 2015. LNCS, vol. 9306, pp. 181–195. Springer, Heidelberg (2015)
9. Knig, D., Laforge, G., King, P., Champeau, C., D'Arcy, H., Pragt, E., Skeet, J.: Groovy in Action. Manning Publications Co., Greenwich (2007)
10. Fischer, R.: Grails Persistence with GORM and GSQL. Apress, Berkeley (2009)
11. Kiselev, I.: Aspect-Oriented Programming with AspectJ. Sams, Indianapolis (2012)
12. McClean, J.: Painless AOP with Groovy. InfoQ, October 2006. http://www.infoq.com/articles/aop-with-groovy. Accessed on 28 March 2016

Cloud Adoption by Fine-Grained Resource Adaptation: Price Determination of Diagonally Scalable IaaS

Kevin Laubis[(✉)], Viliam Simko, and Alexander Schuller

FZI Research Center for Information Technology,
Haid-und-Neu-Straße 10–14, 76131 Karlsruhe, Germany
{laubis,simko,schuller}@fzi.de

Abstract. Cloud computing is a suitable solution for addressing the uncertainty of resource demand by allowing dynamic resource adjustment. However, most IaaS cloud providers offer their services with a limited granularity at rather slow scaling speeds and flat pricing schemes. Diagonal scaling techniques can offer a more adaptive and fine-grained service with a likewise granular pricing model. Before offering such an adaptive service, cloud providers need a comparison between horizontal and diagonal scaling models to estimate how resource prices can be increased while still staying competitive. In this paper we examine the resource reduction potential of diagonal scaling in comparison to conventional horizontal approaches. Given an empirical load pattern of a web application provider we find a CPU allocation reduction potential of 8.05 % compared to the conventional service. Given a more fine-grained pricing model, we find an additional revenue potential for diagonal scaling of 9.01 % when following a competitor based pricing regime.

Keywords: Cloud computing · IaaS · Scaling · Adoption · Pricing

1   Introduction and Background

Cloud computing is an omnipresent concept that is still about to reach its envisioned potential in the business domain [16,20]. Flexible resource adaptation to fluctuating computing demand is one of the main benefits of cloud usage and likewise a main reason for Infrastructure as a Service (IaaS) cloud adoption [1,3].

Resource scaling in cloud computing can be performed horizontally, vertically or diagonally. The former, also currently the most common approach [4,23], adjusts the resource capacity by adding or removing whole virtual machines (VMs) to or from the deployment. Vertical scaling, instead, adjusts the capacity within a VM [6]. Obviously, vertical scaling can be more fine-grained and

This work has been developed in the project CLoUd Services Scalability (CLUSS) that is partly funded by the German ministry of education and research (ref. num.: 01IS13013A-D).

A. Celesti and P. Leitner (Eds.): ESOCC 2015 Workshops, CCIS 567, pp. 249–257, 2016.
DOI: 10.1007/978-3-319-33313-7_19

usually performs much faster than horizontal scaling [18,25]. However, vertical scaling has severe economic and physical limitations compared to its horizontal counterpart. Diagonal scaling, as a combination of both approaches, mitigates the disadvantages of only one scaling dimension [9]. It is capable of increasing the adaptability of IaaS deployments and therefore has the potential to reduce resource allocation under fluctuating loads.

The flexibility of cloud computing requires a fine-grained pricing model. This is especially true, since usage-based pricing is a further important determinant of cloud adoption beside scalability [12,17]. Nevertheless, current usage-based pricing models often have shortcomings in terms of granularity because of their minimum contract duration (e. g. one hour). That makes them quite coarse-granular and in fact nearly flat priced models if shorter time horizons are relevant for the application. Combining diagonal scaling techniques with a real usage-based pricing increases the benefits of IaaS clouds and further fosters cloud adoption. Since there is uncertainty as to which amount the price of such a service could be set, this work presents an approach and preliminary results of determining the upper price limit an IaaS provider could charge for a fine-grained diagonally scaling service.

Following a similar path, Jin et al. describe how the maximum user-accepted price and the optimal billing cycle for a given cloud pricing scheme can be determined [14]. However the approach does not consider different scaling techniques like horizontal and vertical scaling. In [5] a vertical scaling architecture is proposed for overcoming the limitations of coarse-granular pricing. However, no considerations were given to a suitable pricing scheme in connection with this architecture.

The main contribution of this paper is thus the assessment of potential pricing schemes for IaaS providers that implement fine-grained scaling techniques.

The remainder of the paper is structured as follows: in Sect. 2 we introduce the basic scaling model. Section 3 presents the fine-grained pricing model. Thereafter, we evaluate how the scaling model is used to determine the resource reduction potential of diagonal scaling and its price limits in Sect. 4. Section 5 discusses limitations and Sect. 6 concludes on the implications of the results.

2   Scaling Model

To compare horizontal and diagonal scaling alternatives we used a generic scaling model based on threshold-based auto-scaling. The model drives the allocation of VMs and associated virtual CPUs in accordance with the number of requests for a web application. Besides the threshold-based scaling technique, as presented in [9], there are other alternatives based on: reinforcement learning [24], queuing theory [23], control theory [13,15] or time-series analysis [6,10]. Since threshold-based scaling is very popular, as pointed out in [10], and supported by most main IaaS providers such as Amazon Web Services (AWS)[1] or Rackspace[2], we

---

[1] http://aws.amazon.com/autoscaling, last visit 23.06.2015.
[2] http://rackspace.com/cloud/auto-scale, last visit 23.06.2015.

Table 1. Overview of scaling parameters and variables

Parameter	Unit	Description
ϕ	$req \cdot s^{-1} \cdot cpu^{-1}$	Served number of requests per CPU per second
q	%	Common QoS criterion
w_h	s	Decision time window for horizontal scaling
w_v	s	Decision time window for vertical scaling
θ_{h_out}	%	CPU utilization threshold for horizontal scale out
θ_{h_in}	%	CPU utilization threshold for horizontal scale in
θ_{v_up}	%	CPU utilization threshold for vertical scale up
θ_{v_down}	%	CPU utilization threshold for vertical scale down
n_{cpu_max}	cpu	Maximum number of CPUs per VM
d_{prov}	s	Provision duration for scaling up
d_{cont}	s	Minimum contract period
Variable	Unit	Description
n_{req}	$req \cdot s^{-1}$	Number of incoming requests per second
n_{cpu_dem}	cpu	Number of CPUs required to serve requests
n_{cpu_alloc}	cpu	Number of actually allocated CPUs
n_{vm_alloc}	vm	Number of allocated VMs
u	%	CPU utilization

also used this approach for our study. The parameters and variables considered are shown in Table 1.

We considered the CPU demand of a service for making threshold-based scaling decisions [11]. We assume an almost linear relation (ϕ) between the number of requests in a defined period of time (n_{req}) and the number of CPUs (n_{cpu_dem}) required for serving them within a given response time [21]. By applying this constant performance, we are able to calculate the CPU demand at all times of the investigated pattern by the formula: $n_{cpu\_dem}(t) = \lceil n_{req}(t) \cdot \frac{1}{\phi} \rceil$. We consider CPU as the main determinant of VM capacity, thus other aspects such as memory are neglected in this first step.

For simulating the actual resource allocation (n_{cpu_alloc} and n_{vm_alloc}) for a previously determined CPU demand pattern, the scaling model provides continuous monitoring of the CPU utilization (u). A fully utilized CPU is able to serve exactly the amount of requests determined by ϕ while meeting the defined response time for each request. The average CPU utilization of a sliding monitoring window (w_h and w_v) serves as criterion for the scaling thresholds (θ_{h_out}, θ_{h_in}, θ_{v_up} and θ_{v_down}) and is calculated each second. In both techniques, scaling steps always involve a single CPU, i.e. for vertical scenario the unit is a single CPU, while for horizontal scenario the unit is a VM with a single CPU. For distinguishing between horizontal and vertical scaling steps within the diagonal scaling scenario, a maximum number of CPUs per VM (n_{cpu_max}) is taken into account. As mentioned in Sect. 1, the resource reduction potential of diagonal scaling techniques is mainly achieved by shorter provisioning durations (d_{prov}) and can further be increased by shorter contract periods (d_{cont}), reflected by the corresponding parameters. To make a comparison, we chose a common quality of service (QoS) criterion q. Thus, both scenarios have to serve requests within a given response time in a defined fraction of time [19].

3   Pricing Model

In order to define a pricing model based on diagonal scaling techniques that is more usage-based than current IaaS solutions the pricing curve has to be fitted better to the resource consumption curve. Thus, an even closer alignment to the clients' needs can be achieved by avoiding the minimum contract duration which is still common by most of the IaaS providers such as AWS[3] or Rackspace[4]. For achieving a sufficient granularity in terms of time, a pricing model with a resolution of one second and no initial fees has been chosen [2]. Furthermore, for mapping the granularity of diagonal scaling techniques as accurately as possible to the pricing model, the technical scaling units are reflected in the pricing model directly. In case of the proposed scaling model in Sect. 2, scaling units are single CPUs. Since a bundled pricing model was chosen for acceptance and simplicity reasons as discussed in [8], each bundle represents a single CPU. The uniform bundles consist of further corresponding resources such as memory, storage, network, etc. – similar to AWS EC2 instances. To the best authors' knowledge at the time of writing this paper, there is no IaaS provider offering a diagonal scalable and simultaneously real usage-based priced service as described.

4   Evaluation

In this section we first describe how we determined the resource reduction potential of a threshold-based diagonally scalable IaaS compared to a common horizontally scalable IaaS by simulation. Based on this comparison, we show the preliminary results of a competitive price determination for a fine-grained pricing model. The overall approach is outlined in Fig. 1.

Table 2 shows the parameter values for the reduction determination process.

The evaluation was performed by comparing the scenarios, given an eleven-day load pattern (with a one-day heat-up phase) of gloveler[5] – a German web application provider for offering and booking private accommodation. The load pattern is shown in Fig. 1.

We took account of the application tier exclusively [7]. The value of ϕ reflects the performance of an AWS EC2 m3 general purpose instance mapped to the requests of the load pattern. The mapping is based on the CPU performance

---

[3] http://aws.amazon.com/ec2/pricing/, last visit 23.06.2015.

[4] http://rackspace.com/cloud/servers/, last visit 23.06.2015.

[5] http://gloveler.de/, last visit 23.06.2015.

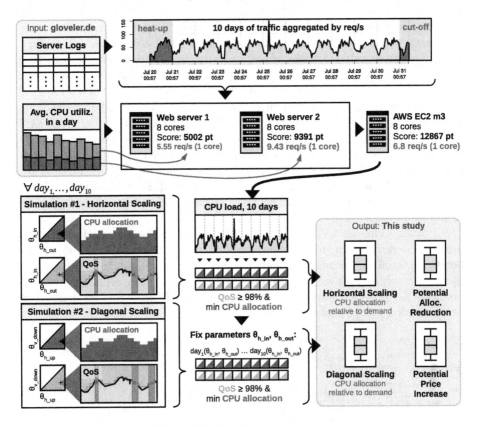

Fig. 1. Outline of our approach

Table 2. Values of scaling parameters used for simulation

Parameter	Value horizontal	Value diagonal	
ϕ	$6.8152\ req \cdot s^{-1} \cdot cpu^{-1}$	$6.8152\ req \cdot 1s^{-1} \cdot cpu^{-1}$	
q	.98	.98	
n_{cpu_max}	$1\ cpu$	$8\ cpu$	
d_{cont}	$1\ min,\ 1\ h$	$1\ s$	
		Horizontal	Vertical
w	$600\ s$	$600\ s$	$30\ s$
d_{prov}	$97\ s$	$97\ s$	$1\ s$

determination[6] of the actual web application servers of gloveler by matching the average CPU utilization per day with the corresponding average CPU load. The CPU performance was chosen for the calculation of the resource demand.

---

[6] http://cpubenchmark.net/compare.php?cmp[]=834&cmp[]=896&cmp[]=1220, last visit 23.06.2015.

Following an example of the AWS Auto Scaling Groups documentation[7] the monitoring window w is 600 s for horizontal scaling and 30 s for vertical scaling. For staying comparable in terms of scaling units the maximum number of CPUs per VM n_{max_cpu} for horizontal scaling is one, which is possible with AWS EC2. For diagonal scaling the maximum number is equal to the biggest AWS EC2 m3 general purpose instances, which currently is eight instances.[8] The provisioning duration d_{prov} for horizontal scaling was determined according to an AWS EC2 Linux VM [18] and according to [25] for diagonal scaling. The minimum contract duration d_{cont} for the horizontal scenario was determined according to the contract duration of AWS EC2 on-demand instances and for a more conservative calculation a duration of one minute was chosen as well. For the diagonal scaling scenario we defined the minimum contract duration of one second since vertical scaling would allow this.

For both scenarios and for each day of the load pattern several simulation runs were performed for different thresholds θ of 5 %, 10 %, 15 %, ..., 95 %. The thereby determined resource allocations and QoS were used for selecting the threshold combinations with the lowest resource consumption while meeting the common QoS criterion q of 98 % for each day [19]. Thus, a fair comparison of both scenarios was possible.

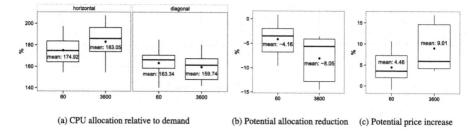

(a) CPU allocation relative to demand   (b) Potential allocation reduction   (c) Potential price increase

Fig. 2. Resource reduction and potential price increase of diagonal scaling for a minimum contract period (d_{cont}) of 60 and 3600 s

Figure 2a shows the average CPU allocation relative to the demand of all ten days and for both scenarios. A mean CPU reduction of 8.05 % was achieved by the diagonal scenario as shown in Fig. 2b. For determining how much an IaaS provider could charge for a single CPU bundle as described in Sect. 3 we calculated a competitive price based on the resource reduction.

A mean price increase potential of 9.01 % per CPU bundle was calculated as shown in Fig. 2c. An IaaS provider of a fine-grained service as described in this paper could charge for a single CPU bundle up to 0.0861 $/h while still being competitive to equivalent AWS EC2 m3 on-demand instances which are priced

[7] http://docs.aws.amazon.com/AWSCloudFormation/latest/UserGuide/
    example-templates-autoscaling.html, last visit 23.06.2015.
[8] http://aws.amazon.com/ec2/instance-types/, last visit 23.06.2015.

with 0.0790 \$/h. Assuming a minimum contract duration of one minute for the horizontal scenario a reduction of still 4.16 % was achieved and a price increase potential of 4.46 % was possible.

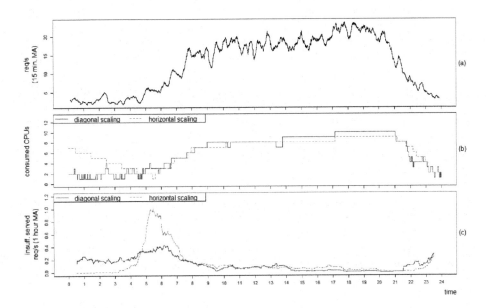

Fig. 3. Allocation and insufficiently served requests of gloveler.de from 24.07.2014 [22]

Figure 3a shows the one-day load pattern of the 24.07.2014 for exemplary reasons. Figure 3b and c show the corresponding resource allocation and the number of requests that were not served in time for both scenarios by using the determined thresholds for this day. Comparing the allocations, a quicker response to load fluctuation for the diagonal scenario is indicated. This increase of elasticity leads to a notable reduction in the violation of the QoS criterion between 5 and 7 a.m.

5   Discussion

We have presented a scenario-independent generic scaling model and a likewise fine-grained pricing model. Using our exemplary real life load pattern, we demonstrated a substantial resource reduction potential. That allows the cloud provider to increase prices while staying competitive. Since the research resulting in the described approach and findings is still in progress, our current work has some limitations. So far, we have covered a rather short load pattern within a single application disregarding long term trends. In addition, we currently neglect different types of requests by applying an averaged load per request to the simulation which can be addressed in further work.

6   Conclusion and Outlook

In this paper we build on an automated diagonal resource scaling procedure and propose an appropriate fine-grained CPU-bundled pricing regime for this case. Such a fine-grained service aims at main determinants of cloud adoption, i.e. adaptation and usage-based pricing. Based on an exemplary real life load pattern of a German web application provider, we compared the resource consumption of a common horizontal scaling approach with a diagonal one. While providing a higher granularity for possible scaling steps, savings in resource consumption of 8.05 % were achieved. With respect to the competitive price range for the CPU bundle price we see that in the analyzed load pattern the upper price limit is 0.0861 \$/h. Compared to an analogous AWS EC2 instance, this means an average increase of 9.01 %.

Next steps in our research will be to consider more uncertainty in the load patterns, and to analyze the impact of the load variations over longer time horizons with the goal of determining a valid corridor for the upper price limit. Further future work can go into various directions. Work with a focus on an improved economic assessment for longer time frames could consider the upfront investment costs of different alternatives. This is also likely to better show the advantages of dynamically and fine-grained scalable resources. Finally, the pricing regime could be evaluated from the perspective of the cloud provider, which in turn has to determine the cost-covering lower price limit.

References

1. Andrade, P., et al.: Improving business by migrating applications to the cloud using cloudstep. In: Proceedings of WAINA 2015, pp. 77–82, March 2015
2. Berndt, P., Maier, A.: Towards sustainable IaaS pricing. In: Altmann, J., Vanmechelen, K., Rana, O.F. (eds.) GECON 2013. LNCS, vol. 8193, pp. 173–184. Springer, Heidelberg (2013)
3. Chebrolu, S.B.: Assessing the relationships among cloud adoption, strategic alignment and information technology effectiveness. JITM **22**(2), 13–29 (2011)
4. Chieu, T., Mohindra, A., Karve, A., Segal, A.: Dynamic scaling of web applications in a virtualized cloud computing environment. In: Proceedings of the ICEBE 2009, pp. 281–286, October 2009
5. Dawoud, W., Takouna, I., Meinel, C.: Elastic virtual machine for fine-grained cloud resource provisioning. In: Krishna, P.V., Babu, M.R., Ariwa, E. (eds.) ObCom 2011, Part I. CCIS, vol. 269, pp. 11–25. Springer, Heidelberg (2012)
6. Dutta, S., Gera, S., Verma, A., Viswanathan, B.: Smartscale: automatic application scaling in enterprise clouds. In: Proceedings of the IEEE CLOUD 2012, pp. 221–228 (2012)
7. Eckerson, W.W.: Three tier client/server architectures: achieving scalability, performance, and efficiency in client/server applications. Open Inf. Syst. **3**(20), 46–50 (1995)
8. El Kihal, S., Schlereth, C., Skiera, B.: Price comparison for infrastructure-as-a-service. In: Proceedings of the ECIS 2012, June 2015, pp. 1–12 (2012)
9. Han, R., Guo, L., Ghanem, M.M., Guo, Y.: Lightweight resource scaling for cloud applications. In: Proceedings of IEEE/ACM CCGrid 2014, pp. 644–651 (2012)

10. Heinze, T., Pappalardo, V., Jerzak, Z., Fetzer, C.: Auto-scaling techniques for elastic data stream processing. In: Proceedings of ICDE 2014, pp. 296–302 (2014)
11. Iqbal, W., et al.: Adaptive resource provisioning for read intensive multi-tier applications in the cloud. Future Gener. Comput. Syst. **27**, 871–879 (2011)
12. Jamshidi, P., Ahmad, A., Pahl, C.: Cloud migration research: a systematic review. IEEE Trans. Cloud Comput. **1**(2), 142–157 (2013)
13. Jamshidi, P., Ahmad, A., Pahl, C.: Autonomic resource provisioning for cloud-based software. In: Proceedings of SEAMS 2014, pp. 95–104. ACM, New York, NY, USA (2014)
14. Jin, H., Wang, X., Wu, S., Di, S., Shi, X.: Towards optimized fine-grained pricing of IaaS cloud platform. IEEE Trans. Cloud Comput. **3**(4), 1 (2014)
15. Kalyvianaki, E., Charalambous, T., Hand, S.: Self-adaptive and self-configured CPU resource provisioning for virtualized servers using kalman filters. In: Proceedings of the ICAC 2009, pp. 117–126. ACM, New York (2009)
16. Leavitt, N.: Is cloud computing really ready for prime time? Computer **42**(1), 15–20 (2009)
17. Lin, G., Fu, D., Zhu, J., Dasmalchi, G.: Cloud computing: IT as a service. IT Prof. **11**(2), 10–13 (2009)
18. Mao, M., Humphrey, M.: A performance study on the VM startup time in the cloud. In: Proceedings of the IEEE CLOUD 2012, pp. 423–430 (2012)
19. Menascé, D.A.: QoS issues in web services. IEEE Internet Comput. **6**(6), 72–75 (2002)
20. Raza, M.H., Adenola, A.F., Nafarieh, A., Robertson, W.: The slow adoption of cloud computing and IT workforce. Procedia Comput. Sci. **52**, 1114–1119 (2015)
21. Sedaghat, M., Hernandez-Rodriguez, F., Elmroth, E.: A virtual machine re-packing approach to the horizontal vs. vertical elasticity trade-off for cloud autoscaling. In: CAC, p. 1 (2013)
22. Sperber, A.P.: Diagonale Skalierung verteilter Webanwendungen am Beispiel von gloveler. Ph.D. thesis, Karlsruhe Institute of Technology (KIT), Karlsruhe (2014)
23. Urgaonkar, B., et al.: An analytical model for multi-tier internet services and its applications. SIGMETRICS Perform. Eval. Rev. **33**(1), 291–302 (2005)
24. Vasić, N., Novaković, D., Miučin, S., Kostić, D., Bianchini, R.: Dejavu: accelerating resource allocation in virtualized environments. In: Proceedings of the ASPLOS 2012, pp. 423–436 (2012)
25. Yazdanov, L., Fetzer, C.: Vertical scaling for prioritized VMs provisioning. In: Proceedings of the CGC 2012, pp. 118–125. IEEE Computer Society, Washington, DC (2012)

IDEA Workshop Papers

Preface of IDEA 2015

Digitization is the use of digital technologies for creating innovative digital business models and transforming existing business models and processes. Information is captured and processed without human intervention using digital means. Digitization creates profound changes in the economy and society. Digitization has both business and technological perspectives. Digital business models and processes are essential for many companies to achieve their strategic goals.

Digitization impacts the product, customer, and the value-creation perspective. Digitized products are dynamic; their functionality can be extended on the fly by using external services. They are capable of reflecting on their own status and thus morph the selling of physical assets to services. Digitization changes the relationships with the customer significantly. Personal interaction is replaced by self-service and proactive action. The customer interacts with the enterprise using a multitude of implicit touch points provided by the Internet of Things. Digitization fosters new models of value creation such as service-dominant logic. Value is also created by platform and network effects.

The goal of the workshop was to identify challenges from digitization for enterprises and organizations and to advance digital enterprise engineering and architecture to cope with these challenges. The workshop allowed us to identify and develop concepts and methods that assist the engineering and the management of digital enterprise architectures and the software systems supporting them.

To achieve the goals of the workshop, the following themes of research were pursued:

- Methods for the design and management of digital enterprises
- Alignment of the enterprise goals and strategies with the digital enterprise architecture
- Digital strategy and governance
- Architectural patterns for value co-creation, dynamic and servitized products
- Service in digital enterprises
- Business process management in digital enterprises
- Advanced analytics for the support of digital enterprises
- Self-service and automation in digital enterprises
- Customer journeys and relationship management in digital enterprises
- Internet of Things and digital enterprises
- Impact of digitization on society and economy
- Security in digital architectures

In the first paper, "Digitization – Perspectives for Conceptualization," Rainer Schmidt, Alfred Zimmermann, Selmin Nurcan, Michael Möhring, Florian Bär, and Barbara Keller develop a framework to conceptualize digitization by introducing several perspectives.

Maurizio Giacobbe, Maria Fazio, Antonio Celesti, Tindara Abbate, and Massimo Villari in their paper – "A Scientometric Analysis of Cloud Computing and QoE Literature to Design a Cloud Platform of Experience for Digital Business" – provide some guidelines to digital business companies for addressing the issues related to QoE that have to be taken into account in order to maximize their business.

In "Enabling Digital Transformation Using Secure Decisions as a Service," Hans-Joachim Hof, Rainer Schmidt, and Lars Brehm introduce a new, secure, and layered architecture that separates the process from the decision model in order to react quickly to changed requirements. It provides flexibility by separating three aspects of decision-making: foundations, methods, and data.

Alexander Smirnov and Andrew Ponomarev collect and analyze all the requirements for crowd computing frameworks that drove the development of these frameworks recently in the paper titled "Exploring Requirements for Multipurpose Crowd Computing Framework."

In the paper "Adaptive Enterprise Architecture for Digital Transformation," Alfred Zimmermann, Rainer Schmidt, Dierk Jugel, and Michael Möhring investigate mechanisms for flexible adaptation and evolution for the next digital enterprise architecture systems in the context of digital transformation. The aim is to support flexibility and agile transformation for both business and related enterprise systems through adaptation and dynamical evolution of digital enterprise architectures.

We wish to thank all the people who submitted papers to IDEA 2015 for having shared their work with us, as well as the members of the IDEA 2015 Program Committee, who made a remarkable effort in reviewing the submissions. We also thank the organizers of ESOCC 2015 for their help with the organization of the event.

Selmin Nurcan
Rainer Schmidt
Alfred Zimmermann

Organization

Program Committee

Said Assar	Institut Mines-Telecom, France
Lars Brehm	Munich University of Applied Science, Germany
Eman El-Sheikh	University of West Florida, USA
Peter Mandl	University of Applied Sciences Munich, Germany
Michael Möhring	Aalen University, Germany
Selmin Nurcan	Université de Paris 1 Panthéon – Sorbonne, France
Gunther Piller	University of Applied Sciences Mainz, Germany
Kurt Sandkuhl	The University of Rostock, Germany
Rainer Schmidt	Munich University of Applied Sciences, Germany
Samira Si-Said Cherfi	CEDRIC – Conservatoire National des Arts et Métiers, France
Alfred Zimmermann	Reutlingen University, Germany

Digitization – Perspectives for Conceptualization

Rainer Schmidt[1(✉)], Alfred Zimmermann[2], Michael Möhring[1], Selmin Nurcan[4],
Barbara Keller[3], and Florian Bär[1]

[1] Munich University of Applied Sciences, Lothstrasse 64, 80335 Munich, Germany
Rainer.Schmidt@hm.edu
[2] Reutlingen University, Reutlingen, Germany
[3] Aalen University of Applied Sciences, Munich, Germany
[4] University Paris 1 Panthéon-Sorbonne, Paris, France

Abstract. Digitization is more than using digital technologies to transfer data
and perform computations and tasks. Digitization embraces disruptive effects of
digital technologies on economy and society. To capture these effects, two
perspectives are introduced, the product and the value-creation perspective. In
the product perspective, digitization enables the transition from material, static
products to interactive and configurable services. In the value-creation perspective, digitization facilitates the transition from centralized, isolated models of
value creation, to bidirectional, co-creation oriented approaches of value creation.

Keywords: Digitization · Value co-creation · Digital business processes · Digital
enterprise

1 Introduction

Digitization has a disruptive impact both on markets and the world of work and social
structures [1]. The impact of digitization on the economy can be observed by the emergence of new companies [2] and the demise of established companies [3]. Therefore, it
does not surprise that digitization is one of the most intensively discussed concepts
today. Digitization is considered as an integral concept of modern management [4] and
in the center of public interest [5]. Digitization is also top-priority topic of IT-Manage-
ment [6] and business process management [7]. Numerous studies from renowned
organizations and companies develop strategies in order to drive digitization [8, 9].
Studies predict enormous benefits through the introduction of digitization [8, 10]. An
economy shaped by digitization, a digital economy, has already been sketched in [11].
Furthermore, digitization shall improve business processes in many industry sectors
outside the information technology like the manufacturing industry [12]. Innovative
approaches using digital technologies can also be found in areas such as tourism [13].

There are many definitions that consider digitization as a primarily technical term
[14]. Technologies often associated with digitization [15] are: cloud computing [16],
big data [17] and [18] advanced analytics, social software [19], and the Internet of things
[20]. Also some new technologies are associated with digitization. For example, deep
learning [21] allows computing to be applied to activities that were considered as

© Springer International Publishing Switzerland 2016
A. Celesti and P. Leitner (Eds.): ESOCC 2015 Workshops, CCIS 567, pp. 263–275, 2016.
DOI: 10.1007/978-3-319-33313-7_20

exclusive to human beings [22]. Digitization is also tightly connected to the flexible execution of business processes [23]. Some authors consider digitization as caused by the exponential growth of computing, storage and networks that have surpassed certain limits [22].

Despite the widespread use of the term digitization there are only few definitions that try to capture the nature of digitization beyond the technological level. Nevertheless, the first approaches to analyze the non-technical perspectives of digitization are also rather old [24]. The definition in [1] identifies two aspects of digitization: the networking of people and things, second the convergence of real and virtual worlds. Other definitions [14] associate digitization with the creation of new opportunities that break down industry barriers and at the same time destroy existing business models [14]. Key elements of digital transformation strategies are described in [25]. In [26] scope, scale, speed and the sources of value creation and capture are identified as key themes for digital business strategy.

Our thesis is, that a definition of the term digitization requires multiple perspectives beyond the technical one. To do so, we introduce two new perspectives, the product and a value-creation perspective into the definition of digitization: Digitization changes the nature of what is called an product. It also transforms value-creation.

Our research method is a conceptual (non empirical) driven research approach [27] based on the current literature in the field of information systems, computer science and management with the focus on digitization. Adapted from the analyzed literature with regards to different influencing factors and basic principles, we create a framework of digitization.

The paper proceeds as follows; first, the technologies enabling digitization are described. Then we introduce two new perspectives for the definition of digitization. First we investigate how digitization impacts the notion of a product. In the following section, the transformation of value-creation will be analyzed. In the following chapter, some effects of the present wave of digitization will be depicted. Finally, an outlook and conclusion is given.

2   Technological Enablers of Digitization

Digital technologies exist since the 1940s. The digital representation of information, its processing and the term digitization, is in use since years [11]. Since the 1960 there is an ongoing exponential growth of the processing, storage and communication skills of modern IT systems [22].

The growth dynamics is described by Moore's law [28] formulated in the 1960s and 1975. It postulates a doubling of chip complexity every two years [28]. Moore's law is still applicable and Intel estimates it will be valid 10 years down to a structure width of 5 nm [29]. Significant economic benefits are associated with these technological advances. For example, an Internet application that caused costs of $150,000 a year of the year 2000, cost only about $1,500 in 2011 [30].

Digitization today is associated with a number of technologies, the most prominent are: Big data [17] and advanced analytics [16, 18] cloud computing [16], social software

[19], and the Internet of things [20]. In the future, it is expected that new potential for digitization is created by the automation of supporting tasks that require dexterity, natural language understanding, pattern recognition and case based problem solving [31].

2.1 Big Data and Advanced Analytics

Big data [17] and advanced analytics [18] have received much attention in industry and research [32]. Big data is not a specific technology or platform such as Hadoop [33], but describes a series of technological advances that made possible a significant improvement of decision support in business. Big Data can help organizations to improve current business processes and to be more competitive [34]. Before the emergence of Big Data, decision support was based on structured data from internal sources, as shown in Fig. 1. This data typically originate from business transactions and are usually maintained in an ERP system. Due to their normalized [35] structure, these data are of limited used for analytics. Therefore approaches such as business analytics [36] and business intelligence [37] move and transform these data using into a data warehouse using an extract, transform and load approach. The use of intermediate data creates considerable latency from the emergence of data to their visibility into the data warehouse. Therefore, the analyses carried out are mainly backwards oriented and have a descriptive perspective. On the contrary, the approach is of limited use for decisions that require an immediate response.

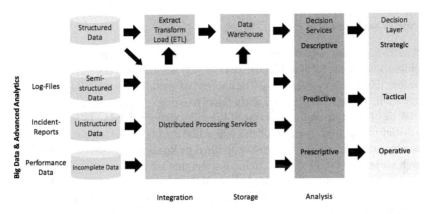

Fig. 1. Big Data extending Volume, Variety and Velocity based on [38]

These constraints and the emergence of always larger sources of unstructured and semi-structured data led to the development of big data and NoSQL technologies [39]. Semi structured data, e.g. log files of Web servers, have no explicit schema as data in a relational database [35]. Unstructured files, e.g. customer comments in a Web blog, have no schema that can be reconstructed. Semantic heterogeneity is another characteristic of semi- and unstructured data.

The processing of semi- and unstructured data is very computing-intensive. Therefore classic database concepts with a centralized architecture [33, 35] are quickly overwhelmed. On the contrary, highly distributed approaches such as Hadoop, allow to process semi- and unstructured data in the Petabyte range [33]. An important effect of distributed computing is the significant reduction of latency between the emergence of the data and the analysis. The inclusion of large amounts of data allows to create also predictive or even recommending analyses. Due to the reduced latency decisions on tactical and even operational level are supported.

2.2   Cloud-Computing

Cloud computing is implementing the vision, that computation and storage is available in the same way as the electricity and water supply, also called "utility computing" [40]. A significant increase in efficiency is achieved by economies of scale. The most widely used definition of cloud-computing from the National Institute of standards (NIST) [16] identifies five characteristics: self-service, a high-performance network access, resource pooling, elasticity, and billing after consumption. The NIST definition distinguishes three service models: software, platform, and infrastructure as a service. In addition, four usage models are defined, namely the private, public, hybrid, and community cloud. Cloud-Computing also generates new economic advantages for enterprises [41] and can be used to be more customer-oriented as well as improve customer relationship management [42].

2.3   Social Software

Social software and its underlying concepts can be found today in many areas, both in the public sector, in the form of social networks [43] as same as in organizations applying approaches like Enterprise 2.0 [44]. The success of social software is based essentially on three basic concepts that significantly reject existing organizational concepts. There are weak ties [45], egalitarian structures [46] and social production [47].

In social production, the role of the individual during production is not defined in advance by management. Instead, the individual makes his contributions in the interest of a high social reputation. No hierarchical structures are necessary to coordinate work or to ensure a high quality. Weak ties [45] are links between people, created by incident outside the established organizational structures. An example is the use of the same blogs. Weak ties can be used to assess the impact of a negative statement about a product. Egalitarian [46] structures assure, that no important contribution is excluded due to a low hierarchical position of the contributor.

2.4   Internet of Things

"Internet of Things" is according to Gartner, the most hyped term 2014 [5]. The basis is that growing miniaturization allows implementing always-richer functionality in a small space. Sensors, actuators and RFID [48] are the starting points of the development of the internet of things. Today powerful processing, storage and communication capabilities have been added, allowing the performance of office PCs of the early 2000s on a credit card to assemble machines such as the raspberry pi 2 [49].

3   Product Perspective

3.1   Digitized Products

Digitized products differ significantly from the physical products shaped by the paradigms of Taylorism [50] and Fordism [51]. An often-standardized hardware captures the environment using sensors and acts through actuators on them. It is controlled via software, which is updatable and in this way customizable and extensible. The device is in connection with other devices or Cloud-based systems via communication networks. The device may use the services provided in the cloud and sends data to these services (Fig. 2).

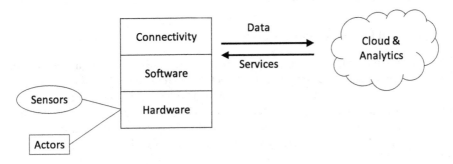

Fig. 2. Digitized products

To enable future extensions, hardware capabilities are designed in a generic way: the functionality of the device is shaped by the software and the cloud services as far as possible. The hardware provides only the necessary processing, storage, and communication skills. Furthermore, external devices are used to complement functionality in quickly evolving technologies. An example is the use of tablets and mobile phones as a substitute for attached displays.

3.2   Digitized Products Are Reflective

Digitized products are constantly in communication with the manufacturer. In this way, the manufacturer can collect genuine information about the use of the product. This collection of data can be done with involvement of the customer. Important information for the development of new products can be obtained. In addition, it is possible to identify up- and cross-selling chances. Based on the data collected higher value offerings or additional offerings can be identified, which are beneficial to customers. The fact that the customer did not realize these needs on its own will also strengthen the relationship of trust with the manufacturer. In the same way, functionality can be identified that is no longer needed by the customer. This information can be used to submit a cheaper deal based on a reduced functionality to the customer. Abstracted from the individual customer, important information can be collected. It is possible to use these data for the segmentation of customers and the identification of customer needs.

3.3 Digitized Products Are Dynamic

The classic industrial products are static [52]. After production, you cannot change the product at all or only to a limited extent. Digitization creates products containing software that can be upgraded via network connections. In addition, digitized products can use external services. Software and especially services are easier to update. New software functions can be added; additional services can be integrated. Therefore, the functionality of products is no longer static, but can be adapted to changing requirements. In particular, it is possible to create step-by-step or temporarily unlockable functionalities of the product. So, customers whose requirements have risen can add functions without hardware modification.

3.4 Digitized Products Are Servitized

The digitization enables products to capture their own state and communicate it to the vendor. By this means, the vendor is able to determine remotely whether the product is still functional and encourage, when appropriate, maintenance and repairs. This is the basis on which the product can be offered as a service, instead of the physical product. This transformation is called servitization [53]. Such services will be measured based on their availability. Examples are guaranteed machine availability, energy savings or crop yields.

By providing a service to the user and not selling a product to a consumer, usage-based billing models can be established (related to public cloud computing [41]). In addition to the usage information also the condition of the product by the manufacturer can be queried and the product informs the manufacturer about critical status changes.

In this context, concepts of preventive maintenance can be developed. These have the objective of to avoid unscheduled stoppages whenever possible. Evaluation of status information and analysis of the history of use of the product allow to predict, when a malfunction of the product is likely. Then, a maintenance or replacement of the product can be performed before the respective date. In this context, the collected data can also be used to provide preparatory information for a repair, so that a high first time solution rate can be achieved. At the same time, storage of spare parts can be minimized.

4 Value-Creation Perspective

To encompass digitization from a value creation perspective, one has to start with the paradigms that governed industrial production before digitization: Taylorism [54] and Fordism [51]. Both paradigms coined the character of industrial products: They are produced isolated from the customer in huge quantities in order to create economies of scale. The single point of interaction between vendor and customer is the exchange of the product against the payment. After the payment the vendor has normally no contact with the product anymore. The product preserves its configuration until it is broken our decommissioned. Products created in such a setting do not communicate either with the producer, among each other or with other objects. Digitized products however, are able to communicate with the producer and their environment. Thus a number of new mechanisms for value creation are provided.

4.1 Platforms

Platforms are complementary products, which cooperate via standardized interfaces [55]. Software platforms support the collection, analysis and exchange of data [52]. Platforms significantly speed-up the development time of new solutions, since the development of new functionality is distributed on different partners [56]. At the same time also a distribution of the development effort and risks takes place [56].

Up- and downward spirals are characteristic of platforms [34]. Attractive platforms attract many customers. This in turn makes the development of additional functionality through new partner attractive. Newly developed capabilities in turn increase the attractiveness of the platform for customers, etc. On the other hand, unattractive platforms lose customers, which, reduce the incentive to develop extensions for these platforms, in turn.

The physical devices in a platform [34] also significantly increase the switching costs for customers. The customer cannot move his equipment to another platform. He loses not only his device, but he must write off the purchases of additional functionalities such as apps. Finally, the customer loses the individual adjustments made by him such as configurations and settings etc.

4.2 Network Effects

By linking devices on networks, benefits are generated from two areas. Both the functionality increases and there are positive effects arising from the overarching data use. Network effects grow exponentially, because they are based on the number of participants, but on the number of possible connections.

The possibility to connect devices of the network increases the possibilities of the individual device, because the number of potential partners increases. By these means, extra value is created that increases faster as the number of devices, since the number of possible connections grows faster as the device number [57]. Furthermore, this makes it easy to provide integrated solutions to the customer that provides solutions over the whole lifecycle. Services provided by a lot of partners with complementary skills [52] may create extra value.

4.3 Networked Intelligence

By linking data from different sources [58], it is possible to detect correlations that would not have been possible to detect with the data of a single device. This effect increases with the number of devices. Therefore, network effects become apparent not only in functionality, but also in the scope of the data. These effects are called network intelligence [24]. Trends can be detected much earlier and more accurately by bringing together data from different network nodes. A characteristic is the involvement of individual product in an information system, which accelerates the learning and knowledge processes across all products [18]. In this way, a number of other beneficial effects can be achieved as network optimization, maintenance optimization, improved restore capabilities, and additional evidence against the consideration of individual systems. Furthermore, extraction of relevant information can be also improved by integrating external data sources.

4.4   Co-creation of Value

The prevalent model of the economy is based on physical goods. Starting point of thinking is the consideration by Adam Smith in his work "The Wealth of Nations" [59]. Here, the market-based exchange of goods enables the specialization and the division of labor production, which leads to a higher overall efficiency. Following this basic orientation also the Taylorism [50] and Fordism [51] are designed.

Central to this thinking is the idea that the producer of goods creates value. The value is determined at the moment of exchange of goods. It had been tried to transfer this idea on services. However, this led to a service definition, which considers services as a negation of physical goods [60]. E.g. services are not material, they are also not divisible, i.e. they must be provided as a whole. Services are also not durable; they cannot be stored and are provided only at the moment of need.

To break this thinking, Vargo and Lusch have developed an alternative design. In the service-dominant logic [61, 62] not goods, but service is the center of economic exchange. Goods hide only the fact that economic exchange actually concerns an exchange of services. Goods are used to materialize services [62]. An example of this is the television set, it used to be for a long time synonymous with television. Today, there are very many different ways to watch TV.

Consequently, the view changed how to determine the value of the service. In contrast to the goods dominant logic the value is determined during use of the service instead of the moment of purchase [62].

Basis for the implementation of service-dominant logic by digitization is the continuous connection of the products with the manufacturer. The manufacturer can win genuine information about the use of the product. Important information for the development of new products can be obtained in this way. The consumer becomes a prosumer [63]. Furthermore, digitization allows collecting information about the customer's preferences. This information can be used to facilitate choice for the customer. An example is Amazon [31] that is offering nearly 10 million different products but enables the customer to quickly find a product and select a vendor by giving recommendations to the customer, collecting evaluations, customer reviews and vendor evaluations. Another example for a sector, which could generate a high advantage is tourism [13]. Modern technologies like VR and also AR could help to improve the service through data driven applications and increase the additional value for the customer [13]. Combining these entire tools enable the customer to find the desired product more easily than in a physical shop (Fig. 3).

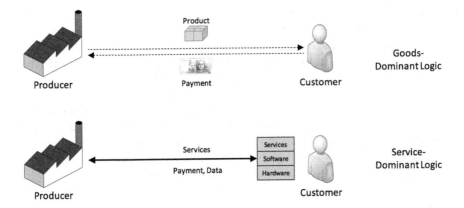

Fig. 3. GD-Logic versus SD-Logic

One could assume that an abundant offer of products and services is valued by the customer. However even small experiments show, that much choice both attracts the customer but also reduces his propensity to make a deal [64, 65]. In general complexity is perceived as negative from a customer's perspective [31]. In consequence, there is a trade-off between complexity and the value created [31]. Digitization is able to reduce complexity especially for the customer and thus increase value-creation by decoupling product and process complexity [31].

In former times, it was assumed, that the direct and personal contact with the customer is the best approach for increasing customer loyalty and revenues. Nowadays an increasing percentage of customer, especially between 20 and 30 years old prefer online touchpoints [31].

5   Conclusion

Digitized products have new capabilities to interact with their environment and the customer. These capabilities embrace sensing, physical interaction, data-exchange and service delivery. We designed a framework for digitization in this paper to get a better understanding. Based on technologies such as Big Data, Cloud-Computing or the Internet of Things, digitization enables the creation of dynamic products that appear more as a service than a device to the customer. Digitized products can be used as data hubs for collecting information about themselves and their environment. The connectivity of digitized products enables network effects and networked intelligence. A significant change of value creation is initiated by digitized products. The so-called Service-Dominant Logic becomes more and more the governing paradigm of economy. Value-creation becomes bidirectional.

We contributed to the current information systems literature in different ways. We defined important aspects of digitization and linked it to each other. Furthermore, researchers can start to empirically evaluate our framework and get a better understanding of digitization. Managers can use our framework to evaluate their business work to become a more competitive organization trough digitization. This is of particular importance because strategy, culture and talent development are more decisive for digitization than technology [66]. Management should focus on reconfiguring the business to take advantage of digital technologies instead of trying to find the most appropriate technology. Winners in this environment will be companies, enable network effects to create value for the customers [52]. Digitization also affects economy and society as a whole [67].

There are some limitations to discuss. Our framework is based on literature work. There is no deep empirical validation until now. Furthermore, industry-specific differences are not described in a detailed way. Therefore, future research should validate our framework trough qualitative and quantitative methods (e.g. expert interviews, experiments, and survey) and explore industry-specific differences.

References

1. Kagermann, P.D.H.: Change through digitization—value creation in the age of industry 40. In: Albach, H., Meffert, H., Pinkwart, A., Reichwald, R. (eds.) Management of Permanent Change, pp. 23–45. Springer Fachmedien Wiesbaden, Wiesbaden (2015)
2. Fortune, Inc.: Fortune 500 firms in 1955 vs. 2014; 89 % are gone, and we're all better off because of that dynamic "creative destruction". http://www.aei.org/publication/fortune-500-firms-in-1955-vs-2014-89-are-gone-and-were-all-better-off-because-of-that-dynamic-creative-destruction/
3. Locker, M.: 8 iconic brands that have disappeared – Fortune. http://fortune.com/2014/11/09/defunct-brands/
4. Manyika, J., McAfee, A.: Why Every Leader Should Care About Digitization and Disruptive Innovation. McKinsey & Company (2014). http://www.mckinsey.com/insights/business_technology/why_every_leader_should_care_about_digitization_and_disruptive_innovation
5. Gartner's 2014 Hype Cycle for Emerging Technologies Maps the Journey to Digital Business. http://www.gartner.com/newsroom/id/2819918
6. Andersson, H., Tuddenham, P.: Reinventing IT to Support Digitization. McKinsey, San Francisco (2014)
7. Markovitch, S., Willmott, P.: Accelerating the Digitization of Business Processes. McKinsey & Company, San Francisco (2014)
8. Capgemini Consulting, MIT Sloan Managment: Digital Transformation: A Road-Map for Billion-Dollar Organizations (2011). http://www.capgemini.com/resources/digital-transformation-a-roadmap-for-billiondollar-organizations
9. Fitzgerald, M., Kruschwitz, N., Bonnet, D., Welch, M.: Embracing digital technology: a new strategic imperative. MIT Sloan Manage. Rev. 55, 1–12 (2013)
10. Manyika, J., Chui, M., Bisson, P., Woetzel, J., Dobbs, R., Bughin, J., Aharon, D.: The Internet of Things: Mapping the Value Beyond the Hype. McKinsey & Company, San Francisco (2015)
11. Brynjolfsson, E.: Understanding the Digital Economy: Data, Tools, and Research: Data, Tools and Research. The MIT Press, Cambridge (2000)

12. Schmidt, R., Möhring, M., Härting, R.-C., Reichstein, C., Neumaier, P., Jozinović, P.: Industry 4.0 - potentials for creating smart products: empirical research results. In: Abramowicz, W. (ed.) BIS 2015. LNBIP, vol. 208, pp. 16–27. Springer, Heidelberg (2015)

13. Keller, B., Möhring, M., Schmidt, R.: Augmented reality in the travel industry: a perspective how modern technology can fit consumer's needs in the service industry. Presented at the Naples Forum on Services 2015, Naples (2015)

14. Weill, P., Woerner, S.: Thriving in an increasingly digital ecosystem. MIT Sloan Manage. Rev. 56(4), 27–34 (2015)

15. Westerman, G., Bonnet, D.: Revamping Your Business Through Digital Transformation. http://sloanreview.mit.edu/article/revamping-your-business-through-digital-transformation/

16. Mell, P., Grance, T.: The NIST Definition of Cloud Computing. http://csrc.nist.gov/groups/SNS/cloud-computing/

17. Agrawal, D., Das, S., El Abbadi, A.: Big data and cloud computing: current state and future opportunities. In: Proceedings of the 14th International Conference on Extending Database Technology, pp. 530–533. ACM (2011)

18. Evans, P.C., Annunziata, M.: Industrial internet: pushing the boundaries of minds and machines. General Electric (2012)

19. Schmidt, R., Nurcan, S.: BPM and social software. In: Ardagna, D., Mecella, M., Yang, J., Aalst, W., Mylopoulos, J., Rosemann, M., Shaw, M.J., Szyperski, C. (eds.) BPM 2008 Workshop. LNBIP, vol. 17, pp. 649–658. Springer, Heidelberg (2009)

20. Atzori, L., Iera, A., Morabito, G.: The Internet of Things: a survey. Comput. Netw. 54, 2787–2805 (2010)

21. Schmidhuber, J.: Deep learning in neural networks: an overview. Neural Netw. 61, 85–117 (2015)

22. Brynjolfsson, E., McAfee, A.: The Second Machine Age: Work, Progress, and Prosperity in a Time of Brilliant Technologies. W. W. Norton & Company, New York (2014)

23. Regev, G., Soffer, P., Schmidt, R.: Taxonomy of flexibility in business processes. In: Proceedings Seventh Workshop on Business Process Modeling, Development, and Support (BPMDS 2006). Requirements for Flexibility and the Ways to Achieve It, Luxemburg, pp. S.90–S.93 (2006)

24. Tapscott, D.: The Digital Economy: Promise and Peril in the Age of Networked Intelligence. McGraw-Hill, New York (1996)

25. Matt, C., Hess, T., Benlian, A.: Digital transformation strategies. Bus Inf. Syst. Eng. 57, 339–343 (2015)

26. Bharadwaj, A., El Sawy, O.A., Pavlou, P.A., Venkatraman, N.: Digital business strategy: toward a next generation of insights. MIS Q. 37, 471–482 (2013)

27. Steenkamp, A.L., Kraft, T.: Integrating conceptual and empirical approaches for software engineering research. In: Research Methodologies, Innovations and Philosophies in Software Systems Engineering and Information Systems, pp. 298–320 (2012)

28. Moore, G.E.: Moore's Law at 40. In: David, C. (ed.) Understanding Moore's Law: Four Decades of Innovation. Chemical Heritage Foundation, Philadelphia (2006)

29. Ever more from Moore (2015). http://www.economist.com/news/business/21648683-microchip-pioneers-prediction-has-bit-more-life-left-it-ever-more-moore?fsrc=scn/tw/te/pe/ed/evermorefromMoore

30. Andreessen, M.: Why Software Is Eating the World (2011). http://www.wsj.com/articles/SB10001424053111903480904576512250915629460

31. Mocker, M., Weill, P., Woerner, S.: Revisiting Complexity in the Digital Age (2015). http://sloanreview.mit.edu/article/revisiting-complexity-in-the-digital-age/

32. LaValle, S., Lesser, E., Shockley, R., Hopkins, M.S., Kruschwitz, N.: Big data, analytics and the path from insights to value. MIT Sloan Manage. Rev. **52**, 21–32 (2011)

33. White, T.: Hadoop: The Definitive Guide. O'Reilly Media, Sebastopol (2012)

34. Schmidt, R., Möhring, M., Maier, S., Pietsch, J., Härting, R.-C.: Big data as strategic enabler - insights from central european enterprises. In: Abramowicz, W., Kokkinaki, A. (eds.) BIS 2014. LNBIP, vol. 176, pp. 50–60. Springer, Heidelberg (2014)

35. Codd, E.F.: Relational Completeness of Data Base Sublanguages. IBM Corporation, San Jose (1972)

36. Davenport, T.: The New World of "Business Analytics". International Institute for Analytics (2010)

37. Kemper, H.-G., Baars, H., Lasi, H.: An integrated business intelligence framework. In: Rausch, P., Sheta, A.F., Ayesh, A. (eds.) Business Intelligence and Performance Management, pp. 13–26. Springer, London (2013)

38. Schmidt, R., Sotzki, M.W., Jugel, D., Möhring, M., Sandkuhl, K., Zimmermann, A.: Towards a framework for enterprise architecture analytics. In: Grossmann, G., Hallé, S., Karastoyanova, D., Reichert, M., Rinderle-Ma, S. (eds.) 18th IEEE International Enterprise Distributed Object Computing Conference Workshops and Demonstrations, EDOC Workshops 2014, Ulm, Germany, 1–2 September 2014, pp. 266–275. IEEE Computer Society (2014)

39. Friedland, A., Hampe, J., Brauer, B., Brückner, M., Edlich, S.: NoSQL: Einstieg in die Welt nichtrelationaler Web 2.0 Datenbanken. Carl Hanser Verlag GmbH & CO. KG, Munich (2011)

40. McCarthy, J.: The Computer Utility Could Become the Basis of a New and Important Industry. MIT Centennial, Harvard (1961)

41. Möhring, M., Koot, C., Schmidt, R., Stefan, M.: Public-Cloud-Angebote: Kostenorientierte Entscheidungskriterien für kleine und mittlere Unternehmen. Controlling - Zeitschrift für erfolgsorientierte Unternehmensteuerung **25**, 619–624 (2013)

42. Härting, R.-C., Möhring, M., Schmidt, R., Reichstein, C., Keller, B.: What drives users to use CRM in a public cloud environment? – insights from European experts. In: Proceedings of the 49th Hawaii International Conference on System Sciences (HICSS), Kauai. IEEE (forthcoming)

43. Facebook: Facebook 2012 Annual Report. Facebook (2012)

44. Andrew, P.: McAfee: Enterprise 2.0: the dawn of emergent collaboration. MIT Sloan Manage. Rev. **47**, 21–28 (2006)

45. Granovetter, M.: The strength of weak ties: a network theory revisited. Sociol. Theor. **1**, 201–233 (1983)

46. Benkler, Y.: The Wealth of Networks: How Social Production Transforms Markets and Freedom. Yale University Press, New Haven (2006)

47. Tapscott, D., Williams, A.: Wikinomics: How Mass Collaboration Changes Everything. Penguin, New York (2006)

48. Welbourne, E., Battle, L., Cole, G., Gould, K., Rector, K., Raymer, S., Balazinska, M., Borriello, G.: Building the Internet of Things using RFID: the RFID ecosystem experience. IEEE Internet Comput. **13**, 48–55 (2009)

49. Richardson, M., Wallace, S.P.: Getting Started with Raspberry Pi. O'Reilly Media, Sebastopol (2012)

50. O'Halloran, D., Kvochko, E.: Industrial Internet of Things: Unleashing the Potential of Connected Products and Services. World Economic Forum

51. Baines, T., Lightfoot, H., Smart, P.: Servitization within manufacturing: exploring the provision of advanced services and their impact on vertical integration. J. Manuf. Technol. Manage. **22**, 947–954 (2011)
52. Taylor, F.W.: The Principles of Scientific Management, vol. 202. Harper & Brothers, New York (1911)
53. Shiomi, H., Wada, K.: Fordism Transformed: The Development of Production Methods in the Automobile Industry. Oxford University Press, Oxford (1995)
54. Baldwin, C.Y., Woodard, C.J.: The architecture of platforms: a unified view. In: Gawer, A. (ed.) Platforms, Markets and Innovation, pp. 19–44. Edward Elgar, Cheltenham (2009)
55. Eisenmann, T.R.: Managing proprietary and shared platforms. Calif. Manage. Rev. **50**, 31–53 (2008)
56. Metcalfe, B.: Invention is a flower, innovation is a weed. Technol. Rev. **102**, 54–57 (1999)
57. Provost, F., Fawcett, T.: Data Science for Business: What You Need to Know about Data Mining and Data-Analytic Thinking. O'Reilly Media, Sebastopol (2013)
58. Smith, A.: An Inquiry into the Nature and Causes of the Wealth of Nations. Methuen, London (1776/1937)
59. Taylor, F.W.: The Principles of Scientific Management. General Books LLC, Memphis (2010)
60. Vargo, S.L., Lusch, R.F.: The four service marketing myths: remnants of a goods-based manufacturing model. J. Serv. Res. **6**, 324–335 (2004)
61. Vargo, S.L., Lusch, R.F.: Evolving to a new dominant logic for marketing. J. Mark. **68**, 1–17 (2004)
62. Vargo, S., Lusch, R.: Service-dominant logic: continuing the evolution. J. Acad. Mark. Sci. **36**, 1–10 (2008)
63. Ritzer, G., Jurgenson, N.: Production, consumption, prosumption the nature of capitalism in the age of the digital "prosumer". J. Consum. Cult. **10**, 13–36 (2010)
64. Iyengar, S.S., Lepper, M.R.: When choice is demotivating: can one desire too much of a good thing? J. Pers. Soc. Psychol. **79**, 995 (2000)
65. Shah, A.M., Wolford, G.: Buying behavior as a function of parametric variation of number of choices. Psychol. Sci. **18**, 369–370 (2007)
66. Technology, C.©.M.I. of, reserved, 1977–2015 All rights: Is Your Business Ready for a Digital Future? http://sloanreview.mit.edu/article/is-your-business-ready-for-a-digital-future/
67. Morozov, E.: Why the internet of things could destroy the welfare state. http://www.theguardian.com/technology/2014/jul/20/rise-of-data-death-of-politics-evgeny-morozov-algorithmic-regulation

A Scientometric Analysis of Cloud Computing and QoE Literature to Design a Cloud Platform of Experience for Digital Business

Maurizio Giacobbe(✉), Maria Fazio, Antonio Celesti,
Tindara Abbate, and Massimo Villari

University of Messina, 98166 Messina, Italy
{mgiacobbe,mfazio,acelesti,abbatet,mvillari}@unime.it
http://mdslab.unime.it

Abstract. Cloud computing is rapidly evolving due to social and cultural influences that are changing the necessary Cloud services. Indeed, an increasing number of application and service providers use Cloud computing to adapt their products to customer needs, by addressing the requirements arisen by the customer Quality of Experience (QoE, QoX or simply QX) evaluation. QoE is a fast emerging multidisciplinary field based on social psychology, cognitive science, management, and engineering science, focused on understanding overall human quality requirements. In order to help Digital Business architects to understand how Cloud computing can help them to increase their business, we present a scientometric analysis of Cloud computing and QoE. Analyzing the current state of the art, we provide some guidelines to Digital Business companies for addressing the issues related to QoE that have to be taken into account in order to maximize their business.

Keywords: Cloud computing · Digital business · Platform of Experience · Quality of Experience · QoE · QoX · QX

1 Introduction

The current financial situation, together with the new market opportunities and the advent of Cloud technologies, has led to major changes both in the Information and Communication Technology (ICT) world and in the consumer's interests over the last few years. Latest economic changes, in fact, have conducted new socio-cultural transformations with great impact on the customer's needs. These changes are significantly influencing also the evolution of Cloud services, and how *digital enterprises* can use Cloud technologies to achieve many advantages both in their internal and external activities. This trend results in a new *digital business* scenario, where Cloud computing play a fundamental role to develop new business strategies by integrating digital and physical worlds. It differs from traditional e-business models thanks to an unprecedented integration of people, business and smart things allowing an optimal convergence with the promising *Internet of Things (IoT)* paradigm [1,2].

© Springer International Publishing Switzerland 2016
A. Celesti and P. Leitner (Eds.): ESOCC 2015 Workshops, CCIS 567, pp. 276–288, 2016.
DOI: 10.1007/978-3-319-33313-7_21

On this regard, *Quality of Experience (QoE, QoX or simply QX)* is a fast emerging multidisciplinary field based on social psychology, cognitive science, management, and engineering science, focused on understanding overall human quality requirements. Traditionally, technology-centric approaches based on QoS parameters have been employed to ensure service quality to end users. QoE expands this horizon to capture people's aesthetic and even hedonistic needs.

In short, QoE provides an assessment of human expectations, feelings, perceptions, cognition and satisfaction with respect to a particular product, service or application [3]. The concept of QoE in computer science is also known as perceived Quality of Service, in the sense of the QoS as it is finally perceived by the end-user adopting software solutions. It is a personal evaluation, that can be expressed through different degrees of appreciation. For example, the evaluation of the perceived QoS for audio-video content provisioning can be expressed by low, medium or high quality level. Then, the service provider can adapt the storage and network resources to obtain a specific level of user satisfaction, thus optimizing resource management.

As an important measure of the end-to-end performance at the services level from the user's perspective the QoE is an important metric for the design of systems and engineering processes. Thus, when designing systems the expected output, i.e. the expected QoE, is often taken into account also as a system output metric. Even though, QoE was originally conceived as concept for several multimedia applications [4], nowadays it becomes a fundamental metric to plan ahead new application and service deployment, with several advantages both for customers and providers. In this context, an increasing number of providers start to adopt Cloud computing services to form a competition market based on customer experience in order to maximize their profits. Customers became active part of a new digital business scenario where Cloud technologies allows them to share their experience to improve services and therefore the same customer experience in a virtuous cycle. A digital enterprise can use Cloud technologies to collect data from its customers devices (e.g., mobile devices, public dashboards). Therefore, data processing allows providers to measure the level of satisfaction of their customers.

In order to help Digital Business architects to understand the impact of Cloud technologies in the assessment of QoE, in this paper, we present a scientometric analysis of Cloud computing strategies in QoE management. The objective of this paper are the following: (1) analyzing the state of the art on QoE and Cloud computing; (2) providing guidelines to digital enterprises to understand how QoE should be taken into account in order to maximize profits; (3) providing a guideline to develop a Cloud based Platform of Experience (PoE) based on a Multi-Input-Multi-Output (MIMO) architecture.

The rest of the paper is organized as follows. Section 2 discusses related work. Section 3 presents a scientometric analysis of Cloud computing and QoE. In Sect. 4, we highlight several relevant aspects related to the topic. Then, in Sect. 5, we present a requirement analysis for the development of an efficient Cloud based Platform of Experience (PoE), describing in Sect. 6 several design aspects. Section 7 concludes the paper.

2   Related Work

This Section introduces several interesting contributions concerning the use of Cloud computing for QoE measurement and evaluation. Wang et al. [5] analyze the factors affecting the Quality of user Experience using the *Cloud Mobile Gaming (CMG)* approach, including the game genres, video settings, the conditions of server and client, and the conditions of the wireless network. Moreover, the authors present a *Mobile Gaming User Experience (MGUE)* model they assert will be helpful for researchers and service providers to develop and assess the performance of future Cloud mobile gaming techniques and services.

Colonnese et al. [6] present a Cloud-assisted procedure to improve the user's Quality of Experience in HTTP Adaptive Streaming (HAS) services. The proposal procedure exploits information on the encoded video content available at the Cloud side to control the client-originated download requests.

Vandenbroucke et al. [7] provide insights for future QoE-aware Cloud services. They refer to what they assert to be the most important mobile contextual factors (e.g., connectivity, location, social, device), and how they affect users' experiences while using such services on their mobile devices. To this end, the authors present the results of a 2-week follow-up study focused on investigating Cloud storage users' Quality of Experience on mobile devices. They use a mobile-based *Experience Sampling Method (ESM)* questionnaire to real-time monitor the mobile Cloud service usage on tablets and smartphones.

Huang et al. [8], by real experiments, demonstrate the potential of network-aware Clouds on improving the QoE of *Massively Multiuser Virtual Environments (MMVEs)*.

Saiz et al. [9] present their *QoXcloud platform*: a Cloud platform for the measurement and evaluation of the Quality of Experience (QoE) which is based on the *QoXphere* model to ensure the user satisfaction. However, this measurement is in terms of QoS, and QoE is included as assessed QoS. The authors also refer to the *Quality of user Perception (QoP)* as a perceived QoS.

Zhang et al. [10] propose a novel Cloud-assisted approach, they name *Cloud-Assisted Drug REcommendation (CADRE)*, for enriching end-user Quality of Experience of drug recommendation.

The above contributions are very interesting to understand the uptrend on the use of Cloud computing for QoE measurement and evaluation, thus to help providers to increase their competitiveness based on customer experience in order to maximize their profits.

3   Scientometric Analysis of Cloud Computing and QoE

In this paper we highlight the importance of the relationship between QoE and Cloud analyzing the *state of the art (sota)* on QoE and Cloud by using the methodological approach organized in the following steps:

- choice of several *keywords* and their meaningful combinations;
- selection of different electronic databases refining our research at *Computer Science* discipline. This last also includes *Engineering, Business and Management, Mathematics and Physics*;
- execution of the research;
- skimming of results of the research on the basis of a correct correspondence of the researched terms;
- download and saving the results in form of Bibtex references;
- survey draft of references.

Each one of the above mentioned combinations results in a different number of references to skim.

Table 1. Highlight on some important numerical results for each selected electronic database.

References	Database	URL	%
91	IEEE xplore	http://ieeexplore.ieee.org	67.41
13	ACM digital library	http://portal.acm.org	9.63
12	Springer link	http://link.springer.com/	8.89
10	ScienceDirect	http://www.sciencedirect.com	7.41
7	ISI web of science	http://apps.webofknowledge.com/	5.18
2	Google scholar	http://scholar.google.com	1.48
0	HCI bibliography	http://hcibib.org	0 (*)
0	Scopus	http://www.scopus.com/	0 (*)
Total = 135	-	-	**100**

(*) The result refers to the added value of the Database compared to the previous ones in the list.

Table 1 shows some important numerical results which are related to each one of the selected electronic database for the following researched terms (i.e. *keywords*) and their meaningful combinations: *'QoE and Cloud', 'Quality of Experience and Cloud', 'QoE' and 'Cloud', 'Quality of Experience' and 'Cloud'*.

Starting from the first row of Table 1, in each row, we consider the contribution of an electronic database in terms of references that are not included in the previous selected databases. More specifically, starting from consider *IEEE Xplore* the first database in our approach, each one of the following (ACM Digital Library is the first one of these considered) does not include the references that are already included in the previously considered database. For example, the HCI database reports a number of ten results, these results are also included in the previous Database (i.e. *ACM Digital Library Link* and to *Digital Content at Springer*). Thus, we consider a zero added value for HCI.

Table 1 consists of the following columns:

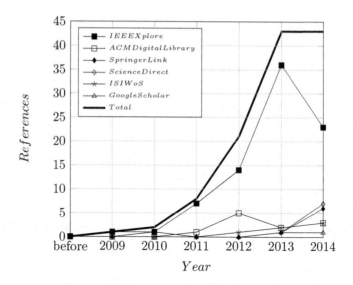

Fig. 1. Trend of the references which are present in the electronic databases in the last years.

- *References*: indicates how many references are resulting from the execution of our method, i.e. form our selection for each electronic database.
- *Database*: shows the names of the electronic databases.
- *URL*: indicates the *Uniform Resource Locator* of each electronic database.
- *%*: shows the percentage quota of the selected references for each electronic database.

The number of references on Cloud and QoS during the last years has the trend drawn in Fig. 1, where we can notice that the electronic Databases report most of references by 2014.

4   QoE Evaluation Based on Cloud Computing Approaches

The *sota* on QoE and Cloud gives us several very interesting hints that are objects of a further in-depth analysis. A first interesting point is the number of references focused on the use of Cloud computing for *measurement and evaluation* of QoE, as shown in Table 2. Compared to the results in Table 1, it means that the most of contributions on Cloud and QoS in literature are not focused on QoE evaluation issues, and, hence, a lot of work can be done.

The uptrend of the scientific literature on the use of Cloud computing for QoE evaluation is shown in Fig. 2, that shows the increasing interest in such kind of application field of Cloud.

Therefore, on the basis of the *sota* and of the above mentioned consideration, we look to a new perspective, where QoS and QoE complement each other and

Table 2. A summary of the references on the use of Cloud computing for QoE measurement and evaluation.

Num.	Database	References
4	ACM digital library	[5–8]
1	IEEE xplore	[9]
1	Springer link	[10]
1	Google scholar	[11]
0	ScienceDirect	-
0	ISI web of science	-
0	HCI bibliography	-
0	Scopus	-
Total = 7 of 135 (5.18 %)	-	-

the user perception is part of the user experience. More specifically, we focus on the design of a Cloud based *Platform of Experience (PoE)* and introduce an approach for the analysis of its requirements.

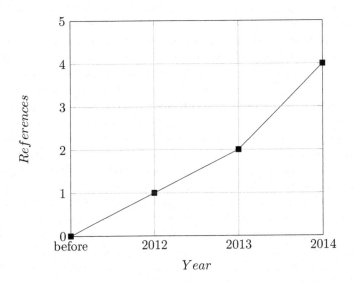

Fig. 2. The uptrend on the use of Cloud computing for QoE measurement and evaluation.

5   Requirements Analysis for a Cloud Based Platform of Experience

In this Section, we focus on the requirements analysis for a Cloud based Platform of Experience (PoE), in prospect of an *experimental marketing*.

5.1   Motivation

Many enterprises equipped with traditional ICT assets have a difficult time delivering customer experiences, this fact due to the unavailability of the necessary connections among ICT systems. For example, customer data storage is often centralized and includes informations from several sources that are often uncorrelated, e.g., social networks, e-mail, web questionnaires and much more. This is a serious problem that prevents a coherent view of customer experiences and can results in an undesirable inconsistency especially in the monitored marketplace context.

Our investigation focus on converting anonymous audiences into known active customers (i.e., members of one or more platforms), whose QoE can be weighted in a digital business context. This goal mainly requires a rich data gathering and a high level of granularity for each customer information, i.e., two requirements which is not always possible to meet with traditional *Information Technology (IT)* systems especially for billion people and devices connected to the Internet.

To this end, we present an approach which is oriented to use *Cloud computing* and *No-SQL databases* [12]. Specifically, a *Cloud Infrastructure-as-a-Service (IaaS)* platform beats the traditional IT systems because it provides web services and not only information, based on best reliability, flexibility and scalability. Moreover, we refer to MongoDB [13] No-SQL database, because the growing interest of the scientific community [14,15] to it. The traditional Relational Data Base Management Systems (RDBMS) analytics, in effect, can get very complicated or rather played out in presence of semi-structured or unstructured data.

Cloud *virtualization* [16] simplifies the use of *virtual contexts*, i.e. a set of virtual devices which are managed by companies with the objective to identify new inputs and ideas to produce new services/products. Virtual contexts act like **experiential providers** in order to develop, enrich and therefore make unique the *user experience*. In this way a company would stimulate several typologies of experiences, such as by involving the five human senses, even though the PoEs would generate great value experiences (e.g., *act, think and relate*). Companies, and therefore the PoEs they refer, concern different market or business sectors, and a comparison between different companies through the results provided by the PoEs would allow to identify significant affinities and differences. These are in turn essentially attributable to the logics and the dynamics which are typical of the respective sectors.

Based on these motivations, through our scientometric analysis we identify the following priorities to investigate to design a Cloud PoE for digital business:

- **Seamless**: a platform without interruption across multiple channels and devices, including mobile.
- **Ad-hoc customized**: Input/Output data, both in terms of right information and context (i.e. marketplace), should be delivered to the right audience at the right time.
- **Coherent**: platform controls information provided by its members to prevent unreliable data, e.g., market attacks by people engaged by possible competitors.
- **Collaborative**: user-to-company and user-to-user relationship and collaboration. This issue involves a stake-holding phase due to many subjects which act as experts and join into the platform through *community* features. A market-oriented approach in which Cloud providers leverage Cloud services from other Cloud providers for seamless provisioning is well discussed in [17].
- **Interactive**: directly and immediately contents exchange between users. This action would provide for *project rooms* (e.g., *social multi-chat rooms*) which are oriented to achieve this issue. The interactive concept [18] should be deepened on the base of two main topics, i.e. *textual interaction* and *personal interaction*, and their possible integration. This is very significant especially for *virtual environments* where it is possible to relate different community members and contemporary to access different contents.
- **Multimedial**: it consists of recognition and involvement actions (i.e. functionalities) [19,20] of new possible PoE members which are handy at web and social networks, thus to simplify the correlation between the PoE members and to increase the PoE quality.
- **Articulate**: well-structured to simplify the information research by platform visual instruments (e.g., the web-interface), thus to speed the procedures.
- **Navigable**: the information research should be executed by combining several search options, such as *keywords, categories* and additional filtering options, thus to maximize the usability, to influence user's first impression and to obtain an appropriate reply as fast as possible. Both this aspect and the above mentioned 'articulate' characteristic, are well discussed in [21].
- **Cloud based**: a flexible and on-demand resource provisioning in a *pay-as-you-go* manner, that is based on *Service Level Agreements (SLAs)* between customers and Cloud providers [22]. Where the world wide web makes information available everywhere and to everyone, Cloud makes storage and computing available everywhere and to everyone and, through Cloud networking mechanisms, without the cost and the constraints of the traditional IT systems.

Moreover, a PoE should be **accessible** for people with disabilities [23]. The above mentioned characteristics can be enhanced on the basis of the human development, and contemporary fulfill new requirements.

As introduced, the in-depth investigation of the above mentioned issues is oriented to set up a Cloud based platform to evaluate its member's experience. Specifically, we think to a Cloud Platform of Experience which is based on a *multi-level platform scale*, i.e. to model a *ranking list r* to evaluate the experience gained at every level.

6   Design of a Cloud Platform of Experience: A Reference Model

Starting from the previous Section where we introduced our requirements analysis, in this Section we present a possible Cloud based PoE reference model for digital business purposes (Fig. 3).

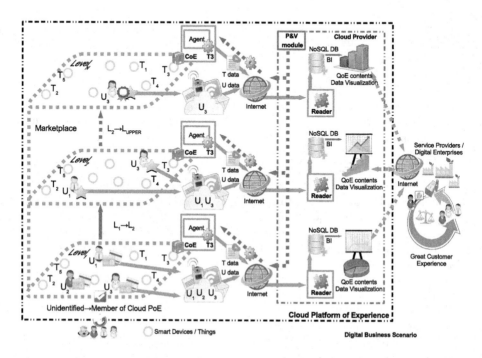

Fig. 3. Cloud Platform of Experience in digital business scenario.

More specifically, we introduce three main figures:

- **Users**, i.e., Customers that uses digital products and provide the evaluation of their experience;
- **Things**, i.e., Smart Sensors/Devices, that provide information on the environment or on the systems where digital products are exploited;
- **Service Providers**, i.e., Digital Enterprises, that provide new digital products.

In particular, both Users and Service Providers are able to use Cloud services with the common goal to improve customer experience, becaming theselves active part of a common Cloud based PoE. Things increase the knowledge of monitored phenomena, by integrating customers experience in the automatic process management.

This mainly results in:

- An 'optimum' level of customer satisfaction, that balances the quality of experience and the costs to provide the product;
- A customer loyalty to assure the maximum profit for digital enterprises.

More specifically, as shown in Fig. 3, Users access the PoE after a preliminary registration step, to became 'Members'. Once logged in, they can interact with other Members, providing several types of feedback, such as replying to questions or quoting ideas. Moreover, Members gradually access to higher Levels of experience evaluation, on the basis of their activity and scores obtained by an evaluation process by the same Members of the PoE. PoE gathers Users experience through a 'Reader' module and compare 'U data' (i.e., data from Members) with 'T data' (i.e., data from Things) in order to verify the coherence of information or to plan automatic activities.

Things can bee considered as 'customizable smart devices' and Cloud can collect data and also dynamically configure smart devices, by using policies of dynamic *provisioning and versioning* of products (P&V module in our digital business scenario). On the basis of a quality of experience evaluation, a digital provider can track and remotely upgrade a *on-device* software component, i.e. the *agent* in Fig. 3. Our approach leverages the dynamic deployment of *virtual containers* [24] to customize the behavior of things. Each agent customize a container as a *Containers of Experience (CoE)*, i.e., an abstraction of the device which collect data from the surrounding environment. For Cloud providers, this also means to assume that computational cost for this operation is strongly related to the availability and performance at the specific smart device.

At the same time, by applying PoE business policies, a QoE evaluation is expressed in terms of numerical value and assigned at each level thus to make experiences available for data visualization. Therefore, each Service Provider that pay-to-use Cloud PoE can access, through Internet, several levels to visualize and use data for its business purposes. For all these reasons, we watch to a Multi-Input-Multi-Output (MIMO) set up where Inputs are several typologies of Users and Things experience contributes and Outputs are several QoE levels and contents for business purpose data visualization. Moreover, if we consider the most general use-case where a marketplace offers several services and interests of end-users and vendors, we can consider a general schema including several platforms.

6.1   Cloud PoE Usability: Discussion of a Use Case

This Section discusses one possible application of a Cloud PoE developed by following our guidelines. It supports *business process management* based on customer experience in a *supermarket chain*.

Monitoring customer experience thus to misure QoE and improve it implies the processing of a set of information useful to characterize the context, both objective and subjective (whose difference has been already explained) with possible correlations. For example, with objectives we refer to the measured temperature of internal areas, presences, motion by Things. With subjectives instead we refer to the comfort level by gathering data from people in terms of customer experience such as availability of sought-after products, perceived temperature (more or less hot or cold), satisfaction level referred to the merchandise allocation, cleaning, prices competitiveness, parking, but not only.

This management process performs three main tasks:

- **Data collection**, to gather data from the supermarket environment and its activities both thanks to Things and Users;
- **Event classification**, to specify which events may be influential and the impact (QoE) on customer experience due to their occurrence;
- **Fulfillment of the customer demand**, to improve QoE for a greater and greater customer experience.

To this end, we have developed a Cloud PoE testbed environment where we emulated several smart devices to gather observations from monitored areas in a supermarket, and contemporary collecting informations from Internet connected Users devices at different levels of experience. Table 3 shows several interesting results, pointing out where improvements are needed on the basis of a threshold of acceptability (i.e., less than 3/5).

Table 3. Several interesting results from our Cloud PoE testbed environment

Event	Obj data	Sbj data	QoE level	Acceptable (Y/N)
Temperature (refrigerated section)	4 °C	'too cold'	1/5	N
Midrange beer price	1,60 €	'too expensive'	1/5	N
Average bread price	3,00 €	'acceptable'	3/5	Y
Average parking lots (10.00–12.00)	10/300 free	'poor'	1/5	N
Employees' courteousness	-	'good'	3/5	Y

For each event (i.e., monitored phenomenon) of the 'Event' column, Table reports, left to right, objective data gathered from sensing (Things), subjective/perceived data from PoE Members, an evaluation of QoE based on the implemented business policies, a Yes/No acceptance rating.

7   Conclusions and Future Developments

In a worldwide competitive market scenario, Cloud computing play a fundamental role to develop new business designs by integrating the digital and physical worlds. An increasing number of Cloud providers deliver services which are oriented to achieve the maximum profit for digital enterprises and contemporary satisfying the user's demand for several marketplaces. Therefore, a best knowledge of the customer experience, through a measurement and evaluation of its quality level is needed.

To meet this goal, we introduce an approach which is oriented to help Cloud architects to clarify this important topic thus to achieve the above mentioned objectives. Specifically, our scientometric analysis of Cloud computing and QoE shows an uptrend on the use of Cloud computing for QoE measurement and evaluation. On the basis of the state-of-the-art like so resulting from our scientometric analysis, we propose a Multi-Input-Multi-Output (MIMO) reference model to design a Cloud based Platform of Experience (PoE).

Both users and service providers are considered part (i.e. members) of the PoE. Our approach allows Cloud providers to 'weigh' customer experiences thus to model a ranking list to evaluate the experience gained at every level. It can be replicated in order to compute several QoE ranking lists for a wide variety of services/products and for several marketplaces.

We think that this research field should be worth considering, because the time is ripe and Cloud computing bodes to efficiently answer to the above mentioned goals in a digital business world, especially due to the increase of mobile devices and contemporary of mobile services customers. We plan to improve our research work through the implementation phase. This step should be shared with the community, by adopting open source technologies, thus to improve business policies and customer quality of experience respecting the main priorities and characteristics indicated in this study.

References

1. Chao, H.-C.: Internet of things and cloud computing for future internet. In: Hsu, C.-H., Yang, L.T., Ma, J., Zhu, C. (eds.) UIC 2011. LNCS, vol. 6905, p. 1. Springer, Heidelberg (2011)
2. Fazio, M., Celesti, A., Villari, M., Puliafito, A.: The need of a hybrid storage approach for IoT in PaaS cloud federation. In: 28th International Conference on Advanced Information Networking and Applications Workshops (WAINA), pp. 779–784 (2014)
3. ur Rehman Laghari, K., Crespi, N., Molina, B., Palau, C.: QoE aware service delivery in distributed environment. In: IEEE Workshops of International Conference on Advanced Information Networking and Applications (WAINA), pp. 837–842 (2011)
4. ITU-T Recommendation P.10. https://www.itu.int/rec/T-REC-P.10
5. Wang, S., Dey, S.: Cloud mobile gaming: modeling and measuring user experience in mobile wireless networks. SIGMOBILE Mob. Comput. Commun. Rev. **16**, 10–21 (2012)
6. Colonnese, S., Cuomo, F., Melodia, T., Guida, R.: Cloud-assisted buffer management for http-based mobilevideo streaming. In: Proceedings of the 10th ACM Symposium on Performance Evaluation of Wireless Ad Hoc, Sensor, & Ubiquitous Networks, PE-WASUN 2013, pp. 1–8. ACM, New York (2013)
7. Vandenbroucke, K., Ferreira, D., Goncalves, J., Kostakos, V., De Moor, K.: Mobile cloud storage: a contextual experience. In: Proceedings of the 16th International Conference on Human-Computer Interaction with Mobile Devices & Services, MobileHCI 2014, pp. 101–110. ACM, New York (2014)

8. Huang, Y.S., Hsu, C.H., El Zarki, M., Erbad, A., Venkatasubramanian, N.: On optimizing MMVEs in network-aware clouds. In: Proceedings of International Workshop on Massively Multiuser Virtual Environments, GPGPU-7, pp. 6:1–6:2. ACM, New York (2014)

9. Saiz, E., Ibarrola, E., Cristobo, L., Taboada, I.: A cloud platform for QoE evaluation: QoXcloud. In: Proceedings of the ITU Kaleidoscope Academic Conference: Living in a Converged World - Impossible Without Standards?, pp. 241–247 (2014)

10. Zhang, Y., Zhang, D., Hassan, M., Alamri, A., Peng, L.: CADRE: cloud-assisted drug recommendation service for online pharmacies. Mob. Netw. Appl. **20**, 1–8 (2014)

11. Hausheer, D., Rückert, J.: Report on initial system architecture. NaDA 1 (2013) G3

12. Dharmasiri, H., Goonetillake, M.: A federated approach on heterogeneous NoSQL data stores. In: International Conference on Advances in ICT for Emerging Regions (ICTer), pp. 234–239 (2013)

13. MongoDB. http://www.mongodb.org/

14. Kanade, A., Gopal, A., Kanade, S.: A study of normalization and embedding in MongoDB. In: IEEE International Advance Computing Conference (IACC), pp. 416–421 (2014)

15. Lawrence, R.: Integration and virtualization of relational SQL and NoSQL systems including MySQL and MongoDB. In: International Conference on Computational Science and Computational Intelligence (CSCI), vol. 1, pp. 285–290 (2014)

16. Celesti, A., Tusa, F., Villari, M., Puliafito, A.: An approach to enable cloud service providers to arrange IaaS, PaaS, and SaaS using external virtualization infrastructures. In: IEEE World Congress on Services (SERVICES), pp. 607–611 (2011)

17. Hassan, M., Huh, E.: Dynamic Cloud Collaboration Platform: A Market-Oriented Approach. Springer Briefs in Computer Science. Springer, Heidelberg (2012)

18. Wilder, B.: Cloud Architecture Patterns. Oreilly and Associate Series. O'Reilly, Sebastopol (2012)

19. Li, Z., Drew, M., Liu, J.: Fundamentals of Multimedia. Texts in Computer Science. Springer, Heidelberg (2014)

20. Hausenblas, M.: Building Scalable and Smart Multimedia Applications on the Semantic Web. GRIN Verlag, Berlin (2011)

21. Casteleyn, S., Rossi, G., Winckler, M. (eds.): ICWE 2014. LNCS, vol. 8541. Springer, Heidelberg (2014)

22. Emeakaroha, V.C., Netto, M.A.S., Calheiros, R.N., De Rose, C.A.F.: Achieving flexible SLA and resource management in clouds. In: Achieving Federated and Self-manageable Cloud Infrastructures Theory and Practice. IGI Global (2012)

23. Henry, S.L., Abou-Zahra, S., Brewer, J.: The role of accessibility in a universal web. In: Proceedings of the 11th Web for All Conference, W4A 2014, pp. 17:1–17:4 (2014)

24. Dua, R., Raja, A., Kakadia, D.: Virtualization vs containerization to support PaaS. In: IEEE International Conference on Cloud Engineering (IC2E), pp. 610–614 (2014)

Enabling Digital Transformation Using Secure Decisions as a Service

Hans-Joachim Hof[1], Rainer Schmidt[2(✉)], and Lars Brehm[3]

[1] MuSe - Munich IT Security Research Group, Munich University of Applied Sciences, Lothstrasse 64, 80335 Munich, Germany
hof@hm.edu
[2] Munich University of Applied Sciences, Lothstrasse 64, 80335 Munich, Germany
Rainer.Schmidt@hm.edu
[3] Munich University of Applied Sciences, Am Stadtpark 20, 81243 Munich, Germany
Lars.Brehm@hm.edu

Abstract. Digital Transformation is of crucial importance for many enterprises and creates new challenges both on the conceptual and architectural level. Therefore, a new, secure, and layered architecture is introduced that separates the process from the decision model in order to quickly react to changed requirements. It provides flexibility by separating three aspects of decision-making: foundations, methods, and data. Security and reliability is achieved by using a reputation system to judge data sources and data contributors. The reputation system offers a score for trustworthiness of a data source that could be used for the selection of appropriate data sources for decisions as well as a basis to calculate a confidence score of a decision.

Keywords: Digital transformation · Business process · Innovation · Decision as a Service · Security

1 Introduction

The Digital Transformation of Enterprise Architectures [1] and business processes is an issue of paramount importance for many enterprises [2]. Enormous benefits by digital transformation are predicted [3, 4]. Digital transformation creates new opportunities for enterprises [5], breaks down industry barriers but also destroys existing business models [5]. Serious disruptions take place, new companies emerge [6] and established companies disappear [7]. A number of strategies have been developed in order to drive digitization [4, 8].

In order to improve the capability of enterprise to react quickly to customer and market requirements, a cornerstone of digital transformation is the improvement of decision support within enterprise. Means both include the speed-up of decisions by automation and the increase of decision precision. To speed up decisions, enterprises replace human decisions by automated decision systems. The precision of decisions is increased by taking into account more data and data from more sources. An example is

© Springer International Publishing Switzerland 2016
A. Celesti and P. Leitner (Eds.): ESOCC 2015 Workshops, CCIS 567, pp. 289–298, 2016.
DOI: 10.1007/978-3-319-33313-7_22

the analysis of data from social software [9] such as social media. It allows measuring the customer sentiment faster and with more precision than traditional means, e.g. surveys.

Big Data receives a great deal of attention in industry and research for improving decision making [10]. The largest benefits of Big Data can be leveraged by companies engaged in the business areas of IT and technology development and marketing [11]. Big Data is not a specific technology or technology platform such as Hadoop [12], but embraces a series of technological advances creating a significant expansion of the analytical capabilities.

Today Big Data technologies are often integrated into Decision as a Service [13] offerings. Decision as a Service relieves companies of duties as the data collection and the continuous improvement of decision models. Additional, companies have the option to select the best offers from an emerging market. A further benefit of Decision as a Service arises from the fact that the service provider who provides the services has access to more data, as the company due to his aggregator role. In this way, the decision quality can be increased and the time to improve decision-making processes can be shortened.

To enable faster and more precise decisions, many enterprises use Big Data [10] to exploit also external data sources. In this approach, data from different sources are combined during decision-making. Unfortunately, this creates a new security threats. Malicious contributors could distort data in order to influence the final decision in their interest.

The contribution of this paper is to introduce a new architecture for decision as a service that includes a reputation system that could be used to protect against these attacks. The reputation system imposes a goodness score on each contributor, judging on the trustworthiness of the contributor.

The paper proceeds as follows, first decision support technologies in digitized enterprise are introduced. Then an architecture for secure decision as a service is introduced. The reputation system that allows evaluating contributors is defined in the following section. The next chapter shows up the use of decision as a service for digital transformation. After discussing related, a conclusion and outlook is given.

2 Basic Architecture for Secure Decision as a Service

The proposed architecture supports decisions using three essential elements. Foundations such as Laws define the basic rules of decisions. Methods define the way to create these decisions. Data are used to make concrete decisions. Foundations, Methods and Data evolve at different speeds. Foundations are the slowest, data are the quickest element. There our architecture differentiates these elements and thus enables their independent evolution (Fig. 1).

Decisions are based on a number of *data sources* in the proposed architecture. Each data source provides data from one or more data *contributors*. For example, a hotel rating website may be a single data source, users writing reviews of hotels are the contributors associated with this data source.

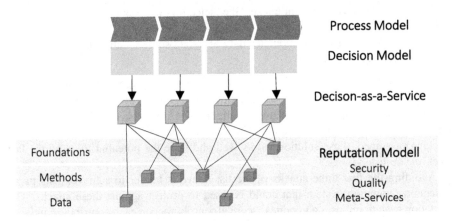

Fig. 1. Layered Decision as a Service

With Decision-as-a-Service models, data from different sources are mixed together to come to a decision. Hence, each data source and each contributor of a data source has the possibility to influence the final decision. In addition, it is expected that the proposed architecture is open and dynamic, i.e. data sources can be added, and contributors are not known in advance. Sources are very likely dynamic, meaning that new content is constantly added to the data source and those new contributors appear and more mature contributors do not contribute anymore to a data source. A Reputation Modell allows to evaluate the Security, Quality and the Meta-Services [14] of services providing foundation, methods or data.

3   Reputation System

Reputation systems are quite common in dynamic and open systems that allow interaction between before unknown parties. A reputation score helps humans to decide whom they will trust. Such a score also allows for automated decisions by machines. One popular example of a reputation system for human interaction is the eBay reputation system (see [15] for a thorough discussion). In [16], a current overview of reputation systems is given. One can notice in [16], that current reputation systems usually only focus on one single domain, hence are limited in their use. The Decision-as-a-Service architecture proposed in this paper however, uses data sources from multiple domains, hence calls for a reputation system that is not limited to one single domain.

For a Decision-as-a-Service provider, it is of crucial importance that decisions are reliable for the customers of the provider. The reliability of a decision can be negatively affected by the following actions:

- Attack 1: A contributor of a data source provides fake data.
- Attack 2: Contributors of a data source cooperate to provide faked data and to discredit other contributors (e.g. a large number of paid reviews at a hotel review site).

- Attack 3: An adversary influences the selection of data sources a Decision-as-a-Service service is based on.
- Attack 4: An adversary manipulates data of a data source, either during storage or during transfer of data.

To avoid the last attack of this list, authenticity and integrity of all data must be guaranteed during transfer and storage. Several methods are available to achieve authenticity and integrity, e.g. secure communication protocols like HTTP over TLS (https, see [17] for details). A correct implementation (including certificate validity checking) assumed, these solution works well and have the potential to avoid the last attack of the list.

Avoiding the first three attacks of the list above is harder to achieve. This paper presents a reputation system that could be used to protect against these attacks. The reputation system imposes a goodness score g(contributor) on each contributor, judging on the trustworthiness of the contributor. For all contributors, it is defined that

$$0 \le g(contributor) \le 1$$

where a goodness store of 0 denotes a totally untrustable contributor whereas a goodness score of 1 means that a contributor is fully trusted.

Using the goodness scores of all contributors of a single data source (one domain), a goodness score for the data source itself can be calculated, e.g. by using a weighted sum of the goodness sources of all n contributors of this data source:

$$g(source) = \sum_{i=1}^{n} (w_i * contributor_i)$$

The weight w_i of a contributor$_i$ expresses the degree a contributor contributes to the data of a data source. For example, the weight could be the number of reviews a contributor has written on a hotel review site. The weights wi should be selected such that

$$\sum_{i=1}^{m} w_i = 1$$

In the hotel review site example, m is the total number of reviews and the w_i for a contributor$_i$ is calculated from the number of reviews (nor) this contributor has written:

$$w_i = \frac{nor}{m}$$

With these definitions, it is ensured that

$$0 \le g(source) \le 1$$

The goodness score of a data source may be enriched using other information about a data source. For example, the identifiability of contributors plays an important role in our model, as it is otherwise not possible to use individual goodness scores to calculate the overall score of a data source. Another aspect is the authentication method used by the data source to authenticate contributors. If the authentication method is weak, it may be easy for an attacker to impersonate other contributors and insert fake data. Yet another aspect is the ease of creating new contributors in a data source. If it is easy for an attacker to create a huge number of new contributors and then only once contribute data to the data source for each created contributor, an attacker can spoil the data of the data source. A quality factor is introduced to address the issues described in this paragraph:

$$g(source) = quality * \sum_{i=1}^{n}(w_i * g(contributor_i))$$

Where

$$quality = \sum_{i=1}^{n}(u_i * qa_i).$$

In this equation, qa_i is one quality aspect that applies for this type of data source and u_i is a weight factor that reflects the importance of the associated quality aspect.
With

$$qa_i \in [0, 1]$$

$$u_i \in [0, 1]$$

$$\sum_{i=1}^{n} u_i = 1$$

it is ensured that

$$0 \leq quality \leq 1,$$

hence

$$0 \leq g(source) \leq 1$$

The knowledge of goodness scores of data sources helps Decision-as-a-Service services to select appropriate data sources for the decision process. Rules may define a lower boundary for the goodness score of data sources to be used. In addition, the goodness score could be used as primary input for a confidence score of a decision. The calculation of the goodness score for a contributor is the heart of the reputation system. All other scores rely on this score. First, it is necessary to have a way to identify reliably the contributors of a single data source. IDs for identification may for example be published (verified) email addresses. If no IDs are available, the only way to use this data source is to assume it is a data source with only one contributor. However, in this case it is very likely that the associated goodness score will be only average or lower.

The goodness score of a contributor should take into consideration that a contributor may appear in more than one data source (domain). For example, a contributor rating hotels on a hotel review website may also rate restaurants on a restaurant review website. A reputation system that works on a potentially unlimited number of domains (data sources) is a significant advance to the state of the art of reputation systems.

To address the problem of multiple data sources, it is necessary, to identify the appearance of one single contributor in multiple data sources. Each data source may use a different ID for this single contributor, for example, one site may use the email address, another site may use a self-selected username (distinct from email addresses), yet another side may use the full name of users. To address this issue, the proposed reputation system associates a randomly chosen GUID (Global Unique ID) with one or more IDs of contributors. For each ID, the confidence that this ID really belongs to the GUID is also stored. This is important in the case of ambiguities. For example, there may be more than one person named "Hans Maier" as the first name Hans and the last name Maier are very common in Germany. In addition, depending of the authentication method and the validation method at registration, it may be possible to impersonate a contributor. The confidence about an association may change over time, hence the goodness score of a contributor may be very dynamic over time. Finding a good and secure way of associating different IDs will be an important part of the proposed reputation system.

Criteria for judgment of the goodness of a contributor are specific for each data source. These criteria may include

- Existing reputation mechanisms from data sources, e.g. user voting systems, user rating systems, ...
- Past behavior of a user.
- Characteristics that are appropriate to detect fake content (e.g. typical wording of paid advertisments).
- ...

The goodness score of a contributor is calculated using the n data sources a user appears in with the best confidence score

$$g(contributor) = \frac{\sum_{i=1}^{n}(confidence_i * g(contributor@source_i))}{n}.$$

The goodness score of a contributor in one single data source is

$$g(contributor@source_i) = \sum_{i=1}^{n}(v_i * gc_i),$$

where gc_i is one criteria for goodness, and v_i reflects the importance of this goodness criteria.

With

$$qc_i \in [0, 1]$$

$$v_i \in [0, 1]$$

$$\sum_{i=1}^{n} u_i = 1$$

it is ensured that

$$0 \leq g(contributor@source_i) \leq 1,$$

hence

$$0 \leq g(contributor) \leq 1.$$

The same semantic (0 = not trustworthy, 1 = fully trustworthy) as above applies.

4   Using Decision as a Service in Digital Transformation

Decision as a service in general and the reputation system in particular are critical elements for the digital transformation of enterprises. Digital transformation is defined according to [4] as "the use of technology to radically improve performance or reach of enterprises" and affects the areas customer experience, operational processes and business models. (see also [18, 19].

Four digital capabilities build the foundation layer for the improvements in these areas and encompass unified processes and data, analytics capability, business and IT integration and solution delivery [4]. While the last two capabilities are more concerned with the realization of effective, solutions for the digital transformation are the first two capabilities directly linked to decision as a service and the reputation system. Unified processes and data are especially difficult to archive in an age of massive volatile processes and unstructured data as described earlier and additionally, it is required to include these processes and unstructured data as sources into the business analytics. The recommended layer architecture for Decision as a service helps to overcome these difficulties.

In the following some potential application of Decision as a service and the reputation system in the areas customer experience, operational processes, and business models will be described.

The area of customer experience provides several opportunities for application.

- Decision as a service can support the customer segmentation by providing relevant information, e.g. from even divers social media contents, to define better customer segments
- In the digital selling process decisions are constantly required to provide customers with individualized marketing information and specific offers with better quality due

to the usage of the reputation system. Additionally, Decision as a service can also support a much leaner, streamlined customer process by eliminating non-relevant alternatives, like in service add-ons, payment options. This also applies to service processes with the customers or retailers.

- Cross-channel coherence can also profit from Decision as a service by ensuring that the marketing content and offers are consistent across the channels.

The area of operational processes is a natural use-case for Decision as a service.

- Process improvements require often decisions within certain activities, but also the decision, which process variant is applicable to a specific case (e.g. case based routing). Decision as a service helps here to include not just company internal, but also external sources with high data quality.
- As performance management needs higher operational transparency and the decision-making process will more and more on data-drive the same reasoning also applies to this building block of digital transformation

Also in the area of business model for Decision as a service can help to support the digital transformation.

- Digital modified business in the form of product/service augmentation or digital wrapper to existing products rely heavily on larger and more divers data sources and high data quality about products, services, customer and other partners to provide the right solution in time. Decision as a service help to fulfill this needs
- New digital business is by definition linked to digital services and with that Decision as a service can also become an import part on new digital products. On example might be trustworthy recommendation in share economy applications.
- With the digital globalization Decision as a service helps to foster a global network and build transparency even for quite distant partners.

These applications show how the recommended layer architecture for Decision as a service helps to successfully digital transform an existing enterprise.

5 Related Work

A more strategic view on Decision as a Service as means for Transformation is discussed in [13]. The positive effects of data-driven decision making on firm performance are analyzed in [20]. Also in [21] the positive effects of analytics are discussed. In [22] the basic concept of Decision as a Service is introduced.

A general introduction into reputation systems is given in [16]. The role of trust in the internet is analyzed in [15]. The first use of reputation as metric for data quality has been defined in [23]. The use of reputation in peer to peer networks is suggested in [24]. The positive effects on separating different aspects of business processes are discussed in [25].

6   Conclusion

Many enterprises and organizations improve their decisions making processes by automation and the integration of more data sources. Although this approach increases the velocity and precision of decision-making, it also creates new risks, because it implies to integrate many more external data sources as before. This creates new challenges to information system security. External data could be forged and leading to false decision. Therefore, a reputation system for Decision-as-a-Service is presented. The reputation system provides a score for the trustworthiness of a data source used for Decision-as-Service. The reputation system is not limited to one domain but can be used on a potentially unlimited number of domains, hence offers a high degree of flexibility for the Decision-as-a-Service service. The output of the reputation system may be used for selection of appropriate data sources as well as for the calculation of a confidence score for the decision of a Decision-as-a-Service service. Future work will have to further detail our reputation model and system architecture.

References

1. Andersson, H., Tuddenham, P.: Reinventing IT to Support Digitization. McKinsey, New York (2014)
2. Markovitch, S., Willmott, P.: Accelerating the Digitization of Business Processes. McKinsey & Company, New York (2014)
3. Manyika, J., Chui, M., Bisson, P., Woetzel, J., Dobbs, R., Bughin, J., Aharon, D.: The Internet of Things: Mapping the Value Beyond the Hype. McKinsey & Company, San Francisco (2015)
4. Capgemini Consulting, MIT Sloan Managment: Digital Transformation: A Road-Map for Billion-Dollar Organizations (2011). http://www.capgemini.com/resources/digital-transformation-a-roadmap-for-billiondollar-organizations
5. Weill, P., Woerner, S.: Thriving in an increasingly digital ecosystem. MIT Sloan Manage. Rev. 56(4), 26–34 (2015)
6. Fortune, Inc.: Fortune 500 firms in 1955 vs. 2014; 89 % are gone, and we're all better off because of that dynamic "creative destruction," http://www.aei.org/publication/fortune-500-firms-in-1955-vs-2014-89-are-gone-and-were-all-better-off-because-of-that-dynamic-creative-destruction/
7. Locker, M.: 8 iconic brands that have disappeared – Fortune. http://fortune.com/2014/11/09/defunct-brands/
8. Fitzgerald, M., Kruschwitz, N., Bonnet, D., Welch, M.: Embracing digital technology: a new strategic imperative. MIT Sloan Manage. Rev. 55, 1–12 (2013)
9. Schmidt, R., Nurcan, S.: BPM and social software. In: Ardagna, D., Mecella, M., Yang, J., Aalst, W., Mylopoulos, J., Rosemann, M., Shaw, M.J., Szyperski, C. (eds.) Business Process Management Workshops, pp. 649–658. Springer, Heidelberg (2009)
10. LaValle, S., Lesser, E., Shockley, R., Hopkins, M.S., Kruschwitz, N.: Big data, analytics and the path from insights to value. MIT Sloan Manage. Rev. 52, 21–32 (2011)
11. Schmidt, R., Möhring, M., Maier, S., Pietsch, J., Härting, R.-C.: Big data as strategic enabler - insights from central European enterprises. In: Abramowicz, W., Kokkinaki, A. (eds.) BIS 2014. LNBIP, vol. 176, pp. 50–60. Springer, Heidelberg (2014)

12. White, T.: Hadoop: The Definitive Guide. O'Reilly Media, Sebastopol (2012)
13. Schmidt, R., Möhring, M., Koot, C.: Data-centered cloud-environments as enabler for decision as a service in small and medium enterprises. In: 2013 NAPLES Forum on Service, Ischia, Napoli (2013)
14. Schmidt, R.: Meta-services as third dimension of service-oriented enterprise architecture. In: Presented at the 2010 14th IEEE International Enterprise Distributed Object Computing Conference Workshops (EDOCW) (2010)
15. Resnick, P., Zeckhauser, R.: Trust among strangers in internet transactions: empirical analysis of ebay's reputation system. Econ. Internet E-commerce 11, 23–25 (2002)
16. Hendrikx, F., Bubendorfer, K., Chard, R.: Reputation systems: a survey and taxonomy. J. Parallel Distrib. Comput. 75, 184–197 (2015)
17. Rescorla, E.: Http Over TLS (2000)
18. Fichman, R.G., Dos Santos, B.L., Zheng, Z.: (Eric): digital innovation as a fundamental and powerful concept in the information systems curriculum. MIS Q. 38(2), 329–343 (2014)
19. Safrudin, N., Rosemann, M., Recker, J.C., Genrich, M.: A typology of business transformations. 360° Bus. Transform. J. 2014, 24–41 (2014)
20. Brynjolfsson, E., Hitt, L., Kim, H.: Strength in numbers: how does data-driven decisionmaking affect firm performance? (2011)
21. Davenport, T.H., Harris, J.G., Morison, R.: Analytics at Work: Smarter Decisions, Better Results. Harvard Business Press, Cambridge (2010)
22. Delen, D., Demirkan, H.: Data, information and analytics as services. Decis. Support Syst. 55, 359–363 (2013)
23. Strong, D.M., Lee, Y.W., Wang, R.Y.: Data quality in context. Commun. ACM 40, 103–110 (1997)
24. Oliver, H., Daanen, J.: Management of peer-to-peer networks using reputation data. Google Patents (2004)
25. Regev, G., Soffer, P., Schmidt, R.: Taxonomy of flexibility in business processes. In: Proceedings Seventh Workshop on Business Process Modeling, Development, and Support (BPMDS 2006), Requirements for Flexibility and the Ways to Achieve It, p. S. 90–93. Luxemburg (2006)

Exploring Requirements for Multipurpose Crowd Computing Framework

Alexander Smirnov[1,2(✉)] and Andrew Ponomarev[1]

[1] St. Petersburg Institute for Informatics and Automation of the Russian Academy of Sciences,
39, 14th Liniya, St. Petersburg 199178, Russia
{smir,ponomarev}@iias.spb.su
[2] ITMO University, 49, Kronverksky Pr., St. Petersburg 197101, Russia

Abstract. Crowd computing is a common name for variety of methods to solve problems with a help of large, undefined groups of people communicating via Internet. It is becoming widely used nowadays, but there still are many questions about how to effectively program distributed scalable systems, employing human information processing abilities. Crowd computing frameworks described in the literature often focus only on several unique features leaving other almost without attention, making it hard to render a systematic view of all the aspects of the design. The goal of this paper is to collect and analyze all the requirements for crowd computing frameworks that drove the development of these frameworks recently. The united and unified set of requirements is meant to provide a basis for further development of crowd computing frameworks and applications and, at the same time, it can serve as a basis for comparison of that kind of products.

Keywords: Crowd computing · Crowdsourcing · Hybrid cloud · Requirements

1 Introduction

Distributed scalable systems allowing humans as one of the elements of information processing loop help to address problems that still cannot be solved in fully automated way. Crowd computing is a research field aimed on development of such systems. It is agreed, that programming for this kind of hybrid human-machine systems requires new approaches and techniques, different from (or extending) classical computer programming [1]. Frameworks for crowd computing provide tools to address the complexity of this new kind of programming.

Crowd computing frameworks described in the literature often focus only on several unique features leaving other almost without attention, making it hard to render a systematic view of all the aspects of the design. The purpose of this paper is to design a complete implementation-independent set of requirements for crowd computing platform. It also aims to explicate and articulate the set of assumptions and reflect on different features that are required for such kind of systems, as well as features that are not required but may be beneficent and why. Each implementation of crowd computing framework is free to implement all of the proposed requirements or a subset of them, and that is a

© Springer International Publishing Switzerland 2016
A. Celesti and P. Leitner (Eds.): ESOCC 2015 Workshops, CCIS 567, pp. 299–307, 2016.
DOI: 10.1007/978-3-319-33313-7_23

design choice that reflects the purpose of the crowd computing platform and allows to position it among other ones.

The proposed set of requirements can also play a role of a comparison framework, a kind of a coordinate system to explore features and characteristics of particular crowd computing frameworks.

The collection of requirements is sometimes referred as a set, however the word "set" does not entirely express the idea, because the artifact that is the aim of this research not only enumerates individual requirements, it also shows different kinds of relationship between them, hence it is more a system of requirements, than a mere set.

Research methodology is the following:

1. Identify the set of research papers about platforms for crowd computing. To perform this step three full-text scientific databases were used: ScienceDirect®, ACM Digital Library, and SpringerLink. These databases were searched for papers published in the last ten years (2005–2014) and presenting frameworks and platforms for crowd computing.
2. Examine the selected papers looking for explicit requirements (e.g. in [2]), design goals (e.g. in [3]) or distinctive features. All found requirements, goals and distinctive features were put into a non-uniform list of objects of obviously varying granularity – a "raw" list of 83 items.
3. Aggregate and conceptualize the list obtained in the previous step.

The approach bears two main limitations. The first one is that primary search keywords in all the explored databases were "crowd computing", however, there are several other terms highly related to human-powered computations: e.g., human computations and crowdsourcing. Extending the list of keywords (by including "crowdsourcing", for example) could have resulted in a more broad set of requirements. The second limitation is the focus on research publications. There are many commercial systems (Amazon Mechanical Turk, CloudFactory, CrowdComputing Systems to name a few) which are closed-source, and no details are available about how they are designed and what kinds of workflows are used. The requirements analysis would benefit a lot if accompanied by that systems examination.

2   Requirements Structure

All the identified requirements are divided into five topics. This mostly follows the accentuation made by the authors of the analyzed papers, who mainly focus on specific issues of human-powered systems. It should be stressed, that this set of topics and requirements beneath each topic do not form a complete set of requirements, as it construed in software engineering, it is a crowd computing-specific template that should be extended for any particular system. The mentioned topics are:

Programming methods and tools. This topic contains all the requirements related to how a program for a crowd computer should be composed, what features need to be implemented by a programming environment to make the process of programming for a crowd-based system versatile, effective and convenient.

Quality. This is the most prominent concern in any crowd-based system [4–6]. This topic covers all the requirements aimed on providing high quality output for crowd-based information processing procedures.

User interface. There are at least two types of user interfaces in most crowd-based systems: one that is exposed to crowd member, participating in some solution process and the other that is used by problem setter and/or system administrator to monitor the process of task execution. Existing crowd computing frameworks and research proto-types on various hardware platforms allow to generalize some common requirements for both types of user interfaces.

Incentivization and rewarding mechanics. The need for incentive is an important distinctive feature of crowd-based systems, as it was highlighted, e.g. by Bernstein et al. in [1].

Interoperability. Versatile and convenient framework for programming and execu-tion of crowd computing tasks is important, but it is useless without access to a large enough pool of human solvers, that will actually accomplish human tasks embedded in the workflow. Currently, there are several platforms (Amazon Mechanical Turk is prob-ably the most well-known) where all crowd resources are concentrated. Building a new crowd pool can be a complex and long process; therefore, in many cases it is reasonable to be able to use existing crowds through an access to the respective platform.

In the rest of this section, each of these requirements topics will be discussed in detail. Key requirements along with papers where they are mentioned are summarized in Table 1.

Table 1. Requirements and references mentioning them

Topic	Requirement	Source
Programming methods and tools	Expressiveness	[2, 3]
	Support for structuring and pattern orientation	[3, 5, 7]
	Conceptual simplicity	[3, 4, 8, 9]
	Adaptability	[7]
Quality	Crowd member selection	[3–5, 10–12]
	Results processing	[5, 6, 9, 10, 13]
	Fraud detection	[4]
User interface	Task execution monitoring and control	[4, 14]
	Crowd member interface for mobile devices	[2, 15]
Incentivization and rewarding	Reward calculation and transfer	[4]
Interoperability	Interface to existing crowd platforms	[3, 8]

2.1 Programming Methods and Tools

This topic organizes requirements to the language (as, for example, Dog in [3], Crowd-Flower Markup Language in [4]), which is provided by the framework to describe tasks and information processing workflows.

Following generic requirements were detected during the analysis of existing systems:

Expressiveness. As programming for a crowd-based system is significantly different from programming for an ordinary hardware/software system, the programming technology itself should be able to define not only the sequence of operations that must be accomplished, but also additional information that is used in assigning a task to specific human solver, his/her incentivization, rewarding and verification of the produced results. Specifically expressiveness includes the ability to define:

Routing policy. The ability to specify crowd member features that are relevant in deciding whether to allow a particular crowd member to try a task or not (e.g., [3, 10]).

Time-to-live specification. The ability to specify a timespan, when the solution of a task is accepted (e.g., [11]).

Incentivization and rewarding. The ability to associate some reward with a task, and describe conditions in which this reward (or its part) can be granted to the task executor and how it is shared among several crowd members participating in task execution if it is the case (for a thorough review of incentivization strategies, see [16]).

Verification rules. The ability to specify a verification procedure for a task.

Support for Structuring and Pattern Orientation. The ability to structure programming code by extracting frequently used pieces of code and pieces of code that accomplish some well-scoped task into separate entities – functions, procedures, methods – is inextricable from any modern programming language. Programming for crowd computing is not much different in this way, it is also convenient to structure program in some way, leaving details in the lower layers of abstraction [2–4]. However, there is more about structure. Much research has been performed about which type of crowd output processing leads to the most reliable result in which task and which crowd platform (crowd platform may matter because of different demography) (e.g., [17–19]). The results of these studies, expressed in some formalized form may result in a library of crowd computing procedures.

Conceptual Simplicity. This general requirement is explicitly declared in [3], other proposals also take it into consideration, for example by sticking to well-known business modeling language (BPMN) for describing an information processing routine for crowd computing [5]. The rationale is, first, to manage the complexity of crowd computing caused by human in the loop, second, to allow non-programmers to compose crowd computing routines, making way for *ad hoc* crowd tasks. One of the already explored ways for conceptual simplicity is graphical representation of the crowd computing routine, implemented, for example, in [4]. It means that workflow composition is performed by some visual diagramming tool (CASE tool). The usage of BPMN (as in [5]) can also be classified as using graphical representation (reusing a well-known one). Another, and almost the opposite in some sense way of reaching conceptual simplicity is sticking to some well-known formal representation, for example, first-order logics [7].

Adaptability. This requirement is less agreed upon than others listed in this section. It means that the program itself can be changed during execution if it occurs that changing some part of it may lead to better quality results or be cheaper maintaining the same quality level. The examples of research work focused on building adaptive crowd computing workflows are [20, 21]. It should be noted, that this requirement matches well with support for structuring and pattern orientation, as adaptability may be implemented as automatic switching implementations of the high-level library of building blocks based on gathered performance metrics.

2.2 Quality

This topic contains all the requirements aimed on providing reliable output from crowd members. The topic itself can also be interpreted as a high-level requirement of making a quality management procedure a part of human-powered computing process.

We distinguish three middle-level requirements clarifying this high-level one: crowd member selection, results processing and fraud detection.

Crowd Member Selection. Crowd member selection means that crowd computing system should accept responses to a task only from some subset of available crowd members, who are most likely to give the correct answer. There are multiple ways to define that subset, and those ways can be seen as possible implementations of crowd member selection requirement. The first branch of member selection implementations leverage rich member profile. Profile here is understood in a wide way and can be described as consisting of two parts: static part and dynamic part. The key difference between them is that static part does not change as a result of task completion by crowd member, whereas dynamic part does. Static part, contrary to literal interpretation, can change; it can be changed by the crowd member himself, or refreshed as a result of some internet robot collecting information about crowd member etc. Important point is that updates of static member profile part are not results of task execution, but happen independently. Examples of information constituting static part of crowd member profile include demographic data, education, location, interests and skills, social relations etc. Dynamic part of crowd member profile contains information about completed tasks and results of their validation if it was performed either in the form of raw data or in the form of some aggregate model. This aggregate model is used to predict how reliable crowd member would be at certain kind of tasks. The concrete structure of the model is out of the scope of this paper, there are many models proposed in the literature (see, e.g., [13, 22, 23]). The second type of crowd member selection is done by addressing crowd members specially prepared questions before assigning task. The answers to these questions are known in advance and if the crowd member gives correct answers, the task (with unknown answer) is assigned to him under the assumption that the crowd member is qualified enough to execute it. This type of crowd member selection is used, for example, by AMT. It is also very similar to the concept of "gold" used by Crowd-Flower [4].

Results Processing. Another middle-level requirement that falls into quality management topic is results processing. In some sense, results processing is opposite to crowd member selection because the aim of the former is to raise the quality of answers received from unreliable crowd members, and the aim of the latter is to assign task only to reliable ones. In reality, however, these two ways of quality management are complementary to each other. On one hand, crowd member selection is always done in uncertainty and may result in false positives, i.e. assigning tasks to crowd members that are not able to accomplish them with the required level of quality; on the other hand, relying only on results processing may be reasonable for some tasks, but may result in significant growth of cost for others, because of excessive duplication needed to overcome absence of specific skill or knowledge from average crowd member. Example methods implementing results processing requirement range from simple ones like majority voting or averaging to elaborate ones like probabilistic models. Special type of results processing is testing through the experiment. This is applicable when it is hard to programmatically find the answer of the task but easy to check.

Fraud Detection. The last middle-level requirement in this topic is fraud detection [4, 24]. It is very close to results processing in that during fraud detection credibility of the results received from crowd members is analyzed. However, difference is that fraud detection tries to distinguish purposeful falsification performed by crowd member in order to increase profit (as a function from the number of completed tasks) from low-quality answer caused by insufficient competence. Implementation can be based on various empirical rules and signals of unfair game (e.g., too quick replies [4]).

2.3   User Interface

There are at least three types of interfaces that should be provided by crowd computing system: for developers, for end users, and for crowd members.

Interface for developers should contain various tools that help to assemble information processing workflow for particular crowd-based application. In several crowd computing frameworks visual workflow construction is advocated as a way to simplify crowd application development and make it available for non-programmers (e.g., [9]).

End user of a crowd computing system is a person who posts a problem (using application). In case of unique problem, an end user may also share the role of a developer, first, building information processing workflow, then, running this workflow with the problem instance. Interface for the end user should include blocks for task definition, result, and task execution monitoring and control.

User interface for crowd members allows to display task description to the crowd member and to receive answer from crowd member. There are two major factors identified during the analysis of existing crowd computing frameworks that influence crowd member interface. First, crowd computing today actively used to process audio and image data, so crowd member interface should be able to display and playback popular media types and formats. Second, geo-enabled types of crowd computing become more and more widespread making a separate class of applications: crowd sensing, participatory sensing applications. The point of this paper is that multipurpose crowd computing framework should be flexible enough to allow building crowd sensing applications, along with more typical data processing applications. That means, that crowd member interface for mobile platforms is necessary. This, however leads to a number of sub-requirements and clarifications related to energy management efficiency of mobile devices, addressed, for instance, in [2].

2.4 Incentivization and Rewarding Mechanics

In a general perspective, an end user should be able to associate some resource with the new problem instance, and this resource is split among the crowd members involved in the process of problem solving. The most popular type of resource in crowd computing (and in social computing in general) systems is money, but other options are available, e.g. reputation points (see, e.g., [16]). This topic is inextricably interwoven with the respective requirement in "Programming methods and tools". The difference is that in "Programming methods and tools" it is required that there should be a way to express incentivization and rewarding policy and associate it with information processing workflow, and here it is required that crowd computing framework should be able to hold and process rewarding information during execution of the workflow.

2.5 Interoperability

Setting aside technological features of the platform, the success of problem solution via crowd computing depends highly on the availability of human solvers with the required skills. There are many services nowadays, each manages its own pool of crowd workers. A newly developed platform may choose a subset of following options: (a) to form its own pool of crowd workers, highlighting its difference from other platforms (e.g., [4]); (b) use programming interfaces (APIs) of existing platforms to have an access to their crowd pools (e.g., [3, 8, 14, 25]). Interoperability, construed here as a possibility to build crowd computing workflows crossing boundaries of single platform is a complex problem. It inevitably affects features of quality and profile management offered by the original system.

3   Conclusion

The paper contains a conceptualization of general high-level requirements for crowd computing frameworks, collected from scientific papers describing original frameworks and arranged into five aggregate topics. These requirements are intended to serve, first, as a template for specific, low-level set of requirements driving the development of some crowd computing framework, second, as a structure that can help to compare different frameworks.

An interesting finding of the performed literature analysis is that there is only one publication [4] that explicitly discusses incentivization and rewarding functionality of the crowd computing framework. It can be explained by a selection bias, as only research crowd computing frameworks (prototypes) were analyzed; commercial frameworks probably pay much more attention to it. The only exception only supports the noticed lack of attention to this topic from the research community, as [4] is actually a publication about commercial system (CrowdFlower).

Major limitations of this paper are the accent on literally "crowd computing" framework descriptions and scientific papers. Relaxing any of these restrictions (for example, considering papers dedicated to *crowdsourcing* framework design or commercial systems) could have resulted in a more complete set of requirements. This is essentially one of two future research directions of the authors. There are several closely connected terms expressing the idea of human-powered computations: crowdsourcing, human computations, crowd computing, and it seems fruitful to analyze existing frameworks in each of those areas. However, it rises the number of papers to analyze to a very high level, demanding a development of the appropriate methodology to deal with it. The other future research direction is to design a crowd computing framework based on the identified requirements.

Acknowledgements. The research was partially supported by projects funded by grants # 13-07-00271, # 14-07-00345, # 14-07-00363 of the Russian Foundation for Basic Research, project 213 (program 8) of the Presidium of the Russian Academy of Sciences, project # 2.2 of the basic research program "Intelligent information technologies, system analysis and automation" of the Nanotechnology and Information Technology Department of the Russian Academy of Sciences, and Grant 074-U01 of the Government of the Russian Federation.

References

1. Bernstein, A., Klein, M., Malone, T.W.: Programming the global brain. Commun. ACM **55**, 41 (2012)
2. Ra, M., Liu, B., Porta, T. La, Govindan, R.: Medusa: a programming framework for crowd-sensing applications categories and subject descriptors. In: Proceedings of the 10th International Conference on Mobile Systems, Applications, and Services, MobiSys 2012, pp. 337–350 (2012)
3. Ahmad, S., Battle, A., Malkani, Z., Kamvar, S.: The jabberwocky programming environment for structured social computing. In: Proceedings of the 24th Annual ACM Symposium User interface Software Technology, UIST 2011, pp. 53–64 (2011)
4. Van Pelt, C., Sorokin, A.: Designing a scalable crowdsourcing platform. In: Proceedings of the 2012 International Conference on Management Data, SIGMOD 2012, p. 765 (2012)
5. Kucherbaev, P., Tranquillini, S., Daniel, F., Casati, F., Marchese, M., Brambilla, M., Fraternali, P.: Business processes for the crowd computer. In: Rosa, M., Soffer, P. (eds.) BPM Workshops 2012. LNBIP, vol. 132, pp. 256–267. Springer, Heidelberg (2013)
6. Dai, P., Mausam, Weld, D.S.: Artificial intelligence for artificial artificial intelligence. In: The 25th AAAI Conference on Artificial Intelligence, pp. 1153–1159 (2011)
7. Morishima, A., Shinagawa, N., Mitsuishi, T.: CyLog/Crowd4U: a declarative platform for complex data-centric crowdsourcing. Proc. VLDB Endow. **5**, 1918–1921 (2012)
8. Franklin, M., Kossmann, D., Kraska, T., Ramesh, S., Xin, R.: CrowdDB: answering queries with crowdsourcing. In: Proceedings of the 2011 ACM SIGMOD International Conference on Management of Data, SIGMOD 2011, pp. 1–12 (2011)

9. Kittur, A., Smus, B., Khamkar, S., Kraut, R.E.: CrowdForge: crowdsourcing complex work. In: Proceedings of the 24th Annual ACM Symposium on User Interface Software and Technology, UIST 2011 (2011)

10. Horowitz, D., Kamvar, S.D.: The anatomy of a large-scale social search engine. In: Proceedings of the 19th International Conference on World Wide Web, WWW 2010, p. 431 (2010)

11. Phuttharak, J., Loke, S.W.: LogicCrowd: A declarative programming platform for mobile crowdsourcing. In: Proceedings of the 12th IEEE International Conference on Trust, Security and Privacy in Computing and Communications, TrustCom 2013, pp. 1323–1330 (2013)

12. Phuttharak, J., Loke, S.W.: Towards declarative programming for mobile crowdsourcing: P2P aspects. In: 1st International Workshop on Mobile Collaborative Crowdsourcing and Sensing (M-CROS) in conjunction with the 15th IEEE International Conference on Mobile Data Management (2014)

13. Dai, P., Lin, C.H., Weld, D.S.: POMDP-based control of workflows for crowdsourcing. Artif. Intell. **202**, 52–85 (2013)

14. Kulkarni, A., Can, M., Hartmann, B.: Collaboratively crowdsourcing workflows with turkomatic. In: Proceedings of the ACM 2012 Conference on Computer Supported Cooperative Work, CSCW 2012, p. 1003. ACM Press, New York (2012)

15. Ra, M., Liu, B., La Porta, T., Govindan, R.: Demo – medusa: a Programming Framework for Crowd-Sensing Applications. In: Proceedings of the 10th International Conference on Mobile Systems, Applications, and Services, MobiSys 2012, pp. 481–482 (2012)

16. Scekic, O., Truong, H.-L., Dustdar, S.: Incentives and rewarding in social computing. Commun. ACM **56**, 72 (2013)

17. Hirth, M., Hoßfeld, T., Tran-Gia, P.: Analyzing costs and accuracy of validation mechanisms for crowdsourcing platforms. Math. Comput. Model. **57**, 2918–2932 (2013)

18. Kazai, G., Kamps, J., Milic-Frayling, N.: Worker types and personality traits in crowdsourcing relevance labels. In: Proceedings of the 20th ACM International Conference on Information and Knowledge Management, CIKM 2011, pp. 1941–1944 (2011)

19. Okubo, Y., Kitasuka, T., Aritsugi, M.: A preliminary study of the number of votes under majority rule in crowdsourcing. Procedia Comput. Sci. **22**, 537–543 (2013)

20. Zhang, H.: Computational Environment Design (2012)

21. Barowy, D., Curtsinger, C., Berger, E., McGregor, A.: AutoMan: a platform for integrating human-based and digital computation. In: Proceedings of the ACM International Conference on Object Oriented Programming Systems Languages and Applications, OOPSLA 2012, pp. 639–654 (2012)

22. Tarasov, A., Delany, S.J., Mac Namee, B.: Dynamic estimation of worker reliability in crowdsourcing for regression tasks: making it work. Expert Syst. Appl. **41**, 6190–6210 (2014)

23. Tran-Thanh, L., Stein, S., Rogers, A., Jennings, N.R.: Efficient crowdsourcing of unknown experts using bounded multi-armed bandits. Artif. Intell. **214**, 89–111 (2014)

24. Yang, Y., Zhu, B.B., Guo, R., Yang, L., Li, S., Yu, N.: A comprehensive human computation framework – with application to image labeling. In: Proceedings of the 16th ACM International Conference on Multimedia Pages, pp. 479–488 (2008)

25. Little, G., Chilton, L.B., Goldman, M., Miller, R.C.: TurKit: human computation algorithms on mechanical turk. In: Proceedings of the 23rd Annual ACM Symposium on User Interface Software and Technology, pp. 57–66. ACM, New York (2010)

Adaptive Enterprise Architecture for Digital Transformation

Alfred Zimmermann[1,2], Rainer Schmidt[1,2(✉)], Dierk Jugel[1,2,3], and Michael Möhring[2,4]

[1] Reutlingen University, Reutlingen, Germany
{alfred.zimmermann,dierk.jugel}@reutlingen-university.de
[2] Munich University, Munich, Germany
Rainer.Schmidt@hm.edu
[3] Rostock University, Rostock, Germany
dierk.jugel@uni-rostock.de
[4] Aalen University, Rostock, Germany
michael.moehring@htw-aalen.de

Abstract. The Internet of Things, Enterprise Social Networks, Adaptive Case Management, Mobility systems, Analytics for Big Data, and Cloud services environments are emerging to support smart connected products and services and the digital transformation. Biological metaphors of living and adaptable ecosystems provide the logical foundation for self-optimizing and resilient run-time environments for intelligent business services and related distributed information systems with service-oriented enterprise architectures. We are investigating mechanisms for flexible adaptation and evolution for the next digital enterprise architecture systems in the context of the digital transformation. Our aim is to support flexibility and agile transformation for both business and related enterprise systems through adaptation and dynamical evolution of digital enterprise architectures. The present research paper investigates digital transformations of business and IT and integrates fundamental mappings between adaptable digital enterprise architectures and service-oriented information systems. We are putting a spotlight with the example domain – Internet of Things.

Keywords: Digital transformation · Internet of Things · Digital enterprise architecture · Architectural integration method · Adaptable services and systems

1   Introduction

Smart connected products and services expand physical components from their traditional core by adding information and connectivity services using the Internet. Smart products and services amplify the basic value and capabilities and offer exponentially expanding opportunities [1]. Smart connected products combine three fundamental elements: physical components, smart components, and connectivity components. A challenging example of digital transformation for smart products results from capabilities of the Internet of Things [2].

© Springer International Publishing Switzerland 2016
A. Celesti and P. Leitner (Eds.): ESOCC 2015 Workshops, CCIS 567, pp. 308–319, 2016.
DOI: 10.1007/978-3-319-33313-7_24

Information, data and knowledge are fundamental concepts of our everyday activities. Social networks, smart portable devices, and intelligent cars, represent only a few instances of a pervasive, information-driven vision [1] for the next wave of the digital economy and the digital transformation. The digital transformation of our society changes the way we live, work, learn, communicate, and collaborate. This disruptive change interacts with all information processes and systems that are important business enablers for the digital transformation since years.

Major trends for the digital enterprise transformation are investigated by [3]: (i) digitization of products and services: products and services are enriched with value-added services or are completely digitized, (ii) context-sensitive value creation: though popularity of mobile devices location contexts are used more frequently and enable on demand customized solutions, (iii) consumerization of IT: one of the challenges is the safe integration of mobile devices into a managed enterprise architecture for both business and IT, (iv) digitization of work: today it is much easier to work together over large distances, which allows often an uncomplicated outsourcing of business tasks, and (v) digitization of business models: businesses need to adapt and have to rethink their business models to develop innovative business models according to employees' current skills and competencies.

Enterprise Architecture Management [4] for Services Computing is the approach of choice to organize, build and utilize distributed capabilities for Digital Transformation [5]. They provide flexibility and agility in business and IT systems. The development of such applications integrates the Internet of Things, Web and REST Services, Cloud Computing and Big Data management, among other frameworks and methods, like architectural semantic support. Today's information systems span a broad range of domains including: intelligent mobility systems and services, intelligent energy support systems, smart personal health-care systems and services, intelligent transportation and logistics services, smart environmental systems and services, intelligent systems and software engineering, intelligent engineering and manufacturing.

The Internet of Things enables a large number of physical devices to connect each other to perform wireless data communication and interaction using the Internet as a global communication environment. Information and data are central components of our everyday activities. Social networks, smart portable devices, and intelligent cars, represent a few instances of a pervasive, information-driven vision of current enterprise systems with IoT and service-oriented enterprise architectures. Social graph analysis and management, big data, and cloud data management, ontological modeling, smart devices, personal information systems, hard non-functional requirements, such as location-independent response times and privacy, are challenging aspects of the above software architecture [6].

Novel technologies demand an increased permeability between "inside" and "outside" of the borders of the classic enterprise system with traditional Enterprise Architecture Management. In this paper we are concentrating on following research questions to support the digital transformation by flexible architectural environments:

RQ1: What are novel architectural elements, compositions, and constraints usable for digitization?

RQ2: What is the blueprint for an extended Enterprise Reference Architecture, which is able to host even new and small types of architectural descriptions, e.g. for the Internet of Things?

RQ3: How can we integrate a dynamically growing number of architectural elements for digitized products and services into an evolutionary architecture?

In our current research we are extending our first version of the Enterprise Services Architecture Reference Cube (ESARC) [4, 7, 8] by mechanisms for architectural integration and evolution to support adaptable information systems and architectural transformations for changing business models. ESARC is an extendable classification framework, which sets a conceptual baseline for digital architectural models. ESARC makes it possible to verify, define and track the improvement path of different business and IT changes considering alternative business operating models, business functions and business processes, enterprise services and systems, their architectures and related technologies. The novelty in our current research about digital enterprise architectures comprises new aspects for architectural evolution and integration methods as an instrument to guide digital transformation endeavors.

The following Sect. 2 sets the architectural context for Digital Transformation with the Internet of Things. Section 3 describes our research platform for Digital Enterprise Architecture, which is a starting point of our mapping approach and scope for agile and adaptable information systems. Section 4 revisits and extends our Architecture Metamodel Integration Method and covers the seeding research for agile adaptable and transformable enterprise architectures and systems. Finally, we summarize in Sect. 5 our research findings and sketch our future research plans.

2 Digital Transformation with the Internet of Things

The Internet of Things maps and integrates real world objects into the virtual world, and extends the interaction with mobility systems, collaboration support systems, and systems and services for big data and cloud environments. Sensors, actuators, devices as well as humans and software agents interact and communicate data to implement specific tasks or more sophisticated business or technical processes. Therefore, smart products as well as their production are supported by the Internet of Things and can help enterprises to create more customer-oriented products. Furthermore, the Internet of Things is an important influence factor of the potential use of Industry 4.0 [9].

In the context of current fast changing markets [2] the Internet of Things (IoT) fundamentally revolutionizes today's digital strategies with disruptive business operating models [10] and holistic governance models for business and IT [Ro06]. Reasons for strategic changes by the Internet of Things [2] are: (i) information of everything – enables information about what customers really demand, (ii) shift from the thing to the composition – the power of the IoT results form the unique composition of things in an always-on always-connected environment, (iii) convergence – integrates people, things, places, and information, and (iv) next-level business – the Internet of Things is changing existing business capabilities by providing a way to interact, measure, operate, and analyze business. With the huge diversity of Internet of Things technologies and products organizations have to leverage and extend previous enterprise architecture efforts to enable business value by integrating the Internet of Things into their classic business and computational environments.

The Internet of Things supports many connected physical devices over the Internet as a global communication platform. The Internet of Things is the result of a convergence of visions [11] like, a Things-oriented vision, an Internet-oriented vision, and a Semantic-oriented vision. A cloud centric vision for architectural thinking of a ubiquitous sensing environment is provided by [12]. The typical configuration of the Internet of Things includes besides many communicating devices a cloud-based server architecture, which is required to interact and perform remote data management and calculations.

A main question of current and further research is, how the Internet of Things architecture fits in a context of a services-based enterprise-computing environment? A service-oriented integration approach for the Internet of Things was elaborated in [13]. The core idea for millions of cooperating devices is, how they can be flexibly connected to form useful advanced collaborations within the business processes of an enterprise. The research in [13] proposes the SOCRADES architecture for an effective integration of Internet of Things in enterprise services. The architecture from [13] abstracts the heterogeneity of embedded systems, their hardware devices, software, data formats and communication protocols. A layered architecture structures following bottom-up functionalities and prepares these layers for integration within an Internet of Things focused enterprise architecture: Devices Layer, Platform Abstraction Layer, Security Layer, Device Management Layer with Monitoring and Inventory Services, and Service Lifecycle Management, Service Management Layer, and the Application Interface Layer.

Today, the Internet of Things includes a multitude of technologies and specific application scenarios of ubiquitous computing [11], like wireless and Bluetooth sensors, Internet-connected wearable systems, low power embedded systems, RFID tracking, smartphones, which are connected with real world interaction devices, smart homes and cars, and other SmartLife scenarios. To integrate all aspects and requirements of the Internet of Things is difficult, because no single architecture can support today the dynamics of adding and extracting these capabilities. A first Reference Architecture (RA) for the Internet of Things is proposed by [14] and can be mapped to a set of open source products. This Reference Architecture covers aspects like: cloud server-side architecture, monitoring and management of Internet of Things devices and services, a specific lightweight RESTful communication system, and agent and code on often-small low power devices, having probably only intermittent connections.

The Internet of Thing architecture has to support a set of generic as well as some specific requirements [14, 15]. Generic requirements result from the inherent connection of a magnitude of devices via the Internet, often having to cross firewalls and other obstacles. Having to consider so many and a dynamic growing number of devices we need an architecture for scalability. Because these devices should be active in a 24×7 timeframe we need a high-availability approach [16], with deployment and auto-switching across cooperating datacenters in case of disasters and high scalable processing demands. Additionally an Internet of Thing architecture has to support automatic managed updates and remotely managed devices. Often connected devices collect and analyze personal or security relevant data. Therefore it is mandatory to support identity management, access control and security management on different levels: from the connected devices through the holistic controlled environment.

Specific architectural requirements [11, 14] result from key categories, such as connectivity and communications, device management, data collection and analysis, computational scalability, and security. Connectivity and communications groups existing protocols like HTTP, which could be an issue on small devices, due to the limited memory sizes and because of power requirements. A simple, small and binary protocol can be combined with HTTP-APIs, and has the ability to cross firewalls. Typical devices of the Internet of Things are currently not or not well managed by device management functions of the current Enterprise Architecture Management.

Desirable requirements of device management [14] include the ability to locate or disconnect a stolen device, update the software on a device, update security credentials or wiping security data from a stolen device. Internet of Things systems can collect data streams from many devices, store data, analyze data, and act. These actions may happen in near real time, which leads to real-time data analytics approaches. Server infrastructures and platforms should be high scalable to support elastic scaling up to millions of connected devices, supporting alternatively as well smaller deployments. Security is a challenging aspect of this high-distributed typical small environment of Internet of Things. Sensors are able to collect personalized data and can bring these data to the Internet.

3   Digital Enterprise Architecture

Our contribution is an extended approach about the systematic composition and integration of architectural data, models, metamodels, and ontologies using adaptable service-oriented enterprise architecture frameworks by means of different integrated service types and architecture capabilities. ESARC - Enterprise Services Architecture Reference Cube, [4, 7, 17] is an integral service-oriented enterprise architecture categorization framework, which sets a classification scheme for main enterprise architecture models, as a guiding instrument for concrete decisions in architectural engineering viewpoints. We are currently integrating metamodels for EAM and the Internet of Things.

The ESARC – Enterprise Services Architecture Reference Cube [4, 7] (see Fig. 1) completes existing architectural standards and frameworks in the context of EAM – Enterprise Architecture Management [18–21] and extends these architecture standards for services and cloud computing in a more specific practical way. ESARC is an original architecture reference model, which provides a holistic classification model with eight integral architectural domains. ESARC abstracts from a concrete business scenario or technologies, but is applicable for concrete architectural instantiations.

Metamodels and their architectural data are the core part of the Enterprise Architecture. Enterprise architecture metamodels [21, 22] should support decision support [23] and the strategic [8] and IT/Business [20] alignment. Three quality perspectives are important for an adequate IT/Business alignment and are differentiated as: (i) IT system

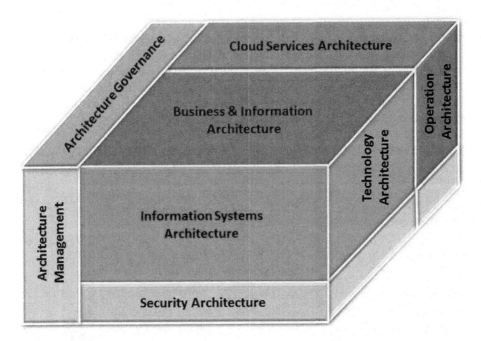

Fig. 1. Enterprise Services Architecture Reference Cube [Zi11], [Zi13b], [Zi14]

qualities: performance, interoperability, availability, usability, accuracy, maintainability, and suitability; (ii) business qualities: flexibility, efficiency, effectiveness, integration and coordination, decision support, control and follow up, and organizational culture; and finally (iii) governance qualities: plan and organize, acquire and implement deliver and support, monitor and evaluate.

Architecture Governance, as in [10] sets the governance frame for well aligned management practices within the enterprise by specifying management activities: plan, define, enable, measure, and control. The second aim of governance is to set rules for architectural compliance respecting internal and external standards. Architecture Governance has to set rules for the empowerment of people, defining the structures and procedures of an Architecture Governance Board, and setting rules for communication.

A layered Reference Architecture for the Internet of Things is proposed in [14] and (Fig. 2). Layers can be instantiated by suitable technologies for the Internet of Things. A current holistic approach for the development for the Internet of Things environments is presented in [15]. This research has a close link to our work about leveraging the integration of the Internet of Things into a framework of digital enterprise architectures. The main contribution from [15] considers a role-specific development methodology, and a development framework for the Internet of Things. The development framework contains a set of modeling languages for a vocabulary language to describe domain-specific features of an IoT application, an architecture language for describing application-specific functionality, and a deployment language for deployment features.

Associated with this language set are suitable automation techniques for code generation, and linking to reduce the effort for developing and operating device-specific code.

The metamodel for Internet of Things applications from [15] defines elements of an Internet of Things architectural reference model like, IoT resources of type: sensor, actuator, storage, and user interface. Internet of Thing resources and their associated physical devices are differentiated in the context of locations and regions. A device provides the capability to interact with users or with other devices. The base functionality of Internet of Things resources is provided by software components, which are handled in a service-oriented way by using computational services.

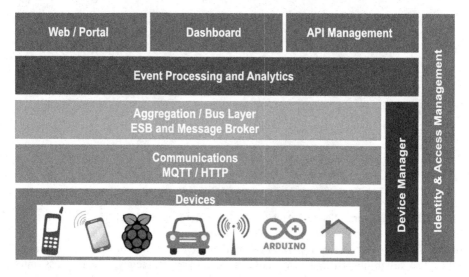

Fig. 2. Internet of Things Reference Architecture [14]

4   Architectural Integration and Adaptation

We have developed the architectural evolution approach to integrate and adapt valuable parts of existing EA frameworks and metamodels from theory and practice [24]. Additionally to a new building mechanism for dynamically extending core metamodels we see a chance to integrate small-decentralized mini-metamodels, models and data of architectural descriptions coming from small devices and new decentralized architectural element, which traditionally are not covert by enterprise architecture environments.

Our focused model integration approach is based on special correlation matrixes (Fig. 3) to identify similarities between analyzed model elements from different provenience and integrate them according their most valuable contribution for an integrated model. According to [25] we are building the conceptualization of EA in 4 steps – from stakeholders' needs, to the concerns of stakeholders, then the extraction of stakeholder relevant concepts, and last but not least the definition of relationships for new tailored architectural metamodels.

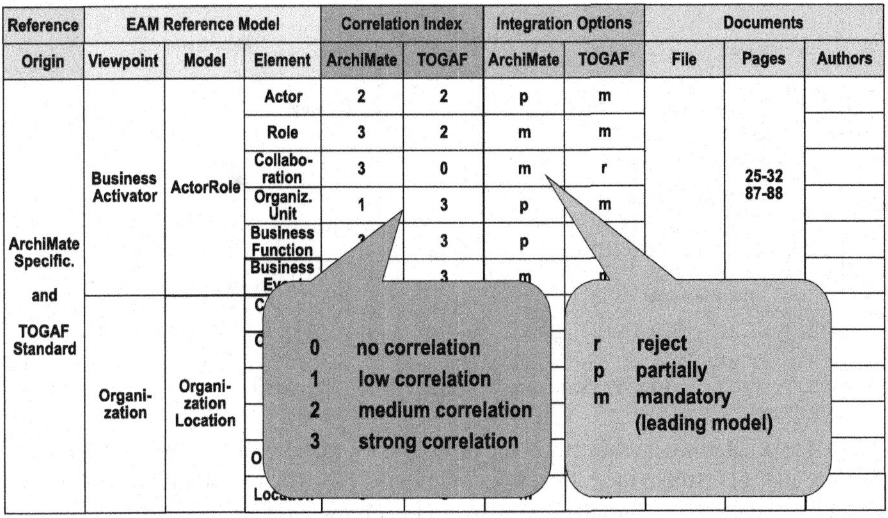

Reference	EAM Reference Model			Correlation Index		Integration Options		Documents		
Origin	Viewpoint	Model	Element	ArchiMate	TOGAF	ArchiMate	TOGAF	File	Pages	Authors
ArchiMate Specific. and TOGAF Standard	Business Activator	ActorRole	Actor	2	2	p	m		25-32 87-88	
			Role	3	2	m	m			
			Collaboration	3	0	m	r			
			Organiz. Unit	1	3	p	m			
			Business Function		3	p				
			Business Event		3	m				
	Organization	Organization Location								

Correlation Index

0 no correlation
1 low correlation
2 medium correlation
3 strong correlation

Integration Options

r reject
p partially
m mandatory (leading model)

Fig. 3. Correlation analysis and integration matrix

First we analyze and transform given architecture resources with concept maps and extract their coarse-grained aspects in a standard way [24] by delimiting architecture viewpoints [20, 26], architecture models [27, 28] their elements, and illustrating these models by a typical example. Architecture viewpoints are representing and grouping conceptual business and technology functions regardless of their implementation resources like people, processes, information, systems, or technologies. They extend these information by additional aspects like quality criteria, service levels, KPI, costs, risks, compliance criteria a. o. We have adopted modeling concepts from ISO/IEC 42010 [26, 29] like Architecture Description, Viewpoint, View, and Model. Architectural metamodels are composed of their elements and relationships, and are represented by architecture diagrams.

To integrate a huge amount of dynamically growing Internet of Things architectural descriptions into a consistent enterprise architecture is a considerable challenge. Currently we are working on the idea of integrating small EA descriptions (Fig. 4) for each relevant IoT object. EA-IoT-Mini-Descriptions consists of partial EA-IoT-Data, partial EA-IoT-Models, and partial EA-IoT-Metamodels associated with main IoT objects like IoT-Resource, IoT-Device, and IoT-Software-Component [14, 15]. Our research in progress main question asks, how we can federate these EA-IoT-Mini-Descriptions to a global EA model and information base by promoting a mixed automatic and collaborative decision process [30, 31]. For the automatic part we currently extend model federation and transformation approaches [32–34] by introducing semantic-supported architectural representations, e.g. by using partial and federated ontologies [35] and associated mapping rules - as universal enterprise architectural knowledge representation, which are combined with special inference mechanisms.

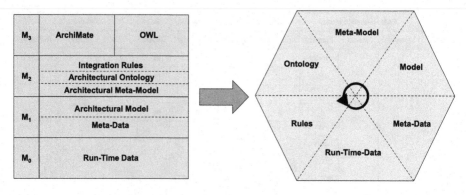

Fig. 4. Structure of EA-IoT-Mini-Description

We are extending architecture metamodels as an abstraction for architectural elements and relate them to architectural ontologies [24, 36]. Ontologies are a base for semantic modeling of digital enterprise architectures in a most flexible way. As mentioned in this section, integration of enterprise architectural elements is a complex task, which is today mainly supported by human effort and integration methodologies, and only additionally by some challenging federated approaches [33, 34] for automated Enterprise Architecture model maintenance. We believe that a part of this manual integration can be automated or additionally supported by human decisions using architectural cockpits, if we better understand the analysis approaches [28] and collaborative architectural decision mechanisms [19, 23, 30, 37] for adaptable digital enterprise architectures as a base for the digital business transformation.

We have adopted an agile manageable spectrum of multi-attribute analysis metamodels and related architectural viewpoints from [20, 23] to support adaptable enterprise architectures. We have extracted the idea of digital ecosystems from [38] and linked this with main strategic drivers for system development and their evolution. Core concepts of ecosystem's enterprise architectures are based in our approach on specific microarchitectures, which are placed in the context of Internet systems. The preferred mechanisms for modularization rely on decoupling and on interface standardization. Architecture governance models show the way to achieve adaptable ecosystems and to orchestrate the platform evolution.

Adaptation drives the survival [38] of enterprise architectures, platforms and application ecosystems. Adapting rapidly to new technology and market contexts improves the fitness of adaptive ecosystems. Volatile technologies and markets typically drive the evolution of ecosystems. Also we have to consider internal factors. Most important for supporting the evolution of ecosystems is the systematic architecture-governance alignment. Both are critical factors, which affect the ecosystem-wide motivation and the ability to innovate ecosystem structures and change processes. The alignment of Architecture-Governance shapes resiliency, scalability and composability of components and services for distributed information systems.

5   Conclusion

From our research in progress work on integrating Internet of Things architectures into Enterprise Architecture Management results some interesting theoretical and practical implications. By considering the context of service-oriented enterprise architecture, we have set the foundation for integrating metamodels and related ontologies for orthogonal architecture domains within our Enterprise Architecture Management approach for the Internet of Things. Architectural decisions for Internet of Things objects (see RQ1), like IoT-Resource, Device, and Software Component, are closely linked with code implementations. Therefore, researchers can use our approach for integrating and evaluating Internet of Things in the field of enterprise architecture management. Our results can help practical users to understand the integration of EAM and Internet of Things as well as can support architectural decision making in this area. Limitations can be found e.g. in the field of practical multi-level evaluation of our approach as well as domain-specific adoptions.

In this paper, we have introduced a new perspective for adaptable digital enterprise architectures (see RQ2), which is model-based and extends main standards, technologies and agile business models. We have developed a metamodel-based EA model extraction and integration approach for enterprise architecture viewpoints, models, standards, frameworks and tools for EAM towards consistent semantic-supported service-oriented reference enterprise architectures in cloud environments.

The presented architectural classification and integration approach (see RQ3) supports new architectural integration aspects for the Internet of Things and other small or mobile environments as well. Our goal is to be able to better support architecture development, assessments, architecture diagnostics, monitoring with decision support, and optimization of the business, information systems, and technologies. We intend to provide a unified and consistent ontology-based EAM-methodology for the architecture management models of relevant information resources, especially for service-oriented and cloud computing systems. Today we additionally observe companies adopting a three level architecture: On the basic level the classic systems of records, on a further level the systems of differentiation, and at the third level new IT opportunities for the systems of innovation. Expanding the classical EAM agenda thru ontology support with business rules and metamodel updating we see the chance for future work and research.

We contribute to the current IS literature by introducing this new perspective for adaptable digital enterprise architectures. EA managers can benefit from new knowledge about adaptable enterprise architectures and can use it for decision support and can reduce operational risks. Some limitations (e.g. use and adoption in different sectors) must be considered. Future research can adopt and evaluate our results for EAM and can take a look at the use in different industry sectors.

References

1. Porter, M.E., Heppelmann, J.E.: How smart connected products are transforming competition. Harv. Bus. Rev. **92**, 64–88 (2014)
2. Walker, M.J.: Leveraging Enterprise Architecture to Enable Business Value With IoT Innovations Today. Gartner Research (2014). http://www.gartner.com/analyst/49943
3. Leimeister, J.M., et al.: Research program "Digital Business Transformation HSG". In: Working Paper Services of University of St. Gallen's Institute of Information Management, No. 1, St. Gallen, Switzerland (2014)
4. Zimmermann, A., et al.: Capability diagnostics of Enterprise Service Architectures using a dedicated Software Architecture Reference Model. In: IEEE International Conference on Services Computing (SCC 2011), Washington DC, USA, pp. 592–599 (2011)
5. Aier, S., et al.: Towards a more integrated EA planning: linking transformation planning with evolutionary change. In: Proceedings of EMISA 2011, Hamburg, Germany, pp. 23–36 (2011)
6. Bass, C., Clements, P., Kazman, R.: Software Architecture in Practice. Addison Wesley, Massachusetts (2013)
7. Zimmermann, A., et al.: Towards service-oriented enterprise architectures for big data applications in the cloud. In: EDOC 2013 with SoEA4EE, Vancouver, BC, Canada, 9–13 September 2013, pp. 130–135 (2013)
8. Schmidt, R., Möhring, M.: Strategic alignment of cloud-based architectures for big data. In: Proceedings of the 17th IEEE International Enterprise Distributed Object Computing Conference Workshops EDOCW, Vancouver, Canada, pp. 136–143 (2013)
9. Schmidt, R., Möhring, M., Härting, R.-C., Reichstein, C., Neumaier, P., Jozinović, P.: Industry 4.0 - potentials for creating smart products: empirical research results. In: Abramowicz, W. (ed.) BIS 2015. LNBIP, vol. 208, pp. 16–27. Springer, Heidelberg (2015)
10. Weill, P., Ross, J.W.: IT Governance: How Top Performers Manage It Decision Rights for Superior Results. Harvard Business School Press, Boston (2004)
11. Atzori, L., et al.: The Internet of Things: a survey. J. Comput. Netw. **54**, 2787–2805 (2010)
12. Gubbi, J., et al.: Internet of Things (IoT): a vision, architectural elements, and future directions. Future Gener. Comput. Syst. **29**(7), 1645–1660 (2013)
13. Spiess, P., et al.: SOA-based integration of the Internet of Things in enterprise services. In: ICWS 2009, pp. 968–975 (2009)
14. WSO2 White Paper: A reference architecture for the Internet of Things. Version 0.8.0 (2015). http://wso2.com
15. Patel, P., Cassou, D.: Enabling high-level application development for the Internet of Things. CoRR abs/1501.05080, J. Syst. Softw. (2015, submitted)
16. Ganz, F., et al.: A resource mobility scheme for service-continuity in the Internet of Things. In: GreenCom 2012, pp. 261–264 (2012)
17. Zimmermann, A., et al.: Adaptable enterprise architectures for software evolution of SmartLife ecosystems. In: Proceedings of the 18th IEEE International Enterprise Distributed Object Computing Conference Workshops (EDOCW), Ulm, Germany, pp. 316–323 (2014)
18. The Open Group: TOGAF Version 9.1. Van Haren Publishing, Zaltbommel (2011)
19. Bente, S., et al.: Collaborative Enterprise Architecture. Morgan Kaufmann, Waltham (2012)
20. Lankhorst, M., et al.: Enterprise Architecture at Work: Modelling, Communication and Analysis. Springer, Heidelberg (2013)
21. The Open Group: Archimate 2.0 Specification. Van Haren Publishing, Zaltbommel (2012)
22. Saat, J., Franke, U., Lagerström, R., Ekstedt, M.: Enterprise architecture meta models for IT/Business Alignment Situations. In: IEEE-EDOC Conference 2010, Vitoria, Brazil (2010)
23. Johnson, P., et al.: IT Management with Enterprise Architecture. KTH, Stockholm (2014)

24. Zimmermann, A., et al.: Towards an integrated service-oriented reference enterprise architecture. In: ESEC/ WEA 2013 on Software Ecosystem Architectures, St. Petersburg, Russia, pp. 26–30 (2013)
25. Buckl, S., et al.: Modeling the supply and demand of architectural information on enterprise level. In: 15th IEEE International EDOC Conference 2011, Helsinki, Finland, pp. 44–51 (2011)
26. ISO/IEC/IEEE: Systems and Software Engineering – Architecture Description. Technical Standard (2011)
27. Iacob, M.-E., et al.: Delivering Business Outcome with TOGAF® and ArchiMate®. eBook BiZZdesign (2015)
28. Buckl, S., Matthes, F., Schweda, C.M.: Classifying enterprise architecture analysis approaches. In: Poler, R., van Sinderen, M., Sanchis, R. (eds.) IWEI 2009. LNBIP, vol. 38, pp. 66–79. Springer, Heidelberg (2009)
29. Emery, D., Hilliard, R.: Every architecture description needs a framework: expressing architecture frameworks using ISO/IEC 42010. In: IEEE/IFIP WICSA/ECSA, pp. 31–39 (2009)
30. Jugel, D., Schweda, C.M., Zimmermann, A.: Modeling decisions for collaborative enterprise architecture engineering. In: 10th Workshop Trends in Enterprise Architecture Research (TEAR), held on CAISE 2015, Stockholm, Sweden (2015)
31. Johnson, P., Ekstedt, M.: Enterprise Architecture – Models and Analyses for Information Systems Decision Making. Studentliteratur, Pozkal (2007)
32. Breu, R., et al.: Living models – ten principles for change-driven software engineering. Int. J. Softw. Inform. 5(1–2), 267–290 (2010)
33. Farwick, M., et al.: A meta-model for automated enterprise architecture model maintenance. In: EDOC 2012, pp. 1–10 (2012)
34. Trojer, T., Farwick, M., Häusler, M., Breu, R.: Living modeling of IT architectures: challenges and solutions. In: De Nicola, R., Hennicker, R. (eds.) Wirsing Festschrift. LNCS, vol. 8950, pp. 458–474. Springer, Heidelberg (2015)
35. Khan, N.A.: Transformation of enterprise model to enterprise ontology. Master thesis, Linköping University, Sweden (2011)
36. Antunes, G., et al.: Using ontologies for enterprise architecture analysis. In: 17th IEEE International Enterprise Distributed Object Computing Conference Workshops 2013, pp. 361–368 (2013)
37. Jugel, D., Schweda, C.M.: Interactive functions of a cockpit for enterprise architecture planning. In: International Enterprise Distributed Object Computing Conference Workshops and Demonstrations (EDOCW), Ulm, Germany, 2014, pp. 33–40 (2014)
38. Tiwana, A.: Platform Ecosystems: Aligning Architecture, Governance, and Strategy. Morgan Kaufmann, San Francisco (2013)

FedCloudNet Workshop Papers

Preface of FedCloudNet 2015

Cloud federation enables cloud providers to collaborate and share their resources to create a large virtual pool of resources at multiple network locations. To support this scenario, it is necessary to research and develop techniques to federate cloud network resources, enabling the instantiation and provision of overlay networks across geographically dispersed clouds, and to derive the integrated management cloud layer that enables an efficient and secure deployment of federated cloud applications. This workshop allowed researchers to present their latest research results on federated cloud networking, including software defined networking (SDN) technology, network overlays, and traffic engineering.

In "BEACON: A Cloud Network Federation Framework," Moreno et al. present the BEACON Framework, which will enable the provision and management of cross-site virtual networks for federated cloud infrastructures in order to support the automated deployment of applications and services across different clouds and data centers.

In "Federated Networking Services in Multiple OpenStack Clouds" Celesti et al. focus on federated cloud networking services considering multiple OpenStack clouds. In particular, they present a preliminary outcome of an innovative design of a federation management system acting as an external service provider dealing with federated networking services among multiple federated OpenStack clouds.

In "Networking Introspection and Analysis for Virtual Machine Migration in Federated Clouds," Andronico et al. explore a way to use dynamically provided resources migrating virtual machines (VMs). In particular, they discuss some reference use cases and required tools and present a concrete implementation of an advanced monitoring agent.

In "SHYAM: A System for Autonomic Management of Virtual Clusters in Hybrid Clouds," Loreti et al. discuss SHYAM, a software layer for the autonomic deployment and configuration of virtual clusters on a hybrid cloud. This system can be used to face the temporary (or permanent) lack of computational resources on the private cloud, allowing cloud bursting in the context of big data applications.

In "A Database-Specific Pattern for Multi-Cloud High Availability and Disaster Recovery," Xiong et al. present an architectural pattern describing the integration of high availability and disaster recovery (HADR). This HADR pattern for database cluster replication implements both synchronous and asynchronous replication concurrently for high availability and disaster recovery purposes. In particular, the authors focus on database cluster replication between private cloud and public cloud environments.

In "An OpenStack-Based Implementation of a Volunteer Cloud," Distefano et al. focus on the intersection between volunteering and cloud computing. In particular they propose a blueprint of a Cloud@Home implementation starting from OpenStack. The reference, layered architecture and the preliminary implementation of a Cloud@Home framework based on OpenStack are discussed.

In "Cloud Services Composition Through Semantically Described Patterns: A Case Study," Di Martino et al. present a methodology, based on the semantic representation of cloud patterns, cloud services, and applications, to support users in developing cloud-oriented software meeting their explicit requirements.

We wish to thank all the people who submitted papers to FedCloudNet 2015 for having shared their work with us, as well as the members of the FedCloudNet 2015 Program Committee, who made a remarkable effort in reviewing the submissions. We also thank the organizers of ESOCC 2015 for their help with the organization of the event.

Antonio Puliafito
Ignacio M. Llorente
Philippe Massonet

Organization

Workshop Organizers

Antonio Puliafito — University of Messina, Italy
Ignacio M. Llorente — Complutense University of Madrid, Spain
Philippe Massonet — CETIC, Belgium

Steering Committee

Philippe Massonet — CETIC, Belgium
Antonio Celesti — University of Messina, Italy

Program Committee

Antonio Puliafito — University of Messina, Italy
Ignacio M. Llorente — Universidad Complutense de Madrid, Spain
Philippe Massonet — CETIC, Belgium
Eduardo Huedo — Universidad Complutense de Madrid, Spain
Francesco Longo — University of Messina, Italy
Jens Jensen — Science and Technology Facilities Council, UK
Rubén S. Montero — Universidad Complutense de Madrid, Spain
Anna Levin — IBM Research, Israel
Rafael Moreno — Universidad Complutense de Madrid, Spain
Luciano Barreto — Federal University of Santa Catarina, Brazil
Tino Vázquez — OpenNebula Systems, Spain
Giovanni Merlino — University of Messina, Italy
Bruno Crispo — University of Trento, Italy
Dean Lorenz — IBM Research, Israel
Zsolt Nemeth — MTA SZTAKI, Hungary
Yaniv Ben-Itzhak — IBM Research, Israel
Chrysa Papagianni — National Technical University of Athens, Greece
Stella Kafetzoglou — National Technical University of Athens, Greece
Luis Muñoz — University of Cantabria, Spain

Publicity Chairs

James Bowater — Flexiant, UK

Sponsors

BEACON: A Cloud Network Federation Framework

Rafael Moreno-Vozmediano[1]([⊠]), Eduardo Huedo[1], Ignacio M. Llorente[1],
Rubén S. Montero[1], Philippe Massonet[2], Massimo Villari[3],
Giovanni Merlino[3], Antonio Celesti[3], Anna Levin[4], Liran Schour[4],
Constantino Vázquez[5], Jaime Melis[5], Stefan Spahr[6], and Darren Whigham[7]

[1] Universidad Complutense de Madrid, Madrid, Spain
{rmoreno,ehuedo,llorente,rubensm}@ucm.es
[2] Centre D'excellence en Technologies de L'information
et de la Communication (CETIC), Charleroi, Belgium
philippe.massonet@cetic.be
[3] Università di Messina, Messina, Italy
{mvillari,gmerlino,acelesti}@unime.it
[4] IBM Israel - Science and Technology Ltd, Petah Tikva, Israel
{lanna,lirans}@il.ibm.com
[5] OpenNebula Systems, Madrid, Spain
{cvazquez,jmelis}@opennebula.systems
[6] Lufthansa Systems, Kelsterbach, Germany
stefan.spahr@lhsystems.com
[7] Flexiant Limited, London, UK
dwhigham@flexiant.com

Abstract. This paper presents the BEACON Framework, which will enable the provision and management of cross-site virtual networks for federated cloud infrastructures in order to support the automated deployment of applications and services across different clouds and datacenters. The proposed framework will support different federation architectures, going from tightly coupled (datacenter federation) to loosely coupled (cloud federation and multi-cloud orchestration) architectures, and will enable the creation of Layer 2 and Layer 3 overlay networks to interconnect remote resources located at different cloud sites. A high level description of the main components of the BEACON framework is also introduced.

1 Introduction

There is a strong industry demand for automated solutions to federate cloud network resources, and to derive the integrated management cloud layer that enables an efficient and secure deployment of resources and services independent of their location across distributed infrastructures. From big companies and large

This research was supported by the European Union's Horizon 2020 Research and Innovation Program under the Grant Agreement No. 644048.

A. Celesti and P. Leitner (Eds.): ESOCC 2015 Workshops, CCIS 567, pp. 325–337, 2016.
DOI: 10.1007/978-3-319-33313-7_25

cloud providers interested in unifying and consolidating multiple datacenters or cloud sites to SMEs building hybrid cloud configurations, federated cloud networking is needed to support the automated deployment of applications across different clouds and datacenters.

Many big companies (e.g. banks, hosting companies, etc.) and also many large Government institutions maintain several distributed datacenters or server farms, for example to serve to multiple geographically distributed offices, to implement HA (High Availability), or to guarantee server proximity to the end user. Federated cloud networking is needed to unify and consolidate datacenters in a virtual way, so that different distributed datacenters can be exposed as a single cloud-like virtual datacenter, and networks of different datacenters can be interconnected in a virtual overlay. Some large cloud providers offer different, geographically dispersed regions, so that users can choose to deploy their infrastructures and services in one particular region attending to different criteria, such as proximity, prices, or available resources. Usually these regions are isolated from other regions inside the same provider, to achieve fault tolerance and stability, and there is no interaction or cooperation between them. Federated cloud networking is needed to support distributed services, and provide the overlay networks needed to interconnect servers on different regions, so freeing the service administrator from manually configuring these remote connections. Many SMEs have their own on-premise private cloud infrastructures to support the internal computing necessities and workloads. These infrastructures are often oversized to satisfy peak demand periods, and avoid performance slowdown. Hybrid cloud (or cloud-bursting) model is a solution to reduce the on-premise infrastructure size, so that it can be dimensioned for an average load, and it is complemented with external resources from a public cloud provider to satisfy peak demands. Federated cloud networking is needed to improve this kind of hybrid configurations, so that local and remote resources can be seen as they belonged to the same cloud, and communication channels between these resources can be automatically configured.

Different types of federation architectures for clouds and datacenters have been proposed and implemented [9] (e.g. cloud bursting, cloud brokering or cloud peering) with different level of resource coupling and interoperation among the cloud resources, from loosely coupled, typically involving different administrative and legal domains, to tightly coupled federation, usually spanning multiple datacenter locations within an organization. In both situations, an effective, agile and secure federation of cloud networking resources is key to impact the deployment of federated applications. An integrated cloud management platform able to leverage a federated cloud network will be able to deliver to applications a reliable and secure access to a large geographically dispersed pool of resources.

This paper presents the BEACON Framework[1], funded by an European project (H2020 Program), which will enable the provision and management of cross-site virtual networks for federated cloud infrastructures, to support the automated deployment of applications and services across different clouds and

---

[1] http://www.beacon-project.eu.

datacenters. BEACON is fully committed to open source software. Cloud networking aspects will be based on OpenDaylight[2], a collaborative project under The Linux Foundation, and specifically it will leverage and extend the Open-DOVE[3] project with new rich inter-cloud APIs to provision cross-site virtual networks overlays. The new inter-cloud network capabilities will be leveraged by existing open source cloud platforms, OpenNebula[4] and OpenStack[5], to deploy multi-cloud applications. In particular, different aspects of the platforms will be extended to accommodate the federated cloud networking features like multi-tenancy, federated orchestration of networking, compute and storage management or the placement and elasticity of the multi-cloud applications.

2 Architectures for Cloud Network Federation

Most cloud federation scenarios can be classified into three main federation architectures: datacenter federation (peer cloud architecture), cloud federation (hybrid cloud architecture), and multi-cloud orchestration (cloud broker architecture). In this section, we describe these three main federation architectures, and introduce some security considerations both at application level and architecture level. The BEACON framework will support these different federation architectures, and will enable the creation of different kind of cross-site virtual networks (e.g. Layer 2 or Layer 3 overlay networks), according to the user needs, to interconnect remote resources located at different cloud sites.

2.1 Datacenter Federation and Interconnection

Datacenter federation architecture (see Fig. 1) corresponds to a tightly coupled federated cloud scenario [10], also called peer cloud federation, consisting of several private cloud premises (or datacenters) usually belonging to the same organization (or closely coordinated), and normally governed by the same Cloud Manager (CM) type, such as OpenNebula or OpenStack. In this scenario, each CM instance can have full control over remote resources (e.g., placement control, full monitoring, or VM life-cycle management and migration control). In addition, other advanced features can be allowed, including the creation of cross-site networks, the support for cross-site migration of Virtual Machines (VMs), the implementation of high-availability techniques among remote cloud instances, the creation of virtual storage systems across site boundaries, etc. The interaction between CM is usually implemented using private cloud interfaces (administration level APIs) and data models (e.g., OpenNebula XML-RPC[6] or OpenStack component APIs[7]). On top of the CM there could be a SM to simplify service definition, deployment and management.

---

[2] http://www.opendaylight.org.
[3] http://wiki.opendaylight.org/view/Open_DOVE.
[4] http://www.opennebula.org.
[5] http://www.openstack.org.
[6] http://docs.opennebula.org/4.4/integration/system_interfaces/api.html.
[7] http://developer.openstack.org/api-ref.html.

Within this architecture, the Network Manager (NM) is responsible for managing virtual networks, both inside and among datacenters. The NM can be integrated with the CM (e.g. OpenNebula Network Manager) or can be a separated component (e.g. OpenDove). NMs in different datacenters interact and cooperate using (possibly private) inter-cloud northbound APIs and protocols (e.g. Open-DayLight Controller REST API[8] or the OpenNebula VirtualNetwork XML-RPC API[9]) that enable the instantiation and management of cross-datacenter networks, mainly based on SDN (Software Defined Networks) and NFV (Network Functions Virtualization) technologies.

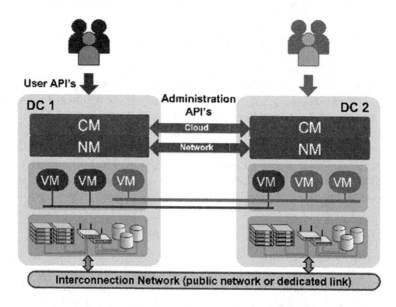

Fig. 1. Architecture for datacenter federation and interconnection.

These cross-site networks are commonly implemented as Layer 2 (L2) or Layer 3 (L3) overlay virtual networks on top of the physical interconnection network, which can be a public network (i.e., a L3 insecure network, such as Internet) or a dedicated high-performance link (usually a private L2 or L3 network). In this context, the most challenging situation is deploying a cross-site secure L2 virtual network over an insecure L3 public connection.

2.2 Cloud Federation and Interconnection

Cloud federation architecture (see Fig. 2) corresponds to a loosely coupled federated cloud scenario that combines multiple independent cloud (both public and

---

[8] http://wiki.opendaylight.org/view/OpenDaylight_Controller:REST_Reference_and_Authentication.

[9] http://docs.opennebula.org/4.12/integration/system_interfaces/api.html#actions-for-virtual-network-management.

private clouds). A typical realization of this architecture is a hybrid cloud [7,11] or inter-cloud federation, also called cloud bursting model, which combines the existing local cloud infrastructure (e.g., a private cloud managed by a CM, such as OpenNebula or OpenStack) with external resources from one or more remote clouds, which can be either public clouds (e.g. Amazon EC2, FlexiScale, Digital Ocean, etc.), or partner clouds (managed by the same or a different CM).

The main goal of this hybrid model is to provide extra capacity to the local cloud to satisfy peak demand periods, and transforming the local data-center in a highly scalable application hosting environment. This architecture is loosely coupled, since the local cloud has no advanced control over the virtual resources deployed in external clouds, beyond the basic operations allowed by these providers. The interaction between the local CM and the various remote clouds is usually implemented using public cloud interfaces (user level APIs) and data models (e.g. Amazon AWS EC2 API[10] or OCCI[11]). As in the previous architecture, on top of the CM there could be a SM.

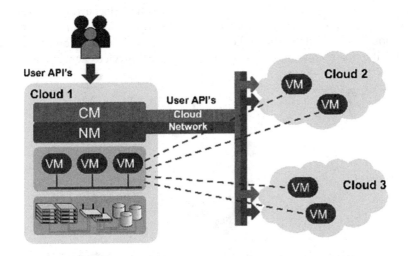

Fig. 2. Architecture for cloud federation and interconnection.

Due to the heterogeneity of network managers (NMs) in different clouds, each cloud can provide different capabilities to interconnect with external resources, regarding the possibility of creating L2 or L3 overlay networks, VPNs, secure channels, or even high level network functions like balancers. In some clouds, VMs are seen as independent resources (e.g., Amazon EC2-Classic platform), that can be accessed using a public IP, so the final user is responsible for configuring the appropriate communication channels (e.g. overlay tunnels or VPNs). Other clouds provide private networking to interconnect VMs inside the cloud

---

[10] http://aws.amazon.com/ec2.
[11] http://occi-wg.org.

(e.g. Amazon EC2-VPC platform) and also some kind of VPN capabilities to implement a L3 overlay between local network and remote resources. However, methods to instantiate and configure these VPNs differ from one provider to another. Regarding the creation of L2 overlay networks between independent clouds, currently there are not any cloud technology offering this kind of capabilities, so this is one of the most important challenges in cloud federation and interconnection.

2.3 Multi-cloud Orchestration and Interconnection

Multi-cloud orchestration architecture (see Fig. 3), also called cloud brokering architecture [6], usually consists of a central broker or orchestrator, which has access to several public independent clouds. This orchestrator can deploy virtual resources in the different clouds, according to criteria specified by the user, such as location restrictions, cost restrictions, etc., and should also provide networking capabilities to enable the interconnection of different resources deployed in geographically dispersed clouds. There could be also decentralized brokering schemes, with several brokers interacting to each other. We assume that, as in the previous architectures, the orchestrator is basically a multi-cloud SM, which is responsible for managing application and network services across clouds.

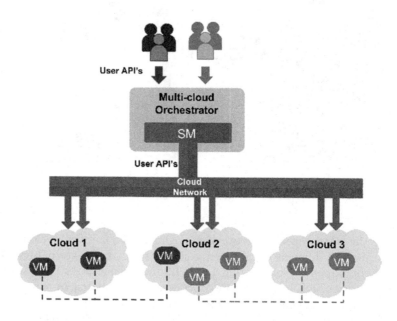

Fig. 3. Architecture for multi-cloud orchestration and interconnection.

Similar to the cloud federation architecture, this architecture is also loosely coupled, since the orchestrator interacts with the different clouds using public cloud interfaces (user level APIs, such as Amazon AWS EC2 API[12] or OCCI[13]), which usually do not allow advanced control over the virtual resources deployed.

Regarding networking issues, the orchestrator must be able to deal with different network managers with different network capabilities, hence it is responsible for creating the required interconnection topologies (e.g. L2/L3 overlay networks) on top of these heterogeneous cloud network services. These overlay networks will be based on virtualized network functions (VNFs) and services, such as bridges, routers, load balancers or firewalls, deployed on the different clouds involved.

2.4 Security Considerations

In BEACON we can have a privileged environment where to enforce and test new security features. Indeed, from the security perspective federated cloud networking provides the opportunity to monitor the virtualized compute, storage and network resources across a federation. This provides opportunities to detect attacks at the federation level that could not be detected at the individual cloud level. We can identify many security issues having a global picture of services deployed and executed in more federated Clouds. The security issues we are considering range from the Intrusion Detections, to vulnerabilities scanning, even to the distributed denial of service (DDoS). For example the DDoS attacks might be difficult to detect by monitoring activity within a single cloud. However DDoS attack patterns could be detected earlier by monitoring data from the cloud federation. Within the BEACON project we will identify opportunities for improving detection of threats thanks to the enhanced monitoring capabilities provided by federated cloud networking.

To summarize the work we are providing in BEACON, in Table 1 we classify our security considerations in four different categories for the BEACON architecture. The table considers security issues at the level of the cloud manager and the network manager on the vertical axis, and distinguishes between application level security and infrastructure level security requirements on the horizontal axis. Application level security deals with the security of the application when it is deployed in a federated cloud. Infrastructure level security deals with securing the cloud infrastructure services, i.e. the cloud manager and the network manager, and protecting them from unauthorized access from applications and users. We review the four categories of security issues identified and then conclude that the requirements from the BEACON case studies indicate that application level security needs to be studied at both the cloud manager and network manager levels.

The requirements from the different case studies of BEACON essentially refer to application level security considerations at both the cloud manager level and the network manager level. The application service manifest should specify required security services to be performed by the cloud manager and the network

---

[12] http://docs.aws.amazon.com/AWSEC2/latest/APIReference/Welcome.html.
[13] http://occi-wg.org/about/specification.

Table 1. Application and infrastructure level security considerations.

Component	Application level security	Infrastructure level security
Cloud manager	Applications should be able to request security services from the cloud manager, e.g., to perform vulnerability analysis on a given VM or to apply application level firewall rules to a given HTTP session.	The cloud manager services must be secured with respect to applications running in the cloud and system administrators.
Network manager	Applications should be able to request security services from the network manager, e.g., to apply firewall rules on one or several network layers, vulnerability analysis at the network level or to apply network intrusion detection.	The network manager services must be secured from unauthorized access, e.g. access to the network controller must be controlled, the communication between the controller and the virtual switches must be encrypted.

managers to ensure that the federated cloud meets the security requirements of the application. To guarantee security at cloud and network management at infrastructure levels, it is necessary to analyze the network managers provided by OpenNebula, OpenStack/Neutron and OpenDaylight/OpenDove, to see how they can be integrated and exchange security policies. It cloud be also interesting to analyze the issues related to the location of the network services, e.g. to decide which firewall NFV must be used when several instances are available. This question of which security function to use will also have to take into account live migration of VM within the cloud federation.

3   The BEACON Framework

The main goal of BEACON project is to define and implement a federated cloud network framework that enables the provision of federated cloud infrastructures, with special emphasis on inter-cloud networking and security issues, to support the automated deployment of applications and services across different clouds and datacenters. The implementation of these new federated cloud networking features, that will leverage on Software Defined Network (SDN) technology, include both, the configuration of overlay networks inside different cloud providers, and the interconnection of these overlays among geographically dispersed sites based on various cloud technologies.

One of the key points of this project is that it is fully driven by real industry uses cases proposed by different cloud actors, such as cloud providers, cloud technology developers, and cloud-user companies and institutions, which are represented by the different partners of the project consortium. These use cases address the different federation architectures described in previous section, such as datacenter federation (peer cloud architecture), cloud federation (hybrid cloud architecture), and multi-cloud orchestration (cloud broker architecture).

Figure 4 depicts a high level view of the BEACON framework architecture, the main components, and the open source projects that will be extended and integrated to implement the BEACON architecture in the case of cloud federation. The proposed network federation model addresses the challenge of federating clouds based on different network technologies in their network backbone as well as in their cloud management platforms.

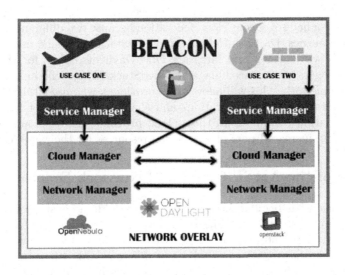

Fig. 4. BEACON federated architecture.

The three main components of the BEACON middleware are the Service Manager, the Cloud Manager and the Network Manager. The Service Manager is responsible for the instantiation of the service application by requesting the creation and configuration of VMs for each service component included in the service definition, using the Cloud interfaces exposed by the cloud manager. The Cloud Manager is responsible for the placement of VMs into physical hosts. It receives requests from the Service Manager through the cloud interface to create and resize VMs, and finds what is the best placement for these VMs that satisfies a given set of constraints (set by the Service Manager) and optimizes a site total utility function. The Cloud Manager is free to place, and move, the VMs anywhere, even on remote sites within the federation, as long as the placement is done within the constraints. The Network Manager is responsible for allocating network resources to manage federated cloud virtual network and overlay networks across geographically dispersed sites. The left and right parts of the figure show two different cloud stacks running on different cloud providers. Together they form a cloud federation with two cloud providers. The middle part of the figure shows that the cloud manager and network managers of the two cloud providers communicate to share resources and manage the cloud federation. The top of the figure shows two application level case studies that are deployed on the cloud federation (a highly scalable airline application distributed over multiple cloud providers, and multi-cloud security use case). The bottom part of the figure shows the open source projects that are used to implement the federated architecture. The cloud provider on the left part of the figure is using OpenNebula to manage its cloud infrastructure. The cloud provider on the right is using OpenStack to manage its cloud infrastructure. The network managers of both cloud providers are both using OpenDaylight to manage the network resources and supports communications between the two cloud providers. This is an example of heterogeneous cloud federation because two different cloud middleware technologies, i.e. OpenNebula and OpenStack, are being used.

BEACON will develop and integrate OpenDaylight drivers for the overlay network managers of OpenNebula and OpenStack. They will be part of the BEACON framework. This will allow cloud providers, who use either OpenNebula or OpenStack, to form federations and share resources. By forming cloud network federations, the users of these cloud providers will thus automatically benefit from an increased pool of virtualized resources for their applications.

4   State-of-the-Art in Cloud and Network Federation

Cloud federation has been an important research field and is still an open issue in cloud computing. Different initiatives have been presented so far regarding energy efficiency [16], storage [17], Assistive Technology [18], dataweb [19] and so on. In the literature, we can find many different realizations, and research works focussed on the different federation architectures. Regarding the tightly coupled peer cloud architecture, some of the most interesting initiatives are the RESERVOIR project [10], which enables the federation and interoperability of infrastructure providers, taking advantage of their aggregated capabilities to provide a seemingly infinite service computing utility, and the Contrail system [2], which provides collaboration, migration, and SLA management across multiple heterogeneous clouds that can be exploited as a single cloud. There are also various research works that show the advantages of hybrid cloud architectures [7,11,12,15], which enable the transformation the local data center in a highly scalable application hosting environment, by combining the existing corporate infrastructure with remote extra resources from one or more public clouds. This is also the case of the StratusLab initiative, which use the hybrid capabilities of the OpenNebula Cloud Manager to support and provision scalable grid services. Finally, cloud brokering has been one of the most explored federation architectures, both in industry and academia. There are various commercial cloud brokers (e.g. RightScale[14], SpotCloud[15] or Kavoo[16], among others), open-source

---

[14] http://www.rightscale.com.
[15] http://www.spotcloud.com.
[16] http://www.kavoo.com.

initiatives (e.g. Aeolus[17] or CompatibleOne[18]), and many other research works [4,6,13,14] and projects [3,5] on cloud brokering, that help cloud customers to cope with a variety of cloud interfaces, instance types, and pricing models, by providing intermediation, arbitrage, and aggregation capabilities. Regarding the networking capabilities of the above mentioned federated platforms (based on peer, hybrid, or broker architectures), most of them rely on public IP addressing to access compute instances deployed in different clouds, or use VPN tunneling mechanisms to improve security that usually are manually configured by the user. However, none of them provides any automatic method or interface to allow a user to instantiate and provision an overlay network across geographically dispersed clouds to interconnect virtual machines deployed in different clouds.

To provide federated networking capabilities, it is necessary a virtual network management system supporting seamless infrastructure, in which services can be deployed on demand across different network platforms and architectures. There are various solutions that provide tools for cloud network management, such as OpenDaylight [8], Contrail controller [2] and federated SDN controller for network virtualization overlays [1]. OpenDaylight is a collaborative project under The Linux Foundation created by leading industry partners with a goal to foster innovation and create an open and transparent approach to Software Defined Networking (SDN). An OpenDaylight controller provides flexible management of both physical and virtual networks. The network management capabilities implemented in OpenDaylight controller allow efficient integration with cloud computing platforms. For example, OpenDaylight is already integrated with Neutron, which provides SDN-based networking solution for OpenStack clouds. In order for OpenDaylight being able to manage heterogeneous networks spread over different cloud computing platforms, it has to be integrated with additional platforms, e.g. OpenNebula. With all the advantages the existing OpenDaylight solution brings to cloud network management, it does not provide a solution for federated cloud network management at its current state. Therefore, it lacks necessary federated cloud management interfaces both to the physical and virtual network elements. In order for the system being able to create and manage simultaneous virtual networks on demand with arbitrary topologies on a loosely coupled federated cloud systems, an additional extension must be defined and implemented in OpenDaylight controller that will allow its integration with federated cloud management systems. This integration should enable virtual network services across federated clouds. The Contrail Controller is a logically centralized but physically distributed SDN controller that is responsible for providing the management of the virtualized network. While the Contrail controller provides control plane, the forwarding plane of the Contrail system is represented by Contrail's virtual routers. Even though Contrail's virtual network management system is integrated with OpenStack, it is limited to the use of the specific virtual routers and does not support commonly deployed open virtual switches (vSwitch). In addition, in order for Contrail controller to

---

[17] http://www.aeolusproject.org.
[18] http://www.compatibleone.com.

provide full solution for federated virtualized cloud network management, it needs to be extended to support additional cloud platforms, such as OpenNebula for example. The federated SDN controller for network virtualization overlays is defined in [1]. It addresses the VXLAN and NVGRE overlays managed by federated SDN controller. This controller definition should be extended to support heterogeneous clouds, in order to be able to work in a federated cloud based on different cloud technologies. Also, the controller must include interfaces to the federated cloud management system, which exposes federated cloud services to applications.

5   Conclusions and Future Work

This paper has analyzed three main types of federation architectures: datacenter federation (peer cloud architecture), cloud federation (hybrid cloud architecture), and multi-cloud orchestration (cloud broker architecture). The paper presented the BEACON federated cloud network framework that enables the provision of federated cloud infrastructures, with special emphasis on intercloud networking and security issues. The challenge is to design and develop a framework that can be integrated into different cloud middleware and yet provide support virtual networking and security for the different federation types mentioned above. Future work first involves integrating the BEACON federated cloud network framework into OpenNebula and OpenStack, and experimenting with OpenNebula and OpenStack based cloud federations. In a second phase experimentation will focus on the heterogeneous case where the BEACON framework provides interoperability between OpenNebula and OpenStack clouds within the same federation.

References

1. Balus, F., Stiliadis, D., Bitar, N.: Federated SDN-based controllers for NVO3 (2012). http://tools.ietf.org/html/draft-sb-nvo3-sdn-federation-00
2. Contrail White Paper. Overview of the contrail system, components and usage (2014). http://contrail-project.eu
3. Ferrer, A., Hernandez, F., Tordsson, J., Elmroth, E., et al.: Optimis: a holistic approach to cloud service provisioning. Future Gener. Comput. Syst. **28**, 66–77 (2012)
4. Guzek, M., Gniewek, A., Bouvry, P., Musial, J., Blazewicz, J.: Cloud brokering: current practices and upcoming challenges. IEEE Cloud Comput. **2**, 40–47 (2015)
5. Kavoussanakis, K., Hume, A., Martrat, J., Ragusa, C., et al.: BonFIRE: the clouds and services testbed. In: 5th IEEE International Conference on Cloud Computing Technology and Science (Cloudcom), pp. 321–326 (2013)
6. Lucas-Simarro, J., Aniceto, I.S., Moreno-Vozmediano, R., Montero, R.S., Llorente, I.M.: A cloud broker architecture for multicloud environments, pp. 359–376. Wiley, Hoboken (2014). Chap. 15
7. Montero, R., Moreno-Vozmediano, R., Llorente, I.: An elasticity model for high throughput computing clusters. J. Parallel Distrib. Comput. **71**, 750–757 (2011)

8. Linux Foundation Collaborative Projects: OpenDaylight - an open source community and meritocracy for software-defined networking (2013). http://www.opendaylight.org
9. Moreno-Vozmediano, R., Montero, R.S., Llorente, I.M.: IaaS cloud architecture: from virtualized data centers to federated cloud infrastructures. Computer **45**, 65–72 (2013)
10. Rochwerger, B., Caceres, J., Montero, R., Breitgand, D., Elmroth, E., Galis, A., Levy, E., Llorente, I., Nagin, K., Wolfsthal, Y.: The reservoir model and architecture for open federated cloud computing. IBM J. Res. Dev. **53**, 4–11 (2009)
11. Sotomayor, B., Montero, R., Llorente, I., Foster, I.: Virtual infrastructure management in private and hybrid clouds. Internet Comput. **13**, 14–22 (2010)
12. Sturrus, E., Kulikova, O.: Orchestrating hybrid cloud deployment: an overview. IEEE Comput. **47**, 85–87 (2014)
13. Tordsson, J., Montero, R.S., Moreno-Vozmediano, R., Llorente, I.M.: Cloud brokering mechanisms for optimized placement of virtual machines across multiple providers. Future Gener. Comput. Syst. **28**, 358–367 (2012)
14. Wang, W., Niu, D., Liang, B., Li, B.: Dynamic cloud instance acquisition via IaaS cloud brokerage. IEEE Trans. Parallel Distrib. Syst. **26**, 1580–1593 (2015)
15. Zhang, H., Jiang, G., Yoshihira, K., Haifeng, C.: Proactive workload management in hybrid cloud computing. IEEE Trans. Netw. Serv. Manage. **11**, 90–100 (2014)
16. Giacobbe, M., Celesti, A., Fazio, M., Villari, M., Puliafito, A.: Towards energy management in cloud federation: a survey in the perspective of future sustainable and cost-saving strategies. Comput. Netw. **91**, 438–452 (2015)
17. Celesti, A., Fazio, M., Villari, M., Puliafito, A.: Adding long-term availability, obfuscation, and encryption to multi-cloud storage systems. J. Netw. Comput. Appl. **59**, 208–218 (2016)
18. Mulfari, D., Celesti, A., Villari, M.: A computer system architecture providing a user-friendly man machine interface for accessing assistive technology in cloud computing. J. Syst. Softw. **100**, 129–138 (2015)
19. Celesti, A., Tusa, F., Villari, M., Puliafito, A.: How the dataweb can support cloud federation: service representation and secure data exchange. In: 2012 Second Symposium on Network Cloud Computing and Applications (NCCA), pp. 73–79 (2012)

Federated Networking Services in Multiple OpenStack Clouds

Antonio Celesti[1]([✉]), Anna Levin[2], Philippe Massonet[3], Liran Schour[2],
and Massimo Villari[1]

[1] DICIEAMA, University of Messina, Messina, Italy
{acelesti,mvillari}@unime.it
[2] HLR, IBM Haifa, Haifa, Israel
{lanna,LIRANS}@il.ibm.com
[3] Cetic, Charleroi, Belgium
philippe.massonet@cetic.be
http://www.beacon-project.eu/

Abstract. Cloud federation refers to a mesh of Cloud providers that are interconnected by using agreements and protocols necessary to provide a decentralized computing environment. Federation is raising many challenges in different research fields but is also creating new business opportunities. Nowadays, the combination between Cloud federation, Software Defined Networking (SDN), and Network Function Virtualization (NFV) technologies offers new business opportunities to Cloud providers that are able to offer new innovative federated Cloud networking services to customers. In this paper, we focus on federated Cloud networking services considering multiple OpenStack Clouds. In particular, we present a preliminary outcome of an innovative design of a Federation Management system acting as an external service provider dealing with federated networking services among multiple federated OpenStack Clouds. More specifically, we describe how virtual resources, virtual networking, and security management can be accomplished.

Keywords: Cloud computing · Federation · SDN · OpenStack

1 Introduction

Cloud federation refers to a mesh of Cloud providers that are interconnected according to agreements and protocols providing a decentralized computing environment. Nowadays, the combination between Cloud federation and Software Defined Networking (SDN) technologies offers new business opportunities to providers that are able to carry out new innovative federated Cloud networking services to customers. However, the development of such an ecosystem is not trivial and many challenges must be addressed.

SDN can enhance Cloud federation scenarios. It is an approach to computer networking that allows network administrators to manage network services through the abstraction of lower-level functionalities. This is done by decoupling

© Springer International Publishing Switzerland 2016
A. Celesti and P. Leitner (Eds.): ESOCC 2015 Workshops, CCIS 567, pp. 338–352, 2016.
DOI: 10.1007/978-3-319-33313-7_26

the system that makes decisions about where traffic is sent (the control plane) from the underlying systems that forward traffic to the selected destination (the data plane). In this way, it is possible to simplify networking. SDN requires some methods for the control plane to communicate with the data plane. Thanks to SDN it is possible to accomplish networking federation between Virtual Machines (VMs) belonging to multiple Cloud providers managed by different administrative domains.

This scientific work took into account interoperability requirements specified by the *IEEE Standard Association* defined in the *P2302 - Standard for Intercloud Interoperability and Federation (SIIF)* project [1] which aims at developing standard methodologies for Cloud-to-Cloud interworking. It represents the basis for new Cloud requirements in federation.

In this paper, we focus on federated Cloud networking services considering multiple OpenStack Clouds. In particular, according to SIIF, we analysed how federated networking services can be instantiated on multiple OpenStack instances belonging to different administrative domains. More specifically, we present a preliminary outcome of an innovative design of a *Federation Management* system acting as an external service provider or Broker dealing with federated networking services among multiple Openstack-based Clouds. More specifically, we describe how virtual resources, virtual networking, and security management can be accomplished. In addition, we discuss how our system suits the requirements of a tightly coupled federation scenario.

The paper is organized as follows. In Sect. 2, we present an overview of the Openstack architecture. The main aspects that have to be considered to design federated Cloud networking services in multiple Openstack Clouds are discussed in Sect. 3. The Federation Management architecture is discussed in Sect. 4. Section 5 summarizes related works. Section 6 concludes the paper.

2   OpenStack Architecture

In this Section, we provide an overview of the OpenStack architecture and we introduce the concepts of tenants, users, and roles.

2.1   Architecture Overview

Openstack provides Cloud Infrastructure as a Service (IaaS) using the cooperation of several services each one dedicated to the provisioning of a specific service. Most of the services are composed by agents that use different plugins to add new features compliant with a specific technologies. Basically the infrastructure provides three kinds of resources: compute, storage, and network. This goal is accomplished with these projects/services:

- Nova (compute service): manages the VMs controlling and supervising the hypervisors distributed in a dedicated compute node with the hardware computational resource.

- Neutron (networking service): provides an API for users to define networks and the attachment to VMs. The agents also provides typical network services such as routing (between VMs and between a VM and an external network), DHCP, firewall, load-balancing.
- Keystone (identity service): provides an authentication and authorization service for the other Openstack service. Every external request (the REST ones) must be validated using a token generated by Keystone in accordance to the role of the user (service or human) who is trying to communicate with the infrastructure.
- Glance (image service): stores and provides the images used as a base for the VMs that are managed by Nova. Those four services represent the main core of Openstack. It means that a minimal Openstack scenario can be created with just Nova, Neutron, Keystone, and Glance.

A more complete and powerful infrastructure can be set up using these other services:

- Horizon (dashboard service): provides a web-based GUI for the administration. It uses the REST API of each service in order to send commands to them in more friendly way.
- Cinder (block storage service): provides and manages the persistent storage by means of volumes that can be directly attached on the running VMs.
- Swift (object storage service): it is a pure storage of object that can be exported using a REST API. It provides mechanisms of redundancy in a scalable architecture.
- Ceilometer (telemetry service): provides the monitoring of the Openstack resources and services for billing, scalability and statistical purposes.
- Heat (orchestration service): provides the orchestration of the resources using a file (HOT template format). With this service, different virtual scenarios and applications can be created, configured and monitored automatically by just editing the file which describes the resources and their interaction.

Trove (database service): provides a Database as a service using both relational and non-relational database engines.

2.2   Tenants, Users, and Roles

The Compute system is designed to be used by different consumers by means of tenants managing shared resources according to role-based access assignments. They consist of an individual VLAN, volumes, instances, images, keys, and users. Roles control the actions that a user is allowed to perform. Tenants are isolated resource containers that form the principal organizational structure within the Compute service. For each tenant, it is possible to use quota controls to limit:

- Number of volumes that can be launched;
- Number of processor cores and the amount of RAM that can be allocated;
- Floating IP addresses assigned to any instance when it launched. This allows instances to have the same publicly accessible IP addresses;

– Fixed IP addresses assigned to the same instance when it launches. This allows instances to have the same publicly or privately accessible IP addresses.

By default, most actions do not require a particular role, but it is possible to configure them by editing policies for user roles. For example, a rule can be defined so that a user must have the admin role in order to be able to allocate a public IP address.

3 Towards OpenStack Federation

Cloud federation is widely considered as a new way for deploying and managing multiple external and internal Cloud computing services to meet business needs. One of the main features of Cloud federation is the ability to share resources allowing providers to maintain their internal administrative policies and rules. In this Section, firstly we present some general concepts related to federation. After that, we discuss the main features of federated Cloud networking services. Then, we describe two possible scenarios of Cloud federation, i.e., loosely coupled and tightly coupled. In the end, we discuss the limits of the current federation features in OpenStack Clouds.

3.1 Main Actors

In the following, we describe the main actors involved in a federated Cloud environment. Starting from the NIST white paper [2] we can consider: *Cloud Service Providers or Cloud Vendor (CV)*, *Cloud Consumers (CCs)* and *Cloud Brokers (CBs)*. CVs includes people, organizations, or entities responsible for making a service available to CCs. Instead, NIST defines a CB as an entity that manages the use, performance, and delivery of Cloud services, as well as the relationship negotiation between CVs. A *Federator and/or Federation Agent* refers to a software module/component inside each CV that is in charge for actuating the federation procedures inside the alliance.

3.2 Loosely and Tightly Coupled Cloud Federation Scenarios

Cloud federation can be seen under many perspectives according to the level of modification and setup that a CV can achieve. To simplify our analysis, in this scientific work, we consider only two scenarios: Loosely and Tightly Coupled federations. The first one guarantees a minimum level of dependency between Cloud Vendors, whereas the second one determines a strong involvement of CVs in terms of low-level functionalities. Figure 1 shows such scenarios. In Fig. 1(a), the *Federator* is able to interact with the APIs of the CV along with a possible hidden Agent installed inside each VM deployed in the CV's virtualisation infrastructure. The VM should provide the Network and Security facilities considering the CV as a *Black Box*. This approach is similar to use the resources delivered by Public Cloud Vendor like Amazon (Cloud bursting). In particular,

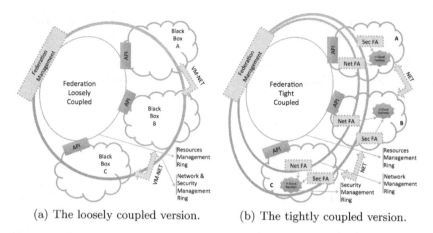

(a) The loosely coupled version.   (b) The tightly coupled version.

Fig. 1. Difference between loosely and tightly coupled federation architectures.

Fig. 1(a) shows two rings of communication through APIs through an ad-hoc channel of communication with VMs deployed in different Clouds. The CV is not aware of the current configuration/deployment of all VMs and their use.

In Fig. 1(b) more rings are depicted. From the smallest to the biggest, the first ring deals with communications through APIs and it is depicted as in the previous case. The second one is related to the possibility to interact with an installed Agent for configuring the Network facilities (look at Network Federation Agent - NetFA), and the third one, an Agent that deals with Security facilities (look at Security Agent - SecA). The NetFA is able to interact with the Network Controller of the CV. In particular, the SecA is able to interact with the infrastructure for both, applying security policies and collecting Data inside the Cloud Vendor useful for security analysis. NetFA and SecA are directly owned/-controlled by CVs. The *Federation Management* module is in charge for orchestrating resources, networks and security features inside the federation among the Cloud Vendors.

3.3   Federated Cloud Networking Services

The reference scenario considered in this paper is depicted in Fig. 2. Looking at the top part of the Figure, three possible tenants are interacting with the Federation Management system of a CB for negotiating/using IaaS Cloud services belonging to different CVs. The CB respectively interacts with CV A, B and C. In this way, by means of the Federation Management system, Tenant 1 is able to control VM instances, indicated with label T.1.A, that are running in CV A. At the same time, Tenant 2 is able to control the VM instances, indicated with label T.2.A, running in CV A and Tenant 3 is able to control VM instances, indicated with label T.3.A, running in CV A. A Similar situation occurs in Cloud Vendors B and C. Considering a Tightly Coupled scenario, the Federation Management system interacting by means of NetFAs can create federated SDN network among

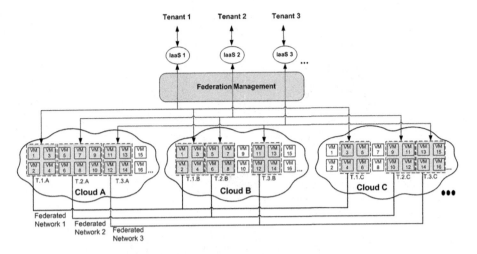

Fig. 2. Reference scenario.

Cloud Vendors A, B and C. In this way Federated Networks 1, 2, and 3 are established respectively for Tenants 1, 2, and 3. In addition, it is possible to observe that each Cloud Vendor is able to manage both internal and external VMs. This means that each Cloud Vendor maintains the full control of its own domain.

3.4   Current Federation Features in OpenStack

In OpenStack [4] a Federation Alliance is defined as reported in [3]. The current OpenStack federation scenario is shown in Fig. 3. Essentially, OpenStack enforces the federation in terms of Identity and Access Management (IAM). Our work follows this approach and uses the outcome of the OpenStack development in order extend the federation facilities in a tightly coupled federation scenario specifically focusing on virtual resources, virtual networking, and security management.

4   Federation Management System

In order to deal with virtual resources, virtual networking and security management in an OpenStack federation, we present a Federation Management system acting between tenants and multiple federated OpenStack CVs. In order to setup federated Cloud networking services in multiple federated OpenStack Clouds it is required to: (I) setup VMs on multiple federated Cloud Vendors; (II) setup networks; (III) enforce security mechanisms. Figure 7 shows the Federation Management architecture. The Federator module inside the Federation Management system consists of three main sub-modules respectively responsible for Virtual Resources, Virtual Networking and Security Management. Inside each Vendor

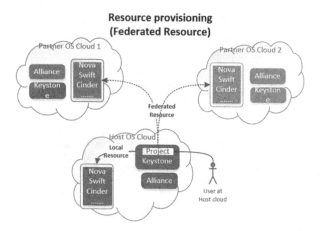

Fig. 3. OpenStack vision on federation (see [3]).

Cloud, the dashed-edge shapes highlights the new modules included in our proposal. Others parts/shapes in Clouds (look at the APIs-rectangle) show the existing modules own/controlled by Cloud Vendors. The *Federation Cloud API* is a RESTful interface the allows tenants to control their assets instantiated in the Cloud Vendor. The secure access is allowed thanks to the in-querying of the security module. The *Federation Coordinator* is responsible for Virtual Resources, Virtual Networking, and Security management. More specifically, it allows tenants to arrange federated Cloud networking services. The Federation Coordinator is the only entity aware of all tenants, their services (i.e., virtual resources), networks and their security requirements. In fact, it store data regarding the configurations of all tenant's federated services. The Federation Management data model adopts a NoSQL approach in order to simplify the management of Big Data related to resources, networks, and security policies. We prefer to use a Big Data approach leveraging a well known No-SQL database such as MongoDB, HBase, Cassandra, etc. In order to simplify the information management, data should be cross-correlated with TAGs and made available for all tenants. As previously described, for each tenant of the Federation Management system a corresponding tenant on multiple Cloud Vendors is created. The Interactions among the Federation Management system and Cloud Vendors is performed by means of Virtual Resource Management, Network Management, and Security Management components respectively using VRM, VNET, and SEC drivers. Drivers allows to control computational/storage resources, networks, and security policies on particular Cloud Vendors. In particular the VRM driver interacts with the APIs of different Cloud Instances. On behalf of each tenant, it is responsible to manage a set of VMs on different Cloud Vendors. The VNM driver interacts with the Network Federation Agents (FAs) of different Cloud Vendors. It is responsible to setup SDN mechanisms among different Cloud Vendors in order to federate the network connecting different VMs. Finally, the Sec driver

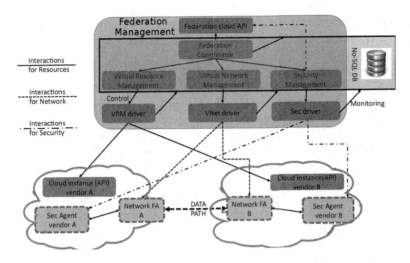

Fig. 4. Internal composition of the Federation Management and its interactions in tightly coupled scenario.

interacts with the Sec Agents of different Cloud Vendors in order to enforce access control policies on each federated Cloud. In a heterogeneous scenario we can have different drives simultaneously (Fig. 4).

4.1 Virtual Resource Management

Considering Cloud federation, OpenStack only supports AIM and several mechanisms for segregating Cloud resources such as cells, regions, availability zones, or host aggregates, as well as Cloud bursting, through either vendor-specific offerings. Instead, the OpenStack networking subsystem (Neutron) does not provide any support for networking federation. This Section, deals with the Virtual Resource Management to setup and manage VMs on multiple OpenStack Clouds. In particular, considering Fig. 7, we discuss a possible VRM driver solution based on jClouds.

Apache JClouds is an open source Multi-Cloud toolkit for the Java platform that gives you the freedom to create applications that are portable across Clouds while giving you full control to use Cloud-specific features. It is an open source library that allows third-party systems to control the specific functionalities of different Virtual Infrastructure Management (VIM) systems by means of a set of APIs. jClouds supports more than 30 cloud providers and pieces of middleware including Abiquo, Amazon, Azure, CloudSigma, CloudStack, DigitalOcean, Docker, Google Cloud Platform, GoGrid, Ninefold, Rackspace, and OpenStack. The key concept of jClouds are:

- **View** are portable abstractions that are designed to allow you to write code that uses cloud services without tying yourself to a specific vendor. Take JDBC as an example: rather than writing code directly for a specific type of database, you can make generic database requests, and the JDBC specification and drivers translate these into specific commands and statements for a certain type of database.

- **APIs** describe the actual calls (often, but not always, HTTP requests) that can be executed against a specific cloud service to "do stuff". In the case of popular APIs, such as the EC2 compute API, or the S3 storage API, there may be multiple vendors with cloud services that support that particular API. For example, EC2 is supported by Amazon and OpenStack, amongst others.
- A **Provider** represents particular Cloud Vendor that supports one or more APIs;
- A **Context** represents a specific connections to a particular provider. From the perspective of our database analogy, this would be broadly similar to a database connection against a specific DB. Once you have created a context via the ContextBuilder and are "connected" to a particular cloud service, you can either get any of the views that are supported by that provider, or go straight to the API or even to the provider level.

Figure 5 shows how the Virtual Resource Management component can interact through JClouds APIs with several Clouds including Openstack. Developing a software layer by means of JClouds Views it is possible to run the same application on multiple Cloud providers. Furthermore, it is possible it is also possible to control specific Cloud providers accessing specific functionalities. The main high-level services include compute and blobstore.

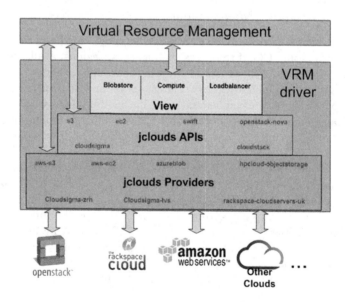

Fig. 5. JClouds scenario.

Furthermore, since JClouds support the Docker container engine, if we consider a Cloud system (for example OpenStack) deployed on container images, it is possible to deploy on physical server an overall Cloud infrastructure.

4.2   Virtual Network Management

Virtual Network Management (VNM) provides tenants an interface and the global view of the whole network spread among the parts of a federated cloud environment. In this section we discuss a possible implementation of the VNet driver. VNM allows Federation Management APIs that allow to configure network specific requirements, such as availability, reliability, isolation, locality, etc. The network view provided by the VNM to tenants may vary from the view of a single virtual network, disregarding of VMs actual deployment, to the exact networks and physical machines deployment at the most detailed level. Lastly, VNM coordinates identities and access control for cross-clouds connectivity, including management and configuration of the control plane entities located at each Cloud Vendor.

Network Federation Agent (NFA) has both control and management roles. In the control plane it receives control requests from the local data plane and replies by communicating with the local SDN controller, such as OVN [5]. It also listens to the local SDN control requests and resolves them by communicating with the other clouds' NFAs. In the management plane, the NFA exports a management API to share virtual networks with other Clouds Vendor. NFA is also responsible to negotiate network sharing with its peers in other Cloud Vendors and pass the tunneling information down to the data plane, configures datapath forwarding rules and controls tunnel establishment commands by specifying tunnel

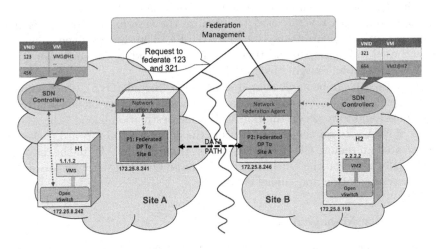

Fig. 6. Internal Virtual Network Management along with the interaction with a federated party.

endpoint locations and the Cloud vendor supported technology (e.g. VXLAN, GRE, GENEVE).

In the following we describe the interfaces between federated network architecture components. Figure 6 summarizes NFA's internal and external interactions with other components, such as SDN controller, datapath and the Federation Management system (by means of the Virtual Network Management and a particular VNM driver). The depicted architecture shows both network configuration and management of network facilities in federated Cloud. For simplicity, the internal component of the Federation Management have been omitted.

The REST-based API between VNM and NFAs allows the Federation Management system to configure the agents with the federated network information, such as tenants' properties in the different sites (e.g., tenant ID, name, credentials), tenant networks (e.g. list of the networks and mapping between their IDs in the sites), and cross site communication parameters (e.g., distant NFA location).

Another REST-based API represents the communication between NFAs located in different Cloud Vendors. The main functions of this communication include handshake between NFAs, which provides a basis to the tunnel establishment and control information exchange, which allows to extend virtual networks across Clouds. During the handshake, NFAs validate the control information which they received from the management and establish communication tunnels between them. In addition, the API between different NFAs is used to exchange control information in order to connect, by means of a single virtual network, two communicating end-points located in different Clouds Vendors.

An additional interface allows NFA to communicate with the network SDN controller. This interface is specific for each SDN controller and may vary depending on technology used in each Cloud. For example, a possible VNET driver implementation can be based on OVN controller. The management plane communication with OVN is used to initialize the system and to register new virtual networks that are being shared by the FA. The control plane communication is used to request the location of VMs and to update the controller about new VMs located on external federated Clouds.

The datapath can be implemented using Open vSwitch (OvS), which employs the data plane of the solution by forwarding packets between Clouds over federation tunnel and towards destination VM inside destination Cloud. The responsibility of NFA is to set the correct flows in the datapath and forward packets to VMs located on remote Clouds via federation tunnels. The API to the datapath are typically based on the OpenFlow protocol and OvS Database for forwarding rules for configuration and tunnel creation.

4.3   Security Management

The main goal of the Security Management of the Federation Management system to enforce authentication, authorization, and accounting tasks by means of particular drivers interacting with Security Agent installed in the Cloud Vendor.

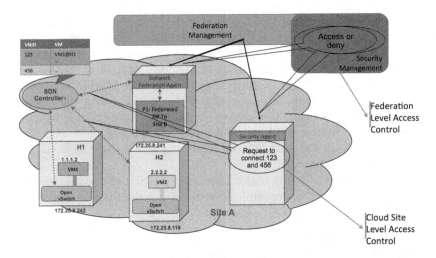

Fig. 7. Security representation in the Architecture: The Security Management in the Federation Management and The Security Agent deployed in each Cloud.

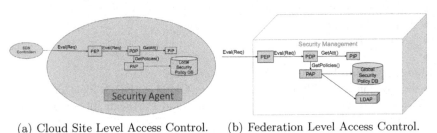

(a) Cloud Site Level Access Control.   (b) Federation Level Access Control.

Fig. 8. Access Control system.

The authentication process can be accomplished by using the federation features available in the keystone component natively integrated in OpenStack.

The Access Control system can be based on the XACML OASIS standard. Policy based management is one of the most widely used approaches followed in network and distributed computing. Access Policy management specifies how to deal with situations that are likely to occur via priorities and access control rules for system resources. The system will have a policy decision point (PDP) for interpreting the policies and a policy enforcement point (PEP) for applying the policies. The XACML directives and policies provide a guideline for formalize all the XML messages and rules necessary to exchange and enforce the access control among the parties. Figure 8 shows how the XACML standard works. The different pictures show the same kind of architecture but at Federation Level and Cloud Level respectively. Both LDAPs in the picture are considered in master-slave configuration. All rules and policies are set at global level (Federation Management) for affecting the local Level (Security Agents).

Regarding the accounting tasks, a flow of data (aggregated and raw) coming from Cloud Vendor is sent to the Federation Management system. Figure 8 shows the overall functionalities of the Security Management. The setup is a master/slave configuration where the global security control of the federation is concentrate in the top part. Security Agents are aware of what is happening internally to Cloud Vendors but only for the part relaying with the federation capabilities. As it is possible to observe, the Security Agent is able to interact with the Network Federation Agent and others elements of the Cloud Vendor system (e.g., the Data Path module) for analysing their behaviour according to security needs and constrains.

In the following, we list the major tasks that the Security Management and the Security Agent have to accomplish for satisfying the security requirements of users, Clouds, and tenants.

- Access Control XACML based:
  - Cloud Site Level Access Control (see Fig. 8(a))
  - Federation Level Access Control (see Fig. 8(b))
- Vulnerability Checks:
  - Vulnerability Scanning
  - Thread Identification
  - Malware Identification
  - ...
- Monitoring and Analysis for Security purposes:
  - Federation Level Monitoring (i.e., Inter-Cloud e., DDoS identification)
  - Cloud Site Level Monitoring (i.e., DDoS and PortScan Intra-cloud identification)
  - Cloud Site Level Data Analysis (raw data and aggregated data).

The list above is susceptible of modifications according new customers needs, however the Agent will be designed for easily changing its behaviour and work.

5   Related Work

Many Intercloud initiatives have been presented so far regarding energy efficiency [6], storage [7], Assistive Technology [8], dataweb [9] and so on. One of the first initiatives in the field of Cloud federation was the FP7 European Project RESERVOIR [10]. RESERVOIR introduced modular, extensible and open Cloud architecture that supports business-driven Cloud federation. The RESERVOIR framework enables Cloud infrastructure providers belonging to different administrative domains, to collaborate with each other in order to create a vast pool of resources while technological and resource management decisions on each domain are made autonomously by the provider. The experience acquired in RESERVOIR leads up to the latest EU initiative known as FI-Ware [11]. In particular, the EC is encouraging a federated framework based on Fi-Ware platform called XI-FI Federation [12]. XI-FI federates homogeneous FI-Ware systems based on OpenStack framework. The above mentioned initiatives are interesting, the not consider federated networking services. Below we mention relevant research in the networking area and emphasize our novelty. In [13] the authors present a cross-communication architecture and protocol. This architecture is based on a distribution layer, which consists of several D-nodes managed by single O-node for each cloud. The D-nodes establish cross-cloud logical communication, configured by the O-nodes. This solution requires the employment of the special nodes at each cloud. Hence, it is restricted and might result in great effort in order to integrate the architecture among the federated clouds. Cloud networking [14] is based-on the SAIL EU-project, and focuses on provisioning virtual infrastructure in a federated-cloud environment. In order to address the delegation of infrastructure provision, the authors introduce a model of virtual networks, termed flash network slice (FNS). The FNS is a network resource type that can be linked across administrative boundaries, providing the ability to partition virtual infrastructures into isolated administrative domains. Another industrial solution is presented by Nuage Networks [15]. Their solution is also closed and consists of Virtualised Services Controllers (VSC), and distributed virtual routing and switching (dVRS) software agents. Moreover, the Virtualised Services Controllers require MP-BGP for synchronization, which complicates the integration of their solution over federated-cloud environments.

However, the aforementioned networking solutions do not consider the emerging SDN technology. In this context, Juniper Networks presents the Contrail system [16], which consists of SDN Controller and vRouter. The Contrail SDN Controller is a logically centralized but physically distributed SDN controller that is responsible for providing the management, control, and analytical functions of the virtualized network. The Contrail solution is closed and proprietary; it is limited to the use of the specific virtual routers and does not support commonly deployed open virtual switches.

6 Conclusion

In this paper we presented an architecture able to create advanced Federated Networks related to OpenStack installations. The design takes into consideration more aspects in terms of resource management than the security constrains of Cloud Costumers. In particular, we presented a Federation Management system that allow tenants to deploy federated Cloud networking services on multiple Cloud Vendors. Drivers connected to Cloud Instance APIs, NF Agents, and Sec Agents allow to achieve a high-level of flexibility and scalability.

Acknowledgment. This research was supported by the European Union's Horizon 2020 Research and Innovation Programme Project BEACON under Grant Agreement No. 644048.

References

1. IEEE: P2302 - The IEEE standards association (2014). http://standards.ieee.org/develop/project/2302.html
2. NIST: Nist cloud computing standards radmap (2013). http://www.nist.gov/itl/cloud/upload/NIST_SP-500-291_Version-2_2013_June18_FINAL.pdf
3. OpenStack Inter Cloud Resource Federation (2015). https://wiki.openstack.org/wiki/InterCloudResourceFederation
4. The Open Source, Open Standards Cloud, Innovative, open source cloud computing software for building reliable cloud infrastructure, January 2015. http://openstack.org/
5. OVN architecture, January 2015. http://openvswitch.org/pipermail/dev/2015-January/050380.html
6. Giacobbe, M., Celesti, A., Fazio, M., Villari, M., Puliafito, A.: Towards energy management in cloud federation: a survey in the perspective of future sustainable and cost-saving strategies. Comput. Netw. **91**, 438–452 (2015)
7. Celesti, A., Fazio, M., Villari, M., Puliafito, A.: Adding long-term availability, obfuscation, and encryption to multi-cloud storage systems. J. Netw. Comput. Appl. **59**, 208–218 (2016)
8. Mulfari, D., Celesti, A., Villari, M.: A computer system architecture providing a user-friendly man machine interface for accessing assistive technology in cloud computing. J. Syst. Softw. **100**, 129–138 (2015)
9. Celesti, A., Tusa, F., Villari, M., Puliafito, A.: How the dataweb can support cloud federation: service representation and secure data exchange. In: 2012 Second Symposium on Network Cloud Computing and Applications (NCCA), pp. 73–79 (2012)
10. Rochwerger, B., Breitgand, D., Epstein, A., Hadas, D., Loy, I., Nagin, K., Tordsson, J., Ragusa, C., Villari, M., Clayman, S., Levy, E., Maraschini, A., Massonet, P., Munoz, H., Toffetti, G.: Reservoir - when one cloud is not enough. Computer **44**, 44–51 (2011)
11. FI-WARE: Open APIs for Open Minds (2015). http://www.fi-ware.org
12. FI-XIFI: Joining the federation scenario exploiting fi-ware framework (2015). http://wiki.fi-xifi.eu/Public:Joining_the_Federation_scenario
13. Lloret, J., Garcia, M., Tomas, J., Rodrigues, J.J.: Architecture and protocol for intercloud communication. Inf. Sci. **258**, 434–451 (2014)
14. Murray, P., Sefidcon, A., Steinert, R., Fusenig, V., Carapinha, J.: Cloud networking: an infrastructure service architecture for the wide area. In: Future Network & Mobile Summit (FutureNetw), 2012, pp. 1–8 (2012)
15. Ferro, G.: Packet pushers white paper. Nuage Networks, White Paper (2013)
16. Contrail Architecture, Juniper Networks, White Paper (2013). http://www.juniper.net/us/en/products-services/sdn/contrail/

Networking Introspection and Analysis for Virtual Machine Migration in Federated Clouds

Giuseppe Andronico[1], Filippo Bua[1], Marco Fargetta[1],
Emidio Giorgio[1], Alessio Guglielmo[1], Salvatore Monforte[1],
Maurizio Paone[1(✉)], and Massimo Villari[2]

[1] Istituto Nazionale di Fisica Nucleare, Sezione di Catania, Catania, Italy
{giuseppe.andronico,flippo.bua,marco.fargetta,emidio.giorgio,
alessio.guglielmo,salvatore.monforte,maurizio.paone}@ct.infn.it
[2] Università degli Studi di Messina, Messina, Italy
mvillari@unime.it

Abstract. Cloud computing demonstrates an effective paradigm to optimise data center management and resources provisioning. A further way to optimize resource exploitation relies on cloud federation. The federation idea introduces into the cloud the possibility to dynamically increase the number of physical resources exploiting external facilities. These are provided by federated cloud providers having different administration domains and access rules but cooperating under the federation regulation.

In this work we explore a way to use dynamically provided resources: migrating Virtual Machines (VMs). We discuss some reference use cases and required tools and we present a concrete implementation of an advanced monitoring agent.

1 Introduction

The business behind the cloud technology has increased at an incredible pace in the last few years creating a huge market with many opportunities for users and companies. Currently, several big companies, operating world-wide, have emerged as market leaders but these work side by side with a myriad of small players specialised in niche markets based on geographical location, specific deployment scenarios, different cloud models or any combination of these elements.

The adoption rate of cloud solutions pushes these small players toward a continuous infrastructure expansion, in order to support peak requests from their customers. They need to satisfy the demand of new resources to avoid the risk of loosing customers who would be seeking for more capable providers. However, to increase the number of available resources can be costly, and can also be complex, considering that configuration of new physical resources within an infrastructure requires a longer time with respect to what is really requested

© Springer International Publishing Switzerland 2016
A. Celesti and P. Leitner (Eds.): ESOCC 2015 Workshops, CCIS 567, pp. 353–362, 2016.
DOI: 10.1007/978-3-319-33313-7_27

and allocated by customers. Physical resources should be prepared in advance and maintained in stand-by until they are requested, resulting in idle resources for the most of the time.

Federation of resources across small providers could be a smart approach for dealing with demand peaks from customers. Federation of resources has to be transparent to users; as they typically have agreement with a single provider, this is responsible to hide aggregation of resources from federated partners.

Cloud federation allows small providers to better support their customers and gives them more flexibility on deciding when and how upgrade their infrastructures like described by the authors in [2]. However, several issues are still associated with the creation and management of a federation. Skipping all the administrative and technical steps involved with the creation, we will focus on how federated providers can maximize the benefit of the federation in terms of customers' support and resources management. In more detail, in this paper we evaluate how and when the resources available in the federation should be used.

When a request for allocation of a new virtual machine (VM) shows up, a federated cloud provider has to consider the possibility to allocate the VM on a partner infrastructure, depending on the current status of its resources. Allocating the VM in a partner could have an impact on the execution in terms of QoS, accessibility, security and so on, and it is difficult to evaluate these in advance. As an example, if the machine has to run a long analysis and requires to access a large data set stored in the provider infrastructure then it is better to have the machine deployed in the same infrastructure. Nevertheless, if the data set is stored in a different place and remotely accessed then the VM could execute in a different cloud without any penalty for the user.

In this paper we provide a different approach to the scheduling in a federated cloud. VMs are always allocated in the *Home* infrastructure but a dedicated daemon is responsible to evaluate the current load of the resources and if needed migrate the VMs towards remote partners (*Foreign Cloud*). This approach makes use of extensive monitoring to identify VMs eligible for the migration. The goal is to identify VMs performing activities not influenced by relocation in a different infrastructure. Of course, the features and settings of the machine have to be maintained and this is part of the federation mechanism put in place.

Additionally, monitoring will collect information from the VMs deployed remotely and these will be used when they have to return back. In a federation, allocate a VM in a partner organisation has a cost and it is important to minimise the number of VMs distributed to the partners in order to better use the own infrastructure and minimise the overall costs. Therefore, when the peak load is over, the VMs should come back from the partner infrastructure.

The remainder of this paper is organised as follows: in Sect. 2 we will present some related work relevant to the presented approach. In order to provide a description of requirements in the VMs' migration process, a very simple technique suitable for this issue is discussed in Sect. 3. In Sect. 4 the mechanism available for the migration and the related penalty for the execution are described. In Sect. 5 the monitoring architecture created to monitor the VMs as long as the more important parameters used by the migration algorithm are presented. Finally, Sect. 6 will provide some conclusion and describe the next steps of this activity.

2   Related Work

In literature different metrics have been proposed to define how to deploy a virtual machine, decide how and when to migrate and the requirements that a migration algorithm should satisfy. All the metrics and approaches examined in this section are related on a single data center.

Many of the available metrics could be used for the federation approach proposed but the impact of each metric into the resource allocation is not the same. Table 1 summarises the most relevant metrics identified which could have a big impact on the allocation. Collecting these metrics, a VM can be characterised in relation to its ability to move. The VMs migration will take this information as input for the decision algorithm.

Table 1. Table of measurements

CPU	Network	Disk
User Space %	Packets/sec	Requests/sec
Kernel %	Bytes/sec	Blocks/sec
I/O Wait %		

For the CPU, it is necessary to consider the percentage of time spent by CPU in user space, in kernel space and I/O waiting, For the network, the parameters to consider are the used bandwidth in terms of both packets and bytes either received and sent. Finally, for the disk, it is only taken in account the number of read/write requests and reads/writes of disk blocks.

The requirements to satisfy with the proposed approach are common in the cloud scenario and they have been well defined by Buyya et al. [3] as follows:

Decentralisation and parallelism: to eliminate SPF (Single Point of Failure) and provide scalability.
High performance: the system has to be able to quickly respond to changes in the workload.
Guaranteed QoS: the algorithms have to provide reliable QoS by meeting SLA.
Independence of the workload type: the algorithms have to be able to perform efficiently in mixed-application environments.

In [1] it is noted that typically a cloud provider establishes agreements with its customers to ensure the agreed **SLA** levels of QoS depending on the established policy whereby you choose the host that takes care of a given VM. These agreements generally are defined as a minimum or maximum function or the highest throughput delay in the response time. Since these may vary depending on the application, cloud providers set different metrics and, according to them, the system rates the number of violations found, named **SLAV** (SLA Violation) which determines when is necessary to proceed with the migration.

In [7] Wood and others define a technique on how to determine overloaded hosts. Once defined metrics (CPU usage, network bandwidth utilization, page faults rate and, if available, memory usage of specific VM, packet drop rate, number of request and request service time) measurements are made on them at regular intervals of time. A mobile observation window is built and used to calculate a probability distribution and a time series. The probability distribution is the probability of resource utilization within the window and it is obtained from the values of use taken at fixed intervals by building the histogram representing observation window. The distribution probability is obtained by histogram normalization within considered window. Differently, the observation series is obtained by collecting all the metric values within the observation window.

The distribution probability is used to know how resource usage probability changes inside the observation window. The series is then used to check whether a system is in an overload state or not. This condition is calculated by checking whether a resource (CPU, network or memory) exceeds a defined threshold. In particular, to avoid the selection of isolated peaks, a system is classified as overloaded if the resource usage exceeds k times the threshold on n observations. By setting the values of k and n is possible to adopt a more aggressive or conservative strategy in the detection process.

An alternative strategy is based on the definition of two threshold values – high and low – for CPU usage [3]. If the CPU usage exceeds the upper threshold, the migration process is started to reduce the risk of **SLA** violations. If the value is underneath than minimum threshold, all VMs are migrated in order to switch off host machine to free memory space and saving energy consumption (**VM Consolidation**). This policy shows excellent results both as energy consumption and as SLA violations inside a single farm.

This policy is very flexible and, entering more permissive **SLA** values, could result in increased energy efficiency and can be adapted to different hardware types and workload of VMs running on. Once established the presence of an host overload, the system must proceed to choose which are best candidates for VM migration to reduce the load. This selection is performed using special algorithms classified according to the technique used:

- Approach based on fixed criteria.
- Approach based on multiple criteria.

The first is based on specific criteria, the most relevant are:

Dynamic Management Algorithm (DMA) which selects the VM with minimal CPU usage.
Minimum Time Migration Policy (MMT) that guarantees the shortest migration time needed.

Random Choice Policy (RC) in which the VM is chosen randomly according to a uniform distribution.

Maximum Correlation Policy (MC) which starts from the consideration that the higher is the correlation between running applications and resource usage on a host, the higher is the probability that host is in overloading state. Therefore, this rule establishes that the VM which will be migrated presents the greatest correlation rate with the considered resource.

The latter uses the **Fuzzy Q-Learning** algorithm that, starting from a set of different strategies, applies fuzzy logic to dynamically choose which is more suitable for each particular case.

Selecting the machine is only the first step in the migration process. The second step is to identify the destination, among all the available candidates, which provide the best distribution according to some parameters. In [4] the host selection takes into account the correlation between the resource usage in the physical machines and the performance of applications running in VM executing on these machines. This approach, using a solution based on knowledge of the application running on a given VM, correlates the performance of application (e.g. for *Apache httpd* daemon it considers the number of requests per second) with some parameters on the physical host, like CPU load, allocated memory, disk reads and writes. The technique used to correlate this information is the canonical correlation analysis. For example you can maximise performance approaching a machine that needs access to the data to run their operations. This approach, reported in [8], allows to reduce the execution time of each task, according to the result of CloudSim based simultations.

3 Migration Technique

In the scenario of federated cloud providers, a VM migration process introduces particular issues that are not experienced in a single-site scenario. Live migration with performance optimization, typically adopted in environments with homogeneous virtualisation infrastructures and overall control of the infrastructure, are hardly exploited in multi-sites scenarios. In these latter, the architectures are heterogeneous in terms of hypervisor implementations (Xen, KVM, VMWare, etc.), hosts OSs, coordinators middleware.

The issues introduced by this heterogeneity do not allow sophisticated memory migration techniques, like *Pure demand-migration* or *Managed migration* implemented by Xen hypervisor (for a brief survey see [5]), then a more limited approach must be used.

Without being exhaustive on this topic, a very simple migration technique is described below, while a more detailed design needs to be investigated. The mechanism is based on (i) hibernation at guest OS level, and (ii) snapshot of VMs images, in order to avoid the adoption of cloud-site specific features. The only requirement that each site must comply with is the capability of managing QCOW images. Each site will be assumed to share the templates of the VMs.

The steps involved in VM migration are:

1. **VM hibernation** - The guest OS saves the memory state and poweroff the VM.
2. **VM image snapshot** - An incremental snapshot of VM instance is created.
3. **Delivery of incremental snapshot** - The original site sends the snapshot to the target site.
4. **VM creation on target site** - A new VM instance on target site is created using the image template and incremental snapshot.
5. **Start of migrated VM** - the target site starts the VM instance and, on success, informs the original site.
6. **Old VM instance destruction** - The original site destroys old VM instance.

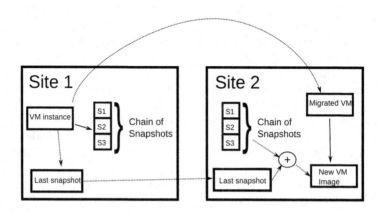

Fig. 1. VM migration scheme. Dotted lines refer to event on VM migration

To optimize the migration process a viable solution consists in sending a *chain* of incremental snapshots, in order to rebuild the VM to be migrated. If a mechanism of shared storage, more precisely a data dissemination system, is available across the cloud sites, an improved algorithm can be adopted (see Fig. 1). In such case each site periodically performs live snapshot of each VM instance image and shares it with all federated sites. In this manner, each site is provided with a chain of incremental snapshots of the VM instances. Thus, in order to create the image of a VM to be migrated, the target site will only need the last VM snapshot, and the migration process will be faster. As a drawback, this approach might require at each site larger storage volumes for maintaining the snapshot chain, if the I/O is particularly relevant. Hence, a trade-off between storage size and migration performance should be found.

Several preliminary trials were performed with QCOW image format, and the results were quite satisfactory.

4   Migration Policy

Our approach is to measure the performance of a host using a mobile window in which the metrics considered are measured at regular intervals. This approach considers at least virtual CPU load, reads and writes on disk and network bandwidth usage. We define two usage thresholds: the former indicates underused host that could be turned off (migrating VMs currently active on it) ensuring smaller energy consumption. The latter indicates that the physical machine is near to an overloading state and implies a migration of VM in order to prevent SLA violations, which happens when a cloud provider allocate on the physical machine multiple VMs making a resource overbooking [6]. More specifically at least k within n observations are needed to start a migration in order to filter temporary situations.

The choice of the VM to migrate can be made through an estimate of the type of operation executed by the VM. Therefore, a virtual machine which has a high CPU usage but low loads of disk and network is a good candidate for migration, being very likely that all the data required for processing are stored in memory and therefore a possible reallocation does not involve a performance degradation due to data access over a wide area network. Vice versa a virtual machine that performs a high network traffic can be a good candidate only if the traffic is directed outside of data center. In this case it does not matter the location of the VM, because data are always accessed via Internet. Instead, the performance of a VM with high network traffic inside the region will be degraded if it is migrated in another one or in federated providers. The last case is a group of VM which collaborate each other to perform some operations. In this situation all VM must be migrated in order to ensure SLA maintenance. This last consideration is also valid in the case of a high use of the block device associated with VM instance.

5   Monitoring

In adopting clouds, users sign an agreement with cloud providers before accessing the resources and this defines the legal and technical condition to be satisfied by the requested resources. The cloud scheduler can use these conditions and the parameters[1] of the resources to estimate if the allocation in a different cloud is acceptable. However, many external factors contribute to the performance of a resource leading to a difference between the estimation and the real use of the resources. This mismatch could create a sub-optimal allocation with the risk of degrading the user experience. For maintaining a good user experience a continuous monitoring of resource status, and related usage metering is required. Indeed, monitoring enhances infrastructure reliability, for instance warning when a resource becomes unavailable. On the other side, usage metering facilitates the optimisation of infrastructure utilisation, for instance providing information about load peaks. This latter scenario is very similar to the one outlined in this paper, where VM usage metering is used as information source to decide which instances have to be migrated under certain conditions. As detailed in Sect. 4,

---

[1] As an example of the difference between condition and parameter it is possible to consider the allocation of a VM. A condition could define the CPU Unit and its tolerance whereas the parameter would be the number of CPU units requested.

migrating VMs are chosen according to their CPU load, disk usage (in terms of read/write request) and their networking activity. CPU load and disk requests are simple to extract from the VM and use for the above mentioned purposes but the network analysis required the development of an additional packet sniffer. This section describes the solution developed to perform the network analysis of the VMs deployed.

The challenge in this work is to link the low level network data with the highest level of services data, adopting a packet sniffer and storing all data on NoSQL database, as it is described in the following section.

5.1   The Packet Sniffer

The VMs network traffic is monitored by means of a packet sniffer implemented using PCAP, that is a library specifically designed on this purpose. In more details, PCAP API is exploited to capture traffic to/from the virtual machine; in order to estimate a specific service usage, captured traffic statistics are filtered according to the specific TCP port number within the matched packets. A prototype version of the sniffer has been implemented in Java using a NoSQL database back-end to store data. MongoDB database has been chosen in order to exploit capabilities such as horizontal scaling, replication facility and high performance. This latter feature is very important in our scenario, because we handle a huge quantity of data which must be quickly copied on persistent storage. For each monitored host, the informations extracted from captured packets are:

- source and destination IP address,
- source and destination TCP ports,
- the packet arrival time and date and,
- the count of packets which belong to same flows.

The latter parameter is the main indicator of a service usage inside a virtual machine. As an example, high traffic on port 80 would very likely indicate the presence of a web server supporting many users. Destination IP address is important as well, because it's used to distinguish whether or not the VM network traffic is directed outside the data center (and the machine would be therefore a suitable candidate for migration).

Figure 2 shows the main parts compounding the sniffer agent. It is possible to identify the Sniffer Class along with a specific implementation where the HTTP traffic is monitored.

5.2   Virtual Machine Monitoring

The monitoring infrastructure is based on Zabbix, a full-featured network monitoring solution, because the high level of customisation and the availability of REST APIs to interact with the server.

For each monitored host, there is a list of items that have to be monitored through agents. A Zabbix agent is a kind of client for the server: it runs on

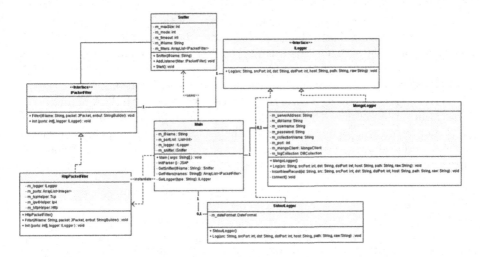

Fig. 2. Zabbix agent class diagram

the monitored host and periodically retrieves from the server the list of checks to be performed, eventually returning check results to the server which store them and trigger associated events. Additionally, Zabbix supports templates and discovery processes, which allows to generically define hosts and related items, and finalise their definition according with the actual host features. In the scenario analysed, a specific template to monitor the VMs has been developed. The template contains items for CPU load, disk I/O requests and prototypes for the network ports. The template is applied to each monitored host (one for each VM); therefore, VMs have to carry out a Zabbix agent and the sniffer. The first time that the Zabbix agent runs on the VM, hooks for CPU load and disk I/O requests are activated, while discovery processes retrieves the network ports being monitored by the sniffer. Furthermore it creates the hooks corresponding to the network traffic ongoing in the monitored ports (each port would logically corresponding to a network service). The discovery process is repeated with a regular pace, such to dynamically capture new traffic flows on different ports, while subsequent runs of the Zabbix agent updates the hooks with the current resources usage. Finally, via the Zabbix API, the controller can check at any time the VM usage details, and use this info for decisions about possible VM migrations. The Zabbix agent is extended with capabilities for aggregating all data retrieved by the sniffer, which are eventually sent to the central Zabbix server.

6 Conclusions

Cloud federation is an important topic for the future of cloud made by a mix of public and private clouds working together as a single entity.

One of the benefit provided by the federation is the possibility of exploiting resources made available from cloud federation by migrating VMs with SLA that are not violated from this operation. We analysed some simple use cases and tools useful to establish policies and define procedures to minimize SLA violations and, at the same time, optimise resource exploitation.

Nevertheless, despite technical refinements yet needed with the VM migration practicality, the power of this procedure in federated cloud emerges clearly.

Future work will focus on extending the use cases to better define migration policies and evaluating the impact of VM migration between federated clouds in a real scenario.

References

1. Abdelsamea, A., Hemayed, E.E., Eldeeb, H., Elazhary, H.: Virtual machine consolidation challenges: a review. Int. J. Innov. Appl. Stud. **8**(4), 1504–1516 (2014). http://www.ijias.issr-journals.org/abstract.php?article=IJIAS-14-245-14
2. Andronico, G., Fargetta, M., Monforte, S., Paone, M., Villari, M.: A model for accomplishing and managing dynamic cloud federations. In: Proceedings of the 2014 IEEE/ACM 7th International Conference on Utility and Cloud Computing, UCC 2014, Washington, D.C., USA, pp. 744–749 (2014). http://dx.doi.org/10.1109/UCC.2014.121
3. Beloglazov, A., Buyya, R.: Energy efficient resource management in virtualized cloud data centers. In: 2010 10th IEEE/ACM International Conference on Cluster, Cloud and Grid Computing (CCGrid), pp. 826–831. IEEE (2010)
4. Do, A.V., Chen, J., Wang, C., Lee, Y.C., Zomaya, A.Y., Zhou, B.B.: Profiling applications for virtual machine placement in clouds. In: 2013 IEEE Sixth International Conference on Cloud Computing, pp. 660–667 (2011)
5. Venkatesha, S., Sadhu, S., Kintali, S.: Survey of virtual machine migration techniques. http://www.academia.edu/760613/Survey_of_Virtual_Machine_Migration_Techniques
6. Tomás, L., Tordsson, J.: Improving cloud infrastructure utilization through overbooking. In: Proceedings of the 2013 ACM Cloud and Autonomic Computing Conference, CAC 2013, pp. 5:1–5:10. ACM, NY (2013). http://doi.acm.org/10.1145/2494621.2494627
7. Wood, T., Shenoy, P., Venkataramani, A., Yousif, M.: Black-box and gray-box strategies for virtual machine migration. In: Proceedings of the 4th USENIX Conference on Networked Systems Design & #38; Implementation, NSDI 2007, p. 17. USENIX Association, Berkeley, CA, USA (2007). http://dl.acm.org/citation.cfm?id=1973430.1973447
8. Yan, J.: A network-aware virtual machine placement and migration approach in cloud computing. In: 2010 9th International Conference on Grid and Cooperative Computing (GCC), pp. 87–92. IEEE (2010)

SHYAM: A System for Autonomic Management of Virtual Clusters in Hybrid Clouds

Daniela Loreti$^{(\boxtimes)}$ and Anna Ciampolini

DISI - Department of Computer Science and Engineering,
Università di Bologna, Viale del Risorgimento 2, Bologna, Italy
{daniela.loreti,anna.ciampolini}@unibo.it

Abstract. While the public cloud model has been vastly explored over the last few years to face the demand for large-scale distributed computing capabilities, many organizations are now focusing on the hybrid cloud model, where the classic scenario is enriched with a private (company owned) cloud – e.g., for the management of sensible data. In this work, we propose SHYAM, a software layer for the autonomic deployment and configuration of virtual clusters on a hybrid cloud. This system can be used to face the temporary (or permanent) lack of computational resources on the private cloud, allowing cloud bursting in the context of big data applications. We firstly provide an empirical evaluation of the overhead introduced by SHYAM provisioning mechanism. Then we show that, although the execution time is significantly influenced by the inter-cloud bandwidth, an autonomic off-premise provisioning mechanism can significantly improve the application performance.

Keywords: Autonomic · Hybrid cloud · Big data · MapReduce

1 Introduction

Offering "the illusion of infinite computing resources available on demand" [5], cloud computing is the ideal enabler for high computing power demanding applications. While the public cloud scenario had been well explored in the past, many organization are now focusing on the hybrid cloud model. Combining both on-premise (company owned) and off-premise (owned by a third party provider) cloud infrastructures, the hybrid scenario can indeed capture a broader use-case [19]. Recently, the exponential increase in the use of mobile devices and the wide-spread employment of sensors across various domains has created large volumes of data that need to be processed to extract knowledge. The pressing need for fast analysis of large amount of data calls the attention of the research community and fosters new challenges in the big data research area [10]. Since data-intensive applications are usually costly in terms of CPU and memory utilization, a lot of work has been done to simplify the distribution of computational load among several physical or virtual nodes and take advantage of parallelism [12]. Nevertheless, the execution

© Springer International Publishing Switzerland 2016
A. Celesti and P. Leitner (Eds.): ESOCC 2015 Workshops, CCIS 567, pp. 363–373, 2016.
DOI: 10.1007/978-3-319-33313-7_28

of data-intensive applications requires a high degree of elasticity in resource provisioning. In this scenario, a widespread choice is to relay on a cloud infrastructure to take advantage of its elasticity in virtual resource provisioning.

In this paper, we focus on the autonomic management of virtual machines (VMs) in the context of hybrid clouds. To this purpose, we present SHYAM (System for HYbrid clusters with Autonomic Management), a system for the autonomic management of VMs in hybrid clouds able to manage virtual clusters using both on-premise (i.e., computing nodes in a private internal cloud IC) and off-premise (i.e. in a public external cloud EC) hardware resources. The system is able to dynamically react to load peaks – due, for instance, to virtual machine (VM) contention on shared computing nodes – by redistributing the VMs on less loaded nodes (either migrating inside IC or crossing the cloud boundaries towards EC). As a case study, we consider the execution of data-intensive applications over clusters of VMs initially deployed on IC. If a physical node hosting a VM for data-processing becomes overloaded in terms of CPU, memory or disk utilization, the performance of the virtual cluster may dramatically decrease, thus slowing down the whole distributed application. In this case, if another less loaded physical machine is available on-premise, the best solution would be to migrate the VM on that physical node. However, the private cloud has a finite amount of resources and it may happen that all the physical machines in IC are too loaded to receive the VM: in this case, we can provide resources on EC and perform application-level load redistribution; in SHYAM we automated this mechanism. As this work tests the SHYAM system on data-intensive applications, it also explores the drawbacks and shortcomings of the hybrid scenario, primarily due to data movement crossing on-/off-premise boundaries. Although data-processing is significantly influenced by the limited inter-cloud bandwidth, our work shows that an autonomic off-premise provisioning mechanism could allow the user to significantly increase the application performance.

The paper is organized as follows. Section 2 presents the architecture of the proposed autonomic system, illustrating the data-processing scenario and management policy adopted, as well as practical details about the implementation. Section 3 discusses the experimental results obtained by testing our solution in the chosen data-intensive scenario. Related work and conclusion follow.

2   Framework Architecture

We focus on a hybrid scenario composed of two separated cloud installations: the on-premise IC, owned and managed by a private company, and the off-premise EC, a collection of resources owned by a cloud provider and rented to customers according to a predefined price plan. Having their own cloud management software and offering their virtualized resources to final users (e.g., customers, company employees, etc.), both IC and EC implement the cloud paradigm at the Infrastructure as a Service (IaaS) level.

As shown in Fig. 1a, the key component of SHYAM is Hybrid Infrastructure as a Service (HyIaaS), a software layer that allows integration between IC and

EC infrastructures. The layer interacts with both on- and off-premise cloud with the goal of providing hybrid clusters of VMs. Each cluster is dedicated to the execution of a particular distributed application (e.g., distributed data-processing). If there are enough resources available, all the VMs of a cluster are allocated on-premise to minimize the costs introduced by the public cloud and the latency of data transferred between the virtual nodes. If on-premise resources are not sufficient to host all the VMs, a part is provisioned on IC and the others on EC. This partitioning should be transparent to the final user of the virtual cluster, allowing her to access all the VMs in the same way, regardless to the physical allocation. We call *hybrid cluster* the result of this operation.

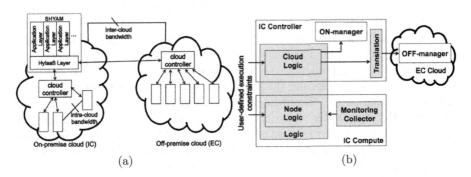

Fig. 1. Figure 1a: Hybrid cloud scenario. SHYAM is an on-premise software component able to collect information about the current status of IC and dynamically add off-premise resources if needed. Figure 1b: Hybrid Infrastructure as a Service layer in detail. Subcomponents are displayed in grey.

HyIaaS is also responsible for autonomously handling to changes in the current utilization level of the on-premise physical machines hosting the VMs of the cluster. To avoid the application slowdown due to the poor performance of these VMs, HyIaaS layer is in charge of dynamically spawning new VMs on EC and providing them to the above Application layer (Fig. 1a). This layer is responsible for installing and configuring a specific distributed application on the newly provided VMs. SHYAM's main goal is to unify on- and off-premise resources while keeping a strong separation between the infrastructure and application levels. It must be installed on IC, so that it can collect monitoring information about the utilization level of the on-premise machines. According to a specific user-defined policy, the HyIaaS layer can perform cloud bursting toward EC by translating generic spawning and scale-down requests into specific off-premise provisioning and de-provisioning commands. If both IC and EC have a centralized architecture, SHYAM makes them able to cooperate by communicating with their central controllers. In the following, we will use the term *compute nodes* to refer all the physical machines (of IC or EC) able to host VMs and not in charge of any cloud management task. HyIaaS layer consists of three components (Fig. 1b): the Monitoring Collector (MC), the Logic and the Translation component. MC is in charge of fetching information about the current resource utilization level of the on-premise *compute node*. The Logic component uses the information read by MC and implements a custom-defined spawning policy. Given the current status of the on-premise cluster and additional constraints possibly introduced by the customer (e.g., deadline for the execution of a certain job), the output of the Logic component is a new allocation of the VMs over the physical nodes, possibly including new VMs spawned off-premise. The Logic component has been split into two subcomponents: Node Logic and Cloud Logic. The Node Logic (one for each *compute*), responsible for analyzing the monitoring data from MC, detecting if a critical situation occurred on that physical machine (e.g., the *compute node* is too loaded) and sending notifications to the Cloud Logic. The Cloud Logic (installed on IC's controller node), in charge of autonomously taking spawning/migration decisions given the monitoring alerts received from Node Logic. The alerts from Node Logic and the policy of Cloud Logic can be defined by the IC system administrator. The rationale behind splitting the Logic component into two parts is to minimize the amount of information exchanged between the on-premise cloud controller and the physical nodes hosting VMs: the Node Logic sends notifications to the Cloud Logic only if a critical condition at node-level is detected. Having a wider vision of the state of the cloud, the Cloud Logic can combine the received information to implement a more elaborate policy. This should be taken into account by the IC system administrator, as she implements the spawning/migration policy. If the new VM allocation produced by the Logic involves EC, the Translation component is used to convert the directives into EC-specific APIs.

2.1 Applicative Scenario

HyIaaS invokes the Application Layer functionalities via a standard interface. In particular, after HyIaaS has produced and deployed a new hybrid cluster structure, it calls the *configure* operation offered by the specific Application Layer involved, which is in charge of installing and configuring the applicative software on the newly provided virtual nodes.

As a case study, we focus on the data-intensive scenario, in which the application load can be distributed among several computing nodes. We adopt MapReduce [12], a widespread programming model to simplify the implementation of data intensive distributed applications. Following this approach, the input dataset is partitioned into an arbitrary number of parts, each exclusively processed by a different computing task, the *mapper*. Each *mapper* produces intermediate results (in the form of *key/value* pairs) that are collected and processed by other tasks, called *reducers*, in charge of calculating the final results by merging the *values* associated to the same *key*. The programs implemented according to this model can be automatically parallelized and easily executed on a distributed infrastructure. The MapReduce model is implemented by several platforms: one of the most popular is Apache Hadoop [1], an open source implementation consisting of two components: Hadoop Distributed File System (HDFS) and MapReduce runtime. The input files for MapReduce jobs are split into fixed size blocks (default is 64 MB) and stored in HDFS. MapReduce runtime follows a master-worker architecture. The master (Job-Tracker) assigns tasks to the worker nodes. Each worker node runs a Task-Tracker that manages the currently assigned tasks. Each worker node can have up to a predefined number of *mappers* and *reducers* simultaneously running. We execute the Hadoop workload over a virtual cluster that can be deployed on the hybrid cloud (partitioned between IC and EC) in case the on-premise resources are not enough. Therefore, the first Application Layer we implement for SHYAM is responsible for installing and configuring Hadoop on the newly provided VMs and allows us to evaluate the performance of operating MapReduce in a hybrid cloud setup.

2.2 Logic Component Policy

We implemented a first example of policy for the Logic component executed on every *compute* node of IC: the SPAN policy (Algorithm 1). The algorithm aims to maintain the load of each *compute* node under a parametric threshold: THR_U. It periodically checks the resource utilization of the *compute* node h (line 2 in Algorithm 1). If the load exceeds THR_U, the procedure selects to move a subset of the VMs currently on h (line 3 in Algorithm 1). The *selectToMove* function is implemented according to Minimization of Migrations algorithm from Beloglazov et al. [6]. This policy ensures to always move the minimum number of VMs that brings h utilization back under THR_U. For each *vm* selected, if there is another on-premise node that can host the VM, a migration is performed (line 7 in Algorithm 1). Otherwise, if no IC's *compute* node can host the VM, a new one is spawned off-premise and the specific application level configuration is performed (line 10 in Algorithm 1). As mentioned in Sect. 2.1, we chose Hadoop as an example of distributed data-processing application. For this reason, the

---

Algorithm 1. SPAN policy

Input: $h, AL, ONmanager, OFFmanager, THR_U, \Delta t$.

1: **while** true **do**
2:    **if** $h.getUtil() > THR_U$ **then**
3:       $vmsToMove = selectToMove(h.getVMs())$
4:       **for each** vm **in** $vmsToMove$ **do**
5:          $d = ONmanager.getAnotherAllocation(vm)$
6:          **if** $d! = null$ **then**
7:             $ONmanager.migrate(vm, d)$
8:          **else**
9:             $vm_{new} = OFFmanager.provideLike(vm)$
10:            $AL.configure(vm, vm_{new})$
11:            $vm_{new} = ONmanager.remove(vm)$
12:          **end if**
13:       **end for**
14:    **end if**
15:    $sleep(\Delta t)$
16: **end while**

---

code of $AL.configure(vm, vm_{new})$ mainly consists of two operations, as show in Algorithm 2. First of all vm_{new} is included in Hadoop virtual cluster (cl in line 1), then the old vm is decommissioned causing its data to be sent to other nodes of the cluster. Focusing on the first operation ($cl.include(vm_{new})$ in line 2), we must consider that Hadoop's Job-Tracker (running on the *master* node) assigns jobs to the workers according to the part of data currently allocated on the worker's portion of HDFS. Having no data initially allocated on the newly provided off-premise workers, they will be scarcely useful for the computation, because the Job-Tracker will not assign any task to them. Nevertheless, our solution relays on a well known Hadoop behavior: when the on-premise vm is decommissioned and its data are replicated, Hadoop prefers the workers with low utilization of HDFS as destinations. Initially having 0 % HDFS utilization, off-premise vm_{new} is likely to be preferred and no other data balancing is needed to give vm_{new} an effective role in computation. Therefore, $cl.exclude(vm)$ in line 3 of Algorithm 2 is enough to trigger the data replication process and avoid the drawbacks of launching Hadoop Balancer process (which is high time-consuming mechanism [1] for equally redistribute data across the workers). It also produces the benefits of an inter-cloud VM migration (i.e., only vm's portion of HDFS is moved to EC) without performing the whole VM snapshot transfer.

Algorithm 2. $AL.configure$ procedure for Hadoop virtual cluster

---

Input: vm, vm_{new}.
1: $cl = vm.getVirtualCluster()$
2: $cl.include(vm_{new})$
3: $cl.exclude(vm)$

2.3 Implementation

We implemented HyIaaS layer by extending OpenStack Sahara [3] component to allow cluster scaling operations in a hybrid scenario. OpenStack [2] is an open source platform for cloud computing with a modular architecture and Sahara is the OpenStack module specific to data processing. It allows the user to quickly deploy, configure and scale virtual clusters dedicated to data intensive applications like MapReduce. We modified the Sahara scaling mechanism to allow the spawning of new VMs on a remote cloud. The MC component is a simple daemon process running on each compute node. It checks the CPU, memory and disk utilization and compares them with THR_U. When the virtual cluster needs to be scaled by providing new off-premise VMs, the command is issued through the Translation component to EC. In our test scenario, the off-premise cloud runs another OpenStack installation, therefore the Translation component simply forwards the provisioning command to EC's Nova component (the central module for VM management in OpenStack infrastructure). Finally, the Application layer configures Hadoop and launches its daemons by connecting to the newly provided VMs.

3   Experimental Results

Our setup is composed of two OpenStack clouds to emulate IC and EC. The on-premise cloud has five physical machines, each one with a Intel Core Duo CPU (3.06 GHz), 4GB RAM and 225 GB HDD. EC is composed of three physical machines, each one with 32 cores Opteron 6376 (1.4 GHz), 32 GB RAM and 2.3 TB HDD. On both IC and EC we provide *adhoc* VMs with two virtual CPUs, 4 GB RAM and 20 GB of disk. The intra-cloud bandwidth of IC and EC is 1000 Mbit/s, while the inter-cloud bandwidth (between the two) is 100 Mbit/s. Our initial scenario is composed of 4 VMs allocated on IC. In order to characterize the performance of the computation on the hybrid cluster, we first analyze the time to provide one or more new Hadoop workers on EC. Figure 2a shows the average time to obtain a single Hadoop worker up and running as we vary the number of VMs spawned at a time on EC. As we expected, the trend of the curve suggests that there is a constant overhead caused by SHYAM provisioning mechanism, but the trend of total time is approximately linear with the number of VMs requested. Furthermore, we can easily verify from the graph in Fig. 2a that provisioning time is independent from the characteristics of the specific VM spawned. Given SHYAM's autonomic provisioning mechanism, we can evaluate the performance of operating MapReduce in a hybrid cloud setup. To this purpose, we assume to have four on-premise VMs already configured to run Hadoop jobs and provided with a certain amount of data D on HDFS, and we consider the time to execute a word count Hadoop job [12] over Wikipedia datasets of different size D [4]. Figure 2b compares the execution time trends of three scenarios. The first one (Te_I in Fig. 2b) represents the ideal situation of having each Hadoop VM allocated on an on-premise dedicated physical machine. Since no other physical or virtual load is affecting the execution, we can obtain good performance (execution time is linear in D). The second scenario (Te_I_{stress} in Fig. 2b) shows the performance degradation when one of the four Hadoop workers is running on a overloaded physical machine and no VM redistribution mechanism is adopted. As we can see in Fig. 2b, the execution time is considerably higher when compared to Te_I because the VM on the stressed physical node sensibly slows down the whole distributed computation. The third scenario (Te_H_{stress} in Fig. 2b) repeats the second scenario and adopts SHYAM redistribution with SPAN policy. THR_U and THR_D are fixed at 90 % and 10 % respectively. In this case, a new VM is spawned off-premise and the on-premise worker running on the stressed machine is decommissioned (i.e., excluded from Hadoop cluster after its data have been copied on other worker nodes). This operation causes a part of data to cross on-/off-premise boundaries. As we can see in Fig. 2b, the adoption of SPAN policy can considerably improve the performance for low values of D. However, the trends show that in the third scenario the execution time is not linear in the volume of data involved and, for high values of D, we can have a lower execution time by avoiding the off-premise spawning. This is mainly due to data movement across the on-/off-premise boundaries, which is usually over a higher latency medium when compared to a fully on-premise computation. Figure 2c shows the gain in execution time obtained with SHYAM.

Although for high volumes of data crossing on-/off-premise boundaries the gain
is low, the graph suggests that the autonomic provisioning and configuration of
VMs on EC can represent a good solution to face critical conditions of stress in
private clouds. In the case of a word count application, the graphic in Fig. 2c
suggests a pseudo linear correlation between the amount of data D and the gain
obtained by providing a new off-premise VM and decommissioning the slow on-
premise worker. This property can be useful to a priori estimate the advantage
of SHYAM's cloud bursting given a certain volume of data D to be processed.

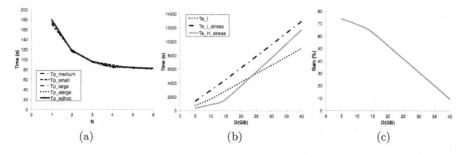

(a)   (b)   (c)

Fig. 2. Figure 2a shows the time to provide a certain number N of new off-premise
VMs with different characteristics (small, medium, large and xlarge are the default
VM configurations offered by OpenStack). Figure 2b compares the time to perform
Hadoop word count on a fully on-premise cluster – with (Te_I) or without (Te_I_stress)
a stressing condition on a physical node –, with the performance on a hybrid cluster
created by the HyIaaS. Figure 2c shows the percentage gain obtained by our solution.

4   Related Work

Cloud computing is currently used for a wide and heterogeneous range of tasks.
According to the classification introduced in [5], in this work we especially focus
on the cloud from the *IaaS* perspective, intending it as an elastic provider of
virtual resources, able to contribute to heavy computing tasks. Data-intensive
applications are an example of resource demanding tasks. A widely adopted
programming model for this scenario is MapReduce [12], whose execution can
be supported by platforms such as Hadoop [1], possibly in a cloud computing
infrastructure. We tested our system with MapReduce applications, choosing
Hadoop as execution engine. Recently, a lot of work has focused on cloud computing for the execution of big data applications: as pointed out in [11], the
relationship between big data and the cloud is very tight, because collecting
and analyzing huge and variable volumes of data require infrastructures able to
dynamically adapt their size and their computing power to the application needs.
The work by Chen et al. [9] presents an accurate model for optimal resource provisioning useful to operate MapReduce applications in public clouds. Similarly,
Palanisamy et al. [17] deal with optimizing the allocation of VMs executing
MapReduce jobs in order to minimize the infrastructure cost in a cloud datacenter. In the same single-cloud scenario, Rizvandi et al. [18] focus on the automatic

estimation of MapReduce configuration parameters, while Verma et al. [20] propose a resource allocation algorithm able to estimate the amount of resources required to meet MapReduce-specific performance goals. However, these models were not intended to address the challenges of the hybrid cloud scenario, which is the target environment of our work.

The choice of primarily relay on a small (e.g., private) cloud and then use the extra-capacity offered by a public cloud for opportunistic scale-out has been investigated by several authors [7,8]. According to the classification in [19], our work mainly deals with the hybrid cloud approach for cloud interoperability, because the main motivation of our system is allowing cloud bursting to EC. However, our proposal could also be classified as a *Federation* mechanism for cloud aggregation because – as in federated clouds – the interoperation between clouds is completely transparent to end-users. The works in [13,16] focus on enabling cloud bursting through inter-cloud migration of VMs, which is generally a time and resource expensive mechanism. In particular, [13] optimizes the overhead of migration using an intelligent pre-copying mechanisms that proactively replicates VMs before the migration. Our work doesn't take into consideration the VM migration, but only the dynamic instantiation of new compute nodes on EC, thus to avoid the unnecessary movement of the whole VM snapshot across the cloud boundaries. As we shown, this technique is particularly suitable for the MapReduce model because the Hadoop provisioning and decommissioning mechanism intrinsically contributes to simplify the cloud bursting process. The hybrid scenario is also investigated in the work by Zhang et al. [21] by focusing on the workload factoring and management across federated clouds. More similarly to our approach, cloud bursting techniques has been adopted for scaling MapReduce applications in the work by Mattess et al. [15], which presents an online provisioning policy to meet a deadline for the Map phase. Differently from our approach, [15] does not consider the time to balance data across the hybrid virtual cluster, which, as we showed, has a consistent role in determining the opportunity of cloud bursting towards the public cloud. Also the work presented by Kailasam et al. [14] deals with cloud bursting for big data applications. It proposes an extension of the MapReduce model to avoid the shortcomings of high latencies in inter-cloud data transfer: the computation inside IC follows the batch MapReduce model, while in EC a stream processing platform called Storm is used. The resulting system shows significant benefits. Differently from [14], we have chosen to keep complete transparency and uniformity in working node allocation and configuration. However, as in [14], our system allows the user to constrain the allocation of *mappers/reducers* in order to optimize the cost of data transfer between these tasks.

5 Conclusion

In this paper we presented SHYAM, a software component to allow VM autonomic management in a hybrid cloud scenario. We illustrated the architecture and the internal structure of the system and we evaluate its performance by executing a Hadoop data-intensive application on a virtual cluster and stressing one of IC's physical machines. In the given scenario, SHYAM autonomously spawns new VMs on EC and configures them as workers of the Hadoop cluster. Our results show that the time to provide a new off-premise worker is not influenced by the characteristics of the VM requested and the hybrid cluster obtained can sensibly improve the performance of a benchmark Hadoop word count application, although the performance of the hybrid cluster decreases as the inter-cloud bandwidth is saturated. Since this drawback could be also influenced by the kind of application executed (e.g., word count in our case study), we plan to further investigate SHYAM performance with different Hadoop workloads. Nevertheless, this work represents a first prototype of an autonomic infrastructure for hybrid clouds able to detect critical conditions on IC and autonomously request resources to EC.

As regards SPAN policy, we trigger the spawning/migration mechanism if the physical machine's CPU utilization exceeds THR_U. However, the policy could be easily modified to take into account the utilization of other resources (RAM, disk, etc.). Furthermore, in case of spawning new VMs towards EC our approach lacks a mechanism for bringing back on IC the off-premise VMs once the critical condition is solved. Therefore, for the future, we plan to enrich the policy with a similar threshold mechanism to detect underloaded hosts in IC. This mechanism will have to be equipped with memory of the past actions taken in order to avoid the continuous provisioning and de-provisioning of VMs (moving data back and forth between IC and EC) due to small variations on the load of the physical machine.

References

1. Apache hadoop. https://hadoop.apache.org/
2. Openstack: Opensource cloud computing software. https://www.openstack.org/
3. Openstack sahara. https://wiki.openstack.org/wiki/Sahara
4. Puma datasets. https://engineering.purdue.edu/puma/datasets.htm
5. Armbrust, M., Fox, O.: Above the clouds: a Berkeley view of cloud computing. Electrical Engineering and CS University of California, Technical report (2009)
6. Beloglazov, A., Abawajy, J., Buyya, R.: Energy-aware resource allocation heuristics for efficient management of data centers for cloud computing. Future Gener. Comput. Syst. **28**(5), 755–768 (2012)
7. Bicer, T., Chiu, D., Agrawal, G.: A framework for data-intensive computing with cloud bursting. In: IEEE International Conference on Cluster Computing (2011)
8. Cardosa, M., Wang, C., Nangia, A., Chandra, A., Weissman, J.: Exploring mapreduce efficiency with highly-distributed data. In: Proceedings of the Second International Workshop on MapReduce and Its Applications. ACM (2011)
9. Chen, K., Powers, J., Guo, S., Tian, F.: Cresp: towards optimal resource provisioning for mapreduce computing in public clouds. IEEE Trans. Parallel Distrib. Syst. **25**(6), 1403–1412 (2014)
10. Chen, M., Mao, S., Liu, Y.: Big data: a survey. Mob. Netw. Appl. **19**(2), 171–209 (2014)
11. Collins, E.: Intersection of the cloud and big data. IEEE Cloud Comput. **1**(1), 84–85 (2014)

12. Dean, J., Ghemawat, S.: Mapreduce: simplified data processing on large clusters. Commun. ACM **51**(1), 107–113 (2008)

13. Guo, T., Sharma, U., Shenoy, P., Wood, T., Sahu, S.: Cost-aware cloud bursting for enterprise applications. ACM Trans. Internet Technol. **13**(3), 10 (2014)

14. Kailasam, S., Dhawalia, P., Balaji, S.: Extending mapreduce across clouds with bstream. IEEE Trans. Cloud Comput. **2**(3), 362–376 (2014)

15. Mattess, M., Calheiros, R., Buyya, R.: Scaling mapreduce applications across hybrid clouds to meet soft deadlines. In: IEEE 27th International Conference on Advanced Information Networking and Applications, pp. 629–636 (2013)

16. Nagin, K., Hadas, D.: Inter-cloud mobility of virtual machines. In: Proceedings of the 4th Annual International Conference on Systems and Storage. ACM (2011)

17. Palanisamy, B., Singh, A., Liu, L.: Cost-effective resource provisioning for mapreduce in a cloud. IEEE Trans. Parallel Distrib. Syst. **26**(5), 1265–1279 (2015)

18. Rizvandi, N., Taheri, J.: A study on using uncertain time series matching algorithms for mapreduce applications. Concurrency Comput. **25**(12), 1699–1718 (2013)

19. Toosi, A.N., Calheiros, R.N., Buyya, R.: Interconnected cloud computing environments: challenges, taxonomy, and survey. ACM Comput. Surv. **47**(1), 7 (2014)

20. Verma, A., Cherkasova, L., Campbell, R.H.: Resource provisioning framework for mapreduce jobs with performance goals. In: Kon, F., Kermarrec, A.-M. (eds.) Middleware 2011. LNCS, vol. 7049, pp. 165–186. Springer, Heidelberg (2011)

21. Zhang, H., Jiang, G., Yoshihira, K.: Proactive workload management in hybrid cloud computing. IEEE Trans. Netw. Serv. Manage. **11**(1), 90–100 (2014)

A Database-Specific Pattern for Multi-cloud High Availability and Disaster Recovery

Huanhuan Xiong[(✉)], Frank Fowley, and Claus Pahl

IC4 - The Irish Centre for Cloud Computing and Commerce,
Dublin City University, Dublin 9, Ireland
h.xiong@cs.ucc.ie

Abstract. High availability and disaster recovery (HADR) are often discussed in highly critical business systems for business function recovery and continuity concerns. With the development of cloud computing, virtual cloud services are perfectly matched to HADR scenarios, and interoperability is a significant aspect to help users to use HADR service across different cloud platforms and providers. In this paper, we present an architectural pattern describing the integration of high availability and disaster recovery. We focus on database cluster replication between private cloud and public cloud environments. This HADR pattern for database cluster replication implements both synchronous and asynchronous replication concurrently for high availability and disaster recovery purposes. To evaluate the effectiveness of this pattern, we simulate a MySQL-database-cluster HADR scenario under three strategies: hot standby, warm standby and cold standby, and analyze the performance, business continuity features and cost.

Keywords: Multi-cloud · Architecture pattern · High availability · Disaster recovery · Clustering · Database replication

1 Introduction

Business continuity (BC) is the capability of a business to withstand outages and continue to operate services normally and without interruption in accordance with predefined SLAs [10]. High availability and disaster recovery are both subsets of business continuity [25]. High availability (HA) is the characteristic of a system to protect against or recover from minor outage in a short time frame with largely automated means. High availability addresses service availability mostly via redundancy and flexible load balancing so that if one infrastructure component (network, servers, and processes) becomes unavailable, overall service remains available. The architecture of a typical HA system is shown in Fig. 1(a). Disaster recovery (DR) is the ability to continue services in the case of outages, often with reduced capabilities or performance, and typically involving manual activities. Disaster recovery addresses service recovery and continuity through two independent environments (primary site and standby site), typically in separate and distinct facilities, each containing their own data and executables. The architecture of a typical DR system is shown in Fig. 1(b).

© Springer International Publishing Switzerland 2016
A. Celesti and P. Leitner (Eds.): ESOCC 2015 Workshops, CCIS 567, pp. 374–388, 2016.
DOI: 10.1007/978-3-319-33313-7_29

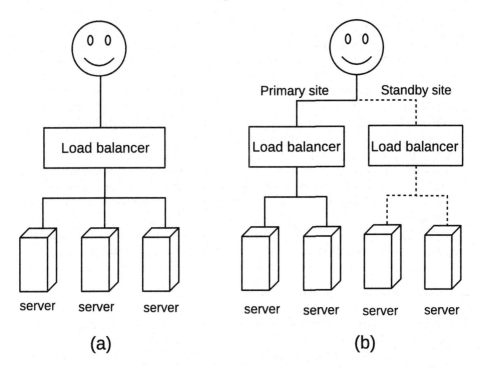

Fig. 1. HA and DR architectures

The effectiveness of BC can be controlled via the key features recovery time objective (RTO) and recovery point objective (RPO) [1]. RTO is the duration of time needed until the service is usable again after a major outage, and RPO refers the point in time from which data will be restored to be usable. To reduce the downtime (RTO) and data loss (RPO) of a system with an outage, it is common to replicate data (e.g., database, application, or system meta-data) to another standby site or another provider. Recently, virtualized cloud platforms have been used to provide scalable HADR solutions. Moreover, the pay-as-you-go pricing mode can reduce the operating cost of infrequently used IT resources over the Internet [4].

A challenge for HADR in the cloud is to implement the system recovery and business continuity across different cloud platforms or providers. A typical use case would be a business has its own private cloud infrastructure for providing services, but does not want to invest in additional infrastructure that is rarely used (e.g., disaster recovery). Taking a public cloud for disaster recovery can help to reduce the capital expenditures. In addition, HADR can happen in different levels, like VMs, storage, or applications. While currently most across-cloud DR solutions focus on infrastructure level, the HADR solution for application data, especially relational databases across multi-cloud is the problem we address here.

We present a database-specific pattern describing the integration of high availability and disaster recovery into a database cluster architecture between private cloud and public cloud environments – addressing a need to look at the cloud from a software architecture perspective [20]. As a case study, we deployed two MySQL database clusters on an OpenStack private cloud as the primary site and Windows Azure public cloud as the backup site separately. We used load balancing to monitor and manage the traffic between the two clouds. The pattern generalizes our specific experience, implementing synchronous replication inside of each database cluster to achieve high availability, as well as asynchronous replication between the primary-database-cluster and the standby-database-cluster to complete fail-over and fail-back.

This paper is organized as follows. We introduce background and related work in Sect. 2, including database clustering and replication techniques, as well as HADR with cloud computing. In Sect. 3, we present the architectural pattern for hybrid database-cluster replication solution for multi-cloud. Then, we implement the HADR pattern based on OpenStack and Windows Azure in Sect. 4 and show the result of the evaluation in Sect. 5. We give the conclusion in Sect. 6.

2   Background and Related Work

A **database cluster** is based on a group of linked computers, working together closely [32]. In the database context, clustering means that the application sees a single database, while under the covers there are two or more computers processing the data. Generally, there are two predominant node configurations for HA clustering: active/passive (master-slave) and active/active (multi-master). The active/passive mode provides a fully redundant instance of each node, which is only brought on-line when its associated primary node fails. The active/active mode is widely used in a homogeneous software configuration, where traffic intended for the failed node is either passed onto an existing node or load balanced across the remaining nodes.

Database replication is frequent data copying from one database to another. Database replication is widely used in distributed database systems – see Table 1. There are two techniques to affect database replication [28]: eager and lazy. In eager replication, updates are propagated within the boundaries of a transaction which usually uses locking for maintaining the data consistency [19], which means all replicas are active and consistent all the time. Lazy replication updates the local copy first and then propagates the update transaction to other database replicas, which is well known for low data consistency and high scalability and performance (short response times) [12].

A **cluster replication** strategy can be selected based on two basic characteristics: when and where [24]. The *when* characteristic is based on when is the data updated, which can be described with replication methods: eager (synchronous) and lazy (asynchronous). The *where* characteristic is based on where the updates can take place, which can be presented by the clustering nodes: master-slave and multi-master.

The primary objective of **high availability and disaster recovery** (HADR) solutions [2,8,14] is disaster recovery to restore critical business system

Table 1. Database replication models

	Master-slave	Multi-master
Synchronous	No updates are made at the primary (master) node until all secondary (slave) nodes have also received the update.	The same data has been updated in different nodes at the same time: using locking techniques to avoid concurrent transactions on the same data or atomic broadcast to determine the total order when conflicting transactions happen.
Asynchronous	When the primary node receives an update transaction, it is executed and committed. Then it propagates a new copy to the secondary nodes.	The same data could have been updated at different nodes at the same time, but a problem during the synchronization might arise, e.g., some decision might need to be made on which transaction to keep and which transaction to undo.

to a normal or near-normal condition following a disruptive incident and high availability management to minimize downtime and help to achieve very low or near-zero RTOs. Popular strategies for recovering systems are high availability cluster [13], remote backup [11] and database replication [28].

Virtual servers have been used in high available clusters [5,6]. A HA cluster has two or more nodes (VMs), each node runs one or more services. When one of the nodes fails, the services or workloads are transparently transferred to other nodes by a load balancer. However, a single load balancer also could become the bottleneck of the system. Thus, virtual IP technology [33] can be used between load balancers for high availability and failure tolerance. Remus [5] is a project that provides a **virtualization-based HA solution** by allowing a group of VMs to be replicated across different data centers over WAN. SecondSite [23] extends high availability to disaster tolerance, allowing the backup VM to take over in a completely transparent manner to implement both fail-over recovery and seamless fail-back. For HADR in cloud environments, Wood et al. [31] analyze the economic benefits and deployment challenges of disaster recovery as a cloud service, exploring the traditional functionality with current cloud platforms in order to minimize cost, data loss and recovery time in cloud based DR services.

There are a number of **commercial HADR solutions**. Amazon (AWS) [7] provides three recovery methods using combination of AWS services: cold DR, pilot-light DR and warm DR. Window Azure [15] offers end-to-end highly available DR using Microsoft virtualization (hyper-v) and failover capabilities complemented by data replication products. VMware Site Recovery Manager (SRM) [27] is widely used for storage-based replication to provide centralized management of recovery plans, enable non-disruptive testing, and automate site recovery and migration processes. Zerto Virtual Replication [32] is a hypervisor-based replication solution for tier-one applications, which can replace traditional array-based DR that was not built for virtual environments. OpenStack also provides both HA and DR as a service [17], HA for continued operations within a single cloud environment (one deployment of OpenStack in a single or multiple locations), DR for continued operations for multiple cloud environments (multiple deployments in various locations). However, these HADR solutions generally focus on backup of applications from on-premise to cloud or between different locations, but for the same cloud platform [22]. Interoperability across different cloud platforms and providers is still a major challenge for HADR.

3   HADR Pattern: Hybrid Multi-cloud Cluster Replication

Generally, as described above, synchronous replication aims at high data consistency, which requires a reliable network and low latency, while asynchronous replication can adapt to long-distance and high network latency environments better at lower cost. The primary purposes of multi-master clustering are increased availability and faster server response time, while master-slave clustering is usually used for failover scenarios rather than high availability purpose.

Thus, for our HADR pattern, we propose synchronous multi-master replication inside of a database cluster to achieve system high availability and data consistency, and use asynchronous master-slave replication between primary and secondary database cluster to ensure the backup/replication operations does not impact the normal performance of primary system.

The presentation of the HADR pattern in this section follows the way architecture patterns are described in [3]: first a definition of problem and context is given, followed by the description of the solution and strategies, and completed with a discussion of comments and limitations. We also discuss concrete technologies to illustrate the implementation of the pattern. The technology discussion extends the pattern and is crucial to demonstrate its feasibility.

3.1   Problem and Context

While both HA and DR strive to achieve business continued operations in the face of failures, HA usually deals with individual component failures based on local area network (LAN) and DR deals with large-scale failures across wide-area network (WAN). Generally, HA and DR would be considered as separate problems and would be addressed separately. We aim at integrating HA and DR into one system, implementing HA across WAN contexts and achieving DR across multi-cloud platforms. As discussed in Sect. 2, most HADR solutions focus on backup of the applications from on-premise to cloud, or between different locations but the same cloud platform. Thus, our HADR pattern addresses:

– Integration of HA and DR. Our HADR pattern integrates the existing HA architectures (i.e., clustering and load balancing) with DR processes

(i.e., backup, fail-over and fail-back), which aims to implement the best-practice to provide the required HA and DR, supporting various degrees of automated fail-over and availability concepts.
– Multi-cloud HADR. Our pattern supports HA and DR across different cloud platforms/providers, such as having the primary HA infrastructure running in a private cloud and implementing DR in a public cloud across the Internet.

We focus the HADR pattern on database clusters, aiming at synchronous replication for local high availability within the primary database cluster, and asynchronous replication for disaster recovery across a remote standby cluster.

3.2 Solution

In our setup, cf. Fig. 2, two virtual server clusters are used to provide HADR for the databases. The primary site could host an OpenStack private cloud, which handles all client requests during the normal operations. The standby site, hosted in the Azure public cloud provides the database service when a failure happens in the primary site. In addition, we use load balancers (active/passive) to manage the workload between these two sites. Note that OpenStack and Azure are used for illustration, but are not part of the actual pattern.

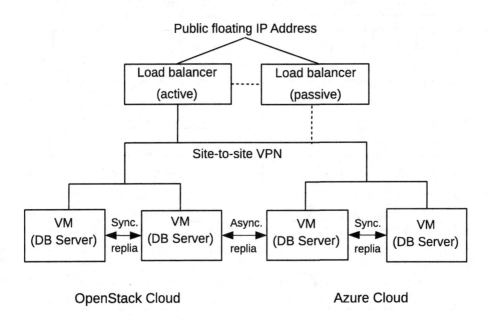

Fig. 2. The architecture of HADR solution

Technically, the HADR pattern architecture includes site-to-site VPN and MySQL cluster replication (synchronous and asynchronous). Here, site-to-site

VPN is a private virtual cloud network that overlays the Internet to connect different cloud infrastructures, which is the networking precondition of the database cluster replication. Then the cluster provides shared-nothing clustering and auto-sharding for the MySQL database system, which consists of multi-master synchronous replication and master-slave asynchronous replication techniques.

- Synchronous replication is implemented using Galera, which a multi-master cluster for MySQL/InnoDB databases. The application can write to any node in a Galera replication [26] cluster, and transaction commits (RBR events) are then applied on all servers, via a certification-based replication using group communication and transaction ordering techniques.
- Asynchronous replication is implemented by Global Transaction Identifiers (GTID) [16], which provides a better master-slave transactions mapping across nodes. The slave can see a unique transaction coming in from several masters, which can easily being mapped into the slave execution list if it needs to restart or resume replication.

The MySQL cluster replication reference architecture is shown in Fig. 3.

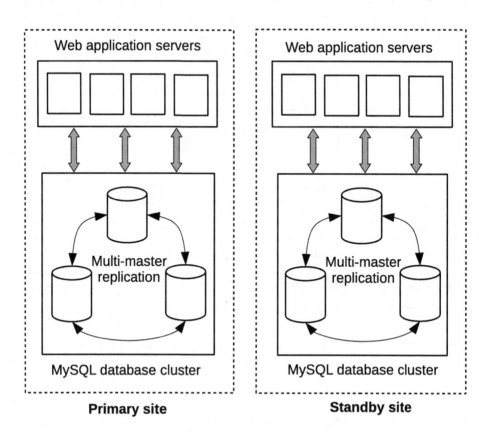

Fig. 3. MySQL cluster replication reference architecture

3.3 Strategies

We selected three use cases to comprehensively match different common DR strategies [29]: hot standby, warm standby and cold standby.

- Hot standby. This is a duplicate of the primary site, with full computer systems as well as near-complete backups of user data. Real-time synchronization between the two sites may be used to completely mirror the data environment of the primary site via VPN.
- Warm standby. This is a compromise between hot and cold, where the basic infrastructures have already been established, though on a smaller scale than the primary production site, e.g., keep one VM running in the backup site, and real-time data synchronization between the two sites via VPN.
- Cold standby. This is the least expensive type of backup site for an organization to operate, which is designed to provide the basic infrastructure needed to run a data center for long-term outages of the primary one. In cold standby, there is no VM running in the backup site, only VM snapshots are transferred from primary site to backup site on a regular basis.

3.4 Comments and Limitations

As discussed in Sect. 2, both synchronous and asynchronous replication are widely used in high availability and fault tolerance for databases. Both of them have pros and cons, as discussed. Our cluster reference architecture in the pattern is integrating synchronous and asynchronous replication into one HADR system, using Galera for local database cluster high availability and applying GTID for remote backup across different platforms as the implementation. In addition, GTID allows a slave to have more than one master, which means if the failure happens at one master, others can continually send the transaction to the slave. This novel master-slave mapping mechanism can help to maximize the flexibility and reduce data loss.

However, the architecture implementation also has some limitations. For example, at the slave side, the Galera cluster service needs to be stopped until the GTID configuration is done, but this only happens in the hot standby scenario where Galera and GTID services are running at the same time. Thus, the most efficient way to handle these two techniques together is to keep only one slave node alive during the normal operations, and start the Galera cluster service only when scaling out to more nodes (e.g., warm standby use case).

4 Pattern Implementation and Evaluation Setup

To implement the HADR pattern, we used, as discussed, an OpenStack private cloud as primary site and an Azure public cloud as the backup site. To prepare an evaluation testbed, in each VM, we used WordPress as the testing application for the evaluation with an Apache web server and a MySQL database on Linux OS (LAMP stack), which can be considered a standard application. Each VM

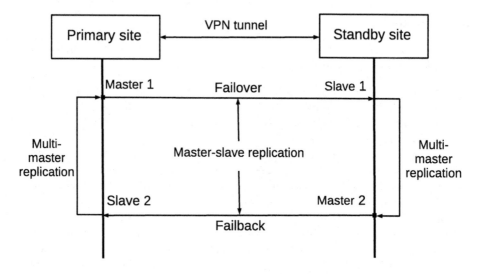

Fig. 4. HADR pattern implementation

is then a web server node as well as a database node. Furthermore, we use the open-source HAproxy as the load balancer, monitoring and controlling the workload between primary site and backup site. The load balancer ensures that the primary cloud is managed and monitored, the HA and DR mode is activated and the update of the backup site is triggered (automated fail-back is enabled). The overall HADR implementation is shown in Fig. 4.

- *VPN tunnel between OpenStack and Azure.* We used Openswan to build up a VPN tunnel between OpenStack and Azure cloud. Openswan is based on the IPsec protocol that encrypts the IP traffic before packets are transferred from source to destination. Since encapsulation, de-capsulation, encryption and decryption take place at the router, the processing overhead and CPU utilization increases would reduce communication speed.
- *Master-slave-master replication.* Global Transaction Identifiers (GTID) released in MySQL 5.6 enables replicated events to be easily tracked through a replication topology of masters and slaves. Thus, any two nodes in primary site and backup site can be configured as master and slave. Rather than the traditional one-to-one mapping mechanism, GTID allows a slave to have more than one master, which helps to maximize the flexibility and reduces data loss. In addition, we implemented bi-directional (master-slave-master) replication between masters and slaves, which achieves automatic fail-over and fail-back between the primary site and backup site.
- *Multi-master replication.* It aims to achieve high availability inside each site. Here, we use the MySQL Galera technique to implement the multi-master synchronous replication in the primary site to enable HA function, as well as in the backup site with the hot standby strategy. In warm standby mode,

there is only one node alive in the backup site during the normal operations, and the Galera service is be started when it scales out to another nodes.

5   Evaluation

We have implemented the pattern as an abstract architectural template through an implementation based on current technologies achieving the desired structural properties. This has been illustrated in Sects. 3 and 4. What needs a further investigation is the demonstration that an implemented pattern actually meets the HA and DR quality requirements and also cost and performance needs. This will also guide the mapping of the pattern to an implementation by selecting the best suitable strategy.

5.1   Objectives and Criteria

For the evaluation of the HADR pattern, we will measure the availability for HA, RPO and RTO for DR, cost (financial constraint) and response time (for system performance) in terms of most company concerns.

The evaluation results vary across to the different DR standby strategies. Selecting an appropriate DR strategy is one of the most important decisions made during the disaster recovery planning (DRP). It is important to carefully consider the specific business needs along with the costs and capabilities (such as RPO and RTO) when identifying the best approach for business continuity.

5.2   Experiment

We carried out experiments with the three different DR strategies on a cloud application service: hot standby, warm standby and cold standby.

- Hot standby. Two VMs run in Azure as the backup, VPN runs and connects with OpenStack, data is asynchronously replicated between two sites and synchronously replicated in the backup site.
- Warm standby. One VM runs in Azure as backup, VPN runs and connects with OpenStack, data is asynchronously replicated between two sites.
- Cold standby. No VM runs in Azure; VPN is created, but not running.

5.3   Results

Availability. Availability can be defined as a ratio of the expected value of the uptime of a system to the aggregate of the expected values of up and down time:

$$A = \frac{E[uptime]}{E[uptime] + E[downtime]} \tag{1}$$

Here, we assure the total time of a functional unit (uptime + downtime) is a year (typical SLA value), which is equal to $365 \times 24 \times 60$ min, while the downtime varies over the different DR strategies. The availability results of hot, warm and cold DR strategies are presented in Table 2.

RTO and RPO. RTO is the period from the disaster happening (the service becoming unavailable) to the service being available again, which is the same as the downtime in availability. RPO is the point in time from that data will be restored, which indicates the period from the latest backup version until the disaster happens. The results of RTO and RPO with hot, warm and cold DR strategies are presented in Table 2.

Cost. To give an indicative costing (according to Windows Azure pricing as of April 2015), we assume the following VM and storage costs for DR resources (cost summaries for the three DR strategies are also shown in Table 2):

- Virtual machine for computing (small size VM): 6.70 Cents per hour or 49 Euros per month
- Networking: virtual network (gateway hours): 2.68 cent per hour or 15.75 euro per month
- Storage: 5 cent per GB per month, or 50 euro per TB per month

Table 2. Performance and business impact analysis results with three DR strategies

	Description	Availability (per year)	RTO	RPO	COST (per month)
Hot standby	Automated	1 (zero downtime)	0 (zero downtime)	0 (no data loss)	113.75 euro
Warm standby	Starting another VM and configure the load balancer and multi-master database cluster	0.99999 (5 min downtime)	5 min	0 (no data loss)	64.75 euro
Cold standby	Creating two VMs based on the latest snapshot, starting VMS, and configuring load balancer and multi-master database cluster	0.99994 (30 min downtime)	30 min	Depends on checkpointing interval	15.75 euro

Response time. For web applications, the response time is the time it takes servers to respond when a user sends a query through a client to the servers. We used jmeter to simulate the workload (including browsing home page, logging in and making comments to our testing application) for the primary site with different DR strategies as well as the response time when the backup site takes over. The response time results of cold, warm and hot DR strategies are shown in Fig. 5.

Here, the top three graphs present the response time (in milliseconds) from the primary site with three common operations of our Wordpress application:

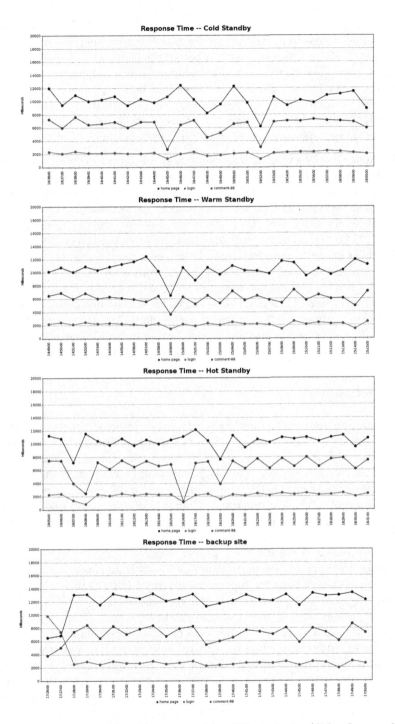

Fig. 5. Response time with cold, warm and hot DR strategies (Color figure online)

browse home page, login and comment, while the last one shows the response time (in milliseconds) from the backup site with the same operations. As we have seen in Fig. 4, the average response times of the different DR strategies from the primary site (see Graphs a,b,c) are similar, which indicates that database replication rarely impacts on response time and user experience. However, the average and maximum response time from the backup site (see Graph d) are slightly higher than the values from the primary site, which is actually expected due to the network latency and cross-cloud load balancing.

Guidelines. For the experimental evaluation, we only run 2 VMs as full-size applications, which makes the differences of recovery time and cost between the three DR strategies not very substantial. However, if we were to run hundreds of VMs for the service, and each VM costs 49 Euros per month, the hot standby would cost significantly more than the warm standby solution. Considering the RPO and RTO, warm standby has the same RPO as the hot standby solution, but the RTO of warm standby depends on the capacity (e.g., cloud bursting and auto scaling) of cloud platforms, ranging from a few minutes to dozens of minutes. In fact, we would not recommend to use cold standby for emergency disaster recovery in real business scenarios, which is quite inexpensive comparing to other two strategies, but extremely inefficient regarding recovery time and data loss. Therefore, warm standby for DR would be an ideal strategy for most organizations in terms of the combination of RPO, RTP and financial concerns.

6   Conclusions

In this paper, we presented a multi-cloud HADR architectural pattern, applied to relational database clusters across different cloud platforms, which targets high availability, reliability and interoperability as quality concerns. We introduced the replication techniques and models for the cloud environment as part of the pattern definition, which helps to minimize cost, data loss and recovery time for business continuity. We suggested a number of core cloud and distributed systems technologies and implemented the abstract HADR pattern based on a real-world cloud environment. As a sample solution, we chose an OpenStack private cloud and a Windows Azure public cloud.

In order to evaluate the pattern and its sample implementation, we simulated three DR scenarios for the commonly used DR strategies hot standby, warm standby and cold standby, and analyzed the availability, RPO and RTO, cost and response time in terms of most SMEs concerns. The system performance results indicate that the database replication rarely impacts the response time and user experience, while the other results show that hot standby is the most expensive and most efficient solution and that cold standby is inexpensive compared to other two strategies, but inefficient for the recovery time and data loss prevention. Warm standby has the same RPO as the hot standby solution, but the RTO of warm standby actually depends on the capacity of the cloud platforms (e.g., depending on cloud bursting and auto scaling strategies). We propose warm standby for DR as an ideal strategy for most organizations in terms of the comprehensive analysis of RPO, RTP and financial issues.

There are a number of cloud providers offering DR as a service (DRaaS), including the DR strategies we discussed. However, they mostly focus on backup of the application or of data from on-premise to the cloud, or in between their own clouds (which means different locations, but the same cloud platforms). In this HADR pattern, we developed a general database-cluster architecture pattern focusing on the interoperability across different clouds, here specifically between an OpenStack and a Windows Azure cloud. In this investigation, we are focused on relational databases, which is still less available than VM-oriented DR solutions. As a next step, we will investigate cloud storage, developing a pattern allowing multi-cloud configurations for managing different cloud storages and a possible (semi-)automated migration between different providers [9,21].

Acknowledgments. The research described here was supported by the Irish Centre for Cloud Computing and Commerce, an Irish national Technology Centre funded by Enterprise Ireland and the Irish Industrial Development Authority.

References

1. Benton, D.: Disaster recovery: a pragmatist's viewpoint. Disaster Recovery J. **20**(1), 79–81 (2007)
2. Bernstein, P.A., Hadzilacos, V., Goodman, N.: Concurrency Control and Recovery in Database Systems. Addison-Wesley, New York (1987)
3. Buschmann, F., Meunier, R., Rohnert, H., Sommerlad, P., Stal, M., Sommerlad, P., Stal, M.: Pattern-Oriented Software Architecture: A System of Patterns, vol. 1. Wiley, New York (1996)
4. Creeger, M.: Cloud computing: an overview. ACM Queue **7**(5), 2 (2009)
5. Cully, B., Lefebvre, G., Meyer, D., Feeley, M., Hutchinson, N., Warfield, A.: Remus: high availability via asynchronous virtual machine replication. In: Proceedings of the USENIX Symposium on Networked Systems Design and Implementation, pp. 161–174 (2008)
6. Fu, S.: Failure-aware resource management for high-availability computing clusters with distributed virtual machines. J. Parallel Distrib. Comput. **70**(4), 384–393 (2010)
7. Robinson, G., Narin, A., Elleman, C.: Using Amazon Web Services for disaster recovery. http://media.amazonwebservices.com/AWS_Disaster_Recovery.pdf. Accessed October 2014
8. Gray, J., Siewiorek, D.P.: High-availability computer systems. Computer **24**(9), 39–48 (1991)
9. Jamshidi, P., Ahmad, A., Pahl, C.: Cloud migration research: a systematic review. IEEE Trans. Cloud Comput. **1**(2), 142–157 (2013)
10. Kandukuri, B.R., Paturi, V.R., Rakshit, A.: Cloud security issues. In: IEEE International Conference on Services Computing, SCC 2009, pp. 517–520 (2009)
11. King, R.P., Halim, N., Garcia-Molina, H., Polyzois, C.A.: Management of a remote backup copy for disaster recovery. ACM Trans. Database Syst. (TODS) **16**(2), 338–368 (1991)

12. Ladin, R., Liskov, B., Shrira, L., Ghemawat, S.: Providing high availability using lazy replication. ACM Trans. on Comput. Syst. (TOCS) **10**(4), 360–391 (1992)
13. Lewis, P.: A high-availability cluster for Linux. Linux J. **64** (1999)
14. Lumpp, T., Schneider, J., Holtz, J., Mueller, M., Lenz, N., Biazetti, A., Petersen, D.: From high availability and disaster recovery to business continuity solutions. IBM Syst. J. **47**(4), 605–619 (2008)
15. Microsoft: High availability and disaster recovery for SQL Server in Azure virtual machines (2014). http://msdn.microsoft.com/en-us/library/azure/jj870962.aspx. Accessed 12 June 2014
16. MySQL: Replication with global transaction identifiers. http://dev.mysql.com/doc/refman/5.6/en/replication-gtids.html
17. Openstack Wiki: Openstack disaster recovery solution. https://wiki.openstack.org/wiki/DisasterRecovery
18. Openswan: Openswan official website. https://www.openswan.org/
19. Pacitti, E., Özsu, M.T., Coulon, C.: Preventive multi-master replication in a cluster of autonomous databases. In: Kosch, H., Böszörményi, L., Hellwagner, H. (eds.) Euro-Par 2003. LNCS, vol. 2790, pp. 318–327. Springer, Heidelberg (2003)
20. Pahl, C., Jamshidi, P.: Software architecture for the cloud – a roadmap towards control-theoretic, model-based cloud architecture. In: Weyns, D., Mirandola, R., Crnkovic, I. (eds.) ECSA 2015. LNCS, vol. 9278, pp. 212–220. Springer, Heidelberg (2015). doi:10.1007/978-3-319-23727-5_17
21. Pahl, C., Xiong, H.: Migration to PaaS clouds - migration process and architectural concerns. In: IEEE International Symposium on the Maintenance and Evolution of Service-Oriented and Cloud-Based Systems (MESOCA 2013), pp. 86–91 (2013)
22. Pahl, C., Xiong, H., Walshe, R.: A comparison of on-premise to cloud migration approaches. In: Lau, K.-K., Lamersdorf, W., Pimentel, E. (eds.) ESOCC 2013. LNCS, vol. 8135, pp. 212–226. Springer, Heidelberg (2013)
23. Rajagopalan, S., Cully, B., O'Connor, R., Warfield, A.: Secondsite: disaster tolerance as a service. In: ACM SIGPLAN Notices, vol. 47, pp. 97–108. ACM (2012)
24. Sapate, S., Ramteke, M.: Survey on comparative analysis of database replication techniques. Int. J. IT Eng. Appl. Sci. Res. (IJIEASR) **2**(3), 72–80 (2013)
25. Schmidt, K.: High Availability and Disaster Recovery. Springer, Heidelberg (2006)
26. Severalnines: ClusterControl for MySql Galera tutorial. http://www.severalnines.com/clustercontrol-mysql-galera-tutorial
27. Vmware: vCenter site recovery manager 5.5 (2014). http://www.vmware.com/files/pdf/products/SRM/VMware_vCenter_Site_Recovery_Manager_5.5.pdf
28. Wiesmann, M., Pedone, F., Schiper, A., Kemme, B., Alonso, G.: Database replication techniques: a three parameter classification. In: Proceedings of the 19th IEEE Symposium on Reliable Distributed Systems, SRDS 2000, pp. 206–215 (2000)
29. Wikipedia: Business continuity planning. http://en.wikipedia.org/wiki/Business_continuity_planning#Business_impact_analysis_.28BIA.29
30. Wikipedia: Virtual private network. http://en.wikipedia.org/wiki/Virtual_private_network
31. Wood, T., Cecchet, E., Ramakrishnan, K., Shenoy, P., Van Der Merwe, J., Venkataramani, A.: Disaster recovery as a cloud service: Economic benefits & deployment challenges. In: Proceedings of the 2nd USENIX Conference on Hot Topics in Cloud Computing, p. 8 (2010)
32. Zerto: Zerto virtual replication. http://www.zerto.com/
33. Zhang, W.: Linux virtual server for scalable network services. In: Ottawa Linux Symposium (2000)

An OpenStack-Based Implementation of a Volunteer Cloud

Salvatore Distefano[1,2]([✉]), Giovanni Merlino[3,4], and Antonio Puliafito[3]

[1] Social and Urban Computing Group, Kazan Federal University, Kazan, Russia
s_distefano@it.kfu.ru
[2] Department of Mathematics and Computer Science,
University of Messina, Messina, Italy
sdistefano@unime.it
[3] Department of Engineering, University of Messina, Messina, Italy
{gmerlino,apuliafito}@unime.it
[4] Department of Engineering, University of Catania, Catania, Italy
giovanni.merlino@dieei.unict.it

Abstract. Recent developments in Cloud computing technology provide capabilities for an extensible, reliable, effective and dynamic infrastructure to technology-enabled enterprises, in order to efficiently leverage (or even monetize) their on-premise equipment. Furthermore, the virtualization technologies powering the Cloud revolution expand their reach by the day, and are nowadays commonly available, nearly household, capabilities. In this light, the intersection between volunteering and Cloud computing may bring massive and ubiquitous compute power for IaaS users. For instance, scientists and researchers, as a category of very demanding users, may benefit from such an enlargement of the pool of resources to tap into for high complexity computational workloads and big data problems without concern for the setup and maintenance of the underlying infrastructure. We have investigated this concept in the past under the Cloud@Home project, aimed at implementing a desktop-powered Cloud. In this paper we propose a blueprint of a Cloud@Home implementation starting from OpenStack, a well-known platform for Cloud solutions, a de-facto standard with variety of features, high interoperability and Open Source support. The reference, layered architecture and the preliminary implementation of a Cloud@Home framework based on OpenStack are discussed in the paper.

Keywords: Cloud · Volunteer computing · Crowd computing · Software Defined Infrastructure

1 Introduction

Cloud computing success is mainly due to capabilities such as the provisioning of a wide range of flexible, customizable, resilient and cost effective infrastructure, platforms and applications, on-demand, QoS guaranteed, as a service.

© Springer International Publishing Switzerland 2016
A. Celesti and P. Leitner (Eds.): ESOCC 2015 Workshops, CCIS 567, pp. 389–403, 2016.
DOI: 10.1007/978-3-319-33313-7_30

Cloud is already an effective technology, plenty of real (business) applications and services have been developed so far and a new digital economy has arisen from it, focused on the utility perspective considering IT resources as commodities, to be provided as a service according to customer needs and wills [12]. Despite the overwhelming success and widespread adoption of Cloud and similar/related paradigms such as service oriented engineering, software defined and virtualized ecosystems, ubiquitous and autonomic computing, there is still room for improving and extending them with novel ideas, towards new directions.

One such avenue is crowdsourcing, as well as resource sharing or volunteer approaches, aimed at exploiting the power and the wisdom of crowds, involving people that may (voluntarily) contribute to a given IT-related project or application by sharing their own (computing, storage, network, sensing, data) resources. Specifically, to adopt this idea in Cloud computing contexts, we have to think about a Cloud system as a collector of resources shared by single contributors, companies, and/or communities contributing to the assembly of an IT infrastructure, bottom-up, following the *volunteer computing* approach [1,9]. This is at the basis of *Cloud@Home* [7], a project aimed at implementing a volunteer Cloud infrastructure on top of resources shared (for free or by charge) by their owners or administrators and to provide those to users through an on-demand, service-oriented interface.

The main challenge of Cloud@Home is to deal with volunteer contributions, requiring mechanisms both at node and at Cloud-infrastructure level for engaging, enrolling, indexing, discovering and managing the contributed nodes as a whole. In particular, the node churn issue due to random and unpredictable join and leave of contributors should be properly addressed. The goal of this paper is to propose a solution to deal with all the above issues at different levels. To this purpose, a reference architecture including the modules of the Cloud@Home software stack providing mechanisms to address these issues is specified. Then, in the design of the Cloud@Home stack, we start from existing solutions already in place and working. In particular we base our implementation on a well-know open source software for creating and managing private and public Clouds, OpenStack [17], a de-facto standard Cloud management software. This way, existing and effective solutions for most of Cloud computing issues, such as security, privacy, accounting, indexing, could be used as they are or anyway extended to the problem at hand, i.e. dealing with the contributor dynamics.

With regard to the existing literature, Cloud@Home was the first and foremost attempt towards a volunteer-based Cloud infrastructure. After that, the idea of volunteer Clouds emerged as one of the most interesting topic in Cloud computing, as for example in [6] where a form of dispersed Cloud or "nebulas" based on voluntarily shared resources is proposed mainly for testing environments. Another interesting attempt in such direction is BoincVM [16], a platform based on BOINC to harness volunteer resources into a computing infrastructure for CPU intensive scientific applications. In P2P Cloud [3,11] a totally distributed, peer-to-peer paradigm is proposed to gather and manage a volunteer Cloud infrastructure. Similarly, Crowd computing [13,14] aims at implementing a computing infrastructure involving "crowds" of contributors, in a crowdsourcing approach. They mainly share their "power", i.e., their computing nodes as in volunteer computing [1] or devices as in participatory, opportunistic and mobile crowdsensing approaches [10]. Anyway, the client-server model is a limitation on the suitability of these paradigms to Cloud computing scenarios.

These works mainly propose new approaches, based on resource sharing, contribution and crowdsourcing, providing some high level directions for dealing with related issues. None of them gets into implementation details. In this paper we go a step beyond towards a real and effective implementation of a volunteer, P2P, desktop Cloud infrastructure, proposing a software stack based on OpenStack, properly customized and extended to deal with contribution issues. To the best of our knowledge this is the first actual attempt in such direction, e.g., a Cloud@Home OpenStack.

Details on that are provided in the remainder of the paper, organized as follows: Sect. 2 provides an overview of preliminary concepts, i.e. Cloud@Home and Openstack. Then, Sect. 3 proposes the Cloud@Home reference architecture identifying main functionalities and modules. The Cloud@Home software stack design though OpenStack is described in Sect. 4, while details on its preliminary implementation are provided in Sect. 5. Some remarks and objectives for future work are reported in Sect. 6.

2 Overview

2.1 Cloud@Home

The Cloud@Home goal is to use *"domestic"* computing resources to build desktop Clouds made of voluntarily contributed resources. Therefore, following the volunteer computing wave [1], across Grid computing and desktop Grids [2,5], we think about desktop Cloud platforms able to engage and retain contributors for providing virtual (processing, storage, networking, sensing) resources as a service, in the Infrastructure as a Service (IaaS) fashion. This novel, revised view of Cloud computing could perfectly fit with private and community needs, but our real, long-term challenge is to exploit it in hybrid and especially in business contexts towards public deployment models.

On this premise, the overall scenario we have in mind is highlighted in Fig. 1. Three actors are identified: the *C@H service provider*, building up the Cloud infrastructure by engaging contributing nodes; *contributors* that share their resources; and *end users*, interacting with the Cloud as customers, submitting requests to "rent" (virtual) resources from C@H.

This way, the infrastructure is mainly made of contributing nodes shared by their owners or admins, acting as Cloud@Home contributors. The C@H provider gathers and collects these resources, managing, abstracting and virtualizing them to be provided as a service, through a specific C@H management system. These resources are therefore provided to end users as virtual ones (machines, storage)

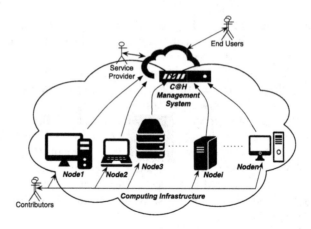

Fig. 1. Cloud@Home scenario.

by the management system. There are no specific boundaries between contributor and end user roles, just different duties, and it is possible a contributor is at the same time end user and vice-versa.

2.2 OpenStack

OpenStack is an OpenSource Cloud computing platform mostly used for development and deployment of IaaS solutions, managed by a non-profit foundation and supported by more than 200 companies and 10,000 community members in

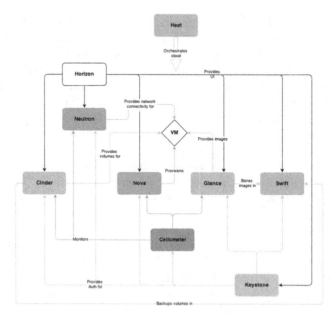

Fig. 2. OpenStack: conceptual architecture.

nearly 100 countries. OpenStack is highly flexible since it supports most of the existing hypervisors thus enabling a variety of virtualization modes and usage scenarios. OpenStack features a growing number of components to build up its services, a core subset of which is depicted in Fig. 2, where arrows describe the relationships and interactions among subsystems. To implement a fully working Cloud environment, to deploy each and every of the depicted components is not strictly required. In particular Swift and Cinder are needed only if object and block storage services are required somehow for the users of the cloud. Same considerations apply for Horizon, if users may do without a Web UI and may recur to a CLI instead of a graphical dashboard. Heat is needed insofar orchestration services are required, and Ceilometer only for billing purposes or other monitoring duties. That leaves only Keystone, Glance, Nova and Neutron as core services, where Keystone provides authentication and authorization facilities, Neutron is in charge of all the networking mechanisms and Nova of the instantiation and lifecycle management of compute virtual machines. Glance provides Nova VMs with the requested images.

3   Cloud@Home Reference Architecture

To implement the Cloud@Home vision, a specific solution framework is required. It has to deal with the interactions among the volunteered resources as well as with the desktop Cloud management and other (federated) Clouds, taking into account their contribution dynamics. Indeed, a contributor can join and leave the system randomly and unpredictably, thus implying node churning. Therefore, a solution should be adaptive to such random events, providing elastic mechanisms promptly reacting to the latter in a transparent way for the end users. Furthermore, *interoperability* [4] is one of the issue to address in Cloud@Home, as well as placement and orchestration also taking into account end-users QoS requirements on resource provisioning.

Apart the basic fuctionalities, the main (non-functional) properties Cloud@Home services have to provide are:

- scalability - the impact of a variation in the number of contributing resources on the performance and the other QoS requirements agreed by the parties has to be hided by the system to the customer;
- adaptability - churn management: the algorithm has to be able to detect changes in the logic organization of nodes and to react to these changes in real-time;
- elasticity - the algorithm has to specify reconfiguration policies to optimize the Cloud@Home infrastructure after contributors' join and leave;
- dependability, resilience, fault tolerance, security and privacy - to deal with the degradation of performance and availability of the whole infrastructure due to unpredictable join and leave of contributors, redundancy techniques and job status tracking and monitoring have to be developed, as well as security

and privacy mechanisms since virtualization provides isolation of services, but does not provide protection from local access, i.e. insider threats and abuses.

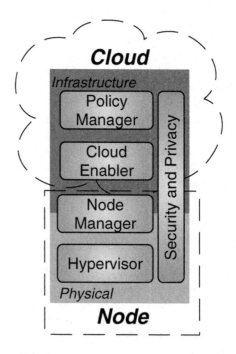

Fig. 3. The Cloud@Home stack reference architecture.

According to these (functional and non-functional) requirements, and based on the well-known Cloud service layering [8,15], the Cloud@Home stack reference architecture shown in Fig. 3 has been identified. Specifically, the Cloud@Home *physical* layer is composed of a *"Cloud"* of geographically distributed contributing nodes. They provide to the upper layers the (physical and virtual) resources for implementing the Cloud@Home infrastructure services. It usually includes the operating system, protocols, packages, libraries, compilers, programming and development environments, etc. Moreover, to adequately manage physical resources a *virtual resource manager* has to be installed into the contributing node for virtualizing physical resources. Abstraction and virtualization of physical resources provide a uniform, interoperable and customizable view of Cloud services and resources. This way, at infrastructure layer, the Cloud@Home stack groups mechanisms and tools for virtualizing physical (computing, storage, sensing, networking, etc.) resources into *virtual resources* (VR).

The *infrastructure* layer provides mechanisms, policies and tools for locally and globally managing the Cloud resources to implement the Cloud@Home service. It mainly provides end users with facilities to manage the Cloud@Home system. Indeed, the infrastructure layer is in charge of the resource and service management (enrolling, discovery, allocation, coordination, monitoring, placement, scheduling, etc.) from the Cloud perspective. It also provides enhanced mechanisms and policies for improving the quality of service (QoS), dealing with churning, managing complex/multiple resource request in an orchestrated way, interacting and brokering with other Clouds.

Specifically, this implements a two-level *Software Defined Infrastructure* (SDI) model, where basic mechanisms and tools at *"data plane"* are provided to the *"control plane"* for implementing advanced management facilities, ranging from orchestration to QoS and churn management.

The core modules of the Cloud@Home Management System are reported in the layered model of Fig. 3. A security and privacy cross-layer module is included into this Cloud@Home reference architecture to provide mechanisms addressing related issues. The core module deployment in either the contributing node or in the infrastructure side is also highlighted and detailed in the following according to the deployment, bottom up.

3.1 Node-Side

Considering a generic Cloud service built on top of a contributing resource, the node-side Cloud@Home framework provides tools for managing virtual resources considering, on one hand, contribution policies from contributors and, on the other, requests and requirements coming from the higher Cloud side. To this purpose, two modules are identified and deployed on the contributing node, at the bottom of the stack: the Hypervisor and the Node Mananager.

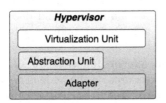

Fig. 4. The Cloud@Home hypervisor modules.

The *Hypervisor* is a core component of Cloud@Home since it introduces layers of abstraction and mechanisms for virtualization in the contributing resource. It mainly provides the primitives, the API for managing a virtual resource. In the case of processing resources, it is the Virtual Machine Manager while in the case of storage resources it could be a distributed file system module, or for sensors and actuators it corresponds to the SAaaS Hypervisor [7]. It is composed of thee main building blocks, i.e. Adapter, Abstraction Unit and Virtualization Unit as reported in Fig. 4.

At the bottom there is the *Adapter*, which plays several distinct roles, such as converting the high-level directives in native commands, processing requests for reconfiguration of the resource and providing mechanisms for establishing an out-of-band channel to the system, for direct interaction with the resources.

The *Abstraction Unit* operates on top of the Adapter, mainly implementing abstraction of underlying physical-hardware resources towards open and well-known standards and interfaces, also dealing with networking issues. The *Virtualization Unit*, name after the Virtual Machine Monitor to highlight its role as a manager of the lifecycle of virtualized resource instances. This includes APIs and functionalities for virtual instance creation, reaping and repurposing, as well as for boot- (defined statically) and run-time (dynamically) parameters discovery and tuning in accordance with contextualization requests. It can work either directly on the Adapter in the case the resource provides generic, standard, abstracted interfaces by itself, or on the Abstraction Unit otherwise.

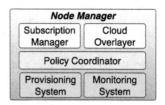

Fig. 5. The Cloud@Home node manager modules.

The other component of the Cloud@Home stack deployed into a node is the *Node Manager*, which can be considered as the brain of a node. Indeed, it implements a first step towards a volunteer Cloud merging local and global mechanisms and policies. It is the bridge between virtual nodes and the Cloud, allowing the node to join a Cloud@Home to expose its resources as services. This is therefore implemented in a collaborative and decentralized way, interacting with neighboring nodes and adopting autonomic self-managing approaches.

This way, the main blocks composing a Node Manager are showed in Fig. 5. The *Provisioning System* implements functions for allocating, managing, migrating and destroying a virtual resource on the node. The *Monitoring System* allows to take under control the local resources. Together with the resource provider they establishes whether a virtual resource allocation request can be satisfied or should be rejected, also alerting the higher Cloud level on crash or shortage of resources in the node.

The *Policy Coordinator* selects and enforces the node management strategy, taking into account Cloud policies coming from the higher level and contribution directives, based on the current status of the node. To perform this task, the Policy Coordinator interacts with the Cloud layer and with the Subscription Manager, coordinating their inputs. Specifically, the *Subscription Manager* is in charge of storing and carrying out the subscriptions of the node to all the Cloud@Home it contributes, since a contributor can be involved in more than one Cloud@Home. For each of them a contribution profile should be specified, also allowing the system to choose the Cloud@Home to contribute in case of overlapped incoming requests from different sources. Moreover, it also locally manages the credits assigned by the different Cloud credit reward systems (if any), transferring and exchanging them as required.

Then, the *Cloud Overlayer* provides mechanisms and tools for joining and leaving a Cloud@Home. From a node perspective the Cloud@Home can be considered as an overlay-opportunistic-P2P network on top of the node resources. A possible way for implementing such mechanism could be through distributed hash tables or similar peer to peer approaches that also provide the concept of neighborhood as well as enrolment, indexing and discovery facilities. This way the Cloud Overlayer is just a client for such kind of systems, also allowing to interact with the high-levele management system, if required. Anyway, different implementations are possible, by choosing the P2P Cloud one the Cloud@Home system is autonomous and can also provide basic Cloud functionalities without requiring advanced, high level mechanisms.

3.2 Cloud Side

This way, on the Cloud side there are mainly mechanisms and tools for managing the Cloud infrastructure as a whole. To this purpose a Software Defined Infrastructure approach has been adopted, splitting basic Cloud mechanisms and functionalities from policies.

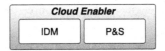

Fig. 6. The Cloud@Home cloud enabler modules.

At the bottom, the *Cloud Enabler* could be considered as the counterpart, server/Cloud-side, of the Cloud Overlayer on the node, implementing basic mechanism and tools for the (centralized) management of the Cloud@Home infrastructure. Its main modules are depicted in Fig. 6: the *Indexing, Discovery and Monitoring (IDM)* service and the *Placement and Scheduling (P&S)* one. The former is in charge of enrolling, indexing, and monitoring contributing nodes. The P&S is a peripheral resource broker of the Cloud@Home infrastructure, allocating a resource to an incoming request, moreover it is in charge of moving and managing services and data (for example VM migrations).

On top of the basic infrastructure mechanisms, advanced ones are implemented in the *Policy Manager*. It is composed of the 5 modules shown in Fig. 7. The Resource Engine is the hearth of Cloud@Home, acing as a resource coordinator at Cloud infrastructure layer. To achieve such goal, the resource engine adopts a hierarchical policy in synergy with the P&S, also interacting with all the other Policy Manager components.

The *Incentive Mechanism* aims at increasing the availability and reliability of volunteered resources by assigning credit and reward or penalties to contributing nodes in a P2P-volunteer fashion. The *SLA Manager* enforces the SLAs negotiated and agreed by the parties (providers and end users), if any. It aims

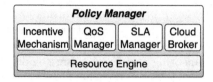

Fig. 7. The Cloud@Home policy manager modules.

at implementing more reliable services on an infrastructure made up of sensors contributed on an otherwise just best-effort basis. Therefore it also specifies the Cloud policies to be actuated in case of SLA violations. The *QoS Manager* provides the service quality management framework at single Cloud level, through metrics and means to measure the underlying Cloud@Home infrastructure, directly interacting with the IDM service and contributing nodes through the latter.

The Cloud broker collects and manages information about the available Clouds and the services they provide (both *functional* and *non-functional* parameters, such as QoS, costs and reliability, *request formats' specifications* for Cloud@Home-foreign Clouds translations, etc.). Moreover, the Cloud broker collaborates with the resource engine to fulfil resource discovery, becoming *"interclouds"*.

4   Cloud@Home OpenStack-Based Architecture

In our effort to extend OpenStack to support the Cloud@Home volunteer-powered Cloud model, we map here the concepts and the modules explored in the previous sections in light of the current status of the OpenStack architecture.

In particular, following a derived logical architecture of Nova as depicted in Fig. 8, starting from the bottom up, we may essentially identify in LibVirt (or other Nova plugin-enabled VMM) the role of the Cloud@Home Hypervisor. Apart from the Hypervisor, also the Queue is depicted in green, to highlight components which are part of the architecture, but not specific of the OpenStack framework. Magenta-colored blocks are instead Nova-specific components. Nova-api, nova-console, nova-consoleauth and nova-cert are not involved in the mapping, because those are either interfaces (-api), authorization-related (-consoleauth for access to the console of any instance, and -cert for client certificates), or specific to certain technologies (-console, as proxy for Xen-based consoles).

The Cloud@Home Provisioning System would be covered by functionalities exposed by the Nova Compute service and the Monitoring system would map to a monitoring subsystem for nodes, which we'll describe later on in the following. It is important to remark that another monitoring subsystem, Ceilometer, is available for OpenStack, but in a different role, i.e., metering for billing purposes, and thus focused on VM-relevant metrics, not on the health of the hosting subsystem, i.e., Compute nodes.

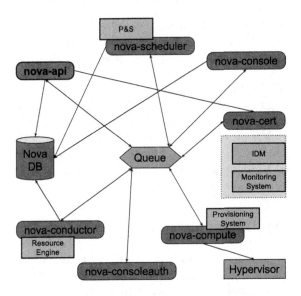

Fig. 8. The Cloud@Home logical architecture.

The Cloud@Home Policy Coordinator instead is not easy to map to the current OpenStack architecture, as it implies some node-mandated restrictions to contribution are in place and need to be mediated with Cloud-level directives, even if a simplified scheme may just be devised where the contributor statically chooses certain constraints, e.g., both temporal ones and resource quotas, and let the subscription phase expose the subset of instance flavors compatible with those, and switch node (or specific resources) availability on or off accordingly. The same considerations apply to the Subscription Manager, which entail for a node to potentially be part of multiple Clouds, and to the Cloud Overlayer as well, in this case implying a different, Controller-less (or distributed Controller), flavor of OpenStack, thus relying on a fully P2P topology.

Within the Cloud@Home Cloud Enabler, the IDM essentially enables the enrollment of volunteering nodes to the Cloud and should actually "enable" nodes to be exploited as Compute ones, i.e., should provision the dynamic pool of resources by deploying essential node-side services, e.g., Nova Compute, on the remote hosts. The Cloud@Home P&S may be considered more or less overlapping with the Nova Scheduler, and the Resource Engine may thus play the role of a (generalized) Nova Conductor. Upwards the Resource Engine, we may consider all components outside the scope of the current (and announced) OpenStack architectural choices and efforts, thus material for future investigations.

A note has to be made about our neglecting more details about the storage/networking subsystems and the corresponding workflows: this is intentional, as our design of the Cloud@Home framework on top of OpenStack is to be considered either totally transparent (in the case of networking) or not relevant, as with storage, considering the choice remains the same, i.e., node-local images or volumes vs.

remote ones, where the only difference lies in the expected performance of remote image/volume-backed instances, thus the need to warn the user about the implications of such a choice when served with volunteered nodes, and to craft suitable SLAs accordingly.

Moreover, while the Scheduler may be left as is, and the policies just implemented by resorting to suitable (reliability/churn-aware) filters and weights, further investigation may point to a more granular mechanism under the guise of a hierarchy of schedulers or, conversely, a specific segregation of the pool of nodes in suitable aggregates, e.g., OpenStack *availability zones* or possibly even *cells*, the latter oriented to more granular pooling, but unfortunately not supporting inter-cell migration yet.

5   Preliminary Implementation

In an effort to not lose generality of the solution where feasible, we envisioned volunteering nodes running heterogeneous *host* Operating Systems (e.g., Windows, MacOS, Linux), thus leading to a nested approach to virtualization, where a VM gets deployed, in the host OS-native (or otherwise preferred) VMM, as Compute Node, in turn able to accomodate the instantiation of either fully virtualized (e.g., Linux KVM-based) VMs as user-requested instances, or even (better) containerized ones, by means of, e.g., Nova LXC/LXD plugin. It is now more clear that the monitoring system needs to actually track the status and health of first-level, remotely hosted, VMs, as exemplified above.

From a deployment perspective, which means that the IDM would operate on what would be abstracted as *remote nodes* but actually consisting of "virtualized" bare metal the host OS VMM (and a suitable virtual network) exposes. We believe Fuel may be a suitable candidate for such automatic deployment and provisioning of the additional compute nodes, as already one of the community-blessed frameworks for whole OpenStack instances deployment on bare metal. In particular, whereas Fuel is especially meant for deployment of an instance from scratch, the setup of additional nodes to any existing (up and running) instance is still possible, as long as it has already been deployed by Fuel itself, in order to have the deployment recipe ready and let the Fuel monitoring subsystem track the availability of the underlying resources, i.e., the virtualized bare metal.

Moreover, Fuel comprises a dashboard for visual point-and-click administration, but its core, Nailgun, exposes REST APIs and a CLI, so interaction on the side of the administrator, graphical or through the APIs, is actually not required after the setup of a Cloud instance by means of an initial configuration phase or the upload of a template.

The node-side core of the Subscription Manager may thus consist in an out-of-band, minimal service running on the host OS, i.e., a bootstrapping executable, which upon first execution: starts up the first-level VM and sets up one TAP-based GRE tunnel between the VMM bridge and each endpoint in the Cloud, corresponding to any unique and essential centralized service behind such endpoint, e.g., at least the Nova Compute in charge of the node, as well as the Neutron Controller, if available on separate machines. Obviously this step includes registering both VM and (at least a control) channel for execution at boot-time for subsequent reboots, as well as to be always-on, via the relevant OS-dependent VMM and networking facilities.

In particular with regard to the *control* channel for command streams and monitoring services, we modeled such a facility as WebSocket-based. *Web Application Messaging Protocol (WAMP)*, our choice of asynchronous transport and delivery system for message-encapsulated commands, is a sub-protocol of Web-Socket, in its turn a standard HTTP-based protocol providing a full-duplex TCP communication channel over a single HTTP-based persistent connection. WAMP specifies a communication semantic for messages sent over WebSocket, and is natively based on WebSocket (even if it also allows for different transport protocols), providing both publish/subscribe (pub/sub) and remote procedure call (RPC) mechanisms. A WAMP router is responsible of brokering pub/sub messages and routing remote calls, together with results/errors.

Figure 9 shows the C@H node-side architecture. The *Subscription Manager* interacts with the Cloud by connecting to a centralized WAMP router through a WebSocket full-duplex channel, sending and receiving data to/from the Cloud and executing commands provided by the users via the Cloud. Such commands are mostly related to the host-level Virtual Machine Monitor subsystem, and in particular about monitoring its state and ensuring the first-level VM is up and running at all times. Moreover, a set of WebSocket tunneling libraries allows the Subscription Manager to also act as a WebSocket reverse tunneling server, connecting to a specific WebSocket server running in the Cloud. This enables internal (host-level) services to be directly accessed by external users through the WebSocket tunnel whose incoming traffic is automatically forwarded to the relevant resident processes, e.g., hypervisor services such as the remote video console, either unmediated or through a specific local proxy service.

The aforementioned GRE tunnels, needed for communication with centralized services, get instantiated over WebSocket-based reverse tunnels which get activated on demand. Outgoing traffic is redirected to the WebSocket tunnel and eventually reaches the relevant Cloud endpoints.

As soon as the setup of the "bare metal" is ready, the Subscription Manager should let the IDM (i.e., Nailgun) mark the new node as ready to be deployed as soon as reachable by polling for its presence through Nailgun APIs, and afterward request the IDM to set its role as a Compute node, and at last trigger deployment of the modifications to the Cloud due to the node just being appended.

Now we can see that Fuel may also tackle churn by an automated node "evacuation" process, i.e., migrating VMs, when some form of advance warning is conveyed from the volunteer to the Cloud ("the node is going to shut down in 10 min from now"), or otherwise instantiating suitable replacements in place of (abruptly) missing ones. Evacuation is an already available primitive in Open-Stack, but it is currently meant to be operated (manually or via scripts) by an administrator. We envision then the design of an extension to Nailgun which monitors the centrally available logs to react on the event of one or more nodes, either signaling imminent churn or outright gone missing, with reaction set as a full evacuation workflow.

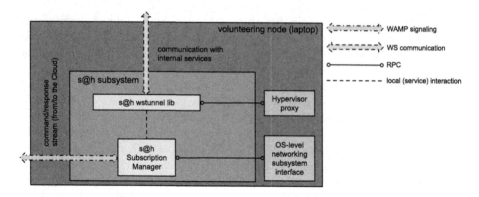

Fig. 9. Stack@Home node-side architecture.

6   Conclusions

In this paper, a novel Cloud paradigm is proposed merging volunteer-crowd computing with service oriented infrastructure. It shifts the traditional Cloud paradigm enabled by the availability of datacenters and server farms a step forward into an ecosystem able to connect any device or node contributing to a complex IT infrastructure by sharing its processing, storage, networking and/or sensing resources. To implement the Cloud@Home paradigm thus proposed, a reference architecture of a software stack has been first defined, and then mapped on top of the OpenStack framework. In the design of the Cloud@Home stack we chose to start from the de-facto standard for IaaS Cloud frameworks, OpenStack, adapting and customizing related modules to the volunteer contribution context. This allowed us to demonstrate the feasibility of the Cloud@Home vision, leveraging off-the-shelf, open source components. Further efforts are thus required to implement a full fledged Cloud@Home system, which have to mainly manage node churn, on one hand improving node reliability by motivating/retaining contributors through specific incentive mechanisms, on the other by implementing mechanisms for dealing with service level agreements and related quality of service guarantees to meet end user/customer requirements.

References

1. Anderson, D.P., Fedak, G.: The computational and storage potential of volunteer computing. In: CCGRID 2006, pp. 73–80 (2006)
2. Andrade, N., Cirne, W., Brasileiro, F., Roisenberg, P.: OurGrid: an approach to easily assemble grids with equitable resource sharing. In: Feitelson, D.G., Rudolph, L., Schwiegelshohn, U. (eds.) JSSPP 2003. LNCS, vol. 2862, pp. 61–86. Springer, Heidelberg (2003)
3. Babaoglu, O., Marzolla, M.: The people's cloud. IEEE Spectr. **51**(10), 50–55 (2014)

4. Buyya, R., Ranjan, R., Calheiros, R.N.: InterCloud: utility-oriented federation of cloud computing environments for scaling of application services. In: Hsu, C.-H., Yang, L.T., Park, J.H., Yeo, S.-S. (eds.) ICA3PP 2010, Part I. LNCS, vol. 6081, pp. 13–31. Springer, Heidelberg (2010)
5. Cappello, F., Djilali, S., Fedak, G., Herault, T., Magniette, F., Néri, V., Lodygensky, O.: Computing on large-scale distributed systems: xtrem web architecture, programming models, security, tests and convergence with grid. Future Gener. Comput. Syst. **21**(3), 417–437 (2005)
6. Chandra, A., Weissman, J.: Nebulas: using distributed voluntary resources to build clouds. In: Proceedings of the 2009 Conference on Hot Topics in Cloud Computing, p. 2. USENIX Association (2009)
7. Cunsolo, V., Distefano, S., Puliafito, A., Scarpa, M.: Volunteer computing and desktop cloud: the cloud@home paradigm. In: 2009 Eighth IEEE International Symposium on Network Computing and Applications, NCA 2009, pp. 134–139, July 2009
8. Distefano, S., Cunsolo, V.D., Puliafito, A.: A taxonomic specification of Cloud@Home. In: Huang, D.-S., Zhang, X., Reyes García, C.A., Zhang, L. (eds.) ICIC 2010. LNCS, vol. 6216, pp. 527–534. Springer, Heidelberg (2010)
9. Fedak, G., Germain, C., Neri, V., Cappello, F.: Xtremweb: a generic global computing system. In: Proceedings of the First IEEE/ACM International Symposium on Cluster Computing and the Grid, pp. 582–587 (2001)
10. Ganti, R.K., Ye, F., Lei, H.: Mobile crowdsensing: current state and future challenges. IEEE Commun. Mag. **49**(11), 32–39 (2011)
11. Graffi, K., Stingl, D., Gross, C., Nguyen, H., Kovacevic, A., Steinmetz, R.: Towards a p2p cloud: Reliable resource reservations in unreliable p2p systems. In: 2010 IEEE 16th International Conference on Parallel and Distributed Systems (ICPADS), pp. 27–34, December 2010
12. Kleinrock, L.: A vision for the internet. ST J. Res. **2**(1), 4–5 (2005)
13. Murray, D.G., Yoneki, E., Crowcroft, J., Hand, S.: The case for crowd computing. In: Proceedings of the Second ACM SIGCOMM Workshop on Networking, Systems, and Applications on Mobile Handhelds (MobiHeld 2010), NY, USA, pp. 39–44 (2010). http://doi.acm.org/10.1145/1851322.1851334
14. Parshotam, K.: Crowd computing: A literature review and definition. In: Proceedings of the South African Institute for Computer Scientists and Information Technologists Conference (SAICSIT 2013), NY, USA, pp. 121–130 (2013). http://doi.acm.org/10.1145/2513456.2513470
15. Mell, P., Grance, T.: The NIST Definition of Cloud Computing. NIST Special Publication 800–145, January 2014
16. Segal, B., Buncic, P., Quintas, D., Gonzalez, D., Harutyunyan, A., Rantala, J., Weir, D.: Building a volunteer cloud. In: Conferencia Latinoamericana de Computación de Alto Rendimiento., September 2009
17. The Openstack Community: OpenStack Cloud Software: open source software for building private and public clouds, November 2011. http://www.openstack.org/

Cloud Services Composition Through Semantically Described Patterns: A Case Study

Beniamino di Martino, Giuseppina Cretella[(✉)], and Antonio Esposito

Second University of Naples, Via Roma 29, Aversa, CE, Italy
beniamino.dimartino@unina.it,
{giuseppina.cretella,antonio.esposito}@unina2.it

Abstract. With the proliferation of Cloud services and the huge number of Cloud offers currently available in the IT market, it can be difficult for customers to understand which one fits their need. Patterns, if correctly applied to the design and development of Cloud applications, can ease programmers' burden and reduce errors and bugs in application implementation. In this paper we use a methodology, based on the semantic representation of Cloud patterns, Cloud services and applications, to support users in developing Cloud oriented software meeting their explicit requirements.

Keywords: Cloud computing · Services composition · Cloud patterns · Semantics · Ontology · OWL

1 Introduction

The Cloud Computing scenario is a plethora of always new and changing Cloud proposals, platforms and capabilities. Furthermore, each provider tends to use its own terminology in order to differentiate itself from others and try to gain new market shares. Thus, it can be difficult for users to clearly understand which services are more suitable for their requirements and needing. In such a situation, also portability and interoperability of Cloud applications and services is badly influenced, making it difficult to make services and resources from different providers to cooperate in order to provide specific functionalities. In this paper we show how, by using a semantic-based representation of Patterns, Cloud services and Virtual appliances, based on the work presented in [16,17,20], it is possible to describe a classical application and support users in deploying it to the Cloud. Such a uniform, integrated and machine-readable representation aims at supporting the migration of applications to the Cloud and at easing the procedures needed to port them across different platforms.

The paper is organized as follows: Sect. 2 reports related works and offers some insight on the technologies used in our representation; Sect. 3 briefly describes the methodology we have applied to the description of patterns and services; Sect. 4 describes the use case and the application of our methodology; finally, in Sect. 5 we report some consideration on the present work and address future directions of research.

© Springer International Publishing Switzerland 2016
A. Celesti and P. Leitner (Eds.): ESOCC 2015 Workshops, CCIS 567, pp. 404–418, 2016.
DOI: 10.1007/978-3-319-33313-7_31

2 State of the Art

The classification and categorization of Cloud Services has been the topic of many research efforts [12,13], which have tried to systematize their exposed functionalities, operations, parameters and service models. A freely navigable online taxonomy has been provided by the OpenCrowd [6] consortium, which categorizes Cloud Services according to both their service model (IaaS, PaaS or SaaS) and application context. Nevertheless the criteria followed to categorize each service are not clear, as well as the limitations and controls under which the taxonomy creation is performed. Machine readable standards for services' representation and orchestration have been proposed and approved: among these, remarkable results have been accomplished by the **Topology and Orchestration Specification for Cloud Applications** (TOSCA - an OASIS standard) and by the orchestration template language **HOT**, developed by **Openstack** [7] within the **HEAT** project. TOSCA describes both a topology of Cloud based web services, consisting in their components, relationships, and the processes that manage them, and the orchestration of such services. HOT is a new template format, compliant with the **CloudFormation** Template defined by Amazon, which details everything that is required for orchestration and it is written in YAML. A Comparison of such formats is available in [19]. Semantic based approaches have been considered and applied in order to overcome limits related to automated processing and reasoning, caused by differences in semantics and syntactic. A semantic ontology is a formal, machine readable knowledge representation of a set of domain-related concepts and the relationships between them. It is used to reason about the properties of that domain and may be used to efficiently describe it by providing a shared vocabulary. The Web Ontology Language (OWL) [30] is a semantic mark-up language for publishing and sharing ontologies on the World Wide Web. A number of ontologies related to cloud computing emerged in the past few years. The authors of [10] provide an overview of Cloud Computing ontologies, their applications and focuses. Some ontologies are used to describe Cloud resources and services, classify the current services and pricing models or define new types of Cloud services [15,34]. Many research efforts have been carried-out to develop ontologies to achieve interoperability among different Cloud providers and their services: different solutions have been discussed in [32]. A remarkable result has been reached by the mOSAIC cloud ontology [31] developed for the mOSAIC platform [21]. Such an ontology has also been adopted by the IEEE P2302 Working Group (Intercloud) [4] for the development of the Intercloud Interoperability and Federation (SIIF). In [11] Bernstein and Vij present the InterCloud Directories and Exchanges mediator to allow collaboration among Cloud vendors which work on an ontology of Cloud Computing resources to deal with providers heterogeneity. In [33], the authors propose a resource selection mechanism based on the users' requirements regardless of where the services are hosted. Han and Sim [25] propose a Cloud service discovery system that uses Cloud ontologies, matchmaking and agents to determine the similarities between and among services. In [14] the author present an ontology-based discovery system to help users in deploying their virtual appliances on the most appropriate IaaS providers, based on their definition of QoS requirements.

2.1 Cloud Patterns

Design Patterns, defined as a general and reusable solution to a common and recurrent problem within a given context [23], have been used for a long time in software design and development. Their objective is to support developers in the design of their application, reducing design and developing time, known errors and bugs. As of today, a number of Design Patterns catalogues exist for several purposes, like ontology creation [5,24] and definition of SOA-oriented applications [8,22]. Recently both Cloud vendors and independent researchers have developed catalogues of Cloud Patterns, which define architectural solutions for designing and developing efficient applications on the Cloud. Remarkable examples are represented by the vendor specific catalogues developed by **Microsoft** [9] for **Azure** and by **Amazon** for **Amazon Web Services** [1]. Independent catalogues are instead retrievable at [2,3]. In the remainder of this paper, we will refer to the formers as to **Vendor Specific** patterns, since they are bound to the specific platform they have been designed for. The latter will be referred to as **Agnostic** patterns, since they provide generic solutions, which are not bound to a specific platform and are therefore more flexible and applicable to different targets. The use of Cloud patterns for the design, implementation and management of Cloud Applications has been widely discussed in the literature [26,27,29].

Our semantic representation focuses on Patterns, and Cloud Patterns in particular, because they can provide the necessary information to build an application's architecture on a platform and, in the case of vendor-specific ones, also to deploy such an application and configure the services which compose it. As an instance, suppose that a user needs to monitor a certain applications, which is running on a server owned by a Cloud Provider. Without knowing which provider hosts the server, it is possible to leverage an agnostic Cloud pattern to know in advance the components needed. The pattern **Usage Monitoring** provided in [3] defines the main components needed to monitor the usage of a simple Cloud Service, by providing access to a set of collected metrics via a portal, which collects information through a ad-hoc monitoring service. The different possible interactions between the user and the system are also described in the pattern, as shown in Fig. 1.

Since the agnostic pattern is extremely general, it is possible to determine a whole set of possible implementations for a certain Cloud platform, each one addressing a specific issue. For example, if we consider the AWS platform and we want to deploy a generic monitoring application on it, the **Monitoring Integration Pattern** describes the architecture and the components needed. As it is shown in Fig. 2, the pattern points out the Amazon services needed to deploy a monitoring application and also shows how to actually connect it to the services to monitor.

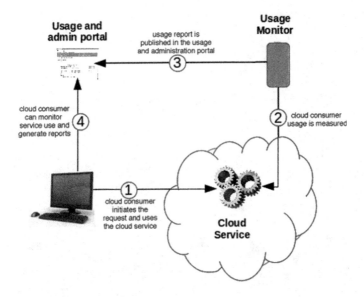

Fig. 1. Usage Monitoring pattern

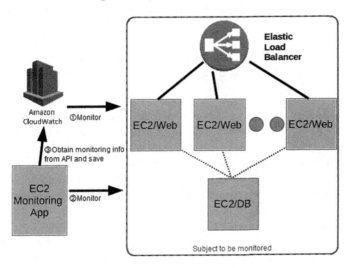

Fig. 2. Monitoring Integration Pattern

3 Methodology Description

In this section we briefly introduce the integrated representation of cloud services, appliances and cloud patterns we have devised. For a more detailed description of such a semantic representation, please refer to [16].

The model we use to describe Cloud related concept is based on a graph representation, which can be divided into five conceptual levels. Each level is

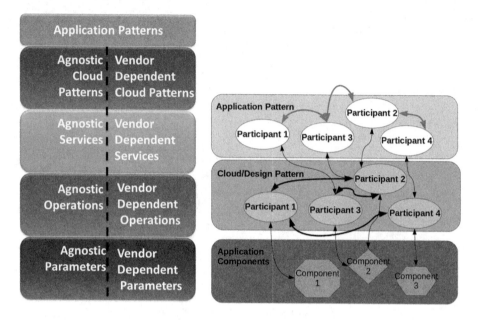

Fig. 3. The Conceptual Layers   **Fig. 4.** Application Pattern Composition

connected to the others through relationships, which enable the Cloud services discovery and composition. Figure 3 reports the layered organization of our representation:

- The **Parameters Level** contains the semantic description of the data types exchanged among Cloud services as input and output of their exposed operations.
- The **Operations Level** provides a syntactic description of the operations and functionalities exposed by a cloud service, in a machine readable format. In this way, it is possible to automatically retrieve information on how to call the service and interact with it.
- The **Services Level** provides a semantic annotation of Cloud services, which are organized according to a hierarchical classification described in [18]. Both vendor specific services and agnostic ones are represented at this level.
- The **Cloud Patterns Level** represents the semantic description of agnostic and vendor dependent Cloud patterns realized through an OWL representation. The patterns described here are composed of services delivered at infrastructure and platform level.
- The **Application Patterns Level** contains information on high level patterns, which describe entire applications with their components. Such patterns are general enough to be applied to different contexts, not necessarily Cloud related: in this way, it is possible to describe a generic application through one or more of Application patterns and then retrieve the components to be used for its implementation using the lower levels of our representation. The

organization of such components and how they should interact to achieve the required functionality in Cloud are described in the Cloud Pattern level.

3.1 Pattern Representation

The core element of our representation is the Application Pattern, which is used to describe general applications with their architectural details and information on the interactions taking place among their components. Application patterns can consist of multiple Design/Cloud patterns, and their components are connected through relationships expressing the equivalence between their participants and potential implementing services. As shown in Fig. 4, each of the application patterns' participants is connected to a Cloud/Design patterns' component: the matching is not necessarily one to one, since two elements of an Application pattern could be embodied by the same participant in a composing Cloud pattern and vice-versa. The same applies to the mapping between Cloud/Design patterns' participants and application components. In the semantic-based representation we use to describe Patterns, the participants are represented by individuals of the OWL class **ComponentTemplate**, while the connections between elements of different layers is obtained via instances of an object property **equivalent**. The connections existing within the same layer, representing workflow and interactions among patterns' participants, are represented via OWL-S [28] native constructs. In order to keep trace of the Patterns involved, of their interconnections and participants, each pattern is represented by an instance of the **Pattern** OWL class, while the object properties **hasParticipant** and **includes** are used to connect a pattern to its owned elements and to other contained patterns, respectively. The representation we use for pattern description is applied to both vendor specific and agnostic patterns, in order to have a homogeneous definition of them. The only difference between agnostic and vendor specific pattern representations resides in the nature of the application components used to realize them: vendor specific patterns will be connected to real components, while agnostic patterns will be composed of agnostic services.

3.2 Services Representation

As we have stated in Sect. 3.1, patterns are connected to application components which can be potentially used to implement them. In particular, since we are addressing a Cloud-oriented implementation, such components will be represented by Cloud Services or Virtual Appliances. Such components are defined in the Services layer, which contains both representation of vendor specific and agnostic services. Agnostic services act as place-holders for services' functionalities, and constitute a hierarchical architecture against which vendor services are annotated. In this way, equivalences between several services and their functionalities can be automatically inferred, through the explicitly declared equivalence with agnostic concepts and logical rules.

Physically, the agnostic services are all defined within a single **Cloud Service ontology**; vendor specific services are organized in self-contained ontologies, independent of each other, which import the agnostic one to annotate their services. The annotation is possible via a set of three object properties:

- **exactEquivalence** defines and exact correspondence between the vendor specific and agnostic service.
- **plugin** is used if a service has not a single correspondence, but it exposes functionalities offered by more than one service.
- **subsumes** represents the inverse situation of *plugin*, that is when the functionality exposed by a service can be obtained only by composing two or more different agnostic or vendor specific services.

All these are sub-properties of a more generic *equivalent* object property. The description of the input and output parameters of vendor specific services relies on OWL-S descriptions, which also leverage an underlying parameter ontology for the disambiguation of similar variable types and the support to logical inferences.

Figure 5 reports a schematic representation of the different ontologies involved in the services representation: the top **Agnostic Service Description Ontology** contains abstract descriptions of services, parameters, operations and resources, which are used as a common ground for comparisons among concepts described in the bottom **Cloud Provider Ontologies** and **Cloud Services OWL-S Descriptions** which, instead, contain platform-specific information. Our knowledge base contains a specific Cloud Provider ontology and OWL-S description for each Cloud platform (AWS, Azure, OpenStack, Google AppEngine, BlueMix) we have considered. Categorization of services is provided by the **Cloud Services Categorization Ontology**, which is used as a bridge between the agnostic descriptions and the OWL-S representations. The connections shown in the figure are obtained through OWL object properties which assess the equivalence among services, parameters and operations. Such properties enable the free navigation of the ontology framework, making it possible to rapidly determine how to replace one or more services and operation calls when necessary.

4   Case Study

The application of Design and Cloud pattern to software development can ease and speed-up programmers' work: common problems that can be encountered in designing and developing a new application can find immediate solutions in the appropriate pattern. The case study we propose in this section aims at showing how, with our semantic base representation, it is possible to effectively support programmers in choosing and applying the needed patterns to the development of a new Cloud-oriented software and/or the migration of an existing application to a Cloud platform.

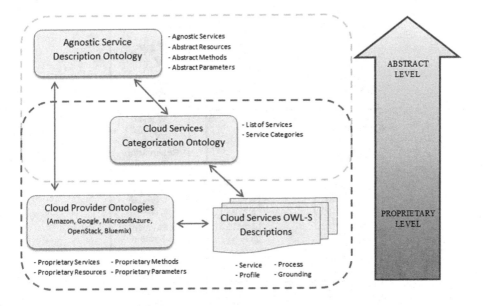

Fig. 5. Ontology Organization

Each of the steps we are showing is executed through a prototype graphical tool, which hides all the SPARQL queries which are automatically run against our knowledge base. Such a tool is still at its early stages of development and will not be shown here.

The example we are taking in consideration regards the complex information system needed to manage a railway reservation web-site. Figure 6 reports a schematic representation of the main components of such a system:

- the **Reservation front-end** that provides a user friendly web interface to customers, allowing them to interact with the system.
- the **Back-end system**, a complex component which in turn consists of an **Availability Checker system** (responsible to check tickets availability), a **Reservation system** (in charge of making the actual reservations) and a **Payment system** (that validates online transactions).
- a **Database** that holds information on trains, stations, timetables, purchased tickets and reservations.

4.1   Step 1: Selection of the Application Pattern

Using a graphical interface, a user can select the type of application she wants to build and deploy on the Cloud: for each application category there will be one or more specific application patterns which will be presented to the user, who can then refine the selection. The software we want to develop in our case study can be easily represented through a very generic Application Pattern, namely the

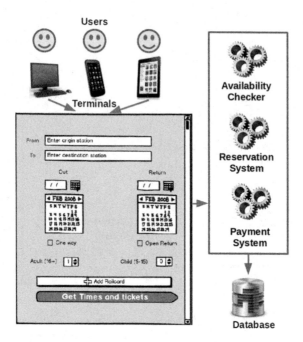

Fig. 6. The railway reservation system example

Reservation System pattern, whose components and correspondence with the agnostic **Three-Tier Cloud Application Pattern** [2] are shown in Fig. 7. The *Reservation System* application pattern can be easily applied to other similar applications, since it is sufficiently general and does not impose specific requirements. Our semantic-based representation can be also extended, so that new patterns can be built from the existing ones to add functionalities.

As soon as the user chooses the application type and a corresponding Application pattern is selected, the system automatically maps its components to an agnostic high-level Cloud pattern, which will represent the starting point for further refinements. The mapping shown in Fig. 7 simply matches the components of the application pattern, corresponding to the Reservation System used as an example, to the three major layers composing a three-tier application on Cloud: the correspondence is not one-to-one, as the Back-end system's components are all automatically matched with the Business Logic layer, where all the processing components belong to. At this point, the user can select one of the components of the high-level Cloud pattern in order to refine it further.

4.2   Step 2: Refinement of the Pattern's Components

Each of the three layers of the selected *Three-Tier Cloud Application Pattern* can be further refined via a mapping to other agnostic Cloud Patterns, which provide better instructions regarding the possible implementation of the needed

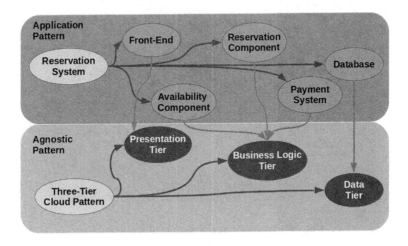

Fig. 7. Mapping between application pattern and agnostic cloud pattern

infrastructure. For each tier a composition of cloud patterns is suggested to implement and improve the single tier performance.

- the presentation tier (Fig. 8) can be implemented using a combination of an Elastic Load Balancer pattern (providing application scalability), a Stateless Component pattern (managing the status of the application's components) and a User Interface pattern (serving as a bridge between the synchronous access of the human user and the asynchronous communications used with other application components).
- the Business Logic tier (Fig. 9) is built via the combination of a **Processing Component Pattern** (providing elaboration capabilities), a **Stateless Component Pattern** and a **Data Access Component Pattern** (which guarantees access to the needed data).
- the Data Tier (Fig. 10) is the simplest of the three different layers as it is composed by a single agnostic patterns, namely the **Data Access Component Pattern**

Composing patterns can be shared among the different layers (the Data Access Component Pattern is used in both the Business Logic and Data tiers) and can also share participants: in the considered Presentation layer the **Elastic Load Balancer** participant is shared among two of its composing patterns.

4.3   Step 3: Selection of a Target Platform

The patterns used to compose the application layers are all agnostic ones: their components are not immediately implemented, as they need to be connected to an existing target platform. By following our pattern-based approach, it is possible to further refine the application composition by identifying vendor specific patterns with more detailed information regarding the implementation of the

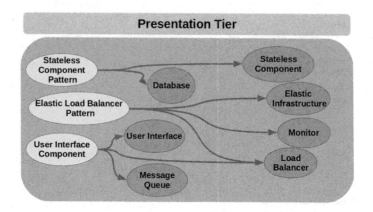

Fig. 8. Presentation tier composing patterns

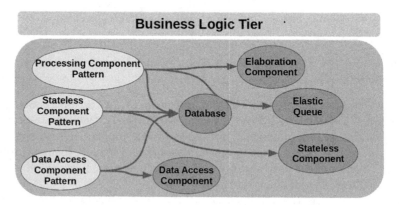

Fig. 9. Business tier composing patterns

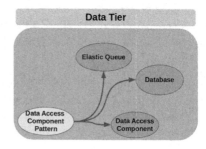

Fig. 10. Data tier composing patterns

different components. In this example, we will refer to Amazon Web Services
as a possible target for the application deployment. By automatically analysing
the semantic-based representation of the Amazon Cloud patterns catalogue [1]

we have devised, it is possible to retrieve equivalent patterns and to determine correspondences between their components. Figure 11 shows how the agnostic patterns and components identified for the Presentation tier are mapped to corresponding Amazon Cloud Patterns and services. In particular:

- Corresponding patterns are connected with black arrows: Stateless Component Pattern with State Sharing Pattern; Elastic Load Balancer Pattern with Scale-out Pattern.
- Blue arrows connect corresponding services/components: Stateless Component, Elastic Infrastructure and User Interface with EC2; Elastic Infrastructure with AutoScaling; Monitor with CloudWatch; Load Balancer with Elastic Load Balancer; Message Queue with Simple Queue Service.

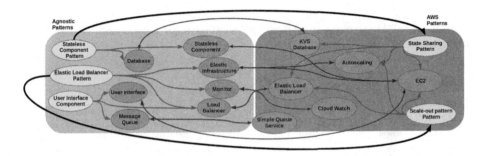

Fig. 11. Implementation of the Presentation tier with AWS patterns

The User Interface pattern does not correspond to any Amazon Cloud pattern, so the system simply identifies suitable services from the target vendor to implement them, without applying a specific pre-defined configuration. In this way, we can avoid the restrictions that the use of vendor specific Cloud patterns could impose to the implementation of an application. Once all the pattern elements have been mapped to a potential implementing Cloud service, the system supports users in making them interact, thanks to the information on the parameters and the operations they expose, which are contained in our semantic-enabled knowledge base. All the correspondences and mappings shown in figures are retrieved by means of SPARQL queries, which are run against our OWL-based knowledge base. Such queries leverage the properties described in Sects. 3.1 and 3.2, and are described in more details in [16]. Here we report, in Listing 1.1, an example of the SPARQL query used to retrieve all the vendor specific services which are equivalent to the agnostic *Elastic Load Balancer* used in the use case. The query first retrieves the category to which the *Elastic Load Balancer* service belongs, using the *equivalent* property defined in the pattern ontology (hence the prefix *patternOntology* we have used). Than, using the service category (*Type* in the query) we retrieve all the corresponding services via the *equivalent* property defined in the Cloud service ontology (hence the *cloudOntology* prefix). The vendor name is retrieved via the **hasVendor** property. Table 1 reports the results of the query. Please note that all the retrieved components are Cloud services, apart from **ZeusExtensibleTrafficManager** which is a Virtual Appliance. The knowledge base contains information on the resource requirements needed to run the virtual appliance on a virtual machine and supports users in selecting the best suited offer on the target platform. The first three Cloud services belong to two different service categories, regarding balancing of application and network loads.

```
SELECT ?Component   ?Vendor ?Type
WHERE {patternOntology:ElasticLoadBalancer
    patternOntology:equivalent ?Type.
        ?Component cloudOntology:equivalent ?Type
        ?Component cloudOntology:hasVendor ?Vendor.
        }
```

Listing 1.1. SPARQL query to retrieve equivalent patterns' components from multiple vendors

Table 1. Partial results from query in Listing 1.1

Component	Vendor	Type
Openstack_Neutron	Redhat	NetworkLoadBalancing, ApplicationBalancing
Azure_Trafficmanager	WindowsAzure	NetworkLoadBalancing, ApplicationBalancing
Amazon_ElasticLoadBalancing	Amazon	NetworkLoadBalancing, ApplicationBalancing
ZeusExtensibleTrafficManager	Riverbed	NetworkLoadBalancing

5   Conclusion and Future Work

In this paper we have applied a semantic-based approach for the description of Cloud Patterns and services to a simple use case, in order to demonstrate the capability of such an approach to support users in developing Cloud oriented applications, without a deep and extensive knowledge of the entire Cloud Computing panorama. The different steps needed to deploy the example application to the Cloud have been described, and an example of the queries run against the proposed semantic knowledge-base has been provided. In the future, we are planning to develop the user friendly graphical interface to ease users' interactions with the system, and to include further services and patterns in our description.

Acknowledgements. This research has been supported by the European Community's Seventh Framework Programme (FP7/2007–2013) under grant agreement n 256910 (mOSAIC Project), by PRIST 2009, "Fruizione assistita e context aware di siti archeologici complessi mediante dispositivi mobili"and CoSSMic (Collaborating Smart Solar-powered Micro-grids - FP7-SMARTCITIES-2013).

References

1. Aws cloud design patterns. http://en.clouddesignpattern.org
2. Cloud computing patterns. http://cloudcomputingpatterns.org
3. Cloud patterns. http://cloudpatterns.org
4. Ieee p2302 working group (intercloud). http://grouper.ieee.org/groups/2302/
5. Ontology design patterns. http://ontologydesignpatterns.org/
6. Opencrowd: Cloud computing vendors taxonomy. http://cloudtaxonomy.opencrowd.com/
7. Openstack services. http://www.openstack.org/software
8. Soa patterns. http://www.soapatterns.org/
9. Windows azure application patterns. http://blogs.msdn.com/b/jmeier/archive/2010/09/11/windows-azure-application-patterns.aspx
10. Androcec, D., Vrcek, N., Seva, J.: Cloud computing ontologies: a systematic review. In: The Third International Conference on Models and Ontology-Based Design of Protocols, Architectures and Services, MOPAS 2012, pp. 9–14 (2012)
11. Bernstein, D., Vij, D.: Intercloud directory and exchange protocol detail using XMPP and RDF. In: 2010 6th World Congress on Services (SERVICES-1), pp. 431–438. IEEE (2010)
12. Buyya, R., Vecchiola, C., Thamarai Selvi, S.: Mastering cloud computing: foundations and applications programming, 1st edn. Morgan Kaufmann Publishers Inc., San Francisco, CA, USA (2013)
13. Catteddu, D.: Cloud Computing: benefits, risks and recommendations for information security. In: Serrão, C., Díaz, V.A., Cerullo, F. (eds.) IBWAS 2009. CCIS, vol. 72, p. 17. Springer, Heidelberg (2010)
14. Dastjerdi, A.V., Tabatabaei, S.G.H., Buyya, R.: An effective architecture for automated appliance management system applying ontology-based cloud discovery. In: 2010 10th IEEE/ACM International Conference on Cluster, Cloud and Grid Computing (CCGrid), pp. 104–112. IEEE (2010)
15. Deng, Y., Head, M., Kochut, A., Munson, J., Sailer, A., Shaikh, H.: Introducing semantics to cloud services catalogs. In: 2011 IEEE International Conference on Services Computing (SCC), pp. 24–31, July 2011
16. Di Martino, B., Esposito, A., Cretella, G.: Semantic representation of cloud patterns and services with automated reasoning to support cloud application portability. IEEE Trans. Cloud Comput. **PP**(99), 1 (2015). doi:10.1109/TCC.2015.2433259
17. Di Martino, B., Cretella, G., Esposito, A.: Semantic and agnostic representation of cloud patterns for cloud interoperability and portability. In: Proceedings of the IEEE Fifth International Conference on Cloud Computing Technology and Science (CloudCom 2013) (2013)
18. Di Martino, B., Cretella, G., Esposito, A.: Towards an unified owl ontology of cloud vendors appliances and services at PaaS and SaaS level. In: Proceedings of the 8th International Conference on Computational Intelligence in Security for Information Systems (CISIS 2014), pp. 570–575 (2014)
19. Di Martino, B., Cretella, G., Esposito, A.: Defining cloud services workflow: a comparison between TOSCA and OpenStack hot. In: Proceedings of the 9th International Conference on Complex, Intelligent, and Software Intensive Systems, July 8th–July 10th 2015. IEEE (2015)
20. Di Martino, B., Esposito, A.: Towards a common semantic representation of design and cloud patterns. In: Proceedings of International Conference on Information Integration and Web-Based Applications & Services, p. 385. ACM (2013)

21. Di Martino, B., Petcu, D., Cossu, R., Goncalves, P., Máhr, T., Loichate, M.: Building a mosaic of clouds. In: Guarracino, M.R., et al. (eds.) Euro-Par-Workshop 2010. LNCS, vol. 6586, pp. 571–578. Springer, Heidelberg (2011)

22. Endrei, M., Ang, J., Arsanjani, A., Chua, S., Comte, P., Krogdahl, P., Luo, M., Newling, T.: Patterns: service-oriented architecture and web services. IBM Corporation, International Technical Support Organization (2004)

23. Catteddu, D.: Cloud Computing: Benefits, Risks and Recommendations for Information Security. In: Serrão, C., Aguilera Díaz, V., Cerullo, F. (eds.) IBWAS 2009. CCIS, vol. 72, p. 17. Springer, Heidelberg (2010)

24. Gangemi, A.: Ontology design patterns for semantic web content. In: Gil, Y., Motta, E., Benjamins, V.R., Musen, M.A. (eds.) ISWC 2005. LNCS, vol. 3729, pp. 262–276. Springer, Heidelberg (2005)

25. Han, T., Sim, K.M.: An ontology-enhanced cloud service discovery system. In: Proceedings of the International Multiconference of Engineers and Computer Scientists, vol. 1, pp. 17–19 (2010)

26. Homer, A., Sharp, J., Brader, L., Narumoto, M., Swanson, T.: Cloud Design Patterns: Prescriptive Architecture Guidance for Cloud Applications. Microsoft Patterns & Practices (2014). ISBN:1621140369 9781621140368

27. Fehling, C., Leymann, F., Retter, R., Schupeck, W., Arbitter, P.: Cloud Computing Patterns Fundamentals to Design, Build, and Manage Cloud Applications. Springer (2014). doi:10.1007/978-3-7091-1568-8, ISBN: 9783709115671, 9783709115688

28. Mark, B., Jerry, H., Ora, L., Drew, M., Sheila, M., Srini, N., Massimo, P., Bijan, P., Terry, P., Evren, S., Naveen, S., Katia, S.: OWL-s: Semantic markup for web services. http://www.w3.org/Submission/2004/SUBM-OWL-S-20041122/

29. Martino, B.D., Cretella, G., Esposito, A.: Semantic and agnostic representation of cloud patterns for cloud interoperability and portability. In: 2013 IEEE 5th International Conference on Cloud Computing Technology and Science (CloudCom), vol. 2, pp. 182–187. IEEE (2013)

30. McGuinness, D.L., Van Harmelen, F., et al.: Owl web ontology language overview. In: W3C Recommendation, vol. 10, no. 10 (2004)

31. Moscato, F., Aversa, R., Di Martino, B., Fortis, T., Munteanu, V.: An analysis of mosaic ontology for cloud resources annotation. In: 2011 Federated Conference on Computer Science and Information Systems (FedCSIS), pp. 973–980. IEEE (2011)

32. Toosi, A.N., Calheiros, R.N., Buyya, R.: Interconnected cloud computing environments: challenges, taxonomy, and survey. ACM Comput. Surv. (CSUR) 47(1), 7 (2014)

33. Xu, B., Wang, N., Li, C.: A cloud computing infrastructure on heterogeneous computing resources. J. Comput. 6(8), 1789–1796 (2011)

34. Youseff, L., Butrico, M., Da Silva, D.: Toward a unified ontology of cloud computing. In: Grid Computing Environments Workshop, GCE 2008, pp. 1–10. IEEE (2008)

EU Projects Track

Preface of EU Projects Track

Following the success of the session devoted to presenting ongoing EU projects on cloud and services, which was held at the ESOCC 2014 SeaClouds Workshop in Manchester, ESOCC 2015 decided to run a "EU Projects Track" on September 15 in Taormina, Italy.

The track was organized in a two-hour general session entirely devoted to presenting the status and perspectives of ongoing EU research projects on cloud and services.

The presentation of the 12 selected ongoing projects – SeaClouds, Panacea, Dice, MODAClouds, CloudWave, AppHub, PaaSage, Broker@Cloud, Beacon, EUBrazil, Clips, and FrontierCities – succeeded in providing an up-to-date view of the achievements and challenges of EU-funded research activities on the cloud and services.

A two-page description of each project presented is included in this volume.

Antonio Brogi
Silvana Muscella

Organization

Program Committee

Antonio Brogi   University of Pisa, Italy
Silvana Muscella   CloudWATCH Coordinator, Italy

Adaptive Application Management over Multiple Clouds

M. Barrientos[1], A. Brogi[2], M. Buccarella[2], J. Carrasco[1], J. Cubo[1],
F. D'Andria[3], E. Di Nitto[4], A. Nieto[1], M. Oriol[2], D. Pérez[4], E. Pimentel[1],
and S. Zenzaro[2]

[1] Departamento de Lenguajes y Ciencias de la Computación,
Universidad de Málaga, Málaga, Spain
[2] Department of Computer Science, University of Pisa, Pisa, Italy
[3] ATOS, Barcelona, Spain
[4] Dipartimento di Elettronica, Informazione e Bioingegneria,
Politecnico di Milano, Milano, Italy

Abstract. SeaClouds is a European FP7 research project, whose goal is
to provide a novel open source platform to enable application developers
to configure, deploy, and manage complex applications across multiple
heterogeneous IaaS and PaaS clouds in an efficient and adaptive way.

The SeaClouds project[1] aims at supporting application developers during all
phases of the cloud application management lifecycle. Users provide as input to
the SeaClouds platform the application they wish to deploy on the cloud together
with different types of requirements — namely, technical, Quality of Service
(QoS) and Quality of Business (QoB) requirements — for the modules composing their application as well as for the whole application. SeaClouds employs
OASIS TOSCA[2] to represent the topology and the requirements of the application to be deployed. SeaClouds users can both interactively specify (in a TOSCA
transparent way) the topology and requirements of their application via a graphical user interface featured by the SeaClouds Dashboard (Fig. 1) and/or directly
provide a TOSCA specification of their application via the SeaClouds API.

Given the application to be deployed, the SeaClouds Planner generates a set
of possible deployment plans satisfying the requirements specified by the user.
To achieve that, the Planner first performs a matchmaking step, to select the
available could offerings (periodically fetched by the Discoverer from different
IaaS and PaaS providers) that satisfy the user requirements. After that, a multi-
objective optimization step is performed to determine the best deployment plans
satisfying the user requirements.

The deployment plan chosen by the user is then passed to the Deployer, that
exploits Apache Brooklyn[3] to perform the actual deployment of all application

---

[1] EU-FP7-ICT-610531 *"Seamless adaptive multi-cloud management of service-based
applications"*. http://www.seaclouds-project.eu.
[2] https://www.oasis-open.org/committees/tosca.
[3] https://brooklyn.incubator.apache.org.

A. Celesti and P. Leitner (Eds.): ESOCC 2015 Workshops, CCIS 567, pp. 422–424, 2016.
DOI: 10.1007/978-3-319-33313-7

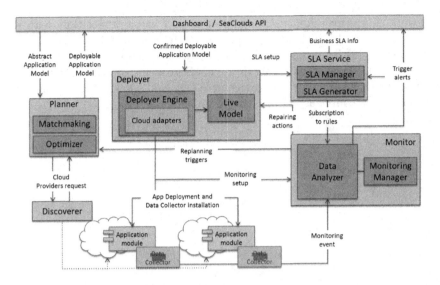

Fig. 1. Main components of the Seaclouds architecture.

modules on the chosen target clouds. Right after the application is deployed, the SeaClouds Monitor starts to perform a distributed monitoring over the target clouds in order to detect possible violations of the application requirements or of the Service License Agreement (SLA) devised by the SLA Service. In case of violations that can be repaired without need to migrate application modules, the Monitor directly triggers the Deployer. In case of violations that require to migrate some application module(s), the Monitor asks the Planner to generate a reconfiguration plan.

SeaClouds features two case studies: A gaming application whose deployment dynamically adapts depending on the number and location of users, and a healthcare application exploiting SeaClouds SLA management and, possibly, cloud bursting.

Besides the aforementioned relations with OASIS TOSCA and Apache Brooklyn, SeaClouds is collaborating also with the MODAClouds project[4]. In particular SeaClouds monitoring relies on and extends the monitoring methodology developed by MODAClouds. Last, but not least, a cross-fertilization effort is currently ongoing with the Alien4Cloud project[5] to assess the feasibility for SeaClouds to use Alien4Cloud TOSCA YAML parser and for Alien4Cloud to use SeaClouds Deployer.

SeaClouds adopted from the very beginning of the project an open source strategy, which includes transparent development and Apache 2.0 licensing. Such strategy is intended to serve as enabler for three main impact paths: (1) To exploit SeaClouds-extended Apache Brooklyn application management

---

[4] http://www.modaclouds.eu.
[5] http://alien4cloud.github.io.

framework as a vehicle for SeaClouds post-project value proposition, with new TOSCA, PaaS and multi-cloud support extending a solution already present in the market, (2) To provide a European platform compliant with the OASIS TOSCA standard that is emerging in the PaaS segment, and (3) To allow industrial SeaClouds members — in particular ATOS and Cloudsoft — to integrate SeaClouds open source assets into their commercial offerings.

TAP: A Task Allocation Platform for the EU FP7 PANACEA Project

Erol Gelenbe and Lan Wang

Intelligent Systems and Networks,
Department of Electrical and Electronic Engineering,
Imperial College, London SW72AZ, UK

Abstract. The EU FP7 PANACEA project has designed a QoS driven smart Task Allocation Platform for varied QoS objectives in the Cloud.

The Cloud [9] supports diverse workloads [1, 2, 6, 7, 10] and simple schemes are needed to allocate jobs with satisfactory QoS and low overhead. The PANACEA project's Task Allocation Platform (TAP) uses on-line observation of the servers in a Cloud system to dynamically allocate tasks. TAP is a Linux kernel module which embeds measurement agents into hosts. We illustrate its usage with a smart algorithm inspired by the Cognitive Packet Network (CPN) [3, 5, 8] which uses reinforcement learning [11], and with a "sensible" policy [4] that probabilistically selects the host whose measured QoS is the best. TAP is a practical system shown in Fig. 1 which exploits several different task allocation algorithms such as the two we mention. It is implemented as a Linux kernel module on PCs with Linux OS.

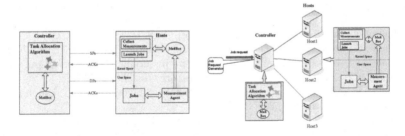

Fig. 1. Architecture of the Task Allocation Platform (left) and its test-bed (right).

A synthetic benchmark is generated, and jobs are sent at fixed intervals denoted by CR, or according to a Poisson process with a fixed rate denoted by EXP. The QoS goals used here are either (i) the minimization of either the execution time on the host, or (ii) the minimization of the response time at TAP, which includes the message sent to activate the job at a host and the time it takes for an ACK to provide information back to TAP. The CPN based

© Springer International Publishing Switzerland 2016
A. Celesti and P. Leitner (Eds.): ESOCC 2015 Workshops, CCIS 567, pp. 425–426, 2016.
DOI: 10.1007/978-3-319-33313-7

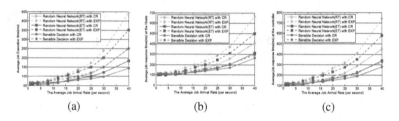

(a)   (b)   (c)

Fig. 2. Average job execution time and average job response time at the hosts, and average job response time at TAP for different job arrival rates.

scheme was tested with both (i) and (ii), whereas the sensible decision approach only used (ii). The experiments are carried out for average job arrival rates of $1, 2, 4, 8, 12, 16, 20, 25, 30, 40$ jobs/sec with each experiment lasting 5 mins. As the average job arrival rates grows, the sensible decision algorithm outperforms the RNN, as shown in Fig. 2. Also the RNN algorithm with online measurement of job execution time performs better than the RNN with the metric of job response time, and the sensible decision is always best under high job arrival rates.

References

1. Berl, A., Gelenbe, E., Di Girolamo, M., Giuliani, G., De Meer, H., Dang, M.Q., Pentikousis, K.: Energy-efficient cloud computing. Comput. J. **53**(7), 1045–1051 (2010)
2. Delimitrou, C., Kozyrakis, C.: Qos-aware scheduling in heterogeneous data-centers with paragon. ACM Trans. Comput. Syst. **31**(4), 12:1–12:34 (2013). http://doi.acm.org/10.1145/2556583
3. Gelenbe, E.: The first decade of g-networks. Europ. J. Operational Res. **126**(2), 231–232 (2000)
4. Gelenbe, E.: Sensible decisions based on qos. CMS **1**(1), 1–14 (2003)
5. Gelenbe, E.: Steps toward self-aware networks. Commun. ACM **52**(7), 66–75 (2009)
6. Gelenbe, E., Lent, R.: Energy-qos trade-offs in mobile service selection. Future Internet **5**(2), 128–139 (2013). http://dx.doi.org/10.3390/fi5020128
7. Gelenbe, E., Lent, R.: Optimising server energy consumption and response time. Theor. Appl. Inform. (4), 257–270 (2013)
8. Gelenbe, E., Timotheou, S.: Random neural networks with synchronized interactions. Neural Comput. **20**(9), 2308–2324 (2008). http://dx.doi.org/10.1162/neco.2008.04-07-509
9. Mell, P., Grance, T.: The nist definition of cloud computing. NIST Spec. Publ. 800–145 (2009)
10. Pradeep, P., Shin, K.G., Zhu, X., Uysal, M., Wang, Z., Singhal, S., Merchant, A., Salem, K.: Adaptive control of virtualized resources in utility computing environments. In: Proceedings of the 2nd ACM SIGOPS/EuroSys European Conference on Computer Systems 2007, pp. 289–302. EuroSys 2007, NY, USA (2007). http://doi.acm.org/10.1145/1272996.1273026
11. Sutton, R.S., Barto, A.G.: Reinforcement Learning: An Introduction. MIT Press (1998)

Towards Quality-Aware Development of Big Data Applications with DICE

Giuliano Casale[1]([⊠]), Elisabetta Di Nitto[2], and Ilias Spais[3]

[1] Imperial College London, London, UK
g.casale@imperial.ac.uk
[2] Politecnico di Milano, Milano, Italy
[3] ATC Technologies, Chalandri, Greece

Abstract. Model-driven engineering (MDE) has been extended in recent years to account for reliability and performance requirements since the early design stages of an application. While this quality-aware MDE exists for both enterprise and cloud applications, it does not exist yet for Big Data systems. DICE is a novel Horizon2020 project that aims at filling this gap by defining the first quality-driven MDE methodology for Big Data applications. Concrete outputs of the project will include a data-aware UML profile capable of describing Big Data technologies and architecture styles, data-aware quality prediction methods, and continuous delivery tools.

Keywords: Quality-driven development · Big Data · UML

1 Overview

Big Data systems [4] are rapidly emerging and their popularity on the ICT market calls for novel software engineering methods to support their development. In particular, independent software vendors (ISVs) need to create novel data-intensive products, but this is complicated by the lack of expertise in technologies such as NoSQL databases, MapReduce/Hadoop analytics, or real-time processing. Pressure to hit the market first can therefore shift the development focus primarily on functional aspects, at the expense of non-functional properties such as reliability, performance or safety of the resulting applications.

The goal of the DICE project is to deliver a methodology and a toolchain to help ISVs develop Big Data applications without compromising on quality. DICE proposes innovations concerning both functional and non-functional properties of data-intensive software systems. For what concerns functional properties, DICE wants to extend model-driven engineering approaches based on UML with a novel profile to annotate properties of data such as volume, velocity, location or data transformations. The traditional ecosystem of models used in MDE,

This paper has been supported by the European Unions Horizon 2020 research and innovation programme under grant agreement No. 644869.

A. Celesti and P. Leitner (Eds.): ESOCC 2015 Workshops, CCIS 567, pp. 427–429, 2016.
DOI: 10.1007/978-3-319-33313-7

which encompasses model ranging from platform-independent to technology-specific, will also consider technologies and architecture styles that are specific to Big data, such as the lambda architecture[1]. The main challenge of this generalization is to develop the model annotations, a consistent methodology, and the underpinning model-to-model transformations. Furthermore, DICE aims at translating such high-level design models into a concrete deployment plan and execute it.

On the non-functional side, the extended UML models will be annotated with performance and reliability requirements using specific annotations, such as the UML MARTE and UML DAM profiles [1, 3], but also with novel annotations that describe the data used by the application. Then, tools will be developed to predict the fulfillment of these requirements before and during application development. In particular, DICE envisions the co-existence of multiple simulation, verification, and testing tools that can guide the developer through the quality assessment of early prototypes of the Big Data application. For example, a developer could initially describe the application architecture, an expected user behaviour, and the technologies to be used; based on this specification, he could then explore the forecasted response times under increasing volumes or rates of data intakes. This information can be helpful to assess if a given architecture design is appropriate to meet customer requirements. The novelty is the explicit accounting for the data volumes or rates in the predictions.

Application Domains. The DICE development environment will offer a general methodology, that can be useful in a number of application domains. In particular, the project plans to develop demonstrators in the areas of *News & Media*, *e-Government*, and *Maritime Operations*. In News & Media, streaming solutions that connect to social platforms will need to be modelled, together with Hadoop/MapReduce processing of the acquired social data. The case of e-Government provides a test scenario for the DICE methodology to apply in an environment with legacy data systems, where decision-making related to the best Big data technologies to adopt is complex. Lastly, Maritime Operations is a sector where streaming data related to vessel movement needs to be processed and analyzed in real-time to guarantee safe and correct port operations.

Future Work. The DICE project has started in February 2015 and a first public release of the DICE MDE tools is scheduled for Spring 2016. News and updates on the project are available at http://www.dice-h2020.eu and a detailed project vision can be found in [2].

References

1. Bernardi, S., Merseguer, J., Petriu, D.C.: Dependability modeling and analysis of software systems specified with UML. ACM Comput. Surv. **45**(1), Article no. 2 (2012)

---

[1] https://en.wikipedia.org/wiki/Lambda_architecture.

2. Casale, G., et al.: DICE: quality-driven development of data-intensive cloud applications. In: Proceedings of the 7th International Workshop on Modeling in Software Engineering (MiSE 2015) (2015)
3. Soley, R., et al.: Modeling and Analysis of Real-Time and Embedded Systems with UML and MARTE. MK/OMG Press (2013)
4. Zikopoulos, P., et al.: Understanding Big Data: Analytics for Enterprise Class Hadoop and Streaming Data. McGraw-Hill Osborne Media (2011)

On MODAClouds' Toolkit Support for DevOps

Elisabetta Di Nitto[1], Giuliano Casale[2], and Dana Petcu[3]

[1] Politecnico di Milano, Milano, Italy
[2] Imperial College London, London, UK
[3] Institute e-Austria Timişoara and West University of Timişoara, Timişoara, Romania

Abstract. We have recently experimented the enhancement of model-driven development with the possibility of exploit models not only as part of design but also as part of the runtime. Through this enhancement the system model becomes a live object that evolves with the system itself and sends back to the designers powerful information that enables a continuous improvement of the system. This approach goes into the direction of offering a valid tool to support development and operation in a seamless way, i.e. to support DevOps concepts. In this short note we present the MODAClouds Toolkit which helps lowering existing barriers between development and operations teams and therefore smooths the way to DevOps practice.

The main goal of MODAClouds project[1] is to provide methods, a decision support system, an open source integrated development environment (IDE) and run-time environment for the high-level design, early prototyping, semi-automatic code generation, and automatic deployment of applications on Multi-Clouds with guaranteed Quality-of-Service (QoS). The concept aligned with this goal was introduced in the early paper [1]. The approach was described in several papers enumerated on the project web site[2].

The MODAClouds model-driven approach is supported by the MODAClouds Toolbox[3]. It consists in there main components (see Fig. 1): (1) Creator4Clouds, an IDE for high-level application design; (2) Venues4Clouds, a decision support system that helps decision makers to identify and select the best execution venue for Cloud applications, by considering technical and business requirements; (3) Energizer4Clouds, a Multi-Cloud run-time environment energized to provide automatic deployment and execution of applications with guaranteed QoS on compatible Clouds.

Creator4Clouds includes plugins focusing on: (i) analysing the QoS/cost trade-offs of various possible application configurations (SpaceDev4Clouds); (ii) mapping high level data models into less expressive but more scalable NoSQL (DataMapping4Clouds); (iii) deploying the resulting application on

---

[1] MODAClouds project, partially funded by the European Commission through the FP7-ICT Grant agreement 318484.

[2] List of publications available at http://www.modaclouds.eu/publications/.

[3] All tools are available as open source, see http://www.modaclouds.eu/software/.

A. Celesti and P. Leitner (Eds.): ESOCC 2015 Workshops, CCIS 567, pp. 430–431, 2016.
DOI: 10.1007/978-3-319-33313-7

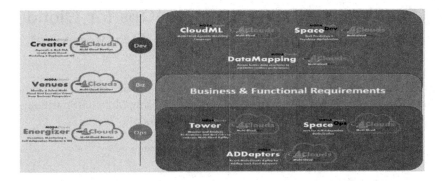

Fig. 1. Main components of the MODAClouds' Toolkit

Multi-Clouds by exploiting the CloudML language. Overall, Creator4Clouds is a unique tool supporting design, development, deployment and resource provisioning for Multi-Cloud applications. It provides features to assess the QoS guarantees required by the application and offers support to the definition of the application SLA.

Energizer4Clouds includes the frameworks to support monitoring (Tower4-Clouds) and self-adaptation (SpaceOps4Clouds), together with utilities that perform ancillary tasks in the platform (ADDapters4Clouds). Energizer4Clouds is one of the few existing solutions that addresses, in a single framework, the needs of operators willing to run their applications in a Multi-Cloud environment. Through Tower4Clouds, operators are able to perform complex monitoring and data analyses from multiple sources. Moreover, thanks to SpaceOps4Clouds, it identifies and actuates proper self-adaptation actions that take into account the current and foreseen state of the system under control.

All three main components of MODAClouds Toolbox are built with the idea to reduce the gap between development and operations teams, according to DevOps philosophy. Therefore, we have included in the design of the MODAClouds architecture what we call Feed-Back Loop technologies that extend capabilities offered by Creator, Venues and Energizer4Clouds. Thanks to the Feed-Back Loop approach, Tower4Clouds connects with Creator4Clouds and Venues4Clouds, respectively. The first connector is responsible for providing developers and the QoS engineers with the perspective of the application behavior at runtime to improve the development process and incorporate DevOps techniques and tools into the process. The second connector allows Venues4Clouds to adapt its knowledge base according to real live data. This helps in offering to users an updated vision of services quality for future recommendations. The capability of the runtime to influence the design time is in line with current research and is a very important feature to empower Multi-Cloud application developers.

Reference

1. Ardagna, D., et al.: A Model-driven approach for the design and execution of applications on multiple clouds. In: Proceedings of MISE 2012, pp. 50–56 (2012)

CloudWave – Leveraging DevOps for Cloud Management and Application Development

Dario Bruneo, Aryan Dadashi, Philipp Leitner, Avi Miron, Boris Moltchanov,
Francesco Javier Nieto De-Santos, Eliot Salant, Amir Molzam Sharifloo,
Karl Wallbom, and Chris Woods

The CloudWave Project Consortium

1 Introduction

DevOps describes the convergence of application development and operation activities. In a DevOps team, software developers and system administrators collaborate in joint task forces and work towards common goals. The vision of the CloudWave project[1] is that a *full-stack DevOps* approach to cloud management can lead to more efficient usage of clouds as well as to better applications. This is achieved by aligning the goals of cloud application developers and cloud operators, and by allowing developers to leverage deeper knowledge of the cloud hosting environment. For cloud operators, the CloudWave model enables *more efficient instance management*, as application developers collaborate with the cloud provider, for example by exposing adaptation enactment points or emitting relevant business metrics. In return, cloud application developers gain deep insight into the internals of the cloud system, and can hence build and tune their application based on *real-time feedback from the cloud*. Similar to DevOps, the collaborative model of CloudWave removes friction between cloud operators and software developers by breaking up the black boxes that clouds and applications traditionally are to each other. CloudWave will provide a reference implementation of these ideas based on Openstack[2].

2 Project Consortium

CloudWave (full title *Agile Service Engineering for the Future Internet*) is an FP7 ICT Call 10 funded European research project. The project is coordinated by Eliot Salant (IBM Research Israel). In addition, the CloudWave consortium consists of SAP SE, Intel Ireland, Telecom Italia, Atos, Cloudmore, University of Duisburg-Essen, University of Messina, Technion, and University of Zurich.

The research leading to these results has received funding from the European Community's Seventh Framework Programme (FP7/2007-2013) under grant agreement no. 610802 (CloudWave).

[1] http://cloudwave-fp7.eu/.
[2] http://www.openstack.org.

A. Celesti and P. Leitner (Eds.): ESOCC 2015 Workshops, CCIS 567, pp. 432–434, 2016.
DOI: 10.1007/978-3-319-33313-7

3   Project Overview

A high-level outline of CloudWave is sketched in Fig. 1. At the heart of the project, monitoring data is generated, analyzed, and aggregated on all levels of the cloud stack, i.e., on physical, virtual, network, and application level. This data is further enriched with information coming from external sources. We refer to this monitoring approach as *3-D monitoring* [1]. 3-D monitoring fuels two primary use cases, coordinated adaptation and feedback-driven development.

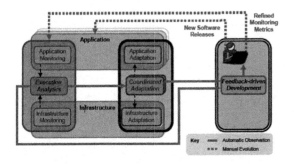

Fig. 1. High-level overview of the CloudWave project

Coordinated adaptation is to improve the quality of adaptation decisions, taken by the infrastructure and application, through reasoning on the global state of the cloud stack provided by 3-D monitoring. By taking decisions in a coordinated manner, more effective adaptations are taken and operated by different components [2]. To this aim, adaptation models of the application (e.g., turning optional application features on or off based on load) and infrastructure (e.g., scaling up or out) are captured by Feature-based models and adaptation plans are derived by an intelligent engine.

Conversely, *feedback-driven development* (FDD) aims to bring 3-D monitoring data to software developers, giving them a better understanding of how the application is actually operated (and adapted) at runtime. This goes way beyond traditional application performance monitoring (APM) solutions, as the CloudWave monitoring solution integrates data from the application stack with infrastructure metrics, information on triggered adaptations, and data from other applications launched by the same tenant. CloudWave demonstrates how this data can provide added value to software developers, for instance via visualizing (and warning about) performance-critical code directly in the Integrated Development Environment (IDE), or by enabling what if analysis of performance and costs for different deployment options [3].

References

1. Marquezan, C.C., Bruneo, D., Longo, F., Wessling, F., Metzger, A., Puliafito, A.: 3-D cloud monitoring: enabling effective cloud infrastructure and application management. In: 10th International Conference on Network and Service Management, pp. 55–63 (2014)

2. Marquezan, C.C., Wessling, F., Metzger, A., Pohl, K., Woods, C., Wallbom, K.: Towards exploiting the full adaptation potential of cloud applications. In: Proceedings of the 6th International Workshop on Principles of Engineering Service-Oriented and Cloud Systems (2014)
3. Cito, J., Leitner, P., Gall, H.C., Dadashi, A., Keller, A., Roth, A.: Runtime metric meets developer - building better cloud applications using feedback. In: Proceedings of the 2015 ACM International Symposium on New Ideas, New Paradigms, and Reflections on Programming & Software. ACM, New York (2015)

AppHub – The European Open Source Market Place

(Extended Abstract)

Peter H. Deussen[1], Majid Salehi Ghamsari[1], Alexandre Lefebvre[2],
Alban Richard[2], Cédric Thomas[3], Olivier Bouzereau[3],
and Catherine Nuel[3]

[1] Fraunhofer Institute for Open Communication Systems, Berlin, Germany
{peter.deussen,majid.salehi.ghamsar}
@fokus.fraunhofer.de
[2] UShareSoft, Grenoble, France
{alexandre.lefebvre,alban.richard}@usharesoft.com
[3] OW2, Paris, France
{cedric.thomas,olivier.bouzereau,
catherine.nuel}@ow2.org

Abstract. This short paper describes the AppHub project, an EU funded initiative that supports open source software providers to facilitate the adoption of their products by making them ready for the cloud.

Keywords: Open source software · Cloud computing

1 A Market Outreach Accelerator

As the current context of IT budget restriction creates business opportunities for open source software (OSS) the market is becoming increasingly competitive. To be successful, vendors must differentiate themselves through their pre-sales services, their ability to quickly deliver operational business solutions. With current information systems migrating toward virtual and cloud environments, vendors must be able to manage several kinds of deployments and cloud technologies. And in the OSS market specifically, vendors must show a community of contributors, and demonstrate adequate project governance. AppHub helps collaborative projects and SMEs meet these demands in a few hours instead of weeks.

AppHub, the European Open Source Market Place, provides a neutral distribution channel for trustworthy software developed by EU-supported projects and OSS SMEs in general. It showcases SMEs and European collaborative projects best practices and pre-sales services to facilitate the adoption of their OSS. It leverages a breakthrough software technology to offer easy-to-download software and online pre-sales services. With AppHub, software vendors and services providers can show suitable Proof-of-Concept to their potential customers very quickly, adapting them to the right physical, virtual or cloud environment. AppHub helps accelerate the adoption of cloud

© Springer International Publishing Switzerland 2016
A. Celesti and P. Leitner (Eds.): ESOCC 2015 Workshops, CCIS 567, pp. 435–436, 2016.
DOI: 10.1007/978-3-319-33313-7

and multi-clouds solutions by both enterprise and cloud service providers. AppHub also helps reduce the learning curve for new cloud infrastructure, and the time required by successive stages of software development, adaptation and testing.

2   The AppHub Platform

AppHub is comprised of three main parts: the Directory, the Factory and the Store:

- The AppHub Directory helps software architects and developers identify the right OSS components for their needs. As of June 2015, the Directory lists 51 projects and 122 assets coming from European SMEs and EC-funded collaborative projects.
- The AppHub Factory provides services to model and build ready-to-deploy and ready-to-use applications for a large diversity of environments. As of June 2015, the Factory supports 12 virtual formats and 12 cloud formats.
- The AppHub Store addresses OSS consumers. It exposes the software either as a template, or as images built with the AppHub Factory. Images can be deployed to any cloud environment, templates can be customized by the consumer if needed.

3   Services That Foster Software Adoption

The AppHub Factory generates image formats suitable for a variety of deployment environments. Because it supports many different environments, AppHub facilitates the migration of OSS applications between them. It enables SaaS software vendors to address the entire market represented by the deployment environments and distributions provided by AppHub.

For cloud service brokers and end-user companies it speeds up the adaptation of any software to any specific environment. With AppHub, they can by quickly customize the complete stack by incorporating additional scripts, easily changing an OS or software package version, adding packages, adding their own middleware, adapting the installation profile of the application, etc.

The AppHub Factory automates the production of images and software clones regardless of the deployment model: private cloud, public cloud or hybrid cloud. The complete stack and its settings can be adapted.

4   The AppHub Project

AppHub is a Horizon 2020 support action funded by the European Commission. The partners that run and promote AppHub, the OW2 open source organization, the Fraunhofer FOKUS research institute and the UShareSoft ISV, combine unparalleled expertise in community management, EU research projects and a breakthrough technology in software asset management. AppHub builds on the experience gained by developing the directory for open source cloud computing during the FP7 OCEAN project.

Cloud Application Modelling and Execution Language (CAMEL) and the PaaSage Workflow

Alessandro Rossini

SINTEF, Oslo, Norway
alessandro.rossini@sintef.no

Model-driven engineering (MDE) is a branch of software engineering that aims at improving the productivity, quality, and cost-effectiveness of software development by promoting models and model transformations as the primary assets in software development. Models can be specified using general-purpose languages like the Unified Modeling Language (UML). However, to fully unfold the potential of MDE, models are frequently specified using domain-specific languages (DSLs), which are tailored to a specific domain of concern.

The PaaSage project[1] delivers a platform to support the modelling, execution, and adaptation of multi-cloud applications (*i.e.*, applications deployed across multiple private, public, or hybrid cloud infrastructures). In order to cover the necessary aspects of the modelling and execution of multi-cloud applications, PaaSage adopts the Cloud Application Modelling and Execution Language (CAMEL) [5].

CAMEL integrates and extends existing DSLs, namely the Cloud Modelling Language (CloudML) [1], Saloon [4], and the Organisation part of CERIF [2]. In addition, CAMEL integrates new DSLs developed within the project, such as the Scalability Rule Language (SRL) [3].

CAMEL enables PaaSage users to specify multiple aspects of multi-cloud applications, such as provisioning and deployment topology, provisioning and deployment requirements, service-level objectives, metrics, scalability rules, providers, organisations, users, roles, security controls, execution contexts, execution histories, etc.

In order to facilitate the integration across the components managing the lifecycle of multi-cloud applications, PaaSage leverages upon CAMEL models that are progressively refined throughout the *modelling, deployment,* and *execution* phases of the PaaSage workflow (see Fig. 1):

- *Modelling Phase*: The PaaSage users design a *cloud-provider independent model* (CPIM), which specifies the deployment of a multi-cloud application along with its requirements and objectives in a cloud provider-independent way.
- *Deployment Phase*: The Profiler component consumes the CPIM, matches this model with the profile of cloud providers, and produces a *constraint problem*. The Reasoner component solves the constraint problem (if possible) and produces a *cloud-provider specific model* (CPSM), which specifies the deployment of a multi-cloud application along with its requirements and objectives

---

[1] http://www.paasage.eu.

© Springer International Publishing Switzerland 2016
A. Celesti and P. Leitner (Eds.): ESOCC 2015 Workshops, CCIS 567, pp. 437–439, 2016.
DOI: 10.1007/978-3-319-33313-7

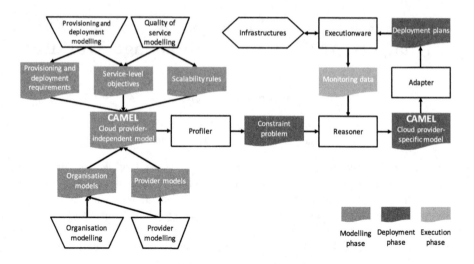

Fig. 1. CAMEL models in the PaaSage workflow

in a cloud provider-specific way. The Adapter component consumes the CPSM and produces *deployment plans*, which specify platform-specific details of the deployment.

– *Execution Phase*: The Executionware consumes the deployment plans and enacts the deployment of the application components on suitable cloud infrastructures. Finally, the Executionware records monitoring data about the application execution, which allows the Reasoner to look at the performance of previous CPSMs when producing a new one.

By leveraging upon CAMEL models not only at design-time but also runtime, PaaSage enables self-adaptive multi-cloud applications (*i.e.*, multi-cloud applications that automatically adapt to changes in the environment).

Acknowledgements. The research leading to these results has received funding from the European Commission's Seventh Framework Programme (FP7/2007–2013) under grant agreement number 317715 (PaaSage).

References

1. Ferry, N., Song, H., Rossini, A., Chauvel, F., Solberg, A.: CloudMF: applying MDE to Tame the complexity of managing multi-cloud applications. In: 7th IEEE/ACM International Conference on Utility and Cloud Computing. UCC 2014, pp. 269–277. IEEE CS (2014)
2. Jeffery, K., Houssos, N., Jörg, B., Asserson, A.: Research information management: the CERIF approach. IJMSO **9**(1), 5–14 (2014)
3. Kritikos, K., Domaschka, J., Rossini, A.: SRL: a scalability rule language for multi-cloud environments. In: 6th IEEE International Conference on Cloud Computing Technology and Science. CloudCom 2014, pp. 1–9. IEEE CS (2014)

4. Quinton, C., Romero, D., Duchien, L.: Cardinality-based feature models with constraints: a pragmatic approach. In: 17th International Software Product Line Conference. SPLC 2013, pp. 162–166. ACM (2013)
5. Rossini, A., Kritikos, K., Nikolov, N., Domaschka, J., Griesinger, F., Seybold, D., Romero, D.: D2.1.3 - CAMEL Documentation. Paasage project deliverable, October 2015

Broker@Cloud: Enabling Continuous Quality Assurance and Optimisation in Future Enterprise Cloud Service Brokers

Simeon Veloudis and Iraklis Paraskakis

South East European Research Centre (SEERC),
International Faculty of the University of Sheffield, CITY College,
24 Proxenou Koromila St, 54622 Thessaloniki, Greece

Abstract. We outline Broker@Cloud – a project which offers methods and mechanisms for facilitating two types of cloud service brokerage, namely Quality Assurance Service brokerage and Service Optimisation brokerage.

Keywords: Cloud computing · Cloud service brokerage · Governance and quality control · Optimisation · Failure prevention and recovery · Service description

1 Setting the Context

The Internet of Services brings about significant advantages for enterprises by reducing upfront investment costs and diminishing risks in pursuing innovative ideas. Nevertheless, at the same time, it transforms the enterprise IT environment into a complex ecosystem of interwoven and variably-sourced infrastructure, platform, and application services. In order to deal effectively with this complexity, future enterprises are anticipated to increasingly rely on cloud service brokerage (CSB). In this respect, the Broker@Cloud project sets out to construct a generic brokerage framework which provides capabilities with respect to two dimensions of CSB, namely *Quality Assurance Service Brokerage*, and *Service Optimisation Brokerage*.

2 Broker@Cloud in a Nutshell

Broker@Cloud offers brokerage mechanisms that provide capabilities that are organised around three general themes: (i) *governance and quality control*; (ii) *failure prevention and recovery*, and (iii) *optimisation*. The 1st theme is concerned with checking the compliance of services with pre-specified policies constraining technical, business and legal aspects of service delivery and deployment. It is also concerned with testing services for conformance with their expected behaviour, and with continuously monitoring their operation for conformance to SLAs. The 2nd theme is concerned with the reactive and proactive detection of cloud service failures, and the selection of suitable adaptation strategies to prevent, or recover, from failures. The 3rd theme is concerned with continuously identifying opportunities to optimise service consumption

© Springer International Publishing Switzerland 2016
A. Celesti and P. Leitner (Eds.): ESOCC 2015 Workshops, CCIS 567, pp. 440–441, 2016.
DOI: 10.1007/978-3-319-33313-7

with respect to such consumer preferences as, for example, cost, quality, and functionality.

Clearly, in the context of a generic CSB framework, such as the one offered by Broker@Cloud, the aforementioned capabilities must be offered orthogonally to any particular cloud service delivery platform. In this respect, a 4th theme is discerned, namely *platform-neutral description of cloud services*. This is concerned with the development of methods underpinning the Broker@Cloud framework and which enable the expression of such artefacts as service descriptions, policies and consumer preferences in a manner generic and platform-agnostic.

3   Broker@Cloud Methods and Mechanisms

We briefly outline progress achieved with respect to the aforementioned themes. Concerning the 1st theme, the Service Completeness-Compliance Checker (SC^3) has been developed. SC^3 is an ontology-driven mechanism which continuously evaluates the quality of services by checking their compliance with pre-specified policies concerning their deployment and delivery; in addition, SC^3 evaluates the correctness of the policies themselves. A governance registry system for dynamically managing the service lifecycle has also been developed. With respect to testing, an XML-based service specification language has been constructed and tools have been created to interpret this language, including verification and validation tools and automatic test-generation tools.

Concerning the 2nd theme, prototype software has been developed to support continuous failure prevention and recovery. The prototype incorporates a CEP engine which derives higher-order events relating to impending service failures from low-level events detected, through monitoring, at the infrastructure level. It also incorporates a reasoner for determining suitable adaptation or recovery actions.

Concerning the 3rd theme, the PuLSaR mechanism has been devised to support continuous optimisation of cloud service delivery, based on the fuzzy AHP (analytic hierarchy process) approach. This offers a unified method for performing an optimal multi-criteria decision making, based on precise (i.e. measurable) and imprecise (i.e. fuzzy) decision criteria. Service consumers may express their preferences for service optimisation using exact numerical or imprecise linguistic terms.

Concerning the 4th theme, an ontological framework has been developed for the generic and platform-agnostic specification of service descriptions, business policies, and consumer preferences. The framework draws upon *Linked USDL*, a lightweight easily-extensible RDF vocabulary for describing services and their pertinent artefacts.

As a means to validate the methods and mechanisms outlined above, two prototype service brokerage platforms have been built. The one is hosted by CAS Software AG (Karlsruhe), as an extension to the *CAS Open* platform, whilst the other is hosted by Singular Logic (Athens), as an extension of the *Orbi* platform.

Acknowledgements. This research is funded by the EU 7th Framework Programme under the Broker@Cloud project (www.broker-cloud.eu), grant agreement n°328392.

BEACON – Enabling Federated Cloud Networking

Philippe Massonet[1] and Craig Sheridan[2]

[1] CETIC, Charleroi, Belgium
Philippe.massonet@cetic.be
[2] Flexiant, Edinburgh, Scotland
csheridan@flexiant.com

Abstract. Cloud federation enables cloud providers to collaborate and share their resources to create a large virtual pool of resources at multiple network locations. Different types of federation architectures for clouds and datacenters have been proposed and implemented. An effective, agile and secure federation of cloud networking resources is key to impact the deployment of federated applications. The main goal of this project is two-fold: research and develop techniques to federate cloud network resources, and to derive the integrated management cloud layer that enables an efficient and secure deployment of federated cloud applications.

Keywords: Cloud computing · Network virtualization · Cloud federation · Security

1 Introduction

The BEACON H2020 project [1] aims at enabling federated cloud networking. The recent development of software defined networking and network virtualization technologies has created the opportunity to fully integrate network virtualization technologies into cloud middleware. This will enable management of advanced hybrid clouds and heterogeneous cloud federations. Network virtualization technologies from the OpenDove project will be integrated with open source cloud middleware Open-Nebula and OpenStack.

2 BEACON Federated Cloud Networking Architecture

The BEACON project aims to enhance cloud middleware market with network virtualization technology to support the management of hybrid clouds and cloud federations. Our proposal will deliver a homogeneous virtualization layer, on top of heterogeneous underlying physical networks, computing and storage infrastructures, providing enablement for automated federation of applications across different clouds and datacenters. The figure below shows the BEACON federated cloud architecture. The service manager is responsible for the instantiation of the application by requesting the creation and configuration of virtual machines for each service component included

© Springer International Publishing Switzerland 2016
A. Celesti and P. Leitner (Eds.): ESOCC 2015 Workshops, CCIS 567, pp. 442–443, 2016.
DOI: 10.1007/978-3-319-33313-7

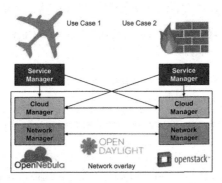

Fig. 1. BEACON Federated cloud networking architecture

in the service definition, using the interfaces exposed by the cloud manager. The Cloud Manager is responsible for the placement of VMs into VM Hosts. It receives requests from the Service Manager through the Cloud interface to create and resize VMs, and finds the best placement that satisfies a given set of constraints. The Cloud Manager is free to place, and move, the VMs anywhere, even on remote sites within the federation, as long as the placement satisfies the constraints. The network manager is responsible for allocating network resources to manage federated cloud virtual network and overlay networks across geographically dispersed sites. The right part of the figure shows a second cloud stack running on a different cloud provider. Together they form a federation with two cloud providers. The middle part of the figure shows that the cloud manager and network managers of the two cloud providers communicate to share resources and manage the federation.

3   Open Source Results

Cloud networking aspects will be based on OpenDove, a collaborative project under The Linux Foundation. We will extend the OpenDOVE project with new rich inter-cloud APIs to provision cross-site virtual network overlays. The new inter-cloud network capabilities will be leveraged by existing open source cloud platforms, OpenNebula and OpenStack, to deploy multi-cloud applications. Different aspects of the platforms will be extended to accommodate the federated cloud networking features like multi-tenancy, federated orchestration of networking, compute and storage management or the placement and elasticity of the multi-cloud applications.

Reference

1. BEACON web site. http://www.beacon-project.eu/

EUBrazil Cloud Connect: A Federated e-Infrastructure for Cross-Border Science

Roberto G. Cascella$^{(\boxtimes)}$, Stephanie Parker, and Silvana Muscella

Trust-IT Services Ltd, Middlesex, UK
{r.cascella,s.parker,s.muscella}@trust-itservices.com

Abstract. EUBrazil Cloud Connect is an international co-operation project aimed at accelerating scientific discovery to advance knowledge on several challenges with high social impact. It provides a user-centric, federated e-infrastructure for European & Brazilian research communities. Major outputs over 24 months include the design and implementation of new programming models and tools enabling the deployment of three scientific use cases on heterogeneous computing resources. It has also deployed multiple **federated cloud** services based on open standards, successfully meeting the needs of scientific users and also analysing business competencies for sustainable usage. Thanks to the high impact results achieved in the project, the scientific community and industry can now benefit from stable components for big data analysis.

1 EUBrazilCC: A Federated Cross-Atlantic Infrastructure

Cloud computing has profoundly changed the way in which business services are created and how we conduct scientific research to tackle challenges of significant socio-economic impact by meeting needs such as intense computation capacity, data access, and elastic management of resources. However, major advances are still needed to create novel cloud technologies applicable to a large set of scientific problems in different fields, such as biodiversity, climate, & medical informatics.

EUBrazil Cloud Connect (EUBrazilCC) (www.eubrazilcloudconnect.eu) is a transatlantic open source project federating heterogeneous cloud resources in Brazil and Europe, and facilitating cross border co-operation by implementing innovative programming models and tools for the development of scientific applications. This new joint cloud infrastructure has built on European and Brazilian excellence in cloud technology, standardisation efforts and scientific applications with the availability of large data sets provided by diverse ecosystems.

EUBrazilCC focuses on an *interoperable-by-design* approach to manage a heterogeneous infrastructure, which includes private clouds, supercomputing and opportunistic desktop resources, using different middleware to manage the IaaS resources. Interoperability is achieved by implementing cloud computing open

This work was supported by the EU FP7 EUBrazilCC Project (Grant Agreement 614048), and CNPq/Brazil (Grant Agreement 490115/2013-6).

A. Celesti and P. Leitner (Eds.): ESOCC 2015 Workshops, CCIS 567, pp. 444–446, 2016.
DOI: 10.1007/978-3-319-33313-7

standards for the design of the architecture, federation and high level services, including customised scientific gateways and programming models to efficiently use the infrastructure and foster data sharing. The implementation of relevant standards, with interoperability testing, eases the integration of the tools in other systems while contributing to standardisation initiatives globally.

EUBrazilCC architecture adopts the European Grid Infrastructure (EGI) federated cloud model by supporting open standards: OCCI for IaaS management and VOMS for resource level authorisation management. These standards are essential for help manage heterogeneous resources and deploy on different cloud middleware, such as OpenStack, OpenNebula, which are federated using *Fogbow*. Fogbow is a middleware that provides a very lightweight business model for the federation of private IaaS providers, based on the exchange of resources. The execution and provision of services can also be performed via the *Infrastructure Manager (IM)* and *CSGrid*. IM provides a high-level service to customise and deploy independently from the underlying platform. CSGrid offers the abstraction of the computational resources to facilitate scientific applications' management and transparent access to supercomputers.

The EUBrazilCC approach to the deployment and execution of large-scope scientific use cases on federated cloud resources mainly focuses on including in the architecture high-level services. *COMPSs* and *e-Science Central* programming frameworks provide functionalities to run complex workflow managers on top of different infrastructures, while reducing the use cases' development cycle. *Parallel Data Analysis Service (PDAS)* manages large volume of scientific data for big data analytics. Data access and transfer is done by means of graphical interfaces developed via the *mc2* framework for scientific gateways.

These tools are the foundation of the EUBrazil Cloud Connect assets that will ensure long-term sustainability through dedicated exploitation plans.

2   Impact and Innovation via Scientific Use Cases

The main impact of EUBrazilCC is the close collaboration between European and Brazilian institutions, in the area of eScience applications on virtualised infrastructures, to demonstrate the efficiency and cost-effectiveness of tools via 3 use cases with high socio-economic impact with mutual benefit to EU & Brazil.

The *Leishmaniasis Virtual Lab* (LeishVL) is a web-based application that offers a dedicated set of tools and services to data sources and powerful computing systems to run experiments for the surveillance of Leishmaniasis, a disease affecting the poorest of the poor. The *Vascular System Simulation* involves simulations of the heart and the arterial system to model pathologies and test therapies under development, which can be examined in-silico, reducing design costs and times. The *Climate Change and Biodiversity* studies the mutual interactions (status and changes) between biodiversity dynamics and climate change, by using earth observation and ground level data together with simulated data.

EUBrazilCC has a high impact to international associations and industries thanks to the use of project assets and establishment of synergies. COMPSs is already adopted in the EGI Federation Cloud, while mc2, e-Science Central, and LeishVL are available on EGI marketplace. The Fogbow component is being considered by RNP, the Brazilian research network, for federating their cloud infrastructure and under testing by SERPRO.

EUBrazilCC has demonstrated a consolidated representation as an important vehicle driving ICT policy dialogue between Europe and Brazil and contributing cloud technologies to interoperability, e-infrastructure and scientific applications.

CLIPS – CLoud Approach for Innovation in Public Services

Roberto Di Bernardo and Marco Alessi

Engineering Ingegneria Informatica SpA, R&D Laboratory, Palermo, Italy
{roberto.dibernardo,marco.alessi}@eng.it

Nowadays, Public Sector is facing two external factors conflicting and apparently irreconcilable: the reduction of budget available and the growing demand for innovation in public services. In this situation, Public Authorities find in the Cloud [1] a valuable ally such as management model of IT infrastructure and SaaS environment [3], but it is not enough. There is the need for new approaches and business models that enable the delivery of value-added IT services for public utility, built on top of those provided by Public Authorities, thanks to the involvement of new actors (e.g. SMEs, Services Providers) [4], so empowering a real, sustainable business ecosystem. Even though the cloud computing advantages are relevant and clear, security and privacy issues are the primary obstacles to wide adoption in public sector [6]. In this frame, the research project CLIPS (www.clips-project.eu), co-funded under CIP-ICT-PSP (Grant 621083), wants to provide city community with a methodology and a set of technological assets that allow public administration, citizens and enterprises to cooperate in the development and provisioning of new and innovative public services. In this way the final aim of CLIPS is to build an ecosystem in which all the actors can play an active role providing a strong cooperation.

In order to support "cloudization" of PA legacy IT systems and the reuse of resources, overcoming the aforementioned obstacles, CLIPS project makes use of the micro-service concept, introduces the micro-proxy one and leverages a hybrid integration approach [2]. More in details (Fig. 1): (1) a micro-service represents a service providing atomic business functionality and is located on the cloud. Being atomic, this maximizes its reusability. All the micro-services deployed in CLIPS ecosystem are resources potentially sharable (building blocks); (2) a micro-proxy represents a service creating the connection between CLIPS cloud environment and PA IT systems. It represents a sort of last mile integration element, on the one hand leaving the full control on personal/sensible data to the single PA and, the other hand, providing access to them according to CLIPS platform dictates.

CLIPS proposes [10]: (1) a Visual Service Mash-up tool, making potentially all stakeholders capable to identify available building blocks (i.e. micro-services and Open Data) and to compose them in a visual way to create new value added services. This represents the adaptative part of the integration approach (called also citizen integration); (2) an integration framework, based on Talend [11], in order to overcome more sophisticated integration (in particular dealing with the creation of micro-proxies). This represents the systematic part of the approach.

A. Celesti and P. Leitner (Eds.): ESOCC 2015 Workshops, CCIS 567, pp. 447–449, 2016.
DOI: 10.1007/978-3-319-33313-7

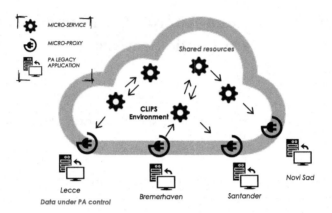

Fig. 1. CLIPS approach

Moreover, to face security issues, CLIPS architecture [4, 10] includes four modules each one operating at different levels: (1) a set of security best practices to be followed by each CLIPS component design; (2) the integration with Secure idenTity acrOss boRders linKed (STORK) [6] framework; (3) the employment of the Remote Attestation [8] (feature provided by the Trusted Computing technology) in order to enforce the trustworthiness of CLIPS infrastructure; (4) a cloud-oriented logging component to monitor the events occurring within the infrastructure.

CLIPS will be piloted in several European cities around a common the scenario of a "family moving across countries/cities" facing with typical complexities such move could entail. CLIPS pilot cities are: Bremerhaven (DE), Lecce (IT), Novi Sad (RS), and Santander (ES). The services to be piloted belong to several fields (e.g. kindergarten registration, payment services, register with administration, get licenses and permissions) and will be run also in cross-border situations paying attention to privacy and ethical issue, being analysed and investigated during the project [9].

References

1. Mell, P., Grance, T.: The NIST Definition of Cloud Computing (2011)
2. Thompson, J.: How to Use Hybrid Integration Platforms Effectively. Gartner (2014)
3. Staten, J.: Hollow Out The MOOSE: Reducing Cost with Strategic Rightsourcing. Forrester Research, Inc. (2009)
4. CLIPS deliverable: D4.1 Security Architecture and API
5. Wojciech, C., Strykowski, S.: E-government based on cloud computing and service-oriented architecture (2009)
6. Marijn, J., Joha, A.: Challenges for adopting cloud-based SAAS in the public sector (2011)
7. STORK Consortium: Stork Project. https://www.eidCstork.eu
8. Trusted Computing Group. https://www.trustedcomputinggroup.org/about_tcg

 9. CLIPS deliverable: D7.1.1 Policy, privacy and technological constraints analysis report
10. CLIPS deliverable: D5.1 CLIPS Architecture and specifications
11. Talend ESB. https://www.talend.com/resource/open-source-esb.html

FrontierCities: Leveraging FIWARE for Advantages in Smart Mobility

Antonio Celesti and Massimo Villari

DICIEAMA, University of Messina, Contrada Di Dio (S. Agata),
98166 Messina, Italy
{acelesti,mvillari}@unime.it

Abstract. FIWARE represents a new European Cloud platform that aims to land on the international ICT market bringing prominent novel advantages for societies. In fact, it provides new compelling and novel software components, available through APIs, able to give developers new valuable Cloud platform functionalities. FrontierCities "European Cities Driving the Future Internet" is an European FP7 founded project related to the FI-PPP Phase 3 CP-CSA call. It aims to leverage the FIWARE technology in order to support SMEs and start-ups in developing new innovative smart mobility applications for the cities of the future.

Keywords: Cloud computing · Internet of Things · FIWARE · Smart mobility

1 FIWARE at Glance

Cloud computing and Internet of Things (IoT) are enabling key technologies for Future Internet (FI). In this context, the European Commission (EC) envisioned the possibility to foster the wide adoption of such technologies, in total openness, avoiding vendor lock-in and simplifying the composition of new services. To this end, the EC has started the Future Internet Private Public Partnership (FI-PPP) program [1] that has brought to the delivery of a new complex European Cloud platform, called FIWARE. The aim of FIWARE is to yield an open standard platform and an open, sustainable, global ecosystem. The FIWARE reference architecture includes a set of general-purpose platform functions called Generic Enablers (GEs) [2]. GEs are related to network and device interfaces, advanced web-based user interfaces, application/service ecosystems and delivery networks, Cloud hosting, data/context management, IoT service enablement, and security. FIWARE provides GE Open Specifications (that are public and royalty-free) and their implementations (GEi). Moreover, FIWARE provides at least one open source reference implementation of each GE (GEri) with a well-known open source license. The advantage in using FIWARE is that software architects can rely on a consolidated set of open source general-purpose platform functions that are supported by a world-wide community. In fact, there are GEs

© Springer International Publishing Switzerland 2016
A. Celesti and P. Leitner (Eds.): ESOCC 2015 Workshops, CCIS 567, pp. 450–451, 2016.
DOI: 10.1007/978-3-319-33313-7

for many specific needs that allow developers to apply agile development strategies. In order to promote the FIWARE Techonogy, the EC has promoted the Future Internet Accelerator Programme including 16 accelerators related to different application fields. FrontierCities [3] is one these 16 accelerators specifically focusing on smart mobility.

2   FrontierCities

FrontierCities "European Cities Driving the Future Internet" is a proposal presented for the FI-PPP Phase 3 CP-CSA call. The project is built on the FI-PPP Phase I and II, and it is directly linked to the work carried out in FI-Phase II instant mobility and outsmart use cases. Mobility and transport are essential for the proper functioning of a city. A smart city should be easily accessible to visitors and residents, and travelling across a city should be problem-free. The aim is to provide a multifaceted, efficient, safe, and comfortable transport system, which is linked to ICT infrastructures and open data. FrontierCities aims to support SMEs and start-ups for the development of innovative smart mobility applications. While building upon Phase II, FrontierCities is however in line with the significant change in focus required under Phase III, and represents an ambitious, market-focussed project. Core objectives are to solicit and select high-calibre grant applications from SMEs and start-ups through a mix of strategies and market the results to a pan-European audience of cities. The main objective of the project is to support grantee projects for a secure market commercialisation of their applications and services considering both cities and wider private sector uptakers and enablers (e.g., corporations and investors). In particular, the project aims to disburse EUR 3.92 million in grant funding to SMEs and start-ups through a streamlined two-step application process. The frontierCities consortium is made up of seven partners (New Frontier Services, Engineering – Ingegneria Informatica SPA, University of Surrey, European Business and Innovation Centre Network, InnovaBic, Energap, Università degli Studi di Messina), each one bringing experience and expertise in management, technology and business development.

3   Preliminary Results

Currently, the assessment of proposals in step 1 is completed. We were thrilled to see such a strong interest in our call with 594 submitted and finalised applications. In particular, we had 201 successful step 1 applicants, who have been invited to participate in step 2.

References

1. FI-Ppp. program. https://www.fi-ppp.eu/projects/fi-ware
2. Generic Enabler (GE) Catalogue. http://catalogue.fiware.org/enablers
3. FrontierCities. http://www.fi-frontiercities.eu/

Author Index

Printed in the United States
By Bookmasters